Y0-DJN-873

RACE AND ETHNIC RELATIONS
94/95

Fourth Edition

Editor

John A. Kromkowski
Catholic University of America

John A. Kromkowski is president of The National Center for
Urban Ethnic Affairs in Washington, D.C., a nonprofit
research and educational institute that has sponsored and
published many books and articles on ethnic relations, urban
affairs, and economic revitalization. He is Assistant Dean of
the College of Arts and Sciences at the Catholic University
of America, and he coordinates international seminars and
internship programs in the United States, England, Ireland,
and Belgium. He has served on national advisory boards for
the Campaign for Human Development, the U.S. Department
of Education Ethnic Heritage Studies Program, the White
House Fellows Program, the National Neighborhood
Coalition, and the American Revolution Bicentennial
Administration. Dr. Kromkowski has edited a series
sponsored by the Council for Research in Values and
Philosophy titled *Cultural Heritage and Contemporary
Change*. These volumes include scholarly findings and
reflections on urbanization, cultural affairs, personhood,
community, and political economy.

Annual Editions
A Library of Information from the Public Press

The Dushkin Publishing Group, Inc.
Sluice Dock, Guilford, Connecticut 06437

Cover illustration by Mike Eagle

The Annual Editions Series

Annual Editions is a series of over 60 volumes designed to provide the reader with convenient, low-cost access to a wide range of current, carefully selected articles from some of the most important magazines, newspapers, and journals published today. Annual Editions are updated on an annual basis through a continuous monitoring of over 300 periodical sources. All Annual Editions have a number of features designed to make them particularly useful, including topic guides, annotated tables of contents, unit overviews, and indexes. For the teacher using Annual Editions in the classroom, an Instructor's Resource Guide with test questions is available for each volume.

VOLUMES AVAILABLE

Africa
Aging
American Foreign Policy
American Government
American History, Pre-Civil War
American History, Post-Civil War
Anthropology
Biology
Business Ethics
Canadian Politics
Child Growth and Development
China
Comparative Politics
Computers in Education
Computers in Business
Computers in Society
Criminal Justice
Drugs, Society, and Behavior
Dying, Death, and Bereavement
Early Childhood Education
Economics
Educating Exceptional Children
Education
Educational Psychology
Environment
Geography
Global Issues
Health
Human Development
Human Resources
Human Sexuality
India and South Asia
International Business
Japan and the Pacific Rim

Latin America
Life Management
Macroeconomics
Management
Marketing
Marriage and Family
Mass Media
Microeconomics
Middle East and the Islamic World
Money and Banking
Multicultural Education
Nutrition
Personal Growth and Behavior
Physical Anthropology
Psychology
Public Administration
Race and Ethnic Relations
Russia, Eurasia, and Central/Eastern
   Europe
Social Problems
Sociology
State and Local Government
Third World
Urban Society
Violence and Terrorism
Western Civilization,
   Pre-Reformation
Western Civilization,
   Post-Reformation
Western Europe
World History, Pre-Modern
World History, Modern
World Politics

Library of Congress Cataloging in Publication Data
Main entry under title: Annual editions: Race and ethnic relations. 1994/95.
    1. Race relations—Periodicals. 2. United States—Race relations—Periodicals. 3. Culture conflict—United States—Periodicals. I. Kromkowski, John A., comp. II. Title: Race and ethnic relations.
ISBN 1–56134–287–4   305.8′073′05

Fourth Edition

Printed in the United States of America

To the Reader

In publishing ANNUAL EDITIONS we recognize the enormous role played by the magazines, newspapers, and journals of the *public press* in providing current, first-rate educational information in a broad spectrum of interest areas. Within the articles, the best scientists, practitioners, researchers, and commentators draw issues into new perspective as accepted theories and viewpoints are called into account by new events, recent discoveries change old facts, and fresh debate breaks out over important controversies.

Many of the articles resulting from this enormous editorial effort are appropriate for students, researchers, and professionals seeking accurate, current material to help bridge the gap between principles and theories and the real world. These articles, however, become more useful for study when those of lasting value are carefully *collected, organized, indexed,* and *reproduced* in a *low-cost format*, which provides easy and permanent access when the material is needed. That is the role played by *Annual Editions*. Under the direction of each volume's *Editor*, who is an expert in the subject area, and with the guidance of an *Advisory Board*, we seek each year to provide in each *ANNUAL EDITION* a current, well-balanced, carefully selected collection of the best of the public press for your study and enjoyment. We think you'll find this volume useful, and we hope you'll take a moment to let us know what you think.

The information explosion and expansion of knowledge about the range of diversity among and within societies has increased awareness of ethnicity and race. During previous periods of history, society was discussed in terms of a universal sense of common humanity. Differences between societies and the arrangements of economic production were noted, but they were usually explained in terms of theories of progressive development or of class conflict that was leading toward a universal and homogenized humanity. Consciousness of the enduring pluralism expressed in ethnic, racial, and cultural diversity that constitutes the human condition has emerged throughout the world. It appears, however, that the dimensions of diversity are significantly, if not essentially, shaped by social, economic, cultural, and, most importantly, political and communitarian processes. Creativity and imagination influence ethnic and racial relations.

The following collection of articles was designed to assist you in understanding ethnic and racial pluralism in the United States of America. Unit 1, for example, illustrates how the most basic legal principles of a society—and especially the U.S. Supreme Court's interpretation of them—are especially significant for the delineation of ethnic groups and for the acceptance of cultural pluralism. Subsequent sections include illustrative articles of ethnic interaction with and within American society. The immigration of persons, the focus of unit 2, into a relatively young society such as America is of particular concern, because the fragility of social continuity is exposed by the recognition of change and differences in the ethnic composition of American society.

The contemporary experiences of indigenous groups including Native Americans are arranged in unit 3. Discussion of the experiences of the descendants of the earliest and the most recently arrived ethnic populations and the legal framework for participating in America are extended in unit 4 on Hispanic/Latino Americans and unit 5 on Asian Americans. Unit 6 explores various dimensions of the African American experience. The ethnicities found in these units form a cluster of concerns addressed in the traditional literature that focused on marginality, minority, and alienation. New voices from within these traditions suggest bridges to the topics included in unit 7, titled "The Ethnic Legacy," which exposes and articulates neglected dimensions of ethnicity derived from the industrial development of America. Unit 8, "The Ethnic Factor: Challenges for the 1990s," and unit 9, "Understanding Cultural Pluralism," broach the national and international implications of exclusivity and the imperatives of new approaches to group relations. The search for a new paradigm and the value of institutional and attitudinal inclusiveness can be found implicitly and explicitly in this cluster of articles.

The American experience, especially those legal protections that are most sacred, has been explained by many as the development of personal freedom. This focus is not entirely valid. For nearly eight decades Americans have become increasingly aware of the ways that group and personal identity are interwoven, and that this process forms a dense network of culture, economy, polity, and sociality. This perspective on the American reality was fashioned from the experiences of the children and grandchildren of post–Civil War immigrants to the United States. Their valuation of a new form of pluralism—one beyond the dichotomous divide of white-Negro/freeman-former slave—became central to a new vision of American society. Thus, the language of ethnic relations has been refashioned from "either-or" logic derived from the race-slavery consciousness of the English American founders, into a vocabulary that reflects a more complex matrix of scores of ethnicities. This new vocabulary retains the components of a divisive legacy, but, more significantly, it also contains the very potential for liberty and justice for all.

Readers may have input into the next edition of *Race and Ethnic Relations* by completing and returning the article rating form in the back of the book.

John A. Kromkowski
Editor

Contents

Unit 1

Race, Ethnicity, and the Law

Five selections in this section consider some of the pivotal Supreme Court decisions regarding citizenship and race in the United States.

Unit 2

Immigration and the American Experience

Five articles in this section review the history of immigration in the social context of the United States.

The concepts in bold italics are developed in the article. For further expansion please refer to the Topic Guide and the Index.

Unit 3

Native American Groups

Nine articles in this section consider some of the issues
and problems faced by indigenous ethnic groups and
Native Americans.

The concepts in bold italics are developed in the article. For further expansion please refer to the Topic Guide and the Index.

Unit 4

Hispanic/Latino Americans

Five articles in this section explore the social and cultural dynamics of Hispanic/Latino Americans.

Unit 5

Asian Americans

Four articles in this section examine the culture of
Asian Americans and their ability to successfully
assimilate.

Unit 6

African Americans

Seven selections in this section review some historical
and current concerns of African Americans.

The concepts in bold italics are developed in the article. For further expansion please refer to the Topic Guide and the Index.

Unit 7

The Ethnic Legacy

Five articles in this section examine some of the neglected dimensions and legacies of traditional ethnic communities in America.

The concepts in bold italics are developed in the article. For further expansion please refer to the Topic Guide and the Index.

Unit 8

The Ethnic Factor: Challenges for the 1990s

Five articles in this section look at the intersections of ethnicity and its impact on international affairs.

The concepts in bold italics are developed in the article. For further expansion please refer to the Topic Guide and the Index.

Unit 9

Understanding Cultural Pluralism

Six articles in this section examine some of the challenges faced by our society as our American culture continues to diversify.

This article uses data that reflects **shifting attitudes toward immigration** to revisit the history of America's concerns as well as current debates about America's identity, its ambivalence about growth and economic change, and the validity of its laws and aspirations in pursuit of justice, as well as the effectiveness of an educational system for a nation of immigrants.

This is a report from the University of North Carolina at Chapel Hill where a proposal to build a black cultural center divided the campus. This account of student attitudes and opinions on everyday issues, as well as their concerns about segregation and double standards, points to the ongoing **intergroup conflict** and the challenges to cooperation among races and ethnic groups.

The authors review and assess the urban mission of the University of Louisville and its attempt to celebrate diversity. This account of the development of a celebrative event and their recommendation for improving and replicating their approach to cooperative action bears witness to the fact that **diversity programs** need not cause separatism and hostility.

Henry Gates's reflective essay on the possible course of integration and fragmentation that will drive history recalls an intellectual tradition that supports his notions of **race and religion.** His forecast of various scenarios for the decades to come indicates the powerful impact of immigration and demography as well as people's options to shape their destiny with symbols of race and religion.

Steven Waldman's article recounts the legislative and administrative maze associated with racial, ethnic, and class factors that collided with President Clinton's hope for a **national service program.** Clinton's dream of a new politics of inclusiveness was smashed by the old politics of race and vested interests.

Irving Howe's analysis of the call for multiculturalism in college studies deepens the discussion of **culture and power.** Critiques of hegemonic cultural forces of the past have become politically correct, but they should challenge us to overcome their shallowness and ideological invocations. He invites a new generation into the process of critical clarification within various traditions and cultures.

The concepts in bold italics are developed in the article. For further expansion please refer to the Topic Guide and the Index.

Topic Guide

This topic guide suggests how the selections in this book relate to topics of traditional concern to students and professionals involved with the study of race and ethnic relations. It is useful for locating articles that relate to each other for reading and research. The guide is arranged alphabetically according to topic. Articles may, of course, treat topics that do not appear in the topic guide. In turn, entries in the topic guide do not necessarily constitute a comprehensive listing of all the contents of each selection.

TOPIC AREA	TREATED IN:	TOPIC AREA	TREATED IN:
Chinese Americans	6. Historical Discrimination 9. Census Bureau 25. Asian Americans 26. Victimization of Asians	**Discrimination (cont'd)**	10. Lifestyle 2000 11. Paupers in a World Their Ancestors Ruled 12. Bolivia's Vice President 14. Return of the Natives 15. Crimes Against Humanity 26. Victimization of Asians 28. Black-Korean Conflict 29. Dramatic Events in African-American History 30. Black Americans 31. Growing Up in Black and White 32. Beyond the Pale 35. Home Ownership 37. New Ethnicity 40. Gates of Nightmare 43. Race and Urban Poverty 44. Ethnic Conflict 45. Walls That Have Yet to Fall 46. America: Still a Melting Pot? 47. Students Talk About Race 48. Diversity 50. 'Ask Not'
Civil Rights	3. *Brown v. Board of Education of Topeka* 4. *University of California Regents v. Bakke* 5. Freedom of Religious Expression 6. Historical Discrimination 7. Immigration Reform 12. Bolivia's Vice President 15. Crimes Against Humanity 20. U.S. Hispanics 24. Not Much Cooking 26. Victimization of Asians 29. Dramatic Events in African-American History 30. Black Americans 31. Growing Up in Black and White 40. Gates of Nightmare 44. Ethnic Conflict 45. Walls That Have Yet To Fall 46. America: Still a Melting Pot? 47. Students Talk About Race		
		Education	3. *Brown v. Board of Education of Topeka* 4. *University of California Regents v. Bakke* 5. Freedom of Religious Expression 9. Census Bureau 22. "La Raza Cosmica" 27. Spicier Melting Pot 30. Black Americans 35. Home Ownership 40. Gates of Nightmare 44. Ethnic Conflict 47. Students Talk About Race 48. Diversity 50. 'Ask Not' 51. Value of the Canon
Class	9. Census Bureau 10. Lifestyle 2000 12. Bolivia's Vice President 14. Return of the Natives 17. American Indians 20. U.S. Hispanics 30. Black Americans 31. Growing Up in Black and White 35. Home Ownership 43. Race and Urban Poverty 44. Ethnic Conflict		
		Elderly	37. New Ethnicity
		Environment	14. Return of the Natives
Courts	1. *Dred Scott v. Sandford* 2. *Plessy v. Ferguson* 3. *Brown v. Board of Education of Topeka* 4. *University of California Regents v. Bakke* 5. Freedom of Religious Expression 15. Crimes Against Humanity	**Family**	8. New Americans Weather and Survive 23. There's More to Racism 31. Growing Up in Black and White 32. Beyond the Pale 34. Politics of Family 35. Home Ownership
Demography	7. Immigration Reform 9. Census Bureau 10. Lifestyle 2000 14. Return of the Natives 17. American Indians 20. U.S. Hispanics 21. What Does "Hispanic" Mean? 24. Not Much Cooking 25. Asian Americans 30. Black Americans 34. Politics of Family 46. America: Still a Melting Pot?	**Identity**	11. Paupers in a World Their Ancestors Ruled 12. Bolivia's Vice President 13. Struggling to Be Themselves 14. Return of the Natives 15. Crimes Against Humanity 16. Gadugi 17. American Indians 18. Lakhota Sioux Hutzel 19. Seeking Lost Culture 20. U.S. Hispanics 21. What Does "Hispanic" Mean?
Discrimination	2. *Plessy v. Ferguson* 5. Freedom of Religious Expression 6. Historical Discrimination		

TOPIC AREA	TREATED IN:	TOPIC AREA	TREATED IN:
Identity (cont'd)	22. "La Raza Cosmica" 24. Not Much Cooking 25. Asian Americans 28. Black-Korean Conflict in Los Angeles 29. Dramatic Events in African-American History 30. Black Americans 31. Growing Up in Black and White 32. Beyond the Pale 37. New Ethnicity 39. Polish American Congress 40. Gates of Nightmare 41. Mirror of the Other 42. Ends of History 44. Ethnic Conflict 45. Walls That Have Yet to Fall 46. America: Still a Melting Pot? 47. Students Talk About Race 48. Diversity 50. 'Ask Not' 51. Value of the Canon	Prejudice	5. Freedom of Religious Expression 6. Historical Discrimination 7. Immigration Reform 10. Lifestyle 2000 11. Paupers in a World Their Ancestors Ruled 12. Bolivia's Vice President 13. Struggling to Be Themselves 14. Return of the Natives 25. Asian Americans 26. Victimization of Asians 28. Black-Korean Conflict 30. Black Americans 31. Growing Up in Black and White 32. Beyond the Pale 34. Politics of Family 37. New Ethnicity 38. Irish Americans 40. Gates of Nightmare 41. Mirror of the Other 42. Ends of History 43. Race and Urban Poverty 44. Ethnic Conflict 45. Walls That Have Yet to Fall 46. America: Still a Melting Pot? 47. Students Talk About Race 48. Diversity 50. 'Ask Not'
Japanese Americans	9. Census Bureau 25. Asian Americans 26. Victimization of Asians 27. Spicier Melting Pot		
Migration	7. Immigration Reform 8. New Americans Weather and Survive 10. Lifestyle 2000 11. Paupers in a World Their Ancestors Ruled 20. U.S. Hispanics 25. Asian Americans 27. Spicier Melting Pot 28. Black Korean Conflict 35. Home Ownership 43. Race and Urban Poverty 46. America: Still a Melting Pot?	Quotas	4. *University of California Regents v. Bakke* 6. Historical Discrimination 7. Immigration Reform 23. There's More to Racism 47. Students Talk About Race
		Refugees	7. Immigration Reform 9. Census Bureau 27. Spicier Melting Pot 43. Race and Urban Poverty 46. America: Still a Melting Pot?
Polish Americans	8. New Americans Weather and Survive 9. Census Bureau 39. Polish American Congress	Segregation	2. *Plessy v. Ferguson* 3. *Brown v. Board of Education of Topeka* 13. Struggling to Be Themselves 26. Victimization of Asians 29. Dramatic Events in African-American History 30. Black Americans 31. Growing Up in Black and White 32. Beyond the Pale 35. Home Ownership 43. Race and Urban Poverty 44. Ethnic Conflict 47. Students Talk About Race 50. 'Ask Not'
Population	7. Immigration Reform 9. Census Bureau 11. Paupers in a World Their Ancestors Ruled 13. Struggling to Be Themselves 14. Return of the Natives 17. American Indians 20. U.S. Hispanics 21. What Does "Hispanic" Mean? 25. Asian Americans 27. Spicier Melting Pot 31. Growing Up in Black and White 46. America: Still a Melting Pot? 47. Students Talk About Race		
Poverty	8. New Americans Weather and Survive 10. Lifestyle 2000 13. Struggling to Be Themselves 14. Return of the Natives 19. Seeking Lost Culture 20. U.S. Hispanics 21. What Does "Hispanic" Mean? 28. Black-Korean Conflict 34. Politics of Family 43. Race and Urban Poverty 50. 'Ask Not'	Slavery	1. *Dred Scott v. Sandford* 15. Crimes Against Humanity
		Ukranian Americans	18. Lakhota Sioux Hutzel
		Vietnamese Americans	8. New Americans Weather and Survive 9. Census Bureau 25. Asian Americans 27. Spicier Melting Pot

Race, Ethnicity, and the Law

The legal framework established by the original U.S. Constitution illustrates the way the American founders handled ethnic pluralism. In most respects, they ignored the cultural and linguistic variety within and between the 13 original states, adopting instead a legal system that guaranteed religious exercise free from government interference, due process of law, and the freedom of speech and the press. The founders, however, conspicuously compromised their claims of unalienable rights and democratic republicanism with regard to the constitutional status of Africans in bondage and the indigenous Native Americans. Even after the Civil War and the inclusion of constitutional amendments that ended slavery and guaranteed equal protection of the laws to all, decisions by the U.S. Supreme Court helped to establish a legal system in which inequality and ethnic discrimination—both political and private—were legally permissible. In fact, it has been only recently that the Court has begun to redress the complex relationship between our constitutional system, our nation's cultural diversity, and assurance of "equal justice under the law" for all persons.

Moreover, the history of American immigration legislation, from the Alien and Sedition Laws at the founding to the most recent statutes, establish a legacy as well as a contemporary framework for governing the ethical, racial, and cultural populations in America. This legal framework continues to mirror the political forces that impose their influence on the definition of citizenship and the very institution and constitution of ethnic identity and ethnic groups in America.

The legacies of African slavery, racial segregation, and ethnic discrimination established by the American constitutional founding and subsequent American legal doctrine developed by the courts are traced in the following abbreviated U.S. Supreme Court opinions.

In the first opinion, *Dred Scott v. Sandford* (1856), the Supreme Court addressed the constitutional status of an African held in bondage who had been moved to a state that prohibited slavery. U.S. Supreme Court chief justice Roger B. Taney attempted to resolve the increasingly divisive issue of slavery by declaring that the "Negro African race"—whether free or slave—was "not intended to be included under the word 'citizens' in the Constitution, and can therefore claim none of the rights and privileges that instrument provides for and secures to citizens of the United States." Contrary to Taney's intentions, however, *Dred Scott* further fractured the nation, ensuring that only the Civil War would resolve the slavery issue.

In the second opinion, *Plessy v. Ferguson* (1896), the Supreme Court upheld the constitutionality of "Jim Crow" laws that segregated public facilities on the basis of an individual's racial ancestry. The Court reasoned that this "separate but equal" segregation did not violate any rights guaranteed by the U.S. Constitution, nor did it stamp "the colored race with a badge of inferiority." Instead, the Court argued that if "this be so, it is not by reason of anything found in the act but solely because the colored race chooses to put that construction upon it." In contrast, Justice John M. Harlan's vigorous dissent from the Court's *Plessy* opinion—also included—contends that "Our Constitution is color-blind, and neither knows nor tolerates classes among citizens."

In the article "Freedom of Religious Expression" (*Shaare Tefila Congregation v. Cobb* and *Saint Francis College v. Al-Khazraji* [1987]), the Supreme Court relied on the intention and legislation debate of Congress that more than a century ago (1866) passed civil rights legislation that protected citizens from discrimination based on racial/ethnic categories. This long ignored and neglected law, and its inclusion in these cases, exposes the variety of racialistic thinking rooted in America's Anglo-Saxon tradition; however, the periodic action of Congress and the rulings of the Supreme Court have supported the rights of persons regardless of their racial/ethnic affiliation.

In *Brown et al. v. Board of Education of Topeka* (1954), the Supreme Court began the ambitious project of dismantling state-supported racial segregation. In *Brown*, a unanimous Court overturned *Plessy v. Ferguson*, arguing that "in the field of public education the doctrine of 'separate but equal' has no place," for "separate educational facilities are inherently unequal."

In *University of California Regents v. Bakke* (1977), the Supreme Court addressed the question of whether a special admissions program to the medical school at the University of California at Davis that guaranteed places for certain ethnic minority groups violated the constitutional

rights of better-qualified, nonminority applicants. In *Bakke*, a splintered Supreme Court upheld a lower court order to admit an applicant who had been denied admission on the basis of his race. The separate opinions of two justices, Lewis F. Powell and Thurgood Marshall, are both included; each presents distinct arguments to the complex issues raised by the case.

Looking Ahead: Challenge Questions

Is the U.S. Constitution color-blind, as Justice Harlan argued in his dissent in *Plessy v. Ferguson*?

Should the constitutional rights and privileges of American citizens be contingent upon racial or ethnic ancestry?

What constitutes an ethnic minority? If laws have shaped a society's image and practice of an ethnic minority, can changes in the law yield changes in ethnic relations?

What role has the Supreme Court played in ending the legacies of slavery, segregation, and discrimination?

What strains are placed on the credibility of a legal system when universal aspirations such as "liberty and justice for all" are proclaimed as its purpose and goal?

Which ethnic minorities are protected under the law? Which are not, and why not?

What criteria for special ethnic claims are warranted and sustainable for the protection of liberty and the defense of equal protection?

Do the Court, Congress, and the executive branch of the national government have an ongoing role in this pursuit? What about state and local governments and their responsibility to enforce the law of the land?

DRED SCOTT V. SANDFORD

December Term 1856.

Mr. Chief Justice Taney delivered the opinion of the court.

This case has been twice argued. After the argument at the last term, differences of opinion were found to exist among the members of the court; and as the questions in controversy are of the highest importance, and the court was at that time much pressed by the ordinary business of the term, it was deemed advisable to continue the case, and direct a re-argument on some of the points, in order that we might have an opportunity of giving to the whole subject a more deliberate consideration. It has accordingly been again argued by counsel, and considered by the court; and I now proceed to deliver its opinion.

There are two leading questions presented by the record:

1. Had the Circuit Court of the United States jurisdiction to hear and determine the case between these parties? And

2. If it had jurisdiction, is the judgment it has given erroneous or not?

The plaintiff in error, who was also the plaintiff in the court below, was, with his wife and children, held as slaves by the defendant, in the State of Missouri; and he brought this action in the Circuit Court of the United States for that district, to assert the title of himself and his family to freedom.

The declaration is in the form usually adopted in that State to try questions of this description, and contains the averment necessary to give the court jurisdiction; that he and the defendant are citizens of different States; that is, that he is a citizen of Missouri, and the defendant a citizen of New York.

The defendant pleaded in abatement to the jurisdiction of the court, that the plaintiff was not a citizen of the State of Missouri, as alleged in his declaration, being a negro of African descent, whose ancestors were of pure African blood, and who were brought into this country and sold as slaves.

To this plea the plaintiff demurred, and the defendant joined in demurrer. The court overruled the plea, and gave judgment that the defendant should answer over. And he thereupon put in sundry pleas in bar, upon which issues were joined; and at the trial the verdict and judgment were in his favor. Whereupon the plaintiff brought this writ of error.

Before we speak of the pleas in bar, it will be proper to dispose of the questions which have arisen on the plea in abatement.

That plea denies the right of the plaintiff to sue in a court of the United States, for the reasons therein stated.

If the question raised by it is legally before us, and the court should be of opinion that the facts stated in it disqualify the plaintiff from becoming a citizen, in the sense in which that word is used in the Constitution of the United States, then the judgment of the Circuit Court is erroneous, and must be reversed.

It is suggested, however, that this plea is not before us; and that as the judgment in the court below on this plea was in favor of the plaintiff, he does not seek to reverse it, or bring it before the court for revision by his writ of error; and also that the defendant waived this defence by pleading over, and thereby admitted the jurisdiction of the court.

But, in making this objection, we think the peculiar and limited jurisdiction of courts of the United States has not been adverted to. This peculiar and limited jurisdiction has made it necessary, in these courts, to adopt different rules and principles of pleading, so far as jurisdiction is concerned, from those which regulate courts of common law in England, and in the different States of the Union which have adopted the common-law rules.

In these last-mentioned courts, where their character and rank are analogous to that of a Circuit Court of the United States; in other words, where they are what the law terms courts of general jurisdiction; they are presumed to have jurisdiction, unless the contrary appears. No averment in the pleadings of the plaintiff is necessary, in order to give jurisdiction. If the defendant objects to it, he must plead it specially, and unless the

From *U.S. Reports*, 1856. Opinion of the Supreme Court, December Term, 1856.

fact on which he relies is found to be true by a jury, or admitted to be true by the plaintiff, the jurisdiction cannot be disputed in an appellate court.

Now, it is not necessary to inquire whether in courts of that description a party who pleads over in bar, when a plea to the jurisdiction has been ruled against him, does or does not waive his plea; nor whether upon a judgment in his favor on the pleas in bar, and a writ of error brought by the plaintiff, the question upon the plea in abatement would be open for revision in the appellate court. Cases that may have been decided in such courts, or rules that may have been laid down by common-law pleaders, can have no influence in the decision in this court. Because, under the Constitution and laws of the United States, the rules which govern the pleadings in its courts, in questions of jurisdiction, stand on different principles and are regulated by different laws.

This difference arises, as we have said, from the peculiar character of the Government of the United States. For although it is sovereign and supreme in its appropriate sphere of action, yet it does not possess all the powers which usually belong to the sovereignty of a nation. Certain specified powers, enumerated in the Constitution, have been conferred upon it; and neither the legislative, executive, nor judicial departments of the Government can lawfully exercise any authority beyond the limits marked out by the Constitution. And in regulating the judicial department, the cases in which the courts of the United States shall have jurisdiction are particularly and specifically enumerated and defined; and they are not authorized to take cognizance of any case which does not come within the description therein specified. Hence, when a plaintiff sues in a court of the United States, it is necessary that he should show, in his pleading, that the suit he brings is within the jurisdiction of the court, and that he is entitled to sue there. And if he omits to do this, and should, by any oversight of the Circuit Court, obtain a judgment in his favor, the judgment would be reversed in the appellate court for want of jurisdiction in the court below. The jurisdiction would not be presumed, as in the case of a common-law English or State court, unless the contrary appeared. But the record, when it comes before the appellate court, must show, affirmatively, that the inferior court had authority, under the Constitution, to hear and determine the case. And if the plaintiff claims a right to sue in a Circuit Court of the United States, under that provision of the Constitution which gives jurisdiction in controversies between citizens of different States, he must distinctly aver in his pleading that they are citizens of different States; and he cannot maintain his suit without showing that fact in the pleadings.

This point was decided in the case of *Bingham v. Cabot*, (in 3 Dall., 382,) and ever since adhered to by the court. And in *Jackson v. Ashton*, (8 Pet., 148,) it was held that the objection to which it was open could not be waived by the opposite party, because consent of parties could not give jurisdiction.

It is needless to accumulate cases on this subject. Those already referred to, and the cases of *Capron v. Van Noorden*, (in 2 Cr., 126) and *Montalet v. Murray*, (4 Cr., 46,) are sufficient to show the rule of which we have spoken. The case of *Capron v. Van Noorden* strikingly illustrates the difference between a common-law court and a court of the United States.

If, however, the fact of citizenship is averred in the declaration, and the defendant does not deny it, and put it in issue by plea in abatement, he cannot offer evidence at the trial to disprove it, and consequently cannot avail himself of the objection in the appellate court, unless the defect should be apparent in some other part of the record. For if there is no plea in abatement, and the want of jurisdiction does not appear in any other part of the transcript brought up by the writ of error, the undisputed averment of citizenship in the declaration must be taken in this court to be true. In this case, the citizenship is averred, but it is denied by the defendant in the manner required by the rules of pleading, and the fact upon which the denial is based is admitted by the demurrer. And, if the plea and demurrer, and judgment of the court below upon it, are before us upon this record, the question to be decided is, whether the facts stated in the plea are sufficient to show that the plaintiff is not entitled to sue as a citizen in a court of the United States. . . .

We think they are before us. The plea in abatement and the judgment of the court upon it, are a part of the judicial proceedings in the Circuit Court, and are there recorded as such; and a writ of error always brings up to the superior court the whole record of the proceedings in the court below. And in the case of the *United States v. Smith*, (11 Wheat., 172) this court said, that the case being brought up by writ of error, the whole record was under the consideration of this court. And this being the case in the present instance, the plea in abatement is necessarily under consideration; and it becomes, therefore, our duty to decide whether the facts stated in the plea are or are not sufficient to show that the plaintiff is not entitled to sue as a citizen in a court of the United States.

This is certainly a very serious question, and one that now for the first time has been brought for decision before this court. But it is brought here by those who have a right to bring it, and it is our duty to meet it and decide it.

The question is simply this: Can a negro, whose ancestors were imported into this country, and sold as slaves, become a member of the political community formed and brought into existence by the Constitution of the United States, and as such become entitled to all the rights, and privileges, and immunities, guarantied by that instrument to the citizen? One of which rights is the privilege of suing in a court of the United States in the cases specified in the Constitution.

It will be observed, that the plea applies to that class of persons only whose ancestors were negroes of the African race, and imported into this country, and sold and held as slaves. The only matter in issue before the court, therefore, is, whether the descendants of such slaves, when they shall be emancipated, or who are born of parents who had become free before their birth, are citizens of a State, in the sense in which the word citizen is used in the Constitution of the United States. And this being the only matter in dispute on the pleadings, the court must be understood as speaking in this opinion of that class only, that is, of those persons who are the descendants of Africans who were imported into this country, and sold as slaves.

The situation of this population was altogether unlike that of the Indian race. The latter, it is true, formed no part of the colonial communities, and never amalgamated with them in social connections or in government. But although they were uncivilized, they were yet a free and independent people, associated together in nations or tribes, and governed by their own laws. Many of these political communities were situated in territories to which the white race claimed the ultimate right of dominion. But that claim was acknowledged to be subject to the right of the Indians to occupy it as long as they thought proper, and neither the English nor colonial Governments claimed or exercised any dominion over the tribe or nation by whom it was occupied, nor claimed the right to the possession of the territory, until the tribe or nation consented to cede it. These Indian Governments were regarded and treated as foreign Governments, as must so as if an ocean had separated the red man from the white; and their freedom has constantly been acknowledged, from the time of the first emigration to the English colonies to the present day, by the different Governments which succeeded each other. Treaties have been negotiated with them, and their alliance sought for in war; and the people who compose these Indian political communities have always been treated as foreigners not living under our Government. It is true that the course of events has brought the Indian tribes within the limits of the United States under subjection to the white race; and it has been found necessary, for their sake as well as our own, to regard them as in a state of pupilage, and to legislate to a certain extent over them and the territory they occupy. But they may, without doubt, like the subjects of any other foreign Government, be naturalized by the authority of Congress, and become citizens of a State, and of the United States; and if an individual should leave his nation or tribe, and take up his abode among the white population, he would be entitled to all the rights and privileges which would belong to an emigrant from any other foreign people.

We proceed to examine the case as presented by the pleadings.

The words "people of the United States" and "citizens" are synonymous terms, and mean the same thing. They both describe the political body who, according to our republican institutions, form the sovereignty, and who hold the power and conduct the Government through their representatives. They are what we familiarly call the "sovereign people," and every citizen is one of this people, and a constituent member of this sovereignty. The question before us is, whether the class of persons described in the plea in abatement compose a portion of this people, and are constituent members of this sovereignty? We think they are not, and that they are not included, and were not intended to be included, under the word "citizens" in the Constitution, and can therefore claim none of the rights and privileges which that instrument provides for and secures to citizens of the United States. On the contrary, they were at that time considered as a subordinate and inferior class of beings, who had been subjugated by the dominant race, and, whether emancipated or not, yet remained subject to their authority, and had no rights or privileges but such as those who held the power and the Government might choose to grant them.

It is not the province of the court to decide upon the justice or injustice, the policy or impolicy, of these laws. The decision of that question belonged to the political or law-making power; to those who formed the sovereignty and framed the Constitution. The duty of the court is, to interpret the instrument they have framed, with the best lights we can obtain on the subject, and to administer it as we find it, according to its true intent and meaning when it was adopted.

In discussing this question, we must not confound the rights of citizenship which a State may confer within its own limits, and the rights of citizenship as a member of the Union. It does not by any means follow, because he has all the rights and privileges of a citizen of a State, that he must be a citizen of the United States. He may have all of the rights and privileges of the citizen of a State, and yet not be entitled to the rights and privileges of a citizen in any other State. For, previous to the adoption of the Constitution of the United States, every State had the undoubted right to confer on whomsoever it pleased the character of citizen, and to endow him with all its rights. But this character of course was confined to the boundaries of the State, and gave him no rights or privileges in other States beyond those secured to him by the laws of nations and the comity of States. Nor have the several States surrendered the power of conferring these rights and privileges by adopting the Constitution of the United States. Each State may still confer them upon an alien, or any one it thinks proper, or upon any class or description of persons; yet he would not be a citizen in the sense in which that word is used in the Constitution of the United States, nor entitled to sue as such in one of its courts, nor to the privileges and immunities of a citizen in the other States. The rights which he would acquire would be restricted to the State which gave them. The Constitution has conferred on Congress the right to establish a uniform rule of naturalization, and this right is evidently exclusive, and has always been held by this court to be so. Consequently, no State, since the adoption of the Constitution, can by naturalizing an alien invest him with the rights and privileges secured to a citizen of a State under the Federal Government, although, so far as the State alone was concerned, he would undoubtedly be entitled to the rights of a citizen, and clothed with all the rights and immunities which the Constitution and laws of the State attached to that character.

It is very clear, therefore, that no State can, by any act or law of its own, passed since the adoption of the Constitution, introduce a new member into the political community created by the Constitution of the United States. It cannot make him a member of this community by making him a member of its own. And for the same reason it cannot introduce any person, or description of persons, who were not intended to be embraced in this new political family, which the Constitution brought into existence, but were intended to be excluded from it.

The question then arises, whether the provisions of the Constitution, in relation to the personal rights and privileges to which the citizen of a State should be entitled, embraced the negro African race, at that time in this country, or who might afterwards be imported, who had then or should afterwards be made free in any State; and to put it in the power of a single State to make him a citizen of the United States, and endue him with the full rights of citizenship in every other State without their consent? Does the Constitution of the United States act upon him whenever he shall be made free under the laws of a State, and raised there to the rank of a citizen, and immediately clothe him with all the privileges of a citizen in every other State, and in its own courts?

The court think the affirmative of these propositions cannot be maintained. And if it cannot, the plaintiff in error could not be a citizen of the State of Missouri,

within the meaning of the Constitution of the United States, and, consequently, was not entitled to sue in its courts.

It is true, every person, and every class and description of persons, who were at the time of the adoption of the Constitution recognised as citizens in the several States, became also citizens of this new political body; but none other; it was formed by them, and for them and their posterity, but for no one else. And the personal rights and privileges guarantied to citizens of this new sovereignty were intended to embrace those only who were then members of the several State communities, or who should afterwards by birthright or otherwise become members, according to the provisions of the Constitution and the principles on which it was founded. It was the union of those who were at that time members of distinct and separate political communities into one political family, whose power, for certain specified purposes, was to extend over the whole territory of the United States. And it gave to each citizen rights and privileges outside of his State which he did not before possess, and placed him in every other State upon a perfect equality with its own citizens as to rights of person and rights of property; it made him a citizen of the United States.

It becomes necessary, therefore, to determine who were citizens of the several States when the Constitution was adopted. And in order to do this, we must recur to the Governments and institutions of the thirteen colonies, when they separated from Great Britain and formed new sovereignties, and took their places in the family of independent nations. We must inquire who, at that time, were recognised as the people or citizens of a State, whose rights and liberties had been outraged by the English Government; and who declared their independence, and assumed the powers of Government to defend their rights by force of arms.

In the opinion of the court, the legislation and histories of the times, and the language used in the Declaration of Independence, show, that neither the class of persons who had been imported as slaves, nor their descendants, whether they had become free or not, were then acknowledged as a part of the people, nor intended to be included in the general words used in that memorable instrument. . . .

PLESSY v. FERGUSON

May 18, 1896
163 U.S. 537 (1896)

MR. JUSTICE BROWN, after stating the case, delivered the opinion of the court.

This case turns upon the constitutionality of an act of the General Assembly of the State of Louisiana, passed in 1890, providing for separate railway carriages for the white and colored races. Acts 1890, No. 111, p. 152.

The first section of the statute enacts "that all railway companies carrying passengers in their coaches in this State, shall provide equal but separate accommodations for the white, and colored races, by providing two or more passenger coaches for each passenger train, or by dividing the passenger coaches by a partition so as to secure separate accommodations: *Provided*, That this section shall not be construed to apply to street railroads. No person or persons, shall be admitted to occupy seats in coaches, other than, the ones, assigned, to them on account of the race they belong to."

By the second section it was enacted "that the officers of such passenger trains shall have power and are hereby required to assign each passenger to the coach or compartment used for the race to which such passenger belongs; any passenger insisting on going into a coach or compartment to which by race he does not belong, shall be liable to a fine of twenty-five dollars, or in lieu thereof to imprisonment for a period of not more than twenty days in the parish prison, and any officer of any railroad insisting on assigning a passenger to a coach or compartment other than the one set aside for the race to which said passenger belongs, shall be liable to a fine of twenty-five dollars, or in lieu thereof to imprisonment for a period of not more than twenty days in the parish prison; and should any passenger refuse to occupy the coach or compartment to which he or she is assigned by the officer of such railway, said officer shall have power to refuse to carry such passenger on his train, and for such refusal neither he nor the railway company which he represents shall be liable for damages in any of the courts of this State."

The third section provides penalties for the refusal or neglect of the officers, directors, conductors and employés of railway companies to comply with the act, with a proviso that "nothing in this act shall be construed as applying to nurses attending children of the other race." The fourth section is immaterial.

The information filed in the criminal District Court charged in substance that Plessy, being a passenger between two stations within the State of Louisiana, was assigned by officers of the company to the coach used for the race to which he belonged, but he insisted upon going into a coach used by the race to which he did not belong. Neither in the information nor plea was his particular race or color averred.

The petition for the writ of prohibition averred that petitioner was seven eighths Caucasian and one eighth African blood; that the mixture of colored blood was not discernible in him, and that he was entitled to every right, privilege and immunity secured to citizens of the United States of the white race; and that, upon such theory, he took possession of a vacant seat in a coach where passengers of the white race were accommodated, and was ordered by the conductor to vacate said coach and take a seat in another assigned to persons of the colored race, and having refused to comply with such demand he was forcibly ejected with the aid of a police officer, and imprisoned in the parish jail to answer a charge of having violated the above act.

The constitutionality of this act is attacked upon the ground that it conflicts both with the Thirteenth Amendment of the Constitution, abolishing slavery, and the Fourteenth Amendment, which prohibits certain restrictive legislation on the part of the States.

1. That it does not conflict with the Thirteenth Amendment, which abolished slavery and involuntary servitude, except as a punishment for crime, is too clear for argument. Slavery implies involuntary servitude—a state of bondage; the ownership of mankind as a chattel, or at least the control of the labor and services of one man for the benefit of another, and the absence of a legal right to the disposal of his own

From *U.S. Reports*, 1896. Opinion of the Supreme Court, May 18, 1896.

person, property and services. This amendment was said in the *Slaughter-house cases*, 16 Wall. 35, to have been intended primarily to abolish slavery, as it had been previously known in this country, and that it equally forbade Mexican peonage or the Chinese coolie trade, when they amounted to slavery or involuntary servitude, and that the use of the word "servitude" was intended to prohibit the use of all forms of involuntary slavery, of whatever class or name. It was intimated, however, in that case that this amendment was regarded by the statesmen of that day as insufficient to protect the colored race from certain laws which had been enacted in the Southern States, imposing upon the colored race onerous disabilities and burdens, and curtailing their rights in the pursuit of life, liberty and property to such an extent that their freedom was of little value; and that the Fourteenth Amendment was devised to meet this exigency.

So, too, in the *Civil Rights cases*, 109 U.S. 3, 24, it was said that the act of a mere individual, the owner of an inn, a public conveyance or place of amusement, refusing accommodations to colored people, cannot be justly regarded as imposing any badge of slavery or servitude upon the applicant, but only as involving an ordinary civil injury, properly cognizable by the laws of the State, and presumably subject to redress by those laws until the contrary appears. "It would be running the slavery argument into the ground," said Mr. Justice Bradley, "to make it apply to every act of discrimination which a person may see fit to make as to the guests he will entertain, or as to the people he will take into his coach or cab or car, or admit to his concert or theatre, or deal with in other matters of intercourse or business."

A statute which implies merely a legal distinction between the white and colored races—a distinction which is founded in the color of the two races, and which must always exist so long as white men are distinguished from the other race by color—has no tendency to destroy the legal equality of the two races, or reestablish a state of involuntary servitude. Indeed, we do not understand that the Thirteenth Amendment is strenuously relied upon by the plaintiff in error in this connection.

2. By the Fourteenth Amendment, all persons born or naturalized in the United States, and subject to the jurisdiction thereof, are made citizens of the United States and of the State wherein they reside; and the States are forbidden from making or enforcing any law which shall abridge the privileges or immunities of citizens of the United States, or shall deprive any person of life, liberty or property without due process of law, or deny to any person within their jurisdiction the equal protection of the laws.

The proper construction of this amendment was first called to the attention of this court in the *Slaughter-house cases*, 16 Wall. 36, which involved, however, not a question of race, but one of exclusive privileges. The case did not call for any expression of opinion as to the exact rights it was intended to secure to the colored race, but it was said generally that its main purpose was to establish the citizenship of the negro; to give definitions of citizenship of the United States and of the States, and to protect from the hostile legislation of the States the privileges and immunities of citizens of the United States, as distinguished from those of citizens of the States.

The object of the amendment was undoubtedly to enforce the absolute equality of the two races before the law, but in the nature of things it could not have been intended to abolish distinctions based upon color, or to enforce social, as distinguished from political, equality, or a commingling of the two races upon terms unsatisfactory to either. Laws permitting, and even requiring, their separation in places where they are liable to be brought into contact do not necessarily imply the inferiority of either race to the other, and have been generally, if not universally, recognized as within the competency of the state legislatures in the exercise of their police power. The most common instance of this is connected with the establishment of separate schools for white and colored children, which has been held to be a valid exercise of the legislative power even by courts of States where the political rights of the colored race have been longest and most earnestly enforced.

One of the earliest of these cases is that of *Roberts v. City of Boston*, 5 Cush. 198, in which the Supreme Judicial Court of Massachusetts held that the general school committee of Boston had power to make provision for the instruction of colored children in separate schools established exclusively for them, and to prohibit their attendance upon the other schools. . . .

Similar laws have been enacted by Congress under its general power of legislation over the District of Columbia, Rev. Stat. D.C. §§ 281, 282, 283, 310, 319, as well as by the legislatures of many of the States, and have been generally, if not uniformly, sustained by the courts. *State v. McCann*, 21 Ohio St. 198; *Lehew v. Brummell*, 15 S. W. Rep. 765; *Ward v. Flood*, 48 California, 36; *Bertonneau v. School Directors*, 3 Woods, 177; *People v. Gallagher*, 93 N.Y. 438; *Cory v. Carter*, 48 Indiana, 327; *Dawson v. Lee*, 83 Kentucky, 49.

Laws forbidding the intermarriage of the two races may be said in a technical sense to interfere with the freedom of contract, and yet have been universally recognized as within the police power of the State. *State v. Gibson*, 36 Indiana, 389.

The distinction between laws interfering with the political equality of the negro and those requiring the separation of the two races in schools, theatres and railway carriages has been frequently drawn by this court. Thus in *Strauder v. West Virginia*, 100 U.S. 303, it was held that a law of West Virginia limiting to white male persons, 21 years of age and citizens of the State, the right to sit upon juries, was a discrimination which implied a legal inferiority in civil society, which lessened the security of the right of the colored race, and was a step toward reducing them to a condition of servility. Indeed, the right of a colored man that, in the selection of jurors to pass upon his life, liberty and property, there shall be no exclusion of his race, and no discrimination against them because of color, has been asserted in a number of cases. *Virginia v. Rives*, 100 U.S. 313; *Neal v. Delaware*, 103 U.S. 370; *Bush v. Kentucky*, 107 U.S. 110; *Gibson v. Mississippi*, 162 U.S. 565. So, where the laws of a particular locality or the charter of a particular railway corporation has provided that no person shall be excluded from the cars on account of color, we have held that this meant that persons of color should travel in the same car as white ones, and that the enactment was not satisfied by the company's providing cars assigned exclusively to people of color, though they were as good as those which they assigned exclusively to white persons. *Railroad Company v. Brown*, 17 Wall. 445.

Upon the other hand, where a statute of Louisiana required those engaged in the transportation of passengers among the States to give to all persons travelling within that State, upon vessels employed in that business, equal rights and privileges in all parts of the vessel, without distinction on account of race or color, and subjected to an action for damages the owner of such a vessel, who excluded colored passengers on account of their color from the cabin set aside by him for the use of whites, it was held to be so far as it applied to interstate commerce, unconstitutional and void. *Hall v. De Cuir*, 95 U.S. 485. The court in this case, however, expressly disclaimed that it had anything whatever to do with the statute as a regulation of internal commerce, or affecting anything else than commerce among the States.

In the *Civil Rights case*, 109 U.S. 3, it was held that an act of Congress, entitling all persons within the jurisdiction of the United States to the full and equal enjoyment of the accommodations, advantages, facilities and privileges of inns, public conveyances, on land or water, theatres and other places of public amusement, and made applicable to citizens of every race and color, regardless of any previous condition of servitude, was unconstitutional and void, upon the ground that the Fourteenth Amendment was prohibitory upon the States only, and the legislation authorized to be adopted by Congress for enforcing it was not direct legislation on matters respecting which the States were prohibited from making or enforcing certain laws, or doing certain acts, but was corrective legislation, such as might be necessary or proper for counteracting and redressing the effect of such laws or acts. In delivering the opinion of the court Mr. Justice Bradley observed that the Fourteenth Amendment

"does not invest Congress with power to legislate upon subjects that are within the domain of state legislation; but to provide modes of relief against state legislation, or state action, of the kind referred to. It does not authorize Congress to create a code of municipal law for the regulation of private rights; but to provide modes of redress against the operation of state laws, and the action of state officers, executive or judicial, when these are subversive of the fundamental rights specified in the amendment. Positive rights and privileges are undoubtedly secured by the Fourteenth Amendment; but they are secured by way of prohibition against state laws and state proceedings affecting those rights and privileges, and by power given to Congress to legislate for the purpose of carrying such prohibition into effect; and such legislation must necessarily be predicated upon such supposed state laws or state proceedings, and be directed to the correction of their operation and effect."

Much nearer, and, indeed, almost directly in point, is the case of the *Louisville, New Orleans & c. Railway v. Mississippi*, 133 U.S. 587, wherein the railway company was indicted for a violation of a statute of Mississippi, enacting that all railroads carrying passengers should provide equal, but separate, accommodations for the white and colored races, by providing two or more passenger cars for each passenger train, or by dividing the passenger cars by a partition, so as to secure separate accommodations. The case was presented in a different aspect from the one under consideration, inasmuch as it was an indictment against the railway company for failing to provide the separate accommodations, but the question considered was the constitutionality of the law. In that case, the Supreme Court of Mississippi, 66 Mississippi, 662, had held that the statute applied solely to commerce within the State, and, that being the construction of the state statute by its highest court, was accepted as conclusive. "If it be a matter," said the court, p. 591, "respecting commerce wholly within a State, and not interfering with commerce between the States, then, obviously, there is no violation of the commerce clause of the Federal Constitution. . . . No question arises under this section, as to the power of the State to separate in different compartments interstate passengers, or affect, in any manner, the privileges and rights of such passengers. All that we can consider is, whether the State has the power to require that railroad trains within her limits shall have separate accommodations for the two races; that affecting only commerce within the State is no invasion of the power given to Congress by the commerce clause."

A like course of reasoning applies to the case under consideration, since the Supreme Court of Louisiana in the case of the *State ex rel. Abbott v. Hicks, Judge, et al.*, 44 La. Ann. 770, held that the statute in question did not apply to interstate passengers, but was confined in its application to passengers travelling exclusively within the borders of the State. The case was decided largely upon the authority of *Railway Co. v. State*, 66 Mississippi, 662, and affirmed by this court in 133 U.S. 587. In the present case no question of interference with interstate commerce can possibly arise, since the East Louisiana Railway appears to have been purely a local line, with both its termini within the State of Louisiana. Similar statutes for the separation of the two races upon public conveyances were held to be constitutional in *West Chester &c. Railroad v. Miles*, 55 Penn. St. 209; *Day v. Owen*, 5 Michigan, 520; *Chicago &c. Railway v. Williams*, 55 Illinois, 185; *Chesapeake &c. Railroad v. Wells*, 85 Tennessee, 613; *Memphis &c. Railroad v. Benson*, 85 Tennessee, 627; *The Sue*, 22 Fed. Rep. 843; *Logwood v. Memphis &c. Railroad*, 23 Fed. Rep. 318; *McGuinn v. Forbes*, 37 Fed. Rep. 639; *People v. King*, 18 N.E. Rep. 245; *Houck v. South Pac. Railway*, 38 Fed. Rep. 226; *Heard v. Georgia Railroad Co.*, 3 Int. Com. Com'n, 111; *S.C.*, 1 Ibid. 428.

While we think the enforced separation of the races, as applied to the internal commerce of the State, neither abridges the privileges or immunities of the colored man, deprives him of his property without due process of law, nor denies him the equal protection of the laws, within the meaning of the Fourteenth Amendment, we are not prepared to say that the conductor, in assigning passengers to the coaches according to their race, does not act at his peril, or that the provision of the second section of the act, that denies to the passenger compensation in damages for a refusal to receive him into the coach in which he properly belongs, is a valid exercise of the legislative power. Indeed, we understand it to be conceded by the State's attorney, that such part of the act as exempts from liability the railway company and its officers is unconstitutional. The power to assign to a particular coach obviously implies the power to determine to which race the passenger belongs, as well as the power to determine who, under the laws of the particular State, is to be deemed a white, and who a colored person. This question, though indicated in the brief of the plaintiff in error, does not properly arise upon the record in this case, since the only issue made is as to the unconstitutionality of the act, so far as it requires the railway to provide separate accommodations, and the conductor to assign passengers according to their race.

It is claimed by the plaintiff in error that, in any mixed community, the reputation of belonging to the dominant race, in this instance the white race, is *property*, in the same sense that a right of action, or of inheritance, is property. Conceding this to be so, for the purposes of this case, we are unable to see how this statute deprives him of, or in any way affects his right to, such property. If he be a white man and assigned to a colored coach, he may have his action for damages against the company for being deprived of his so called

property. Upon the other hand, if he be a colored man and be so assigned, he has been deprived of no property, since his is not lawfully entitled to the reputation of being a white man.

In this connection, it is also suggested by the learned counsel for the plaintiff in error that the same argument that will justify the state legislature in requiring railways to provide separate accommodations for the two races will also authorize them to require separate cars to be provided for people whose hair is of a certain color, or who are aliens, or who belong to certain nationalities, or to enact laws requiring colored people to walk upon one side of the street, and white people upon the other, or requiring white men's houses to be painted white, and colored men's black, or their vehicles or business signs to be of different colors, upon the theory that one side of the street is as good as the other, or that a house or vehicle of one color is as good as one of another color. The reply to all this is that every exercise of the police power must be reasonable, and extend only to such laws as are enacted in good faith for the promotion for the public good, and not for the annoyance or oppression of a particular class. Thus in *Yick Wo v. Hopkins*, 118 U.S. 356, it was held by this court that a municipal ordinance of the city of San Francisco, to regulate the carrying on of public laundries within the limits of the municipality, violated the provisions of the Constitution of the United States, if it conferred upon the municipal authorities arbitrary power, at their own will, and without regard to discretion, in the legal sense of the term, to give or withhold consent as to persons or places, without regard to the competency of the persons applying, or the propriety of the places selected for the carrying on of the business. It was held to be a covert attempt on the part of the municipality to make an arbitrary and unjust discrimination against the Chinese race. While this was the case of a municipal ordinance, a like principle has been held to apply to acts of a state legislature passed in the exercise of the police power. *Railroad Company v. Husen*, 95 U.S. 465; *Louisville & nashville Railroad v. Kentucky*, 161 U.S. 677, and cases cited on p. 700; *Daggett v. Hudson*, 43 Ohio St. 548; *Capen v. Foster*, 12 Pick. 485; *State ex rel. Wood v. Baker*, 38 Wisconsin, 71; *Monroe v. Collins*, 17 Ohio St. 665; *Hulseman v. Rems*, 41 Penn. St. 396; *Orman v. Riley*, 15 California, 48.

So far, then, as a conflict with the Fourteenth Amendment is concerned, the case reduces itself to the question whether the statute of Louisiana is a reasonable regulation, and with respect to this there must necessarily be a large discretion on the part of the legislature. In determining the question of reasonableness it is at liberty to act with reference to the established usages, customs and traditions of the people, and with a view to the promotion of their comfort, and the preservation of the public peace and good order. Gauged by this standard, we cannot say that a law which authorizes or even requires the separation of the two races in public conveyances is unreasonable, or more obnoxious to the Fourteenth Amendment than the acts of Congress requiring separate schools for colored children in the District of Columbia, the constitutionality of which does not seem to have been questioned, or the corresponding acts of state legislatures.

We consider the underlying fallacy of the plaintiff's argument to consist in the assumption that the enforced separation of the two races stamps the colored race with a badge of inferiority. If this be so, it is not by reason of anything found in the act, but solely because the colored race chooses to put that construction upon it. The argument necessarily assumes that if, as has been more than once the case, and is not unlikely to be so again, the colored race should become the dominant power in the state legislature, and should enact a law in precisely similar terms, it would thereby relegate the white race to an inferior position. We imagine that the white race, at least, would not acquiesce in this assumption. The argument also assumes that social prejudices may be overcome by legislation, and that equal rights cannot be secured to the negro except by an enforced commingling of the two races. We cannot accept this proposition. If the two races are to meet upon terms of social equality, it must be the result of natural affinities, a mutual appreciation of each other's merits and a voluntary consent of individuals. As was said by the Court of Appeals of New York in *People v. Gallagher*, 93 N.Y. 438, 448, "this end can neither be accomplished nor promoted by laws which conflict with the general sentiment of the community upon whom they are designed to operate. When the government, therefore, has secured to each of its citizens equal rights before the law and opportunities for improvement and progress, it has accomplished the end for which it was organized and performed all of the functions respecting social advantages with which it is endowed." Legislation is powerless to eradicate racial instincts or to abolish distinctions based upon physical differences, and the attempt to do so can only result in accentuating the difficulties of the present situation. If the civil and political rights of both races be equal one cannot be inferior to the other civilly or politically. If one race be inferior to the other socially, the Constitution of the United States cannot put them upon the same plane.

It is true that the question of the proportion of colored blood necessary to constitute a colored person, as distinguished from a white person, is one upon which there is a difference of opinion in the different States, some holding that any visible admixture of black blood stamps the person as belonging to the colored race, (*State v. Chavers*, 5 Jones, [N.C.] 1, p. 11); others that it depends upon the preponderance of blood, (*Gray v. State*, 4 Ohio, 354; *Monroe v. Collins*, 17

Ohio St. 665); and still others that the predominance of white blood must only be in the proportion of three fourths. (*People v. Dean*, 14 Michigan, 406; *Jones v. Commonwealth*, 80 Virginia, 538.) But these are questions to be determined under the laws of each State and are not properly put in issue in this case. Under the allegations of his petition it may undoubtedly become a question of importance whether, under the laws of Louisiana, the petitioner belongs to the white or colored race.

The judgment of the court below is, therefore,

Affirmed.

MR. JUSTICE HARLAN dissenting.

By the Louisiana statute the validity of which is here involved, all railway companies (other than street-railroad companies) carrying passengers in that state are required to have separate but equal accommodations for white and colored persons, "by providing two more passenger coaches for each passenger train, or by dividing the passenger coaches by a partition so as to secure separate accommodations." Under this statute, no colored person is permitted to occupy a seat in a coach assigned to white persons; nor any white person to occupy a seat in a coach assigned to colored persons. The managers of the railroad are not allowed to exercise any discretion in the premises, but are required to assign each passenger to some coach or compartment set apart for the exclusive use of his race. If a passenger insists upon going into a coach or compartment not set apart for persons of his race, he is subject to be fined, or to be imprisoned in the parish jail. Penalties are prescribed for the refusal or neglect of the officers, directors, conductors, and employés of railroad companies to comply with the provisions of the act.

Only "nurses attending children of the other race" are excepted from the operation of the statute. No exception is made of colored attendants traveling with adults. A white man is not permitted to have his colored servant with him in the same coach, even if his condition of health requires the constant personal assistance of such servant. If a colored maid insists upon riding in the same coach with a white woman whom she has been employed to serve, and who may need her personal attention while traveling, she is subject to be fined or imprisoned for such an exhibition of zeal in the discharge of duty.

While there may be in Louisiana persons of different races who are not citizens of the United States, the words in the act "white and colored races" necessarily include all citizens of the United States of both races residing in that state. So that we have before us a state enactment that compels, under penalties, the separation of the two races in railroad passenger coaches, and makes it a crime for a citizen of either race to enter a coach that has been assigned to citizens of the other race.

Thus, the state regulates the use of a public highway by citizens of the United States solely upon the basis of race.

However apparent the injustice of such legislation may be, we have only to consider whether it is consistent with the constitution of the United States. . . .

In respect of civil rights, common to all citizens, the constitution of the United States does not, I think, permit any public authority to know the race of those entitled to be protected in the enjoyment of such rights. Every true man has pride of race, and under appropriate circumstances, when the rights of others, his equals before the law, are not to be affected, it is his privilege to express such pride and to take such action based upon it as to him seems proper. But I deny that any legislative body or judicial tribunal may have regard to the race of citizens when the civil rights of those citizens are involved. Indeed, such legislation as that here in question is inconsistent not only with that equality of rights which pertains to citizenship, national and state, but with the personal liberty enjoyed by every one within the United States. . . .

The white race deems itself to be the dominant race in this country. And so it is, in prestige, in achievements, in education, in wealth, and in power. So, I doubt not, it will continue to be for all time, if it remains true to its great heritage, and holds fast to the principles of constitutional liberty. But in view of the constitution, in the eye of the law, there is in this country no superior, dominant, ruling class of citizens. There is no caste here. Our constitution is color-blind, and neither knows nor tolerates classes among citizens. In respect of civil rights, all citizens are equal before the law. The humblest is the peer of the most powerful. The law regards man as man, and takes no account of his surroundings or of his color when his civil rights as guaranteed by the supreme law of the land are involved. It is therefore to be regretted that this high tribunal, the final expositor of the fundamental law of the land, has reached the conclusion that it is competent for a state to regulate the enjoyment by citizens of their civil rights solely upon the basis of race.

In my opinion, the judgment this day rendered will, in time, prove to be quite as pernicious as the decision made by this tribunal in the Dred Scott Case.

It was adjudged in that case that the descendants of Africans who were imported into this country, and sold as slaves, were not included nor intended to be included under the word "citizens" in the constitution, and could not claim any of the rights and privileges which that instrument provided for and secured to citizens of the United States; that, at the time of the adoption of the constitution, they were "considered as a subordinate and inferior class of beings, who had been subjugated by the dominant race, and, whether emancipated or not, yet remained subject to their authority, and had no rights or privileges but such as those who held the power and the government might choose to grant them" 17 How. 393, 404. The recent amendments of the constitution, it was supposed, had eradicated these principles from our institutions. But it seems that we have yet, in some of the states, a dominant race,—a superior class of citizens,—which assumes to regulate the enjoyment of civil rights, common to all citizens, upon the basis of race. The present decision, it may well be apprehended, will not only stimulate aggressions, more or less brutal and irritating, upon the admitted rights of colored citizens, but will encourage the belief that it is possible, by means of state enactments, to defeat the beneficent purposes which the people of the United States had in view when they adopted the recent amendments of the constitution, by one of which the blacks of this country were made citizens of the United States and of the states in which they respectively reside, and whose privileges and immunities, as citizens, the states are forbidden to abridge. Sixty millions of whites are in no danger from the presence here of eight millions of blacks. The destinies of the two races, in this country, are indissolubly linked together, and the interests of both require that the common government of all shall not permit the seeds of race hate to be planted under the sanction of law. What can more certainly arouse race hate, what more certainly create and perpetuate a feeling of distrust between these races, than state enactments which, in fact, proceed on the ground that colored citizens are so inferior and degraded that they cannot be allowed to sit in public coaches occupied by white citizens? That, as all will admit, is the real meaning of such legislation as was enacted in Louisiana.

The sure guaranty of the peace and security of each race is the clear, distinct, unconditional recognition by our governments, national and state, of every right that inheres in civil freedom, and of the equality before the law of all citizens of the United States, without regard to race. State enactments regulating the enjoyment of civil rights upon the basis of race, and cunningly devised to defeat legitimate results of the war, under the pretense of recognizing equality of rights, can have no other result than to render permanent peace impossible, and to keep alive a conflict of races, the continuance of which must do harm to all concerned. This question is not met by the suggestion that social equality cannot exist between the white and black races in this country. That argument, if it can be properly regarded as one, is scarcely worthy of consideration; for social equality no more exists between two races when traveling in a passenger coach or a public highway than when members of the same races sit by each other in a street car or in the jury box, or stand or sit with each other in a political assembly, or when they use in common the streets of a city or town, or when they are in the same room for the purpose of having their names placed on the registry of voters, or when they approach the ballot box in order to exercise the high privilege of voting. . . .

The arbitrary separation of citizens, on the basis of race, while they are on a public highway, is a badge of servitude wholly inconsistent with the civil freedom and the equality before the law established by the constitution. It cannot be justified upon any legal grounds.

If evils will result from the commingling of the two races upon public highways established for the benefit of all, they will be infinitely less than those that will surely come from state legislation regulating the enjoyment of civil rights upon the basis of race. We boast of the freedom enjoyed by our people above all other peoples. But it is difficult to reconcile that boast with a state of the law which, practically, puts the brand of servitude and degradation upon a large class of our fellow citizens,—our equals before the law. The thin disguise of "equal" accommodations for passengers in railroad coaches will not mislead any one, nor atone for the wrong this day done. . . .

I am of opinion that the statute of Louisiana is inconsistent with the personal liberty of citizens, white and black, in that state, and hostile to both the spirit and letter of the constitution of the United States. If laws of like character should be enacted in the several states of the Union, the effect would be in the highest degree mischievous. Slavery, as an institution tolerated by law, would, it is true, have disappeared from our country; but there would remain a power in the states, by sinister legislation, to interfere with the full enjoyment of the blessings of freedom, to regulate civil rights, common to all citizens, upon the basis of race, and to place in a condition of legal inferiority a large body of American citizens, now constituting a part of the political community, called the "People of the United States," for whom, and by whom through representatives, our government is administered. Such a system is inconsistent with the guaranty given by the constitution to each state of a republican form of government, and may be stricken down by congressional action, or by the courts in the discharge of their solemn duty to maintain the supreme law of the land, anything in the constitution or laws of any state to the contrary notwithstanding.

For the reason stated, I am constrained to withhold my assent from the opinion and judgment of the majority.

BROWN et al.

v.

BOARD OF EDUCATION

OF TOPEKA et al.

347 U.S. 483 (1954)

MR. CHIEF JUSTICE WARREN delivered the opinion of the Court.

These cases come to us from the States of Kansas, South Carolina, Virginia, and Delaware. They are premised on different facts and different local conditions, but a common legal question justifies their consideration together in this consolidated opinion.[1]

In each of the cases, minors of the Negro race, through their legal representatives, seek the aid of the courts in obtaining admission to the public schools of their community on a nonsegregated basis. In each instance, they had been denied admission to schools attended by white children under laws requiring or permitting segregation according to race. This segregation was alleged to deprive the plaintiffs of the equal protection of the laws under the Fourteenth Amendment. In each of the cases other than the Delaware case, a three-judge federal district court denied relief to the plaintiffs on the so-called "separate but equal" doctrine announced by this Court in *Plessy v. Ferguson,* 163 U.S. 537. Under that doctrine, equality of treatment is accorded when the races are provided substantially equal facilities, even though these facilities be separate. In the Delaware case, the Supreme Court of Delaware adhered to that doctrine, but ordered that the plaintiffs be admitted to the white schools because of their superiority to the Negro schools.

The plaintiffs contend that segregated public schools are not "equal" and cannot be made "equal," and that hence they are deprived of the equal protection of the laws. Because of the obvious importance of the question presented, the Court took jurisdiction.[2] Argument was heard in the 1952 Term, and reargument was heard this Term on certain questions propounded by the Court.[3]

Reargument was largely devoted to the circumstances surrounding the adoption of the Fourteenth Amendment in 1868. It covered exhaustively consideration of the Amendment in Congress, ratification by the states, then existing practices in racial segregation, and the views of proponents and opponents of the Amendment. This discussion and our own investigation convince us that, although these sources cast some light, it is not enough to resolve the problem with which we are faced. At best, they are inconclusive. The most avid proponents of the post–War Amendments undoubtedly intended them to remove all legal distinctions among "all persons born or naturalized in the United States." Their opponents, just as certainly, were antagonistic to both the letter and the spirit of the Amendments and wished them to have the most limited effect. What others in Congress and the state legislatures had in mind cannot be determined with an degree of certainty.

An additional reason for the inconclusive nature of the Amendment's history, with respect to segregated schools, is the status of public education at that time.[4] In the South, the movement toward free common schools, supported by general taxation, had not yet taken hold. Education of white children was largely in the hands of private groups. Education of Negroes was almost nonexistent, and practically all of the race were illiterate. In fact, any education of Negroes was forbidden by law in some states. Today, in contrast, many Negroes have achieved outstanding success in the arts and sciences as well as in the business and professional world. It is true that public school education at the time of the Amendment had advanced further in the North, but the effect of the Amendment on northern States was generally ignored in the congressional debates. Even in the North, the conditions of public education did not approximate those existing today. The curriculum was usually rudimentary; ungraded schools were common in rural areas; the school term

From *U.S. Reports,* 1954. Opinion of the Supreme Court, 1954.

17

was but three months a year in many states; and compulsory school attendance was virtually unknown. As a consequence, it is not surprising that there should be so little in the history of the Fourteenth Amendment relating to its intended effect on public education.

In the first cases in this Court construing the Fourteenth Amendment, decided shortly after its adoption, the Court interpreted it as proscribing all state-imposed discriminations against the Negro race.[5] The doctrine of "separate but equal" did not make its appearance in this Court until 1896 in the case of *Plessy v. Ferguson, supra,* involving not education but transportation.[6] American courts have since labored with the doctrine for over half a century. In this Court, there have been six cases involving the "separate but equal" doctrine in the field of public education.[7] In *Cumming v. County Board of Education,* 175 U.S. 528, and *Gong Lum v. Rice,* 275 U.S. 78, the validity of the doctrine itself was not challenged.[8] In more recent cases, all on the graduate school level, inequality was found in that specific benefits enjoyed by white students were denied to Negro students of the same educational qualifications. *Missouri ex rel. Gaines v. Canada,* 305 U.S. 337; *Sipuel v. Oklahoma,* 332 U.S. 631; *Sweatt v. Painter,* 339 U.S. 629; *McLaurin v. Oklahoma State Regents,* 339 U.S. 637. In none of these cases was it necessary to reexamine the doctrine to grant relief to the Negro plaintiff. And in *Sweatt v. Painter, supra,* the Court expressly reserved decision on the question whether *Plessy v. Ferguson* should be held inapplicable to public education.

In the instant cases, that question is directly presented. Here, unlike *Sweatt v. Painter,* there are findings below that the Negro and white schools involved have been equalized, or are being equalized, with respect to buildings, curricula, qualifications and salaries of teachers, and other "tangible" factors.[9] Our decision, therefore, cannot turn on merely a comparison of these tangible factors in the Negro and white schools involved in each of the cases. We must look instead to the effect of segregation itself on public education.

In approaching this problem, we cannot turn the clock back to 1868 when the Amendment was adopted, or even to 1896 when *Plessy v. Ferguson* was written. We must consider public education in the light of its full development and its present place in American life throughout the Nation. Only in this way can it be determined if segregation in public schools deprives these plaintiffs of the equal protection of the laws.

Today, education is perhaps the most important function of state and local governments. Compulsory school attendance laws and the great expenditures for education both demonstrate our recognition of the importance of education to our democratic society. It is required in the performance of our most basic public responsibilities, even service in the armed forces. It is

the very foundation of good citizenship. Today it is a principal instrument in awakening the child to cultural values, in preparing him for later professional training, and in helping him to adjust normally to his environment. In these days, it is doubtful that any child may reasonably be expected to succeed in life if he is denied the opportunity of an education. Such an opportunity, where the state has undertaken to provide it, is a right which must be made available to all on equal terms.

We come then to the question presented: Does segregation of children in public schools solely on the basis of race, even though the physical facilities and other "tangible" factors may be equal, deprive the children of the minority group of equal educational opportunities? We believe that it does.

In *Sweatt v. Painter, supra,* in finding that a segregated law school for Negroes could not provide them equal educational opportunities, this Court relied in large part on "those qualities which are incapable of objective measurement but which make for greatness in a law school." In *McLaurin v. Oklahoma State Regents, supra,* the Court, in requiring that a Negro admitted to a white graduate school be treated like all other students, again resorted to intangible considerations: " . . . his ability to study, to engage in discussions and exchange views with other students, and, in general, to learn his profession." Such considerations apply with added force to children in grade and high schools. To separate them from others of similar age and qualifications solely because of their race generates a feeling of inferiority as to their status in the community that may affect their hearts and minds in a way unlikely ever to be undone. The effect of this separation on their educational opportunities was well stated by a finding in the Kansas case by a court which nevertheless felt compelled to rule against the Negro plaintiffs:

> "Segregation of white and colored children in public schools has a detrimental effect upon the colored children. The impact is greater when it has the sanction of the law; for the policy of separating the races is usually interpreted as denoting the inferiority of the negro group. A sense of inferiority affects the motivation of a child to learn. Segregation with the sanction of law, therefore, has a tendency to [retard] the educational and mental development of negro children and to deprive them of some of the benefits they would receive in a racial[ly] integrated school system."[10]

Whatever may have been the extent of psychological knowledge at the time of *Plessy v. Ferguson,* this finding is amply supported by modern authority.[11] Any language in *Plessy v. Ferguson* contrary to this finding is rejected.

We conclude that in the field of public education the doctrine of "separate but equal" has no place. Separate educational facilities are inherently unequal. Therefore, we hold that the plaintiffs and others similarly situated for whom the actions have been brought are, by reason of the segregation complained of, deprived of the equal protection of the laws guaranteed by the Fourteenth Amendment. This disposition makes unnecessary any discussion whether such segregation also violates the Due Process Clause of the Fourteenth Amendment.[12]

Because these are class actions, because of the wide applicability of this decision, and because of the great variety of local conditions, the formulation of decrees in these cases presents problems of considerable complexity. On reargument, the consideration of appropriate relief was necessarily subordinated to the primary question—the constitutionality of segregation in public education. We have now announced that such segregation is a denial of the equal protection of the laws. In order that we may have the full assistance of the parties in formulating decrees, the cases will be restored to the docket, and the parties are requested to present further argument on Questions 4 and 5 previously propounded by the Court for the reargument this Term.[13] The Attorney General of the United States is again invited to participate. The Attorneys General of the states requiring or permitting segregation in public education will also be permitted to appear as *amici curiae* upon request to do so by September 15, 1954, and submission of briefs by October 1, 1954.[14]

It is so ordered.

NOTES

1. In the Kansas case, *Brown v. Board of Education*, the plaintiffs are Negro children of elementary school age residing in Topeka. They brought this action in the United States District Court for the District of Kansas to enjoin enforcement of a Kansas statute which permits, but does not require, cities of more than 15,000 population to maintain separate school facilities for Negro and white students. Kan. Gen. Stat. § 72-1724 (1949). Pursuant to that authority, the Topeka Board of Education elected to establish segregated elementary schools. Other public schools in the community, however, are operated on a nonsegregated basis. . . .

In the South Carolina case, *Briggs v. Elliott*, the plaintiffs are Negro children of both elementary and high school age residing in Clarendon County. They brought this action in the United States District Court for the Eastern District of South Carolina to enjoin enforcement of provisions in the state constitution and statutory code which require the segregation of Negroes and whites in public schools. . . .

In the Virginia case, *Davis v. County School Board*, the plaintiffs are Negro children of high school age residing in Prince Edward County. They brought this action in the United States District Court for the Eastern District of Virginia to enjoin enforcement of provisions in the state constitution and statutory code which require the segregation of Negroes and whites in public schools. . . .

In the Delaware case, *Gebhart v. Belton*, the plaintiffs are Negro children of both elementary and high school age residing in New Castle county. They brought this action in the Delaware Court of Chancery to enjoin enforcement of provisions in the state constitution and statutory code which require the segregation of Negroes and whites in public schools. . . .

2. technical footnote deleted.
3. technical footnote deleted.
4. technical footnote deleted.
5. technical footnote deleted.
6. technical footnote deleted.
7. technical footnote deleted.
8. technical footnote deleted.
9. technical footnote deleted.
10. technical footnote deleted.
11. K. B. Clark, Effect of Prejudice and Discrimination on Personality Development (Midcentury White House Conference on Children and Youth, 1950); Witmer and Kotinsky, Personality in the Making (1952), c. VI; Deutscher and Chein, The Psychological Effects of Enforced Segregation: A Survey of Social Science Opinion, 26 J. Psychol. 259 (1948); Chein, What are the Psychological Effects of Segregation Under Conditions of Equal Facilities?, 3 Int. J. Opinion and Attitude Res. 229 (1949); Brameld, Educational Costs, in Discrimination and National Welfare (MacIver, ed., 1949), 44–48; Frazier, The Negro in the United States (1949), 674–681. And see generally Myrdal, An American Dilemma (1944).
12. technical footnote deleted.
13. technical footnote deleted.
14. technical footnote deleted.

UNIVERSITY OF CALIFORNIA REGENTS v. BAKKE

428 U.S. 269 (1977)

Mr. Justice Powell announced the judgment of the Court.

This case presents a challenge to the special admissions program of the petitioner, the Medical School of the University of California at Davis, which is designed to assure the admission of a specified number of students from certain minority groups. The Superior Court of California sustained respondent's challenge, holding that petitioner's program violated the California Constitution, Title VI of the Civil Rights Act of 1964, 42 U.S.C. § 2000d *et seq.*, and the Equal Protection Clause of the Fourteenth Amendment. The court enjoined petitioner from considering respondent's race or the race of any other applicant in making admissions decisions. It refused, however, to order respondent's admission to the Medical School, holding that he had not carried his burden of proving that he would have been admitted but for the constitutional and statutory violations. The Supreme Court of California affirmed those portions of the trial court's judgment declaring the special admissions program unlawful and enjoining petitioner from considering the race of any applicant.† It modified that portion of the judgment denying respondent's requested injunction and directed the trial court to order his admission.

For the reasons stated in the following opinion, I believe that so much of the judgment of the California court as holds petitioner's special admissions program unlawful and directs that respondent be admitted to the Medical School must be affirmed. For the reasons expressed in a separate opinion, my Brothers The Chief Justice, Mr. Justice Stewart, Mr. Justice Rehnquist, and Mr. Justice Stevens concur in this judgment.

I also conclude for the reasons stated in the following opinion that the portion of the court's judgment enjoining petitioner from according any consideration to race in its admissions process must be reversed. For reasons expressed in separate opinions, my Brothers Mr. Justice Brennan, Mr. Justice White, Mr. Justice Marshall, and Mr. Justice Blackmun concur in this judgment.

Affirmed in part and reversed in part.

Opinion of Powell, J.

I‡

The Medical School of the University of California at Davis opened in 1968 with an entering class of 50 students. In 1971, the size of the entering class was increased to 100 students, a level at which it remains. No admissions program for disadvantaged or minority students existed when the school opened, and the first class contained three Asians but no blacks, no Mexican-Americans, and no American Indians. Over the next two years, the faculty devised a special admissions program to increase the representation of "disadvantaged" students in each Medical School class[1] The special program consisted of a separate admissions system operating in coordination with the regular admissions process.

Under the regular admissions procedure, a candidate could submit his application to the Medical School beginning in July of the year preceding the academic year for which admission was sought. Record 149. Because of the large number of applications,[2] the admissions committee screened each one to select candidates for further consideration. Candidates whose overall undergraduate grade point averages fell below 2.5 on a scale of 4.0 were summarily rejected. *Id*, at 63. About one out of six applicants was invited for a personal interview. *Ibid.* Following the interviews, each candidate was rated on a scale of 1 to 100 by his interviewers and four other members of the admissions committee. The rating embraced the interviewers' summaries, the candidate's overall grade point average, grade point average in science courses, scores on the Medical College Admissions Test

20

From *U.S. Reports*, 1977. Opinion of the Supreme Court, 1977.

(MCAT), letters of recommendation, extracurricular activities, and other biographical data. *Id.*, at 62. The ratings were added together to arrive at each candidate's "benchmark" score. Since five committee members rated each candidate in 1973, a perfect score was 500; in 1974, six members rated each candidate, so that a perfect score was 600. The full committee then reviewed the file and scores of each applicant and made offers of admission on a "rolling" basis.[3] The chairman was responsible for placing names on the waiting list. They were not placed in strict numerical order; instead, the chairman had discretion to include persons with "special skills." *Id.*, at 63–64.

The special admissions program operated with a separate committee, a majority of whom were members of minority groups. *Id.*, at 163. On the 1973 application form, candidates were asked to indicate whether they wished to be considered as "economically and/or educationally disadvantaged" applicants; on the 1974 form the question was whether they wished to be considered as members of a "minority group," which the Medical School apparently viewed as "Blacks," "Chicanos," "Asians," and "American Indians." *Id.*, at 65–66, 146, 197, 203–205, 216–218. If these questions were answered affirmatively, the application was forwarded to the special admissions committee. No formal definition of "disadvantaged" was ever produced, *id*, at 163–164, but the chairman of the special committee screened each application to see whether it reflected economic or educational deprivation.[4] Having passed this initial hurdle, the applications then were rated by the special committee in a fashion similar to that used by the general admissions committee, except that special candidates did not have to meet the 2.5 grade point average cutoff applied to regular applicants. About one-fifth of the total number of special applicants were invited for interviews in 1973 and 1974.[5] Following each interview, the special committee assigned each special applicant a benchmark score. The special committee then presented its top choices to the general admissions committee. The latter did not rate or compare the special candidates against the general applicants, *id.*, at 388, but could reject recommended special candidates for failure to meet course requirements or other specific deficiencies. *Id.*, at 171–172. The special committee continued to recommend special applicants until a number prescribed by faculty vote were admitted. While the overall class size was still 50, the prescribed number was 8; in 1973 and 1974, when the class size had doubled to 100, the prescribed number of special admissions also doubled, to 16. *Id.*, at 164, 166.

From the year of the increase in class size—1971—through 1974, the special program resulted in the admission of 21 black students, 30 Mexican-Americans, and 12 Asians, for a total of 63 minority students. Over the same period, the regular admissions program pro-

duced 1 black, 6 Mexican-Americans, and 37 Asians, for a total of 44 minority students.[6] Although disadvantaged whites applied to the special program in large numbers, see no. 5, *supra*, none received an offer of admission through that process. Indeed, in 1974, at least, the special committee explicitly considered only "disadvantaged" special applicants who were members of one of the designated minority groups. Record 171.

Allan Bakke is a white male who applied to the Davis Medical School in both 1973 and 1974. In both years Bakke's application was considered under the general admissions program, and he received an interview. His 1973 interview was with Dr. Theodore C. West, who considered Bakke "a very desirable applicant to [the] medical school." *Id.*, at 225. Despite a strong benchmark score of 468 out of 500, Bakke was rejected. His application had come late in the year, and no applicants in the general admissions process with scores below 470 were accepted after Bakke's application was completed. *Id.*, at 69. There were four special admissions slots unfilled at that time, however, for which Bakke was not considered. *Id.*, at 70. After his 1973 rejection, Bakke wrote to Dr. George H. Lowrey, Associate Dean and Chairman of the Admissions Committee, protesting that the special admissions program operated as a racial and ethnic quota. *Id.*, at 259.

Bakke's 1974 application was completed early in the year. *Id.*, at 70. His student interviewer gave him an overall rating of 94, finding him "friendly, well tempered, conscientious and delightful to speak with." *Id.*, at 229. His faculty interviewer was, by coincidence, the same Dr. Lowrey to whom he had written in protest of the special admissions program. Dr. Lowrey found Bakke "rather limited in his approach" to the problems of the medical profession and found disturbing Bakke's "very definite opinions which were based more on his personal viewpoints than upon a study of the total problem." *Id.*, at 226. Dr. Lowrey gave Bakke the lowest of his six ratings, an 86; his total was 549 out of 600. *Id.*, at 230. Again, Bakke's application was rejected. In neither year did the chairman of the admissions committee, Dr. Lowrey, exercise his discretion to place Bakke on the waiting list. *Id.*, at 64. In both years, applicants were admitted under the special program with grade point averages, MCAT scores, and benchmark scores significantly lower than Bakke's.[7]

After the second rejection, Bakke filed the instant suit in the Superior Court of California.[8] He sought mandatory, injunctive, and declaratory relief compelling his admission to the Medical School. He alleged that the Medical School's special admissions program operated to exclude him from the school on the basis of his race, in violation of his rights under the Equal Protection Clause of the Fourteenth Amendment,[9] Art. I, § 21, of the California Constitution,[10] and § 601 of Title VI of the Civil Rights Act of 1964, 78 Stat. 252,

42 U.S.C. § 2000d.[11] The University cross-complained for a declaration that its special admissions program was lawful. The trial court found that the special program operated as a racial quota, because minority applicants in the special program were rated only against one another, Record 388, and 16 places in the class of 100 were reserved for them. *Id.*, at 295–296. Declaring that the University could not take race into account in making admissions decisions, the trial court held the challenged program violative of the Federal Constitution, the State Constitution, and Title VI. The court refused to order Bakke's admission, however, holding that he had failed to carry his burden of proving that he would have been admitted but for the existence of the special program.

Bakke appealed from the portion of the trial court judgment denying him admission, and the University appealed from the decision that its special admissions program was unlawful and the order enjoining it from considering race in the processing of applications. The Supreme Court of California transferred the case directly from the trial court, "because of the importance of the issues involved." 18 Cal. 3d 34, 39, 553, P. 2d 1152, 1156 (1976). The California court accepted the findings of the trial court with respect to the University's program.[12] Because the special admissions program involved a racial classification, the Supreme Court held itself bound to apply strict scrutiny. *Id.*, at 49, 553 P. 2d, at 1162–1163. It then turned to the goals the University presented as justifying the special program. Although the court agreed that the goals of integrating the medical profession and increasing the number of physicians willing to serve members of minority groups were compelling state interests, *id.*, at 53, 553 P. 2d, at 1165, it concluded that the special admissions program was not the least intrusive means of achieving those goals. Without passing on the state constitutional or the federal statutory grounds cited in the trial court's judgment, the California court held that the Equal Protection Clause of the Fourteenth Amendment required that "no applicant may be rejected because of his race, in favor of another who is less qualified, as measured by standards applied without regard to race." *Id.*, at 55, 553 P. 2d, at 1166.

Turning to Bakke's appeal, the court ruled that since Bakke had established that the University had discriminated against him on the basis of his race, the burden of proof shifted to the University to demonstrate that he would not have been admitted even in the absence of the special admissions program.[13] *Id.*, at 63–64, 553 P. 2d, at 1172. The court analogized Bakke's situation to that of a plaintiff under Title VII of the Civil Rights Act of 1964, 42 U.S.C. § § 2000e–17 (1970 ed., Supp. V) see, *e.g., Franks v. Bowman Transportation Co.*, 424 U.S. 747, 772 (1976). 18 Cal. 3d, at 63–64, 553 P. 2d, at 1172. On this basis, the court initially ordered a remand for the purpose of determining whether, under the newly

allocated burden of proof, Bakke would have been admitted to either the 1973 or the 1974 entering class in the absence of the special admissions program. App. A. to Application for Stay 48. In its petition for rehearing below, however, the University conceded its inability to carry that burden. App. B. to Application for Stay A19–A20.[14] The California court thereupon amended its opinion to direct that the trial court enter judgment ordering Bakke's admission to the Medical School. 18 Cal. 3d, at 64, 553 P. 2d, at 1172. That order was stayed pending review in this Court. 429 U.S. 953 (1976). We granted certiorari to consider the important constitutional issue. 429 U.S. 1090 (1977). . . .

V
A

It may be assumed that the reservation of a specified number of seats in each class for individuals from the preferred ethnic groups would contribute to the attainment of considerable ethnic diversity in the student body. But petitioner's argument that this is the only effective means of serving the interest of diversity is seriously flawed. In a most fundamental sense the argument misconceives the nature of the state interest that would justify consideration of race or ethnic background. It is not an interest in simple ethnic diversity, in which a specified percentage of the student body is in effect guaranteed to be members of selected ethnic groups, with the remaining percentage an undifferentiated aggregation of students. The diversity that furthers a compelling state interest encompasses a far broader array of qualifications and characteristics of which racial or ethnic origin is but a single though important element. Petitioner's special admissions program, focused *solely* on ethnic diversity, would hinder rather than further attainment of genuine diversity.[50]

Nor would the state interest in genuine diversity be served by expanding petitioner's two-track system into a multitrack program with a prescribed number of seats set aside for each identifiable category of applicants. Indeed, it is inconceivable that a university would thus pursue the logic of petitioner's two-track program to the illogical end of insulating each category of applicants with certain desired qualifications from competition with all other applicants.

The experience of other university admissions programs, which take race into account in achieving the educational diversity valued by the First Amendment, demonstrates that the assignment of a fixed number of places to a minority group is not a necessary means toward that end. An illuminating example is found in the Harvard College program:

"In recent years Harvard College has expanded the concept of diversity to include students from disadvantaged economic, racial and ethnic groups. Harvard College now recruits not only Californians or Louisianans but also blacks and Chicanos and other minority students. . . .

"In practice, this new definition of diversity has meant that race has been a factor in some admission decisions. When the Committee on Admissions reviews the large middle group of applicants who are 'admissible' and deemed capable of doing good work in their courses, the race of an applicant may tip the balance in his favor just as geographic origin or a life spent on a farm may tip the balance in other candidates' cases. A farm boy from Idaho can bring something to Harvard College that a Bostonian cannot offer. Similarly, a black student can usually bring something that a white person cannot offer. . . .

In such an admissions program,[51] race or ethnic background may be deemed a "plus" in a particular applicant's file, yet it does not insulate the individual from comparison with all other candidates for the available seats. The file of a particular black applicant may be examined for his potential contribution to diversity without the factor of race being decisive when compared, for example, with that of an applicant identified as an Italian-American if the latter is thought to exhibit qualities more likely to promote beneficial educational pluralism. Such qualities could include exceptional personal talents, unique work or service experience, leadership potential, maturity, demonstrated compassion, a history of overcoming disadvantage, ability to communicate with the poor, or other qualifications deemed important. In short, an admissions program operated in this way is flexible enough to consider all pertinent elements of diversity in light of the particular qualifications of each applicant, and to place them on the same footing for consideration, although not necessarily according them the same weight. Indeed, the weight attributed to a particular quality may vary from year to year depending upon the "mix" both of the student body and the applicants for the incoming class.

This kind of program treats each applicant as an individual in the admissions process. The applicant who loses out on the last available seat to another candidate receiving a "plus" on the basis of ethnic background will not have been foreclosed from all consideration for that seat simply because he was not the right color or had the wrong surname. It would mean only that his combined qualifications, which may have included similar nonobjective factors, did not outweigh those of the other applicant. His qualifications would have been weighed fairly and competitively, and he would have no basis to complain of unequal treatment under the Fourteenth Amendment.[52] . . .

B

In summary, it is evident that the Davis special admissions program involves the use of an explicit racial classification never before countenanced by this Court. It tells applicants who are not Negro, Asian, or Chicano that they are totally excluded from a specific percentage of the seats in an entering class. No matter how strong their qualifications, quantitative and extracurricular, including their own potential for contribution to educational diversity, they are never afforded the chance to compete with applicants from the preferred groups for the special admissions seats. At the same time, the preferred applicants have the opportunity to compete for every seat in the class.

The fatal flaw in petitioner's preferential program is its disregard of individual rights as guaranteed by the Fourteenth Amendment. *Shelley v. Kraemer*, 334 U.S., at 22. Such rights are not absolute. But when a State's distribution of benefits or imposition of burdens hinges on ancestry or the color of a person's skin, that individual is entitled to a demonstration that the challenged classification is necessary to promote a substantial state interest. Petitioner has failed to carry this burden. For this reason, that portion of the California court's judgment holding petitioner's special admissions program invalid under the Fourteenth Amendment must be affirmed.

C

In enjoining petitioner from ever considering the race of any applicant, however, the courts below failed to recognize that the State has a substantial interest that legitimately may be served by a properly devised admissions program involving the competitive consideration of race and ethnic origin. For this reason, so much of the California court's judgment as enjoins petitioner from any consideration of the race of any applicant must be reversed. . . .

NOTES

†. technical footnote deleted.
‡. technical footnote deleted.
1. technical footnote deleted.
2. technical footnote deleted.
3. technical footnote deleted.
4. technical footnote deleted.
5. technical footnote deleted.
6. technical footnote deleted.
7. technical footnote deleted.
8. technical footnote deleted.
9. technical footnote deleted.
10. technical footnote deleted.
11. technical footnote deleted.
12. technical footnote deleted.
13. technical footnote deleted.
14. technical footnote deleted.
50. technical footnote deleted.
51. technical footnote deleted.
52. technical footnote deleted.

Opinion of Marshall, J.

MR. JUSTICE MARSHALL.

I agree with the judgment of the Court only insofar as it permits a university to consider the race of an applicant in making admissions decisions. I do not agree that petitioner's admissions program violates the Constitution. For it must be remembered that, during most of the past 200 years, the Constitution as interpreted by this Court did not prohibit the most ingenious and pervasive forms of discrimination against the Negro. Now, when a State acts to remedy the effects of that legacy of discrimination, I cannot believe that this same Constitution stands as a barrier.

I
A

Three hundred and fifty years ago, the Negro was dragged to this country in chains to be sold into slavery. Uprooted from his homeland and thrust into bondage for forced labor, the slave was deprived of all legal rights. It was unlawful to teach him to read; he could be sold away from his family and friends at the whim of his master; and killing or maiming him was not a crime. The system of slavery brutalized and dehumanized both master and slave.[1] . . .

II

The position of the Negro today in America is the tragic but inevitable consequence of centuries of unequal treatment. Measured by any benchmark of comfort or achievement, meaningful equality remains a distant dream for the Negro.

A Negro child today has a life expectancy which is shorter by more than five years than that of a white child.[2] The Negro child's mother is over three times more likely to die of complications in childbirth,[3] and the infant mortality rate for Negroes is nearly twice that for whites.[4] The median income of the Negro family is only 60% that of the median of a white family,[5] and the percentage of Negroes who live in families with incomes below the poverty line is nearly four times greater than that of whites.[6]

When the Negro child reaches working age, he finds that America offers him significantly less than it offers his white counterpart. For Negro adults, the unemployment rate is twice that of whites,[7] and the unemployment rate for Negro teenagers is nearly three times that of white teenagers.[8] A Negro male who completes four years of college can expect a median annual income of merely $110 more than a white male who has only a high school diploma.[9] Although Negroes represent 11.5% of the population,[10] they are only 1.2% of the lawyers and judges, 2% of the physicians, 2.3% of the dentists, 1.1% of the engineers and 2.6% of the college and university professors.[11]

The relationship between those figures and the history of unequal treatment afforded to the Negro cannot be denied. At every point from birth to death the impact of the past is reflected in the still disfavored position of the Negro.

In light of the sorry history of discrimination and its devastating impact on the lives of Negroes, bringing the Negro into the mainstream of American life should be a state interest of the highest order. To fail to do so is to ensure that America will forever remain a divided society.

III

I do not believe that the Fourteenth Amendment requires us to accept that fate. Neither its history nor our past cases lend any support to the conclusion that a university may not remedy the cumulative effects of society's discrimination by giving consideration to race in an effort to increase the number and percentage of Negro doctors. . . .

IV

While I applaud the judgment of the Court that a university may consider race in its admissions process, it is more than a little ironic that, after several hundred years of class-based discrimination against Negroes, the Court is unwilling to hold that a class-based remedy for that discrimination is permissible. In declining to so hold, today's judgment ignores the fact that for several hundred years Negroes have been discriminated against, not as individuals, but rather solely because of the color of their skins. It is unnecessary in 20th-century America to have individual Negroes demonstrate that they have been victims of racial discrimination; the racism of our society has been so pervasive that none, regardless of wealth or position, has managed to escape its impact. The experience of Negroes in America has been different in kind, not just in degree, from that of other ethnic groups. It is not merely the history of slavery alone but also that a whole people were marked as inferior by the law. And that mark has endured. The dream of America as the great melting pot has not been realized for the Negro; because of his skin color he never even made it into the pot. . . .

It is because of a legacy of unequal treatment that we now must permit the institutions of this society to give consideration to race in making decisions about who will hold the positions of influence, affluence, and prestige in America. For far too long, the doors to those positions have been shut to Negroes. If we are ever to become a fully integrated society, one in which the color of a person's skin will not determine the opportunities available to him or her, we must be willing to take steps to open those doors. I do not believe that anyone can truly look into America's past and still find that a remedy for the effects of that past is impermissible.

It has been said that this case involves only the individual, Bakke, and this University. I doubt, however, that there is a computer capable of determining the number of persons and institutions that may be affected by the decision in this case. For example, we are told by the Attorney General of the United States that at least 27 federal agencies have adopted regulations requiring recipients of federal funds to take " '*affirmative action* to overcome the effects of conditions which resulting in limiting participation . . . by persons of a particular race, color, or national origin.' " Supplemental Brief for United States as *Amicus Curiae* 16 (emphasis added). I cannot even guess the number of state and local governments that have set up affirmative-action programs, which may be affected by today's decision.

I fear that we have come full circle. After the Civil War our Government started "affirmative action" programs. This Court in the *Civil Rights Cases* and *Plessy v. Ferguson* destroyed the movement toward complete equality. For almost a century no action was taken, and this nonaction was with the tacit approval of the courts. Then we had *Brown v. Board of Education* and the Civil Rights Acts of Congress, followed by numerous affirmative-action programs. *Now,* we have this Court again stepping in, this time to stop affirmative-action programs of the type used by the University of California.

NOTES

1. technical footnote deleted.
2. technical footnote deleted.
3. technical footnote deleted.
4. technical footnote deleted.
5. technical footnote deleted.
6. technical footnote deleted.
7. technical footnote deleted.
8. technical footnote deleted.
9. technical footnote deleted.
10. technical footnote deleted.
11. technical footnote deleted.

Freedom of Religious Expression

The Historical and Legal Origins of Racial Categories and
the Protection of Civil Liberties of American Citizens

SHAARE TEFILA CONGREGATION v. COBB

Cite as 107 S.Ct. 2019 (1987)

Justice White delivered the opinion of the Court.

On November 2, 1982, the outside walls of the synagogue of the Shaare Tefila Congregation in Silver Spring, Maryland, were sprayed with red and black paint and with large anti-Semitic slogans, phrases and symbols. A few months later, the Congregation and some individual members brought this suit in the Federal District Court, alleging that defendants' desecration of the synagogue had violated 42 U.S.C. § § 1981, 1982, 1985(3) and the Maryland common law of trespass, nuisance, and intentional infliction of emotional distress. On defendants' motion under Fed. Rule Civ.Proc 12(b)(1) and (6), the District Court dismissed all the claims. The Court of Appeals affirmed in all respects. 785 F.2d 523 (CA4 1986). Petitioners petitioned for writ of certiorari. We granted the petition, 479 U.S. _____, 107 S.Ct. 62, 93 L.Ed.2d 21 (1986), and we now reverse the judgment of the Court of Appeals.

[1] Section 1982 guarantees all citizens of the United States, "the same right . . . as is enjoyed by white citizens . . . to inherit, purchase, lease, sell, hold, and convey real and personal property." The section forbids both official and private racially discriminatory interference with property rights, *Jones v. Alfred H. Mayer Co.*, 392 U.S. 409, 88 S.Ct. 2186, 20 L.Ed.2d 1189 (1968). Petitioners' allegation was that they were deprived of the right to hold property in violation of § 1982 because the defendants were motivated by racial prejudice. They unsuccessfully argued in the District Court and Court of Appeals that Jews are not a racially distinct group, but that defendants' conduct is actionable because they viewed Jews as racially distinct and were motivated by racial prejudice. The Court of Appeals held that § 1982 was not "intended to apply to situations in which a plaintiff is not a member of a racially distinct group but is merely *perceived* to be so by defendants." 785 F.2d, at 526 (emphasis in original). The Court of Appeals believed that "[b]ecause discrimination against Jews is not racial discrimination," *id.*, at 527, the District Court was correct in dismissing the § 1982 claim.

[2] We agree with the Court of Appeals that a charge of racial discrimination within the meaning of § 1982 cannot be made out by alleging only that the defendants were motivated by racial animus; it is necessary as well to allege that defendants' animus was directed towards the kind of group that Congress intended to protect when it passed the statute. To hold otherwise would unacceptably extend the reach of the statute.

[3–5] We agree with petitioners, however, that the Court of Appeals erred in holding that Jews cannot state a § 1982 claim against other white defendants. That view rested on the notion that because Jews today are not thought to be members of a separate race, they cannot make out a claim of racial discrimination within the meaning of § 1982. That construction of the section we have today rejected in *Saint Francis College v. Al-Khazraji*, _____ U.S., at _____, 107 S.Ct., at _____. Our opinion in that case observed that definitions of race when § 1982 was passed were not the same as they are today and concluded that the section was "intended to protect from discrimination identifiable classes of persons who are subjected to intentional discrimination solely because of their ancestry or ethnic characteristics." At _____, 107 S.Ct., at 2028. As *St. Francis* makes clear, the question before us is not whether Jews are considered to be a separate race by today's standards, but whether, at the time § 1982 was adopted, Jews constituted a group of people that Congress intended to protect. It is evident from the legislative history of the section reviewed in *Saint Francis College*, a review that we need not repeat here, that Jews and Arabs were among the peoples then considered to be distinct races and hence within the protection of the statute. Jews are not foreclosed from stating a cause of action against other members of what today is considered to be part of the Caucasian race.

The judgment of the Court of Appeals is therefore reversed and the case is remanded for further proceedings consistent with this opinion.

From *U.S. Reports*, 1987. Opinion of the Supreme Court, 1987.

SAINT FRANCIS COLLEGE v. AL-KHAZRAJI

Cite as 107 S.Ct. 2022 (1987)

JUSTICE WHITE delivered the opinion of the Court.

Respondent, a citizen of the United States born in Iraq, was an associate professor at St. Francis College, one of the petitioners here. In January 1978, he applied for tenure; the Board of Trustees denied his request on February 23, 1978. He accepted a 1-year, nonrenewable contract and sought administrative reconsideration of the tenure decision, which was denied on February 6, 1979. He worked his last day at the college on May 26, 1979. In June 1979, he filed complaints with the Pennsylvania Human Relations Commission and the Equal Employment Opportunities Commission. The State agency dismissed his claim and the EEOC issued a right to sue letter on August 6, 1980.

On October 30, 1980, respondent filed a *pro se* complaint in the District Court alleging a violation of Title VII of the Civil Rights Act of 1964 and claiming discrimination based on national origin, religion, and/or race. Amended complaints were filed, adding claims under 42 U.S.C. §§ 1981, 1983, 1985(3), 1986, and state law. The District Court dismissed the 1986, 1985(3) and Title VII claims as untimely but held that the §§ 1981 and 1983 claims were not barred by the Pennsylvania 6-year statute of limitations. The court at that time also ruled that because the complaint alleged denial of tenure because respondent was of the Arabian race, an action under § 1981 could be maintained. Defendants' motion for summary judgment came up before a different judge, who construed the pleadings as asserting only discrimination on the basis of national origin and religion, which § 1981 did not cover. Even if racial discrimination was deemed to have been alleged, the District Court ruled that § 1981 does not reach claims of discrimination based on Arabian ancestry.[1]

The Court of Appeals rejected petitioners' claim that the § 1981 claim had not been timely filed. Under the court of Appeals' holding in *Goodman v. Lukens Steel, Co.*, 777 F.2d 113 (CA 2 1985), that the Pennsylvania 2-year statute of limitations governed § 1981 cases, respondent's suit would have been barred. The Court of Appeals, however, relying on *Chevron Oil Co. v. Huson*, 404 U.S. 97, 92 S.Ct. 349, 30 L.Ed.2d 296 (1971), held that *Goodman* should not be retroactively applied and that this suit was timely under its pre-*Goodman* cases which had borrowed the State's 6-year statute.

Reaching the merits, the Court of Appeals held that respondent had alleged discrimination based on race and that although under current racial classifications Arabs are Caucasians, respondent could maintain his § 1981 claim.[2] Congress, when it passed what is now § 1981, had not limited its protections to those who today would be considered members of a race different from

the race of the defendant. Rather, the legislative history of the section indicated that Congress intended to forbid "at the least, membership in a group that is ethnically and physiognomically distinctive." 784 F.2d 505, 517 (CA 3 1986). Section 1981, "at a minimum," reaches "discrimination directed against an individual because he or she is genetically part of an ethnically and physiognomically distinctive sub-grouping of *homo sapiens.*" *Ibid.* Because respondent had not had full discovery and the record was not sufficient to determine whether he had been subjected to the sort of prejudice § 1981 would redress, respondent was to be given the opportunity to prove his case.[3]

We granted certiorari. 479 U.S. _____, 107 S.Ct. 62, 93 L.Ed.2d 21 (1986), limited to the statute of limitations issue and the question whether a person of Arabian ancestry was protected from racial discrimination under § 1981, and now affirm the judgment of the Court of Appeals.

I

[1] We agree with the Court of Appeals that respondent's claim was not time barred. *Wilson v. Garcia*, 471 U.S. 261, 105 S.Ct. 1938, 85 L.Ed.2d 254 (1985), required that in selecting the applicable state statute of limitations in § 1983 cases, the lower federal courts should choose the state statute applicable to other personal injury torts. Thereafter, the Third Circuit in *Goodman* held that *Wilson* applies to § 1981 cases as well and that the Pennsylvania 2-year statute should apply. The Court of Appeals in this case, however, held that when respondent filed his suit, which was prior to *Wilson v. Garcia*, it was clearly established in the Third Circuit that a § 1981 plaintiff had six years to bring an action and that *Goodman* should not be applied retroactively to bar respondent's suit.

Insofar as what the prevailing law was in the Third Circuit, we have no reason to disagree with the Court of Appeals. Under controlling precedent in that Circuit, respondent had six years to file his suit, and it was filed well within that time. See 784 F.2d, at 512–513. We also assume but do not decide that *Wilson v. Garcia* controls the selection of the applicable state statute of limitations in § 1981 cases. The Court of Appeals, however, correctly held that its decision in *Goodman* should not be retroactively applied to bar respondent's action in this case. The usual rule is that federal cases should be decided in accordance with the law existing at the time of decision. *Gulf Offshore Co. v. Mobil Oil Corp.*, 453 U.S. 473, 486, n. 16, 101 S.Ct. 2870, 2879, n. 16, 69 L.Ed.2d 784 (1981); *Thorpe v. Durham Housing*

Authority, 393 U.S. 268, 281, 89 S.Ct. 518, 526, 21 L.Ed.2d 474 (1969); *United States v. Schooner Peggy,* 1 Cranch 103, *110, 2 L.Ed. 49 (1801). But *Chevron Oil Co. v. Huson, supra,* counsels against retroactive application of statute of limitations decisions in certain circumstances. There, the Court held that its decision specifying the applicable state statute of limitations should be applied only prospectively because it overruled clearly established circuit precedent on which the complaining party was entitled to rely, because retroactive application would be inconsistent with the purpose of the underlying substantive statute, and because such application would be manifestly inequitable. The Court of Appeals found these same factors were present in this case and foreclosed retroactive applications of its decision in *Goodman.* We perceive no good reason for not applying *Chevron* where *Wilson* has required a Court of Appeals to overrule its prior cases. Nor has petitioner persuaded us that there was any error in the application of *Chevron* in the circumstances existing in this case.

II

Section 1981 provides:

> "All persons within the jurisdiction of the United States shall have the same right in every State and Territory to make and enforce contracts, to sue, be parties, give evidence, and to the full and equal benefit of all laws and proceedings for the security of persons and property as is enjoyed by white citizens, and shall be subject to like punishment, pains, penalties, taxes, licenses, and exactions of every kind, and to no other."

[2]   Although § 1981 does not itself use the word "race," the Court has construed the section to forbid all "racial" discrimination in the making of private as well as public contracts. *Runyon v. McCrary,* 427, U.S. 160, 168, 174–175, 96 S.Ct, 2586, 2593, 2596–2597, 49 L.Ed.2d 415 (1976). The petitioner college, although a private institution, was therefore subject to this statutory command. There is no disagreement among the parties on these propositions. The issue is whether respondent has alleged *racial* discrimination within the meaning of § 1981.

[3]   Petitioners contend that respondent is a Caucasian and cannot allege the kind of discrimination § 1981 forbids. Concededly, *McDonald v. Sante Fe Trail Transportation Co.,* 427 U.S. 273, 96 S.Ct. 2574, 49 L.Ed.2d 493 (1976), held that white persons could maintain a § 1981 suit; but that suit involved alleged discrimination against a white person in favor of a black, and petitioner submits that the section does not encompass claims of discrimination by one Caucasian against another. We are quite sure that the Court of Appeals properly rejected this position.

Petitioner's submission rests on the assumption that all those who might be deemed Caucasians today were thought to be of the same race when § 1981 became law

in the 19th century; and it may be that a variety of ethnic groups, including Arabs, are now considered to be within the Caucasian race.[4] The understanding of "race" in the 19th century, however, was different. Plainly, all those who might be deemed Caucasian today were not thought to be of the same race at the time § 1981 became law.

In the middle years of the 19th century, dictionaries commonly referred to race as a "continued series of descendants from a parent who is called the *stock,*" N. Webster, An American Dictionary of the English Language 666 (New York 1830) (emphasis in original), "[t]he lineage of a family," N. Webster, 2 A Dictionary of the English Language 411 (New Haven 1841), or "descendants of a common ancestor," J. Donald, Chambers's Etymological Dictionary of the English Language 415 (London 1871). The 1887 edition of Webster's expanded the definition somewhat: "The descendants of a common ancestor; a family, tribe, people or nation, believed or presumed to belong to the same stock." N. Webster, Dictionary of the English Language (W. Wheeler ed. 1887). It was not until the 20th century that dictionaries began referring to the Caucasian, Mongolian and Negro races, 8 The Century Dictionary and Cyclopedia 4926 (1911), or to race as involving divisions of mankind based upon different physical characteristics. Webster's Collegiate Dictionary 794 (1916). Even so, modern dictionaries still include among the definitions of race as being "a family, tribe, people, or nation belonging to the same stock." Webster's Third New International Dictionary Mass.1870 (1971); Webster's Ninth New Collegiate Dictionary 969 (Springfield, Mass. 1986).

Encyclopedias of the 19th century also described race in terms of ethnic groups, which is a narrower concept of race than petitioners urge. Encyclopedia Americana in 1858, for example, referred in 1854 to various races such as Finns, vol. 5, p. 123, gypsies, 6 *id.,* at 123, Basques, 1 *id.,* at 602, and Hebrews, 6 *id.,* at 209. The 1863 version of the New American Cyclopaedia divided the Arabs into a number of subsidiary races, vol. 1, p. 739; represented the Hebrews as of the Semitic race, 9 *id.,* at 27, and identified numerous other groups as constituting races, including Swedes, 15 *id.,* at 216, Norwegians, 12 *id.,* at 410, Germans, 8 *id.,* at 200, Greeks, *id.,* at 438, Finns, 7 *id.,* at 513, Italians, 9 *id.,* at 644–645 (referring to mixture of different races), Spanish, 14 *id.,* at 804, Mongolians, 11 *id.,* at 651, Russians, 14 *id.,* at 226, and the like. The Ninth edition of the Encyclopedia Britannica also referred to Arabs, vol. 2, p. 245 (1878), Jews, 13 *id.,* at 685 (1881), and other ethnic groups such as Germans, 10 *id.,* at 473 (1879), Hungarians, 12 *id.,* at 365 (1880), and Greeks, 11 *id.,* at 83 (1880), as separate races.

These dictionary and encyclopedic sources are somewhat diverse, but it is clear that they do not support the claim that for the purposes of § 1981,

Arabs, Englishmen, Germans and certain other ethnic groups are to be considered a single race. We would expect the legislative history of § 1981, which the Court held in *Runyon v. McCrary* had its source in the Civil Rights Act of 1866, 14 Stat. 27, as well as the Voting Rights Act of 1870, 16 Stat. 140, 144, to reflect this common understanding, which it surely does. The debates are replete with references to the Scandinavian races, Cong.Globe, 39th Cong., 1st Sess., 499 (1866) (remarks of Sen. Cowan), as well as the Chinese, *id.*, at 523 (remarks of Sen. Davis), Latin, *id.*, at 238 (remarks of Rep. Kasson during debate of home rule for the District of Columbia), Spanish, *id.*, at 251 (remarks of Sen. Davis during debate of District of Columbia suffrage) and Anglo-Saxon races, *id.*, at 542 (remarks of Rep. Dawson). Jews, *ibid.*, Mexicans, see *ibid.*, (remarks of Rep. Dawson), blacks, *passim*, and Mongolians, *id.*, at 498 (remarks of Sen. Cowan), were similarly categorized. Gypsies were referred to as a race. *Ibid.*, (remarks of Sen. Cowan). Likewise, the Germans:

> "Who will say that Ohio can pass a law enacting that no man of the German race . . . shall ever own any property in Ohio, or shall ever make a contract in Ohio, or ever inherit property in Ohio, or ever come into Ohio to live, or even to work? If Ohio may pass such a law, and exclude a German citizen . . . because he is of the German nationality or race, then may every other State do so." *Id.*, at 1294 (Remarks of Sen. Shellabarger).

There was a reference to the Caucasian race, but it appears to have been referring to people of European ancestry. *Id.*, at 523 (remarks of Sen. Davis).

The history of the 1870 Act reflects similar understanding of what groups Congress intended to protect from intentional discrimination. It is clear, for example, that the civil rights sections of the 1870 Act provided protection for immigrant groups such as the Chinese. This view was expressed in the Senate. Cong.Globe, 41st Cong., 2d Sess., 1536, 3658, 3808 (1870). In the House, Representative Bingham described § 16 of the Act, part of the authority for § 1981, as declaring "that the States shall not hereafter discriminate against the immigrant from China and in favor of the immigrant from Prussia, nor against the immigrant from France and in favor of the immigrant from Ireland." *Id.*, at 3871.

[4–6]   Based on the history of § 1981, we have little trouble in concluding that Congress intended to protect from discrimination identifiable classes of persons who are subjected to intentional discrimination solely because of their ancestry or ethnic characteristics. Such discrimination is racial discrimination that Congress intended § 1981 to forbid, whether or not it would be classified as racial in terms of modern scientific theory.[5] The Court of Appeals was thus quite right in holding that § 1981, "at a minimum," reaches discrimination against an individual "because he or she is genetically part of an ethnically and physiognomically distinctive sub-grouping of *homo sapiens.*" It is clear from our holding, however, that a distinctive physiognomy is not essential to qualify for § 1981 protection. If respondent on remand can prove that he was subjected to intentional discrimination based on the fact that he was born an Arab, rather than solely on the place or nation of his origin, or his religion, he will have made out a case under § 1981.

The Judgment of the court of Appeals is accordingly affirmed.

NOTES

1. technical footnote deleted.
2. technical footnote deleted.
3. technical footnote deleted.
4. There is a common popular understanding that there are three major human races—Caucasoid, Mongoloid, and Negroid. Many modern biologists and anthropologists, however, criticize racial classifications as arbitrary and of little use in understanding the variability of human beings. It is said that genetically homogeneous populations do not exist and traits are not discontinuous between populations; therefore, a population can only be described in terms of relative frequencies of various traits. Clear-cut categories do not exist. The particular traits which have generally been chosen to characterize races have been criticized as having little biological significance. It has been found that differences between individuals of the same race are often greater than the differences between the "average" individuals of different races. These observations and others have led some, but not all, scientists to conclude that racial classifications are for the most part sociopolitical, rather than biological, in nature.
5. technical footnote deleted.

Immigration and the American Experience

The peopling of the Americas during the eighteenth and nineteenth centuries because the United States was a locus of economic development was probably perceived by indigenous people as the extension and intensification of conflict and the final stage of their conquest. Africans brought in bondage probably viewed the opening of America to the "wretched refuse" of Europe as a strategy designed to exclude them from prosperity and as a threat to their full enfranchisement.

To the European and Asian immigrant, America represented freedom from the constraints of state-bound societies whose limits could not be overcome except through emigration. Yet this historical pathway to liberty, justice, and opportunity came to be perceived as a "tarnished door" when the deep impulses of exclusion and exclusivity came to the fore. The victims were aliens who, ironically, achieved the American promise but were denied the reward of acceptance and incorporation into the polity, economy, and culture they fashioned. The following articles describe the immigrant experience, and raise once again the issues that every large-scale multiethnic regime must address: How can unity and diversity be channeled into political, economic, and cultural well-being?

The history of immigration laws does not champion American ethnic groups. Immigration laws include the Chinese Exclusion Acts of the 1880s, the National Origins Quota System of the 1920s, the Mexican Repatriation Campaign of the 1950s, and the McCarran-Walter Act. A new era began with the inclusiveness of the mid-1960s. The findings of the 1990 U.S. Census indicate a range of demographic, economic, and social indicators as well as the legal status of the most recent era of immigration in the United States. The immediate impact, as well as the long-term developments and changes in America that can be attributed to the conflicts and the contributions related to newcomers, appears to be a facet of nearly every contemporary issue.

The changing nature of immigration can be discerned more clearly through the experiences of recent immigrant families. These stories of new immigrants from Afghanistan, Ireland, Poland, Vietnam, and Mexico give firsthand accounts of their adaptation. The stories suggest challenges and opportunities that growth provides, while offering support for arguments that immigrants need not be sources of fear and suspicion. Change and growth

pose great potential for the well-being and economic development of the United States. Nevertheless, the challenges to polity and social systems that this large influx of persons and cultures brings will require awareness of our cultural diversity and common humanity, as well as energy, mutual openness to talent, and participation of all in the experience of being and becoming an American.

Full employment and social-economic mobility in countries and economies from which persons are coming to the United States would decrease incentives for migration. Political and religious freedom in other countries would negate another cause for the movement of people from oppressive regimes to democratic and liberal societies.

Changes in the immigration laws of the United States in 1965 contributed to the growing number of Central American, South American, and Asian immigrants who have entered the country. The flow of population also includes persons who have entered without governmental authorization. Extreme violence and political turmoil have contributed to the number of refugees seeking asylum in the United States.

As the unit articles make clear, immigration not only impacts on the receiving country, but also affects nations that lose talent, skill, and the loyalty of disaffected migrants. Immigration, moreover, contributes to an already complex process of intergenerational relationships and the socialization of persons whose experiences of profound cultural change are intensified by competition, patterns of settlement, options for mobility, and the consciousness of ethnic traditions that conflict with dominant cultural and education institutions.

Dr. Michael Piore's assessment of children born to immigrant workers suggests an interesting lens through which the following articles may be read. Dr. Piore writes:

There is nothing in the immigration process that ensures that this second generation will be able to move up to higher level jobs toward which they aspire. Indeed, historically industrial societies appear consistently to disappoint the expectations of the second generation in this regard. That disappointment has in turn been the source of enormous social tensions. The sit-down strikes in the late thirties which sparked the industrial unions movement in the United States may in large measure be attributed to the reaction of the children of pre–World War I European immigrants to their labor market conditions. Similarly, the racial disturbances in Northern urban ghettos in the middle and late 1960s may be looked upon as a revolt of the black migrants against a society bent upon confining them to their parents' jobs.

As a guide for your own study, the U.S. Commission on Civil Rights has noted that increased immigration raises the following issues for both recent arrivals and Americans by birth:

Employment: The areas of occupation selected by or imposed upon various ethnic populations trace ethnic group mobility strategies and ethnic succession in the workplace, especially in manufacturing, hospitals, restaurants, and maintenance and custodial positions. Some ethnic populations appear to have greater numbers of highly educated persons in professional or semiprofessional positions.

Institutional and societal barriers: The job preferences and discrimination against the ethnic enclave and persons in small communities that are isolated from mainstream English-speaking society suggest the value of second-language competencies. Mutual accommodation is required to minimize the effect of inadequate language skills and training and difficulties in obtaining licenses, memberships, and certification.

Exploitation of workers: The most common form is the payment of wages below minimum standards. Alien workers have been stereotyped as a drain on public services cost. Such scapegoating is insupportable.

Taking jobs from Americans: Fact or fiction?: The stunning fact is that immigrants are a source of increased productivity, and a significant, if not utterly necessary, addition to the work force as well as to the consumer power that drives the American economy.

Looking Ahead: Challenge Questions

Why do periods of economic crisis appear to exacerbate tensions and strain relations between ethnic groups?

Does clustering of ethnic populations in occupational grouping utterly contradict the notion of a homogenized society—i.e., one with a random mixing of persons in various occupations?

What remedies for language diversity are acceptable in a democratic society?

Is discussion of immigration issues as if they were a matter of protecting American borders a fruitful form of policy analysis?

Historical Discrimination in the Immigration Laws

The Early Years

During the formative years of this country's growth, immigration was encouraged with little restraint. Any restrictions on immigration in the 1700s were the result of selection standards established by each colonial settlement. The only Federal regulation of immigration in this period lasted only 2 years and came from the Alien Act of 1798, which gave the President the authority to expel aliens who posed a threat to national security.[1]

Immigrants from northern and western Europe began to trickle into the country as a result of the faltering economic conditions within their own countries. In Germany, unfavorable economic prospects in industry and trade, combined with political unrest, drove many of its nationals to seek opportunities to ply their trades here.[2] In Ireland, the problems of the economy, compounded by several successive potato crop failures in the 1840s, sent thousands of Irish to seaports where ships bound for the United States were docked.[3] For other European nationals, the emigration from their native countries received impetus not only from adverse economic conditions at home but also from favorable stories of free land and good wages in America.[4]

The Nativist Movements

As a result of the large numbers of Catholics who emigrated from Europe, a nativist movement began in the 1830s.[5] It advocated immigration restriction to prevent further arrivals of Catholics into this country. Anti-Catholicism was a very popular theme, and many Catholics and Catholic institutions suffered violent attacks from nativist sympathizers. The movement, however, did not gain great political strength and its goal of curbing immigration did not materialize.

Immigrants in the mid-19th century did not come only from northern and western Europe. In China, political unrest and the decline in agricultural productivity spawned the immigration of Chinese to American shores.[6] The numbers of Chinese immigrants steadily increased after the so-called Opium War, due not only to the Chinese economy, but also to the widespread stories of available employment,

good wages, and the discovery of gold at Sutter's Mill, which filtered in through arrivals from the Western nations.[7]

The nativist movement of the 1830s resurfaced in the late 1840s and developed into a political party, the Know-Nothing Party.[8] Its western adherents added an anti-Chinese theme to the eastern anti-Catholic sentiment.[9] But once again, the nativist movement, while acquiring local political strength, failed in its attempts to enact legislation curbing immigration. On the local level, however, the cry of "America for Americans" often led to discriminatory State statutes that penalized certain racially identifiable groups.[10] As an example, California adopted licensing statutes for foreign miners and fishermen, which were almost exclusively enforced against Chinese.[11]

In the mid-1850s, the Know-Nothing Party lost steam as a result of a division over the question of slavery, the most important issue of that time.[12] The nativist movement and antiforeign sentiment receded because of the slavery issue and the Civil War. It maintained this secondary role until the Panic of 1873 struck.

Chinese Exclusion

The depression economy of the 1870s was blamed on aliens who were accused of driving wages to a substandard level as well as taking away jobs that "belonged" to white Americans. While the economic charges were not totally without basis, reality shows that most aliens did not compete with white labor for "desirable" white jobs. Instead, aliens usually were relegated to the most menial employment.[13]

The primary target was the Chinese, whose high racial visibility, coupled with cultural dissimilarity and lack of political power, made them more than an adequate scapegoat for the economic problems of the 1870s.[14] Newspapers adopted the exhortations of labor leaders, blaming the Chinese for the economic plight of the working class. Workers released their frustrations and anger on the Chinese, particularly in the West.[15] Finally, politicians succumbed to the growing cry for exclusion of Chinese.

From *The Tarnished Golden Door*, Civil Rights Issues in Immigration, September 1980, pp. 7-12. Reprinted by permission of The U.S. Commission on Civil Rights, Washington, D.C.

Congress responded by passing the Chinese Exclusion Act of 1882.[16] That act suspended immigration of Chinese laborers for 10 years, except for those who were in the country on November 17, 1880. Those who were not lawfully entitled to reside in the United States were subject to deportation. Chinese immigrants were also prohibited from obtaining United States citizenship after the effective date of the act.

The 1882 act was amended in 1884 to cover all subjects of China and Chinese who resided in any other foreign country.[17] Then in 1888, another act was enacted that extended the suspension of immigration for all Chinese except Chinese officials, merchants, students, teachers, and travelers for pleasure.[18] Supplemental legislation to that act also prohibited Chinese laborers from reentering the country, as provided for in the 1882 act, unless they reentered prior to the effective date of the legislation.[19]

Senator Matthew C. Butler of South Carolina summed up the congressional efforts to exclude Chinese by stating:

> [I]t seems to me that this whole Chinese business has been a matter of political advantage, and we have not been governed by that deliberation which it would seem to me the gravity of the question requires. In other words, there is a very important Presidential election pending. One House of Congress passes an act driving these poor devils into the Pacific Ocean, and the other House comes up and says, "Yes, we will drive them further into the Pacific Ocean, notwithstanding the treaties between the two governments."[20]

Nevertheless, the Chinese exclusion law was extended in 1892[21] and 1902,[22] and in 1904 it was extended indefinitely.[23]

Although challenged by American residents of Chinese ancestry, the provisions of these exclusion acts were usually upheld by judicial decisions. For example, the 1892 act[24] mandated that Chinese laborers obtain certificates of residency within 1 year after the passage of the act or face deportation. In order to obtain the certificate, the testimony of one credible white witness was required to establish that the Chinese laborer was an American resident prior to the passage of the act. That requirement was upheld by the United States Supreme Court in *Fong Yue Ting* v. *United States.* [25]

Literacy Tests and the Asiatic Barred Zone

The racial nature of immigration laws clearly manifested itself in further restrictions on prospective immigrants who were either from Asian countries or of Asian descent. In addition to extending the statutory life of the Chinese exclusion law, the 1902 act also applied that law to American territorial possessions, thereby prohibiting not only the immigration of noncitizen Chinese laborers from "such island territory to the mainland territory," but also "from one portion of the island territory of the United States to another portion of said island territory."[26] Soon after, Japanese were restricted from free immigration to the United States by the "Gentleman's Agreement" negotiated between the respective governments in 1907.[27] Additional evidence would be provided by the prohibition of immigration from countries in the Asia-Pacific Triangle as established by the Immigration Act of 1917.[28]

During this period, congressional attempts were also made to prevent blacks from immigrating to this country. In 1915 an amendment to exclude "all members of the African or black race" from admission to the United States was introduced in the Senate during its deliberations on a proposed immigration bill.[29] The Senate approved the amendment on a 29 to 25 vote,[30] but it was later defeated in the House by a 253 to 74 vote,[31] after intensive lobbying by the NAACP.[32]

In 1917 Congress codified existing immigration laws in the Immigration Act of that year.[33] That act retained all the prior grounds for inadmissibility and added illiterates to the list of those ineligible to immigrate, as a response to the influx of immigrants from southern and eastern Europe. Because of a fear that American standards would be lowered by these new immigrants who were believed to be racially "unassimilable" and illiterate, any alien who was over 16 and could not read was excluded. The other important feature of this statute was the creation of the Asia-Pacific Triangle, an Asiatic barred zone, designed to exclude Asians completely from immigration to the United States. The only exemptions from this zone were from an area that included Persia and parts of Afghanistan and Russia.

The 1917 immigration law reflected the movement of American immigration policy toward the curbing of free immigration. Free immigration, particularly from nations that were culturally dissimilar to the northern and western European background of most Americans, was popularly believed to be the root of both the economic problems and the social problems confronting this country.

The National Origins Quota System

Four years later, Congress created a temporary quota law that limited the number of aliens of any nationality who could immigrate to 3 percent of the United States residents of that nationality living in the country in 1910.[34] The total annual immigration allowable in any one year was set at 350,000. Western Hemisphere aliens were exempt from the quota if their country of origin was an independent nation and the alien had resided there at least 1 year.

The clear intent of the 1921 quota law was to confine immigration as much as possible to western and northern European stock. As the minority report noted:

The obvious purpose of this discrimination is the adoption of an unfounded anthropological theory that the nations which are favored are the progeny of fictitious and hitherto unsuspected Nordic ancestors, while those discriminated against are not classified as belonging to that mythical ancestral stock. No scientific evidence worthy of consideration was introduced to substantiate this pseudoscientific proposition. It is pure fiction and the creation of a journalistic imagination. . . .

The majority report insinuates that some of those who have come from foreign countries are non-assimilable or slow of assimilation. No facts are offered in support of such a statement. The preponderance of testimony adduced before the committee is to the contrary.[35]

Notwithstanding these objections, Congress made the temporary quota a permanent one with the enactment of the 1924 National Origins Act.[36] A ceiling of 150,000 immigrants per year was imposed. Quotas for each nationality group were 2 percent of the total members of that nationality residing in the United States according to the 1890 census.[37] Again, Western Hemisphere aliens were exempt from the quotas (thus, classified as "nonquota" immigrants). Any prospective immigrant was required to obtain a sponsor in this country and to obtain a visa from an American consulate office abroad. Entering the country without a visa and in violation of the law subjected the entrant to deportation without regard to the time of entry (no statute of limitation). Another provision, prohibiting the immigration of aliens ineligible for citizenship, completely closed the door on Japanese immigration, since the Supreme Court had ruled that Japanese were ineligible to become naturalized citizens.[38] Prior to the 1924 act, Japanese immigration had been subjected to "voluntary" restraint by the Gentleman's Agreement negotiated between the Japanese Government and President Theodore Roosevelt.

In addition to its expressed discriminatory provisions, the 1924 law was also criticized as discrimina-

tory against blacks in general and against black West Indians in particular.[39]

The Mexican "Repatriation" Campaign

Although Mexican Americans have a long history of residence within present United States territory,[40] Mexican immigration to this country is of relatively recent vintage.[41] Mexican citizens began immigrating to this country in significant numbers after 1909 because of economic conditions as well as the violence and political upheaval of the Mexican Revolution.[42] These refugees were welcomed by Americans, for they helped to alleviate the labor shortage caused by the First World War.[43] The spirit of acceptance lasted only a short time, however.

Spurred by the economic distress of the Great Depression, Federal immigration officials expelled hundreds of thousands of persons of Mexican descent from this country through increased Border Patrol raids and other immigration law enforcement techniques.[44] To mollify public objection to the mass expulsions, this program was called the "repatriation" campaign. Approximately 500,000 persons were "repatriated" to Mexico, with more than half of them being United States citizens.[45]

Erosion of Certain Discriminatory Barriers

Prior to the next recodification of the immigration laws, there were several congressional enactments that cut away at the discriminatory barriers established by the national origins system. In 1943 the Chinese Exclusion Act was repealed, allowing a quota of 105 Chinese to immigrate annually to this country and declaring Chinese eligible for naturalization.[46] The War Brides Act of 1945[47] permitted the immigration of 118,000 spouses and children of military servicemen. In 1946 Congress enacted legislation granting eligibility for naturalization to Pilipinos[48] and to races indigenous to India.[49] A Presidential proclamation in that same year increased the Pilipino quota from 50 to 100.[50] In 1948 the Displaced Persons Act provided for the entry of approximately 400,000 refugees from Germany, Italy, and Austria (an additional 214,000 refugees were later admitted to the United States).[51]

The McCarran-Walter Act of 1952

The McCarran-Walter Act of 1952,[52] the basic

law in effect today, codified the immigration laws under a single statute. It established three principles for immigration policy:
(1) the reunification of families,
(2) the protection of the domestic labor force, and
(3) the immigration of persons with needed skills.

However, it retained the concept of the national origins system, as well as unrestricted immigration from the Western Hemisphere. An important provision of the statute removed the bar to immigration and citizenship for races that had been denied those privileges prior to that time. Asian countries, nevertheless, were still discriminated against, for prospective immigrants whose ancestry was one-half of any Far Eastern race were chargeable to minimal quotas for that nation, regardless of the birthplace of the immigrant.

"Operation Wetback"

Soon after the repatriation campaigns of the 1930s, the United States entered the Second World War. Mobilization for the war effort produced a labor shortage that resulted in a shift in American attitudes toward immigration from Mexico. Once again Mexican nationals were welcomed with open arms. However, this "open arms" policy was just as short lived as before.

In the 1950s many Americans were alarmed by the number of immigrants from Mexico. As a result, then United States Attorney General Herbert Brownell, Jr., launched "Operation Wetback," to expel Mexicans from this country. Among those caught up in the expulsion campaign were American citizens of Mexican descent who were forced to leave the country of their birth. To ensure the effectiveness of the expulsion process, many of those apprehended were denied a hearing to assert their constitutional rights and to present evidence that would have prevented their deportation. More than 1 million persons of Mexican descent were expelled from this country in 1954 at the height of "Operation Wetback."[53]

The 1965 Amendments

The national origins immigration quota system generated opposition from the time of its inception, condemned for its attempts to maintain the existing racial composition of the United States. Finally, in 1965, amendments to the McCarran-Walter Act abolished the national origins system as well as the Asiatic barred zone.[54] Nevertheless, numerical restrictions were still imposed to limit annual immigration. The Eastern Hemisphere was subject to an overall limitation of 170,000 and a limit of 20,000 per

country. Further, colonial territories were limited to 1 percent of the total available to the mother country (later raised to 3 percent or 600 immigrants in the 1976 amendments). The Western Hemisphere, for the first time, was subject to an overall limitation of 120,000 annually, although no individual per-country limits were imposed. In place of the national origins system, Congress created a seven category preference system giving immigration priority to relatives of United States residents and immigrants with needed talents or skills.[55] The 20,000 limitation per country and the colonial limitations, as well as the preference for relatives of Americans preferred under the former selections process, have been referred to by critics as "the last vestiges of the national origins system" because they perpetuate the racial discrimination produced by the national origins system.

Restricting Mexican Immigration

After 1965 the economic conditions in the United States changed. With the economic crunch felt by many Americans, the cry for more restrictive immigration laws resurfaced. The difference from the 19th century situation is that the brunt of the attacks is now focused on Mexicans, not Chinese. High "guesstimates" of the number of undocumented Mexican aliens entering the United States, many of which originated from Immigration and Naturalization Service sources, have been the subject of press coverage.[56]

As a partial response to the demand for "stemming the tide" of Mexican immigration, Congress amended the Immigration and Nationality Act in 1976,[57] imposing the seven category preference system and the 20,000 numerical limitation per country on Western Hemisphere nations. Legal immigration from Mexico, which had been more than 40,000[58] people per year, with a waiting list 2 years long, was thus cut by over 50 percent.

Recent Revisions of the Immigrant Quota System

Although the annual per-country limitations have remained intact, Congress did amend the Immigration and Nationality Act in 1978 to eliminate the hemispheric quotas of 170,000 for Eastern Hemisphere countries and 120,000 for Western Hemisphere countries. Those hemispheric ceilings were replaced with an overall annual worldwide ceiling of 290,000.[59]

In 1980 the immigrant quota system was further revised by the enactment of the Refugee Act. In addition to broadening the definition of refugee, that statute eliminated the seventh preference visa category by establishing a separate worldwide ceiling for refugee admissions to this country. It also reduced the annual worldwide ceiling for the remaining six preference categories to 270,000 visas, and it increased the number of visas allocated to the second preference to 26 percent.[60]

[1] Ch. 58, 1 Stat. 570 (1798).
[2] Carl Wittke, *We Who Built America* (rev. 1964), p. 67.
[3] Ibid., pp. 129–33.
[4] Ibid., pp. 101–10.
[5] Ibid., pp. 491–97.
[6] Li Chien-nung, *The Political History of China, 1840–1928* (1956), pp. 48–49; Stanford Lyman, *Chinese Americans* (1974), pp. 4–5.
[7] Mary Roberts Coolidge, *Chinese Immigration* (1909), pp. 16–17.
[8] Wittke, *We Who Built America*, pp. 497–510.
[9] Coolidge, *Chinese Immigration*, p. 58.
[10] Ibid., pp. 69–82. Some municipalities also adopted ordinances that discriminated against Chinese. As an example, a San Francisco municipal ordinance, subsequently held unconstitutional in Yick Wo v. Hopkins, 118 U.S. 356 (1886), was enacted regulating the operation of public laundries but in practice was enforced almost exclusively against Chinese.
[11] Ibid., pp. 33–38, 69–74.
[12] Wittke, *We Who Built America*, pp. 509–10.
[13] As one author noted, "[b]efore the late 1870's the Chinese engaged only in such work as white laborers refused to perform. Thus the Chinese not only were noninjurious competitors but in effect were benefactors to the white laborer." S.W. Kung, *Chinese in American Life: Some Aspects of Their History, Status, Problems, and Contributions* (1962), p. 68.
[14] Carey McWilliams, *Brothers Under the Skin* (rev. 1951), pp. 101–03.
[15] Coolidge, *Chinese Immigration*, p. 188.
[16] Ch. 126, 22 Stat. 58 (1882).
[17] Ch. 220, 23 Stat. 115 (1884).
[18] Ch. 1015, 25 Stat. 476 (1888).
[19] Ch. 1064, 25 Stat. 504 (1888).
[20] 19 Cong. Rec. 8218 (1888).
[21] Ch. 60, 27 Stat. 25 (1892).
[22] Ch. 641, 32 Stat. 176 (1902).
[23] Ch. 1630, 33 Stat. 428. (1904).
[24] Ch. 60, 27 Stat. 25 (1892).
[25] 149 U.S. 698 (1893).
[26] Ch. 641, 32 Stat. 176 (1902).
[27] The Gentleman's Agreement of 1907, U.S. Department of State, *Papers Relating to the Foreign Relations of the United States 1924* (1939), vol. 2, p. 339.
[28] Ch. 29, 39 Stat. 874 (1917).
[29] 52 Cong. Rec. 805 (1914).
[30] *Id.* at 807.
[31] *Id.* at 1138–39.
[32] See *Crisis*, vol. 9 (February 1915), p. 190.
[33] Ch. 29, 39 Stat. 874 (1917).
[34] Ch. 8, 42 Stat. 5 (1921).
[35] As reprinted in the legislative history of the INA [1952] U.S. Code Cong. and Ad. News 1653, 1668.
[36] Ch. 190, 43 Stat. 153 (1924).
[37] That act provided, however, that:

> The annual quota of any nationality for the fiscal year beginning July 1, 1927, and for each fiscal year thereafter, shall be a number which bears the same ratio to 150,000 as the number of inhabitants in continental United States in 1920 having that national origin (ascertained as hereinafter provided in this section) bears to the number of inhabitants in continental United States in 1920, but the minimum quota of any nationality shall be 100.

Ch. 190, 43 Stat. 153, 159, §11(b).

[38] Early congressional enactments restricted eligibility for naturalization to free white persons (ch. 3, 1 Stat. 103 (1790)) and to persons of African nativity or descent (Rev. Stat. §2169 (1875)). But when Congress passed the Naturalization Act of June 29, 1906 (ch. 3592, 34 Stat. 596), persons of Japanese ancestry began submitting petitions to become naturalized citizens under the procedures established by that act. The Supreme Court, however, held that the 1906 act was limited by the prior congressional enactments and thus Japanese were ineligible for naturalization. Ozawa v. United States, 260 U.S. 178 (1922).
[39] "West Indian Immigration and the American Negro," *Opportunity*, October 1924, pp. 298–99.
[40] Under the Treaty of Guadalupe Hidalgo, many Mexican citizens became United States citizens after the annexation of territory by the United States following the Mexican War. Leo Grebler, Joan W. Moore, and Ralph C. Guzman, *The Mexican American People* (1970), pp. 40–41. The Treaty of Guadalupe Hidalgo is reprinted in Wayne Moquin, *A Documentary History of the Mexican Americans* (1971), p. 183.
[41] Grebler, Moore, and Guzman, *The Mexican American People*, pp. 62–63.
[42] Ibid.
[43] Ibid., p. 64.
[44] Ibid., pp. 523–26.
[45] Moquin, *A Documentary History of the Mexican Americans*, p. 294.
[46] Ch. 344, 57 Stat. 600 (1943).
[47] Ch. 591, 59 Stat. 659 (1945).
[48] 60 Stat. 1353.
[49] Ch. 534, 60 Stat. 416 (1946).
[50] Presidential Proclamation No. 2696, [1946] U.S. Code Cong. and Ad. News 1732.
[51] Ch. 647, 62 Stat. 1009 (1948).
[52] Ch. 477, 66 Stat. 163 (1952).
[53] Grebler, Moore, and Guzman, *The Mexican American People*, pp. 521–22. Mark A. Chamberlin *et al.*, eds., "Our Badge of Infamy: A Petition to the United Nations on the Treatment of the Mexican Immigrant," in *The Mexican American and the Law* (1974 ed.), pp. 31–34.
[54] Pub. L. No. 89–236, 79 Stat. 911 (1965).
[55] The 1965 amendments to the Immigration and Nationality Act provided the following seven category preference system:

> First preference: unmarried sons and daughters of U.S. citizens. (20 percent)
> Second preference: spouses and unmarried sons and daughters of lawful resident aliens. (20 percent plus any visas not required for first preference)
> Third preference: members of the professions and scientists and artists of exceptional ability and their spouses and children. (10 percent)
> Fourth preference: married sons and daughters of U.S. citizens and their spouses and children. (10 percent plus any visas not required for first three preferences)
> Fifth preference: brothers and sisters of U.S. citizens and their spouses and children. (24 percent plus any visas not required for first four preferences)
> Sixth preference: skilled and unskilled workers in occupations for which labor is in short supply in this country, and their spouses and children. (10 percent)
> Seventh preference: refugees. (6 percent)

Spouses and minor children of American citizens are exempt from the preference system.

[56] "6–8 million," *New West Magazine*, May 23, 1977; "4–12 million," *Los Angeles Times*, Aug. 7, 1977.
[57] Pub. L. No. 94–571, 90 Stat. 2703 (1976).
[58] In 1976 there were 57,863 immigrants from Mexico; in 1975, 62,205. U.S., Immigration and Naturalization Service, *Annual Report 1976*, p. 89.
[59] Pub. L. No. 95–412, 92 Stat. 907 (1978).
[60] Refugee Act of 1980, Pub. L. No. 96–212 (to be codified in scattered sections of 8 U.S.C.). The Refugee Act also increased the allocation of refugee visas to 50,000 annually for the first three fiscal years under the statute and provided that the number of refugee admissions in the following years would be determined by the President after consultation with Congress.

IMMIGRATION REFORM

OVERVIEW OF RECENT URBAN INSTITUTE IMMIGRATION POLICY RESEARCH

The past five years have been a time of unusual ferment in immigration law and policy. In 1986 Congress passed the landmark Immigration Reform and Control Act (IRCA), which was intended to give the government the tools required to bring illegal immigration under control. Four years later Congress enacted the Immigration Act of 1990, which increased the number of visas to be awarded and substantially transformed the legal immigration system by revising the labor, family, and other grounds for admitting immigrants into the United States.

With a Ford Foundation grant, The Urban Institute and The RAND Corporation embarked on a joint Immigration Research Program in 1988 to address continuing issues and problems pertaining to immigration and immigration policy. Some of their findings on changes introduced by the 1986 and 1990 legislation are presented in this special section on immigration.

New Tools

Taken together, the 1986 and 1990 immigration laws have introduced major new tools and approaches for U.S. immigration policy. IRCA, for example, established employer sanctions, the penalizing of employers hiring undocumented immigrants or committing associated violations. IRCA also authorized a series of legalization programs intended to regularize the immigration status of undocumented aliens residing in the United States.

New Enforcement Policies and Pressure for Compliance

The new laws substantially expanded the reach of immigration law and policy. The legislation assigned new responsibilities to the Immigration and Naturalization Service (INS) and mandated that

> The articles that follow place the 1986 and 1990 immigration laws in historical perspective. They also provide information about the effectiveness of the legalization and employment sanction programs of IRCA; and the projected effects of the 1990 Immigration Act on the size and composition of the immigrant population in the United States. An article on the changing role of the INS, and a review of immigrant policies in Western Europe round out this special section on immigration reform.

the business community comply with IRCA. IRCA's employer sanctions brought all U.S. employers under a new regime of labor regulation; and the legalization provisions of the law altered the status of several million immigrants residing in the United States.

New Influx of Immigrants

These laws have contributed to increased migration to the United States. More than 2. 5 million people have attained legal status under

IRCA's amnesty provisions. The Immigration Act of 1990 not only increases the number of annual legal admissions by 40 percent, it also provides several avenues for regularizing the legal status of many in the United States who remain undocumented. As these demographic changes occur, the question arises whether the nation needs an immigrant policy that better protects newcomers' social and economic integration to complement immigration reform initiatives.

New Rationale

The new laws also alter the rationale used for selection of immigrants. Perhaps the most notable change is the gradual shift in emphasis that the 1990 legislation embodies. It moves away from the social goal of family unification to the economic goal of meeting the labor force requirements of employers. At the same time, though, the 1990 immigration law counterbalances this trend by increasing the number of family members admitted through the creation of a temporary "safe haven" for undocumented Salvadorans already in the United States.

New Problems

But recent legislation has inadvertently introduced a number of new immigration-related problems. Most debated has been the expansion in discrimination against foreign-sounding or -looking job applicants. Another less noticed problem involves the proliferation of taxing new responsibilities assigned to an already overburdened INS and a diffusion of the agency's mission. These emerging areas of concern are the focus of Institute research now underway.

From *Policy and Research Report*, Winter/Spring 1991, pp. 11-20. Reprinted by permission of The Urban Institute, 2100 M Street, NW, Washington, D.C., 20037.

RECENT TRENDS AND LEGISLATIVE RESPONSES

Although other nations may receive larger numbers of immigrants in relation to their population, no other nation willingly accepts as many new settlers as does the United States. Significant changes in U.S. immigration law in 1986 and 1990 have reaffirmed this country's openness to immigrants. The legislative acts address significant changes in the numbers, origins, and legal status of the nation's immigrant population that have occurred in the past three decades. Recent work by Urban Institute researchers Michael Fix and Jeffrey S. Passel puts both laws into historical context and assesses the likely effects of the 1990 legislation.

Legal immigration to the United States has increased steadily over the past five decades, from about 1 million immigrants in the 1940s to some 6 million in the 1980s. More immigrants live in the United States now than at any time in history— more than 17 million. But the rate of immigration in the 1980s was not the highest our nation has experienced. The number of arriving immigrants peaked at 8.8 million in the first decade of the twentieth century, when our population was about one-third of what it is today.

Moreover, while recently the proportion of foreign-born persons in the United States has been increasing steadily, from about 4.9 percent in 1970 to about 7 percent in 1990, this does not even approach the levels of the nineteenth century. Then, about 1 person in 7, or almost 15 percent of the population, was foreign-born. This ratio of foreign-born to native-born began a steady decline in 1932. The immigration cutbacks can be traced to a number of factors, including the restrictive immigration laws of 1921 and 1924, the inhibiting effect of the great depression and world war II, and the aging of earlier groups of immigrants.

1986 IMMIGRATION ACT IN HISTORICAL PERSPECTIVE

The impact of immigrants on the labor force also is less today. In 1907 alone, for example, the number of immigrants who found jobs when they arrived added about 3 percent to the U.S. labor force. An equivalent amount of immigration today would mean an annual flow of 9 million persons into the United States — more than ten times current numbers.

In the nineteenth century, virtually all immigration to the United States was from Europe and Canada; this trend continued into the 1950s. By the 1980s, however, only 14 percent originated from Europe and Canada.

The most dramatic change is an increase in the proportion of Asian immigrants, which rose from 13 percent in the 1960s to 44 percent in the 1980s. In this same period, immigration of Mexicans and other Latin Americans remained steady, at 14 percent and 26-27 percent, respectively.

The explosive increase in the immigration of Asians to the United States—2.6 million arrived in the 1980s—can be traced to the legal changes incorporated into the Immigration Act of 1965. That law put immigrants from all countries on essentially equal footing and eased restrictions in force since 1885 against immigration from Asia.

As total immigration increased during the 1980s, so did the number of illegal immigrants. The estima-

ted number of illegal aliens in this country rose from 2.5 to 3.5 million in 1980 to 3 to 5 million by 1986.

Enactment of the Immigration Reform and Control Act (IRCA) in 1986 authorized legalization of immigrants who had resided illegally in the United States since before January 1, 1982. Since the law's passage, some 2.5 million formerly illegal aliens have attained legal status; the estimated number of illegal aliens remaining is 1.8 to 3 million.

These estimates of the undocumented population are lower than might be expected, considering recent media publicity given to apprehensions of illegal aliens along the U.S.-Mexico border. Such publicity, however, obscures two important factors: First, much of the inflow from Mexico consists of temporary labor migrants; and second, there is a large, unreported reverse flow from this country back into Mexico.

The impact of immigration, both legal and illegal, is uneven across the country. Three-quarters of all immigrants who arrived in the United States in the 1980s came to only six states—California, New York, Texas, Florida, Illinois, and New Jersey. During this period two states— California and New York—received more than half, about 3.3 million of the total 6 million. Of these, 2.3 million arrived in California and 1 million in New York.

This uneven impact played a key role in the redistribution of U.S. population during the 1980s, a decade of considerable population growth. For example, California's huge population increase, confirmed in the 1990 census, was fueled mainly by immigrants. Texas received significant numbers of both immigrants and internal migrants. But the arrival of large numbers of immigrants in New York and Illinois nevertheless failed to offset the exodus of residents out of these states in the 1980s.

These shifts in the numbers, origins, and geographical distribution of immigrants provided the impetus for the Immigration Act of 1990, which addresses primarily the issue of legal immigration. The act defines the family unit, labor, and other criteria for admitting immigrants to the United States.

1990

IMMIGRATION

ACT AND ITS

LIKELY

EFFECTS

The Immigration Act of 1990 was enacted at a time of extreme economic uncertainty, when the nation was poised on the brink of a recession and the outbreak of war in the Persian Gulf. In an era when other industrialized countries are making their immigration laws more restrictive, the 1990 act authorizes an *increase* in legal immigration to the United States. In so doing, it complements the 1986 attempt of the Immigration Reform and Control Act (IRCA) to close the "back door" of illegal immigration with a legislative strategy for keeping open the "front door" of legal immigration.

This liberalization allows entry of many more family members of immigrants and creates a temporary "safe haven" for as many as 500,000 undocumented Salvadorans already in the United States. Thus, it stands in sharp contrast to IRCA, which focused primarily on limiting illegal immigration.

Passage of the 1990 act was driven by three imperatives:

• **Economic**—to forge a closer link between immigration and human resources policy, in order to avoid the anticipated mismatch between the numbers and skill requirements of future U.S. jobs and the numbers and skill levels of future immigrants.

• **Cultural**—to encourage more diversity in the immigrant stream.

• **Social**—to promote family unity.

The provisions of the 1990 law, according to Fix and Passel, signal two important conceptual shifts in U.S. immigration policy: a stronger focus on labor market concerns and an interest in diversifying the immigrant stream, principally by increasing the number of immigrants from Europe.

Cap on Immigration. The new law places a yearly cap on total immigration for the first time since the 1920s. For 1992-95 the limit is 700,000 persons; for the years thereafter, 675,000.

The cap, however, may be more symbolic than real because the law allows an unlimited number of visas for immediate relatives of U.S. citizens (now about 220,000 per year), while at the same time setting a floor of 226,000 visas for other family-based immigration.

Employment-Related Immigration. The number of visas reserved for workers under the new law will increase significantly—from the current level of 58,000 per year to 140,000. However, only about 40 percent of the total is expected to be workers; the others are likely to be members of workers' families. The new law emphasizes admission of skilled workers by capping the number of visas for unskilled workers at 10,000, about half the number allowed under previous law.

Diversity. Perhaps the most interesting innovation in the Immigration Act of 1990 is the class of diversity visas it creates to "seed" immigration from countries that have sent comparatively few migrants to the United States in recent years. However, the diversity criteria are not demanding enough to ensure such an outcome. In fact, during the three years following the law's enactment, national origin and not human capital considerations will largely determine who obtains a visa.

Family-Based Immigration. An important sign of the new law's pro-immigrant character is its approach to family-based immigration. These provisions are driven by congressional interest in promoting the nuclear family, by an interest in eventually diversifying the immigrant stream, and by a less publicized interest in reducing the size of the nation's illegal population.

The provisions increase the number of persons who may enter based on the family categories. Admissions of immediate family members of United States citizens remain unlimited under the act; the preexisting preference system has been updated; and 55,000 visas per year for three years will go to immediate family members of immigrants who have attained legal status under IRCA's so-called amnesty programs.

Thus, despite public attention given to the increase in employment-based immigration, the bill did not increase workers at the expense of family-based admissions.

Reducing the size of the Undocumented Population. Several lesser-known provisions of the new law best demonstrate its generous, inclusionary nature. The legislation, for instance, prohibits the deportation of, and grants work authorization to, all spouses and children of the 2.5 to 2.8 million persons who will eventually attain legal status under IRCA, if the spouses and children were in the United States before May 5, 1988.

Another provision creates a temporary "safe haven" for a minimum of 18 months for an estimated 350,000 to 500,000 Salvadorans who, although living in the United States, were generally ineligible for legalization and remain undocumented.

Agencies in Charge of the Implementation. The liberal values that characterize the bill are striking, especially in areas related to public health. Whereas in IRCA the principal agency of enforcement was the Immigration and Naturalization Service, under the 1990 bill responsibility for implementation is assigned to Health and Human Services, which is given the authority to determine whether a person "has a communicable disease of public health significance" or "has a physical or mental disorder that could or has in the past posed a threat to others." The former made possible a recently announced, sweeping revision of the nation's policy on immigration and AIDS. The latter substantially eliminates most grounds for excluding those with a physical or mental disability.

Passage of the 1990 act should quiet the concerns of many who feared that enactment of IRCA in 1986 signaled a new, restrictive era of immigration policy. The various programs have the power to change the legal status and work eligibility of more than 1 million persons. In terms of sheer numbers, immigrants in the United States under the legalization and safe-haven provisions clearly outnumber the 34,000 new skilled workers admitted annually under the bill.

Future Research Focus

Urban Institute demographers and immigration analysts are taking a close look at the impact of the 1990 law on the size and makeup of the immigrant stream entering the United states. This work in turn will contribute to Institute assessments of the future effects of immigration on the composition of the U.S. population. Another focus will be the family structure of different immigrant groups both within the United States and within the immigrants' countries of origin in order to predict future immigration trends.

Institute research is also addressing a broad range of economic impacts. For example, how do new immigrants fare economically? What impact do they have on the native-born work force? An analysis of the community impacts of immigrants is forthcoming, with research addressing the fiscal and other costs engendered by recent immigration.

Finally, another set of under-researched issues—those relating to immigrant policy—is an area of focus. Should the United States have a deliberate policy for integrating immigrants into society and for providing them specialized services? The Institute's program on immigration policy is developing a taxonomy of state and local immigrant policy and trying to determine how the state and local governments respond to increases in the number of immigrants and reductions in federal support for immigrant services.

A conference in summer 1991 will examine some of these issues, specifically immigrant integration, adaptation, and policy.

For further information see "The Door Remains Open: Recent Immigration to the United States and a Preliminary Analysis of the Immigration Act of 1990," by Michael Fix and Jeffrey S. Passel, available from the Institute's Research Paper Sales Office for $8.00.

ILLEGAL IMMIGRATION: ARE EMPLOYER SANCTIONS WORKING?

Newly available research on undocumented immigration indicates that one of the major goals of the 1986 Immigration Reform and Control Act (IRCA)—to reduce the flow of undocumented migrants into the United States—was achieved, at least in the short term. Border apprehensions and undocumented immigration declined substantially in the years immediately following enactment of the legislation.

However, much of the decrease in the flow of undocumented immigrants through 1989 appears to result from the 1986 IRCA legislation *legalizing* formerly illegal residents, not from the legislatively mandated employer sanctions. The legalization of more than 1 million agricultural workers and 1.7 million other illegal immigrants removed many individuals from the flow. Yet, recent evidence of a resurgence in illegal immigration in 1990 calls into question the effectiveness of employer sanctions. If the number of illegal aliens is rising, even after successful implementation of legalization efforts, are the IRCA sanctions working?

The Paper Curtain, a book of essays edited by Institute researcher Michael Fix, helps answer this question. It provides a series of perspectives on the impact of these sanctions, their implementation, and potential reforms in light of the growing controversy about employer sanctions and whether they should be retained and reformed, or repealed.

In a concluding chapter, Fix summarizes three arguments for repealing employer sanctions:

1. *Flows of illegal immigrants.* The analysis of flows, based on apprehensions along the southern border of the United States, indicates that the comparatively steep decline in illegal immigration through FY89 reversed itself sharply in FY90, when the number of apprehensions per linewatch hour rose 22 percent. The reversal tends to reinforce the contention of co-researcher Jeffrey S. Passel and others that the decrease before 1990 was largely due to the

effects of the legalization program and would continue to erode over time.

2. *Farm labor stability*. If sanctions were having their intended effect, there would have been less worker turnover and more regular employment of authorized workers in California agriculture. Philip Martin and Edward Taylor demonstrate in one of the book's chapters that this has not been the case. Instead, turnover among farm workers is increasing, not decreasing, as new immigrant workers continue to be drawn to seasonal farm work, largely through the recruitment of farm labor contractors.

3. *National origin and citizenship discrimination.* Given supporting evidence in numerous studies, it is reasonable to conclude that some new employer discrimination can be tied to IRCA.

Overall, sanctions appear to be ineffective in reducing undocumented immigration, stabilizing turnover in low-wage industries such as California agriculture, and avoiding the unintended costs of additional discrimination. The case against sanctions is strengthened further by recent regulatory developments that will increase the burden borne by law-abiding employers.

Proponents of employer sanctions, on the other hand, claim that they reflect a consensus, at least among lawmakers, that tolerates increased admission of immigrants as long as the perception of control remains in place. Moreover, they contend that there is no good policy alternative to sanctions and that sanctions are a necessary part of any long-term strategy to control illegal immigration, albeit one that may need to be reformed.

Among the book's suggested reforms:

• Substantially increased resources for employer education regarding discrimination.

• A federally funded follow-up study of sanctions-related discrimination, using both audits and surveys.

• More systematic oversight of sanction practices and penalties, together with expedited development of a national data base that permits enforcement officials to monitor implementation for fairness and consistency.

• Rapid transition to requiring two identification documents for immigrants (reducing the potential for fraud).

• Substantial expansion of the Department of Labor's role in enforcing employer sanctions.

The last reform is the most challenging and potentially far-reaching. It is based on European success in linking sanctions to labor law enforcement, and would permit enforcement of workplace regulations by an experienced inspection staff. The strategy also has the advantage of identifying employers who violate both immigration and labor laws and coordinating their prosecution. Shifting responsibility to the Department of Labor may help link the administration of employer sanctions with a broad and effective employer education campaign and antidiscrimination mandates.

For further information see Undocumented Migration to the United States: IRCA and the Experience of the 1980s, *edited by Frank D. Bean, Barry Edmonston, and Jeffrey S. Passel, Urban Institute Press, 1990, $18.75;* The Paper Curtain: Employer Sanctions' Implementation, Impact, and Reform, *edited by Michael Fix, Urban Institute Press, summer 1991.*

LEGALIZATION PROGRAMS: A CAUTIOUS WELCOME

Implementing the legalization programs created by the Immigration Reform and Control Act of 1986 (IRCA) presented a multifaceted challenge to the Immigration and Naturalization Service (INS).

Congress authorized two temporary, one-time legalization programs—a general one for immigrants who had resided in the United States continuously since 1982, and the Special Agricultural Worker (SAW) program for undocumented agricultural workers who had resided in the United States for at least six months.

The INS was responsible for implementing both programs, each with its own requirements. The administrative burden was compounded by the fact that in each program some of the required steps for obtaining legal status posed complicated questions, including how to ensure both availability of and funding for the services.

The INS responded slowly, beginning its outreach effort only one month before the start of the application period for temporary residence (Phase I) under the general program, and publishing proposed regulations only four days before the program started. The regulations for Phase II—receipt of permanent resident status—were issued nine months after the first applicants became eligible for it. When the perception grew that the legalization program was not working, immigrant advocacy groups prodded the INS both through litigation and by working more closely with local INS officials. As a result of the legalization programs created by IRCA, more than 2.5 million undocumented immigrants have achieved legal status.

Former Institute researcher Susan González Baker reviewed INS implementation of legalization programs and analyzed remaining implementation problems as well as successes. Her findings are based on interviews with government and private officials and agencies responsible for program implementation and on first-hand observation by Urban Institute and RAND Corporation researchers at eight study sites: Los Angeles, San Jose, San Antonio, El Paso, Houston, Chicago, New York, and Miami.

The general legalization program has been more successful in processing applicants than the SAW program for undocumented agricultural workers, which has been plagued by charges of fraud as well as by a lack of resources.

Nationally, approval rates for the general program exceed 90 percent. But, two years after the close of the SAW program, over 400,000 of the 1.4 million applicants remain in limbo awaiting resolution of their petitions.

Although approval rates for the general program were high, turnout varied widely by region and city. Of the 1.7 million applicants, 1 million filed their petitions in the eight study cities, nearly 700,000 of them in Los Angeles. Aggressive publicity by Los Angeles INS officials and high-profile advocacy from immigrants' rights groups contributed to the city's large turnout.

By contrast, only 100,000 applications, half of the expected turnout, were filed in New York City. González Baker attributes this low turnout both to the difficulty of conducting publicity and outreach activities in areas with a more diverse immigrant population and to the commitment of fewer resources by the New York INS.

Turnout was heaviest among Mexican undocumented immigrants. Although a little more than 50 percent of the total undocumented population was of Mexican origin, about 75 percent of the immigrant population with legal status reported Mexico as their country of citizenship. Such heavy turnout is attributed at least in part to the INS Spanish language publicity campaign. When other ethnic groups also were mobilized through aggressive outreach strategies, early turnout was substantial, as evidenced by the 16,000 Polish applicants in Chicago.

Advocacy groups played a crucial and often under-appreciated role in sustaining the INS commitment to legalization. Even in communities where INS officials made legislation a top priority, immigrant advocates continued to play an important role. This included forging cooperative relationships with the agency, counseling applicants on how to file petitions, and filing class action lawsuits on behalf of applicants.

Assistance to newly arrived immigrants, particularly at the community level, will continue to be important as the United States shifts some of its focus from legalization efforts to ways to integrate newcomers more effectively into society.

For further information see The Cautious Welcome: The Legalization Programs of the Immigration Reform and Control Act, *by Susan González Baker, 1990, from The Urban Institute Press in association with The RAND Corporation, $19.00.*

THE CHANGING ROLE OF THE INS

In 1986, the landmark Immigration Reform and Control Act (IRCA) charged the Immigration and Naturalization Service (INS) with implementing two complex programs: Employer sanctions, subjecting 7 million firms to regulation by the INS for the first time, and legalization, offering amnesty to several million illegal immigrants. The reform law also expanded the INS Border Patrol, required states to use an INS data base to verify the legal status of immigrants applying for public benefits, and increased the INS budget.

How well has the agency coped with these dual responsibilities and expanded tasks? Urban Institute researcher Jason Juffras, whose recent study examined IRCA's effect on the INS, reports that the generally positive impact of IRCA on the INS was weakened by two developments.

First, the INS responded to congressional pressure to increase efforts to deport criminal aliens and interdict drugs. While these programs may have been worthwhile, they overstrained the INS staff and precipitated a budget crisis in the agency in 1989.

Second, because the agency grew so rapidly, the decentralized management structure of INS—consisting of a central office, four regional offices, 33 district offices, and 22 Border Patrol sectors—was unable to provide sufficient oversight and ensure consistent implementation of the new programs.

Effects on INS Enforcement

Juffras noted that the INS implemented employer sanctions mostly in a measured and cooperative way, emphasizing the education of employers and voluntary compliance. Sanctions represented a major stride for the INS toward becoming a regulatory agency controlling incentives instead of a police agency controlling people. These sanctions have promoted an enforcement process that is fairer, more predictable, and less intrusive than the workplace raids the INS had formerly employed. However, as described below, sanctions have been a less important enforcement priority for the INS than IRCA sponsors might have imagined.

The INS did a creditable job in implementing sanctions largely because Congress imposed constraints on the agency even as it expanded its enforcement power. The "sunset" provision ensuring three annual reviews of the impact of sanctions on employment discrimination was the most important constraint. Another factor in the successful implementation effort was the willingness of the INS to recruit special agents—the plainclothes officers who take the lead in enforcing sanctions—from outside the agency. The new agents made it easier for the INS to switch from a policy emphasizing workplace raids to one stressing employer education and voluntary compliance.

Yet sanctions were only one of several important changes in INS enforcement policy between 1986 and 1989. IRCA also set the target of a 50 percent increase in the Border Patrol. The cost of such an expansion, as well as the political appeal of the Border Patrol, ultimately meant that most of the added enforcement resources the INS received to implement IRCA were devoted to border control and not to employer sanctions. During the same period, two major antidrug bills enacted in 1986 and 1988 mandated that the INS do more to remove criminal aliens from the United States and interdict drugs at the border. Staff and money were funneled into these responsibilities, leaving sanctions with only one-third of INS's extra enforcement money in 1987 and 1988.

As a result of these changes in enforcement policy, the INS entered the 1990s as a diversified and more versatile law enforcement agency. INS investigators typically divided their time among sanctions, criminal alien removal, and antifraud efforts. The Border Patrol has also broadened its role and become more specialized. The patrol now serves as

both the leading drug interdictor along the land border and as a participant in more antidrug task forces with other agencies.

The downside of this growth in enforcement responsibilities is that it outstripped the agency's capacity for effective oversight. Regional and district offices had to be given considerable latitude, resulting in different priorities and procedures around the country. District offices and Border Patrol sectors often operated independently in pursuing sanctions and criminal alien cases. Overall, concern about sanctions seemed to decline as INS managers decided to stress criminal alien removal and drug interdiction.

The 1989 INS budget crisis reflected the inability of this agency to meet all of its new enforcement responsibilities. In trying to reach the target of 50 percent expansion of the Border Patrol, the INS exceeded its budget by $50 million, forcing an agency-wide hiring freeze and cuts in other programs.

Effects on INS Services

INS services also benefited from IRCA, although the positive impact of the legislation on INS services was the result of a long and difficult learning process. From the outset of the legalization programs, the INS was criticized for insufficient outreach services to illegal immigrants and for overly restrictive regulations on eligibility. Despite these problems, the INS eventually improved its outreach services, eased its regulations under pressure from advocacy groups, and gradually learned which groups immigrants tend to trust and how to target outreach to different ethnic communities. This learning process should help the INS communicate more effectively with immigrant groups in the future.

To implement legalization programs, the INS had to hire hundreds of new staff members and transfer staff from other divisions into the program. Many of the new staff received praise for their willingness to serve immigrants, and the expo-

sure of long-time employees to a service program provided them with the experience and increased the commitment needed for the INS to improve its other service programs.

Finally, the sheer challenge of the legalization program, which involved processing 3 million people through a two-step procedure—permanent residency and then citizenship—spurred the INS to improve the infrastructure and funding mechanisms for its service programs. To assist with these efforts the INS computerized its regional and district legalization offices, an important step for an agency criticized for its lack of automation. The INS also paid for legalization entirely through applicant fees. This experience with user fees led Congress to grant the INS authority to switch its services to user-fee funding, a change that will put the INS on firmer financial footing in the future.

Overall, IRCA increased the importance of service programs in the INS while retaining the dominance of enforcement programs. As the INS almost doubled its budget—from $570 million in 1986 to $1.12 billion in 1990—the service programs fared quite well, increasing by 166 percent. Yet, service programs still account for only 12 percent of the INS budget. In other respects, such as the allocation of attorneys to INS programs, enforcement continues to take precedence over services.

For further information see Impact of the Immigration Reform and Control Act on the Immigration and Naturalization Service, *by Jason Juffras, January 1991, from The Urban Institute Press in association with The RAND Corporation, $10.25.*

THE EUROPEAN EXPERIENCE WITH IMMIGRANT POLICIES

As the numbers of immigrants and refugees arriving on European and American soil increase, the need for a coherent set of policies addressing their specific needs takes on heightened importance. This is especially true for Western Europe, where the reunification of East and West Germany, dramatic changes in Eastern Europe, and the movement toward a single European market in 1992 prompt urgent consideration of immigrant and refugee issues.

The increasing cultural and linguistic diversity of the new arrivals is expected to expand the immigration debate beyond such traditional issues as the criteria for admission to

> *"While these countries have developed explicit immigrant policies [implementation] has been less than successful."*

a particular country. Equally important will be the ability of the host countries to meet the educational and social service needs of various immigrant groups. What models exist for developing such a coherent approach and how relevant are they to the U.S. experience?

Three European countries—Germany, France, and the United Kingdom—have all received large numbers of immigrants since the turn of the century and will probably receive substantially more over the next ten years. Each of these countries has established policies aimed at integrating the immigrants and refugees already there, while pursuing other policies to restrict new arrivals.

Immigration to these countries began mostly as temporary labor recruitment that evolved into permanent immigration through ad

hoc but deliberate integration policies over time. Institute researcher Wendy Zimmermann and colleague Charles Calhoun, now at Fannie Mae, look at the experiences of France, Germany, and the United Kingdom and draw lessons, where possible, for U.S. immigrant policy.

Zimmermann and Calhoun base their findings on a series of interviews conducted during May and June of 1990 with immigrant officials, immigration researchers, and representatives from immigrant organizations in France, Great Britain, and the former Federal Republic of Germany. The interviews have been supplemented with a selective review of published research and current reporting on immigration and immigrant policy in Europe.

Despite differences in attitudes toward immigration, the fundamental principle governing policymaking in all three countries is to restrict newcomers while integrating those already in the country. Immigrants are generally granted access to education, housing, and social services by law, but in practice are often denied equal access to services, either because of political conflicts, discrimination, or competition for resources. For instance:

• In Germany, immigrants have equal legal access to government-subsized low-income housing; but the combination of a quota system, a general housing shortage, and the practice of giving priority to former East German migrants and ethnic Germans coming from Eastern Europe has in practice limited availability of housing.

• In the United Kingdom, local districts are less likely to build schools in low-income, heavily immigrant areas for fear of being perceived as pro-immigration.

• In France, although the government has developed language and integration programs in schools, these programs reach only a few

and often are not of high quality.

Thus, while these countries have developed explicit immigrant policies, even as they have followed a restrictionist approach to the admission of new immigrants, implementation of those policies has been less than successful. Moreover, increasing illegal immigration, a growing population of refugees and people seeking asylum, and political and economic developments in Eastern Europe have also begun to divert the attention and resources of the European governments away from integration and toward a policy of greater immigration control.

Despite different immigration histories and varying attitudes toward immigration and immigrants in Europe and in the United States, some comparisons can be made. For instance, although access to permanent residence and citizenship is somewhat easier in the United States, access to social services is more complex and restrictive. The best example of this is the five-year ban in the United States on eligibility for benefits facing the undocumented population that recently attained legal status.

Zimmermann and Calhoun suggest that U.S. policymakers turn their attention to creating deliberate policies and programs that meet the diverse needs of the country's immigrants and refugees. These policies will need to address, among other issues, immigrant education, housing, public benefits, employment, and vocational training. While the European countries may not provide the best example of how immigrant policies should be implemented, they offer a model for making integration and immigrant programs an explicit goal of public policy.

For further information see "Immigrant Policies in Western Europe," by Wendy Zimmermann and Charles Calhoun, available from the Institute's Research Paper Sales Office for $8.00.

New Americans weather and survive

Al Santoli

Al Santoli is the son of an Italian immigrant and is married to a Vietnamese refugee. A veteran of the Vietnam war, he has been active in refugee affairs for the past six years. He lives in New York City and is a contributing editor of Parade *magazine. His book,* New Americans: An Oral History, *from which these excerpts were taken, was published in 1988 by Viking Press.*

Since the 1960s, American society has been undergoing a transformation that is dynamic and at the same time challenges the very ideals that the nation was founded and built upon. We are a culture of immigrants whose sweat, visions and schemes have fueled the evolution of industry and technology and augmented the freedoms of faith, enterprise and expression still denied to most areas of the world. We are now experiencing the most awesome surge of immigrants and refugees in modern times. The newcomers, mostly Asians, Latins, Creoles, Africans, Moslems, Jews and Slavs are not only changing the ethnic makeup of America, but also creating a dramatic impact in many communities.

[Here are four stories from refugees from diverse parts of the globe and their struggles adapting to their adopted homeland.]

From Kabul, Afghanistan to Eastham, Mass.

Of the 16 million people in Afghanistan before the 1979 invasion, more than a million have been killed, and at least five million have fled — nearly half of the world's total refugee population. A select few—fewer than 20,000—have been allowed into the United States.

Mohammad Daud Nassery (called Dowd by his American friends) had been a pediatrician in Afghanistan. Two years earlier, he escaped twice from his ravaged homeland. After surviving a dangerous journey across the Hindu Kush Mountains, he returned to Kabul with a small group of freedom fighters to rescue his wife and three small daughters. They arrived penniless at the Pakistan frontier, joining 3 million other destitute Afghani refugees.

For Daud and his family, freedom has not come easily. Although he is a competent physician, refugee doctors are unable to practice in America until they complete a grueling series of medical examinations in the English language. While waiting to take the exams, Daud took a job in a hardware store to support his growing family. [They settled in Cape Cod, Mass. with the help of Edward and Bernice Brown, the family with whom Daud had lived as a foreign exchange student 15 years earlier. The community contributed to a fund for their expenses.]

Mohammad Daud Nassery: *The Browns had found a house for us, even before we arrived. . . . The house was in pretty run-down shape. So the Browns made an agreement*

Reprinted with permission from *State Government News*, Vol. 32, No. 1, January 1989, pp. 11-15. © 1989 by The Council of State Governments.

with the landlord that, in exchange for repairing the house, my family could live rent-free for 12 months. During the first three weeks, we lived with the Browns while our friends helped us to renovate our new home.

We put in new windows, repaired the electrical and heating systems, replaced the water pump, painted the walls and varnished the exposed wood. With the help of our friends, we put in hundreds of work hours. Truly a labor of love.

With money that was left in the fund, I bought a refrigerator, a television, a gas stove and other appliances. Mrs. Brown was just like a mother to us. Whenever we needed something, I would talk with her and she'd provide it from the fund. Most of the lamps and furniture were donated by friends and local people.

After I arrived in Eastham, it wasn't five or six days before I began working in Mr. Baskin's hardware store. I work five days a week, usually 47 hours, with Wednesdays and Sundays off. I earn around $250 a week after taxes, which comes to around $12,000 a year. It is a good job — steady work providing service for the community. I've learned to do anything that the job requires. But I am not very happy, because it's not my profession. I would rather be at a hospital or medical institute, where I could be learning new things while I wait to take my certification exam.

Sometimes, I think that I am not going to be able to go back into medicine. I'm trying to save at least $10,000 so I can support my family while I take the medical refresher course I need before I take the certification exam.

To be honest, I have some of the medical texts that I need to study, but I'm so exhausted when I get home from work that I don't have the energy. And I have responsibilities to my family. My kids have all kinds of questions about life here. My wife and I try to maintain communication with family and friends inside Afghanistan and scattered around the world. And we have to do the shopping. If the kids are sick, I am not allowed to write out a pre-scription, so we have to take them to another doctor. I always go because my wife can't speak English.

Even though she was a high school teacher in Kabul, here she is helpless because she doesn't know the language. To regain a teaching certification, it will cost a lot of time and money to go back to school. In this part of the Cape, there are no adult English-language classes for foreigners.

[In 1987, Daud began the medical certification study program in Amherst, Mass.]

From Trzebinia, Poland to Providence, R.I.

Jozef Patyna was a coal miner in southern Poland in 1980 when a grassroots movement for workers' rights and national independence spread throughout the country. The nonviolent uprising led by farmers, students and blue-collar workers gave birth to the Solidarity Union, led by a humble electrician named Lech Walesa. Solidarity, with 10 million members — almost a third of Poland's total population — became the first independent labor union in Soviet-controlled Eastern Europe.

During Solidarity's first national Congress, Jozef was elected to the union's executive committee. His task was to mediate disputes between workers and government officials. By December 1981, a growing crescendo of student demonstrations and labor strikes indicated the demand for true democracy in the upcoming national elections. In response, Soviet and East German troops massed along Poland's borders.

Solidarity's leaders called an emergency meeting in Gdansk, a northern port city, to attempt peace talks with the government. In the predawn hours of Sunday, Dec. 12, a group of Solidarity organizers informally gathered in Jozef's hotel room to discuss conciliatory promises by the government. They didn't realize that heavily armed militia were surrounding their building. Without warning, police stormed into Jozef's room. Within hours, secret jails throughout the country were filled with Solidarity activists.

Hundreds of other people were killed or disappeared.

Jozef endured six months of brutal incarceration before suffering a heart attack. Released to his hometown, he was under constant police surveillance. A government blacklist made him unemployable. He faced three choices: suicide, a return to prison or fleeing with his wife and two children out of the country. In late 1983, following thousands of Polish patriots who had already fled, the Patyna family arrived in the United States.

Jozef: *We arrived in Rhode Island from West Germany on Dec. 21, 1983. It was a very cold Wednesday night, 10 p.m. We were four people, including my wife, Krystyna; our teen-age daughter, Magdalena; and our 11-year-old son Przemyslaw (Shem). We were exhausted from the time change — it was 4 a.m. European time — and the long flight.*

Our American sponsor, who met us at Providence Airport, was a stranger. She was a middle-aged woman who volunteered to sponsor us through a refugee-assistance agency. She didn't speak Polish and had no translator. We couldn't understand what she was talking about because we couldn't speak English. We felt very awkward using sign language. We just gestured with our hands.

Krystyna: *Now we can laugh about it. But at the time we were very confused and frustrated.*

Jozef: *She drove us to a building in Central Falls, just outside of Providence. We were in a second-floor apartment with three bedrooms. The heat was shut off. We couldn't make tea or hot coffee because the gas was off in the stove. No electricity. She dropped us off in the dark and said, "Wait for me. I'll be back."*

We waited . . . all day Thursday, all day Friday. Nobody came. We had no water for baths, no heat. In the combined kitchen-living room there was a table and three chairs for the four of us. No radio or television. We had to keep our coats on because of the cold.

Our sponsor returned on Saturday. That was an emotional time because it was Christmas Eve, which is a big holiday in Poland. She gave us $50 for shopping.

I was very angry. I didn't care about myself — I had lived in worse conditions during one year in jail in Poland. But I was worried about my wife and children. I tried to tell our sponsors, "We only want a job. And find us a decent apartment." I said, "When I have a job and am earning money, I will pay you back for everything. I don't want to be on welfare or receiving financial aid."

Krystyna: Besides needing food, we didn't have anything in the kitchen to eat with. We had to buy silverware, dishes and cooking materials, too. Nobody took us to the market to show us how to compare food prices, and we couldn't read English or speak the language to ask questions in the stores. Our sponsor one time drove us to Star Market, which is more expensive than other stores. Fortunately, we had brought enough clothes from Poland.

Jozef: To be honest with you, the first month here, we were hungry much of the time. Only $110 the four of us had to live on for three weeks! Our sponsor was unbelievable. We came from a culture in Poland, not a jungle. I can't imagine the problems with sponsors that refugees from non-Western societies have when they arrive here. . . .

The sponsoring agency found us that apartment and nothing more. After the New Year holiday, my wife and the kids and I walked to the school by ourselves. It was the middle of winter, and the sidewalks were covered with snow. We only knew how to say "Good morning," "Goodbye," and "Thank you." But the principal and teachers were very kind to us. They couldn't understand Polish, but they knew what our children needed. My daughter went to high school and my son was in middle school.

Krystyna and I were anxious to find work. After a month, a Polish man told us about a local factory. We walked to the office and filled out applications. Soon the factory called my wife to work. The next day they called me. We are still working there, making safety belts for cars, parachutes and other uses.

From South Vietnam to Uptown Chicago

In the years after North Vietnamese tanks rolled into Saigon in 1975, waves of frightened and disoriented Vietnamese "boat people" began arriving in Chicago. Overwhelmed by the size and rhythm of the city, they had no relatives or ethnic community to welcome them. Their sponsors, relief agencies, were nearly as penniless as the refugees. The only affordable housing was Uptown. The refugees had left one war zone to enter another. Unable to speak English and defenseless, they became the neighborhood's easiest prey.

Today, Uptown is one of Chicago's up-and-coming neighborhoods. A dynamic rivalry between the refugees and a group of ambitious Chinese-American businessmen has transformed the once-abandoned Argyle Street business district into a flourishing Oriental market. On weekends, suburban tourists who used to lock their car doors if they had to drive through the neighborhood, now stand in line outside of popular Vietnamese restaurants to enjoy delicately spiced cuisine. Uptown has been rediscovered. The lure of "Little Saigon" has drawn a new generation of Chicagoans to visit and live and restore some of the neighborhood's former elegance. . . . The name of Trong Nguyen, [47], was most often mentioned as that of a "hero" who organized the refugee community and coordinated efforts with community agencies to transform the neighborhood. For 10 years, he's operated out of a cramped second-floor office at Travelers and Immigrants Aid.

On week nights and throughout the weekend, Trong manages his own struggling business, the Song Huong Restaurant.

Trong Nguyen: I have always believed that if you just stay home and do nothing, you are not a person whom others will respect. Since I came to Chicago in 1976, I've been involved in building the Vietnamese community. Of the 12,000 Vietnamese who live in this city, more than half live in a 14-block area around the Argyle Street busi-

ness strip, between Broadway and Sheridan roads.

Uptown is called the Ellis Island of Chicago. Some 30 languages are spoken in the area. Besides the Vietnamese, there are 1,000 Cambodians, 200 Laotians and some Hmong. But most of the people are American blacks, Appalachian whites who came from the coal mines of Kentucky and West Virginia, Mexicans and some American Indians.

In 1975, when the refugees first began arriving, the area was a dumping ground for derelicts, mental patients and everyone else the city didn't want. Drug addicts, gangs and prostitutes hung out in abandoned buildings owned by absentee landlords. Some refugee families with children lived in transient hotels alongside winos. Large multistory housing projects like on the corner of Argyle and Sheridan were very dangerous. Refugees were constantly robbed and beaten.

When my wife and I came to Chicago, our major concern was to feed our five small children. We had Vietnamese pride and did not want to take public aid. We wanted the American community and authorities to respect us.

In Uptown, we felt like we were thrust from one war zone to another. Local community organizations strongly opposed the refugees. People talked about a "Yellow Horde invasion." They started a lawsuit campaign against the city for bringing Indochinese into their area. They said, "Because the refugees are moving in, rents are going higher."

The absentee landlords in the neighborhood were horrible. The (community) organizations had started a boycott against them before the refugees arrived. This created a lot of vacancies in some of the run-down buildings. The voluntary agencies who sponsored the refugees saw the cheap rents and placed refugee families in those apartments. That allowed slumlords to stay in business.

At the height of the tension, the city brought the community associations, some refugee leaders and voluntary agency representatives into a room to talk. Commander

"To pick a bag of oranges, you have to climb up and down a 30-foot ladder. On a very good day, where the condition of the fruit on the trees and the weather are just right, the average person can hope to pick around $40 worth."

— Father Frank O'Loughlin

Howard Patinkin of the police department moderated the session because it was getting to the point of violence. At the meeting, the community groups realized that the refugees were good people, and an agreement was made for the voluntary agencies to coordinate with local residents.

Just trying to begin a new life here, we had so many difficulties. When I worked as a janitor at Water Tower Place, a co-worker told me, "Trong, do you know that America is overpopulated? We have more than 200 million people. We don't need you. Go back where you belong." I was shocked to hear people trying to chase us out. I thought, "Who is going to feed the children?" In America, a single income can never feed the family. Even though our youngest was just a baby, my wife had to find work.

In 1978, just before the boat-people crisis began, I found a job as a caseworker with Travelers and Immigrants Aid. My goal was to help those in need. After seven years in that job, when the Vietnamese community had become stabilized, I decided to open a restaurant. For my wife, working in a factory was such a heavy job. She tried so hard to stay with that type of work to help feed our family, but she was laid off on different occasions. When friends sometimes came to our home, they enjoyed my wife's cooking. They said, "Maybe one day open a restaurant, so we can eat your cooking more often."

They were joking, but it gave us the idea to open our own business. In June 1985, we opened this res-taurant. We named it Song Huong, after the Perfume River in my home area of central Vietnam.

As a social worker, I've never made much money. I didn't qualify to borrow from the bank. To open the restaurant, we had to borrow from friends. To keep our operating expenses down, my son and two oldest daughters help out. I know that isn't professional in terms of building a reputation for a good restaurant, but we have no other choice.

My life here has been working for the community. I never thought about making a lot of money for my own use. Sometimes my wife says, "It seems that you care more about the community than your own family."

My children here are my 19-year old son and my 15-, 14-, 12- and 11-year-old daughters. Sometimes the children have expressed disappointment that I'm not home very often. I explain to them that when you have a bowl of rice, no matter how small, you have to think about those people who don't have any rice to eat.

Father Frank O'Loughlin: Migrant advocate

Ten miles east of Lake Okeechobee, on the edge of the humid Everglades marshlands near Florida's largest citrus grove, a sleepy one-stoplight town was built on the campsite of a Seminole Indian hunting ground. The main street is a two-lane highway that traverses sandy clusters of pine trees and fanlike palmetto bushes on either side of the Saint Lucie Canal.

Every year, from November until spring, while tourists visit nearby Palm Beach resorts, Indiantown's 3,000 resident population is doubled by migrant farm laborers who stream in to pick thousands of acres of oranges and limes and fields of winter vegetables. Legal and illegal Mexicans, Haitians, Jamaicans, Puerto Ricans, and hard-luck black and white Americans sleep in old cars and ramshackle trailers or crowd into stuffy cinderblock houses, matchbox wooden shacks and huge barrack-like apartment complexes called "camps."

Beginning in 1982, entire families of small brown people with Asiatic eyes began straggling into Indiantown, speaking an incomprehensible language. They are descendants of the ancient Mayan civilization, displaced by civil war and poverty in the mountains of Guatemala. Unfamiliar with electricity and indoor plumbing, and unable to read or write in their obscure Kanjobal dialect, most of the Indians had never heard of the United States before they fled massacres in their remote villages. Many had bellies bloated from malnutrition, and swollen feet and legs from the long journey through Mexico.

Today, close to 1,000 Kanjobal men, women and children are trying to make a home in Indiantown. One attraction is the availability of low-paying, back-breaking agricultural jobs. But, more important, hearing that immigration officials will deport them back to the killing grounds of their homeland, they've found a safe haven where a small Catholic church led by an Irish priest is defending them.

Father Frank O'Loughlin, pastor of Holy Cross Church, has fought for 20 years to bring hope and dignity to migrant farm workers. Tall and thin with blue eyes, reddish-brown hair receding high on his forehead, and a warm baritone brogue, he has comforted the rural poor and challenged labor bosses and government authorities. Although Father Frank has adopted some unconventional tactics to remedy the wretched living conditions of parishioners, he maintains the traditional black shirt and jack-et outfit of an old-school Catholic priest.

Father Frank: *I'm off the boat myself. Twenty years ago, I arrived from Ireland, newly ordained, at the West Palm Beach parish. I became involved with migrant farm workers almost immediately.*

The first time I ever had a knock on my door in the middle of the night to anoint the sick was a call to the shack of a migrant Mexican family. No electricity, no water, a large bed filled the only room. I had to climb on this bed to reach the woman who was dying. There were five or six kids sleeping with her as she died. I couldn't get over this.

I started going back to that desolate part of town, into those shacks. There was a wonderful kind of Mother Teresa, a nun called Sister Aquinas, a gritty, tiny woman who was the only one paying attention to these people. She went around browbeating parishioners for money and food to feed the migrants. I'd go around with her.

I had a hell of a time when I went into the houses or shacks. The interiors were so grimy that I'd stick to the chair where I sat. I could hardly breathe from the smell of urine. I'd be afraid for my life that they would offer me something to eat.

Very often, what passes for a house is a hovel that is open for two or three months of the year, while the farm labor is needed. It's rat-infested, roach-infested. Just a place for workers to lay down between long days of picking fruit or vegetables.

In the famous book about migrant farm workers in the Lake Okeechobee area, Uprooted Children, Robert Coles says, "Even animals have a place where they belong. But these people don't." I used to read that passage over and over again, and choke on it. That's one of the reasons why, after I became pastor in Indiantown, we started a housing office. And we started a sewing co-op, directed by Sister Teresa Auagd. I wanted people to have a place.

I made a deal with the first nuns that came to work in Indiantown that they would stay to work for a long time. I told them, "The point is to become a landmark, so no matter how much the migrants travel, when they finally swing back this way, you'll be here. Something will be stable in their lives." That's how the Holy Cross Service Center started.

Indiantown only has 7 percent of the county's population, but we have 20 to 100 percent of the various intestinal diseases. That's because of the squalor. I got phone calls at the church from farm workers beginning to break out in blisters across their necks and chests because they'd been exposed to pesticides. Their kids got into the bathtub and got the rash, too. They were beginning to have respiratory problems and starting to panic.

We went running over to them. Nobody knew what to do. We say, "Let's go to the emergency room." And they say, "We've got a bill at the emergency room, so we can't go there." I go talk to the ambulance crew. I say, "There's a poison control center at Good Samaritan Hospital. Let's go to Good Sam." The drivers say, "Good Sam is C.O.D. — Cash or Die."

The growth of the agricultural industry in Florida skyrocketed with the formula for orange-juice concentrate. Self-made Florida farming entrepreneurs made vast fortunes from scratch. They made it on the backs of farm workers. The picking rate paid to workers when I came to Indiantown was 55 cents for a 95-pound bag of oranges.

To pick a bag of oranges, you have to climb up and down a 30-foot ladder. On a very good day, where the condition of the fruit on the trees and the weather are just right, the average person can hope to pick around $40 worth.

If you go into the groves and meet some of the black farm workers, they are some of the finest athletes you'll ever see. These men are big and strong, with huge hands. They are the fathers of professional athletes. Tremendous physical ability. But who do the growers want to hire? The little five-foot-tall Mexicans or Guatemalans, who can hardly maneuver up a 30-foot ladder with a 95-pound sack of oranges hanging around their necks. Yet they are the most desired employees, simply because they are vulnerable to every kind of exploitation.

Until the early 1980s, the majority of the migrants were Mexican. When the Guatemalans began to arrive, they were illegal and worked cheaper than the Mexicans, so they got the jobs. Mexicans who had legal papers and wanted a little higher wage were displaced. They shifted up to Fort Pierce.

Farming in the area is largely corporate. Among the big employers are Coca-Cola and Minute Maid Orange Juice. Concerns like Mutual of New York and Metropolitan Life are major shareholders in these big farms. They hire farm managers who are fairly enlightened "Joe College" types. They like to separate themselves from the "Old Boy" generation. The fact is, they don't effectively run different operations.

In one of the corporate groves, I helped file a lawsuit by John Robinson, who is the only black ever to become a foreman. It was made clear to him every day that his promotion was a token gesture. One morning his boss told him, "John, climb over the transformers and fix that thing." John said, "If I climb over the transformer, I'll be electrocuted." He refused.

We filed a civil-rights suit in his behalf. A whole lot of workers signed one, including a crew of women. The females, mostly Hispanic, had tractor-driving jobs. They'd be sent out to some remote part of the grove. A boss would follow and sexually molest them. They'd say to the guy, "How long is this going to continue?" And he'd say, "How long do you want to keep your job?"

The whole migrant-labor system replicates conditions in the Third World. The poverty, the social stratification with big growers, foremen and classes of serfs. I remember one of the big sugar barons complaining about the setting up of a day-care center. She said, "Where are we going to find our ignorant workers?"

CENSUS BUREAU FINDS SIGNIFICANT DEMOGRAPHIC DIFFERENCES AMONG IMMIGRANT GROUPS

Susan Lapham

A new report released today by the Commerce Department's Census Bureau on the nation's foreign-born population shows sharply varying levels of social-economic well-being among the various groups.

Susan Lapham, author of the report, *The Foreign Born Population in the United States: 1990 (CP-3-1)*, says, "An analysis of 1990 census information on recent immigrants (citizens and non-citizens) indicates that nearly 90 percent of African-born residents had a high school education or higher, compared with 76 percent of Asian-born and 46 percent of Central American-born residents. This report also shows that the per capita income of African immigrants was $20,117 in 1989, compared with $16,661 for Asian immigrants and $9,446 for foreign-born Central Americans. Family poverty rates for these same groups varied from 11.7 percent for foreign-born Africans to 13.1 percent for foreign-born Asians to 20.9 percent for foreign-born Central Americans.

The following additional highlights, extracted from the report's 400 pages of statistical tables, provide comparisons between foreign-born and natives:

- In 1990, about 20 million of the nation's total population were foreign-born and 229 million native-born. About 6 percent of immigrants entering the country between 1987 and 1990 were naturalized, compared with 10 percent of those entering between 1985 to 1986, 19 percent between 1982 to 1984, 27 percent from 1980 to 1981, and 61 percent before 1980.

- About 1 out of 5 adults, whether foreign born or native born, had a Bachelor's degree or higher in 1990. The ratio was 1 in 4 among immigrants who arrived after 1980 and 1 in 5 for those who arrived before 1980.

- About two-thirds of naturalized citizens had a high school diploma or more education in 1990, compared with slightly more than one-half of non-citizens. The gap was narrower for persons with a Bachelor's degree or more: 23 percent for naturalized and 19 percent for non-citizens.

- About 19 percent of families with a foreign-born householder had three or more workers in the family in 1990, compared with 13 percent among native-born families.

- About 19 percent each of naturalized and non-citizens had three or more workers in the family in 1990.

- Although the foreign born had a higher per capita income than the native born ($15,033 versus $14,367) in 1989, their median family income was almost $4,000 less than the native born ($31,785 versus $35,508).

- Although naturalized ($20,538) persons had a higher per capita income than non-citizens ($11,293) in 1989, their median family incomes were about the same at $31,754 and $31,943 respectively.

- The unemployment rate for foreign-born persons aged 16 and over was 7.8 percent in 1990, compared with 6.2 percent for the native born. Immigrants who entered since 1980 had an unemployment rate of nearly 10 percent, while those entering before 1980 had a rate of 6.4 percent.

- The unemployment rate for naturalized citizens (5.4 percent) was 4 percentage points lower than that for non-citizens (9.4 percent) in 1990.

- About 15 percent of families with a foreign-born householder were living in poverty in 1989, compared with nearly 10 percent of families with a native-born householder. Nearly 1 in 4 families with a foreign-born householder who entered the United

States since 1980 were living in poverty--about twice the proportion (11 percent) of families with a foreign-born householder who entered before 1980.

- The poverty rate of families with a naturalized householder (8.7 percent) was 12 percentage points lower than that of comparable non-citizens (20.7 percent) in 1990.
- About 8 out of 10 of the foreign born (5 years and older) speak a language other than English at home. Nearly 9 out of 10 of those who have arrived since 1980 speak a language other than English at home, compared with 7 out of 10 of those who arrived before 1980.
- About 7 out of 10 naturalized citizens (5 years and older) speak a language other than English at home in 1990, compared with more than 8 out of 10 non-citizens.

Since data in this report are from the sample portion of the decennial census, they are subject to sampling variability.

Editor's Note: One-page demographic profiles (CPH-L-148) for 47 countries of origin and regions as well as tables that rank 38 of the countries by selected characteristics are available on request. In addition, a five-page summary of social and economic highlights for foreign-born persons now living in the U.S. who were born in Europe, the Soviet Union, Asia, North and South America, Africa or Oceania, also are available.

Other reports planned for release by the bureau in this series (CP-3) include ancestry, persons of Hispanic origin and Asian and Pacific Islanders.

The bureau has also started releasing, on a flow basis, subject summary tape files (SSTFs). The tapes include the same types of data shown in the reports, but provide additional geographic detail. These files are designed to meet the data needs expressed by users who have a special interest in selected subjects or subgroups of the population.

Media representatives may obtain copies of the report on the foreign population from the bureau's Public Information Office on 301-763-4040. Subject Summary Tape Files can be ordered from the bureau's Customer Services Office on 301-763-4100. Non-media orders for any of these products should go to the Customer Services Office.

born elderly than the respective native born populations.

More foreign born men than women have entered the country since 1980 resulting in a sex ratio of 110 males per 100 females. Foreign born who entered prior to 1980 had a sex ratio of 86 males per 100 females. Foreign born Africans have the highest sex ratio, 146 males per 100 females, while foreign born Canadians have the lowest sex ratio of 70 males per 100 females.

On average, foreign born women have 2,254 children ever born per 1,000 women, compared with 1,927 children ever born per 1,000 women for native born women.

Nativity, place of birth, and year of entry	Median age	Children ever born[1]	Sex ratio[2]
Native born	32.5	1,927	94.9
Foreign born	37.3	2,254	95.8
Entered 1980 to 1990	28.0	2,200	110.3
Entered before 1980	46.5	2,282	85.8
Naturalized	36.3	2,098	87.0
Entered 1980 to 1990	29.5	2,062	113.2
Entered before 1980	45.3	2,104	83.0
Not a citizen	38.0	2,371	102.3
Entered 1980 to 1990	27.8	2,230	110.0
Entered before 1980	51.2	2,512	90.3
Europe	53.2	1,865	77.8
Soviet Union	54.6	1,690	82.3
Asia	35.4	1,997	96.1
North America	33.2	2,718	104.2
Canada	52.9	1,772	70.3
Mexico	29.9	3,289	122.9
Caribbean	39.0	2,144	88.3
Central America	30.5	2,518	96.1
South American	35.1	1.931	93.4
Africa	33.9	2,202	145.6
Oceania	36.1	2,187	83.5

[1]Per 1,000 women 35 to 44 years old.
[2]Males per 100 females.

Source: Bureau of the Census, 1990 Census of Population and Housing, CP-3-1, The Foreign-Born Population in the United States: 1990.

Demographic Characteristics of the Foreign-Born

On average, the foreign born population is about 5 years older than the native born population. However, those who have entered the country since 1980 have a median age which is about 5 years younger than the median age for the foreign born.

About half the native born population is concentrated among the working ages (25 to 64 years old), compared with 64 percent of the foreign born. There are relatively fewer foreign born children or foreign

Language Ability of the Foreign Born

About 79 percent of the foreign born (5 years old and over) speak a language other than English in their homes and about 28 percent of the foreign born live in households which are linguistically isolated.

About 88 percent of those foreign born who have arrived since 1980 do not speak English at home, compared with about 72 percent of those who arrived before 1980.

Nearly 42 percent of the foreign born who have

2. IMMIGRATION AND THE AMERICAN EXPERIENCE

arrived since 1980 are linguistically isolated, compared with only 18 percent of those who arrived before 1980.

Over 96 percent of foreign born Mexicans speak a language other than English at home, while about 60 percent of foreign born Europeans speak a language other than English at home.

Just over 70 percent of the native born workers held skilled occupations, compared with 60 percent of foreign born workers.

Thirteen percent of families with a native born householder, compared with 19 percent of families with a foreign born householder had 3 or more workers in the family.

Nativity, place of birth, and year of entry	Speak a language other than English	Do not speak English "very well"	Linguistically isolated[1]
Native born	7.8	2.3	1.2
Foreign born	79.1	47.0	28.2
Entered 1980 to 1990	88.0	59.9	41.6
Entered before 1980	72.4	37.2	18.0
Naturalized	70.6	32.7	16.8
Entered 1980 to 1990	86.9	49.9	31.8
Entered before 1980	67.6	29.6	14.1
Not a citizen	85.0	56.8	36.0
Entered 1980 to 1990	88.2	61.6	43.3
Entered before 1980	79.7	48.8	24.0
Europe	59.5	26.1	13.4
Soviet Union	81.1	52.1	39.9
Asia	91.6	49.9	30.0
North America	81.6	56.8	35.1
Canada	19.2	5.0	2.4
Mexico	96.1	70.7	43.5
Caribbean	67.8	42.8	25.5
Central America	92.7	63.3	41.4
South American	82.8	48.1	27.3
Africa	74.9	23.4	12.4
Oceania	46.1	17.5	7.3

[1]Linguistic isolation refers to persons in households in which no one 14 years old or over speaks only English and no one who speaks a language other than English speaks English "very well."

Source: Bureau of the Census, 1990 Census of Population and Housing, CP-3-1, The Foreign-Born Population in the United States: 1990.

Nativity, place of birth, and year of entry	Unemployed	Employed in skilled occupations[1]	3 or more workers in family
Native born	6.2	70.5	12.8
Foreign born	7.8	59.5	18.5
Entered 1980 to 1990	9.6	51.2	16.6
Entered before 1980	6.4	65.3	19.4
Naturalized	5.4	69.6	18.5
Entered 1980 to 1990	7.5	56.7	18.6
Entered before 1980	5	72.1	18.5
Not a citizen	9.4	52.3	18.6
Entered 1980 to 1990	10	50.1	16.2
Entered before 1980	8.5	55.3	20.9
Europe	4.8	71.4	18.6
Soviet Union	13.3	76.7	10.2
Asia	5.6	71.8	19.1
North America	10.1	45.7	20.8
Canada	4.2	80.8	11.1
Mexico	11.3	34.3	23.5
Caribbean	9.4	59.7	18.6
Central America	10.2	43.2	21.9
South American	7.5	60.3	19.6
Africa	6.8	71.5	11.6
Oceania	5.5	70.5	14.6

[1]Skilled occupations include the general categories of managerial and professional speciality; technical, sales, and administrative support; and precision production, craft and repair occupations.

Source: Bureau of the Census, 1990 Census of Population and Housing, CP-3-1, The Foreign-Born Population in the United States: 1990.

Employment and Occupation Characteristics of the Foreign Born

The unemployment rate for native born persons 16 years and over was 6.2 percent, compared with 7.8 percent for the foreign born.

Foreign born who have entered since 1980 have an unemployment rate of nearly 10 percent. Those foreign born who entered before 1980 have unemployment rates more similar to the native born population.

Foreign born from the Soviet Union had the highest unemployment rate, about 13 percent, while foreign born Canadians had the lowest unemployment rate at 4.2 percent.

Educational Attainment of the Foreign Born

One of every four foreign-born adults (25 years old and over) had less than a 9th grade education in 1990, compared with less than 1 of every 10 native born adults.

About 59 percent of the foreign born adults had a high school diploma or higher, compared with 77 percent of native born adults. However, foreign born and native born adults had nearly the same proportion who had a bachelor's degree or higher in 1990. And, the foreign born had a higher proportion than the native born of adults who had graduate degrees or higher, 3.8 percent versus 2.4 percent.

Estimated Resident Illegal Alien Population: October 1992

State of residence	Number	Pct.	Country or area of origin	Number	Pct.
U.S. TOTAL	3,200,000	100	N. America	2,100,000	66
			Asia	335,000	10
			Europe	310,000	10
California	1,275,000	40	S. America	200,000	10
New York	483,000	15	Africa	120,000	4
Florida	345,000	11	Oceania	15,000	–
Texas	320,000	10			
Illinois	170,000	5			
New Jersey	125,000	4	Mexico	1,002,000	31
Massachussetts	48,000	2	El Salvador	258,000	9
Arizona	47,000	1	Guatemala	121,000	4
Virginia	37,300	1	Canada	104,000	3
Georgia	28,000	1	Poland	102,000	3
			Philippines	101,000	3
Maryland	27,500	1	Haiti	98,000	3
Washington	26,200	1	Nicaragua	76,000	2
Pennsylvania	18,800	1	Colombia	75,000	2
Connecticut	17,000	1	The Bahamas	72,000	2
Oregon	16,600	1			
Nevada	16,400	1	Honduras	69,000	2
New Mexico	16,000	1	Italy	67,000	2
North Carolina	15,500	–	Ecuador	53,000	2
Colorado	14,500	–	Dom. Rep.	51,000	2
D.C.	14,500	–	Jamaica	50,000	2
			Trinidad	41,000	1
All other	136,700	4	Iran	37,000	1
			Ireland	37,000	1
Michigan, Oklahoma, Rhode Island, Utah, Louisiana, Ohio, and Hawaii.	6,000–9,900		Pakistan	33,000	1
			Portugal	32,000	1
			All other	681,000	21
Kansas, Wisconsin, Idaho, S. Carolina, Indiana, Minnesota, Tennessee, Missouri and Alabama.	3,000–5,500		India, Peru, Israel, China, Dominica, and Nigeria	24,000–30,000	
Nebraska, Arkansas, Iowa, Delaware, Alaska, Kentucky, Mississippi, and New Hampshire.	1,200–2,400		Yugoslavia, Lebanon, Guyana, Belize and France	15,000–19,000	
Wyoming, West Virginia, Montana, Maine, Vermont, North Dakota, and South Dakota.	100–700		All countries not listed above	Less than 15,000	

Source: INS Office of Strategic Planning, Statistics Division.

Foreign born Africans have the highest proportion of high school graduation or higher, 88 percent. This is about 12 percentage points higher than foreign born Asians, and about 15 percentage points higher than foreign born Canadians. Africans also have a higher proportion of bachelor's degrees or higher than any other immigrant group. Over 47 percent of foreign born Africans completed at least a bachelor's degree, compared with about 38 percent of foreign born Asians. On average, foreign born from Central American and Caribbean countries and Mexico were less educated than those from Africa, Asia, or Europe.

Nativity, place of birth, and year of entry	Per capita income	Median family income	Family poverty
Native born	$14,367	$35,508	9.5
Foreign born	$15,033	$31,785	14.9
Entered since 1980	$ 9,408	$24,595	23.4
Entered before 1980	$19,423	$35,733	11.0
Naturalized	$20,538	$31,754	8.7
Entered 1980 to 1990	$12,100	$29,257	18.0
Entered before 1980	$22,102	$36,028	7.5
Not a citizen	$11,293	$31,943	20.7
Entered 1980 to 1990	$ 8,954	$23,576	24.6
Entered before 1980	$15,274	$33,748	16.9
Europe	$20,904	$40,428	5.1
Soviet Union	$15,012	$28,799	18.5
Asia	$16,661	$39,395	13.1
North America	$11,225	$24,963	21.5
Canada	$21,904	$39,995	4.9
Mexico	$ 8,483	$21,585	27.4
Caribbean	$14,225	$29,464	16.4
Central America	$ 9,446	$23,587	20.9
South American	$14,955	$32,750	11.7
Africa	$20,117	$36,783	11.7
Oceania	$19,200	$39,775	11.6

Source: Bureau of the Census, 1990 Census of Population and Housing, CP-3-1, The Foreign-Born Population in the United States: 1990.

Nativity, place of birth, and year of entry	High school diploma or higher	Bachelor's degree or higher
Native born	77.0	20.3
Foreign born	58.8	20.4
Entered since 1980	59.4	23.7
Entered before 1980	58.5	18.7
Naturalized	65.4	22.5
Entered since 1980	65.6	23.6
Entered before 1980	65.3	22.3
Not a citizen	53.1	18.5
Entered since 1980	58.3	23.7
Entered before 1980	47.1	12.5
Europe	63.5	18.0
Soviet Union	64.0	27.1
Asia	75.8	38.4
North America	41.6	9.1
Canada	72.6	22.1
Mexico	24.3	3.5
Caribbean	56.9	13.6
Central America	45.7	8.5
South American	71.3	20.0
Africa	87.9	47.1
Oceania	77.0	24.2

Source: Bureau of the Census, 1990 Census of Population and Housing, CP-3-1, The Foreign-Born Population in the United States: 1990.

Income and Poverty of the Foreign Born

Although the foreign born have a higher per capita income than the native born population, their median family income was almost $4,000 less than the native born.

About 15 percent of families with a foreign born householder were below the poverty rate, compared with nearly 10 percent of native born families.

The per capita income of foreign born who have entered since 1980 is less than half the per capita income of foreign born who entered this country before 1980.

Nearly 1 of 4 families with a foreign born householder who entered the country since 1980 were living in poverty, compared with just over 1 of 10 families with a foreign born householder who entered before 1980.

LIFESTYLE 2000:

New Enterprise and Cultural Diversity

*How will dramatic demographic changes in business ownership
affect America's social, political, and economic direction in the 21st century?*

Jerry Feigen

Mr. Feigen is adjunct professor, Georgetown University Law Center, Washington, D.C.

THE SOCIAL, economic, and political dynamics of a society will depend greatly on its economic system and the wealth accumulation of its citizens. In particular, the diversity and creativity of its population will serve to expand the horizons of those that have economic self-sufficiency and make it possible for those individuals and families who are not in the mainstream to be given realistic opportunities to achieve such independence. With this comes the basis for social and political stability and growth. The evidence is clear today as the daily papers report that the dramatic changes in Europe, Latin America, and Asia are driven by former totalitarian regimes not being able to answer and provide the basic needs of their people. Suppressing the individual creative and economic drives of a nation's populace dooms that country's ability to survive and meet the challenges of the future.

The U.S. was created through the ideas and needs of people from diverse cultures fleeing the oppressive political regimes of their homelands. The opportunity associated with expansion of this new nation created freedom and wealth for some and hardship and slavery for others. From the early 1600s to the early 1800s, more than 1,800,000 immigrants entered the country,

mostly from England and Ireland. The 1790 census showed that 4,000,000 persons lived in the U.S.

As the nation expanded, new industries and wealth were created. Wealth from the soil proliferated as oil, gold, grains, tobacco, and cotton served a growing population as well as overseas markets. Rather than cultural diversity, however, Manifest Destiny subsumed those who couldn't assimilate fast enough. Whether Native Americans, African slaves, or Asian coolies, individual rights and cultural roots were severed as irrelevant in the scheme of things.

From 1820 to 1889, Germany, Ireland, Canada, Sweden, and France sent the most immigrants, fleeing from poor harvests and political unrest. Between 1841 and 1860, the U.S. accepted more than 4,300,000 newcomers. During the 1840s and 1850s, about 1,500,000 Irish came; between the 1840s and 1880s, approximately 4,000,000 Germans arrived; and 1,500,000 people from Scandinavian countries settled in America between the 1870s and 1900s. Public high school education in the U.S. was just getting off the ground by 1850 to accommodate those families that couldn't afford private lessons.

Railroads, steel, new power sources, and financial services were the main generators of economic, social, and political activity and control, but a new middle class of entrepreneurs also was being spun off in great numbers in the form of farmers, jobbers, wholesalers, retailers, and manufacturers. Owners and workers of these enterprises combined new skills with cheap (and often abused) labor, looking to this economic ex-

pansion as the means to achieve financial, social, and political self-sufficiency for the future.

During the last half of the 19th century, many issues of cultural diversity came to a head. Native Americans, Hispanics, and Asians were forced into trying to survive in an economic roller coaster that was clearly beyond their physical and cultural control. With the Emancipation Proclamation, Pres. Abraham Lincoln signaled the necessity for the U.S. to have a free and diverse society. However, he freed indentured individuals with little education and skills to compete in a socially biased, economically competitive society. There were nearly 4,000,000

It was the diversity, creativity, and perseverance of the massive immigration of people to the United States that drove the U.S. economic engine into and through the 20th century.

black slaves in 1860, representing more than one-third of the population of the southern slave states.

The approach of the 20th century triggered still additional social and economic clashes as pogroms in eastern Europe brought boatloads of Jews seeking economic and social justice. Nearly 2,500,000 Jews arrived from eastern Europe, with about 1,000,000 non-Jewish Poles entering the U.S. between the 1880s and 1920s. Approximately 4,000,000 Austrians, Hungarians, Czechs, and Slovaks sought a better life in America during this same period.

In 1907, the U.S. admitted a record 1,300,000 immigrants, 70% from southern and eastern Europe. About 4,500,000 Italians also came between the 1880s and 1920s to flee famine and poverty, accepting whatever duties others wouldn't perform. These individuals—lacking formal learning and clashing with existing Americans for the most menial, lowest-paying tasks—tried to blend and assimilate into the new culture. The U.S. population was placed at more than 75,000,000 in 1900.

Dealing with presumed ignorant Native Americans, immigrants, and former slaves from Africa—all with different cultures, colors, and/or physical appearances—became an anathema for those whose forefathers came to the U.S. only generations before, but had the good fortune, education, and drive to be at the starting gate of a unique economic expansion. It would be hard to imagine that the well-being of subsequent generations of these *nouveau riche* Americans would be tied to the successful evolution of these same peoples into the U.S. economic mainstream. The Depression years brought out the staying power and resiliency of these new Americans, contributing to the arts as well as labor and industry.

Yet, even though there were assimilation efforts by those striving to be included as upwardly socially mobile Americans, it was their diversity, creativity, and perseverance that drove the U.S. economic engine into and through the 20th century. The social, cultural, and political nature of the country and the world changed as the U.S. became *the* major power.

The immigrants and emigres strove to educate themselves and become accepted. New industries emerged out of these fertile and sometimes desperate minds. Movies, radio, television, electronics, ship building, housing, newspapers, entertainment, and new sciences and scientific theories, as well as small retail shops and restaurants, became the basis by which wealth would accumulate for these first- or second-generation Americans. The need to build economic security and equity for future family generations sometimes would interfere with what was appropriate for the present. The economic aftermath of World

War II expanded these potentials exponentially.

The war also slowly spun out economic and social opportunities previously closed to many minority Americans. Sports opened up to blacks, creating wealth and role models that would lead to new business creation on a small and shaky scale. Government policies created educational opportunities for minority Americans to help them compete after 200 years of being held back from fulfilling their latent potential. Minority families accumulated sufficient income through an 18-hour day in low-skill jobs or by operating their own lifestyle business to pay for the schooling of the newest generation. Music and entertainment businesses became growth industries for minorities with or without formal education.

Throughout the 1960s and 1970s, the U.S. was dominant in new venture creation in scientific fields—computers, health, electronics, etc. The development of an American venture capital industry during this time frame permitted creativity and growth in technical and nontechnical areas. Funds directed toward minority business enterprises also rose. Generations of technically gifted young Americans began to create opportunities. Many businesses emerged from these scientific advancements, including a number created by skilled minority entrepreneurs. In addition, nontechnical growth businesses were created in the franchise, entertainment, and communications fields, as well as retail, wholesale, and manufacturing areas. New wealth accumulation occurred for owners, investors, and employees of these growth firms.

The new immigrants

During this time, waves of immigrants began flooding U.S. shores for the same reasons as prior groups had. Asians and Hispanics were trying to escape from the poverty, war, and tyranny in Southeast Asia and Latin and Central America. Between the 1960s and 1980s, more than 700,000 Cubans fled their island to avoid the communist takeover. Vietnamese emigres during the 1960s and 1970s numbered about 500,000. Moreover, between the 1970s and 1980s, 900,000 immigrants from the Caribbean fled unemployment and poverty.

Clashes and confrontation occur when new groups vie for the most menial jobs with existing job-seekers. Again, wealth, independence, and economic status accumulate more rapidly for these families through business ownership than from the low wage rates they may receive. Also, as has been seen in prior first- and second-generation emigres, social acceptance, while never total, is closest to reality when economic independence is assured.

During the 1980s, the U.S. began to lose

its position as the world's economic leader. Automobiles, electronics and semiconductors, financial services, and manufacturing of durable goods all were given up to foreign competitors. The U.S. venture capital industry no longer invested in ideas, but in bailouts and reorganizations, with many deals occurring overseas. At the same time, communist and other such regimes began to topple in favor of free market economies and private enterprise. A wave of Russian emigres came to the U.S. with highly specialized scientific knowledge, but naivete about the world of freedom and private enterprise. Sources for new wealth creation opportunities dried up, yet minority-owned businesses grew rapidly.

Cultural diversity for the next century will be greater than any time in American history.

The latest available data from the Commerce Department is revealing. The number of black businesses with paid employees grew 87% between 1982 and 1987, generating receipts of more than $14,000,000,000, up 147% over 1982. This figure jumps to nearly $20,000,000,000 if firms without paid employees are included. Equivalent data for Hispanics show firms with paid employees increased 111% from 1982 to 1987, with sales and receipts of $17,700,000,000, up 138% from 1982. Receipts for all Hispanic companies, including those without paid employees, amounted to nearly $25,000,000,000 in 1987. Women-owned businesses with paid employees grew to 618,000, up 98% from 1982. They had sales and receipts of $224,000,000,000, an increase of 245% over 1982 figures. Receipts for all such firms (with and without paid employees) amounted to $278,000,000,000. To place this data in perspective, the total 1987 sales and receipts for all U.S. firms was 1.7 trillion dollars, representing 3,500,000 businesses with paid employees, and nearly two trillion dollars in receipts, representing 13,700,000 (with and without paid employees).

Projected population figures indicate that, by the year 2010, total U.S. population will increase to around 282,500,000, or 12.8% over 1990. The white population will reach 229,000,000, with a modest nine percent increase, while there will be approximately 40,000,000 blacks, a 29% rise from 1990, and Hispanics will total more than 38,000,000, nearly an 80% jump.

Cultural diversity for the next century will be greater than any time in American history. According to some Japanese writings, Japan will increase its dominance in the economic world because of its similarity of culture and population, while the U.S. will continue to lose its economic share because of growing American diversity. History has shown U.S. strength to rest in the creativity and drive of its multicultural society.

As the nation nears the 21st century burdened with the economic difficulties of the 1990s and a rapidly changing world arena, the following questions must be addressed: How will the U.S. sustain itself and its people without calling on the diversity inherent in a free people? Can the multiple cultures of the next generation cope better with some of the social ostracism of the past than its predecessors? Will the entrepreneurial role models of the next century overcome the inherent biases and insecurity found at the beginning of this one or will the same mistakes be made? Will wealth accumulation through business ownership for minority population be the fastest way out of the 20th-century poverty and education maelstrom? Will women's roles as business owners radically revise management and labor concepts? How will the dramatic increases in minority- and female-owned enterprises affect the U.S.'s worldwide economic competitive position? How will these dramatic demographic changes in business ownership and independent wealth accumulation affect the social, political, and economic direction of the U.S. in the 21st century?

Native American Groups

- Indigenous Ethnic Groups (Articles 11–14)
- Native Americans (Articles 15–19)

The contemporary issues and images of Native Americans as well as the descendants of conquered indigenous peoples add their voices to the forum that addresses the claims for cultural justice, equal protection, and due process in America. As North and South America marked the 500th anniversary of Christopher Columbus's voyage of discovery, the indigenous people of the Americas explored their roots and new remedies for the conquest that turned many into a permanent underclass.

The following collection of materials is a composite of findings. Though they represent only a current cross section of the images and expressions of the Native American community, these articles give voice to the world of Native Americans. They express their forced accommodation in the modern era, the environmental and cult challenges of rapid change, and the renewal of tradition and its curious relationship to legalized gambling. The Native American populations remember and invite us to recall their changes and struggles, to find ways of shaping and sharing the new sense of pluralism offered within the American experience and the spiritual sources of ethnic identity that persons encounter as the legitimacy of ancient practices widens.

Native American communities have been plagued, often inflicted, with a complex array of historical, social, cultural, and economic factors. As a result, this time within the drama of the late twentieth century, the traditions of Native Americans have been renegotiated by yet another generation. The U.S. economy and pluralistic culture are a challenging stage for their quest for self-sufficiency as well as their aspirations for the preservation of a unique cultural legacy. Current Native American leaders challenge past perceptions. Native American leaders find it increasingly difficult to strike a balance between traditional values and new demands. Native Americans' challenge of the American legal system is part of this current redefinition. Finally, however, they are challenging themselves to be themselves.

Ethnicity is built upon the truth and strength of a tradition. Senses of family and community, and an unwillingness to give up, has led to standoffs with many forces and aspects of America. In this light, this section details some efforts of how an ethnic group retrieves their rights and their heritage to preserve an ancient culture from amnesia and extinction.

Looking Ahead: Challenge Questions

What are the most compelling issues that face Native American communities?

What social, economic, and political conditions will affect the next Native American generation?

Because of the strides of the current Native American community, will the next generation enter the middle class of America? Is that, or should that be, a goal?

How will the American public and private bureaucratic systems address the challenges of pluralistic constituencies?

Unit 3

Paupers in a World Their Ancestors Ruled

South American Indians still live under the thumb of the conquistadors

Eugene Robinson

Washington Post Foreign Service

LIMA, Peru—As South America prepares to mark the 500th anniversary of Christopher Columbus's voyage of discovery, the people he found when he arrived—and insisted on calling "Indians"—are at the bottom of the social and economic ladder, an underclass in lands their forebears ruled.

Throughout the continent, whites of European ancestry constitute the wealthiest and most powerful class, while Indians are among the poorest and most disenfranchised.

The gap is so wide, and dates so far back, that many people do not perceive it in those terms. Officials in South American countries talk of the need for programs to aid "peasants" or "poor people" in words that obscure the powerful role that race and ethnicity play in determining who is rich and who is poor.

"People like myths," says Maria Rostworowski, a noted Peruvian historian. "The Spanish had their myths; we have ours. To confront the reality of race is disturbing and at times painful. So people tell themselves stories."

One of the myths is that South American societies are mostly, if not entirely, colorblind—that after centuries of coexistence a truly hybrid culture has emerged, one that draws from both worlds.

"There has been a process of mixing, but there is also racism, discrimination and domination," says Jose Diego Condorcanqui, a leading Argentine advocate for Indian rights. Condorcanqui, 55, a self-taught sociologist and anthropologist, is a Kolla Indian born in the Andean province of Jujuy. Elders have named him an *amauta*, or guardian of his ancestors' cultural heritage.

"In the workplace, those of us with brown skin, no matter how qualified, have no real hope of advancement," Condorcanqui says. "Our young people go to the discotheques in Buenos Aires and find that if they do not look Italian or Spanish, they cannot get in. Our youth consider themselves Indian inside the home, but outside they have to abandon their identity."

The theme has regional variations. In Argentina, a country populated mostly by Europeans who arrived at the turn of the century, hundreds of thousands of Indians live out of sight, and out of mind, in the tropical northeast and mountainous northwest. There they endure grinding poverty and a rate of infant mortality twice that of the rest of the country.

Residents of cosmopolitan Buenos Aires can be overheard referring to people of Indian heritage, including the many who live in suburban slums, as "those blacks" or "those greasers."

As Indians in the rest of South America do, Argentina's estimated 3 million Indians enjoy full political rights but practically no representation on the national level. A comprehensive Indians' rights law passed in 1985 remains an empty shell. Its promises of land, development and better education for Indian communities have fallen victim to economic crisis. The government has yet to change an article of the constitution that commits leaders to "Christianize" indigenous populations.

In Brazil, forest Indian communities fight a losing battle against the steamrolling encroachment of the modern world. Their population of up to 5 million when whites arrived has been reduced to around 220,000 today. In the state of Mato Grosso do Sul, more than two dozen members of the Guarani-Kaiowa tribe, mostly young girls, have killed themselves over the past year in apparent despair over the invasion of their reservation lands by ranchers and farmers.

In Bolivia, the Indian majority in the high plains and valleys around La Paz, clinging to traditional clothing and customs, remains desperately poor and increasingly receptive to populist politicians trying to unite them into an electoral force. Last year [1990], hundreds of Indians from the eastern lowlands crossed the Andes on foot to demand that Bolivian officials recognize their claims for hunting and fishing lands.

In Pisaq, Peru, some villagers bring crafts to town to sell at a market, but tourists—fearing terrorism and cholera—are few.

In Ecuador, Indians fed up with centuries of ethnic discrimination have staged angry protests over the past year, blocking roads, occupying lands and attempting to sabotage elections.

In Paraguay, the racial pecking order exists as elsewhere, but there is more of an attempt to integrate Indian culture into the mainstream. Paraguay has two official languages—Spanish and Guarani, an Indian language—and more than nine out of 10 Paraguayans, including the president, speak both.

Nowhere are the issues of race more complex than in Peru. The seat of the mighty Inca empire, and later the proud headquarters of the Spanish viceroyalty, has been reduced to near-chaos by terrorism, disease, privation and economic catastrophe.

Cuzco, the Inca capital high in the southern Andes, once efficiently organized the care and feeding of millions. Today, the city is ringed by sad shantytowns populated almost exclusively by people of Indian descent—desperate people.

"We see malnutrition in 70 percent of the children under 5 in the shantytowns," says Jorge Silva Sierra, a psychologist who works with a government relief agency in Cuzco. "I spoke to a woman last week who sold her baby for adoption for $1,000."

The overwhelming majority of those struck by the cholera epidemic filling Peruvian hospitals are poor and dark. "Cholera is a poor person's disease," the director of a Lima-area hospital said recently. Up to 20,000 children, mostly Indian, die of diarrheal disease each year.

The streets of Lima are filled with at least a half-million *ambulantes*, or walking vendors, a brown-skinned army selling everything from socket wrenches to toilet paper in an attempt to eke out a living.

Estimates are that well over four-fifths of Peru's population of around 22 million are either Indian or *mestizo*, those of mixed blood. Here, as in other countries, numbers and even individuals are hard to pin down.

When Peruvians come from the countryside to Lima—as hordes have done, swelling the city's population from 700,000 to 7 million in the past 50 years—almost immediately they abandon the traditional rural costume. Long skirts and pigtails give way to stone-washed blue jeans, Michael Jackson T-shirts and curly permanents. Self-image also changes: Indians become mestizos.

The Peruvian state encourages this process of transformation. In a country where at least a third of the population grows up speaking a language other than Spanish—generally Quechua, the tongue of the Incas—there is essentially no bilingual education.

"When the Indian comes to the city and dresses like a mestizo, speaks Spanish instead of Quechua, goes to school and all that, he ceases being an Indian," says Diego Garcia-Sayan, head of the Andean Commission of Jurists, a human rights lobby. "The Indian is forced to whiten himself. . . . This is just part of the discrimination that runs throughout the society."

In Peru and elsewhere on the continent, those ambiguities of racial identification have helped inhibit the development of any broad-based consciousness movement that might unite Indians into a coherent political force. But there are indications that in some places this may be changing.

Last year [1990], for the first time, racial consciousness—and anger—played a significant role in a Peruvian presidential election, helping political novice Alberto Fujimori defeat novelist Mario Vargas Llosa in a vote that sent analysts scrambling for answers.

Vargas Llosa had held a substantial lead throughout the campaign, but he came to be identified with the traditional elite—the fair-skinned Peruvian oligarchy. The monied classes backed him with their checkbooks and influence, helping Vargas Llosa's message of free-market sacrifice dominate the airwaves.

Fujimori, who is of Japanese descent, railed against "the little whites" who had selfishly run the country into the ground at the expense of the *campesinos* and the *pobladores*, code words for the dark-skinned majority. He told voters in the shantytowns around Lima and in the mountain villages that he would be "a president like you."

In working-class and poor neighborhoods, voters were almost gleeful as they cast their ballots for Fujimori, giving him an impressive victory. "Democracy has lost," television commentator Cesar Hildebrandt, a Vargas Llosa supporter, grumbled on election night.

Fujimori said after the election, "When I put on traditional dress, I look a lot more like most Peruvians than Mario Vargas Llosa ever will."

The racial divide is so striking that many have begun to see the Maoist insurgency called Shining Path—which has provoked the government into putting more than half the country under a state of emergency—as what amounts to an armed Indian revolt.

In reality, Shining Path is primarily led by whites and its doctrines pay little more than lip service to racial issues. About 90 percent of the guerrilla war's 20,000-plus victims over the past decade have been Indians and mestizos from the countryside or the shantytowns.

The Peruvian military is also commanded mostly by whites—just like the armed forces of other South American countries. Descending through the ranks, skin color darkens.

"Indians are just cannon fodder to Shining Path," says Garcia-Sayan, the human rights activist. "But Indians are also the army's cannon fodder. The myth of Shining Path as the voice of the oppressed Indian is simply wrong, but racial discrimination is so great that Shining Path is able to take advantage of the issue and use race to their advantage."

People like Antonia Saga are caught in the middle.

Saga, who is in her late forties, is from the mountain town of Huanta, just north of Ayacucho, the birthplace of Shining Path. The guerrillas moved into Huanta shortly after beginning their armed struggle in 1980, and attempted to establish a stronghold. The armed forces quickly followed in an attempt to root out the guerrillas. The battle for Huanta has been raging ever since.

Saga's husband, Alejandro Huanahuana, disappeared in 1983. Human rights advocates say there have been nearly 6,000 such disappearances over the past decade.

Frightened for her own safety and that of her eight children, Saga says, she moved to Lima, settling in Canto Grande, an archipelago of shantytowns stretching out from the city's northern suburbs. Like many other such *desplazados*, or displaced persons, she was unable to find work. She could not even afford to buy a cart to make money selling food in the street, she says, so she lived by the kindness of friends.

Last year, Saga says, she went back to Huanta to see what kind of life she could rebuild there. "My home had been searched and they had taken everything," she says. "I went to the army to report it, and they said I was a terrorist. They took me to jail."

She said she was released on condition that she join an antiguerrilla militia sponsored by the armed forces. It was an impossible position to be caught in: participate and become a certain target for Shining Path; refuse and be harassed by the army.

Saga says she fought the guerrillas for a while, witnessing several brutal killings by the militia of people suspected of being guerrillas—"they treat us like animals," she says—and then slipped away and came back to Lima.

"Now I am back in Canto Grande," she says. "The neighbors, bless them, give us food to eat. There is nothing for us, nothing."

Even in Lima, people who fled the highlands to get away from political violence find themselves caught in the middle. The shantytown of Huaycan, for example, has been infiltrated by Shining Path supporters who cover the walls with Maoist graffiti and occasionally drape the main street in red banners.

Whenever there is a high-profile terrorist attack in Lima, police raid places like Huaycan and arrest thousands of people, mostly brown-skinned young men. Citywide round-ups of 20,000 or more are not uncommon.

The flood of people like Antonia Saga coming to Lima has transformed the "City of the Kings," as named by conquistador Francisco Pizarro, from a European-flavored metropolis of wide boulevards and parks into something more Andean, more Indian.

Already, the social and political center of Lima is not the posh traditional suburbs of San Isidro and Miraflores, nor even the newer upscale residential re-

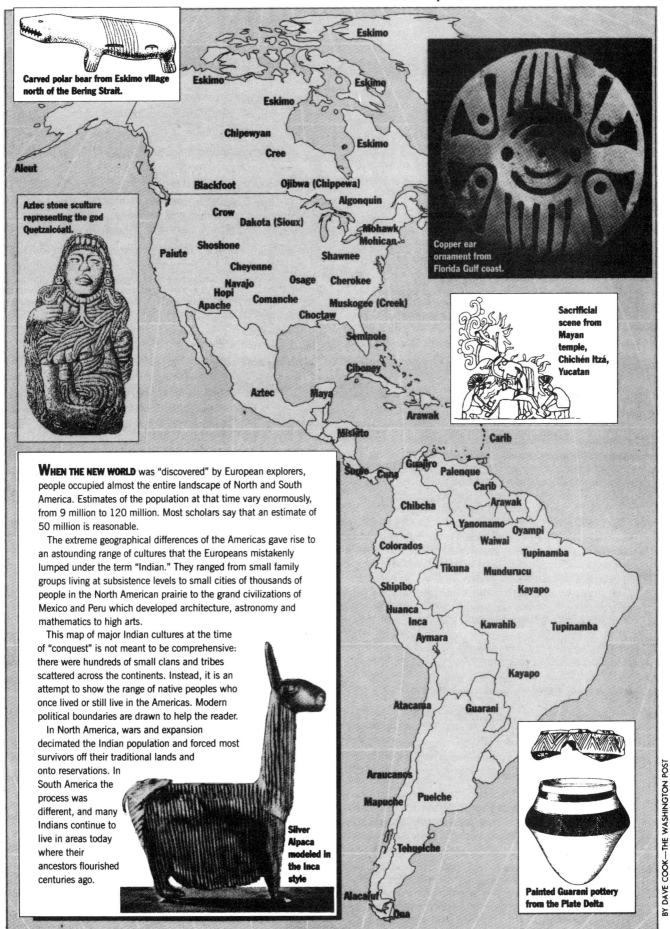

Carved polar bear from Eskimo village north of the Bering Strait.

Aztec stone sculture representing the god Quetzalcóatl.

Copper ear ornament from Florida Gulf coast.

Sacrificial scene from Mayan temple, Chichén Itzá, Yucatan

WHEN THE NEW WORLD was "discovered" by European explorers, people occupied almost the entire landscape of North and South America. Estimates of the population at that time vary enormously, from 9 million to 120 million. Most scholars say that an estimate of 50 million is reasonable.

The extreme geographical differences of the Americas gave rise to an astounding range of cultures that the Europeans mistakenly lumped under the term "Indian." They ranged from small family groups living at subsistence levels to small cities of thousands of people in the North American prairie to the grand civilizations of Mexico and Peru which developed architecture, astronomy and mathematics to high arts.

This map of major Indian cultures at the time of "conquest" is not meant to be comprehensive: there were hundreds of small clans and tribes scattered across the continents. Instead, it is an attempt to show the range of native peoples who once lived or still live in the Americas. Modern political boundaries are drawn to help the reader.

In North America, wars and expansion decimated the Indian population and forced most survivors off their traditional lands and onto reservations. In South America the process was different, and many Indians continue to live in areas today where their ancestors flourished centuries ago.

Silver Alpaca modeled in the Inca style

Painted Guarani pottery from the Plate Delta

BY DAVE COOK—THE WASHINGTON POST

63

doubts such as Casuarinas—an exclusive, well-guarded hillside neighborhood that is home only to "white people and drug traffickers," in the words of one resident.

Rather, Lima's critical mass lies in the shantytowns that ring the periphery. The biggest and best-known of these in Villa El Salvador, which in less than 20 years has grown from a woebegone outpost clinging to the barren sand dunes south of the city into a makeshift community of more than 300,000 people.

Here, as in other such settlements, migrants from the same Andean region cling together—in social clubs and especially food cooperatives. Peru's economic crisis has forced families to band together to buy food and prepare meals. There are more than 1,000 such cooperatives in Villa El Salvador, comprising around two-thirds of the shantytown's population.

The sectors set aside for new arrivals are easily distinguished by the impermanence of the dwellings—most of them are made exclusively of straw mats—and by the sounds of spoken Quechua. Some older women still wear traditional long skirts and aprons, although immigrant youths quickly adopt the fashions of their city-born playmates.

But there is impermanence of a different kind in evidence in Lima's shantytowns of late—the fleeting dreams of immigrant Indians that a better life can be found in the city. The roads leading out of Lima are now full of return travelers forced by deprivation to seek their future in the places of their past.

"A great many people are having second thoughts," says Jose Rodriguez Aguirre, mayor of Villa El Salvador. "People came here believing that their problems of employment and housing would be solved. Now they realize that it just isn't so. We see an increasing number of people returning to the countryside, or trying to, after they see that Lima is no paradise."

But for many, such as Antonia Saga, a return to the highlands is impossible. Shining Path has extended its influence along the spine of the Andes, occupying some areas and forcing the government to turn others into armed camps.

One area that the armed forces have been able to keep relatively free from guerrilla influence is Cuzco, the gateway to Machu Picchu and focal point of Peru's tourism industry. Magnificent ruins attest to the glories of the past—but Cuzco's present is moribund. Neither Shining Path nor cholera is much in evidence in Cuzco, but nonetheless their specters have combined to keep the tourists away.

An hour outside the city is the Sacred Valley of the Incas, as Peruvians refer to the temple-filled valley of the Urubamba River. Some of the old traditions are still observed. In the town of Urubamba, an occasional house features a long pole crowned with a bunch of flowers or a puff of colored paper—a sign that the proprietor is offering chicha, Andean moonshine.

But the villages are shrinking. Some have seen their populations cut by half, as people moved to the shantytowns around Cuzco or Lima. On Sundays, some villagers dress in colorful traditional outfits and bring handicrafts to the town of Pisaq to sell at a weekly market, but it is an empty gesture as long as there are no tourists.

A few of the old Inca agricultural terraces are still in use, as is an old Inca salt mine. Inca bridges, fortresses, cemeteries and temples abound, most of them barely excavated and some completely untouched—there is little money for such undertakings.

At the end of the valley lies Ollantaytambo, perhaps the town in Peru most unchanged from the days when the Incas ruled. Here, amid narrow streets that lead uphill to an impressive fortress, the leader Manco Inca made a desperate stand against the Spaniards in 1536 before fleeing into the mountains. Today, barefoot children play among the ruins while their parents wait beside the road with trays of bargain-priced trinkets.

"This valley has a history that goes far back beyond the Incas," says Pedro Taca, who supervises the ruins at Ollantaytambo for the National Institute of Culture. "This is a heritage that we should all be proud of, that we should all celebrate. Sadly, we do not."

Conversations/*Víctor Hugo Cárdenas*

Bolivia's Vice President, First Indian In High Office, Waits for Change

Nathaniel C. Nash

LA PAZ, Bolivia

There are many things that Víctor Hugo Cárdenas laments about his youth—the poverty of his Aymara village on the windy banks of Lake Titicaca, his father's inability to get a state-approved teaching job because he was an Indian, being forbidden to speak his native language in school and that his name really should not be Cárdenas.

"My father's name was Chokewanka," Mr. Cárdenas said. "But he gave his two sons a Spanish name—the name of my maternal grandmother—so that we would not have to suffer the discrimination that he did."

The gentle, mournful eyes reveal only a touch of bitterness. More, they show the serenity that has enabled the Aymara to survive for the 500 years since they were conquered by the Spanish, and the quiet resistance that has prevented the assimilation of their culture and religion.

He folds his hands almost reverently as he talks of Bolivia's 4.7 million Indians: Aymara, Quechua, Guaraní, Mojeño, Chimane and smaller groups—more than 70 percent of the population.

But the 41-year-old Mr. Cárdenas, who speaks three Indian languages, plus Spanish, English and French, is not just another tribal leader hoping the world will pay attention.

As of last month, he became Vice President of Bolivia, and suddenly was thrust into the forefront of the movement of indigenous peoples throughout Latin America who seek to reclaim their rights and the region's respect.

Never since independence came to this continent in the early 19th century has an Indian held such a high national office. To be sure, many, including himself, think he will be treated as a token. He is still visibly uncomfortable in office, staying to the side during cabinet meetings and diplomatic gatherings. But political analysts here say that Bolivia's new President, Gonzalo Sánchez de Lozada, is well aware that Mr. Cárdenas brought him many votes in June's elections, and will not forget the debt.

Mr. Cárdenas began as an educator and is thought of by his people as a philosopher, but he moved into politics in 1985 when he founded the Tupac Katari Revolutionary Movement of Liberation, named after the Aymara rebel leader who was dismembered by the Spanish in 1781. Other political parties had tried to appeal to his constituency, but had been led by non-Indians.

ODD COUPLE ON TICKET

Many consider it a brilliant stroke to have him on the ticket. They made an odd couple, since Mr. Sánchez de Lozada is not only a multimillionaire mining entrepreneur, but was raised in the United States and speaks Spanish with a heavy accent. Neither candidate spoke it as a first language, and the two were often referred to as "the gringo and the indio." Some even less polite critics called them "the Lone Ranger and Tonto."

On a cold afternoon here, Mr. Cárdenas sits in the sparsely furnished living room of the home he worked 15 years to build. The sofa and two easy chairs are new, obviously bought to accommodate his new flow of visitors. He is angry but does not threaten, plain-spoken but not a demagogue. His main hope is that modern colonialism, in its visible and invisible forms, comes to an end.

The votes he brought probably elected the President. But his wife still cannot legally teach school without cutting her braids and changing her Indian skirt.

"When they founded the republic, we were excluded, even though we had suffered from the beginning under Spanish conquest and even though we fought from the beginning for independence," he said. "For 168 years we have been excluded from democracy. For us we went from Spanish colonialism to internal colonialism. Before, it was oppression from one state to another. Now it is oppression within the country. From our point of view, we never have been a real democracy.

"Only a small elite group has had democracy, what I would call an exclusively criollo democracy," he said, referring to the mixed-race ruling class. "My responsibility is to show we are opening a road to create a society that can be truly called democratic. This is part of an awakening of the indigenous movement. And it is the expression of something normal, that the indigenous people should also be capable and permitted to rule."

If there is a place to record such discrimination, Bolivia is as graphic as any in Latin America—the rights of a majority of its people are repeatedly denied.

Mr. Cárdenas's wife, Lydia, is an Aymara who wears traditional dress—long black braids with black tassels on the end, a colorful multilayered skirt that accentuates the girth of the female body, felt shoes and a bowler hat.

She is a trained teacher, he said, but cannot work in a state school because of the way she dresses. Nor can she teach in the Aymara tongue, in a country where almost 40 percent speak it as their first language.

Government workers and medical students are not permitted to dress in traditional clothes.

"For Lydia to teach in a school, she has to cut her hair and take off her skirt,"

Mr. Cárdenas said, "even if she was teaching Aymara children."

CHANGING NAMES

There are other forms of open discrimination: None of the Indian organizations are sanctioned by the state, and so cannot get bank financing for projects. Anyone caught practicing the elaborate and sometimes highly effective folk medicines is subject to arrest. The jobs most indigenous people can get are at the lowest social rung and pay scale—street sweepers, maids, gardeners, laundry ladies and nannies.

Widespread discrimination is taking a toll, Mr. Cárdenas says. Many are changing their names, just as his father did. Mannaní becomes Martínez. Quispe becomes Gisbert. And Jang'o becomes Blanco.

He has an ambitious program for change that he hopes the President will slowly put in place. It includes bilingual education, eliminating dress restrictions and changing voting laws to permit half the Congress to be elected from regions throughout the country, where much of the Indian population lives.

Perhaps the hardest task, he said, will be to change education textbooks and teacher training to change the portrayal of the Indian "from an individual on the margin of society that does not count for much to someone who is in the mainstream of Bolivian life and makes up most of the country."

"The idea is not to separate us from the state," he said. "We are not groups that want independence. We want to be part of the process of government."

He plans to push for more Government spending in the countryside. Now, less than 5 percent of public funds are spent there. And he will seek government recognition of all indigenous organizations.

The work, he said, will not go quickly. But his option is not violence, like that seen in neighboring Peru, where the Shining Path guerrillas draw much of their support from indigenous peoples.

"The Indian people want to solve our problems but within a democratic system, instead of through violent methods," he said. "We want to solve our tragic poverty within the limits of democracy. We have the right to be governed, but also the right to govern. We want to elect, but we also want to be elected."

And he is not a man in a hurry.

"We have waited 500 years," he said. "And we can wait another five, another 15, another 50 years."

STRUGGLING TO BE THEMSELVES

MICHAEL S. SERRILL

ELIJAH HARPER, A CREE-OJIBWAY Indian and legislator in the province of Manitoba, became a hero to Canadian Indians and Inuit two years ago when he brought the machinery of national constitutional reform to a halt. His decisive no in the Manitoba legislative assembly not only doomed a complex pact designed to put the Canadian confederation on a new footing but also sent the country's political leadership back to the drawing board. Spurred in part by the Manitoban's stubborn stand, federal and provincial leaders agreed for the first time that a revised constitution must recognize native peoples' "inherent right to self-government."

But native rights lost ground when a broad majority of Canadians rejected the new constitution last week. Ovide Mercredi, chief of the Assembly of First Nations, warned of new confrontations as indigenous peoples sought redress through roadblocks and public protests instead. Still, Canada's attempts to codify native self-government was the latest sign that the struggle for political recognition by native peoples across North and South America is bearing some fruit. From the Yukon to Yuma to Cape Horn, indigenous peoples are using new strategies to recover some of the land, resources and sovereignty they lost in the past 500 years. They have negotiated, sued, launched international campaigns, occupied land and, in a few cases, taken up arms to press their cause, marking in their own way the quincentennial of Christopher Columbus' arrival in the New World—an event Native Americans rank as the greatest single disaster in their history.

History cannot be reversed, but historic change seems to be in the making. In Canada the commitment to native self-determination followed another major

CANADA

Native population: 1.5 million
Percent of total population: 6%
Number of bands: 633

Native peoples have made great strides in recovering their lands and political power. Since constitutional recognition has failed, they must seek self-government through legislation.

step: the creation of a self-governing entity called Nunavut out of the vast Northwest Territories, effectively turning a fifth of Canada's 4 million-sq.-mi. territory over to 17,500 Inuit. In the province of Quebec, persistent agitation by 10,000 Inuit and Cree Indians against the second phase of an $11 billion hydroelectric project at James Bay, which would flood thousands more acres of Indian and Inuit lands, has placed the enterprise's future in doubt.

In South America large areas of the Amazon Basin have been reserved for the exclusive use of Brazilian, Ecuadorian, Peruvian and Venezuelan Indians. The rights of tribes to conduct their own affairs, form their own councils and receive royalties for mining activities on Indian lands are gradually being recognized.

In the U.S., Indian tribes are trying to get government to honor promises of autonomy that go back 150 years. Some tribes fund the effort with dollars earned from gambling operations on Indian land, where state writ generally does not apply.

The fate of 40.5 million indigenous people—37 million in Latin America, 2 million in the U.S. and 1.5 million in Canada—has become a focus for discussion at the U.N. and in the councils of the European Community. Environmental groups have declared native peoples to be model conservators of

the earth's increasingly fragile ecology. Native activism is entering a multinational phase. Over the past year, representatives of dozens of tribes in the hemisphere have held dozens of meetings to discuss common action to regain land and at least a measure of self-government. In some cases, they have called for recognition of their right to preserve their cultural identities.

Such assertiveness cannot come too soon for most of the Americas' original inhabitants, whose plight, more often than not, is desperate. The U.S.'s poorest county, according to the 1990 census, is the one encompassing the Pine Ridge Reservation of the Oglala Sioux in South Dakota, where 63% of the people live below the poverty line. Death from heart disease occurs at double the national rate; from alcoholism, at 10 times the U.S. average. Similarly, in Canada, aboriginals, as they are called, are among the poorest of the poor, afflicted by high rates of alcoholism and suicide. In Latin America the descendants of the Maya, Aztecs and Incas have been relegated to the lowest rung of society.

Neglect is not the worst that native peoples have suffered. "For centuries governments have often treated the rights of indigenous people with contempt—torturing and killing them in the tens of thousands and doing virtually nothing when others murder them," charges Amnesty International in a report issued last month. The depth of discrimination, poverty and despair makes some of the recent strides by the Americas' native peoples all the more remarkable:

CANADA. Sixty miles north of Vancouver, a group of 700 Sechelt Indians, self-governing since 1986, have established themselves on 3,000 acres of waterfront and forest land. They own a salmon hatch-

UNITED STATES

Indian population: 2 million
Percent of total population: 0.8%
Number of tribes: 515

Nominally autonomous since 1831, U.S. tribes have made real progress only in the past 25 years. They now control 40% of the Indian Affairs budget and fund some social programs through gambling.

---

ery and earn revenue from a gravel-quarrying business; the profits have helped build a community center and provide social benefits, including low-cost housing for the elderly. The Sechelt gained autonomy by giving up their claim to an additional 14,250 acres of British Columbia, for which they have asked $45 million in compensation. Though other natives have criticized the deal, Chief Thomas Paul, 46, says the settlement "will give us a large economic base to make us self-sufficient."

Canada's rejected constitutional changes would have given the natives a "third order of government," with status analogous to the federal and provincial governments. Indians would have gained full jurisdiction over such natural resources as oil and gas, minerals and forests, their own local or regional administrations, justice and education systems, and the administration of much of the $4.5 billion in federal social-welfare funds that flow to the tribes.

Such sweeping guarantees would have been an enormous step forward, but in practical ways Canada is already engaged in enormous land settlements and a broad transfer of local power to native peoples. In many cities as well as in the northern territories, administrative powers and tax money can be turned over to the natives, and Justice Minister Kim Campbell promised after the vote that this will be done. Although some Indians were just as glad the constitutional changes failed, both yes and no voters insisted that the referendum last week did not mean a permanent rejection of native rights.

THE U.S. On the Ak-Chin Indian reservation south of Phoenix, Arizona, self-government and self-sufficiency are taken for granted. The Ak-Chin broke away from the paternalistic U.S. Bureau of Indian Affairs, the federal agency that still controls much of Indian life from cradle to grave, in 1961 when the tribe insisted on farming its own lands rather than leasing them out to non-Indians for negligible revenues. Today the 600-member tribe takes in profits of more than $1 million a year by growing crops on 16,500 acres. About 175 Ak-Chins work on the land or in commu-

nity government; the tribal unemployment rate is 3%. The Ak-Chins accept federal funds only for housing loans. To become even more self-sufficient, the tribe has plans to start manufacturing operations and perhaps casinos.

On paper at least, the 2 million Indians and Eskimos in the U.S. have had more autonomy—and have had it longer—than their Canadian or Latin American counterparts; in 1831 the U.S. Supreme Court declared that the tribes were "domestic dependent nations" entitled to limited self-government. That status was largely fiction for the next 140 years, however; not until 25 years ago did an Indian-rights movement begin agitating to claim what had been guaranteed. Since then the movement has scored some notable gains:

▶ In 1971 Congress awarded the 60,000 native peoples of Alaska $962 million and 40 million acres to settle their land claims. Natives have used the funds to invest in companies involved in everything from timber to broadcasting.

▶ In 1988 the Puyallup Indians in Tacoma, Washington, received $66 million and 300 acres of prime land in the port of Tacoma based on an 1854 treaty. The tribe will build a marina and container-shipping facility on the land—and will celebrate each member's 21st birthday with a $20,000 gift.

▶ In 1990 the Shoshoni-Bannock people of the Fort Hall reservation in Idaho secured their right to use 581,000 acre-feet of water flowing through the Snake River under an 1868 treaty. The tribe will use the water for farming and sell any excess.

Ever since passage of the 1975 Indian Self-Determination Act, the tribes can take back from federal authorities the administration of education and other social programs; as a result, Indian governments now control about 40% of the Bureau of Indian Affairs' $1.9 billion budget. Self-government without development, however, has merely given many Indians the responsibility to administer their own poverty: they still have the shortest life-spans, highest infant-mortality rate, highest high school dropout rate and most extensive health problems of any U.S. ethnic group.

In some places that situation is changing slowly with the spin of roulette wheels. Empowered by a series of court decisions and a 1988 federal law, about 140 Indian tribes across the country operate 150 gambling operations. Revenue has grown from $287 million in 1987 to more than $3.2 billion and is making some tribes rich.

LATIN AMERICA. The protest was unlike anything Ecuadorians had ever seen. In June 1990, responding to a call from the Confederation of Indigenous Nationalities of Ecuador to demand title to their lands, more than half a million native Ecuadorians marched out of their isolated vil-

LATIN AMERICA

Indian population: 37 million
Percent of total population: 8%
Number of tribes: 589

Indians are demanding political rights and the return of lands lost centuries ago. Amazonian tribes have been most successful in obtaining millions of acres, but mineral rights and self-government are proving elusive.

---

lages to block roads, occupy churches and city halls, and stage noisy demonstrations. The sudden upheaval, which lasted a week and virtually shut down the country, shocked the European and mixed-race élites that have ruled Ecuador for centuries—but it also produced results. Last May, then President Rodrigo Borja agreed to hand over legal title to more than 2.5 million acres of Amazon land to 109 communities of Quichua, Achuar and Shiwiar peoples in the eastern province of Pastaza.

"We believe in our capacity to organize, not in the government's goodwill," says Valerio Grefa, leader of the Indians of the Ecuadorian Amazon. Similar sentiments have stirred tribes from Mexico to Chile and have even inspired some armed guerrilla movements that make the struggle for Indian rights part of their ideology. After initial anger and confusion, governments have begun to respond. In Peru, Amazonian Indians have reclaimed 5 million acres of traditional lands, using $1.3 million in assistance from Denmark. Colombia's 60 Indian tribes have won title to more than 2.5 million acres.

In Brazil, with 240,000 Indians in a population of 146 million, the government last year set aside 37,450 sq. mi. for 9,500 Yanomami, a fragile Amazon tribe whose way of life had been virtually destroyed by migratory gold miners. In the past 2½ years, Brasília has created 131 reserves covering 120,000 sq. mi. in 19 states that are home to 100,000 Indians. It is a beginning—but it does not come close to ending the threat to the tribes, whose lands are frequently invaded by aggressive miners and ranchers and who receive little help from the Indian-protection agency.

Cycles of destruction and rebirth are hardly unknown to the Americas' native peoples. The Aymara people of Bolivia have a word for times of war, enslavement and privation: *pachakuti,* or the disruption of the universe. But *pachakuti* also contains the assumption that the cosmic order will be restored, ushering in a period of peace and harmony, or *nayrapacha.* Though their struggle has a far way to go, the native peoples of the two continents are hoping that *nayrapacha* is within their reach. *—Reported by Nancy Harbert/ Albuquerque, Ian McCluskey/Rio de Janeiro and Courtney Tower/Ottawa*

Return of the Natives

The Kayapó sell Brazil-nut oil to The Body Shop and use video
cameras to record politicians' promises. Just one
of the indigenous peoples who work with outsiders—and organize
themselves—to get off the world's endangered list.

Alan Thein Durning

Salmon from the Pacific Northwest may be simply a passing pleasure for gourmets, but it is the very bedrock of Native American culture in that rugged region. When non-Indians took more and more salmon away from them, the Lummi, Tulalip, Muckleshoot, and other Northwestern tribes faced the loss of what they held most dear. Many peoples—among the world's nearly 5,000 distinct indigenous cultures—have faced similar losses, whether through commerce, disease, or environmental degradation. A handful have found out how to save their

heritage. That handful includes the salmon tribes, who depend on the mysterious instincts of creatures that return from years in the ocean and fight their way up cascading rivers to spawn.

A century ago the US government demanded territorial concessions from the Pacific Northwest Indians. In exchange, the government promised them permanent access to their customary fishing grounds, both on and off reservations. But, starting early in this century, non-Indian fishers began to take most of the catch, leaving little for Indians.

ALAN THEIN DURNING ("Environment: What Sid Did (and You Can Do)," WM, August 1992), senior researcher at the Worldwatch Institute in Washington, D.C., adapted this article from his latest Worldwatch Paper, "Guardians of the Land: Indigenous Peoples and the Health of the Earth." His book "How Much Is Enough? The Consumer Society and the Future of the Earth" was published by W.W. Norton & Co.

The native fishing industry dwindled, and by mid-century had almost died—until the Indians organized themselves to demand their rights. Eventually, in a series of landmark legal rulings in the 1970s, US courts interpreted the treaties as reserving half of all disputed fish for Indians.

Their rights secured, the tribes have once again become accomplished fishery managers—rejuvenating their traditional reverence for salmon and training themselves in modern approaches with the help of supportive non-Indians. As stipulated under the court rulings, state and federal fisheries regulators have agreed with qualified tribes to manage fish runs jointly. Today those Lummi, Tulalip, Muckleshoot, and other Northwestern tribes are managing the salmon runs that nourished their ancestors.

All the globe's indigenous people—hundreds of millions of them, from Africa to Australia to the Philippines to the Americas—have ancient ties to the land,

water, and wildlife of their ancestral domains. All are endangered by the onrushing force of the outside world. They have been decimated by plagues and violence. Their cultures have been altered by missionaries and exploited by entrepreneurs. Their subsistence economies have been dismantled by the agents of national development. And their homelands have been overrun by commercial resource extractors and landless peasants.

It's not only in America's Northwest that the future has begun to brighten. In Ecuador, for example, Indians have mounted a dramatic and effective campaign to claim their due. After centuries of second-class citizenship, they want to secure not only rights to the lands they have worked since time immemorial, but also constitutional recognition of their distinct cultures.

In June 1990, after decades of grassroots organizing, Ecuador's Indian federations called their people to march peacefully on the cities, to blockade the nation's highways, and to refuse to sell food outside their communities. For three days, a million Indians brought the country to a standstill. Enraged as they were, the ruling classes had no choice but to take heed as the Indians enumerated their priorities. High on the list were 72 land claims languishing in the bureaucracy.

Negotiations with the government, begun during that watershed week in 1990, continued with little progress until a new march began in 1992. This time 2,500

From *World Monitor,* March 1993, pp. 54-56, 58, 60, 62. Originally "Native Americans Stand Their Ground," by Alan Thein Durning, November/December 1991. © 1991 by Worldwatch Institute, Washington, DC.

marchers set out from the jungle lowlands of Pastaza province, heading for the mountain capital of Quito. As the marchers gained altitude, they gained support, swelling to 10,000 when they reached the seat of government in April. There, with the weight of national opinion behind them, they won rights to almost 3 million acres of their forest homeland.

"The reason why in recent times the indigenous peoples have been having so much success is that indigenous peoples from many different places have come together and united to fight a common battle, to stand together," observes Albino Pereira Cece of the Kinikinau people of Brazil in a statement that applies equally to Ecuador.

A similar case can be found in Namibia, where most of the San (Bushmen)—after a century in which their population declined by 80% and their land base shrank by 85%—are now day laborers on cash-crop plantations. In the 1980s, however, some 48 bands of San, totaling about 2,500 individuals, organized themselves to return to the desert homes they had tenuous rights over. There they have created a modified version of their ancient hunting and gathering economy. With the help of anthropologists, they have added livestock and drip-irrigated gardens to the daily foraging trips of their forebears, fashioning a way of life that is both traditional and modern.

Perhaps because natural-resource rights are best recognized in the Americas, indigenous groups there are the furthest advanced in adapting traditional resource management arrangements to the modern setting.

• In northern Canada, the Inuvialuit people have created management plans for grizzly and polar bears and for beluga whales.

• In southern Mexico, the Chinantec Indians are gradually developing their own blend of timber cutting, furniture making, butterfly farming, and forest preservation in their retreat in the Juarez mountains.

• The Miskito Indians of Nicaragua's Atlantic Coast, meanwhile, are forming local management groups to police the use of forests, wetlands, and reefs in the extensive Miskito Coast Protected Area they helped create in 1991.

Another positive thrust comes from "alternative traders"—organizations committed to cultural survival and environmental sustainability. They now market millions of dollars worth of indigenous

They want rights to the lands they have worked— and to be recognized.

peoples' products in industrial countries. The Mixe Indians of southern Mexico, for example, sell organic coffee to US consumers through the Texas-based alternative-trade organization Pueblo to People. The Kayapó sell Brazil-nut oil for use in hair conditioners to the British-based Body Shop chain.

By eliminating links from the merchandising chain, such alternative traders keep more of the product value flowing back to indigenous producers. The potential for alternative trade to expand is enormous, given the growing purchasing power of environmentally conscious consumers and the abundance of plant products hidden in indigenous lands.

Is all the effort to protect endangered cultures too little, too late—a case of closing the barn door after the barn has burned? Indigenous peoples get little attention in the mainstream media, and what little they get often implies that there are just a few remaining holdouts for a way of life that is, in any case, now largely gone.

Those perceptions are mistaken. Indigenous people are far from disappearing, and their cause is far from hopeless.

There are two compelling reasons for the world's dominant societies to heed the voices of indigenous peoples more seriously than they ever have. These reasons bear not only on the lives—and ways of life—of the threatened peoples, but on those of the dominant ones as well.

1. Indigenous peoples are the sole guardians of vast, little-disturbed habitats that modern societies depend on more than they may realize—to regulate water cycles, maintain the stability of the climate, and provide valuable plants, animals, and

Indigenous cultures by region...

AFRICA AND MIDDLE EAST: Great cultural diversity throughout the continent. "Indigenous" share of land hotly contested. Some 25 million to 30 million nomadic herders in East Africa, Sahel, and Arabian peninsula include Bedouin, Dinka, Masai, and Turkana. San (Bushmen) of Namibia and Botswana and pygmies of central African rain forest, both traditionally hunter-gatherers, have occupied present homelands for at least 20,000 years. 2,000 languages spoken.

AMERICAS: Native Americans concentrated near centers of ancient civilizations: Aztec in Mexico, Mayan in Central America, and Incan in Andes. In Latin America, most farm small plots; in North America, 2 million Indians live in cities and reservations. 900 languages spoken.

ARCTIC: Inuit (Eskimo) and other Arctic peoples of North America, Greenland, and Siberia traditionally fishers, whalers, and hunters. Sami (Lapp) of arctic Scandinavia traditionally reindeer herders. 50 languages spoken.

EAST ASIA: Chinese indigenous peoples, numbering up to 82 million, mostly subsistence farmers such as Bulang of south China or former pastoralists such as ethnic Mongolians of north and west China. Ainu of Japan and aboriginal Taiwanese now largely industrial laborers. 150 languages spoken.

OCEANIA: Aborigines of Australia and Maoris of New Zealand, traditionally farmers, fishers, hunters, and gatherers. Many now raise livestock. Islanders of South Pacific continue to fish and harvest marine resources. 500 languages spoken.

SOUTH ASIA: Gond, Bhil, and other adivasis, or tribal peoples, inhabit forest belt of central India. Adivasis of Bangladesh concentrated in Chittagong hills on Burmese border; several million tribal farmers and pastoralists in Afghanistan, Pakistan, Nepal, Iran, and central Asian republics of former USSR. 700 languages spoken. Tribal Hmong, Karen, and other forest-farming peoples form ethnic mosaic covering uplands. Indigenous popula-

(continued next page)

tion proportional to distribution of forest: Laos has most forest and tribal peoples, Myanmar and Vietnam have less of each, and Thailand and mainland Malaysia have least. Tribal peoples concentrated at ends of Philippine and Indonesian archipelagoes. Island of New Guinea mostly indigenous tribes. 1,950 languages spoken.

...and how they tend their ecosystems

FOREST: Lacondon Maya of southern Mexico plant intricate tree gardens, mimicking the diversity of natural rain forests. Tribal peoples of India revere and protect certain trees as sacred. Gorowa of Tanzania, like the Gabra of Kenya, reserve ancient forest groves as sacred sites dedicated for coming-of-age rituals, men's and women's meeting places, and burials. Karen tribal elders in Thailand carefully regulate community use of forested watersheds.

GRASSLAND: Sukuma, south of Africa's Lake Victoria, rotate grazing on a 30- to 50-year cycle. Zaghawa of Niger move their camels and sheep north to wet-season Saharan pastures in separate, parallel paths, leaving ungrazed strips for the return trek. Fulani orchestrate the orderly return of thousands of head of livestock to the Niger delta in early dry season to avoid overgrazing.

WATERS: Temple priests in highlands of Bali distribute irrigation water to farmers through networks of channels, with synchronized rotation ensuring fairness, maximum yields, and minimum pest damage. In mountains of Iran, long-lived gravity-powered quanat system provides irrigation water through elaborate excavations and recharging of groundwater.

FISHERIES: In South Pacific, ritual restrictions based on area, season, and species prevent overfishing; religious events often open and close fishing seasons. In Marquesas islands, chieftains forbid the consumption of certain fish and enforce the ban, in extreme cases, by expulsion from island. Wet'suwet'en and Gitksan of Canadian Pacific believe salmon spirits give their bodies to humans for food but punish those who waste fish, catch more than they can use, or disrupt habitats.

genes. These homelands may harbor more endangered plant and animal species than all the world's nature reserves.

2. Indigenous peoples possess, in their ecological knowledge, an asset of incalculable value: a map to the biological diversity of the earth on which all plant, animal, and human life depends. Encoded in indigenous languages, customs, and practices may be as much understanding of nature as is stored in the libraries of modern science.

It was little appreciated in past centuries of exploitation, but it is undeniable now, that the world's dominant cultures cannot sustain Earth's ecological health without the aid of the world's endangered cultures. Biological diversity—of paramount importance both to sustaining viable ecosystems and to improving human existence through scientific advances—is inextricably linked to cultural diversity.

Indigenous peoples are "the 'miner's canary' of the human family," says Guajiro Indian writer José Barreiro. Their cultures, existing in direct and unmediated dependence on nature, are the first to suffer when it is poisoned, degraded, or exhausted. Yet in a world threatened by mass species extinction, catastrophic climate change, and industrial contamination of land, air, and water, no culture can afford to be complacent.

In the words of Guarani holy man Pae Antonio, whose Argentine village was burned to the ground in 1991 to make way for a casino, "When the Indians vanish, the rest will follow."

What are the conditions in which traditional systems of ecological management can persist in the modern world? Based on the diverse experience of indigenous peoples, three necessary conditions stand out.

1. Traditional stewardship's persistence depends on indigenous peoples having secure rights to their subsistence base— rights that are not only recognized but enforced by the state and, ideally, backed by international law. Latin American tribes such as the Shuar of Ecuador, when threatened with losing their land, have cleared their own forests and taken up cattle ranching, because in Latin America these actions prove ownership. If Ecuador had defended the Shuar's land rights, the ranching would have been unnecessary.

2. Indigenous ecological stewardship can survive the onslaught of the outside world if indigenous peoples are organized politically and the states in which they reside allow democratic initiatives. The Khant and Mansi peoples of Siberia, like most indigenous people in the former Soviet Union, were nominally autonomous in their customary territories under Soviet law, but political repression precluded the organized defense of that terrain until the end of the '80s. Since then, the peoples of Siberia have begun organizing themselves to turn paper rights into real local control. In neighboring China, in contrast, indigenous homelands remain nothing more than legal fictions because the state marginalizes all representative organizations.

3. If they are to surmount the obstacles of the outside world, indigenous communities need access to information, support, and advice from friendly sources. The tribal people of Papua New Guinea know much about their local environment, for example, but they know little about the impacts of large-scale logging and mining. Foreign and domestic investors have often played on this ignorance, assuring remote groups that no lasting harm would result from leasing parts of their land to resource extractors. If the forest peoples of Papua New Guinea could learn from the experience of threatened peoples elsewhere— through supportive organizations and indigenous peoples' federations—they might be more careful.

As they struggle to adapt their natural resource stewardship to modern pressures, indigenous peoples are beginning to pool their expertise.

• The Native Fish and Wildlife Service in Colorado, formed by a coalition of North American tribes, serves as an information clearinghouse on sustainable management.

• The Kuna of Panama—whose tribal regulations on hunting turtles and game, catching lobsters, and felling trees fill thick volumes—have convened international conferences on forest and fisheries management, with the aid of environmental funders.

• The Inuit Circumpolar Conference representing Inuit peoples from Canada, Greenland, Russia, and the United States, has developed an Inuit Regional Conservation Strategy that includes tight controls on wildlife harvesting and resource extraction, and collaborative arrangements for sharing ecological knowledge.

Such instances are still exceptional, but they blaze a trail for indigenous peoples everywhere.

A newer route to assuring indigenous peoples a basic income is through intellectual property rights—proprietary rights to ideas, designs, or information most commonly typified by patents and copyrights.

With the explosive growth in biotechnology since 1980, the demand for new genetic material is burgeoning. Many of the world's genes are in the millions of species in the endangered places known only to endangered peoples. Indeed, some indigenous leaders think of the rush to codify and exploit their people's knowledge of biological diversity as the latest in the long history of resource grabs perpetrated against them.

"Today," says Adrian Esquina Lisco, spiritual chief of the National Association of Indigenous Peoples of El Salvador, "the white world wants to understand the native cultures and extract those fragments of wisdom which extend its own dominion."

Still, supporters of indigenous peoples are developing legal strategies to turn the gene trade to native advantage by demanding recognition that indigenous communities possess intellectual property rights as valid as those of other inventors and discoverers.

Legal cases play an important part in native movements in places where the rule of law is strong. North American tribes now have a generation of talented lawyers who turn what they call "white man's law" to Indian advantage, winning back ancestral land and water rights. Maori organizations in New Zealand catalyzed the creation of a special tribunal to investigate violations of the century-old Waitangi treaty, which guaranteed Maori land rights. The tribunal is charged with sifting through claims that cover 70% of the country and many of its offshore fisheries.

All in all, from the smallest tribal settlements to the UN General Assembly, indigenous peoples' organizations are making themselves felt. Their grassroots movements have spread quickly since 1970, strengthening their political skills, recruiting ever more members, adapting their cultural techniques of self-defense to the political circumstances in which they find themselves.

Some indigenous movements have also mastered use of communications media. Brazil's Kayapó tribe takes video cameras to meetings with politicians to record the promises they make. Aboriginal groups in Australia publish newspapers reflecting their culture. And 2 million Aymara Indians in Bolivia, Peru, and Chile tune their radios to Radio San Gabriel for Aymara language news, music, and educational programming.

Regional and global meetings on the rights of indigenous peoples are now commonplace. In June 1992, for example, three separate conferences of native peoples were held in Rio, one preceding and two coinciding with the UN Conference on Environment and Development.

The longest-lived series of meetings, and perhaps the most important, has been the annual sessions of the Geneva-based UN Working Group on Indigenous Populations. Established by the UN Human Rights Commission in 1982, the Working Group is drafting a Universal Declaration on the Rights of Indigenous Peoples. The version of late 1992 stated: "Indigenous peoples have the collective and individual right to own, control and use the lands and territories they have traditionally occupied or otherwise used. This includes the right to full recognition of their own laws and customs, land tenure systems and institutions for the management of resources, and the right to effective measures by States to prevent any interference with or encroachment on these rights."

The end of the Cold War has unfrozen systems of governance, allowing a shifting of political authority from central governments both downward to local bodies and upward to international ones. It has also allowed the protection of the global environment to rise to a prominent place on the international agenda.

Some of the unfreezing of governance will undoubtedly play itself out in increased nationalism, as it has with tragic effects in the former Yugoslavia in the early '90s. Declarations of national independence have come at a frenzied pace in recent years, to the astonishment of most students of international affairs. Between 1988 and October 1992, the UN membership rolls added 16 new names, totalling 178.

Such a trend tends to reinforce itself. If Latvians, Czechs, and Eritreans deserve national recognition, peoples everywhere are bound to ask themselves, Why not us too? The Oromos of Ethiopia, the Tibetans, the Karen of northern Myanmar, and the Papuans and Timorese of eastern Indonesia have been struggling for autonomy or independence for decades. Scores of other peoples may eventually voice similar demands. Given the underlying cultural divisions that scar Africa and Asia in particular, the number of states could continue to rise swiftly for some time to come.

Such a scenario—involving the dissolution of China and various multi-ethnic African states—would have seemed farfetched in the late '80s. In 1993, it is at least conceivable.

A global tapestry of diverse cultures must still have some binding threads. The rapid degradation of the global environment suggests that one of these universal values should be the objective of passing on to future generations a planet undiminished by the present generation's actions. As this value gains political support worldwide, indigenous cultures could benefit. Their qualifications as stewards of ecosystems could increase their prominence and win them long-deserved respect. They may finally be seen as part of the future, as well as of the past.

These peoples also offer the world's dominant culture—a consumerist and individualist culture born in Europe and bred in the United States—living examples of ancient values that may be shared by everyone: devotion to future generations, ethical regard for nature, and commitment to community among people.

For environmentalists, indigenous peoples represent the best hope for preserving the vast, little-degraded habitats encompassed by ancestral homelands. For indigenous peoples, environmentalists are powerful allies, sometimes better skilled in the thrust and parry of modern resource politics. Both sides of this alliance are somewhat wary of the other, divided sometimes by culture, race, and priorities. Still, in the end, indigenous peoples and the environmental movement have much in common. In the words of a young man from the Banwa'on tribe of the Philippines: "Our skins might not be the same color, but our dreams are the same."

Crimes Against Humanity

*If nifty little "pep" gestures like the "Indian Chant" and the "Tomahawk Chop"
are just good clean fun, then let's spread the fun around, shall we?*

Ward Churchill

During the past couple of seasons, there has been an increasing wave of controversy regarding the names of professional sports teams like the Atlanta "Braves," Cleveland "Indians," Washington "Redskins," and Kansas City "Chiefs." The issue extends to the names of college teams like Florida State University "Seminoles," University of Illinois "Fighting Illini," and so on, right on down to high school outfits like the Lamar (Colorado) "Savages." Also involved have been team adoption of "mascots," replete with feathers, buckskins, beads, spears and "warpaint" (some fans have opted to adorn themselves in the same fashion), and nifty little "pep" gestures like the "Indian Chant" and "Tomahawk Chop."

A substantial number of American Indians have protested that use of native names, images and symbols as sports team mascots and the like is, by definition, a virulently racist practice. Given the historical relationship between Indians and non-Indians during what has been called the "Conquest of America," American Indian Movement leader (and American Indian Anti-Defamation Council founder) Russell Means has compared the practice to contemporary Germans naming their soccer teams the "Jews," "Hebrews," and "Yids," while adorning their uniforms with grotesque caricatures of Jewish faces taken from the Nazis' anti-Semitic propaganda of the 1930s. Numerous demonstrations have occurred in conjunction with games—most notably during the November 15, 1992 match-up between the Chiefs and Redskins in Kansas City—by angry Indians and their supporters.

In response, a number of players—especially African Americans and other minority athletes—have been trotted out by professional team owners like Ted Turner, as well as university and public school officials, to announce that they mean not to insult but to honor native people. They have been joined by the television networks and most major newspapers, all of which have editorialized that Indian discomfort with the situation is "no big deal," insisting that the whole thing is just "good, clean fun." The country needs more such fun, they've argued, and "a few disgruntled Native Americans" have no right to undermine the nation's enjoyment of its leisure time by complaining. This is especially the case, some have argued, "in hard times like these." It has even been contended that Indian outrage at being systematically degraded—rather than the degradation itself—creates "a serious barrier to the sort of intergroup communication so necessary in a multicultural society such as ours."

Okay, let's communicate. We are frankly dubious that those advancing such positions really believe their own rhetoric, but, just for the sake of argument, let's accept the premise that they are sincere. If what they say is true, then isn't it time we spread such "inoffensiveness" and "good cheer" around among *all* groups so that *everybody* can participate *equally* in fostering the round of national laughs they call for? Sure it is—the country can't have too much fun or "intergroup involvement—so the more, the merrier. Simple consistency demands that anyone who thinks the Tomahawk Chop is a swell pastime must be just as hearty in their endorsement of the following ideas—by the logic used to defend the defamation of American Indians—should help us all really start yukking it up.

First, as a counterpart to the Redskins, we need an NFL team called "Niggers" to honor Afro-Americans. Half-time festivities for fans might include a simulated stewing of the opposing coach in a large pot while players and cheerleaders dance around it, garbed in leopard skins and wearing fake bones in their noses. This concept obviously goes along with the kind of gaiety attending the Chop, but also with the actions of the Kansas City Chiefs, whose team members—prominently including black team members—lately appeared on a poster looking "fierce" and "savage" by way of wearing Indian regalia. Just a bit of harmless "morale boosting," says the Chiefs' front office. You bet.

So that the newly-formed Niggers sports club won't end up too out of sync while expressing the "spirit" and "identity" of Afro-Americans in the above fashion, a baseball franchise—let's call this one the "Sambos"—should be formed. How about a basketball team called the "Spearchuckers?" A hockey team called the "Jungle Bunnies?" Maybe the "essence" of these teams could be depicted by images of tiny black faces adorned with huge pairs of lips. The players could appear on TV every week or so gnawing on chicken legs and spitting watermelon seeds at one another. Catchy, eh? Well, there's "nothing to be upset about," according to those who love wearing "war bonnets" to the Super Bowl or having "Chief Illiniwik" dance around the sports arenas of Urbana, Illinois.

And why stop there? There are plenty of other groups to include. "Hispanics?" They can be "represented" by the Galveston "Greasers" and San Diego "Spics," at least until the Wisconsin "Wetbacks" and Baltimore "Beaners" get off the ground. Asian Americans? How about the "Slopes," "Dinks," "Gooks," and "Zipperheads?" Owners of the latter teams might get their logo ideas from editorial page cartoons printed in

the nation's newspapers during World War II: slant-eyes, buck teeth, big glasses, but nothing racially insulting or derogatory, according to the editors and artists involved at the time. Indeed, this Second World War-vintage stuff can be seen as just another barrel of laughs, at least by what current editors say are their "local standards" concerning American Indians.

Let's see. Who's been left out? Teams like the Kansas City "Kikes," Hanover "Honkies," San Leandro "Shylocks," Daytona "Dagos," and Pittsburgh "Polacks" will fill a certain social void among white folk.

Cleveland "Indians"

Have a religious belief? Let's all go for the gusto and gear up the Milwaukee "Mackerel Snappers" and Hollywood "Holy Rollers." The Fighting Irish of Notre Dame can be rechristened the "Drunken Irish" or "Papist Pigs." Issues of gender and sexual preference can be addressed through creation of teams like the St. Louis "Sluts," Boston "Bimbos," Detroit "Dykes," and the Fresno "Fags." How about the Gainesville "Gimps" and Richmond "Retards," so the physically and mentally impaired won't be excluded from our fun and games?

Now, don't go getting "overly sensitive" out there. None of this is demeaning or insulting, at least not when it's being done to Indians. Just ask the folks who are doing it, or their apologists like Andy Rooney in the national media. They'll tell you—as in fact they *have* been telling you—that there's been no harm done, regardless of what their victims think, feel, or say. The situation is exactly the same as when those with precisely the same mentality used to insist that Step 'n' Fetchit was okay, or Rochester on the Jack Benny Show, or Amos and Andy, Charlie Chan, the Frito Bandito, or any of the other cutsey symbols making up the lexicon of American racism. Have we communicated yet?

Let's get just a little bit real here. The notion of "fun" embodied in rituals like the Tomahawk Chop must be understood for what it is. There's not a single non-Indian example used above which can be considered socially acceptable in even the most marginal sense. The reasons are obvious enough. So why is it different where American Indians are concerned? One can only conclude that, in contrast to the other groups at issue, Indians are (falsely) perceived as being too few, and therefore too weak, to defend themselves effectively against racist and otherwise offensive behavior.

Fortunately, there are some glimmers of hope. A few teams and their fans have gotten the message and have responded appropriately. Stanford University, which opted to drop the name "Indians" from Stanford, has experienced no resulting drop-off in attendance. Meanwhile, the local newspaper in Portland, Oregon recently decided its long-standing editorial policy prohibiting use of racial epithets should include derogatory team names. The Redskins, for instance, are now referred to as "the Washington team," and will continue to be described in this way until the franchise adopts an inoffensive moniker (newspaper sales in Portland have suffered no decline as a result).

Such examples are to be applauded and encouraged. They stand as figurative beacons in the night, proving beyond all doubt that it is quite possible to indulge in the pleasure of athletics without accepting blatant racism into the bargain.

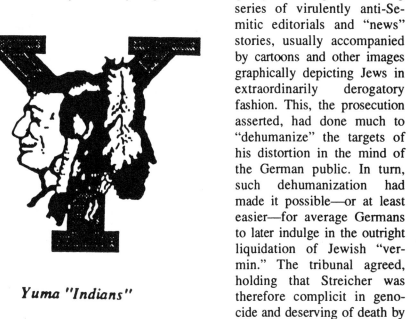

Yuma "Indians"

Nuremberg Precedents

On October 16, 1946, a man named Julius Streicher mounted the steps of a gallows. Moments later he was dead, the sentence of an international tribunal composed of representatives of the United States, France, Great Britain, and the Soviet Union having been imposed. Streicher's body was then cremated, and—so horrendous were his crimes thought to have been—his ashes dumped into an unspecified German river so that "no one should ever know a particular place to go for reasons of mourning his memory."

Julius Streicher had been convicted at Nuremberg, Germany of what were termed "Crimes Against Humanity." The lead prosecutor in his case—Justice Robert Jackson of the United States Supreme Court—had not argued that the defendant had killed anyone, nor that he had personally committed any especially violent act. Nor was it contended that Streicher had held any particularly important position in the German government during the period in which the so-called Third Reich had exterminated some 6,000,000 Jews, as well as several million Gypsies, Poles, Slavs, homosexuals, and other untermenschen (subhumans).

The sole offense for which the accused was ordered put to death was in having served as publisher/editor of a Bavarian tabloid entitled *Der Sturmer* during the early-to-mid 1930s, years before the Nazi genocide actually began. In this capacity, he had penned a long series of virulently anti-Semitic editorials and "news" stories, usually accompanied by cartoons and other images graphically depicting Jews in extraordinarily derogatory fashion. This, the prosecution asserted, had done much to "dehumanize" the targets of his distortion in the mind of the German public. In turn, such dehumanization had made it possible—or at least easier—for average Germans to later indulge in the outright liquidation of Jewish "vermin." The tribunal agreed, holding that Streicher was therefore complicit in genocide and deserving of death by hanging.

During his remarks to the Nuremberg tribunal, Justice Jackson observed that, in implementing its sentences, the participating powers were morally and legally binding themselves to adhere forever after to the same standards of conduct that were being applied to Streicher and the other Nazi leaders. In the alternative, he said, the victorious allies would have committed "pure murder" at Nuremberg—no different in substance from that carried out by those they presumed to judge—rather than establishing the "permanent benchmark for justice" which was intended.

Yet in the United States of Robert Jackson, the indigenous American Indian population had already been reduced, in a process which is ongoing to this day, from perhaps 12.5 million in the year 1500 to fewer than 250,000 by the beginning of the 20th century. This was accomplished, according to official sources, "largely through the cruelty of [EuroAmerican] settlers," and an informal but clear governmental policy which had made it an articulated goal to "exterminate these red vermin," or at least whole segments of them.

Bounties had been placed on the scalps of Indians—any Indians—in places as diverse as Georgia, Kentucky, Texas, the Dakotas, Oregon, and California, and had been maintained until resident Indian populations were decimated or disappeared altogether. Entire peoples such as the Cherokee had been reduced to half their size through a policy of forced removal from their homelands east of the Mississippi River to what were then considered less preferable areas in the West.

Others, such as the Navajo, suffered the same fate while under military guard for years on end. The

United States Army had also perpetrated an long series of wholesale massacres of Indians at places like Horseshoe Bend, Bear River, Sand Creek, the Washita River, the Marias River, Camp Robinson, and Wounded Knee.

Through it all, hundreds of popular novels—each competing with the next to make Indians appear more grotesque, menacing, and inhuman—were sold in the tens of millions of copies in the U.S. Plainly, the Euro-American public was being conditioned to see Indians in such a way as to allow their eradication to continue. And continue it did until the Manifest Destiny of the U.S.—a direct precursor to what Hitler would subsequently call Lebensraumpolitik (the politics of living space)—was consummated.

By 1900, the national project of "clearing" Native Americans from their land and replacing them with "superior" Anglo-American settlers was complete; the indigenous population had been reduced by as much as 98 percent while approximately 97.5 percent of their original territory had "passed" to the invaders. The survivors had been concentrated, out of sight and mind of the public, on scattered "reservations," all of them under the self-assigned "plenary" (full) power of the federal government. There was, of course, no Nuremberg-style tribunal passing judgment on those who had fostered such circumstances in North America. No U.S. official or private citizen was ever imprisoned—never mind hanged—for implementing or propagandizing what had been done. Nor had the process of genocide afflicting Indians been completed. Instead, it merely changed form.

Between the 1880s and the 1980s, nearly half of all Native American children were coercively transferred from their own families, communities, and cultures to those of the conquering society. This was done through compulsory attendance at remote boarding schools, often hundreds of miles from their homes, where native children were kept for years on end while being systematically "deculturated" (indoctrinated to think and act in the manner of Euro Americans rather than as Indians). It was also accomplished through a pervasive foster home and adoption program—including "blind" adoptions, where children would be permanently denied information as to who they were/are and where they'd come from—placing native youths in non-Indian homes.

Westminster "Warriors"

The express purpose of all this was to facilitate a U.S. governmental policy to bring about the "assimilation" (dissolution) of indigenous societies. In other words, Indian cultures as such were to be caused to disappear. Such policy objectives are directly contrary to the United Nations 1948 Convention on Punishment and Prevention of the Crime of Genocide, an element of international law arising from the Nuremberg proceedings. The forced "transfer of the children" of a targeted "racial, ethnical, or religious group" is explicitly prohibited as a genocidal activity under the Convention's second article.

Article II of the Genocide Convention also expressly prohibits involuntary sterilization as a means of "preventing births among" a targeted population. Yet, in 1975, it was conceded by the U.S. government that its Indian Health Service (IHS) then a subpart of the Bureau of Indian Affairs (BIA), was even then conducting a secret program of involuntary sterilization that had affected approximately 40 percent of all Indian women. The program was allegedly discontinued, and the IHS was transferred to the Public Health Service, but no one was punished. In 1990, it came out that the IHS was inoculating Inuit children in Alaska with Hepatitis-B vaccine. The vaccine had already been banned by the World Health Organization as having a demonstrated correlation with the HIV-Syndrome which is itself correlated to AIDS. As this is written, a "field test" of Hepatitis-A vaccine, also HIV-correlated, is being conducted on Indian reservations in the northern plains region.

The Genocide Convention makes it a "crime against humanity" to create conditions leading to the destruction of an identifiable human group, as such. Yet the BIA has utilized the government's plenary prerogatives to negotiate mineral leases "on behalf of" Indian peoples paying a fraction of standard royalty rates. The result has been "super profits" for a number of preferred U.S. corporations. Meanwhile, Indians, whose reservations ironically turned out to be in some of the most mineral-rich areas of North America, which makes us, the nominally wealthiest segment of the continent's population, live in dire poverty.

By the government's own data in the mid-1980s, Indians received the lowest annual and lifetime per capita incomes of any aggregate population group in the United States. Concomitantly, we suffer the highest rate of infant mortality, death by exposure and malnutrition, disease, and the like. Under such circumstances, alcoholism and other escapist forms of substance abuse are endemic in the Indian community, a situation which leads both to a general physical debilitation of the population and a catastrophic accident rate. Teen suicide among Indians is several times the national average.

The average life expectancy of a reservation-based Native American man is barely 45 years; women can expect to live less than three years longer.

Such itemizations could be continued at great length, including matters like the radioactive contamination of large portions of contemporary Indian Country, the forced relocation of traditional Navajos, and so on. But the point should be made: Genocide, as defined in international law, is a continuing fact of day-to-day life (and death) for North America's native peoples. Yet there has been —and is—only the barest flicker of public concern about, or even consciousness of, this reality. Absent any serious expression of public outrage, no one is punished and the process continues.

A salient reason for public acquiescence before the ongoing holocaust in Native North America has been a continuation of the popular legacy, often through more effective media. Since 1925, Hollywood has released more than 2,000 films, many of them rerun frequently on television, portraying Indians as strange, perverted, ridiculous, and often dangerous things of the past. Moreover, we are habitually presented to mass audiences one-dimensionally, devoid of recognizable human motivations and emotions; Indians thus serve as props, little more. We have thus been thoroughly and systematically dehumanized.

Nor is this the extent of it. Everywhere, we are used as logos, as mascots, as jokes: "Big Chief writing tablets, "Red Man" chewing tobacco, "Winnebago" campers, "Navajo and "Cherokee" and "Pontiac" and "Cadillac" pickups and automobiles. There are the Cleveland "Indians," the Kansas City "Chiefs," the Atlanta "Braves" and the Washington "Redskins" professional sports teams—not to mention those in thousands of colleges, high schools, and elementary schools across the country—each with their own degrading caricatures and parodies of Indians and/or things In-

dian. Pop fiction continues in the same vein, including an unending stream of New Age manuals purporting to expose the inner works of indigenous spirituality in everything from pseudo-philosophical to do-it-yourself styles. Blond yuppies from Beverly Hills amble about the country claiming to be reincarnated 17th century Cheyenne Ushamans ready to perform previously secret ceremonies.

In effect, a concerted, sustained, and in some ways accelerating effort has gone into making Indians unreal. It is thus of obvious importance that the American public begin to think about the implications of such things the next time they witness a gaggle of face-painted and war-bonneted buffoons doing the "Tomahawk Chop" at a baseball or football game. It is necessary that they think about the implications of the grade-school teacher adorning their child in turkey feathers to commemorate Thanksgiving. Think about the significance of John Wayne or Charleton Heston killing a dozen "savages" with a single bullet the next time a western comes on TV. Think about why Land-o-Lakes finds it appropriate to market its butter with the stereotyped image of an "Indian princess" on the wrapper. Think about what it means when non-Indian academics profess—as they often do—to "know more about Indians than Indians do themselves." Think about the significance of charlatans like Carlos Castaneda and Jamake Highwater and Mary Summer Rain and Lynn Andrews churning out "Indian"

Lamar High School
"Home of the Savages"

bestsellers, one after the other, while Indians typically can't get into print.

Think about the real situation of American Indians. Think about Julius Streicher. Remember Justice Jackson's admonition. Understand that the treatment of Indians in American popular culture is not "cute" or "amusing" or just "good, clean fun."

Know that it causes real pain and real suffering to real people. Know that it threatens our very survival. And know that this is just as much a crime against humanity as anything the Nazis ever did. It is likely that the indigenous people of the United States will never demand that those guilty of such criminal activity be punished for their deeds. But the least we have the right to expect—indeed, to demand—is that such practices finally be brought to a halt.

Gadugi: A Model of Service-Learning for Native American Communities

Mr. Hall shows how, by combining the best of the education reform movement with traditional Native American values, the National Indian Youth Leadership Project has pioneered the spread of service-learning into Native American communities.

McCLELLAN HALL

McCLELLAN HALL is director of the National Indian Youth Leadership Project, Gallup, N.M.

MANY OF THE concepts that are the foundation of the outdoor/experiential education movement — service-learning, self-directed learning, mentoring, challenge-based learning, and so on — have parallels in Native American traditions. The National Indian Youth Leadership Project (NIYLP) has identified and implemented several traditional Native American approaches to teaching and learning that both affirm the group identity of our people and can help rebuild our communities through the efforts of our young people.

One example of a Native American concept that can be usefully developed by the schools is the Cherokee tradition of *Gadugi*. Among the Tsa-la-gi (Cherokee) people, the call for a *Gadugi* is a call to bring people together to help one another, much as the early European settlers came together for barn raisings. As Cherokees, we are connected to one another through a clan system that defines our relationships. This system of interdependence and mutual obligation has helped us maintain our identity and culture to the present day, and similar concepts exist in all Native American traditions. For example, Bernie Bearskin of the Winnebagos was quoted by Studs Terkel as saying, "I think that perhaps my early training in the home impressed me with the philosophy of our forebears. It was taught to us that if one could be of service to his people, this is one of the greatest honors there is."*

For young people to become involved in service to others is thus a natural extension of Native Americans' traditional sense of communal responsibility. At the same time, learning through providing service to others can be a significant step toward breaking the cycle of dependence in which many Native Americans feel themselves trapped.

Service-learning has been a key ingredient in the evolution of the NIYLP as a model program in Native American communities. The group of people who would later form the nucleus of the

*Studs Terkel, *Division Street, America* (New York: Avon Books, 1967).

NIYLP came together in 1981 in northeastern Oklahoma, where dropout rates for Cherokee students were as high as 70% in some public school systems. In those early discussions, we were confident that the traditional Native American concept of "leader as servant" would work well with the idea of service-learning to help reunite the Cherokee people in the 14-county area that makes up the Cherokee Nation of Oklahoma. We weren't at all sure that contemporary Cherokee young people would recognize and accept such traditional values and commit themselves to this unique effort. Nor were we sure how such traditional values could be made relevant to and practiced in the 1980s and beyond. However, we were optimistic that it could be done, and the spiritual leaders of the Cherokee Nation encouraged our efforts.

As director of the Cherokee Nation's alternative high school from 1981 to 1983, I spent many hours in conversation with Cherokee spiritual leaders — primarily Crosslin Smith, grandson of Redbird Smith, hereditary Chief of the Keetoowah Cherokees (an extremely traditional faction of the tribe that still practices the ancient religion). In response to my concerns about what was happening to contemporary Cherokee youth, Crosslin replied that long ago the spiritual leaders had fasted and gone through prayer and rituals to see into the future and had already seen this situation coming. The lesson I drew from this discussion — though it was never articulated — was that we should view the plight of our young people as a challenge and see what could be done, rather than accept it as something beyond our control. From these conversations, the NIYLP philosophy began to take form.

In the early 1980s none of us had heard of Kurt Hahn and William James, and we were only vaguely aware of the experiential education movement. But we didn't have to look far for examples of the service ethic.

Before she became Principal Chief of the Cherokee Nation of Oklahoma, Wilma Mankiller was quietly attracting national attention through her work with self-help community service projects in isolated Cherokee communities. The most dramatic of these involved the tiny community of Bell, where local Cherokees designed and carried out a project that became a catalyst for bringing their community together. The project could have been done *for* the people (the approach usually taken by government agencies) rather than *by* the people, but that wasn't what Mankiller had in mind.

As is customary among the Cherokee people, a process of consensus building, in the form of a painstakingly thorough grassroots needs assessment, was undertaken in the community to find out exactly what the people felt were priorities. As it became evident that what people really wanted was running water in their homes, the skills and resources of the Bell residents proved to be impressive. Wilma and her husband, Charlie Soap, were told repeatedly that the project wouldn't work. But when the families were asked to put in the hours required to bring the water lines to their homes, they did their share and more. Much more was actually accomplished than just the creation of a water system; a community based on the concept of *Gadugi* came to life.

A further challenge faced the founders of the NIYLP: how replicable would a model developed in Cherokee country prove to be with other tribes that have different cultures, governmental structures, and historical experiences? In late 1984 a small-scale project was started on the Navajo reservation in New Mexico to test the effectiveness of the model with southwestern tribes. Since 1985 the Indian Youth Leadership Camp has been held in New Mexico, and a number of tribes (Navajo, Zuni, Acoma, Laguna, Santa Clara, Hopi, Passamaquoddy, Colville, and Lakota) have taken part over the years.

Under the auspices of the National Youth Leadership Council, the NIYLP has also conducted similar camps in Native American communities from Alaska to Maine and has provided training nationwide in the basics of the model. As more tribes became involved and as the reputation of the project grew, the NIYLP was incorporated as a private, Indian-led, nonprofit organization and has been recognized by the U.S. Office of Indian Education as a model program.

TRADITIONAL VALUES FOR THE 1990s

The NIYLP focuses on key values common to Native Americans. We believe that these values can be practiced today, in spite of the tremendous changes that have taken place in our tribes and communities. These critical values are listed and briefly described below.

Family. The most important unit in Native American culture has always been the family. In these times of rapid change and social fragmentation, special attention and concerted effort are needed to restore the strength of the family and to develop in young people a strong sense of commitment to family values.

Service to others. Service to others has been highly valued in Native American cultures from the earliest times. Cultivating the spirit of service and generosity provides young people with an opportunity to transcend self-centeredness, to develop genuine concern for others, and to put into action positive attitudes and skills. Service permeates the approach of the NIYLP.

Spiritual awareness. Traditional spiritual teachings of Native Americans often complement many Christian beliefs (e.g., the belief in a supreme being, in the concept of brotherhood, in the existence of a moral code, in the value of prayer and fasting, and so on). In modern times, a return to spiritual values — be they Christian or traditional — will provide young people with a constant

source of inner strength, self-knowledge, love for others, and the feeling of gratitude for the gifts of life.

Challenge. There is value in involving young people in risk-taking activities that call on them to tap their sources of strength and to stretch their capabilities. In such activities, they experience directly the relationship between their own performance and success or failure.

Meaningful roles. Young people must have meaningful roles in the life of the family and the community if they are to develop positive social skills and a sense of self-worth.

Recognition. It is critically important that we recognize the accomplishments and transitions in the lives of our young people. These turning points are often referred to as "rites of passage" and need to be acknowledged and celebrated.

Responsibility. As young people mature and as their roles expand, their responsibilities increase. A strong sense of personal responsibility is a vital element in the development of capable young people.

Natural consequences. Young people need to understand that actions are followed by consequences. Nature is often the best teacher, and young people must not be overprotected from reality.

Respect. In order to develop a sense of their relationship with the universe, young people must learn to respect the traditions, values, and customs of their heritage, as well as those of other individuals, generations, races, and cultures.

Dialogue. Traditionally, there was a high level of intimate communication between adults and the young in Native American culture, and this contact provided a strong foundation for a child's education. The key to getting the most from learning experiences is "processing" those experiences through meaningful dialogue. Talking about *what* happened, analyzing *why* it's important, and generalizing to determine *how* we can learn from the experience helps young people

> # SERVICE OPPORTUNITIES CAN PROVIDE A LEGITIMATE WAY TO REINTEGRATE ALIENATED STUDENTS.

to internalize the lessons of their experience and thereby to become empowered to apply them in other situations.

SOME EXAMPLES

Our research has identified alienation and social isolation as contributing factors in the cycle of substance abuse and school failure into which all too many young Native Americans fall. Service opportunities can provide a legitimate way to reintegrate alienated students.

I once took a group of three boys and three girls from the Cherokee Nation alternative school to visit Anna, an elderly woman of mixed blood, who lived alone several miles from Stillwell, Oklahoma. She grew a large strawberry patch, raised cattle that her son looked after, and did some trapping. When we arrived, we decided first to split and stack firewood for her, since it was fall and starting to get cold at night. After some time had passed, I realized that the three girls had wandered off. We finished our splitting and took the load of wood to the house to stack it in the yard. When I went inside, I found the three missing students sitting at the table engaged in lively conversation with Anna.

These three girls were known for fighting and stealing and generally had very negative reputations in the community. They had been expelled from the public school and had been recruited by the alternative school. In this setting, however, they knew intuitively that they could provide a much more valuable service than splitting and stacking firewood.

As we made ready to leave, Anna offered us $5 to help pay for our gas. I explained that we couldn't take her money because we were volunteers. She insisted and slipped the $5 bill into my pocket. As we began to move toward the door, the young woman with unquestionably the worst reputation in the group walked over to me, discreetly pulled the $5 bill from my pocket, and quickly slipped it under the sugar bowl on her way out the door.

When we got back to school I gave her a hug and let her know how impressed I was with what I had seen. I think that day was a turning point for her, and it certainly restored my confidence in a group of young people that most community members had given up on.

There have been many success stories over the years as students have carried out a number of projects, including the following:

• Students assisted the Pueblo of Picuris in rebuilding a 250-year-old adobe church. In one day, we made nearly 1,000 adobe bricks by hand, mixing straw and mud, pouring the mixture into molds, and cleaning molds — and we transported about 3,000 dry bricks to the church site.

• Students painted the administrative offices of the Jemez Pueblo Social Services complex, including the governor's office. One group taught songs and games to children in a summer lunch program while the larger group painted.

• Students worked for the National Park Service at El Morro National Monument, repairing existing trails and building new ones, cleaning and weeding the Anasazi ruins, working to contain erosion on trails, and so on.

• In 1988 our entire camp group (approximately 80 people) went to Canyon de Chelly, one of the most scenic locations on the Navajo reservation. Our Navajo guide told stories about the history of the canyon, including the infamous roundup of the Navajos by Kit Carson and the U.S. Army in the 1860s. We heard about the burned houses, the trampled corn fields, and the fruit trees chopped down in an attempt to drive the Navajos from the canyon. One student came up with the idea that we should begin to replant peach trees in the canyon to make up for Kit Carson's destruction. That year we began with a single peach tree, and we have continued the tradition ever since.

YEAR-ROUND PROGRAM

At the request of school administrators, parents, and students, the NIYLP has evolved into a year-round program, with our camp serving as the "ignition" experience. While at the camp, the students learn valuable skills and plan projects that they can implement in their home communities during the school year. A teacher or another adult must accompany students to the camp, where the adults go through an intensive orientation to the model to prepare them to work with students in the follow-up program.

NIYLP staff members serve as facilitators in an effort to cultivate volunteers from among the parents and others in the home communities. Incoming sixth-graders take part in the Pathfinders program, which uses a skill-building and prevention approach; seventh- and eighth-graders focus on "leadership for service"; high school students are currently testing the Community Response Corps in the Zuni Pueblo. The high school program works cooperatively with the United World College to offer search and rescue training and training for service with volunteer fire departments. Training for parents and inservice training for teachers are also provided by the NIYLP. The Zuni Youth Council provides an opportunity for young people to have genuine input into programs in their community.

One of our long-range goals is to develop a core group of Native American youths who have attended our camps and are positive role models who can serve as staff members and leaders. At present, our key "service staff" members are all former participants with an average involvement of three years. One student, who attended our first camp in 1983 as an eighth-grader, will graduate from the University of Notre Dame in the spring of 1991 and plans to join our full-time staff.

Currently we have projects under way in the school systems in Ramah (Navajo) and in Zuni, Acoma, and Santa Clara Pueblos in New Mexico, plus a new project on the Upper Peninsula of Michigan. Our projects are both school- and community-based and operate only in communities to which we have been invited.

To support our efforts to introduce service-learning into schools serving Native American students, NIYLP works collaboratively with the National Youth Leadership Council under a grant from the Kellogg Foundation. Also under this grant, we are working closely with the American Indian Science and Engineering Society to provide teacher training. Initially, a small number of teachers, NIYLP staff members, and a group of respected Native Americans will come together to develop a curriculum that will then be used to train teachers who will go back to teach in Indian communities.

The NIYLP has pioneered the spread of service into Native American communities, and we are confident that our traditional values — key concepts that once held our tribes and communities together — will combine with the best efforts of the education reform movement to offer our young people what they deserve: the best of both worlds.

American Indians in the 1990s

The true number of American Indians may be unknowable, but a rapidly growing number of Americans are identifying with Indian culture. The Anglo appetite for Indian products is creating jobs on poverty-plagued reservations. Gambling and tourism are the most lucrative reservation businesses. Meanwhile, the middle-class Indian's urge to "go home" is growing.

D a n   F o s t

Dan Fost is a contributing editor of American Demographics *in Tiburon, California.*

When Nathan Tsosie was growing up in the Laguna Pueblo in New Mexico, he was not taught the Laguna language. The tribe's goal was to assimilate him into white society.

Today, Tsosie's 9-year-old son Darren learns his ancestral language and culture in the Laguna schools. He speaks Laguna better than either of his parents. "They're trying to bring it back," says Darren's mother, Josephine. "I'm glad he's learning. I just feel bad that we can't reinforce it and really teach it."

The strong bonds American Indians still feel to their native culture are driving a renaissance in Indian communities. This cultural resurrection has not yet erased the poverty, alcoholism, and other ills that affect many Indians. But it has brought educational and economic gains to many Indians living on and off reservations. A college-educated Indian middle class has emerged, American Indian business ownership has increased, and some tribes are creating good jobs for their members.

The census counted 1,878,000 American Indians in 1990, up from fewer than 1.4 million in 1980. This 38 percent leap exceeds the growth rate for blacks (6 percent) and non-Hispanic whites (13 percent), but not the growth of Hispanics (53 percent) or Asians (108 percent).

The increase is not due to an Indian baby boom or to immigration from other countries. Rather, Americans with Indian heritage are increasingly likely to identify their race as Indian on census forms. Also, the Census Bureau is doing a better job of counting American Indians.

Almost 2 million people say that their race is American Indian. But more than 7 million people claim some Indian ancestry, says Jeff Passel at the Urban Institute. That's about 1 American in 35.

"A lot of people have one or more ancestors who are American Indian," says Passel. "There's a clear trend over the last three censuses for increasing numbers of those people to answer the race question as American Indian. But it doesn't tell you how 'Indian' they are in a cultural sense.

"The strength of this identification in places that are not Indian strongholds is transitory. If it becomes unfashionable to be American Indian, it could go down."

People who try to count American Indians employ many different means that often confound demographers. Tribes keep tabs on enrollment, but the rules vary on how much Indian blood makes one a member. Some tribes are not recognized by the federal government. Local health services may keep one set of records, while federal agencies like the Bureau of Indian Affairs will keep another. Some Indians are nomadic; Navajos, for example, may maintain three residences. Rural Indians can be hard to find, and minorities are always more prone to census undercounts. A growing number of mixed marriages blurs the racial boundaries even further.

"I don't know what an Indian is," says Malcolm Margolin, publisher of the

3. NATIVE AMERICAN GROUPS: Native Americans

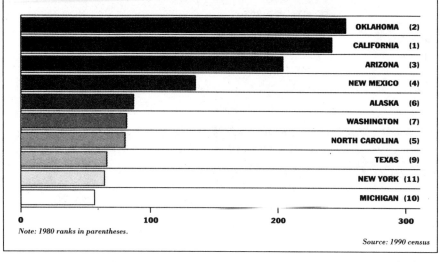

INDIAN STATES

During the 1980s, Oklahoma replaced California as the state with the largest American Indian population. South Dakota dropped off the top ten list as New York moved into ninth place.

(population of the ten states with the largest American Indian populations, in thousands)

OKLAHOMA (2)
CALIFORNIA (1)
ARIZONA (3)
NEW MEXICO (4)
ALASKA (6)
WASHINGTON (7)
NORTH CAROLINA (5)
TEXAS (9)
NEW YORK (11)
MICHIGAN (10)

0   100   200   300

Note: 1980 ranks in parentheses.

Source: 1990 census

monthly *News from Native California.* "Some people are clearly Indian, and some are clearly not. But the U.S. government figures are clearly inadequate for judging how many people are Indian."

Even those who can't agree on the numbers do agree that Indians are returning to their roots. "In the early 1960s, there was a stigma attached to being American Indian," Passel says. These days, even Anglos are proud of Indian heritage.

IDENTIFYING WITH INDIANS

When white patrons at Romo's restaurant in Holbrook, Arizona, learn that their host is half Navajo and half Hopi, they frequently exclaim, "I'm part Cherokee!" The host smiles and secretly rolls his eyes. More *bahanas* (whites) are jumping on the Indian bandwagon.

"In the last three years, interest in Indian beliefs has really taken off," says Marzenda McComb, the former co-owner of a New Age store in Portland, Oregon. To celebrate the sale of her store, a woman performed an Indian smudging ritual with burnt cedar and an eagle feather. Most of McComb's customers were non-Indian.

Controversy often accompanies such practices. Some Indians bristle at the

sharing of their culture and spiritual practices with whites. But others welcome people of any race into their culture. And many tribal leaders recognize that Indian art and tourism are hot markets.

Anglos are not the only ones paying more attention to Indian ways. Indian children are showing a renewed interest in their culture. Jennifer Bates, who owns the Bear and Coyote Gallery in California, says her 9-year-old son has taken an independent interest in Northern Miwok dance. "It's nice, knowing that we're not pushing it on him," she says. "He wanted to dance and make his cape. It's up to us to keep things going, and if we don't, it's gone."

The oldest generation of California Indians "grew up among people who recalled California before the arrival of whites," says Malcolm Margolin. These people have "something in their tone, their mood, their manners—a very Indian quality." Younger generations are more comfortable in the white world, he says, but they sense "something very ominous about the passing of the older generation. It's the sense of the younger generation that it's up to them."

The Zuni tribe is trying to revive an-

cient crafts by opening two tribal-owned craft stores—one in their pueblo in New Mexico, and one on San Francisco's trendy Union Street. The most popular items are fetishes—small stone carvings of animals that serve as good-luck charms. "After *Dances with Wolves* came out, we weren't able to keep the wolf fetishes in stock," says Milford Nahohai, manager of the New Mexico store.

JOBS ON RESERVATIONS

Many Indians on and off the reservation face a well-established litany of problems, from poverty and alcoholism to unemployment. Many tribal leaders say that only jobs can solve the problem. Promoting Indian-owned businesses is their solution.

The number of Indian-owned businesses increased 64 percent between 1982 and 1987, compared with a 14 percent rise for all U.S. firms, according to the Census Bureau. "A whole new system of role models is being established," says Steven Stallings, president of the National Center for American Indian Enterprise Development in Mesa, Arizona. "Indians see self-employment as a viable opportunity."

In boosting reservation-based businesses, Stallings aims to create sustainable, self-reliant economies. In some areas, 92 cents of every dollar earned on a reservation is spent outside the reservation, he says. Non-Indian communities typically retain as much as 85 cents.

Stallings's center hopes to start by attracting employers to Indian country. The next step is to add retail and service businesses that will "create a revolving economy on the reservation."

This strategy is at work in Laguna, New Mexico. The Laguna Indians were hit hard in 1982, when the price of uranium plummeted and the Anaconda Mineral Company closed a mine located on their reservation. But the Lagunas have bounced back with several enterprises, including Laguna Industries, a tribal-owned manufacturing firm that employs 350 people.

Laguna Industries' clients include the Department of Defense, Raytheon, and Martin Marietta. Its flagship product is a communications shelter that U.S. forces

INDIAN INDUSTRIES

American Indian specialty contractors had receipts of $97 million in 1987.
But automotive and food-store owners may earn higher profits.

(ten largest industry groups in receipts for firms owned by American Indians and Alaska Natives)

rank	industry group	firms	receipts (in thousands)	receipts per firm (in thousands)
1	Special trade contractors	2,268	$97,400	$43
2	Miscellaneous retail	1,799	85,400	47
3	Agriculture services, forestry, and fishing	3,128	84,000	27
4	Automotive dealers and service stations	222	65,300	294
5	Food stores	301	54,300	180
6	Business services	2,532	48,600	19
7	Eating and drinking places	464	35,300	76
8	Construction	461	34,200	74
9	Trucking and warehousing	590	32,200	55
10	Personal services	1,719	26,500	15

Source: 1987 Economic Censuses, Survey of Minority-Owned Business Enterprises

INDIAN MARKETS

The 1990 census showed rapid increases among American Indians who live in large metropolitan areas. Some of the increases reflect an increasing willingness to declare one's Indian heritage.

(top ten metropolitan areas, ranked by American Indian, Eskimo, and Aleut population in 1990; and percent change in that population, 1980–90)

rank	metropolitan area	1990 population	percent change 1980–90
1	Los Angeles-Anaheim-Riverside, CA	87,500	5%
2	Tulsa, OK	48,200	41
3	New York-Northern New Jersey-Long Island, NY-NJ-CT	46,200	101
4	Oklahoma City, OK	45,700	82
5	San Francisco-Oakland-San Jose, CA	40,800	19
6	Phoenix, AZ	38,000	66
7	Seattle-Tacoma, WA	32,100	42
8	Minneapolis-St. Paul, MN-WI	24,000	49
9	Tucson, AZ	20,300	36
10	San Diego, CA	20,100	37

Source: 1990 census

used in the Gulf War. "It's pretty nice to see your own people getting involved in high-tech stuff," says welding supervisor Phillip Sarracino, 44.

Laguna Indians are given first priority for jobs at the plant, but several middle managers are white. Conrad Lucero, a plant group leader and former tribal governor, says that non-Indian supervisors are often retirees who lend their expertise until Indians can run things on their own.

"I have an 8-year-old daughter," says Sabin Chavez, 26, who works in the quality control division. "I'm hoping to keep this company going, so our kids can live on the reservation. It's a long shot, but we have to believe in long shots."

High morale at Laguna Industries is tempered by the risks of relying on the government. The Lagunas realize that their dependence on military contracts makes them vulnerable to cuts in the de-

fense budget. And in August 1994, the tribe's right to bid on minority set-aside contracts will expire—partly because the business has been so successful.

"We have to be able to meet and beat our competitors on the open market," Lucero says. The Lagunas may succeed: Martin Marietta Corporation has already awarded Laguna Industries a contract based on price and not minority status, says Martin Marietta customer representative Michael King.

Laguna Industries has not solved all the tribe's problems, however. Tribal planner Nathan Tsosie estimates that unemployment runs as high as 35 percent on the reservation. Much of the housing is substandard, water shortages could impede future development, and alcoholism still tears Indian families apart. But Tsosie has an answer: "We just need to develop more. People leave the reservation to get jobs. If there were jobs here, they'd stay."

GAMBLING AND TOURISM

Indians bring some real advantages to the business world. The Lagunas show that a cohesive community can be organized into an efficient production facility. Other reservations have rich natural resources. But the biggest benefit may be "sovereignty," or the suspension of many local, state, and federal laws on Indian territory. Reservations have no sales or property tax, so cigarettes, gasoline, and other items can be sold for low prices. They can also offer activities not permitted off-reservation.

Like gambling.

"Bingo is a way for tribes to amass funds so they can get into other economic development projects," says Frank Collins, a Mescalero Apache from San Jose who specializes in development.

Bingo can be big business. One parlor on the Morongo reservation, just north of Palm Springs, California, draws 5,000 people a week and employs more than 140 people. The Morongo tribe's main objective is to develop as a major resort destination, says bingo general manager Michael Lombardi.

Lombardi won't say how much money bingo generates for the Morongos. He will

THE BEST STATES FOR

Indians in Business

This table shows how the states rank on the basis of business ownership among American Indians. States in the South may offer the most opportunity for American Indians, while midwestern states may offer the least.

The number of Indian-owned businesses in a state is not closely related to the business ownership rate. Business ownership rates are calculated by dividing the number of Indian-owned businesses by the number of Indians and multiplying by 1,000. The top-ranked state, Alaska, is one of only five states with more than 1,000 Indian-owned firms. But the state that ranks last, Arizona, has the seventh-highest number of Indian-owned businesses.

Statistical analysis also indicates that the pattern of business ownership among American Indians is not driven by the rate of growth in a state's Indian population during the 1980s, or by a state's overall level of business ownership.

There appear to be strong regional biases in patterns of Indian business ownership. The business ownership rate was 12.2 Indian-owned firms per 1,000 Indians in the South, 10.3 in the West, 9.6 in the Northeast, and only 7.4 in the Midwest.

One clue to a state's business ownership rate among Indians could be the share of its Indian population living on reservations. The lowest-ranking state, Arizona, contains seven of the ten most populated reservations in the U.S., including a large share of the huge Navajo reservation (1990 Indian population of 143,400 in Arizona, New Mexico, and Utah). South Dakota, ranking 47th, contains the large and economically troubled Pine Ridge, Rosebud, and Standing Rock reservations. Indians living on a reservation have limited entrepreneurial opportunities. Another factor that may be related to the Indian business rate is the state's general economic health: several states near the bottom of the ranking, Kentucky, Nebraska, and Michigan, have experienced weak economic growth during the 1980s.

But the most powerful predictor is probably the business skill of a state's Indian tribes. Third-ranking North Carolina is home to one branch of the Cherokee tribe, which has large investments in lumber and tourism. And Alaska may rank first because its native American, Eskimo, and Aleut population received billions of dollars in a federal land claim settlement. These data do not contain businesses owned by Eskimos or Aleuts. But many of Alaska's Indians live in isolated towns where small businesses have a captive, all-native audience.

—William O'Hare

William O'Hare is Director of Population and Policy Research Program, University of Louisville.

INDIAN OPPORTUNITY

(states with more than 100 American Indian-owned businesses in 1987, ranked by business ownership rate)

rank	state name	number of firms 1987	American Indian population 1987	business ownership rate*
1	Alaska	1,039	28,700	36.2
2	North Carolina	1,757	75,600	23.2
3	Texas	872	57,500	15.2
4	Virginia	188	13,300	14.1
5	Colorado	343	24,600	13.9
6	California	3,087	225,600	13.7
7	Louisiana	221	16,600	13.3
8	Massachusetts	132	10,700	12.4
9	Kansas	225	20,000	11.3
10	Florida	348	30,900	11.3
11	Maryland	123	11,300	10.9
12	Pennsylvania	139	12,800	10.8
13	Georgia	122	11,400	10.7
14	New Jersey	131	12,800	10.3
15	New Mexico	1,247	126,400	9.9
16	Illinois	182	19,600	9.3
17	Montana	405	44,700	9.1
18	Oklahoma	2,044	229,300	8.9
19	Oregon	306	34,500	8.9
20	North Dakota	208	24,300	8.6
21	Wisconsin	306	36,300	8.4
22	Ohio	149	17,700	8.4
23	Washington	602	72,300	8.3
24	Nevada	146	17,700	8.3
25	New York	425	54,800	7.8
26	Missouri	133	17,500	7.6
27	Minnesota	333	45,400	7.3
28	Michigan	304	50,900	6.0
29	South Dakota	267	49,000	5.5
30	Utah	109	22,700	4.8
31	Arizona	843	189,100	4.5

* Number of American Indian-owned firms per 1,000 Indians.
Source: Bureau of the Census, 1987 economic census, and author's estimates of 1987 Indian population

say that 113 reservations allow some form of gaming, and he attributes bingo's popularity to the effects of Reagan-era cutbacks in the Bureau of Indian Affairs budget. Lombardi says then-Secretary of the Interior James Watt told Indians, "Instead of depending on the Great White Father, why don't you start your own damn business?"

Indian culture also can create unique business opportunities. On the Hopi reservation in northern Arizona, Joe and Janice Day own a small shop on Janice's ancestral property. They swap elk hooves and cottonwood sticks, useful in Indian rituals, for jewelry, and baskets to sell to tourists.

The Days would like to credit their success to their shrewd sense of customer service. But they confess that the difference between profit and loss may be their wildly popular T-shirts, which read "Don't worry, be Hopi."

Not long ago, Hopis had to leave the reservation to go to school or find work. Today, the tribe has its own junior and senior high school and an entrepreneurial spirit. But small schools and small businesses won't keep people on the reservation. The Days still make a two-hour drive to Flagstaff each week to do their banking, laundry, and shopping. "The first Hopi you can get to build a laundromat is going to be a rich man," says Joe Day.

The Days lived in Flagstaff until their children finished high school. At that point, they decided to come "home." Janice's daughter is now an accountant in San Francisco, and she loves the amenities of the big city. "But who knows?" Janice says. "She may also want to come home someday. No matter where you are, you're still going to end up coming home."

THE URGE TO GO HOME

"Going home" may also mean renewing a bond with one's Indian heritage. While the population in 19 "Indian states" grew at predictable levels during the 1980s, the Urban Institute's Jeff Passel says it soared in the non-Indian states.

For example, Passel estimated the 1990 Indian population in Arizona at 202,000 (the 1980 population of 152,700, plus the intervening 58,600 births and minus the intervening 10,300 deaths)—a figure close to the 1990 census number (203,500). But in Alabama, a non-Indian state, Passel found a huge percentage increase that he could not have predicted. Alabama's Indian population grew from 7,600 in 1980 to 16,500 in 1990, a 117 percent increase. Higher birthrates, lower death rates, and migration from other states do not explain the increase.

Passel explains the gap this way: "The people who are Indians always identify themselves as Indians. They tell the census they are Indians, and they register their newborns as Indians." These people are usually found in the Indian states.

"People who are part Indian may not identify themselves as American Indians. But they don't do that consistently over time."

Today, for reasons of ethnic pride, part-Indians may tell the Census Bureau they

> "Instead of depending on the Great White Father, why don't you start your own damn business?"

are Indian. At the hospital, they may identify themselves as white to avoid discrimination. This is most common in non-Indian states, which Passel generally defines as having fewer than 3,000 Indians in 1950.

California ranks second only to Oklahoma in its Indian population, but its mixture of tribes is unique in the nation. Some Indian residents trace their roots to native California tribes, says Malcolm Margolin. Others came west as part of a federal relocation program in the 1950s. In California cities, Cherokees, Chippewas, and other out-of-state Indians congregate in clubs.

"What has happened is the formation of an inter-tribal ethic, a pan-Indian ethic," Margolin says. "People feel that America has a lot of problems. That cultural doubt causes them to look for their ethnic roots, for something they can draw strength from. And for Indians, it's right there. It's ready-made."

Lakhota Sioux Hutsul

Myron B. Kuropas

Her father is a Boyko. Her grand-mother and mother were Hutsuls. Her grandfather was Lakhota Sioux from South Dakota.

Today, Jean Szewczyk (nee Benyk), married to a Ukrainian, raised in a Ukrainian family, a graduate of St. Nicholas Ukrainian Catholic Cathedral School in Chicago, is rediscovering her Native American roots.

For years she denied knowledge of her Indian background because her mother never believed it was necessary to say anything more than to mention that her grandfather was "not a Ukrainian." But within Little Jean Benyk's soul, there was a spiritual hunger that was pulling her towards Native American culture. "As a kid watching cowboys and Indians, I'd always root for the Indians, not knowing why," she said. "I had fantasies of growing up an Indian maiden in moccasins."

Jean was born in Hanover, Germany, to Mykola and Maria Benyk (nee Samar), both displaced persons who later immigrated to the United States, settling eventually in Chicago where Jean grew up.

"For me, growing up Ukrainian was difficult," she told me. "I didn't have many friends. I just felt odd, different from the people I was growing up with."

She married Stan Szewczyk and later moved to Gurnee, Ill. "We took the opportunity to leave Chicago," she told Greg Miller, a report for Lakelife, a local periodical. Later, the family moved to Spring Grove, in the wide-open spaces of McHenry County.

As a young girl, Jean learned to make Ukrainian Easter eggs, becoming quite good at it. Later she was introduced to Trypillian art, and it became her passion. Mychailo Humeniak, a Ukrainian ceramic artist, suggested she explore the art of America's southwest Indian tribes, and as soon as she did, she was hooked. Deciding to become a professional potter, she attended classes at the College of Lake County and was soon producing pottery with Indian motifs. "I had this strong affection and devotion to Indian art," she explained. "I could never understand why . . . It seems that I have always been very fond of the Indian people." The more involved she became with Indian art, the more doors seem to open for her.

Perfecting her craft, Jean was one of a select group of artists invited to display work at the annual Washington (D.C.) Craft Show in 1992. Sponsored by the Smithsonian Institute Women's Committee, the show featured just 100 artists from among thousands who applied nationwide.

It was not until her mother, believing she was on her death bed following cardiac arrest, that Jean Szewczyk, already married with two children, discovered how different she really was from most Ukrainian Americans.

Her grandfather, Jean learned from her mother, was an American Indian. He came to Europe in the early part of the century as a member of some kind of Wild West exhibition. During the crossoceanic voyage he became violently ill. Petrified of the return sea voyage, he roamed around Europe, eventually settling in the Transcarpathia region of Ukraine where he adopted the surname Samar and married Jean's grandmother. When Jean's mother was only 3, her father fell from a horse and never recovered.

When I asked how she felt when she learned of her Indian heritage, Jean answered: "Relief! At first I thought I was going bonkers, that it was all a delusion, a part of wanting to be an Indian so badly that I was imagining all of the feelings I had. Now I knew there was a purpose and a reason behind it all."

Responding to her natural instincts, Jean later traveled to the Standing Rock Reservation in South Dakota. "My heart told me to go there, that there was something waiting for me out there."

She was right. She met a spiritual leader (medicine man) who told her the story of a Lakhota Sioux who had remained in Europe because of his fear of seasickness. His name was Bad Moccasin. "I have told you his name," he told Jean, "now it is up to you to discover the rest of the story." Returning home, she told her mother what she had learned, and together they tried to piece it all together.

Towards the end of her life, Jean's mother also accepted her Indian heritage. Stricken by diabetes, she asked to be taken to the Indian reservation. "They will cure me there," she told Jean. She passed away before she could make the trip.

Jean Szewczyk, meanwhile, continues to cultivate her Lakhota Sioux heritage. Her grandfather, she has learned, was a member of the Hunkpapas, one of the seven sub-tribes of the Lakhota Sioux nation. She believes that he was attracted to the Carpathians because they reminded him of the sacred Black Hills of South Dakota where he grew up.

In December of 1991, Jean and her husband rented a truck, loaded it with clothes and food, and drove to the Pine Ridge Reservation in South Dakota. (Pine Ridge was used for the filming of "Dances with Wolves.") "It was just wonderful out there," Jean told Mr. Miller. "It looks like it hasn't been touched by man since the beginning of time."

"The people are very poor," she continued. "It's sad to see that the arrival of food is the highlight of their week or

From *The Ukrainian Weekly*, September 12, 1993, pp. 7, 17. Reprinted by permission.

month. Instead of having the government send funds all over the world, I think we should take care of our own first."

Jean visits the reservation every summer now and is fully accepted by most of the Indians. Some, however, especially those who are full-blooded, are still not sure about her. No one questions her heritage, but she still needs to obtain the paperwork that will prove that her grandfather was really a Lakhota Sioux. Because she doesn't have a registered number, something only the government can grant, Jean can't advertise that her pottery is "Indian-made." The Department of Interior informed her of this when she had her exhibition in Washington.

There have been times when she has been shunned by both the Whites and the Indians. Shopping in a reservation store, she said she has been followed around by the owner who seemed afraid "I would steal something." In Chicago, where she is active in the Indian Center, some full-blooded Indians look down upon her because she lacks the necessary paperwork.

Following Indian tradition, Jean Szewcyzk has been legally adopted by Archie White, an Indian spiritual director. The adoption is recognized by the State of Minnesota and is one of the eight "rites of passage" Indians

believe they received from God. The rite is part of a process that leads to expanding relations with others.

Jean believes her facial features are becoming more Indian. "People I've known all my life from the old Ukrainian neighborhood will pass me by, not recognizing me until I say 'Dobryi Den.' Then they stop and look at me and hesitatingly say, Genia? Genia Benyk?"

Although Jean and her two daughters, Alana and Tania, were raised Ukrainian Catholic, they no longer practice their faith. "Out of respect for my mother and father, I sent my children to religion classes," she told me. "They have been baptized and they received their First Holy Communion. But they see too many negative aspects" of that religion. They have accepted Indian beliefs because Indian ways "are very wholesome. There are no contradictions between beliefs and behavior, and its natural," she said.

Still, Jean has not given up all of her Ukrainian ways. "Before she died, my mother asked that I never forget who I am," Jean explained. Her family still prepares the traditional Ukrainian Christmas Eve dinner and bring a basket to be blessed at Easter time. "I do it for my father and mother," she told me.

Today, Jean and her daughters are very

involved with the Indian Center in Chicago where they learned traditional Indian dances. Jean also attends Native American Educational Services, a college where she is learning the Lakhota Sioux language. Recently, she adopted Camilla, a Danish girl she met while attending Indian heritage classes.

Jean has received numerous awards for her pottery in recent years, which is in demand at shows and galleries throughout Chicagoland. Low-fire white talc clay is her primary medium. In a variation of the above process, Jean fires the piece in burning sawdust, giving it a polished, black-stone-like appearance

She also makes jewelry, does beadwork, and creates Native American artifacts from buckskin. She makes ceremonial masks complete with feathers, and her pottery includes the same kind of seed pots formerly used by Indians at planting time.

Jean believes that art is a good way to generate awareness. "I think you can reach people through art. Even if they don't buy a piece, they may be mesmerized by it. Maybe in some small way, it raised their consciousness about what's happening in the world."

Jean Szewczyk's search for her Indian roots continues. She still hopes to discover more about her grandfather, the Lakhota Sioux who became a Hutsul.

Seeking Lost Culture at a Powwow

Pequots Draw Ritual Dancers Across U.S. With Rich Prizes

Kirk Johnson

Special to The New York Times

HARTFORD, Sept. 17—Michael Thomas stands at the arched entryway to the Hartford Civic Center arena, watching the parade of Indian dancers and clutching his cellular phone as the relentless ONE-two-ONE-two of the drums thunders out of the public address system. Men who seem almost made of feathers shimmer past; women in Chippewa Jingle Dresses heel-and-toe to the beat, each step a symphony of tiny bells.

Next year, Mr. Thomas vows, there will be a Mashantucket Pequot Indian out there. Maybe, in fact, it will be he. Then, his brief reverie over, he's back to business, barking orders into his phone, consulting with security guards, racing off on his own private dance as a coordinator for perhaps the largest traditional powwow ever held on the East Coast.

This is a Pequot production, all the way, but without the Pequots.

The tiny 260-member tribe, which introduced big-stakes casino gambling to Connecticut last year, has become enormously wealthy and influential, making tens of millions of dollars a month in profits. But it is a society, its members say, with no real living culture: the traditions are almost all gone, eroded after 350 years of dispersion, along with most of its language and the important ceremonial dances.

Now, armed with the casino millions, the Pequots have begun a sometimes awkward, sometimes poignant effort to bring Indian culture back to Connecticut. This week's powwow, which instantly vaulted the tribe into the major leagues of Indian dance competition, drew about 1,200 American Indian performers from all across North America, some attracted by the $200,000 offered by the Pequots—by far the richest purse on the competition powwow circuit—others invited by the tribe to come and share their traditional ways and skills, all expenses paid.

The Indians who have come, from Canada, Washington, Iowa and elsewhere—including two young men who drove 32 hours straight from Bismarck, N.D., for the first competitions on Thursday night—say that the Pequot festival, called Schemitzun, is a singular event. The big prize money is part of it—double the $100,000 purse at Pine Ridge, S.D., long the reigning World Series of powwows.

The setting is unusual too, smack downtown in the largest arena in the capital of a state not known for its elaborate Indian ceremony. For some participants, who have heard of the Pequots but have never met one, the enigmatic nature of the hosts, and their search, is a draw as well.

"We're helping out just by being here," said Tomme Roubideaux, a Lakota from Saskatchewan who is pursuing a doctorate in social work at Washington University in St. Louis. "Some of us are not here to go for the prize money, but just to show that there's a presence and that they have support: political support and social support from all the tribes in the country."

WORLDS WITHIN WORLDS

Mr. Roubideaux, clad in a startling combination of red, white and blue flag material and feathers, also confesses to a private agenda. He sheds coat and tie and hits the powwow circuit to save his sanity.

"If not for this I'd probably be listening to Bly and going through some male ritual somewhere," he said.

There are other agendas and worlds-within-worlds here, too. From the deeply traditional Lakota dancers with their slow-speaking dignity, to the giggly vivacity of a suburban Oneida hairdresser who came here to sell her shell jewelry, to the wild drumming of the Grey Horse Singers from Oklahoma, the Connecticut tribe has opened a door to a new world for them and for the state. In their effort to revive a culture of their own, the Pequots say, they will borrow and adapt what they can from other tribes—but the point, ultimately, is self-knowledge.

"It's the rebirth of a nation, and you can't do everything all at once," said Judy Bell, a tribe member also known as Little Flower. "You're learning a little at a time, but unfortunately by having to unearth our culture, it's going to take us a while before we know as much about ourselves as other tribes know about themselves."

FEAST OF GREEN CORN

Curiosity cuts both ways at Schemitzun (pronounced Ski-MET-zen), a Pequot word for the Feast of Green Corn and Dance.

"Any time anybody can offer the money they're offering here, it's a topic of discussion—it's *the* topic of discussion," said Orval L. Kirk, a Kickapoo from Oklahoma who makes his living officiating and announcing at powwows around the country. "This is going to end up being the biggest event like this in the world, and a lot of us never even heard of the Pequots until a year ago."

And there an undercurrent of debate, as there is among tribes everywhere, about whether the business of gambling is good for Indians or simply one of the few business niches available. Federal law allows recognized Indian tribes to conduct gambling if the state they live in allows some form of gambling off the reservation. In Connecticut, the state allowed nonprofit "casino nights" for fund raising, and it is through that opening that the Pequots have built what they say is now the largest gambling center in the Western hemisphere, in Ledyard, in the southeast corner of the state.

"This is one of the tribes we'll probably have to take a look at, to see how it is," said Anthony Tail, a 34-year-old Lakota from Pine Ridge, S.D. Mr. Tail, who said he speaks "Lakota first and English second," says he opposes gambling because he thinks it will erode traditions and make people forget who they are. "Look forward maybe 20–30 years, you know—where are we going to be at?" He asked. "You lose the values."

WHAT'S NATURAL TO OTHERS

For their part, the Pequots are trying, almost from scratch, to learn arts and skills that people in other tribes can absorb effortlessly from early childhood—how in traditional dance, for example, some judges watch everything from the movement of a dancer's eyes to whether the feathers are in constant motion with the beat or not, while other judges watch only feet. Experts say the essence of grass dance is just as easy to state and just as loaded with endless subtleties, in making the body and costume mimic the fluid, undulating motions of the prairie.

And there are secrets to the trade as well, like learning just how dry and hot to make the drumhead in searching for the right tone, and how to do it. (Ken Scabbyrobe of the Yakima Blood Tribe in Washington uses a blow dryer.)

This tribe can afford the prizes. What it wants is the rituals.

"I have to take my hat off to them," Mr. Kirk, the announcer, said of the Pequots. "They're learning."

Mr. Thomas, the Pequot organizer who eventually wants to participate as a singer, said that the social songs and dances of the type done at powwows will be the easiest and most appropriate to borrow. Since they were designed to be shared at social, inter-tribal gatherings, those dances are almost generic.

'THIS IS THE EASY STUFF'

"The ceremonial songs and dances—those are the ones that have really been lost to the Pequots; those are the ones that will be much more difficult to recapture," he said. "This is the easy stuff," he added, referring to the powwow inside the arena hall. "Because when we lost it, everyone else still had it."

The success that the Pequots have had in Connecticut, with $20 million a month in gross profits on just slot machines this summer—and presumably millions more from table games, which they do not

have to report—is being assiduously studied by people who would borrow from that new tradition.

Members of the Oneida tribe from upstate New York, for example, who opened their own casino in July near Syracuse, said here that the Pequot casino, known as Foxwoods, was the inspiration in how to do it right.

"Our design is based on theirs," said Gigi Winder, a tribe member who travels the powwow circuit selling her hand-made jewelry. "They know what they're doing."

The Survivors of a Massacre

The disaster that shaped modern Pequot history occurred in 1637, when a colonial militia nearly wiped out the tribe in a single massacre at the Pequot fort in Mystic.

Many of the survivors were sold as slaves and shipped, with other Indian captives, to the Caribbean for servitude.

The tribe's informal name, the Fox People, was adopted soon afterward as Connecticut survivors rallied around a charismatic leader named Robin Cassasinnamon, who negotiated with the colonists for a reservation of 3,000 acres.

By the early 1970's, the land had dwindled to 214 acres, the population to about 50.

Hispanic/Latino Americans

The following collection of materials on Hispanic/Latino Americans is a composite of findings about ethnicities. The clustering of ethnicities and nationalities, as well as the relationship to the Spanish language, seems to be sufficient evidence of the commonalities that constitute the shared expression of this complex of memory and contemporary politics. Yet the interchangeable use of "Hispanic" and "Latino" as nominative of the differentiation and distance from the Anglo-America founding and institutionalization, as well as the social imagination expressed in the search for a cultural and political terrain, are but the surface of the process of intergroup dynamics in the United States.

The articles in this unit propose angles of vision that enable us to view the process of accommodation and change that is articulated in political practice, scholarship, advocacy, and art. The issues presented provocatively shift traditional perspectives from the eastern and midwestern mind-set toward the western and southwestern analysis of the peopling of the United States.

The Immigration Act of 1965 induced a process of peopling America not unlike the period of large-scale eastern and southern European immigration between 1880 and 1924. This immigration includes scores of various ethnic groups. Cultural geographic descriptions are not the clearest form of ethnic identity.

Hispanic/Latino Americans are not a single ethnic group. The designation of various ethnic populations—migrants and persons whose ancestry is derived from Spanish-speaking countries—by the words "Hispanic" and "Latino" is a relatively recent phenomenon in the United States. The cultural, economic, and political differences and similarities of various Hispanic communities, as well as the wide dispersal of these communities, suggest the need for care in generalization about Hispanic American populations.

The reality of these groups, whether they are political refugees, migrant workers, settled residents prior to territorial incorporation into the United States, long-settled immigrants, recent arrivals, or the children and grandchildren of immigrants, presents interesting and varied patterns of enclave community, assimilation, and acculturation, as well as isolation and marginalization. Hispanic/Latino American linkages to other Latin countries, the future of their emerging political power, and their contributions to cultural and economic change within the United States are interesting facets of the Hispanic/Latino American experience.

The Hispanic/Latino experience is a composite of groups seeking unity while interacting with the larger arena of ethnic groups that constitute American society. Convergent issues that bridge differences, as well as those that support ideological and strategic differences, bode a future of both cooperation and conflict.

What issues bind Hispanic groups together? What values cause cleavages among Hispanic populations? What does bilingualism mean? Is bilingualism a freedom of speech issue? Is bilingualism a concern of non–Spanish-speaking persons in the United States? What are the implications of establishing an official public language policy?

Competition and conflict over mobility into mainstream leadership positions are aspects of American society that may be exacerbated by the misuse of ethnic indicators. Nonetheless, indicators of social cohesion and traditional family bonds are apparently noncompetitive and nonconflictual dimensions of robust ethnic experiences. Thus, fears that Hispanic/Latino Americans may not relish competitive pressures are assuaged by the capacities of family and community to temper the cost of any such failure. This complex dynamic of personal and group interaction is a fascinating and fruitful topic for a society seeking competitiveness and stronger community bonds. Cast in this fashion, the American dilemma takes on a new and compelling relevance.

Looking Ahead: Challenge Questions

Does attention to historical background and its expression in current culture promote both understanding and tolerance?

Does the United States Census and its various publications regarding ethnic and racial issues foster understanding and tolerance?

What strengths and weakness do strong bonds of ethnic communities posses?

In what respects are Hispanic/Latino American culture becoming part of mainstream American culture?

To what do you attribute the popularity of Mexican, Italian, and Chinese foods in the marketplace?

Unit 4

US Hispanics:
To Be *and* Not to Be

*Mexican-Americans in southern California balance assimilation and
preserving their cultural heritage*

Daniel B. Wood

Staff writer of The Christian Science
Monitor

POMONA, CALIF.
"They'll love it in Pomona." These
words, uttered by William Holden in
"Sunset Boulevard," suggest how
the 1950s film industry gauged mid-
dle-American tastes for their latest
cinematic offerings.

Now this city of 140,000, about 60
miles east of Los Angeles, is 51 percent Hispanic according to the 1990
census, and some say the Hispanic
population will reach 60 percent this
year. In April voting, the town elected its first Hispanic mayor, and four
of seven City Council members are
also Hispanic.

What is developing in Pomona and
dozens of nearby towns is being
called the clearest example in the
United States of fringe-suburban
outposts known as "exurbs" or edge
cities. From 1980 to 1990, Riverside
County was one of the nation's fastest growing, and its Hispanic population—80 percent of whom are of
Mexican origin—increased 38 percent over the decade.

Experts say this demographic pattern makes the county an illustrative
example of how Hispanics are assimilating into American culture, politics, and economy.

"Suburban areas like Riverside are
where Hispanics move most naturally
into the American mainstream," says
Alan Heslop, director of the Rose
Institute at Claremont McKenna College in Claremont, Calif. Assimilation, according to Dr. Heslop, a
political demographer, does not
mean that Hispanics or other minority groups abandon a sense of cultural identity, but rather that they are
free to choose where to live for reasons other than a community's ethnic identity.

"For reasons of support and security, Hispanics have tended to remain far more congregated in rural
and urban settings," Heslop says.
Under his definition, Pomona's 51-
percent Hispanic makeup makes it a
city where ethnicity still exerts a
powerful influence over choice of
residence. But the small towns that
ring it—such as Duarte, Glendora,
San Dimas, Laverne, Sierra Madre,
West Covina, and others—are the
kinds of communities where Hispanics are making the jump out of
the barrio and into the American
middle class.

In each of these towns over the
past decade, Hispanic populations have grown from very low
numbers to concentrations of 5 to 30
percent.

"You see it in the number of Hispanic service corporations, law offices,
dentists, businesses, counselors, teachers in high schools," says Rudy
Acuna, a professor of Chicano
studies at California State College,
Northridge. He notes a similar pattern in the San Fernando Valley,
where Hispanics are moving beyond
such traditional barrios as Pacoima
and Arleta to North Hollywood, Syl-
mar, and Chatsworth.

The access card to bigger, better,
and more affluent suburbia, according to new Pomona Mayor Eddie
Cortez, is education.

"As they become more educated,
Hispanics position themselves to
move out of their de facto segregation that has served as a sense of
security," he says. "They begin to
see that what they want is not necessarily tied to the community that
spawned them."

This issue, say ethnographers and
Hispanic leaders, is forcing confrontation within the ranks. Should the
barrio's most able—those who clear
hurdles of language, culture, education—move out of primarily Hispanic
areas, or reinvest the fruits of their
success in their own neighborhoods?

Having 51 percent of the population of Pomona is not the issue," says
Tomas Arsua, a former city council
member who was defeated by Mr.
Cortez for mayor in April. "How do

you get that 51 percent to move forward is the question."

Mr. Arsua would like to reverse what he calls "brain drain," as successful Hispanic professionals, business people, and scholars leave their familiar neighborhoods for middle-class suburban life.

"The media focus on the 10 percent of us who are new Hispanic political stars or the Harvards and Yalies who are smart enough to become just like every other American," Arsua says. "But the broad trend for Hispanics for the next two decades is that we are becoming the major labor force that will drive the Southwest economy. We need people who will address needs back in the barrios—of education, housing, business opportunity."

WHAT'S IN A NAME

■ *Hispanic* is an umbrella term for anyone of Spanish or Portuguese descent, in or outside the US. It extends broadly also to those in the US of Latin American origin, but for this group alone, *Latino* is preferred. *Anglo* may distinguish between non-Hispanic and Hispanic or Latino whites. *Chicano(s)* (fem., *Chicana*) is a short synonym for a *Mexican-American*.

—From the Monitor Stylebook

Arsua's plan to reverse Hispanic exodus from Pomona is a broad-based, grass-roots restructuring of the community, addressing housing needs, educational curriculum, and business inequities. But the four-year city council member and defeated mayoral candidate says that those supporting his ideas are an "extreme minority."

Much more at the forefront, observers say, is Mayor Cortez. Born in Texas to Mexican migrant workers, Cortez started an auto business with his parents' life savings 20 years ago. One of nine children, Cortez says his father's religious background taught him to detest segregation and to find ways to embrace opportunities.

"Where else but America can a family that grew up picking grapes blossom to produce a mayor, a businessman, a pharmacist, and a teacher?" he asks.

"What Does Hispanic Mean?"

SUMMARY

Hispanic Americans are a united market in some ways, but not in others. Those who share the same language, culture, religion, and television programs can be approached as a single market, but economic, political, and other differences divide the market into several distinct segments. Becoming American is an essential part of the dynamic of the Hispanic marketplace.

Patricia Braus

Patricia Braus is a contributing editor of American Demographics.

Business interest in Hispanic customers continues to heat up. So does the level of confusion surrounding this market. Some marketers claim that it is possible to market to Hispanic Americans as a single group. Others contend that looking at 22 million people as one market ignores a considerable amount of cultural and demographic diversity. But the brightest minds in Hispanic marketing steer clear of all generalizations. They know that sometimes it's best to divide the Hispanic market, and sometimes it's better to take the Hispanic market as a whole.

"How different we are depends on the goal of the individual who wants to work with this market," says Nilda Anderson, a Puerto Rican woman who is president of the research firm Hispanic Market in New York City. In other words, how you define the Hispanic market depends on what you want to accomplish, how much money you have, and the level of precision you need.

Hispanics are expected to become America's largest minority group in as little as 15 years. In the 1990s, they will account for 40 percent of U.S. population growth. "If you don't try to market to [them], you're not going to get a share of that growth," says Roger Sennott, general manager for Market Development in San Diego.

SAME LANGUAGE, SINGLE MARKET

Hispanics are united in some important ways. The Spanish language, for example, is "the primary motivating factor behind Hispanic marketing," according to Sennott. Many analysts believe that a shared language creates the potential for a single market.

Frito-Lay treats Hispanic Americans as a single market because the company tries to project a consistent national image, says spokesman Tod MacKenzie. The company advertises on Spanish-language television, and local advertisements occasionally address local populations—but in general, the company aims "at the broadest possible target," he says.

Not all Hispanics speak Spanish. In fact, 30 percent of Hispanics do not speak Spanish as their primary language at home, according to a recent survey by the Hispanic MONITOR.

Most immigrant groups become more "American" as time passes. But high levels of immigration may be pushing Hispanics away from the Anglo mainstream. Hispanic Americans are more likely to speak Spanish at the dinner table than they were four years ago. Seventy percent of Hispanics speak Spanish at home in 1992, up from 57 percent in 1988, according to the MONITOR, produced jointly by Market Development Inc. of San Diego, California, and Yankelovich Partners of Westport, Connecticut. The survey found that 72 percent of Hispanic Americans were born outside the U.S., and 40 percent of nonnative Hispanics have been in the country for less than ten years.

The increasing importance of Spanish also reflects the increasingly established nature of America's Spanish-speaking communities. "You can live in many metropolitan areas in this country completely in Spanish," says Gary Berman, president of Market Segment Research in Coral Gables, Florida. "You can have a rich life in Spanish—socially, economically, and politically. This was not true for earlier immigrants."

Another reason for the growth of Spanish-speaking Hispanics is cultural pride. Three-quarters of those surveyed by the Hispanic MONITOR say that the Spanish language is more important to them now than it was five years ago.

Marketers are taking advantage of Hispanics' renewed commitment to their native language. *Tradiciones de Familia* magazine was distributed free of charge to an estimated 2 million Hispanics across the United States from October 1992 to January 1993 by Segmented Marketing Services of Winston-Salem, North Carolina. The 20-page magazine is essentially an advertising vehicle. Procter & Gamble was its sole sponsor in 1992, and in one issue, a full-page advertisement for Scope faces an article discussing the danger of "a foul-smelling mouth."

The magazines are distributed through churches, and each recipient gets a bag of product samples. Its editors, from three different Spanish-speaking countries, were chosen in part because they could remove regional variations in the Spanish language, says Lafayette Jones, president of Segmented Marketing Services. Jones hopes to produce the magazine twice a year.

The magazine's approach reflects the care marketers must take when they look at the Hispanic market as one group. "Our clients always try to test their promotional

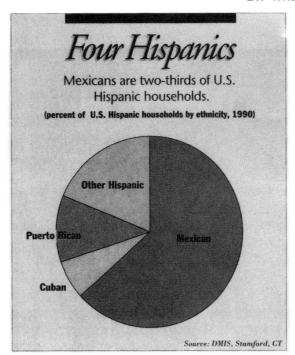

Four Hispanics

Mexicans are two-thirds of U.S. Hispanic households.

(percent of U.S. Hispanic households by ethnicity, 1990)

Source: DMIS, Stamford, CT

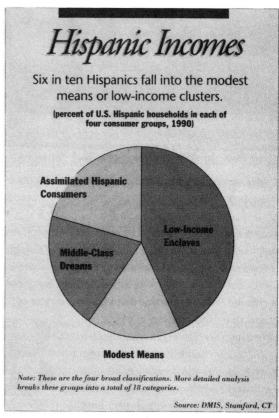

Hispanic Incomes

Six in ten Hispanics fall into the modest means or low-income clusters.

(percent of U.S. Hispanic households in each of four consumer groups, 1990)

Note: These are the four broad classifications. More detailed analysis breaks these groups into a total of 18 categories.

Source: DMIS, Stamford, CT

materials with all the main [Hispanic] groups," says Felipe Korzenny, president of Hispanic Marketing Communication Research in Belmont, California. "They make sure all groups understand the language and that none of them are offended by any of the language used."

The success of Spanish-language television in the U.S. is another shared cultural experience for Spanish speakers—and a ripe opportunity for marketers. Hispanics watch more television than the general population: an average of 3.6 hours on weekdays, compared with 3.2 hours for all Americans, according to the Hispanic MONITOR. And more than three-quarters of Hispanics surveyed spend most of their television or radio time with Spanish-language programming.

Spanish-language television creates national cultural figures within the Hispanic community, as loyal viewers from Miami to Los Angeles see the same celebrities. "It's something they share," says Jay Gangi, senior associate for Yankelovich Partners. "Certain people have come into the limelight, like Gloria Estefan and Paul Rodriguez." Marketers are now using these celebrities to build commercial bridges between Puerto Ricans, Cubans, Mexicans, and other ethnic groups. For example, actor/comedian Paul Rodriguez and his son appeared on the first cover of *Tradiciones de Familia*.

Shared cultural attitudes also make a single-Hispanic-market approach possible. When Nilda Anderson did a study for a hospital to learn why Hispanics don't use prenatal care, she found that "it doesn't matter if you're Mexican, Cuban, or other. What matters are cultural Latino attitudes. A man does not like another man, a stranger, to touch his wife."

Religion is a strong cultural value shared by most Hispanics, says Berman. Seventy percent of Hispanics are Roman

> **More than three-quarters of Hispanics surveyed spend most of their television or radio time with Spanish-language programming.**

Catholics, according to Market Segment Research's 1993 Minority Market Report.

Another unifying factor is family size. Hispanic families are larger than the average U.S. family. In fact, 27 percent of Hispanic households have five or more people, compared with 11 percent of the general population. The average size for Hispanic families is 3.4 people, compared with 2.6 for all families. "Families are very important—for all Hispanic groups," says Berman.

SEVERAL DISTINCT SEGMENTS

To reach Hispanics successfully, a business must capitalize on shared traits. But there are also profound differences

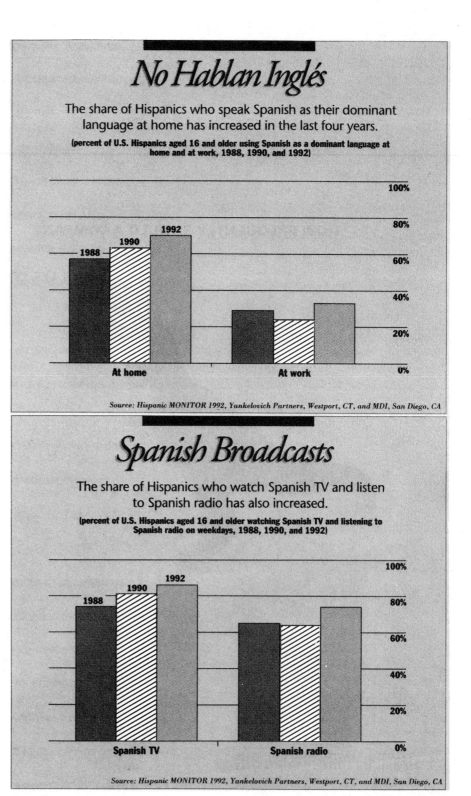

No Hablan Inglés

The share of Hispanics who speak Spanish as their dominant language at home has increased in the last four years.

(percent of U.S. Hispanics aged 16 and older using Spanish as a dominant language at home and at work, 1988, 1990, and 1992)

Source: Hispanic MONITOR 1992, Yankelovich Partners, Westport, CT, and MDI, San Diego, CA

Spanish Broadcasts

The share of Hispanics who watch Spanish TV and listen to Spanish radio has also increased.

(percent of U.S. Hispanics aged 16 and older watching Spanish TV and listening to Spanish radio on weekdays, 1988, 1990, and 1992)

Source: Hispanic MONITOR 1992, Yankelovich Partners, Westport, CT, and MDI, San Diego, CA

between Hispanic groups that cannot be ignored. "I think you can [market to Hispanics] with one overall campaign by being sensitive to the needs of constituents," says Berman. "But if you have the budget and the time, you can do it more effectively in subgroups."

Hispanics tend to be more religious than other Americans, but their church-going habits vary considerably. Market Segment Research found that 51 percent of Hispanics in San Francisco attend church at least once a week, compared with just 27 percent of Hispanics in Phoenix and Tucson.

Family size also differs among Hispanic groups. The average Hispanic household in heavily Mexican Los Angeles has 4.4

people, compared with 3.2 in Miami's predominantly Cuban Hispanic households. "Their sizes are different and their ages are different," says Berman. "Mexicans are younger than Cubans."

Being aware of differences is crucial to neighborhood businesses and those who market specific products and services. Sponsoring sporting events has long been a popular way for companies to gain name recognition in Hispanic communities, for example. But the fabled Hispanic love of sports is not a unified passion. "Mexicans play soccer, but Cubans and Puerto Ricans play baseball," says Berman. "You don't want to have a soccer tournament among Caribbean-based Hispanics."

Differences in sports, religion, and family size are just three of many differences among Hispanic groups. Some experts consider these differences too great for marketers to overcome. "You can't have the same marketing program for Hispanics in Los Angeles and in New York," says Jorge Del Pinal, Branch Chief of the Census Bureau's Ethnic and Hispanic Statistics Branch. "It doesn't make sense to have a strategy that you try to uniformly apply everywhere." Pinal

> To reach Hispanics successfully, a business must capitalize on shared traits. But there are also profound differences.

questions how businesses can effectively market in a single stroke to Mexicans who have just arrived in the U.S. and to those who have been here for decades.

Some firms are helping businesses approach the Hispanic market by dividing it extensively with a sharp knife. Donnelley Marketing Information Services (DMIS) of Stamford, Connecticut, recently introduced a marketing tool that splits U.S. Hispanics in no fewer than 18 ways. Its Hispanic Portraits system ranges from "Puerto Rican, high income, younger, established with single/multi-family homes" (3 percent of U.S. Hispanic households) to "Mexican, lowest income,

younger, low mobility, Hispanic neighborhoods" (16 percent of Hispanic households).

The system is designed to help businesses target market to Hispanics. "There are nuances within the market. People have different music. People have different cultures. People have different holidays," says Barbara Guthrie, product manager of analytic services for DMIS. "You have to understand that [Hispanics] are different."

Businesses can use DMIS's geographically based cluster system for such tasks as site location. For example, knowing that a neighborhood is 60 percent Mexican with many middle-class residents could encourage a franchiser to open a pizza parlor and hire a Mexican manager.

Segmenting the Hispanic market also reveals opportunities for marketers of luxury goods. As a whole, the Hispanic market does not look affluent. The median household income for Hispanics was $23,300 in 1990, compared with $30,500 for non-Hispanic households. Yet 14 percent of Hispanic households have an annual income of $50,000 or more. That adds up to 2.9 million affluent Hispanic households nationwide.

Marketers of luxury goods should focus on income, not country of origin, says Anderson of Hispanic Market. "I could define the Hispanic market . . . by people who have a lot of money and people who

> Hispanic support for the Republican party should increase as Hispanics become more affluent.

don't. If you want to sell Rolls Royces, it doesn't matter what country people are from. Money is the great equalizer."

Addressing Hispanics as a single political group is also perilous, according to a recent study of 4,900 Hispanics. "They look like other Americans," says Barry Kosmin, co-author of the study with Ariela Keysar. "As [Hispanics] get richer, they get more conservative."

Forty-one percent of Hispanics said they identified with Democrats, and 24

percent said they identified with Republicans. Yet Kosmin, director of the Bermain Institute for Survey Research at City University of New York Graduate Center, says that Hispanics demonstrate major regional differences in their political affiliation. Those in the South are less likely to be Democrats, while those in the West and Midwest are less likely to be Republicans and more likely to register as Independents. Hispanic America resembles white America more than black America in the ways class and local political cultures influence patterns of party support. Kosmin suggests that Hispanic support for the Republican party should increase as Hispanics become more affluent.

BECOMING AMERICAN

When Hispanic immigrants first arrive in the U.S., they generally gravitate to brands they knew in their native country. Yet this loyalty can be challenged by advertising to new arrivals before their American habits form.

Colgate toothpaste holds a 70 percent market share among newly arrived immigrants, according to a Market Segment Research survey. This stems from Colgate's dominance in Latin America, where it is the leading brand. The leading competitor, Crest, has only 15 percent of this group's market share. But among more acculturated Hispanics, Crest claims nearly one-fourth of the market.

Newcomers don't stay newcomers forever. A great majority of Hispanics (73 percent) agree with the statement that immigrants to this country should be prepared to adopt the American way of life, according to the Hispanic MONITOR. Four in ten agree that within 50 years, Hispanics will lose their culture and language and become like everyone else.

As ethnic market consultants stress their ability to understand the complicated needs of Hispanics, others warn that many U.S. Hispanics don't need translators and don't want to be addressed in Spanish. Rodolfo O. de la Garza urges businesses to keep the needs of U.S.-born Hispanics in mind when they develop marketing campaigns.

4. HISPANIC/LATINO AMERICANS

"A major component of the Latino population is an American population. You have to separate that population out," says de la Garza, a Mexican American who is professor of government at the University of Texas in Austin. Hispanics born in the U.S. are more likely than foreign-born Hispanics to be affluent, well educated, and bilingual, says de la Garza, who was principal investigator for the recent Latino National Political Survey.

De la Garza's survey found that most Hispanics do not have a particular interest in Latin America and do not support increased immigration. He also objects to generalizations that Hispanics can't or won't learn English. His data suggest they learn the language relatively quickly.

Perhaps the safest way of attracting U.S.-born Hispanics is by placing references to Latino culture in English-speaking advertisements. Such advertisements appeal to Hispanics who primarily speak English but still have pride in their culture, says Korzenny of Hispanic Marketing Communication Research. "The more sensitive you are to their needs and desires, the more they will respond to your services," he says.

Marketing to the many faces of Hispanic Americans may seem overwhelming, but experts say the profit is well worth the risks and potential pitfalls. "It is a social and political land mine," says Lafayette Jones. "But you can win big if you take the time and resources to understand."

TAKING IT FURTHER
The Bureau of the Census defines "Hispanic" as a person of any race who either speaks Spanish or has a Spanish-speaking ancestor. For this reason, *American Demographics* also uses Hispanic.

For more information on the Hispanic MONITOR, contact Jay Gangi, Yankelovich Partners, 8 Wright Street, Westport, CT 06880; telephone (203) 227-2700, or Roger Sennott, Market Development, Inc., 1643 Sixth Avenue, San Diego, CA 92101; telephone (619) 232-5628. For more about Hispanic Portraits, contact Barbara Guthrie, Donnelley Marketing Information Services, 70 Seaview Avenue, Stamford, CT 06904; telephone (203) 353-7207.

American Demographics and *The Number News* have published extensively on Hispanics, recently compiled into a reprint package called "Hispanic Americans." To order, call (800) 828-1133.

"La Raza Cosmica"

Richard Rodriguez

—————————— A journalist with Pacific News Service and author of Hunger of Memory *and the upcoming* Mexico's Children (Viking), *Richard Rodriguez is an incisive and compassionate commentator on the unique struggles faced by the "troubled people in between" – the Mexican who comes to America to live or just to work; who crosses a border of time, of pronouns and faith; who must come to terms with the land he is ancestrally connected to but which he no longer owns.*

The following is adapted from a conversation with NPQ's Marilyn Berlin Snell. ——————————

There is an extraordinary sign scrawled on a wall near the point where hundreds of Mexicans make their escape from Tijuana across the border into the US every night. It says: "Vete pero non me olvidas" – Go, but do not forget me – and it captures a particularly haunting dilemma for the Mexican emigrant: in order to survive, he must forsake his culture, which is based on memory and intimacy – a mother, an embrace, a family name, an ancestral cemetery, a patch of sky – and enter a culture of amnesia, a culture that is almost totally constructed on the future and the first-person singular pronoun.

As the Mexican makes his way across the border, he assures himself that he is not going to forget Mexico, that he is not going to become a "gringo." He is only going for the job. The problem with this formulation is that the job is key to the identity that the US will offer him. When the Mexican starts earning more money than his father ever dreamed of earning, the culture of memory loses its authority to the cul-

ture of possibility – the culture of individuality and initiative which we call the United States. The Mexican suddenly finds himself immersed in a culture where people do not ask about his family name; they want to know what he does for a living. Then slowly, haltingly, he begins to have American expectations: that he can really escape his father's fate; that he can put away his father's eyes; that he can become someone new.

Gradually, the Mexican begins to change and is bewildered by the change. He goes back to Mexico, taking money back to his family as he promised, but he is no longer at ease. He is living out an ancient drama: the struggle of a man caught between two impulses. In this case, the struggle between the future tense of America and the past tense of Mexico.

Troubled People in Between | Mexico and the US are more or less agreed that Mexican migrants to the US are "troubled people in between." The US takes note of the fact that for many Mexicans, their first act in America is a criminal act. They steal into the US under the cover of night.

Mother Mexico's feelings are more ambivalent. On the one hand, migrants to the US have long been given a protective regard by the Mexican government which has not hesitated to voice her concern over the Mexicans' working conditions in the US, their harassment by US immigration authorities, etc. Yet Mexican travelers to the US have also been traditionally regarded by Mexico as a kind of peasant class – people who could not "make it" in their homeland.

Though much has been written – both positively and negatively – about the Mexican migrants' influence on the US, their enormous influence on Mexico is rarely noted. Yet for years and from hundreds of Mexican villages, men

> Mexico and the US are more or less agreed that Mexican migrants to the US are "troubled people in between."

have been leaving for US cities and towns, and these same men have returned with their seductive stories. The grandfather returns and then takes his sons and grandsons, who then return with their own tales. And so the path between the two countries has been well worn over time. Mexicans have left Mexico with dreams and have returned with stereo equipment, t-shirts and dollars. In the process, we have unsettled Mexico.

In the state of Michoacán there is a village called Jaripo. Each year men and women who work in Stockton and Hollister or in the San Fernando Valley return to Jaripo. They pack their suitcases with black suits and evening gowns and each night in Jaripo they have a procession at sunset – the factory worker in an elegant suit, his teenage daughters and wife in prom gowns and high heels.

In an obvious way, the journey to Jaripo is an homage to memory. But in a more subtle way it is also a showing off of the US to Mexico. They come back to Mother Mexico and say, "Look at what we have accomplished." And their procession creates a foreign glamor in Jaripo, with its old plaza and its dusty streets. The ostensible homage to memory is at least also an homage to America's culture of desire. Perhaps most importantly, it is an homage to change.

In a very real way, these Mexicans who have travelled to America embody in blood and soul what the Mexican philosopher Jose Vasconcelos called *"La Raza Cosmica"* – the Cosmic Race. Most Mexicans are people of mixed race; Mexico's culture is a culture of mixture. In her official nationalism, however, Mexico has denied her own richness. Mexico has been afraid of the invader; since Independence, Mexican nationalists have portrayed Mexico as raped mother – put upon by Spain, by France, and of course by the US. Poor Mexico!

But this is nonsense. Mexico is not to be pitied. Mexico has been, since the 18th century, the first modern country of the world. Mexico has torn down the borders of the old world. Mexicans carry the blood of at least two continents. Mexico's true genius, her survival, has been due to her absorbancy. Indeed, if the Mexican is famous, it is not for giving up his gods but for taking the enemy's gods as his own. Mexico is a place of rape which became marriage, European

> The tragedy of Mexico was not her rape. The tragedy of Mexico has been that she does not have an idea of herself as rich as her blood.

intrigue which became romance. And so I – who carry Mexico's blood – I come out looking five shades darker than my brother who is mistaken in California for being Italian.

La Raza Reviled | The tragedy of Mexico was not her rape. The tragedy of Mexico has been that she does not have an idea of herself as rich as her blood. When I go to Mexico, even the waitress lets me know with her voice that I displease her because I don't speak Spanish well. I have betrayed Mother Mexico; I have betrayed memory.

On this side of the border, there is the same Mexican resistance to mixture by people who are the creatures of mixture. The Chicano movement of recent decades has become famous for its resistance to assimilation, the idea of the melting pot. And in the US I am accused by all sorts of people of having "lost my culture." My answer: Culture is not static. If I am not my father, it is because I did not grow up in Mexico. I did not grow up speaking Spanish into my adulthood.

My detractors seem to think I somehow "left my culture" at the Greyhound bus station; I forgot it somewhere. I lost it as though it were something independent of me. But one doesn't lose one's culture. I am my culture. Lucille Ball is my culture. And Walt Disney is my culture. A California freeway is my culture.

A Mexican-American bishop in Sacramento once pointed to a mosaic of Our Lady of Guadalupe – the Virgin Mary in the guise of an Indian Maiden – and said, "That is what I am and I want America to be. We are pieces of glass and we combine to make a beautiful mosaic." I disagree. I am not a piece of glass. I am not static. I have a soul. And souls are not static. We are not stone. We are fluid; we are human; we are experience. And within that experience we are transformed by our contact with each other. I am Chinese because I live in San Francisco, a Chinese city. I became Irish in America. I became Portuguese in America.

Of course, many Mexicans don't feel the way I do. Indeed, I don't believe any group scolds its own more than the Mexicans. We brood over our children and tell them that they are going to lose their culture; that they must not be ashamed of their culture; that they must hold onto their culture. There are all kinds of historical reasons why we do this in the US, since Mexico has been mocked and trivialized here for a very long time. Nevertheless, in our admonitions against change, we turn our children against their culture in very deep ways. We should be telling them, "Don't be afraid of becoming Chinese. Go to France next year and don't apologize for learning French. Don't apologize for becoming what you always have been – children of assimilation. Assimilation is what your ancestors did, and that is how the Indians not only survived but flourished to the point where we frighten the environmentalists of North America with our "overpopulation."

In the end, we trivialize Mexico by proclaiming ourselves separate from the US mainstream. By insisting on our unique heritage, we deny our heritage.

Looking back on the Chicano movement of the sixties, I believe that if Mexican Americans had really wanted to be revolutionary in Protestant America, they would have asserted themselves as a culture of marriage and union, a Catholic culture of half-breeds, a culture rich in all the things puritan America most feared.

Individuality and separatism are North American traits, not Mexican traits. Americans, not wanting to admit that we create one another, continue to insist on the primacy of individuality. The rejection of the "we" has been particularly destructive to Mexican Americans because in denying Mexico's genius, we end up a puzzle to ourselves. As second- and third-generation Americans, we do not know why we are so Americanized when we don't want to be. We do not understand that our wanting to be Mexican is, in fact, a perversion of Catholic Mexico and of our Indian heritage.

Discovering the Discoverers | The problem is that we haven't made up our minds about the Indian. We don't understand who the Indian was or is. We don't understand the Indian's genius. We accept the white writers of Latin America – with their French wives and their brittle continental wit – as being the voice of the Indian. But they are not the voice of the Indian.

I believe I heard it once. I was travelling earlier this year throughout Mexico, working on a documentary for the BBC. For days we travelled, the London crew getting pink under the Mexican sun. Finally, one day, we arrived in an Indian village around noon and we heard singing from the inside of a church. As we approached we could see a group of dark old women, who looked like Greek furies singing at the foot of the altar. They were singing in Spanish but with a voice, a calm that translated the European words into an Indian temperament. They were reforming the language of Europe as they sang, and they were making Spanish an Indian language.

Now the great world is preparing for 1992 – the 500th anniversary of the Columbus voyage. And the neo-Marxists and the effete liberal Europeans and the American environmentalists are already organizing themselves to remember the "shame" of the Conquest. Once again the Indian will be required to play the role of victim. And the European will be the actor who tramples through the Americas, stealing the Indian's language and stealing the Indian's gods and ravishing innocence.

Such a view of history fails to give any stature to the Indian. My own view is that the Indian was at least curious when Columbus approached. European vocabularies do not have a rich enough word to describe this curiosity – the active principle within contemplation. Asia would probably better understand the Indian because the Indian is kin to Asia. What Columbus and his activist European tradition met when he arrived in "India" was an absorbing glance that swallowed him up.

I regard my own insistent curiosity about the US as an Indian curiosity, not a Spanish one. I see this quality coming from a Mexican rather than a Spanish inheritance. Indeed, as an educated Mexican-American I am engaged exactly as the Indian of the 16th century was engaged – in the discovery of the new world. I want nothing less than the world. I warn the US that if you think you are going to get tacos and nachos from me, you are going to be very surprised. I want the United States of America. I want to swallow you up. I have already swallowed your language and now it is mine.

In Shakespeare's *Tempest* there is a prophetic description of the Mexican – of me – in the figure of the Indian, Caliban. Shakespeare understood that if the European, Prospero, let Caliban loose, Caliban would turn and steal Prospero's books. Caliban was always plotting to get Prospero's books because he understood that those books would give him power. And now I have stolen

> What Columbus and his activist European tradition met when he arrived in "India" was an absorbing glance that swallowed him up.

your books, I have stolen Prospero's language, I have stolen his power.

The Price of Change | I wish I could tell Mexican children that they have nothing to lose by acquiring a new culture. But in some very basic and often tragic way, the child who comes from Mexico to Los Angeles must change, must move away from the language of parents and grandparents, the intimate pronoun of *tu* – toward the stranger's world, the realm of *usted*.

The popular educational ideology of the movement (masquerading as bilingual education) encourages children to imagine that there is no price to be paid. It is said you can speak your "family language" in the classroom while you learn English. But this is nonsense! Family language exists only within the family. What children need to learn in a classroom is public language and unless they learn it, they will miss the point of the classroom.

Mexicans come from a culture that prizes intimacy. But finally, in the Los Angeles classroom, the dilemma faced by the Mexican-American child is no different than that faced by children in Appalachia or in Bedford Stuyvesant. The child returns home after having heard public language in school and hears another language being spoken by family members. In that instant, the child knows that there is a difference between the public language of school and family language.

The bilingualism I care about is the ability to speak to two very different societies, public and private. The problem for many working-class Hispanic children in the US is that they speak neither a public Spanish nor a public English. They lack a public imagination of themselves.

I understood language very well as a child. At home I heard my father speak differently than my teacher. I was well aware of the implications of that difference. At school I knew I was being called to a different identity. The Irish nun at my Catholic elementary school in Sacramento said, "Richard, speak in a loud voice, repeat your name after me." She was asking me to use language publicly – the first lesson in school. And it wasn't that I could not say what she asked, that I could not make those sounds. I didn't want to make those sounds. I didn't want to speak her language, your language. I didn't want to speak to "all the boys and girls."

Language must always be the beginning of any discussion of education. The question is how children understand the language they are using and what that language is doing to their souls. The psychic, cultural and familial price a working-class child must pay, necessarily pay, for the transition from private to public language is very high. In California, 50 percent of Hispanics drop out of high school.

America's Forgotten Canon | I am concerned by the renewed movement toward a 60s-style ethnic separatism on the college campus. Higher education is retreating from the notion that there is an American canon. In a cruel way, American educators betray their newest non-white students.

It is very important for the university to say to the newcomer that there is a history here. It is crucial that the newcomer understand that America exists. And there is a difference between knowing about Plymouth Rock and knowing about Santa Fe. Something happened at Plymouth Rock that implicates the immigrant and will make him quite unlike his Confucian grandmother. The immigrant will become the new Protestant, the new Puritan. That is why he needs to know more about a mad British king of the 18th century than about Mexican revolutionaries of the 19th century. As an American, I have more to do with Paul Revere and Thomas Jefferson than with Benito Juarez.

The notion that there is nothing here, that the immigrant can bring his culture whole and set up his own private tent, is foolishness. America exists, and the professors who don't want to admit this fact are those same people who are most afraid of having to deal with the immigrant's inclusion in the American landscape. Easier to say: "Do your own thing."

At a time of spectacular ethnic diversity in this country, higher education is unable to come to terms with the common identity of Americans. Ultimately, those who will be blamed for this travesty will be the so-called ethnic radicals, but this is not where blame belongs. It belongs primarily with the distinguished, graying faculty members of Stanford and Harvard and all the other institutions of higher learning who can no longer define what it is we know or what we should know in common.

> I wish I could tell Mexican children that they have nothing to lose by acquiring a new culture. But in some very basic and often tragic way, the child who comes from Mexico to Los Angeles must change.

There's More to Racism Than Black and White

Elizabeth Martinez

The small brown woman with a serious face stood on the curb almost motionless as thousands of people marched by her in a line that stretched 22 blocks. Amidst huge banners and hundreds of big colorful signs, her hand-lettered words on corrugated paper had a haunting simplicity:

We were here
We are here
This was our land
is still our land
Stand up for your rights.

It was August 25, 1990, in Los Angeles and people—mostly Mexican American—were marking the 20th anniversary of the Chicano Moratorium against the war in Vietnam. We assembled at the same park as we did two decades ago and marched the same route to the same park for a rally. As the *señora*'s sign indicated, the struggle goes on and in many ways conditions have worsened for Latinos—La Raza-over the past 20 years. At the same time, the Moratorium reflected important, complex, and often positive new developments. Finally, for the U.S. left in general, the event carried a message that cannot be ignored.

On August 29, 1970, some 20,000 mostly Chicano people came from all over the country to protest the Vietnam war and especially the fact that our casualties were running at a much higher rate than the Mexican American proportion of the U.S. population. As the rally began around midday, a minor scuffle near the edge of the park served as the excuse for a massive police attack. Tear gas filled the air as 500 officers charged the youth, families, and elderly who had been sitting on the grass and drove out the panicked crowd. I remember running with a dozen other people into a nearby house to get away from the tear gas. Friends and relatives were scattered; my daughter, for one, could not be located until ten o'clock in the evening.

Three Chicanos died that day as a result of the police repression: Angel Diaz, Ruben Salazar and Lynn Ward. The best-known was journalist Salazar, who had been investigating and writing a series of articles on recent cases of police brutality for *The Los Angeles Times;* he had reportedly become radicalized in the process. After the attack in the park he had stopped with a friend at the nearby Silver Dollar cafe and was sitting at the bar. From the sidewalk outside, a sheriff's deputy fired a 10-inch tear-gas projectile into the cafe, which almost blew off Salazar's head. Later claiming they had received reports of an armed man in the bar, police said that before firing they had told all occupants to leave; witnesses said they heard no such warning.

That evening the sky over East Los Angeles turned black with smoke as protesters selectively torched many buildings. Sirens wailed for hours; barricades everywhere made "East Los," as it's called, look like an occupied territory. In the weeks that followed, the District Attorney refused to prosecute Salazar's killer despite an inquest damaging to the Sheriff's Department. Protesters demonstrated over the next few months; at one event, when officers again fired on the crowd with tear gas, some people hurled objects at them. Police killed one man, an Austrian student who looked Chicano, and left 19 wounded by buck-shot.

At this year's Moratorium police seemed to keep a relatively low profile. News reports said 6,000 people came, mostly from the Southwest with a sprinkling of Chicago and New York participants. It looked like more, and it certainly felt like more because of the high spirits and energized mood. Was it yet another Day of Nostalgia in the current era of 1960s anniversaries? Yes, but mostly no.

Moratorium organizers had said the day's goal was not just to commemorate a historic event but to protest conditions now facing the overwhelming majority of La Raza. The excellent, thoughtful tabloid *L.A. Moratorium*, published by the organizing committee, pointed to the elimination of Chicano studies, attacks on bilingual education, "English Only" laws, terror from police and immigration officers, attacks by the Klan and skinheads, youth killing one another, the dumping of toxic wastes in Raza communities, and CIA/FBI imported drugs. (One might add a recent statistic: the infant mortality rate among Latinos in Los Angeles County has risen by over a third since 1987.) At the same time, the tabloid said, "the ability of the Movement to defend its people's rights is extremely limited or nonexistent" and the lack of organization also prevents effective support for Native American struggles and against U.S. colonialism in Central America.

The rally program sustained these themes. Although activists with long histories of struggle were featured, like Dolores Huerta of the United Farm Workers and Professor Rudy Acuña, they never lingered on "the wonderful 1960s." This was no mere pep rally. Instead they and other speakers talked eloquently about domestic issues as well as U.S. militarism and intervention, democracy in Mexico, and opposition to the 1992 quincentenary to "celebrate" Christopher Columbus's arrival in 1492.

What about lessons to be drawn from the past, or a long-range strategy and developed vision for the future? The rally itself did not go much beyond calling for greater activism. Still something was being born, something new and very young was in the air.

About half the Moratorium participants seemed to be under 25, including many college as well as high school students. A major force in mobilizing the youth was MEChA (Movimiento Estudiantil Chicano de Aztlan, the Chicano Student Movement of Aztlan). Born in 1969, its strength ebbed in later years. By 1985, according to one MEChA leader, much of the organization was splintered by ideological debate; activism revived in response to worsening socioeconomic conditions. Today divisions still exist on such issues as a strictly Chicano vs. broader Latino focus, and the merits of affiliation with nonstudent, left organizations. Still, MEChA has lasted far longer than most student groups and retains a certain moral authority.

Many of the Chicano youth marching on August 25 were not even born when the first Moratorium took place, and most schools teach little about the extraordinary struggles of the 1960s worldwide. At its best MEChA helps to fill this void, serving as a transmission belt from past to present, with faculty members who were 1960s activists sometimes providing continuity as well as inspiration. The youth on the march seemed to be learning their history and respecting it. You could feel a thrill ripple through the crowd when one speaker said: "20 years ago they tried to destroy the Chicano movement. 20 years later we are here to tell them that they failed!"

All that week and through September, events related to the Moratorium took place in Los Angeles: several days of extensive TV coverage; a photo exhibit; two plays, one of them a re-enactment of the killing of Salazar staged in the Silver Dollar itself and another called "August 29." A major exhibition, "Chicano Art: Resistance and Affirmation" (CARA) from 1965–1985 opened at the University of California, with many special cultural events scheduled around it.

"We want to pass on our history," said one student at the Moratorium and the spirit that visibly animated the youth that day was indeed nationalist. Dozens of times the 1960s cry of "Chicano Power!" rang out. But the words seem to have a different meaning today—more concrete and more complex than yesterday's generalized rhetoric.

"'Chicano Power' is different now because people realize we will be the majority in a few years," said a young Chicana from Fresno. "The next step will be to turn those numbers into political and economic power, to take over our communities. For example, in the valley in Fresno the people are 80 percent Chicano and Mexicano. The mayor and the school board should reflect that. When it happens, it will be a real affirmation of Chicano Power."

A second meaning of Chicano Power today lies in its implicit rejection of "Hispanic" as a label imposed by the dominant society and adopted by many Latinos themselves—specially those sometimes called Chuppies or Buppies—Chicano or Brown yuppies. "Hispanic" is a fundamentally racist term which obliterates the Native American and African American heritages of La Raza in favor of the white European component from Spain. The August 25 march countered this distortion with a contingent of Native Americans at the head of the line. Others carried signs rejecting "Hispanic" and affirming "Chicano."

That message also came across while people assembled to march, when the group Culture Clash performed and "Slick Rick" did his bilingual Chicano rap songs. He chided: "Chicanos who are wearing blue contact lenses today—forget it, you're Chicano. Don't try to be white, they do it better!" And: "The 1980s were supposed to be the 'Decade of the Hispanic' but that turned out to be an event sponsored by Coors beer." In other words: the concept "Hispanic" emerged as a marketing tool to conveniently target all Spanish-speaking cultures at once.

The Chicano/Latino/Raza versus "Hispanic" debate is about more than terminology or even racism. It also concerns values, politics, and class: the Raza tradition of collectivity and sharing versus the individualism and consumerism that intensified during the 1980s. In that decade, for example, we saw one "Hispanic" art exhibit after another, often with corporate sponsors and usually apolitical in content. But the new exhibit, CARA, is consciously entitled "Chicano Art" and is not by chance much more political than its predecessors. CARA organizers also say they sought to avoid commercialization and cultural homogeneity. Further, the show was organized by means of an unusually collective approach—regional committees rather than a single curator—so as to promote the empowerment of community people rather than professional elitism.

In these and other ways, the nationalism that ran strong on August 25 has an implicitly or overtly anti-capitalist thrust. Any denunciation of capitalist exploitation brought strong cheers from the rally audience. The presence of organized labor at this year's Moratorium also seemed stronger than 20 years ago, in part because of militant struggles that have been recently waged by workers like Janitors for Justice. Mostly Central Americans, they have attracted wide support from many groups with their courage, determination, imaginative tactics—and by winning a major victory. The extremely brutal police attack on their peaceful demonstration at Century Plaza earlier this year further generated solidarity.

A NEW INTERNATIONALISM

Above all, the Moratorium emanated an internationalism much stronger than 20 years ago. Some of us had wondered if it would address current U.S. policy in the Persian Gulf. We need not have doubted. Signs everywhere, and not just from predominantly white left formations, called for an end to U.S. militarism in the Middle East. "The oil belongs to the people, not Texaco!" got some of the loudest applause at the rally.

There was also a much stronger Mexican presence than in 1970, which speaks to the ever-growing Mexican population. Their numbers are rising so rapidly that formerly Chicano neighborhoods are now Mexican (the different terms here meaning, simplistically, born in the U.S. as opposed to born in Mexico). A well-known Mexican socialist leader, Heberto Castillo of the Democratic Revolutionary Party (PRD), spoke eloquently at the rally, stressing the crucial links between today's struggle for democracy in Mexico and action by Mexican-origin people here.

In another kind of internationalism not seen 20 years ago, a group from the Nation of Islam attended the rally and one of the best-received speakers came from the African People's Socialist Party. This spirit may be drawing encouragement from cross-cultural developments like the black-inspired Chicano rap music from Culture Clash, Kid Frost's *Hispanic Causing Panic* album, and other singers. Finally, a small Korean contingent marched in the Moratorium—a welcome sight.

The National Chicano Moratorium Committee, which worked on the event for many months at the national and regional levels, deserves much credit for its success. "The most democratic mobilization effort in my memory," Professor Rudy Acuña called it, despite having disagreed with members at times. Its commitment to combat sectarianism paid off well, judging by the wide variety of politics represented. The banner of the Mothers of East Los Angeles, a strong community organization, could be seen not far from a small sign proclaiming "Mao—hoy mas que nunca" (Mao, today more than ever). Although the "Principles of Unity" limited membership on the organizing committee to Chicano/Mexican organizations, anti-white feeling seemed absent.

When it came to gender roles, the committee showed little progress over 20 years ago. Women held the posts of—guess what—secretary and treasurer, plus one youth coordinator. All four media liaisons were men. Rally speakers had a better balance: far from equal but solid, and women's participation in the movement was not trivialized by tokenistic recognition. In addition to Dolores Huerta, Nita Gonzales of Denver (longtime community organizer and daughter of "Corky" Gonzales) spoke as did Juana Gutierrez of the Mothers of East Los Angeles and Patricia Marin of Orange County MEChA.

On the march itself you could see a Chicana women's consciousness that was absent 20 years ago. Signs like "Vote Chicano—Vote Chicana" may not have been numerous, but they wouldn't have been seen at all before. Activist women agree it's time for the decline of the "CPMG," a species identified by several Chicanas talking in the Silver Dollar after the Moratorium: the Chicano Person Movement Guy. The generation of women now in college may bring major changes. In recent years, for example, it has not been unusual to find a woman heading a MEChA chapter or women outnumbering the men on a MEChA board. A future Moratorium organizing committee should find more women with experience, in their 30s and 40s like much of the current committee, and ready at least to run more of the show.

HOW SHALL WHITE LEFTISTS RELATE TO A NEW MOVIMIENTO?

Some of us felt a new Chicano movement being born last Aug. 25. The day made it clear that sooner or later this will happen—a Latino movement, I would hope. An old question then arises: how will leftists relate to it? Past experience has been so poor that for many Latinos—not to mention other people of color in the U.S.—"the left" has often come to mean white folks. In the next era, will so much of the Anglo left continue to minimize the Mexican American struggle?

At the heart of the problem is a tendency to see race relations and the struggle against racism primarily or exclusively in terms of black and white. Every week articles or books appear that claim to address racial issues like Affirmative Action but contain not a single word about any population except the African American. In the histories of the 1960s by white authors, although the treatment of black struggle is never adequate one can at least find Martin Luther King, the Black Panthers, and a few other references. But in 25 such books reviewed by this writer, the massive Chicano movement of the 1960s and early 1970s might never have happened. (See "That Old White (Male) Magic," *Z*, July–August 1989.)

To criticize this blindness is not to deny the primacy of African American struggle: the genocidal nature of enslavement, the constant resistance by slaves, the "Second Reconstruction" of the 1960s and its extraordinary leaders, and today's destruction of black youth if not black males in general. Also, African Americans up to now remain the largest population of color in this country. I began my own political work in the black civil rights movement because it was so obviously on the cutting edge of history for all people of color, for the whole society. Many white progressives also gave support, sometimes even their lives, to that movement. But somehow, while combating the symbolism of blacks as "the Invisible Man" they overlooked new "invisible" men—and women—of other colors.

One apparent exception to the left's myopia about Mexican Americans surfaced during the party-building movement of the 1970s. A flurry of Marxist-Leninist position papers about Chicanos descended, telling us that we were a nation and should secede from the U.S. (wha?), or that we were a national minority whose goal should be regional autonomy (wha?), or that we were nothing more than part of the U.S. working-class (wha?), or that we were a racial but not a national minority (hunh?!). Those we called the Alphabet Soup came to visit Chicano groups in New Mexico at different times. Their organizational positions were unrelated to the realities we knew, concoctions that seemed to have sprung full-grown from their heads, nourished by theory alone. This could only leave us feeling a lack of respect for our history, culture, and struggle.

Earlier the Communist Party had done better and provided courageous leadership to labor struggles involving Mexican or Chicano workers. But here too Raza who were in the party have their stories to tell of an alienating chauvinism. All in all, left organizations too often use that demeaning stock phrase: "African Americans and other minorities" or "African Americans and other Third World people" or "African Americans and other people of color."

Even when Anglo leftists do study Raza culture and history, the problem remains of demonstrating support for Latinos abroad rather than at home. Many Anglos have worked hard on solidarity with Central America and against U.S. intervention. They learn Spanish, embrace the culture, pass hard and often dangerous time in Central American countries. But, except for the issue of refugees and sanctuary, this has rarely translated into support for domestic struggles by Latino peoples—for example, Chicanos/Mexicans or Puerto Ricans in the U.S. Intentions aside, a romanticized and in the end paternalistic view of Latinos tends to prevail all too often.

Anglos are not alone in showing little effort to understand the history, culture, and struggles of Mexican Americans. Peoples of color can also be blind. Among blacks, for example, author Manning Marable is one of the few who regularly brings Latinos into his worldview. Even within the same population, class differences make some Chicanos want racism exposed, while others prefer to maintain a pretense of "No problem." Some will affirm their brownness proudly while others prefer to pass for white if possible.

Up to now the dominant society has had no interest in teaching our unknown histories to anyone and preferred to leave in place the melting-pot model. The burden then falls on the rest of us to work for internationalism inside—not just outside—U.S. borders. We have to teach and learn from each other, we have to develop mutual knowledge of and respect for all our cultures. A new kind of U.S. left will not be born otherwise, as activist/author Carlos Muñoz emphasized in a recent hard-hitting *Crossroads* article.

1992: A CHANCE TO SING "DE COLORES" AS NEVER BEFORE

The upcoming quincentenary offers a once-in-500-years chance to pull our colors together in common protest. Christopher Columbus's arrival on this continent has meaning, usually deadly, for all people of color and many others. In the face of what will be constant, repugnant official celebrations of 1492, we can together mount educational events and demonstrations of all kinds with great scope and impact. The symbolism begs for sweeping protest, a protest that will not merely say "No" to what happened 500 years ago but affirm the infinite treasure-house of non-European cultures and histories, then and now.

For Native Americans, of course, Columbus's arrival meant instant genocide. Today indigenous peoples all over the continent are already planning domestic and international actions. Europe's colonization also paved the way for the enslavement of Africans by the million, brought here to build vast wealth for others with their blood and sweat. At the same time, colonialism launched the birth—by conquest and rape—of a whole new people, La Raza, who combine the red, white, and black in what we may still call a bronze people.

On the backs of all these colors was constructed the greatest wealth ever seen in the world, a wealth that soon came to need more slaves of one kind or another. This time it drew them from the East: Chinese, Japanese, Filipino, Pacific peoples, and many others. Ultimately the whites failed to protect many of their own children from an inhuman poverty and contempt.

So we can come together on this, if we choose. We can make 1992 a year that THEY will remember. We can, in gentler terms, make it the year of "De Colores," of new alliances, in the spirit of the old song by that name: *Y por eso los grandes amores de muchos colores me gustan a mi"* (*"And so the loves of many colors are pleasing to me."*)

N O T   M U C H
COOKING
WHY THE VOTING RIGHTS ACT IS NOT EMPOWERING MEXICAN AMERICANS

Peter Skerry

Peter Skerry, staff associate with the Brookings Governmental Studies program, is director of Washington programs at the UCLA Center for American Politics and Public Policy. This article is drawn from his book, Mexican Americans: The Ambivalent Minority *(The Free Press, 1993).*

Although most of the controversy surrounding the Voting Rights Act has focused on the benefits it affords black Americans, they are hardly its only beneficiary. Since 1975 Hispanics have also been covered. And though arguments for and against the Voting Rights Act's extraordinary provisions are routinely assumed to apply to blacks and Hispanics alike, in actuality the law does not work the same way for the two groups. Arguably, it hinders the political empowerment of Hispanics, Mexican Americans in particular. Certainly, the effect of the Voting Rights Act on Mexican Americans raises fundamental questions about using policies directed at racial barriers faced by black Americans to address the problems of a group composed primarily of recently arrived immigrants.

Census data on how Mexican Americans define themselves racially offer one widely overlooked reason for asking these questions. Despite the pervasive tendency to treat Mexican Americans, and Hispanics generally, as a nonwhite racial minority (as in routine references to "whites, blacks, and Hispanics"), in the 1990 census 50.6 percent of all Mexican Americans identified themselves as racially "white," while 1.2 percent said they were "black," and 46.7 percent identified themselves as "other race."

Another indicator that challenges the uncritical eagerness with which Mexican Americans are regarded as racially isolated from the mainstream is intermarriage. While blacks rarely marry outside their group, Mexican Americans frequently do. Indeed, exogamy rates for Mexican Americans have long been at least as high as those for European immigrant groups earlier this century.

Mexican Americans who grew up in Los Angeles during the 1950s and 1960s typically complain today that they were encouraged by their parents and teachers to "act like Anglos" and raised without much knowledge of their people's culture and language. In the late 1970s David Lopez surveyed 1,100 Mexican households in Los Angeles and concluded, "Were it not for new arrivals from Mexico, Spanish would disappear from Los Angeles nearly as rapidly as most European immigrant languages vanished from cities in the East."

The influx of Spanish-speaking immigrants to Los Angeles County since 1980 has been so great that 50 percent of Hispanics there told 1990 census takers that they do not speak English "very well." But if previous patterns of language assimilation prevail, they—and certainly their offspring—will learn English. Indeed, in recent years a persistent lament in the barrios of Los Angeles has been that Mexican grandmothers who speak little English have a hard time communicating with grandchildren who speak no Spanish.

Meanwhile, at the University of California, researchers with the Berkeley-based Diversity Project document "the corrosive impact of cultural assimilation" on Mexican-American undergraduates. Often the first from their families to attend college, these young people typically do not speak Spanish and consider themselves "white," only to discover on campus they are "Chicano," that is, members of a discriminated against racial minority. As one such youth put it, he was "born again at Berkeley." Ironically, for many Mexican Americans today the biggest difficulty is not obstacles to assimilation, but its unsettling consequences.

These trends may be slowed by the influx of Mexican immigrants in the past 10 to 15 years, not to mention the recent recession, especially in California. But there is no reason to believe that the basic assimilative processes have been stymied—or that the basic difference with black Americans has changed. Indeed, one manifestation of this difference that is particularly relevant politically is the residential mobility of Mexican Americans, who follow the classic immigrant pattern of gradually moving up and out of initially settled urban enclaves. A Rand Corporation study of 1980 census data found that "unlike the patterns for blacks, an influx of Latinos into an area does not appear to precipitate an outflow of Anglos. Thus, with increasing exposure to U.S. society and continued upward mobility, Latinos blend into the larger society."

Because compactness is one of the criteria in drawing legislative districts, such residential mobility and dispersion have increased the difficulty of drawing Hispanic-majority districts under the Voting Rights Act. In Los Angeles, for example, a historic 1990 federal court decision, *Garza v. County of Los Angeles,* created an Hispanic seat on the powerful five-person county board of supervisors. To construct the district, demographers focused on what they called "the Hispanic Core," an area composed of 229 contiguous census tracts, all but three of which had a majority of Hispanics. The Core contained 81 percent of all census tracts in the county with Hispanic population majorities in 1980, and 72 percent of its total population was Hispanic. But Hispanics were so widely scattered throughout Los Angeles County that the Core contained only 40 percent of the total Hispanic population there, and just 36 percent of all voting-age Hispanic citizens.

Years of Exclusion

Do such indicators of assimilation mean that Mexican Americans have experienced no discrimination whatsoever? Not at all. Many harbor bitter memories of the way they or their forebears have been treated in this country. Indeed, in the rural towns and ranches of the Southwest, particularly in Texas, Mexican Americans endured virtual caste status. Early this century in Gonzales County, Texas, Mexican contract laborers were chained to posts and guarded by men with shotguns. Until rather recently Mexican Americans in South Texas often went to separate and inferior schools, worshipped at the back of churches, were excluded from Anglo neighborhoods by restrictive covenants, or were refused burial in public cemeteries. In politics, Texas Anglos used poll taxes, burdensome candidate filing fees, restrictive voter registration procedures, and, when necessary, intimidation and violence to ensure that "Meskins," as they were contemptuously called, wielded little power.

On the other hand, whenever Democratic candidates found it advantageous to mobilize the Mexican vote, local "*jefes*" were provided with the necessary "walking around money" to get their families, friends, neighbors, and subordinates to the polls. Poll taxes would be paid en masse; campaign rallies organized; and beer and tamales liberally supplied. On their way into the voting booths, the illiterate would be given strings tied with knots, indicating where their x's should be put on the ballot, and poll watchers would make sure Mexicans voted as they were told. Election supervisors would routinely violate the law by entering voting booths—when there *were* voting booths.

Such practices were recounted in great detail in 1975, when Congress brought the entire state of Texas under the Voting Rights Act. Undeniably, Mexican Americans in Texas, and elsewhere, have had to face offensive and humiliating forms of discrimination. Yet it must also be said that the barriers they encountered have been decidedly less overwhelming than those confronting blacks. Treated in law as "Caucasians," Mexican Americans met barriers more enforced by custom than enshrined in law.

As a result, the caste status of Mexican Americans was more porous and negotiable than Jim Crow. For example, while the Texas constitution of 1876 *required* separate schools for blacks, the segregation of Mexican Americans practiced in Texas until after World War II was a matter of local policy. And local attitudes varied widely. As David Montejano observes in his recent book, *Anglos and Mexicans in the Making of Texas, 1836–1986,* "In some counties, Mexicans and Anglos were completely separate. In others, there was an easy mingling among the two 'races' and few social distinctions were drawn between them." And those in oppres-

sive circumstances had escape routes. One was the military during World War II, which, unlike for blacks, did not mean serving in segregated units. Another was the migrant labor stream. For with dependable sources of wages up north, where Mexicans were often treated relatively well, migrant families were less susceptible to Anglo social controls when they returned home at the end of the growing season.

Nor were Mexicans totally excluded from the political process, as were blacks, who were subjected to the infamous Texas "white primaries" struck down by the Supreme Court in 1944. Clifton McCleskey, perhaps the leading student of Texas politics, observes that "though local rules and informal discouragement" sometimes hampered Mexican American participation in politics, "in some respects Mexican Americans have traditionally had a place in Texas politics long denied to blacks."

Narrow though this foundation was, Mexican Americans used it to build up their political strength. Long before the Voting Rights Act, Texas was an incubator of Mexican-American political talent. President Clinton's first and most visible Hispanic cabinet appointee, HUD Secretary Henry Cisneros, is merely the latest in a long line of nationally visible Mexican-American leaders to have emerged from the state. And Texas has been the point of origin for virtually every important Mexican-American organization this century: the League of United Latin American Citizens (LULAC), the American G.I. Forum, the Raza Unida Party, the Mexican American Legal Defense and Educational Fund, and the Southwest Voter Registration Education Project.

The obvious contrast is with California, where, despite a much more benign social and economic environment, Mexican Americans have enjoyed far less political success in terms of officeholding, public sector employment, and the number and quality of leaders and organizations. Greater social and economic opportunities in California have meant that fewer energies have been channeled into collective political efforts there, more into individual advancement. Moreover, the money- and media-dominated politics of California have long made it harder for a disadvantaged group like Mexican Americans to break into the political system.

The ironies are manifest. Although it was Texas's history of discrimination against Mexican Americans that laid the basis for including Hispanics under the Voting Rights Act in 1975, and although that year the law (section 5) covered Hispanics throughout Texas, while covering Hispanics in only a few rural counties in California, Mexican Americans in Texas were much more potent politically than their California cousins.

With the 1982 amendments, all of California (indeed, all of the nation) was brought under the Voting Rights Act. Since then, several new Hispanic seats across the Southwest can be attributed to it. Yet the relative political weakness of Mexican Americans in California has not changed. In Texas, the Voting Rights Act took the lid off a pot that was already boiling, allowing Mexican Americans there to achieve their political potential. In California, by contrast, that potential was much less developed. The lid may be off, but there is not much cooking.

Voting Rights Success Stories?

To be sure, the Voting Rights Act has increased the number of Mexican-American officeholders throughout Texas. The threat of a Voting Rights Act suit caused the San Antonio City Council to shift from at-large to single-member districts, resulting in an enlarged and stable Mexican-American plurality on that body. And a suit in Houston led to a reorganized city council and a gain of seats by Mexican Americans. Similar stories unfolded in other cities and towns across Texas. Yet many of those changes were already pending, because of the growing political clout of Mexican Americans.

In California the Voting Rights Act has also added to the number of Mexican-American officeholders, including breakthroughs onto the Los Angeles City Council and County Board of Supervisors. But the gains so achieved are less than meets the eye. For example, in the newly created district from which Gloria Molina was elected to become the first Mexican-American county supervisor since 1875, less than 5 percent of the approximately 1.8 million residents voted. Reflecting surprisingly low interest in an election that received national and world attention, this figure also reflects the low proportion of Hispanics eligible to vote in Los Angeles. When created in 1990, Molina's First District had 707,651 voting-age citizens, compared with the predominantly Anglo Third District, which had 1,098,663. Hispanics constituted 71 percent of Molina's district's overall population and 59 percent of its voting-age citizens, but just 51 percent of its registered voters. Indeed, barely 27 percent of the Hispanic Core from which Molina's district was created were voting-age citizens.

The problem is that such districts are so packed with illegal immigrants and other noncitizens ineligible to vote that they are virtual rotten boroughs. To be sure, the result is more Hispanic elected officials. But these officials are certainly not viewed by their Anglo counterparts as colleagues capable of delivering substantial blocks of voters. Indeed, by concentrating noncitizens in such highly visible districts, the problem of low Hispanic political participation gets highlighted, and the stereotype of Hispanics as politically passive gets reinforced. Moreover, by fostering the impression that significant political power is being acquired, these districts reduce the pressure for more gains, both political and substantive.

Many argue that more Mexican-American officeholders result in increased rank-and-file participation. But the evidence from Los Angeles suggests otherwise. For Voting Rights Act–fostered districts seduce Mexican-American officeholders into a numbers game. Habituated to the passivity of their many nonvoting constituents, but unable to rest content with their relatively weak positions in a dynamic social and political system, such officials have come to rely on increasing numbers of Hispanics (regardless of their eligibility to vote) as the means of maximizing their influence. For, according to the affirmative-action logic that now pervades our political culture, steadily increasing numbers of Mexican immigrants automatically translate into demands for more Hispanic employees and elected officials.

Yet high levels of immigration are not necessarily in the interest of Mexican Americans generally. Immigration from Mexico certainly undercuts them economically, especially those with low skills and wages. And immigrants create political problems. They are certainly not easy to organize for political goals, and massive immigration creates so much instability and transience that political efforts become far more difficult. In precincts where noncitizens equal or outnumber potential voters, registration drives resemble the proverbial hunt for a needle in a haystack. The search soon becomes as tiresome as it is inefficient—and expensive.

The resulting dynamic is precisely the opposite of what is often argued—that Mexican-American leaders seek to control their constituents by isolating them in barrio enclaves. On the contrary, these leaders understand the powerful forces that are drawing their

people into America's mainstream. Their goal is therefore not control over constituents, but over agendas. And for those seeking to portray Mexican Americans as a disadvantaged, discriminated-against minority, the continuing arrival of poor, uneducated immigrants serves precisely this purpose.

In sum, the political weakness of Mexican Americans today, especially in California, but also in Texas and elsewhere, is explained less by the historical grievances on which the Voting Rights Act is predicated than by the group's high proportion of noncitizens.

The Wrong Answer to the Real Problem

But if noncitizenship is the critical barrier to Mexican-American political advancement, how have we come to rely so singlemindedly on the Voting Rights Act? In the first instance, it responds to Mexican Americans who feel that their grievances against this society are every bit as pressing as those of black Americans. More mundanely, in a complicated and often intractable world, elective posts have become one of the tangible, measurable goods that Mexican-American leaders can deliver to their people.

Moreover, the Voting Rights Act serves the needs of various Anglo elites. Republicans, for example, support implementation of the act because packing Hispanics into specified districts results in safer Anglo—that is, Republican—districts. And Voting Rights Act–induced rotten boroughs permit Democratic leaders to respond to the aspirations of a disadvantaged group without much risk of mobilizing tens of thousands of new voters who would complicate the difficulty of assembling successful coalitions.

Even among those motivated by genuine concern, the Voting Rights Act, as applied to Mexican Americans, smacks of a legalistic quick fix for elites impatient with the real obstacles to this group's political advancement. The impatience of Mexican-American leaders is understandable. That of Anglo elites is more perplexing, but traceable to a lesson absorbed during the civil rights turmoil of the 1960s: if tolerance is a virtue, so is impatience. At least, having once been roundly, and justifiably, criticized for counseling patience to victims of racial discrimination, such elites are determined not to make the same mistake again.

Yet impatience may be ill advised when dealing with the problems of recent immigrants. It inevitably leads to comparative victimology, which unfortunately risks exacerbating tensions among all groups, especially between blacks and Latinos. Moreover, impatience communicates the wrong message to new arrivals and risks raising unrealistic expectations, which may have been reflected among the Latino rioters last year in Los Angeles. Not only does the Voting Rights Act falsely teach that political power can be willed into being by well-meaning elites, it leads all of us to forget what a long and arduous process it is for immigrants to become full participants in American life. Indeed, we now seem incapable of even waiting for these immigrants to settle in and adapt to their new home before declaring them to be victims of a regime that fails to include them.

For Mexican Americans the Voting Rights Act is at best a palliative. At worst, it reflects the most egregious opportunism of the 1980s, when we refused to consider the consequences, political or economic, of unlimited immigration. But now that all these people are here, and their numbers continue to grow, we need to find more effective, and less divisive, ways of bringing them into our political system.

Asian Americans

The following collection of articles on Asian Americans invites us to reflect on the fact that the United States is related to Asia in ways that would seem utterly amazing to the worldview of the American founders. The expansion of the American regime across the continent, the importation of Asian workers, and the subsequent exclusion of Asians from the American polity are signs of the tarnished image and broken promise of refuge that America extended and then revoked. The Asian world is a composite of ethnicities and traditions ranging from the Indian subcontinent northeastward to China and Japan. Thus the engagement of the United States beyond its continental limits brought American and Asian interests into a common arena now called the Pacific Rim. The most recent and perhaps most traumatic episode of this encounter was the conflict that erupted in 1941 at Pearl Harbor in Hawaii. Thus examining the Asian relationship to America begins with the dual burdens of domestic exclusion and war.

The cultural roots and current interaction between the United States and Asia form a complex of concerns explored in the unit articles. Understanding the culture matrices of Asian nations and their ethnicities and languages initiates the process of learning about the Asian emigrants and the peopling of America by persons that for many reasons decided to leave Asia to seek a fresh beginning in the United States.

The population growth of Asian Americans since the immigration reform of 1965, the emergence of Japan and other Asian nations as international fiscal players, and the image of Asian American intellectual and financial success have heightened interest in this ethnic group in the United States. Recent devastation of Korean American neighborhood stores in urban centers and the strategies of political, economic, and professional mobility chosen by Asian Americans are debated within these communities and in various public forums. This aftermath of conflict and plethora of analysis has riveted attention to the ethnic factor.

The details of familial and cultural development within Asian American communities comprise worlds of meaning that are a rich source of material from which both insights and troubling questions of personal and group identity emerge. Pivotal periods of conflict appear to be moments in the drama of the American experience that provide an occasion for learning as much about ourselves and about one of the newest clusters of ethnicities—the Asian Americans.

Looking Ahead: Challenge Questions

The public passions generated during World War II have subsided and anti-Japanese sentiment is no longer heard. Is this statement true? Why?

Under what circumstances and toward which nations could the snarls of ethnic hatred be renewed?

What are the attitudinal and institutional obstacles to inclusions?

Can inclusiveness as an American value be taught? What approaches are most promising?

Unit 5

Asian Americans Don't Fit Their Monochrome Image

Moon Lee

Special to The Christian Science Monitor

BOSTON

Demographers project that by the year 2000, 10 million people of Asian and Pacific Islander descent will live in the United States. By 2020, the number is expected to reach 20 million. Yet many Americans know little about the fastest growing segment of the population.

Ironically, the relative invisibility of Asian Americans is exacerbated by their widespread image as the "model minority"—hard-working, intelligent people who have made it in America.

The model-minority image is often misleading, however. It is a myth that has hurt the Asian population, says J. D. Hokoyama, president of Leadership Education for Asian Pacifics (LEAP), a Los Angeles organization founded to develop new leaders in the Asian and Pacific Islander community.

A sizable percentage of the Asian American population is facing poverty, joblessness or underemployment, and lack of access to needed social services, according to a report this year by the LEAP Asian Pacific American Public Policy Institute and the UCLA Asian American Studies Center.

Asian Americans are not always treated in a model way. "Contrary to the popular perception that Asian Americans are a 'model minority,' . . . [they] face widespread prejudice, discrimination, and denials of equal opportunity," says a 1992 report of the US Commission on Civil Rights.

'Portrayal [of Asians as a model minority] has not been very fair because the community is so complex.'
—**Diane Yen-Mei Wong**

Monona Yin, director of development and public policy for the Committee Against Asian American Violence, based in New York City, says that 131 cases of bias-related crime against Asian Americans in New York were reported between 1987 and 1992. Many other hate-crime incidents go unreported, Ms. Yin says.

LEAP's Mr. Hokoyama sees, in part, a hidden agenda behind the positive stereotyping of Asian Americans. The model-minority image emerged, he contends, in the mid-1960s—a time of racial unrest, when some whites wanted to discredit the growing militancy and demands for social justice by African Americans.

"In general, the portrayal [of Asians as a model minority] has not

been very fair because the community is so complex, and it's much easier to just resort to stereotypes than to deal with the reality of those complexities," says Diane Yen-Mei Wong, former executive director of the Asian American Journalists Association and a consultant to Unity '94, a coalition of four national minority journalism associations.

Stereotypes are always based upon some aspect of truth that is blown out of proportion, says Henry Der, a San Francisco activist and executive director of Chinese for Affirmative Action.

For instance, while it is true that many Asian American youths are successful in school, many other Asian students drop out, Ms. Wong says.

Phuong Do, leadership-program coordinator for the Indo China Resource Action Center, an advocacy and community-resource organization for Southeast Asian refugees in Washington, says schools do not pay attention to the needs of Asian students. "They don't see them as people in need," she says.

There are also differences in socioeconomic levels between the established Asian minorities and the recent immigrants and refugees, Hokoyama says.

Recent arrivals, such as the Southeast Asian refugees—Vietnamese, Cambodians, Laotians, and Hmongs—tend to be in a much more precarious economic and psychological state than established groups such as the Japanese, Chinese, Filipinos, and Koreans. Most members of the established Asian groups emigrated to America willingly, Hokoyama points out; whereas many members of the more recent groups fled to the US to save their lives, with only the possessions they could carry.

"Refugees have an even more difficult time . . . understanding this new system. It's the same as if we [Americans] had to move to Ethiopia," he says.

Yet both groups face the same problem when it comes to violence, Wong says. "Hit us with a baseball bat and it doesn't matter if you're a Japanese American, Korean American, or a foreigner, if you are a target of some kind of [anti-]Asian hatred."

Hokoyama says many people think that all Asians are the same. Yet the term Asian and Pacific Islander—a government classification—embraces 59 groups, each with its own language, customs, and culture, he notes.

Mr. Der says society has changed from 25 to 30 years ago, when Asians felt they had to assimilate in order to be accepted. The melting pot theory

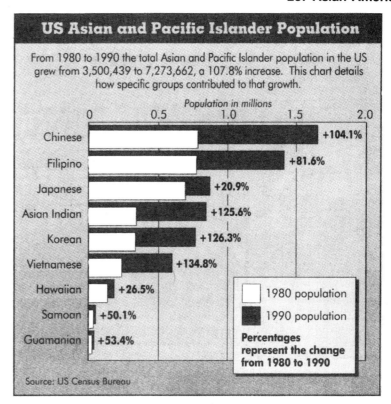

US Asian and Pacific Islander Population

From 1980 to 1990 the total Asian and Pacific Islander population in the US grew from 3,500,439 to 7,273,662, a 107.8% increase. This chart details how specific groups contributed to that growth.

Population in millions

Chinese	+104.1%
Filipino	+81.6%
Japanese	+20.9%
Asian Indian	+125.6%
Korean	+126.3%
Vietnamese	+134.8%
Hawaiian	+26.5%
Samoan	+50.1%
Guamanian	+53.4%

☐ 1980 population
■ 1990 population

Percentages represent the change from 1980 to 1990

Source: US Census Bureau

has "gone down the tube," he says. "To be an American, you don't have to shed your culture," he says.

Yet Hokoyama says that, although Asians have been in the US a long time, they are not considered American. The third-generation Japanese American says people ask him, "Where are you from?" When he answers, "Los Angeles," he says they ask again, meaning "What foreign country are you from."

THE VICTIMIZATION OF ASIANS IN AMERICA

Gary Y. Okihiro

Gary Y. Okihiro is associate professor of history and director of the Asian American Studies Program at Cornell University in Ithaca, New York.

Asked which of the country's ethnic minorities has been subjected to the most discrimination and the worst injustices," observed sociologist William Petersen in 1966, "very few persons would even think of answering: 'The Japanese Americans.' Yet, if the question refers to persons alive today, that may well be the correct reply. Like the Negroes, the Japanese have been the object of color prejudice. Like the Jews, they have been feared and hated as hyperefficient competitors. And more than any other group, they have been seen as the agents of an overseas enemy. Conservatives, liberals and radicals, local sheriffs, the federal government and the Supreme Court have cooperated in denying them their elementary rights—most notoriously in their World War II evacuation to internment camps."

Writing in the aftermath of the 1965 Watts riot in Los Angeles, Petersen noted that normally the treatment accorded to America's Japanese would have created a "problem minority," like blacks, characterized by low incomes, poor health and education, high crime rates, and unstable families. Race prejudice, inferior schools, and social ostracism, common wisdom argued, tended to produce a "cumulative degradation" such that even after a formal end to segregation and discrimination, "the minority's reaction to them is likely to be negative—either self-defeating apathy or a hatred so all-consuming as to be self-de-

structive. For all the well-meaning programs and countless scholarly studies now focused on the Negro, we barely know how to repair the damage that the slave traders started."

But the history of Japanese Americans, countered Petersen, challenges that generalization about America's minorities. "Every attempt to hamper their progress resulted only in enhancing their determination to succeed. Even in a country whose patron saint is the Horatio Alger hero, there is no parallel to this success story." Moreover, Petersen claimed, "by any criterion of good citizenship that we choose, the Japanese Americans are better than any other group in our society including native-born whites." In an allied report some five years after Petersen, *Newsweek* declared that Japanese Americans had "outwhited the whites."

Indeed, Asian Americans as a whole—not just Japanese Americans— have been held up as America's "model minority." In an article published in the same year as Petersen's essay, *U.S. News & World Report* praised Chinese Americans' success: "Visit Chinatown U.S.A.," the report contended, "and you find an important racial minority pulling itself up from hardship and discrimination to become a model of self-respect and achievement in today's America." And more recent articles—in *Newsweek, Time,* the *New Republic,* the *New York Times Magazine,* and *Fortune*—add Koreans, Asian Indians, and Southeast Asians to the list of Asian Americans who have succeeded in overcoming adversity and prejudice.

All those reports are built upon the

basic argument that although Asian Americans were victims of war and inhumanity, race prejudice and hatred, poverty and injustice, they overcame those obstacles through their culture—their family and ethnic solidarity, religion and work ethic, morals and values. As put by Petersen, the Japanese "could climb over the highest barriers our racists were able to fashion in part because of their meaningful links with an alien culture. Pride in their heritage and shame for any reduction in its only partly legendary glory— these were sufficient to carry the group through its travail." Asians, because of their physical appearance, their single-minded drive to succeed, their willingness to defer immediate gratification for future gains, their ethnic solidarity, their ties to Asia, were victimized in America by racists, white workers, labor leaders, politicians, and the yellow press.

INSTANCES OF ANTI-ASIAN ACTIVITY

When the first Chinese migrants arrived in the mid-nineteenth century, various laws and ordinances were passed to restrict their economic, political, and social advancement. California, where most of America's Asians lived and worked, passed in 1850 the Foreign Miner's Tax, which, although applied equally to all noncitizen miners, was directed especially at the Chinese, who paid nearly all of the $5 million raised through that tax between 1850 and 1870. Cities and counties passed a number of anti-Chinese measures, such as the 1870 "pole ordinance" in San Francisco, which prohibited the use of poles on sidewalks to carry objects, and the 1874 "laundry ordinance" which taxed Chinese laundries fifteen dollars per quarter for not using horse-drawn vehicles. California's 1879 constitution gave power to cities and towns to segregate Chinese residences and denied employment to Chinese for any state, county, or city public works projects. In 1913, California passed the alien land law, which denied Asians the ability to own land, and during the 1920s tightened those restrictions, prohibiting Asians from renting land or engaging in sharecropping.

Those economic constraints were backed by political disabilities and sanctions. In 1854, the California Supreme Court ruled that Asians, like American Indians and African Americans before them, could not testify in court for or against whites, who, according to the court, had to be protected from the "corrupting influences of degraded castes." Perhaps most importantly, Asians were denied naturalization rights for about one hundred years, from the 1850s to 1952, and as perpetual aliens could neither participate in nor have a voice in the governing of their lives. And in a series of laws and agreements, Asian immigration was curtailed in 1882 for Chinese, 1908 for Japanese, 1924 for Koreans and Asian Indians, and 1934 for Filipinos.

Through antimiscegenation laws that prohibited marriage between Asians and whites, actions that initiated separate "Oriental" schools, and codes that enforced residential segregation, the social separation and inferiority of Asians was sanctioned and applied by state and local government. Even in Hawaii where intermarriage was commonplace among certain classes of Hawaiians, whites, and Asians, a system of segregated schools beginning in 1920 provided unequal education for Asians and whites. And in San Francisco, where Asian parents saw the classroom as the gateway to success for their children, the board of supervisors warned: "Meanwhile, guard well the doors of our public schools, that they [the Chinese] do not enter. For however hard and stern such a doctrine may sound, it is but the enforcement of the law of self-preservation ... [to] defend ourselves from this invasion of Mongolian barbarism."

PRÉCIS

Bigotry against Asian Americans has been a noisome undercurrent in U.S. history that has generally been masked by the tide of discrimination against blacks and Jews.

During the nineteenth and twentieth centuries, Asians were discriminated against through laws that restricted their economic and sociopolitical advancement, through antimiscegenation ordinances that prohibited marriage between Asians and whites, through actions that initiated separate "Oriental" schools, and through codes that enforced residential segregation.

But Asian Americans fought back through the courts. Their vigorous challenge of separate-but-equal schooling, for example, was part of the reason for the dismantling of segregation spearheaded by the historic 1954 *Brown v. Board of Education* Supreme Court ruling.

Sadly, anti-Asian feeling is not a thing of the past. It has been manifested in contemporary America in such ways as the racially motivated 1982 murder of Vincent Chin, a Chinese American, outside a Detroit bar; the 1990 beating and killing of fifteen-year-old Vietnamese American Hung Truong in Houston by two white teenagers who shouted "white power" as they chased Truong; and the apparent informal quota set in the admission of Asian American students at universities including Harvard, Yale, Princeton, Brown, and Stanford.

It is valuable to remember that the victimization of any group reduces the humanity and hence freedoms of both victims and victimizers.

Those institutionalized barriers erected for "self-preservation" encouraged and reflected social practices such as consumer boycotts against Asian restaurants and Asian-produced goods made in America like cigars and shoes, and job discrimination that led to the underemployment of highly qualified Asian Americans. College graduates with education and engineering degrees could not find work in the professions for which they had trained, causing discouragement among some of those trapped within the ethnic economic ghetto. "I am a fruitstand worker," wrote a Japanese American in 1937. "It is not a very attractive nor distinguished occupation. ... I would much rather it were doctor or lawyer ... but my aspiration of developing into such [was] frustrated long ago. ... I am only what I am, a professional carrot washer."

Politicians and political parties gained electoral support by anti-Asian rhetoric and platform planks, as in the

5. ASIAN AMERICANS

1910 California elections when the Democratic, Republican, and Socialist parties all ran campaigns featuring anti-Japanese positions, leading one historian to declare that Asians were the "indispensable enemy." Similarly, Asians supplied newspaper editors, novelists, and filmmakers with caricatures of derision such as the obsequious John Chinaman and of villainy such as "the yellow peril incarnate," the evil genius Fu Manchu. A white moviegoer during the 1920s described the impact of those popular images: "A picture whose name I have forgotten comes back to me often, or rather just one part, that of the villain, a sleek, treacherous Chinese. He was employed to do the 'dirty work.' A white man had been murdered, and the picture showed the Chinese with a knife going into the man's room. Shortly after, he came out, with a villainous, bloodthirsty, satisfied look that haunts me now, ten or more years after. Then the American, stabbed, dead, was shown."

Physical violence was perhaps the logical end result of institutionalized and practiced racism. The objects of our fear were reduced to mere animals, nonhumans, the "degraded castes"—"Chinks,"

"Japs," "gooks"—who could be removed with scant legal or moral consequences. A California legislative committee reported in 1862: "Your committee was furnished with a list of eighty-eight Chinamen, who are known to have been murdered by white people, eleven of which number are known to have been murdered by Collectors of Foreign-Miner's License Tax—sworn officers of the law. But two of the murderers have been convicted and hanged. Generally they have been allowed to escape without the slightest punishment."

A white mob descended on Los Angeles' Chinatown in 1871, looted and burned businesses, and lynched about eighteen Chinese, and in 1885, whites in Rock Springs, Wyoming, massacred about thirty Chinese workers. Filipinos were threatened with mob violence from Washington to California, and in 1930, whites rioted in Watsonville, California, and killed one Filipino. Chinese were forcibly driven en masse from mining areas in California during the 1850s and from that state's Shasta County in 1855 and Humboldt County in 1885; Japanese workers were expelled from Turlock, California, in 1921; Filipinos were encour-

aged by the U.S. government to "repatriate" to the Philippines in 1935; and all of the Japanese along the West Coast were removed from their homes in 1942.

Asians were indeed victimized, or at least marked, by both individual whites and groups of them. They were the objects of institutionalized and practiced economic, political, and social repression, and they were the targets for physical violence and expulsion. But all that seems to have been a thing of the past. Like all immigrants, Asians encountered initial misunderstanding and hostility that over time was resolved as they adapted to the new environment and whites learned to accept them. Thus, today we rarely think of Asians as victims in America, except perhaps as the targets of looters in Los Angeles this past year, and we even believe that Asian Americans have become so successful in overcoming the barriers of race prejudice that they no longer bear the stigma of "minority." Asian Americans, accordingly, are not usually included within affirmative action programs or special assistance grants and contracts. They are the latest arrivals, in a long string of such arrivals, in America's promised land. The dream lives on.

■ **The McCarran-Walter Immigration Act of 1952 removed bars to citizenship for first-generation Japanese.**

THE ASIANS PROTEST THE BIGOTRY AGAINST THEM

But the arrival of Asians was less a matter of time than a consequence of intense and conscious effort. Asians were not simple victims of exclusion; they actively and, yes, loudly protested their victimization in their struggle to secure the promise of American democracy. Too easily Asians were dismissed as quiet and long-suffering in their repression. Too readily their angry voices and raised fists were ignored. Too comfortably they were contrasted with African Americans and Hispanics, whose responses to victimization have been characterized as "either self-defeating apathy or a hatred so all-consuming as to be self-destructive." Asians, like other minorities, resisted the binds that constrained them.

"No nation can afford to let go its high ideals," warned Yan Phou Lee in 1889, writing about the 1882 Chinese Exclusion Act, continuing,

The founders of the American Republic asserted the principle that all men are created equal, and made this fair land a refuge for the whole world. Its manifest destiny, therefore, is to be the teacher and leader of nations in liberty. Its supremacy should be maintained by good faith and righteous dealing, and not by the display of selfishness and greed. But now, looking at the actions of this generation of Americans in their treatment of other races, who can get rid of the idea that that Nation, which Abraham Lincoln said was conceived in liberty, waxed great through oppression, and was really dedicated to the proposition that all men are created to prey on one another? How far this Republic has departed from its high ideal and reversed its traditional policy may be seen in the laws passed against the Chinese.

In 1909, on the Hawaiian island of Oahu, about seven thousand Japanese sugar plantation workers went on a four-month-long strike against the racial and wage hierarchies of the white planters. Japanese, for instance, were paid $18 a month, while Portuguese and Puerto Ricans doing the same work received monthly salaries of $22.50. "Is it not a matter of simple justice, and moral duty to give [the] same wages and same treatment to laborers of equal efficiency, irrespective of race, color, creed, nationality, or previous condition of servitude?" they reasoned. And eleven years later, during the 1920 sugar strike, some three thousand Japanese and Filipino men, women, and children marched through the streets of downtown Honolulu, carrying portraits of President Abraham Lincoln, who symbolized to them the liberator of other plantation workers and the personification of freedom and equality. Hawaii's white oligarchy drew a different conclusion to the protest march, as articulated by the *Honolulu Star-Bulletin*: "Americans do not take kindly to the spectacle of several thousand Asiatics parading through the streets with banners flaunting their hatred of Americanism and American institutions and insulting the memory of the greatest American president since Washington."

Japanese and Mexican sugar beet field workers in Oxnard, California, joined to form the historic Japanese-Mexican Labor Association (JMLA) in 1903. Under a Japanese president and Mexican secretary, the union struck for higher wages and an end to labor contractor commissions and the company store monopoly. During the monthlong confrontation, a Mexican striker was shot and killed and two Japanese were wounded. The JMLA ultimately won all of its demands and applied for a charter from the American Federation of Labor. Despite a membership that exceeded thirteen hundred or 90 percent of the entire work force in Oxnard, the JMLA was offered a charter on the condition that it expelled all Asians from its membership. The union's secretary, J.M. Lizarras, censured the AFL's Samuel Gompers: "We would be false [to the Japanese] and to ourselves and to the cause of Unionism, if we … accepted privileges for ourselves which are not accorded to them [Asians]." Workers should unite, wrote Lizarras, "without regard to their color or race."

In addition to confronting racism and inequality in the workplace, Asians used the courts to protect whatever rights were afforded to them by the constitutional guarantee of equal protection. The Chinese, like African Americans barred from schools for whites, were segregated into "colored" or "Oriental" schools. Some, however, tried to obtain an equal education by integrating the public schools. In 1884, two years after passage of the Chinese Exclusion Act, Mamie, the American-born daughter of Chinese migrants Joseph and Mary McGladery Tape, attempted to enroll at the Spring Valley Primary School in San Francisco. Principal Jennie Hurley turned away the eight-year-old, and Mamie, her brother, and four other Chinese boys had to attend the Chinese Primary School under a state mandate that read: "Trustees shall have power to exclude children of filthy or vicious habits, or children suffering from contagious or infectious diseases, and also to establish separate schools for children of Mongolian or Chinese descent. When such separate schools are established Chinese or Mongolian children must not be admitted to any other schools."

Although San Francisco's school superintendent praised the legislation as "not a question of race prejudice," Mary McGladery Tape disagreed. In a letter to the board of education, she wrote:

I see that you are going to make all sorts of excuses to keep my child out off the Public Schools. Dear sirs, Will you please tell me! Is it a disgrace to be born a Chinese? Didn't God make us all!!! What right! have you to bar my children out of the school because she is a Chinese Descend.… I will let the world see sir What Justice there is When it is govern by the Race prejudice men! Just because she is of the Chinese descend, not because she don't dress like you because she does. Just because she is descended of Chinese parents I guess she is more of a American then a good many of you that is going to prevent her being Educated.

About three decades later, nine-year-old Martha Lum was turned away from the white school in Bolivar County, Mississippi. The school superintendent required that she attend the school for "colored" children, but Gong Lum, Martha's father, challenged that decision through the courts. The case reached the U.S. Supreme Court, where in 1927 Chief Justice William Howard Taft wrote for a unanimous court that states were within their power to institute segregated facilities for their citizens as decided in the landmark 1896 decision of *Plessy v. Ferguson*, which affirmed the "separate but equal" doctrine. That central tenet of segregation would be overturned in the 1954 *Brown v. Board of Education* ruling, wherein both *Plessy v. Ferguson* and *Gong Lum v. Rice* played prominent roles.

Meanwhile, in 1920 Hawaii's legislature authorized the Department of Public Instruction to issue and revoke operating permits to foreign-language schools; to test and certify language school teachers, who were required to have knowledge of the "ideals of democracy, American history and institutions and the English language"; and to regulate the curriculum, textbooks, and hours of operation of those schools. Moving beyond the act's regulatory intent, the department sought to eliminate the territory's 143 Japanese-language schools, and on December 28, 1922, some 87 language schools joined in a petition testing the constitutionality of the legislative mandate.

The constitutional challenge reached the U.S. Supreme Court, where the Japanese-language school petitioners won a unanimous decision in their favor on February 21, 1927. Despite the "grave problems" of a "large alien population in the Hawaiian Islands," the court ruled, parents had the right to determine the education of their children and the state had to observe limits in curtailing the rights and power of individuals. At a mass meeting the following month, five thousand test-case supporters passed a series of resolutions, including: "We reaffirm our confidence in the friendship and good-will of the American people, and reassert our pride in the fact that our children are American citizens"; and "we emphatically reaffirm our continued loyalty to America and our desire to rear our children as loyal, patriotic and useful citizens of the United States." Kinzaburo Makino, a leader in that successful challenge, told the gathering that the litigation was "the right of a people living in a free democracy to seek legal clarification regarding constitutionality of their laws," but cautioned, "we must never forget that we have to stand up for our rights as guaranteed under the Constitution."

The Asian American civil rights move-ment—as we might characterize the drive for inclusion—mainly sought to ensure and expand the guarantees of equal protection under the Fourteenth Amendment. In 1879, because of a suit filed by Ah Kow Ho, the U.S. Supreme Court ruled that equal protection applied to citizen as well as to noncitizen, but the watershed case in the application of equal protection was *Yick Wo v. Hopkins,* rendered by the Supreme Court in 1886. Between 1873 and 1884, the San Francisco board of supervisors enacted fourteen "laundry ordinances" that employed neutral language for licensing and regulating laundries in the city but were meant for and applied directly to Chinese-owned businesses. Associate Justice Stanley Matthews, writing for a unanimous court, declared that although the laws appeared neutral, their administration discriminated against the Chinese minority and thus violated the equal protection clause of the Fourteenth Amendment. *Yick Wo*, by subjecting to scrutiny the intent and application of the law in determining discrimination, became one of the most cited decisions in considerations of equal protection under the Constitution.

In 1879, because of a suit filed by Ah Kow Ho, the U.S. Supreme Court ruled that equal protection applied to noncitizen as well as to citizen.

THE STRUGGLE FOR CITIZENSHIP

Perhaps more basic than the application of equal protection was the civil rights movement's struggle for the inclusion of Asians within the category of citizen, in the face of sentiment that sought to "whiten" America. Benjamin Franklin, for instance, wrote in 1751 that since whites cleared America of its forests and thereby made it "reflect a brighter light ... why should we ... darken its people? Why increase the sons of Africa, by planting them in America, where we have so fair an opportunity, by excluding all Blacks and Tawneys [aboriginal inhabitants of Asia and the Americas], of increasing the lovely White ...?" Similarly, the Native Sons of the Golden West, a fraternal order of California-born whites, pledged themselves to preserve the state "as it has always been and God Himself intended it shall always be—the White Man's Paradise."

Asians, as we have noted, were "aliens ineligible to citizenship" and as such most could never become naturalized citizens, until 1952. Those born in America, however, were citizens by birth as guaranteed by the Constitution, but even that birthright was questioned and threatened. In 1895, Kim Ark Wong, an American citizen by birth, was refused entry into the United States on the ground that he was not a citizen, having been born to parents who were "aliens ineligible to citizenship." Wong petitioned the courts, and in 1898 the U.S. Supreme Court reaffirmed that "all persons," including Asians, were covered by the Fourteenth Amendment's provision that everyone born within America was a citizen.

The definition and meaning of citizenship and equal protection were severely strained during World War II, when an international contest polarized the domestic positions over nationality and race. Despite their birthright of citizenship, Japanese Americans were always Japanese—a race apart—and bore the blood of the enemy. A February 1942 *Los Angeles Times* editorial explained: "A viper is nonetheless a viper wherever the egg is hatched—so a Japanese-American, born of Japanese parents—grows up to be Japanese, not an American." Lt. Gen. John L. De Witt, the commander in charge of the Army's Western Defense Command, subscribed to that view when in early 1942 he recommended the mass detention of both aliens and citizens, because "the Japanese race is an enemy race and while many second and third generation Japanese born on United States soil, possessed of United States citizenship, have become 'Americanized,' the racial strains are undiluted." A year later, he put it more succinctly: "A Jap is a Jap."

While some in government might have shared the view of Assistant Secretary of War John McCloy that the Constitution was "just a scrap of paper" when the nation's security was at stake, Japanese Americans who formed the Fair Play Committee (FPC) at Heart Mountain concentration camp in Wyoming took seriously the document's guarantees. Begun by Hawaii-born Kiyoshi Okamoto, the committee held open forums to discuss the racism of some camp administrators, the curtailment of free speech, the substandard wages and living conditions, and the injustice of the entire detention program. When Japanese Americans became subject to the draft in January 1944, the committee organized public meetings to discuss the implications of the program.

country as set forth in the Constitution and the Bill of Rights, for on its inviolability depends the freedom, liberty, justice, and protection of all people including Japanese-American and all other minority groups. But have we been given such freedom, such liberty, such justice, such protection? NO!! Without any hearings, without due process of law as guaranteed

such actions are opposed *NOW*, and steps taken to remedy such injustices and discriminations, *IMMEDIATELY*, the future of all minorities and the future of this democratic nation is in danger.

Members of the committee accordingly resolved to refuse to comply with the physi-

■ Japanese Americans, "potential enemies," arrive at an Alien Reception Center in California, 1942.

After the debate, the some two hundred members of the committee agreed that the drafting of *nisei* (or second generation Japanese) from the camps, "without restoration of their civil rights and rectification of the tremendous economic losses suffered by them, was not only morally wrong, but legally questionable." Despite the risk of federal prosecution, the committee defiantly declared:

We, the Nisei have been complacent and too inarticulate to the unconstitutional acts that we were subjected to. If ever there was a time or cause for decisive action, IT IS NOW!

We, the members of the FPC are not afraid to go to war—we are not afraid to risk our lives for our country. We would gladly sacrifice our lives to protect and uphold the principles and ideals of our

anteed by the Constitution and Bill of Rights, without any charges filed against us, without any evidence of wrongdoing on our part, one hundred and ten thousand innocent people were kicked out of their homes, literally uprooted from where they have lived for the greater part of their lives, and herded like dangerous criminals into concentration camps with barb wire fence and military police guarding it, AND THEN, WITHOUT RECTIFICATION OF THE INJUSTICES COMMITTED AGAINST US NOR WITHOUT RESTORATION OF OUR RIGHTS AS GUARANTEED BY THE CONSTITUTION, WE ARE ORDERED TO JOIN THE ARMY THRU *DISCRIMINATORY PROCEDURES* INTO A *SEGREGATED COMBAT UNIT*! Is that the American way? NO! The FPC believes that unless

cal examination or induction notices, to test the constitutionality of their detention.

Branded "disloyal" by the camp administrators, Okamoto and other FPC leaders were removed from Heart Mountain and taken to the Tule Lake concentration camp in California, where dissidents and disloyals were detained. They charged the sixty-three draft resisters and seven members of the FPC's executive council with draft evasion and conspiracy to violate the law. Federal District Judge Blake Kennedy found all sixty-three guilty, sentenced them to three years' imprisonment, and questioned their loyalty. "If they are truly loyal American citizens," he wrote, "they should ... embrace the opportunity to discharge the duties [of citizenship] by offering themselves in the cause of our National Defense." The seven leaders were likewise found guilty by federal District Judge Eugene Rice, who sentenced them to four years at Leavenworth Federal Penitentiary. After the war with Japan had ended, the 10th U.S. Circuit Court of Appeals reversed the convictions of the seven, and on Christmas Eve, 1947, President Harry Truman granted a presidential pardon to all nisei draft resisters. Guntaro Kubota, one of the seven, perhaps best summed up the feelings of the draft resisters, when he told Frank Emi, an FPC member, one day while sitting together in a Leavenworth prison cell: "Emi, I'm really proud to be here with you fellows. If I don't ever do anything else in my life, this will be the proudest thing I ever did because I had a part in your fight for a principle." Remembered Emi, "I will never forget his words. Mr. Kubota passed away at the age of sixty-two."

During testimony before Congress in 1910, Hawaiian Sugar Planters' Association secretary Royal Mead boasted: "The Asiatic has had only an economic value in the social equation. So far as the institutions, laws, customs, and language of the permanent population go, his presence is no more felt than is that of the cattle on the ranges." But Asian Americans, in their drive for civil rights, contested Mead's claim. Exploited, Asian American workers organized themselves into unions "without regard to their color or race," unlike the American Federation of Labor, and went on strike for equal pay "irrespective of race, color, creed, nationality, or previous condition of servitude." Segregated into "colored" schools, Asian American students and their parents challenged the institution and, to paraphrase Mary McGladery Tape, found themselves to be more American than those who would deny children an equal education on the basis of race. Their refusal to accept the undemocratic idea of "separate but equal" would result in the eventual dismantling of segregation, led by the historic 1954 *Brown v. Board of Education* decision, widely remembered today as a triumph only for African Americans.

The Asian American struggle for inclusion within the American community, as migrants and citizens, was principally based upon the constitutional guarantee of equal protection. As neither white nor black, Asians were deemed "aliens ineligible to citizenship" and were denied the privileges of life, liberty, and property, exemplified by their exclusion from the

white courtroom, restrictions placed upon their language and their choice of spouses and livelihoods, and land laws that limited their access to real property. But Asians contested the intent and application of discriminatory legislation, epitomized by *Yick Wo*, and affirmed their birthright of citizenship, as in *Kim Ark Wong*. The language school challenge was an exercise in citizenship and taught Asian Americans that they had to stand up for their rights as guaranteed under the Constitution. The antidemocratic concentration camps spawned the demand for "fair play," with its proponents citing President Abraham Lincoln's statement that "if by the mere force of numbers a majority should deprive a minority of any Constitutional right, it might in a moral point of view justify a revolution" as inspiration for their act of resistance.

THE CONTEMPORARY STRUGGLE AGAINST ANTI-ASIAN PREJUDICE

If Asian Americans are no longer victimized in quite the same way as in the past, it is in large measure because they protested against injustice and inequality in countless fields and factories, courts and legislatures, schools and street corners. And that contest over their civil liberties continues to this day, despite the popular and widespread notion of the "model minority." On a late afternoon in June 1982, in a Detroit bar, two white autoworkers called Vincent Chin, a Chinese American, "Jap," and, according to one account, said: "It's because of you motherf—s that we're out of work." Chin confronted his accusers, a fist fight broke out, and Chin, his two friends, and his antagonists were expelled from the bar. Outside, the autoworkers went to their car, took out a baseball bat, and chased Chin and his companions for about twenty minutes. Once they caught Chin, one of them pinned his arms as the other beat him in the head, chest, and knees with the bat. Chin, who had gone to the bar with friends to celebrate his upcoming wedding, instead died of his wounds four days later.

Vincent, the only son of Lily and Hing Chin, had worked as a draftsman. His father was a World War II veteran, and his great-grandfather on his mother's side had been a railroad worker in the nineteenth century. "I don't understand how this could happen in Ameri-

ca," cried Lily. "My husband fought for this country. We always paid our taxes and worked hard. Before, I really loved America, but now this has made me very angry." She was not alone. When Judge Charles Kaufman sentenced Chin's assailants to three years' probation, a fine of $3,000, and $780 in fees, Asian Americans in large numbers shared her anger. "Three thousand dollars can't even buy a good used car these days," lamented a Chinese American, "and this was the price of a life."

"What kind of law is this? What kind of justice?" asked Lily. "This happened because my son is Chinese. If two Chinese killed a white person, they must go to jail, maybe for their whole lives. ... Something is wrong with this country."

"What disturbs me," observed a Chinese American trade unionist, "is that the two men who brutally clubbed Vincent Chin to death in Detroit in 1982 were thinking the same thoughts as the lynch mob in San Francisco Chinatown one hundred years ago: 'Kill the foreigners to save our jobs! The Chinese must go!' When corporate heads tell frustrated workers that foreign imports are taking their jobs, then they are acting like an agitator of a lynch mob."

Members of the Asian American community formed the American Citizens for Justice, demanded a retrial, and asked the Justice Department to investigate whether Vincent Chin's civil rights had been violated. Based on evidence amassed by the FBI, a grand jury indicted both men in 1983. Only one of Chin's assailants was found guilty by a trial jury the following year; he received a twenty-five-year prison sentence but was released for alcohol abuse treatment after posting a $20,000 bond. Without having spent a single night in jail, Chin's killer was freed on appeal on a technicality that the prosecutors had improperly coached the witnesses, and at a retrial, after a change in venue, he was declared to be innocent.

Despite the defeat, Asian Americans throughout the country had rallied behind the campaign for Vincent Chin, and the lessons they learned from that drive led them to monitor and combat hate crimes and racially motivated attacks and killings. Some of those included the 1987 bludgeoning death of Asian Indian Navroze Mody in Hoboken, New Jersey, by a gang of eleven youths as they chanted "Hindu, Hindu"; the 1989 massacre of five Southeast Asian children in the playground of a Stockton, California, school by a gunman dressed in military garb firing an AK47 assault rifle; the 1989 Raleigh, North Carolina, murder of Chinese American Ming Hai Loo, taken to be a Vietnamese by two whites who had lost a brother in the Vietnam War; the 1990 kicking, beating, and killing of fifteen-year-old Vietnamese American Hung Truong in Houston by two white teenagers who had shouted "white power" as they chased Truong; and the 1992 beating death of nineteen-year-old Vietnamese American Luyen Phan Nguyen at the hands of about fifteen men in Coral Springs, Florida, after he had protested racial slurs made during a party.

The very site of Asian American success—college and university campuses—has also been the site of conflict. On a December 1987 evening, eight Asian American students boarded a University of Connecticut bus to attend a university-sponsored dance. Feona Lee, dressed in a full-length, blue silk gown that she had brought from her home in Hong Kong, felt something land on her hair. "At first I thought it was just water dripping from the bus," she recalled. "Then I felt something warm and slimy hit me in the face."

The object, she realized, was spit. As she looked around to identify her attacker, she was hit again in the eye. "Who did that?" she screamed. About six students, two of whom were football players, continued spitting at her and the other Asian American students who had risen to her defense. "Chinks!" "Gooks!" and "Oriental faggots!" they taunted. A scuffle broke out, and the bus driver yelled, "Sit down and shut up!" The harassment, however, continued for about forty-five minutes until the bus pulled up to the dance hall.

At the dance, the racial insults continued, along with "animal sounds" made by a tormentor as he elbowed his way between the Asian American partners. When they complained to the university resident assistants who were in charge of the dance, the victims were told "not to spoil a good time" or face being "written up," and when they tried to file a complaint with the police, it was lightly dismissed. Laughing, a state trooper exclaimed, "Boy, this guy must have been drunk out of his mind," when one of the students told how a harasser had "mooned" her at the dance. "He asked me, did I see [the man] pull his pants down, and did I see his penis?" she remembered. "I said I did, and he asked

me, do I really know what a penis looks like?" Only after the students threatened to report the incident to the press did the university take seriously their complaint. One of the guilty was expelled from school for a year, and the other, a star football player, was barred from living in the dormitories but allowed to continue playing for the university. That act of racism and the administration's slow and ineffectual response prompted Paul Bock, an Asian American professor, to fast for eight days in protest, and after a faculty investigation into the racial and sexual climate at the university found "deep-seated prejudice," the president issued sterner measures for dealing with those found guilty of harassment.

On another front within the halls of ivy, Asian Americans protested against what they determined to be an informal quota set in the admission of Asian American students at universities, including Harvard, Yale, Princeton, Brown, Stanford, and the University of California at Berkeley and Los Angeles. Beginning in the late 1960s, after the civil rights movement had opened the doors for minorities, Asian American students in large numbers applied to elite institutions. For example, whereas Asian Americans repre-

■ **Refugees leaving Vietnam, 1989.**

sented only 2–4 percent of the total applicants at Harvard, Yale, Princeton, and Brown in the early 1970s, they comprised 10–15 percent a decade later. The admissions protest was sparked by data that revealed that despite their strong record, Asian Americans were admitted at a lower rate than any other group. Following investigations, and while denying discriminatory intent, Brown conceded that Asian Americans had been "treated unfairly," Stanford admitted the possibility of "unconscious bias," and Berkeley's chancellor publicly apologized for "disadvantaging" Asian Americans in the admissions process.

A *Wall Street Journal* and NBC News poll conducted in the spring of 1991 showed that a majority of Americans believed that there was no discrimination against Asian Americans. In fact, some held that Asian Americans received "too many special advantages." Among those "special advantages," no doubt, is the racial privilege of culture whereby Asians are programmed to succeed, especially in economic affairs, as purported by a number of current popular books. But a 1992 report of the U.S. Commission on Civil Rights concluded that "bigotry and violence against Asian Americans remains a serious national problem today," and contrary to popular opinion, "Asian Americans still face widespread prejudice, discrimination, and denials of equal opportunity." Contributory to that anti-Asianism, explained the report, were race prejudice, economic competition, misunderstanding, and resentment over the real or imagined success of Asian Americans. The idea that Asian Americans posed an exemplar to other minorities, the idea that Asians had overcome all barriers to succeed in America, the idea that Asian Americans had even "outwhited the whites," was the very idea that fueled hatred of and denied equal opportunity to that vaunted group.

A prominent aspect of the notion of contemporary success is that despite past victimization, Asian Americans have, through quiet fortitude, patience, and hard work, attained their heralded status. They did not become a "problem minority," nor did they manipulate their victimization for economic or political advantage, or so the argument goes. But the historical record shows that Asians, like African Americans and Latinos, worked the edges, insofar as they were permitted, and struggled mightily to make inroads toward the center and the full promise of American democracy. Asian Americans enjoined the civil rights movement, broadly construed, for legal, economic, and social equality—for inclusion within the definition of America. That effort for inclusion was not a self-serving drive for gain at the expense of others, but expanded the meaning and application of the American creed, and helped to protect and guarantee the civil liberties of all Americans. This we must remember. The victimization of any group reduces the humanity and hence freedoms of both victims and victimizers; equally, the struggle against victimization secures the humanity and freedoms of both victims and victimizers. And therein rests the true significance of minorities, of Asians in America.

Spicier Melting Pot

Asian Americans come of age politically

Susumu Awanohara in Los
Angeles

City schoolboard member Warren Furutani got help from the Blacks and Hispanics he had worked with back in his days as an activist protester. City councilman Mike Woo even learned to speak a few words of Armenian to woo a segment of his electorate.

Business-as-usual for the new breed of Asian American politicians, but unthinkable for many of their parents' generation. To court outsiders, to forge a "vote bank" by making common cause with other Asian American groups, even to stand for election in the first place and risk the "face" loss of defeat—these are all new ideas for many ethnic Asians in the US.

The gambles are starting to pay off, though election results earlier this month showed it is not an easy process. Asian Americans lost in two high-profile state-wide races, but gained a few county and city seats in California. They also made headway in Nevada, taking the secretary of state's office and a state assembly seat. Progress like this makes the two mainstream national parties wake up to Asian Americans as a political factor.

With their economic and social success already established, Asian Americans are now aiming at political "empowerment." Ethnic Asians in the US hotly debate whether it makes sense to construe their disparate communities as a cohesive block. But, taken as a group, they comprise the fastest growing minority in the country.

As such, they are bound to have increasing say in the "minority agenda" in American politics. Yet much of the "agenda" set by the established minorities now devolves upon problems of economic and cultural disadvantage. Blacks press for preferential "affirmative action" access to jobs and schools. Hispanics demand more lenient treatment of illegal immigrants. They also want public education systems to offer Spanish-medium instruction in "core" subjects like science and maths.

Many Asian Americans, at least from the more upwardly mobile "Confucian" cultures and the Indian Subcontinent, feel they have "graduated" beyond such coddling. They advocate strict meritocracy and view concessionary quotas as obstacles, rather than aids to their aspirations.

But the demographics of the Asian Americans themselves are shifting (*see table*). The fastest growing groups are also the most "disadvantaged"—Americans of Philippine and Indochinese extraction, who may be likelier to align with Blacks and Hispanics on "underdog" issues. And Asian Americans of whatever ethnic stripe are quickly mastering the arts of trade-off, compromise and mutual back-scratching which are the essence of US communal politics.

To bolster their political clout, Asian Americans will have to overcome discriminatory obstacles set up against them by American society, as well as cultural inhibitions brought over from their Asian homelands. They must also target those issues on which they can make common cause and downplay the issues that divide them.

But the US political establishment, for its part, is starting to take them seriously. Both major parties now vie for Asian American favour with "outreach" programmes to tap into their potential as a source of votes, campaign financing and—eventually—political talent.

Not that all Asian Americans are political novices. As early as the 1930s, the old China Lobby of Chiang Kai-shek's Kuomintang regime was a force to reckon with in Washington. Japanese Americans waged a long campaign to win an official apology and financial redress for their wartime internment in US detention camps. Three out of the five Asian American federal lawmakers (two Californian congressmen and a senator from Hawaii) are of Japanese extraction.

Still, Asian American activists feel that their group is glaringly under-represented compared with other minorities such as the Blacks, Hispanics and the highly successful Jews. President George Bush has appointed a record number of Asian Americans to federal jobs, but few of them have achieved a high profile.

At the state and local levels, Hawaii has many Asian American elected and appointed officials. But that is only to be expected in the one state where Whites are a minority and Asian Americans account for nearly half the population.

In other major centres of Asian American settlement—California, New York, Illinois, Texas, Washington and Virginia—their political clout still lags far behind their demographic weight. Even in California, whose 3 million Asian Americans comprise nearly a tenth of the population, they account for barely 3% of the voting rolls.

Fewer still actually turn out to vote. No wonder they have yet to put one of their own into the state legislature and boast just a few slots on city and county councils. The top-ranking Asian American in the California administration is the secretary of state, who is in the influential position of supervising elections.

The sheer heterogeneity of Asian Americans makes it hard for them to consolidate political power. They are divided into at least half a dozen major ethnic groups, each of which is further subdivided according to time of arrival, social origins, religious and factional affiliations.

Then, too, Asian Americans still suffer the residual effects of systematic exclusion from the US political process due to racially discriminatory US laws and

From *Far Eastern Economic Review,* November 22, 1990, pp. 30, 32-36. Reprinted by permission of *Far Eastern Economic Review,* Hong Kong.

5. ASIAN AMERICANS

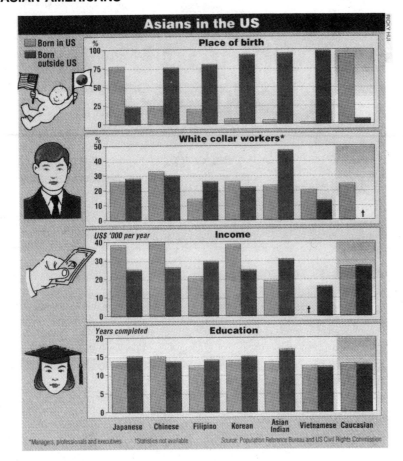

Asians in the US

Born in US
Born outside US

Place of birth

White collar workers*

Income
US$ '000 per year

Education
Years completed

Japanese Chinese Filipino Korean Asian Indian Vietnamese Caucasian

*Managers, professionals and executives   †Statistics not available   *Source*: Population Reference Bureau and US Civil Rights Commission

practices—long since repealed—barring them from naturalised citizenship and franchise.

What is more, many Asian Americans have brought with them from their ancestral lands a tradition of political non-involvement. The Asian immigrant typically fears putting his name to any political programme and would never risk the shame of a defeated candidacy. He thinks politics dirty, but dreads offending those in power.

Politically reticent and splintered though the Asian American community may be, some common concerns have emerged—anti-Asian hate crime, immigration, education, social and occupational discrimination (*see box*). To press their agenda, Asian American leaders emphasise, the community will need much broader participation in US politics.

Asian Americans are kidding themselves if they feel they have "made it" in the US, says Washington state legislator Gary Locke. Until they achieve political parity, their economic and social costs and benefits will be allocated to them by other groups, he says. And in an economic downturn,

such as now looms, an unorganised and powerless minority may be pounced on as an easy scapegoat.

To fend off these hazards, the current buzz-word is "empowerment." How to attain it is the subject of conclaves of Asian American students and voters' organisations. More and more of the Asian American community's best and brightest are now prepared to run for office.

Furutani describes himself as "a protester turned politician." He made the switch, he explains, when he "got tired of demonstrating on the outside, being anti-this or anti-that. You have to go inside to have any clout."

Other Asian American office-holders launched their political careers on more of an inside track, serving as legislative staffers before launching candidacies of their own. "Whispering advice to those who make decisions," says Woo, "I saw I could do at least as well as those whom we served."

These new-breed politicians have become "role models," rasing the community's self-esteem and shattering negative stereotypes. Asian Americans remain touchy about hackneyed characterisations of them as "reserved," "smiling," "myopic," "passive" or "inscrutable."

After the Korean influence-buying scandals of the 1980s, journalist Lee writes, US newspapers "depicted Koreans as sinister aliens. Then almost overnight, we were called a model minority. Now we are taunted and jeered as the exploiters of hapless blacks. We are none of these."

Even more damaging are occupational stereotypes of Asian Americans as good accountants, engineers and doctors, but never as administrators or leaders. US Congressman Robert Matsui recounts how his white peers tried to keep him "in his place" at every stage.

Democrats and Republicans are scrambling over each other to persuade Asian Americans that they can best do what they want to do within the ranks of their respective parties. The "outreach" programme of the Grand Old Party (or GOP, as Republicans like to call themselves) has been particularly active, putting Democrats—traditional champions of minorities—on the defensive.

Among Asian American groups Japanese and Filipinos have been predominantly Democratic, while Korean and Vietnamese, for ideological reasons, have gone largely Republican. In between, Indian Americans lean more toward the Democrats, while Chinese Americans split roughly equally between the two parties. (In presidential elections, Asian Americans tend to back incumbents of whatever party.)

Republicans appeal to conservative Asian Americans with their anti-communism, disdain for welfarism and advocacy of entrepreneurship. They have established the outreach office in GOP national headquarters explicitly aimed at stealing Asian American voters from the Democrats and recruiting Republican candidates from the Asian American community.

One of their most promising recruits is Matthew Fong, a young lawyer running for California state controller. Son of prominent Democrat March Fong, California's secretary of state, the younger Fong enjoyed lavish assistance from the GOP—campaign stumping by federal cabinet members and a full time aide from the national office.

Even so, Fong lost, as predicted, to the Democratic incumbent in November. But the Republicans succeeded in showcasing their commitment to the Asian American community. And insiders tip Fong to bounce back as a possible candidate in the 1992 Congressional elections.

Democrats will not take such challenges lying down. They can point to an undeniably better record on such minority issues as civil rights, immigration, redress for Japanese American internees, equal employment opportunities and health care.

But the party realises it can hardly rest on its laurels. Maeley Tom, a Chinese American and dean of California legislative aides, now sits on the executive committee of the Democratic National Committee. The party also recruited a prominent activist from the Organisation of Chinese Americans to handle its Asian American outreach programme. State assembly candidate Lon Hatamiya got some campaign help from the Democrats in his unsuccessful bid in last month's elections to become California's first Asian American legislator.

California is shaping up as a crucial battleground, both for the national parties and for Asian American aspirations. After the 1990 census results are in, the state will gain seven or eight Congressional seats through reapportionment and redistricting. Given the tenacity of congressional incumbents, the best hope for increased Asian American representation would seem to be creating new districts where they would have an easier time getting elected.

That means targeting areas with high concentrations of Asian American voters and guarding against dilution by other groups. The deadline is fast approaching for specific district line proposals to the state legislature.

Some Asian American groups have already identified two or three possible districts where a third of the population would be ethnically Asian. In the redistricting that followed the 1980 census, Blacks and Hispanics made benchmark gains. Asian Americans now want the same, but in the process, they could clash with other minorities' interests and stir up communal tensions.

The dilemma underscores the delicacy of the balancing act of US ethnic politics for Asian American candidates. It is seldom enough to appeal only to one's own ethnic group for support, particularly for higher level offices with larger constituencies where voters of any particular Asian ancestry cannot account for more than a few percent of the total.

The next best thing is to seek the support of other Asian American groups. But even the block support of all Asian Americans would not be enough to carry the day in most cases. "You just can't win as an Asian candidate" per se, says Hatamiya. In his northern California district of rich farmers, for instance, Asian Americans accounted for only 2% of the votes. Most of the rest were Whites.

Nevertheless, ethnic Asian candidates will continue to play to the Asian American galleries, if for no other reason than to secure the generous campaign finance they provide. At the same time, Asian American politicians must transcend parochial interest to get elected. And once in office, they must attend to the concerns of the different groups which put them there. Too much focus on Asian American causes will earn the ire of non-Asian American supporters, and vice versa.

The answer, says Furutani, is to "bust a gut" and try to satisfy all groups. Scrupulously pursued, this approach could nurture Asian American politicians as truly national, rather than parochial, leaders.

Agreeing on agenda
Rallying point or stumbling block

If Asian Americans are to emerge as a political force, they will need to nurture common concerns around which to rally. Some existing issues have been natural meeting grounds for diverse Asian American groups. Others are potentially divisive.

But, to gain political clout, Asian American groups know they must trade favours with each other and build coalitions. And there is already evidence that they are mastering these political arts. Among the top issues on the Asian American agenda are:

• Redress for the Japanese Americans interned in relocation camps during World War II. Not only Asian Americans, but even Black and Hispanic civil rights groups rallied around this question because the Japanese were able to present it as a constitutional issue of bypassing due process of law on racial grounds.
• Anti-Asian violence and hate crimes, typified by the 1982 murder of Vincent Chin, a Chinese American, in Detroit.

Two white auto plant workers, mistaking Chin for a Japanese, vented their frustration about the plight of the US auto industry by bludgeoning him to death with a baseball bat. Asian Americans, outraged by what it saw as lenient punishment, sought heavier sanctions against the murderers.

National attention has also focused on the boycott of Korean American shopowners by New York City Blacks. Less publicized cases of verbal harassment, vandalism, arson, beatings and killings fill the columns of Asian American newspapers. And things could get worse as recession sets in and the public mood grows uglier. Prodded by Asian American and other minority groups, Congress passed a Hate Crimes Statistics Act this year, requiring the Justice Department to track racially motivated crimes.
• Immigration curbs on Asians is something that all Asian American groups can readily unite against. In the debate leading to the recent passage of the 1990 immigration act, mainstream politicians tried to bridle the tide of Asian and Hispanic arrivals by reviewing the immigration privileges of relatives of naturalised US citizens. Asian American groups, mainly led by Chinese Americans, made common cause with Jews and Mexicans to keep family-based immigration opportunities open.
• Job discrimination for Asian American professionals takes the form of a "glass ceiling"—an invisible barrier that keeps them from ever reaching the topmost rungs of the corporate or social ladder. Studies also suggest that, adjusting for occupation and industry, highly educated, US-born Asian American males earn less than similarly qualified white men.

"Glass ceilings" are, by definition, hard to legislate against. But, at least, measures now before Congress would minimise discrimination against foreign-trained doctors (of whom there are many from India).

Thanks to legal victories in the 1970s, Asian Americans are entitled to "affirmative action" benefits—preferential hiring by such employers as police forces, the media and trade unions where they were adjudged to be under-represented. They are also eligible, as minorities and small businessmen, for "affirmative action" quotas in government procurement.

Getting the traditionally reticent Asians to use the quotas they are entitled to is another matter, but Asian American activists are now taking up the theme. Even the independent Equal Employment Opportunity Commission now includes an Indian American appointee.

• Education is an issue with more divisive potential. Some groups are battling racial college admission ceilings designed to prevent Asian American "over-representation," while others seek preferential "affirmative action" access to schools.

High achievers advocate a strict merit system on the grounds that hard work is the only way to beat societal discrimination. But some groups who feel disadvantaged—Filipino and Vietnamese students at some California campuses, for instance—find it doubly ironic to be excluded from affirmative action programmes on the grounds that Asian Americans are already doing quite well.

Susumu Awanohara

On an uptick
'Model minority' or ethnic grab-bag?

Diverse as they are, statistically, it is debatable whether it makes any sense to speak of Asian Americans as any sort of cohesive group at all. But, if taken in the aggregate, they comprise by far the fastest growing US minority.

Experts project their numbers to grow by the end of the century to around 10 million, or 4% of the US population. By 2010, they will number nearly 13.4 million, or 5% of the population; and 18 million (or 6.4%) by 2050.

The Chinese were the first to arrive in the 19th century to work in the mines, lay down the rail tracks and perform assorted domestic services. The Japanese, Filipinos, and a few Koreans followed, despite laws and practices excluding Asians from civil rights and citizenship.

Fuelled by a 1965 liberalisation of US immigration laws and the refugee backwash of Indochinese wars, Asian immigration has surged again in recent years. The Asian share of US legal immigration soared from 5% in 1931–60 to nearly 50% in the 1980s, exceeding legal immigrants from Latin America.

The 1965 law abolished the national origin quotas (heavily stacked against Asians) in favour of preferences for workers with needed skills and relatives of US residents. Some 120,000 immigrants a year were to be admitted from the Western Hemisphere and 170,000 from the Eastern Hemisphere, with a 20,000 ceiling on nationals of any one country (exclusive of immediate family members of already naturalised immigrants as well as refugees).

Most Asian Americans are clustered in just a few states. Three out of five of them live in California, Hawaii or New York. They comprise nearly half of Hawaii's population and are the second largest minority group in California (after Hispanics). Lately there also has been an influx of Asians into cities like Chicago, Washington DC, Philadelphia, Seattle and Houston.

The academic achievements of Asian American students have stirred both admiration and envy. One estimate has it that nearly half of all US graduate students are Asian Americans. Aside from family pressure and bookish cultural traditions, Asian Americans' scholastic distinction might represent a bid to overcome discrimination through good grades, some experts suggest.

Not all Asian American students are successful, though. Many Indochinese refugees, for instance, faced with a formidable English-language barrier, drop out of school to find only dead-end jobs.

Unemployment, however, is relatively low among all Asian American groups. US-born Asian Americans work in much the same occupations as their White counterparts. But foreign-born Asian American immigrants show different patterns.

On the one hand, immigrants from India, the Philippines and Japan had a higher ratio of top-paying jobs as managers, professionals and executives. On the other hand, a greater proportion of immigrants from China, Vietnam and South Korea found their way into low-paying service jobs.

The average family income for most Asian American groups is at least as high, and usually higher, than that of Whites. One explanation might be that more family members, working longer hours, contribute to the family till. A notable exception has been the Vietnamese, whose average family income is only 60% that of white families.

Susumu Awanohara

Textbook tussle
Demographic shift forces historical reassessment

California is the belwether state where the future of other American states can be observed today. With the influx of Asian Americans and Hispanics, white students have already become a minority in California public schools.

Within the next 15 years, whites are likely to become a minority population in the state. Experts project that whites will eventually become a minority nationwide—perhaps by the mid-21st century.

As the US continues to accept non-European immigrants until no one group commands a majority, minorities are bound to grow stronger and more assertive. But, in its efforts to accommodate the demands of diverse groups, the US risks undermining its commitment to common ideals.

What this could mean for the American self-image is suggested by a recent controversy in California over a new set of history textbooks. A quarter century ago, Sacramento enacted laws requiring all teaching materials to reflect the state's ethnic diversity. But it hardly seemed to make much difference, at least at first: history textbooks continued to focus on the white experience.

Liberal educators and minority advocates complained that the books were increasingly out of touch with the demographic reality of California. By omitting the non-whites' contribution to US nation-building, they argued, the textbooks distorted history, failed to instil pride in minority students and may have fed negative stereotypes of non-whites.

So this year, California invited publishers to submit new history textbooks prepared strictly according to a new set of guidelines. Among other things, the new textbooks were to foster "cultural literacy," so that students could grasp the nation-building contributions of various ethnic groups.

The object was to strike a balance between emphasis on traditional American democratic values, on the one hand, and a new awareness of the racial, cultural and ethnic roots of those who make up the nation.

Seven years ago, the last time the state renewed its history textbooks, 22 publishers sought a piece of California's US$170 million textbook market, the nation's largest. But this year, unwilling to spend the money for new books to meet the state's stringent requirements, all but nine publishers dropped out of the running.

Public hearings and a panel of state-appointed experts (including minorities)

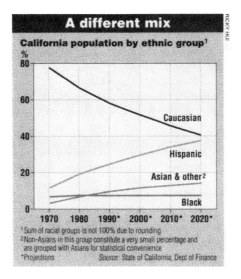

A different mix

California population by ethnic group[1]

Caucasian

Hispanic

Asian & other[2]

Black

1970 1980 1990* 2000* 2010* 2020*

[1] Sum of racial groups is not 100% due to rounding
[2] Non-Asians in this group constitute a very small percentage and are grouped with Asians for statistical convenience
*Projections   Source: State of California, Dept of Finance

further narrowed the short-list down to two: offerings from Houghton Mifflin and Holt Rinehart & Winston, respectively. These are impressive history textbooks by any standard—certainly by any Asian standard. They bend over backwards to be honest, accurate and sensitive.

For example, the eighth grade book by Houghton Mifflin suggests that the teacher challenge students with the question: "How did the treatment of [early] immigrants—ridicule, hostility, violence, job and housing discrimination—compare with the ideals of the Declaration of Independence and the Constitution?"

Later on, the book invites students to comment on the incongruity of a World War II photograph of young Japanese Americans being drafted into the US Army from an internment camp where they were being held on suspicion of disloyalty.

The books elicited a storm of controversy before they were approved. All sorts of interests—women and gays, as well as assorted religious and ethnic groups—wanted their stories told their way, and at length. On the other side of

the spectrum, some critics argued that the new books had already gone too far.

The frantic attempt to include everybody, the critics argued, amounted to effective ethnic and gender quotas on public school curricula. The end result, they warned, could be a "Balkanised" California, splintered into self-centred and mutually hostile groups.

Indeed, Asian Americans can come in conflict with other groups—particularly the larger, more homogeneous and also fast-growing Hispanic community—as they compete for scarce resources. For example, Asian Americans and Hispanics are united in their opposition to a radical English Only movement, led by white conservatives and insisting that all official business must be conducted solely in English. The movement's extremists have tried to suppress the use of foreign languages even in commercial signs and opposed public libraries carrying Asian-language books. But while most minorities uphold bilingualism in principle, Asian American students living in areas with large Hispanic populations often complain that their schools offer Spanish (along with French, German and so on) as a second language but not Korean or Vietnamese.

Optimists counter that California and the nation will hold together and evolve into a harmonious microcosm of the world as it should be—"A More Perfect Union" (as one of the books is entitled, borrowing language from the preamble to the US Constitution). To reach that goal, though, will require a lot more debate on how much multiculturalism is desirable, versus how much—and what sort—of a common American culture.

But, as Asian Americans gain political clout and increasingly assert themselves, the evolving American culture will inevitably incorporate more of their inputs and become "Asianised."

Susumu Awanohara

Scapegoats no more
Japanese Americans caught in trade war cross-fire

Half a century after the US, at the start of World War II, incarcerated Japanese Americans in detention camps without due process of law, the government has acknowledged

its mistake and begun paying compensation to surviving internees. That bittersweet victory was a reminder of how far Japanese Americans have come.

Today, they are arguably the best-as-

similated Asian American community. Still, some of them worry that Japanese Americans could be victimised once again, now that US–Japan relations are deteriorating.

5. ASIAN AMERICANS

The institutions and self-perceptions of the Japanese American community were profoundly affected by the struggle to redress wartime internment. Unorganised demand for redress arose early, but picked up momentum in the radical atmosphere of the civil rights and anti-Vietnam War movements of the 1960s and early 1970s.

Encouraged by official admissions at that time that the World War II internments had been an error, Japanese American activists—notably those of the Japanese American Citizens League (JACL)—began a concerted campaign for more concrete "redress and reparations."

The struggle was painful and divisive for the Japanese American community itself. Accusations were traded on who turned in whom to the FBI as dangerous aliens. Debate was revived on whether Japanese American draft resisters among the internees deserved condemnation or praise. Yet the struggle was also cathartic, particularly for those who spoke of their wartime experiences and feelings for the first time. The fight for redress also renewed the ties between Japanese Americans and other US ethnics: Asian American, Black, Hispanic and Jewish groups supported it.

The humiliation of internment probably made the Japanese Americans more eager to join the US mainstream and become like *hakujin,* or Whites. In this, they have succeeded, more or less.

The assimilationist trend was reinforced by the dwindling of Japanese immigration to the US. As a result, the ratio of US-born Japanese Americans is much higher than for other Asian American groups.

The Japanese Americans enjoy impressive educational achievements, an enviable occupational profile and the highest average family income of all Asian American groups. No wonder they have fewer grievances than newer Asian American arrivals—a possible cause for the occasional Asian American complaint that the Japanese Americans are aloof and fail to make common cause politically.

Many Japanese Americans fret that mounting US–Japan friction over trade investment, technology and security issues could damage relations between Japanese Americans and the mainstream population.

Some alarm bells went off in the community a few years ago when Hawaii, worried about rising Japanese investment in the state's real estate, tried (unsuccessfully) to pass legislation restricting land ownership.

For the most part, though, Japanese Americans have tried to steer clear of US–Japan disputes. Some Japanese Americans may feel they understand Japan's positions on issues and can help articulate them to mainstream America. In the past, they might have been more inclined to serve as a bridge between the two countries. Nowadays, it is riskier.

Besides, Japanese Americans have long nurtured a grudge that Japanese from Japan tend to treat them as inferiors and ignore them when doing business in the US. This gap may have narrowed as the Japanese Americans have gained respectability back in the ancestral homeland through their success.

But, at the same time, younger Japanese Americans have grown more distant from things Japanese. Many of them share the mainstream American exasperation at Japan's perceived "intransigence."

Self-preservation instincts might also help explain some of the Japanese American coolness to the motherland. To seem to be doing Tokyo's bidding is an increasingly risky business, particularly for a Japanese American with any political ambitions.

Whatever latent sympathy they may retain for the Japanese side on bilateral issues, hardly any Japanese Americans can forgive the racist remarks of some Japanese officials. In this, they are motivated not only by fear of racial backlash. As beneficiaries of the US civil rights movement, many Japanese Americans are truly indignant.

How else to react to comments like Japanese Justice Minister Seiroku Kajiyama's recent comparison of foreign prostitutes in Tokyo with Blacks moving into white US neighbourhoods? Both influxes, Kajiyama quipped, "ruin the atmosphere."

Japanese Americans still wince at the recollection of former prime minister Yasuhiro Nakasone's 1986 pronouncement that American knowledge levels trail Japan's because of the admixture of Blacks, Puerto Ricans and Mexicans in the US population. In the same vein is the more recent assertion by Michio Watanabe, a leading politician, that American Blacks have few qualms about defaulting on debts.

Bruce Iwasaki, a member of the National Coalition for Redress and Reparations, wrote in the *Los Angeles Times* lately that "Japanese American progress could not have occurred without the civil rights movement led by African Americans.

"The most heinous single violation of civil liberties inflicted by the US Government in this century was the incarceration of 120,000 Japanese Americans in World War II concentration camps . . . In the decades [since], the Black-led movement against segregation altered America's attitude toward racial bigotry.

"Members of the Congressional Black Caucus were the first to support reparations [for the internees]. Japanese Americans have [Black leaders] to thank for winning redress."

Perhaps the time has now come for Japanese Americans to lend a hand in the re-education of the ancestral homeland, muses JACL president Cressy Nakagawa. Tokyo's abject apologies for ministerial wise-cracks are not enough, he says. They must be accompanied by legislative and educational programmes to overcome racial bigotry and discrimination.

"The difference between the US and Japan is that the US has these programmes and Japan doesn't," Nakagawa points out. He hopes the JACL, with the help of US minority organisations and the Japanese Government, can develop a curriculum on the subject for Japanese schools. He has already approached Japanese Ambassador in Washington Ryohei Murata with the idea.

Susumu Awanohara

BLACK-KOREAN CONFLICT IN LOS ANGELES

DARRELL Y. HAMAMOTO

Darrell Y. Hamamoto teaches at the University of California, Irvine Program in Comparative Culture.

OF THE estimated 820,000 Koreans in the United States, over 164,000 reside in Los Angeles County. One in five Koreans in the Southern California region live in the district of Los Angeles known as "Koreatown." Koreans represent 10 percent of the population of Koreatown with African Americans and Latinos predominating. Along with South-Central Los Angeles, Crenshaw, Hollywood, Mid-Wilshire, Echo Park, and Silver Lake, the Koreatown community bore the brunt of the recent urban rebellion, perhaps the worst civil disturbance of the 20th century.

Prior to 1965, when discriminatory barriers against Asian immigration were lifted, the Korean population in the United States was small. But from 1970 to 1990 the numbers of Koreans soared from 70,598 to 820,000. Since 1980, 33,000 Koreans have entered the country each year, a rate of growth exceeded only by Filipinos and Hispanics. Middle class in origin and highly educated as a group, Korean immigrants have made their mark on the local Los Angeles economy. Although composing only 10 percent of the Koreatown population, Koreans own 42 percent of the commercial lots, 40 percent of office buildings, and 41 percent of all shopping centers within an area ten times larger than Chinatown and Little Tokyo combined. Throughout the 1970s to the present, the Korean American ethnic sub-economy in Los Angeles has flourished in comparison to the sluggish performance of the county at large. But such economic strides have earned the enmity of many Blacks and Latino, while winning the praise of commentators who point to Korean Americans

as a shining example of entrepreneurial capitalism at work.

Nationally, Black-Korean tensions have often escalated into violent incidents. In Brooklyn, New York the Family Red Apple grocery store operated by Bong Jae Jang was boycotted for 16 months by protesters after it was claimed that store employees beat an African American customer they had accused of stealing. The city of Los Angeles was the site of the March 16, 1991 shooting death of 15-

From New York to Los Angeles, the Korean American shopkeeper has been portrayed as the principal antagonist of the ethnic underclass composed of Blacks and Hispanics.

year-old Latasha Harlins by the proprietor of a family-run market, Soon Ja Du. The following November, when Compton Superior Court Judge Joyce A. Karlin sentenced Soon Ja Du to five years probation, the African American community was outraged.

In the popular imagination, the

drama of Black-Korean conflict is played out at mom and pop food and liquor stores. In truth, Korean-owned businesses comprise a diverse range of enterprise including manufacturing, finance, insurance, retail and wholesale trade, construction, and real estate. The popular association of the retail food and liquor trade with Korean Americans no doubt stems from their over representation in this area of business activity. As of 1980, 3.5 percent of all businesses that sell liquor were owned by Koreans although they represented only 0.8 percent of the population in Los Angeles County.

Prior to the mid-1960s, the liquor store trade in South-Central Los Angeles was dominated by Jewish American merchants. The Watts Riots of 1965 precipitated the flight of Jewish American proprietors, who sold their stores cheaply to Blacks. African American proprietors in turn dominated the retail liquor store trade from the late 1960s through the 1970s. The deregulation of liquor prices in 1978 made it difficult for small store owners to maintain already marginal profits. As a consequence, many African American owners sold their stores, often at a good profit, to Korean immigrants who saw small-scale family proprietorships as a point of entry into the economy.

From New York to Los Angeles, the Korean American shopkeeper has been portrayed as the principal antagonist of the ethnic underclass composed of Blacks and Hispanics. A classic example of what sociologists refer to as a "middleman minority," Korean American small business owners serve as an effective buffer between absentee Euro-American capitalist owners and non-white residents living in core urban areas. The Korean American business person is often held up as "proof" of social mobility in a class-bound society, a living denial that race prejudice works as a barrier to economic success. Yet it is a combination of social discrimination and lack of English language competence that forces Korean immigrants into the ethnic enclave economy in the first place.

The myth-making potential of Asian immigrants in the service of U.S. capital already has been exploited by government officials. In June of last year, President Bush addressed a crowd of an estimated 40,000 Asian Americans at Mile Square Park in Fountain Valley, California. The event was billed by the White House as being the first such address delivered specifically to an Asian American audience. Over the past several years, the GOP has sensed a strengthening ideological linkage between its attacks on the welfare state and the growing Asian American immigrant community. Many recent Asian immigrants to the United States embrace such Republican verities as "free enterprise," family-based entrepreneurialism, self-help, and a minimalist definition of government. The anticommunism of Republican leaders and pro-business policies of the conservative regime are additional lures to this rapidly emerging constituency.

As part of the attack on the welfare state, the forces of conservative reaction point to Asian immigrant families as exemplars of the entrepreneurial ideal which eschews federal support in favor of a self-sufficient "localism." It is not uncommon for newspaper accounts to write of "Asian newcomers" who have "provided a fresh injection of economic investment and ingenuity for their new communities." Vietnamese and Korean merchants in particular are praised for their bringing about the "revitalization" of areas that were once in economic decline.

But as Ivan Light and Edna Bonacich observe in their exhaustive study *Immigrant Entrepreneurs: Koreans in Los Angeles 1965-1982* (1991), large-scale U.S. capital looms in the background through the sales and service of national business franchises and by subcontracting piece-work to Korean American manufacturing concerns. The highly competitive garment manufacturing industry is but one example of unequal economic exchange between

Historically, the responses to Asian immigration to the U.S. has ranged from enthusiastic acceptance to violent rejection depending on a given group's relationship to capital.

Korean small business and large U.S. corporations. More importantly, Korean American small businesses provide indirect benefits to large-scale capital by distributing national brand-name products to under served urban populations, reducing labor standards and costs, pioneering new areas of enterprise for eventual takeover by big capital, and perpetuating the myth of ethnic entrepreneurial success within class society.

The calamitous events that followed the not-guilty verdict in the Rodney King trial gives lie to the myth of Asian American entrepreneurial success currently being trumpeted by a number of journalists and academics, including Joel Kotkin, James Fallows, Peter L. Berger, Thomas Sowell, and Dinesh D'Souza. Koreatown was especially hard hit by firebomb attacks and looting, two days and nights of terror which were interpreted by the news media as the almost inevitable result of ongoing conflict between Blacks and Korean Americans. The estimated loss of about 850 Korean-owned businesses at a cost of up to $300 million during the rebellion graphically illustrates the daily risks taken by merchants who do business in urban areas deemed too unprofitable by corporate chains.

In the popular culture, the tension-fraught relationship between the Korean store owner and his Black clientele in Spike Lee's *Do the Right Thing* was emblematic of the Black-Korean conflict, with the climactic scene prefiguring the much larger conflagration that was to later engulf large sections of Los Angeles. Rap artist Ice Cube added fuel to the fire by his 47-

second diatribe "Black Korea" on *Death Certificate*, which advised disrespectful "chop suey ass" merchants to "pay respect to the Black fist, or we'll burn your store right down to a crisp."

Placed in its historical context, the recent attack on L.A.'s Koreatown is consistent with 150 years of hostility and overt acts of violence against Asian American communities. Sucheng Chan in *Asian Americans: An Interpretive History* (1991) divides anti-Asian hostility into several distinct but related categories: prejudice, economic discrimination, political disenfranchisement, physical violence, immigration exclusion, social segregation, and incarceration. The irony of this most recent attack against the Korean American community lies in the fact that it came during a time when immigration laws no longer discriminate against Asians, *de jure* discrimination has ceased, and legislation exists to preserve civil rights. But such formal gains over the past 25 years have been rendered virtually meaningless because 12 years of regressive social and economic policies under Reagan/Bush has fragmented cities such as Los Angeles into mutually antagonistic groups for whom survival means ongoing struggle against one another with little regard to the abstract principles of liberal democracy.

The first recorded attack on an Asian community in Los Angeles took place in 1871, when a mob invaded Chinatown and attacked its residents. By the end of the melee, fifteen Chinese had been hanged, four shot, and two wounded. As in the case of many crimes committed against Asians, the perpetrators were never fully punished by white civil authorities. The historical record is filled with many more accounts of violent attacks against Asian communities of which the Koreatown siege is but the latest example.

Historically, the responses to Asian immigration to the U.S. has ranged from enthusiastic acceptance to violent rejection depending on a given group's relationship to capital. For example, Leland Stanford, whose Central Pacific railroad was in dire need of cheap, exploitable labor, welcomed Asian immigration while the Irish working class was noteworthy for its virulent opposition to Chinese workers viewed as economic competitors. According to David R. Roediger in *The Wages of Whiteness: Race and the Making of the American Working Class* (1991), the anti-Chinese campaign was national and spearheaded by Irish American immigrant workers for whom "whiteness" was their ticket for inclusion into a *herrenvolk* republican order where class divisions were elided by a common Anglo-Saxon racial heritage.

In the latter 19th century when anti-Asian hysteria was at a high, Asian immigrants, Mexicans, Indians, and African Americans were lumped together as equally ineligible for full participation in the economy. Yet in 1992 we are treated to the specter of non-white minorities battling each other for the few crumbs that have fallen from the well-set tables of capitalists who live in homogeneous communities patrolled by private security forces.

Fully 122 years separate the first recorded attack on an Asian community in Los Angeles and the April 1992 outbreak of violence in Koreatown. While the faces of the Koreatown attackers were predominantly Black and brown, the underlying causes of their anger, hostility, and resentment against Asians are not so dissimilar from that of their white working class counterparts who also have been blinded to the subtle mechanisms of a capitalist society that divides disenfranchised groups into warring camps. The current Black-Korean conflict is at bottom a displacement of the more fundamental problem: the profoundly disruptive effects of economic inequality. The Black-Korean conflict is not likely to abate unless this nation moves in the direction of greater economic democracy.

African Americans

A 1988 *New York Times* editorial suggests an appropriate introductory focus to the following collection of articles about an ethnic group that traces its American ancestry to initial participation as "three-fifths" persons in the U.S. Constitution and to its later exclusion from the polity altogether by the U.S. Supreme Court's *Dred Scott* decision. The editors of the *Times* write in the article "Negro, Black and African American" (December 22, 1988):

> The archaeology is dramatically plain to older adults who, in one lifetime, have already heard preferred usage shift from *colored* to *Negro* to *black*. The four lingual layers provide an abbreviated history of civil rights in this century.

Perhaps the fact of renaming this ethnic group "African American" may produce fresh vision needed to understand and transcend the deep racism that infects society. The following glimpses of the African American reality, its struggles for freedom, its tradition and community, its achievements, and the stresses of building bridges between worlds reveal a dense set of problems. More importantly, they suggest pieces of authentic identity rather than stereotype. Becoming a healthy ethnic society involves more than the end of ethnic stereotyping. The basis of ethnic identity are sustained by authentic portrayal of positive personal and group identity. The cultivation of ethnicity that does not encourage disdain against and self-hatred among members and groups is an important psychological and social artifice.

Progress or lack of progress on issues of race involves examination of a complex of historical, social, cultural, and economic factors. Analysis of this sort requires assessment of the existence of deep racism in the American mentality—that is, the cultural consciousness and the institutions that transmit images and practices that shape the foundations and configurations of social reality.

Discrimination and prejudice based on skin color are issues rarely broached in mainstream journals of opinion. Ethnic and racial intermarriage and the influence and impact of skin hue within the African American community raise attendant issues of discrimination and consciousness of color. This concern is ultimately traced to the eighteenth and nineteenth century—its origins in laws and practices of defining race that shaped the ongoing mentalities of color consciousness, prejudice, and racism

in America. Other dimensions of the African American experience can be found in this section's accounts of African American traditions and experiences of self-help and the family, in addition to the African roots of music that have been incorporated into the general culture.

Obviously, what some see as strengths and positive contributions, others argue are merely romantic diversions from more compelling social, economic, and political issues. Though this debate continues, patterns of change within African American populations have compelled discussion of the emerging black middle class. The purpose and influence of the historically black university and the reopening of the discussion of separate but equal in the courts and in the renewed attention to Afrocentric education are clear evidence of the ambivalence and ambiguity inherent in the challenges of a multicultural society. Earlier dichotomies—slave/free, black/white, poor/rich—are still evident, but a variety of group relations based on historical and regional as well as institutional agendas to preserve cultural and racial consciousness have complicated the simple hope for liberty and justice that was shared by many Americans. Issues of race and class are openly addressed by several articles in this section as are the ideological and psychological aspects of the complicated journey of African Americans toward full participation in the promises of liberty and justice, as well as the enjoyment of cultural freedom in a multiethnic America.

Looking Ahead: Challenge Questions

What are the most compelling issues that face African American communities?

What social, economic, and political conditions have supported the expansion of an African American middle class?

What explains the persistence of an African American underclass?

What effect does the media have on shaping the consciousness of ethnic group identity?

In what respect is attention to pluralism diminished by the economic and social plight and isolation of African Americans?

Does the name "African Americans" augment the development of pluralism?

Unit
6

10 Most Dramatic Events In African-American History

Lerone Bennett Jr.

1. *The Black Coming*

A YEAR before the arrival of the celebrated *Mayflower*, 244 years before the signing of the Emancipation Proclamation, 335 years before *Brown* vs. *Board of Education*, a big, bluff-bowed ship sailed up the river James and landed the first generation of African-Americans at Jamestown, Va.

Nobody knows the hour or the date of the official Black coming. But there is not the slightest doubt about the month. John Rolfe, who betrayed Pochohontas and experimented with tobacco, was there, and he said in a letter that the ship arrived "about the latter end of August" in 1619 and that it "brought not anything but 20 and odd Negroes." Concerning which the most charitable thing to say is that John Rolfe was probably pulling his boss' leg. For no ship ever called at an American port with a more important cargo. In the hold of that ship, in a manner of speaking, was the whole gorgeous panorama of Black America, was jazz and the spirituals and the black gold that made American capitalism possible.* Bird was there and Bigger and King and Malcolm and millions of other Xs and crosses, along with Mahalia singing, Duke Ellington composing, Gwendolyn Brooks rhyming and Michael Jordan slam-dunking. It was all there, illegible and inevitable, on that day. A man with eyes would have seen it and would have announced to his contemporaries that this ship heralds the beginning of the first Civil War and the second.

As befitting a herald of fate, the ship was nameless, and mystery surrounds it to this day. Where did this ship come from? From the high seas, where the crew robbed a Spanish vessel of a cargo of Africans bound for the West Indies. The captain "ptended," John Rolfe noted, that he needed food, and he offered to exchange his cargo for "victualle." The deal was arranged. Antoney, Pedro, Isabella and 17 other Africans with Spanish names stepped ashore, and the history of Africans in America began.

And it began, contrary to what almost all texts say, not in slavery but in freedom. For there is indisputable evidence that most of the first Black immigrants, like most of the first White immigrants, were held in indentured servitude for a number of years and then freed. During a transitional period of some 40 years, the first Black immigrants held real property, sued in court and accumulated pounds and plantations.

This changed drastically in the sixth decade of the century when the White founding fathers, spurred on by greed and the unprotected status of African immigrants, enacted laws that reduced most Africans to slavery. And so, some 40 years after the Black coming, Black and White crossed a fatal threshold, and the echo of that decision will reverberate in the corridors of Black and White history forever.

2. *The Founding of Black America*

WHEN, on a Sunday in November 1786, the little band of Black Christians arrived at Philadelphia's St. George's Methodist Episcopal Church, the sexton pointed to the gallery. The Blacks paused and then started up the rickety stairs with downcast eyes and heavy hearts. To the leaders of this group, Richard Allen and Absalom Jones, this was the ultimate indignity—to be shunted from the first floor to the gallery in a church Black men had helped build.

The group had barely reached the top of the stairs when a voice from the pulpit said, "Let us pray." Without thinking, the men plopped down where they were—in the *front* of the gallery. Allen was praying as hard as he could when he heard loud voices. He opened his eyes and saw a white sexton trying to pull Absalom Jones from his knees.

"You must get up; you must not kneel down here!" the White sexton said.

"Wait until the prayer is over," Jones replied.

The voices echoed through the church, and people looked up and beheld the incredible scene of a Black Christian and a White Christian wrestling in the house of the Lord over the color of God's word.

"Get up!" the sexton said. "Get up!"

"Wait until the prayer is over," Jones replied wearily, "and I will not trouble you any more."

Four or five White Christians rushed to the sexton's aid, and the struggle spread over the gallery. Before the issue was resolved, the prayer ended. The Black men stood up then and, without a word, streamed out of the church in the first mass demonstration in Black American history.

Richard Allen added a mournful postscript:

". . . And they were no more plagued by us in the church."

They were no more plagued by Blacks in a lot of places. For the Philadelphia demonstration was the focal point of a national movement that created the foundations of Black America. On April 12, 1787, Richard Allen and Absalom

*The Shaping of Black America

Jones created the Free African Society which DuBois called "the first wavering step of a people toward a more organized social life."

Similar societies were formed in most major Northern cities. And on this foundation rose an intricate structure of independent Black churches, schools and cultural organizations. The movement climaxed in the 1820s and 1830s with the founding of Freedom's Journal, the first Black newspaper, and the convening of the first national Black convention.

3. Nat Turner's War

GOD was speaking, Nat Turner said later.

There was, he remembered, thunder and lightning and a "loud voice" in the sky. And the voice spoke to him, telling him to take up the yoke and fight against the serpent "for the time was fast approaching when the first should be last and the last should be first."

Nat Turner was numbered among the last. And although he was a slave in Southampton County, Va., it would be said of him later that he "made an impact upon the people of his section as great as that of John C. Calhoun or Jefferson Davis." A mystic with blood on his mind and a preacher with vengeance on his lips, he was an implacable foe of slaveholders. He had believed since he was a child that God had set him aside for some great purpose. And he decided now that God was calling him to rise up and "slay my enemies with their own weapons."

To this end, Turner, who was about 30 years old, chose four disciples and set his face towards Jerusalem, the county seat of Southampton.

On Sunday morning, Aug. 21, 1831, the disciples gathered on the banks of Cabin Pond on the property of Joseph Travis, who had married the widow of Turner's last master and who had therefore inherited Turner and death. Nat, who appreciated the value of a delayed and dramatic entrance, appeared suddenly late in the afternoon and announced that they would strike that night, beginning at the home of his master and proceeding from house to house, killing every man, woman and child.

At 1 a.m., Nat Turner and his army crept through the woods to the home of the luckless Joseph Travis. They were seven men, armed with one hatchet and a broadax. Twenty-four hours later, they would be seventy and at least fifty-seven Whites would be dead.

When, on Monday morning, the first bodies were discovered, a nameless dread seized the citizens. Men, women and children fled to the woods and hid under the leaves until soldiers and sailors arrived from Richmond and Norfolk. Some Whites left the county; others left the state.

Defeated in an engagement near Jerusalem, Turner went into hiding and was not captured until six weeks later. On Nov. 11, 1831, the short Black man called the Prophet was hanged in a field near the courthouse. Before climbing the gallows, he made one last prophecy, saying there would be a storm after his execution and that the sun would refuse to shine. There was, in fact, a storm in Jerusalem on that day, but Turner was not talking about the weather—he was predicting a major disturbance in the American psyche. The storm he saw came in the generation of crisis that his act helped precipitate.

4. Free at Last!

TO Felix Haywood, who was there, it was the Time of Glory when men and women walked "on golden clouds."

To Frederick Douglass, it was a downpayment on the redemption of the American soul.

To Sister Winny in Virginia, to Jane Montgomery in Louisiana, to Ed Bluff in Mississippi, to Black people all over the South and all over America, it was the Time of Jubilee, the wild, happy, sad, mocking, tearful, fearful time of the unchaining of the bodies of Black folks. And the air was sweet with song.

Free at last!
Free at last!
Thank God Almighty!
We're free at last.

W.E.B. Dubois was not there, but he summed the whole thing up in phrases worthy of the ages. It was all, he said, "foolish, bizarre, and tawdry. Gangs of dirty Negroes howling and dancing; poverty-stricken ignorant laborers mistaking war, destruction, and revolution for the mystery of the free human soul; and yet to these Black folk it was the Apocalypse." And he added:

"All that was Beauty, all that was Love, all that was Truth, stood on the top of these mad mornings and sang with the stars. A great human sob shrieked in the wind, and tossed its tears upon the sea—free, free, free."

Contrary to the common view, the emancipation of Blacks didn't happen at one time or even in one place. It started with the first shot fired at Fort Sumter. It continued during the war and in the Jubilee summer of 1865, *and it has not been completed.* For the slaves, who created the foundation of American wealth, never received the 40 acres of land that would have made freedom meaningful.

It was in this milieu that African-Americans embarked on a road called freedom. As the road twisted and turned, doubling back on itself, their enemies and their problems multiplied. But they endured, and endure.

5. Booker T. Washington vs. W. E. B. DuBois

THERE was a big parade in Atlanta on Wednesday, Sept. 18, 1895, and a huge crowd gathered in the Exposition Building at the Cotton States Exposition for the opening speeches. Several Whites spoke and then former Gov. Rufus Bullock introduced "Professor Booker T. Washington." The 39-year-old president of Tuskegee Institute moved to the front of the platform and started speaking to the segregated audience. Within 10 minutes, reporter James Creelman wrote, "the multitude was in an uproar of enthusiasm — handkerchiefs were waved . . . hats were tossed into the air. The fairest women of Georgia stood up and cheered."

What was the cheering about?

Metaphors mostly—and words millions of Whites wanted to hear. Washington told Blacks: "Cast down your buckets where you are." To Whites, he offered the same advice: "Cast down your bucket [among] the most patient, faithful, law-abiding and unresentful people the world has seen . . . ."

Suddenly, he flung his hand aloft, with the fingers held wide apart.

"In all things purely social," he said, "we can be as separate as the fingers, yet [he balled the fingers into a fist] one as the hand in all things essential to mutual progress."

The crowd came to its feet, yelling.

Washington's "Atlanta Compromise" speech made him famous and set the tone for race relations for some 20 years. One year after his speech, the Supreme Court rounded a fateful fork, endorsing in *Plessy* vs. *Ferguson* the principle of "separate but equal."

Washington's refusal to make a direct and open attack on Jim Crow and his implicit acceptance of segregation brought him into conflict with W.E.B. DuBois and a group of Black militants who organized the germinal Niagara Movement. At its first national meeting at Harpers Ferry in 1906, the Niagara militants said, "We claim for ourselves every single right that belongs to a freeborn American, political, civil, and social; and until we get these rights we will never cease to protest and assail the ears of America."

So saying, the Niagara militants laid the foundation for the National Association for the Advancement of Colored People which merged the forces of Black militancy and White liberalism.

6. The Great Migration

HISTORY does not always come with drums beating and flags flying.

Sometimes it comes in on a wave of silence.

Sometimes it whispers.

It was like that in the terrible days of despair that preceded the unprecedented explosion of hope and movement that is called The Great Migration.

This event, which was the largest internal migration in American history and one of the central events of African-American history, started in the cracks of history, in the minds and moods of the masses of Blacks, who were reduced to the status of semi-slaves in the post-Reconstruction period. Pushed back toward slavery by lynchings, segregation and the sharecropping systems, they turned around within themselves and decided that there had to be another way and another and better place. The feeling moved, became a mood, an imperative, a command. Without preamble, without a plan, without leadership, the people began to move, going from the plantation to Southern cities, going from there to the big cities of the North. There, they found jobs in wartime industries and sent letters to a cousin or an aunt or sister or brother, saying: Come! And they came, hundreds and hundreds of thousands. The first wave (300,000) came between 1910 and 1920, followed by a second wave (1,300,000) between 1920 and 1930, and

third (500,000) and fourth (2,500,000) waves, even larger, in the '30s and '40s.

In the big cities of the North, Blacks emancipated themselves politically and economically and created the foundation of contemporary Black America.

7. Brown vs. Board of Education

THE marshal's voice was loud and clear.

"Oyez! Oyez! Oyez! All persons having business before the Honorable, the Supreme Court of the United States, are admonished to draw near and give their attention, for the Court is now sitting."

The marshal paused and intoned the traditional words:

"God save the United States and this Honorable Court!"

It was high noon on Monday, May 17, 1954, and the Supreme Court was crammed to capacity with spectators. Among the dozen or so Blacks present was Thurgood Marshall, chief counsel of the NAACP, who leaned forward in expectation.

Cases from four states (South Carolina, Virginia, Delaware, Kansas) and the District of Columbia were before the Court, which had been asked by Marshall and his associates to overturn the *Plessy* vs. *Ferguson* decision and declare segregation in public schools unconstitutional. All America awaited the long-expected decision which would come on a Monday. But which Monday? No one knew, and there was no sign on the faces of the justices that the issue was going to be settled on this day.

The Court disposed of routine business and announced decisions in several boring cases involving the sale of milk and the picketing of retail stores. Then Chief Justice Earl Warren picked up a document and said in a firm, quiet voice: "I have for announcement the judgment and opinion of the Court in No. 1—*Oliver Brown et al. v. Board of Education of Topeka*. It was 12:52 p.m. A shiver ran through the courtroom, and bells started ringing in press rooms all over the world.

Warren held the crowd in suspense, reviewing the history of the cases. Then, abruptly, he came to the heart of the matter:

"Does segregation of children in public schools solely on the basis of race, even though the physical facilities and

other "tangible" factors may be equal, deprive the children of the minority group of equal educational opportunities?" Warren paused and said: "We believe that it does." The decision was unanimous: 9-0.

The words raced across the country and were received by different people according to their different lights. Southern diehards like Herman Talmadge issued statements of defiance and promised a generation of litigation, but the implications of the decision were so enormous that many Americans were shocked into silence and wonder. In Farmville, Va., a 16-year-old student named Barbara Trent burst into tears when her teacher announced the decision. "We went on studying history," she said later, "but things weren't the same and will never be the same again."

8. Montgomery and the Freedom Movement

IT was a quiet, peaceful day in Montgomery, Ala., the Cradle of the Confederacy—but it was unseasonably hot for December 1.

The Cleveland Avenue bus rolled through Court Square, where Blacks were auctioned in the days of the Confederacy, and braked to a halt in front of the Empire Theater. There was nothing special about the bus or the day; neither the driver nor the passengers realized that a revolution was about to begin that would turn America and the South upside down.

Six Whites boarded the bus at the Empire Theater, and the driver stormed to the rear and ordered the foremost Blacks to get up and give their seats to the White citizens. This was an ancient custom, sanctioned by the peculiar mores of the South, and it excited no undue comment. Three Blacks got up immediately, but Rosa Parks, a mild-mannered seamstress in rimless glasses, kept her seat. For this act of defiance, she was arrested. Local leaders called a one-day bus boycott on Monday, Dec. 5, 1955, to protest the arrest. The one-day boycott stretched out to 381 days; the 381 days changed the face and heart of Black America, creating a new leader (Martin Luther King Jr.), and a new movement. There then followed in quick succession a series of movements (the Sit-ins and Freedom Rides) and dramatic events (Birmingham, Selma, Watts, the March on Washington) that constituted Black America's finest hour and one of the greatest moments in the history of the Republic.

9. Little Rock

THE GIANT C-119 flying boxcars circled the field, like grim birds.

One by one, they glided into the Little Rock, Ark., airport and debouched paratroopers in full battle gear. There were, in all, more than 1,000 soldiers, Black and White; and they were in Little Rock to enforce the orders of a federal court. For the first time since the Reconstruction era, the United States of America was deploying federal troops to defend the rights of Black Americans.

Escorted by city police cars, a convoy of olive-drab jeeps and trucks sped to Central High School where a howling mob had prevented the enrollment of nine Black students. The troops deployed on the double to block all entrances to the schools, and signalmen strung telephone lines and set up command posts.

Wednesday morning, Sept. 25, 1957, dawned bright and clear, and nine Black teenagers gathered at the ranch-style home of Daisy Bates, president of the Arkansas NAACP. At 8:50 a.m., there was a rumble of heavy wheels. The teenagers rushed to the window.

"The streets were blocked off," Daisy Bates recalled later. "The soldiers closed ranks . . . Oh! It was beautiful. And the attitude of the children at that moment: the respect they had. I could hear them saying, 'For the first time in my life I truly feel like an American.' I could see it in their faces: Somebody cares for me—*America cares.*"

At 9:45, U.S. soldiers with drawn bayonets escorted six Black females and three Black males into Central High School, and the Rev. Dunbar H. Ogden, president of the Greater Little Rock Ministerial Association, said: "This may be looked back upon by future historians as the turning point—for good—of race relations in this country."

10. Memphis and the Triumph of the Spirit

THERE had never been a moment like this one.

Time stopped.
Everything stopped.

And every man and woman living at that terrible time would be able to tell you until the end of their time what they were doing and where they were on Thursday, April 4, 1968, when word came that Martin Luther King Jr. had been assassinated on the balcony of the Lorraine Motel in Memphis, Tenn.

The response in Black and White America was tumultuous. Performances, plays, meetings, baseball games were cancelled, and men and women walked aimlessly through the streets, weeping.

There were tears, rivers of tears, and there was also blood. For Black communities exploded, one after another, like firecrackers on a string. Some 46 persons were killed in uprisings in 126 cities, and federal troops were mobilized to put down rebellions in Chicago, Baltimore and Washington, D.C.

To counteract this fury, and to express their sorrow, Americans of all races and creeds joined forces in an unprecedented tribute to a Black American. President Lyndon B. Johnson declared a national day of mourning and ordered U.S. flags to fly at half-mast over U.S. installations at home and abroad. On the day of the funeral—Tuesday, April 9—more than 200,000 mourners followed King's coffin, which was carried through the streets of Atlanta on a wagon, borne by two Georgia mules.

Eighteen years later, the spirit and the truth of Martin Luther King Jr. triumphed when he became the second American citizen (with George Washington) to be celebrated in a personal national holiday.

BLACK AMERICANS: THE NEW GENERATION

Generational Shift of Black Leaders

Detroit's Best Days Are Still Ahead, Say City's Young Black Activists

Keith Henderson

Staff writer of The Christian Science Monitor

DETROIT

Detroit has the largest proportion of African-Americans of any major city in the United States. Nearly 80 percent of its residents are black. The same black mayor, Coleman Young, has run the city for the past 20 years. His tenure has been a constant struggle to rescue Detroit from the economic decline caused by shrinkage in the US automobile industry.

Twenty-five years after riots scattered many white residents to the suburbs, the city is typically described as a shriveled core surrounded by relative prosperity. Crime in Detroit is endemic; gun-toting youngsters regularly kill each other.

According to some of its most prominent young leaders, however, Detroit is not inexorably collapsing in on itself. They have a determined optimism about the city that defies the statistics about population loss and unemployment, as well as the boarded-up store fronts, weed-filled lots, and other daily reminders of decay.

The Rev. Wendell Anthony, a United Church of Christ minister who was recently elected president of the De-troit branch of the National Association for the Advancement of Colored People (NAACP), says "Detroit has not seen its best days." The "media image" of the city, Mr. Anthony says, does not account for the substantial talents and abilities of its citizens.

Anthony's point is bolstered by Melvin J. Hollowell, Jr., a lawyer in his mid-30s who puts in 12 hours or more of pro bono (unpaid) work for the NAACP each week. Mr. Hollowell's firm—Lewis, White & Clay—is the largest black-owned law firm in the country, he says, with 35 lawyers at its Detroit headquarters and in Washington.

While his professional specialty is bond counseling for cities, Hollowell's passion is clearly civil rights. He is currently shepherding a discrimination lawsuit against the car-insurance industry through the state courts. "I believe people should be charged based on how they drive, not where they live," he says.

The case plunges into what Mr. Hollowell calls "the new civil rights arena." Such cases "will make us get into the guts of how things work," says the attorney. He sees banking practices, which put hurdles before black homeowners or businesspeople who want loans, as another part of this "arena."

Hollowell has an eye on the politi-cal arena, too. He is "in the hunt" to become US attorney in Detroit. Unlike many other young black professionals—"Buppies"—Hollowell and his wife live in the city, where he grew up. Their five-year-old son attends a private school in the city called Nataki Talibah. Like most of the Detroit public schools, it emphasizes African culture.

From the one-story, gold-buff rectangle of his Fellowship Chapel on McNichols Road, Anthony runs his own African-flavored youth programs—*Isuthu* and *Intonjani*, Xhosa (African) terms for coming into manhood and womanhood. The programs, which include some 275 youngsters aged 6 to 18, put a premium on helping the elderly and serving the community.

Despite the low incomes of most Detroit residents, the city's African-American community manages some impressive fund raising. Each year the local NAACP—with 20,000 members, by far the largest branch in the US—holds a Freedom Fund dinner for some 10,000 guests. The event, which attracts wide corporate support, brings in more than $1 million for scholarships and other NAACP programs. But that should only be a start, says Anthony. "If we have a Freedom Fund dinner, we must have a grass-roots breakfast."

He worries about a gap between prominent leaders in the community and the mass of people struggling to stay afloat in Detroit's economic turbulence. To solve the city's problems, Anthony says, "we must work in coalition with others"—businesspeople, government, people of all races. But the prerequisite for progress, he says, is a drawing together of the city's black population itself.

Institutions of government may have to change. Keith Butler, another prominent young black minister before he became the first Republican elected to Detroit's City Council in decades, says the city has to lighten its tax burden before it can hope to retain the businesses it has, much less attract new ones.

Also, the crime problem has to be attacked with a larger, revitalized police force, Mr. Butler says—something that could be possible, he adds, if inefficiency were rooted out of city government.

Butler hopes for a changing of the guard in City Hall this year. After 20 years, he says, the Young administration "has run out of steam."

Anthony defends the mayor, while noting that "within any group, you always have another generation coming up." "I don't like the old-guard, new-guard split," he says. "There's only one guard, guarding against racism and deprivation, regardless of age, gender, or ethnicity."

The Rising Generation of Leaders Comes From Diverse Backgrounds

James H. Andrews

Staff writer of The Christian Science Monitor

BOSTON

When Benjamin Hooks retires this month as executive director of the National Association for the Advancement of Colored People (NAACP), the event will mark another milestone in a generational shift that is taking place in black leadership in the United States. Those mentioned to succeed him—including Randall Robinson, executive director of Trans-

Africa, and Jesse Jackson—are half a generation younger than Mr. Hooks, who is 68.

Hooks belongs to a generation of black Americans who wrought a historic civil rights revolution in the country. Now, many major figures of that generation either are gone (Thurgood Marshall most recently) or—like Hooks—are what Washington Post columnist Juan Williams calls "graying revolutionaries."

As their ranks thin, a new genera-

tion of African-Americans is assuming positions of leadership not only in civil rights organizations, but also in politics, business, academia, and the arts.

While black scholars agree that this transition is occurring, they point out that the leadership structure in black America is changing in other respects as well.

"The civil rights movement embedded reforms in political and legal institutions," says Prof. Ron Walters,

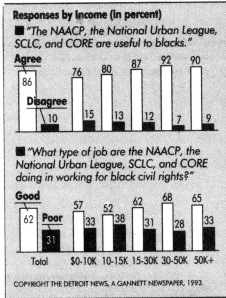

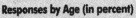

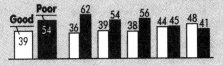

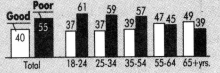

WHO SPEAKS FOR BLACK AMERICANS?

■ How blacks regard the National Association for the Advancement of Colored People (NAACP), the National Urban League, the Southern Christian Leadership Conference (SCLC), and the Congress of Racial Equality (CORE):

Rich or poor, black Americans believe that the major civil rights organizations are useful to blacks and do a good job to fight discrimination. **(See charts at left.)**

But many African-Americans, especially younger ones, believe that the organizations should do more to help blacks get jobs and to build unity within the black community. **(See charts at right.)**

Source: Survey of 1,211 black Americans conducted for The Detroit News and Gannett News Service, Nov. 11-25, 1991.

chairman of the political science department at Howard University in Washington. "Consequently, black leadership has shifted in part from ministers and civil rights activists to government officials."

Arvarh Strickland, a professor of history at the University of Missouri, Columbia, similarly notes that whereas the earlier black leaders came heavily from churches, today many leaders are coming from business and the professions as blacks have found greater opportunity in those fields. "The leadership spectrum has broadened," Dr. Strickland says.

Some black scholars say that, in contrast to many generational shifts, younger black leaders today largely share the perspectives of their predecessors. "The ideas [regarding the

place of blacks in America] being brought forward by younger leaders are not that different," says political science Prof. Ron Brown of Wayne State University in Detroit. "Incorporation is still the goal."

According to Professors Brown, Walters, and Strickland, such developments as blacks' growing focus on African culture, the creation of magnet schools designed to appeal to black students, and the growth of black suburbs do not betoken a retreat from the goal of integration.

"Blacks, like other groups, enjoy being with their own people," Walters notes. "But they still want free access to all aspects of the American culture and economy."

But if younger African-Americans generally share common ideals with

their elders, many young blacks say that black leaders should focus somewhat less on civil rights and more on economic and social issues like jobs, education, and drug abuse. (See charts.)

While the civil rights leaders opened doors for black people throughout American life, Mr. Williams says their triumphs also "slowed development of the next generation of black leaders. . . . The new generation has been inhibited from putting itself forward for fear of appearing to contravene the honor due to the older leaders."

Today, however, with the changing of the guard, younger African-Americans are putting their own imprint on the black experience in America.

Georgia Congresswoman Empowers 'Voiceless' Blacks

Clara Germani

Staff writer of The Christian Science Monitor

WASHINGTON
Black, female, and young, newly seated Congresswoman Cynthia McKinney is part of the forward guard of a new generation infiltrating the corridors of traditionally white male power.

Her reception at the Capitol is perhaps the clearest example of how unusual the Georgia Democrat's presence here is: Guards at staff entrances and staff elevators still try to turn her away because she doesn't *look* like a member of Congress, she says.

But then, says Ms. McKinney, she's not trying to fit into a status quo that has traditionally left her constituents "voiceless and oftentimes voteless as well."

Instead, she wants Washington to adjust to where she's coming from: the newly drawn majority-black 11th District of Georgia. Extending through urban, suburban, and rural areas

with high concentrations of poverty, unemployment, illiteracy, and teen pregnancy, the district that McKinney fought to create while she was a state representative is full of people "who have never seen a congressperson, never knew what Congress was," she says.

"Because I go into these meetings and hearings [here] and am invited to sit at the table, [my constituents] have a seat at the table where decisions are being made that will impact their lives. And that's what is new and different and exciting [about my being here]," she says.

Small behind her big government-issue desk, McKinney wore braids, a batik dress, and a Mickey Mouse watch during a recent interview. But her voice—fiercely pointed at times—fills her Capitol Hill office with authority. She is most vehement when explaining the needs of the black community.

McKinney, a 37-year-old divorced single mother of a seven-year-old

boy, is the daughter of longtime State Rep. Billy McKinney, one of Atlanta's first black policemen. She grew up in Atlanta accompanying her father to civil rights demonstrations.

She bridles at questions of whether there is a new agenda—broader than that of the civil rights era of the 1960s—for a new generation of black leaders.

"The agenda for civil rights never stops," she says. "In fact in the 11th Congressional District, where we have black people who are [still] denied their right to vote, we have elections that have turned on blacks who have been turned away from the polls. No, I can't say that the civil rights era is over."

While the black agenda may have broadened to include economic questions, she says that basic civil rights remains a core issue that may sometimes be obscured by the growing success of many blacks.

"Certainly you've had those blacks who've been able to take advantage of the system as it is, and that's a good thing," she says. "But we need to have more blacks who are able to move up, and to do that we need to have a government that's more sensitive to the needs of the rest of us."

Black-community problems such as teenage pregnancy, limited access to health care, joblessness, and inferior education are all ultimately rooted in limits to civil rights, McKinney says.

And how much are these problems due to white racism? "Racism is sort of the structural construct around which our society today operates. . . . We have a lot of right-thinking, good-hearted white Americans who understand that there's a problem . . . but nobody seems to know the answer. . . ."

McKinney credits her career in politics and as a college instructor working on her doctorate in international affairs to being a "child of affirmative action." But, she adds, that doesn't mean that blacks have completely achieved the civil rights they are due.

She points to her own experience campaigning in rural Georgia as an example of how racism can still bar access to basic civil rights. She describes how local officials in one rural town escorted her out of the county rather than have her spend the night there, because of fears that Ku Klux Klan members, upset about being put into a majority-black district, might do her harm.

But she says the fact that the area elected her as the first black congresswoman from Georgia shows that things *are* changing. And getting "more people of color elected to city councils and county commissions and school boards" is a major part of the minority agenda for the 1990s, McKinney says.

But as a black leader, can she represent the interests of the 45 percent of her constituents who are not black?

"That was the fallacy all along of those who led white backlash movements: that there was some danger in incorporating blacks into the mainstream of whatever it was to be an American," McKinney says.

She adds: "[I] provide an opportunity for them to redeem themselves in a way that is tolerant of people who are different and accepting of differences of opinions."

Community Activist in Los Angeles Stresses Economic Clout for Blacks

Daniel B. Wood

Staff writer of The Christian Science Monitor

LOS ANGELES
"In the civil rights era, African-Americans should have been looking for economic power instead of the political power which we thought was the answer," says Mark Whitlock, executive director of L.A. Renaissance.

The 38-year-old founder of this new grass-roots response to the Los Angeles riots says that such fundamental misdirection resulted in a long-term impoverishment for blacks in South Central Los Angeles that has remained largely unchanged in the quarter century since Watts exploded here in 1965.

"Instead of taking government money and investing it in homes and urban development, we should have put it into black businesses," Mr. Whitlock says. "We would now be employing ourselves, doing business with ourselves, and we would have our own economy that would ensure our place at the decisionmaking tables."

The lesson needs to be learned in every large city in America, says Whitlock, a St. Louis native who went to L.A., later became a Chicago businessman, and now is a Los Angeles father of two. If blacks controlled a more proportional slice of each community's economic pie, he says, clout would extend naturally into politics, culture, and education. Since they do not, he says, "the American dream is still a dream deferred for most African-Americans."

To emphasize his fundamental difference in approach, Whitlock has been creating an alternative to the more well-known consortium of city, state, and federal bodies known here as "Rebuild L.A." That organization is attempting mere patchwork from the top down, he says, and is doomed to repeat past failures.

"You can't rebuild something that was built wrong in the first place," Whitlock says. "We need to build anew, from the community up."

Enter L.A. Renaissance, an umbrella organization for about seven programs intended for African-Americans to break their cycle of financial and psychological dependency and poverty.

To get low-interest loans of $2,000 to $20,000 to start a business in the community, for instance, applicants must first complete a 10-week entrepreneurial program. A job-creation and employment section focuses on career development and promotion, developing skills for particular industries. Another program provides mentoring for young men and women about discipline, self-esteem, and getting on successful educational tracks early.

Other ideas include breakfasts to hear national and community leaders, and sports activities to provide alternatives to gangs and the drug culture.

"This is a response to the total reversal of the Great Society programs of the '60s," says the Rev. John Cager, an L.A. Renaissance project manager. "CETA [the Comprehensive Employment and Training Act], JTPA [the Job Training Partnership Act], Job Corps—you don't hear about [federal] programs like that anymore. They failed because they just threw money at the problems until things quieted down. So we're starting our own."

By most accounts, credit for the success of L.A. Renaissance in securing nearly $5 million in underwriting from such companies as the Disney Company, Reebok, and ARCO goes to Whitlock. A self-described ex-drug user and dealer, formerly a gang member and a homeless person, Whitlock broke that cycle through his involvement with the leading African-American church in Los Angeles, First African Methodist Episcopal (FAME).

After rising to vice president of a Chicago insurance firm, Whitlock wanted to harness his experience for struggling blacks back on the streets of his former community. "I learned how millions of dollars were advancing the goals of my employers from real estate to banking," says Whitlock. "I thought, why not translate my experience directly to the African-American community?"

"Mark has come to Los Angeles as a CARE package," says Cecil Murray, head pastor of FAME. "He is equally comfortable in the boardroom, on the gang streets, or in the pulpit. He helps African-Americans believe in themselves because they believe in him."

The wall of Whitlock's office bears tributes to his civic accomplishments. Certificates from the police department, the mayor, and the city attorney recognize such programs as one he spearheaded four years ago to rid the local community of gangs, crack houses, and prostitution. Fifty to 200 men walked the streets for

months serving notice that such behavior would not be tolerated. Fourteen crack houses were closed.

"I want everything I do to send a message to African-Americans that you cannot blame the system for what has happened," Whitlock says. "If you do, you will continue to remain a victim."

African-Americans are still "denied the same financial opportunity, fair housing, and education" as whites, he says. But he adds that the time is ripe to reverse the pattern. His clarion call for African-Americans in the 1990s: Harness the best and brightest, not for the Fortune 500 companies, but back in the 'hood where they can help the brothers pull themselves up by the bootstraps.

"Many have had an employee mentality for so long they don't know how to break it," Whitlock says. "Well, it's the employer who creates the rules, and it's time for us to create our own rules."

GROWING UP IN BLACK AND WHITE

For African-American children, learning to love themselves is a tough challenge

Jack E. White

"Mommy, I want to be white."

Imagine my wife's anguish and alarm when our beautiful brown-skinned three-year-old daughter made that declaration. We thought we were doing everything right to develop her self-esteem and positive racial identity. We overloaded her toy box with black dolls. We carefully monitored the racial content of our TV shows and videos, ruling out *Song of the South* and *Dumbo,* two classic Disney movies marred by demeaning black stereotypes. But we saw no harm in *Pinocchio,* which seemed as racially benign as *Sesame Street* or *Barney,* and a good deal more engaging. Yet now our daughter was saying she wanted to be white, to be like the puppet who becomes a real boy in the movie. How had she got that potentially soul-destroying idea and, even more important, what should we do about it?

That episode was an unsettling reminder of the unique burden that haunts black parents in America: helping their children come to terms with being black in a country where the message too often seems to be that being white is better. Developing a healthy self-image would be difficult enough for black children with all the real-life reminders that blacks and whites are still treated differently. But it is made even harder by the seductive racial bias in TV, movies and children's books, which seem to link everything beautiful and alluring with whiteness while often treating blacks as afterthoughts. Growing up in this all pervading world of whiteness can be psychologically exhausting for black children just as they begin to figure out who they are. As a four-year-old boy told his father after another day in the overwhelmingly white environment of his

Connecticut day-care facility, "Dad, I'm tired of being black."

In theory it should now be easier for children to develop a healthy sense of black pride than it was during segregation. In 1947 psychologists Kenneth and Mamie Clark conducted a famous experiment that demonstrated just how much black children had internalized the hatred that society directed at their race. They asked 253 black children to choose between four dolls, two black and two white. The result: two-thirds of the children preferred white dolls.

The conventional wisdom had been that black self-hatred was a by-product of discrimination that would wither away as society became more tolerant. Despite the civil rights movement of the 1960s, the black-is-beautiful movement of the '70s, the proliferation of black characters on television shows during the '80s and the renascent black nationalist movement of the '90s, the prowhite message has not lost its power. In 1985 psychologist Darlene Powell-Hopson updated the Clarks' experiment using black and white Cabbage Patch dolls and got a virtually identical result: 65% of the black children preferred white dolls. "Black is dirty," one youngster explained. Powell-Hopson thinks the result would be the same if the test were repeated today.

Black mental-health workers say the trouble is that virtually all the progress the U.S. has made toward racial fairness has been in one direction. To be accepted by whites, blacks have to become more like them, while many whites have not changed their attitudes at all. Study after study has shown that the majority of whites, for all the commitment to equality they espouse, still consider blacks to be inferior, undesirable and dangerous. "Even though race relations have changed

for the better, people maintain those old stereotypes," says Powell-Hopson. "The same racial dynamics occur in an integrated environment as occurred in segregation; it's just more covert."

Psychiatrists say children as young as two can pick up these damaging messages, often from subtle signals of black inferiority unwittingly embedded in children's books, toys and TV programs designed for the white mainstream. "There are many more positive images about black people in the media than there used to be, but there's still a lot that says that white is more beautiful and powerful than black, that white is good and black is bad," says James P. Comer, a Yale University psychiatrist who collaborated with fellow black psychiatrist Alvin F. Poussaint on *Raising Black Children* (Plume).

The bigotry is not as usually as blatant as it was in Roald Dahl's *Charlie and the Chocolate Factory.* When the book was published in 1964, the New York *Times* called it "a richly inventive and humorous tale." Blacks didn't see anything funny about having the factory staffed by "Oompa-Loompas," pygmy workers imported in shipping cartons from the jungle where they had been living in the trees.

Today white-controlled companies are doing a better job of erasing racially loaded subtexts from children's books and movies. Yet those messages still get through, in part because they are at times so subtle even a specialist like Powell-Hopson misses them. She recently bought a book about a cat for her six-year-old daughter, who has a love of felines. Only when Powell-Hopson got home did she discover that the beautiful white cat in the story turns black when it starts behaving badly. Moreover, when the products are not objectionable, they are sometimes promoted in ways that unintentionally drive home the theme of black inferiority. Powell-Hopson cites a TV ad for dolls that displayed a black version in the background behind the white model "as though it were a second-class citizen."

Sadly, black self-hatred can also begin at home. Even today, says Powell-Hopson, "many of us perpetuate negative messages, showing preference for lighter complexions, saying nappy hair is bad and straight hair is good, calling other black people 'niggers,' that sort of thing." This danger can be greater than the one posed by TV and the other media because children learn so much by simple imitation of the adults they are closest to. Once implanted in a toddler's mind, teachers and psychologists say, such misconceptions can blossom into a full-blown racial identity crisis during adolescence, affecting everything from performance in the classroom to a youngster's susceptibility to crime and drug abuse. But they can be neutralized if parents react properly.

In their book, Comer and Poussaint emphasize a calm and straightforward approach. They point out that even black children from affluent homes in integrated neighborhoods need reassurance about racial issues because from their earliest days they sense that their lives are "viewed cheaply by white society." If, for example, a black little girl says she wishes she had straight blond hair, they advise parents to point out "in a relaxed and unemotional manner . . . that she is black and that most black people have nice curly black hair, and that most white people have straight hair, brown, blond, black. At this age what you convey in your voice and manner will either make it O.K. or make it a problem."

Powell-Hopson, who along with her psychologist husband Derek has written *Different and Wonderful: Raising Black Children in a Race-Conscious Society* (Fireside), takes a more aggressive approach, urging black parents in effect to inoculate their children against negative messages at an early age. For example, the authors suggest that African-American parents whose children display a preference for white dolls or action figures should encourage them to play with a black one by "dressing it in the best clothes, or having it sit next to you, or doing anything you can think of to make your child sense that you prefer that doll." After that, the Hopsons say, the child can be offered a chance to play with the toy, on the condition that "you promise to take the very best care of it. You know it is my favorite." By doing so, the Hopsons claim, "most children will jump at a chance to hold the toy even for a second."

White children are no less vulnerable to racial messages. Their reactions can range from a false sense of superiority over blacks to an identification with sports superstars like Michael Jordan so complete that they want to become black. But if white parents look for guidance from popular child-care manuals, they won't find any. "I haven't included it because I don't feel like an expert in that area," says T. Berry Brazelton, author of *Infants and Mothers* and other child-care books. "I think it's a very, very serious issue that this country hasn't faced up to." Unless it does, the U.S. runs the risk of rearing another generation of white children crippled by the belief that they are better than blacks and black children who agree.

As for my daughter, we're concerned but confident. As Comer says, "In the long run what children learn from their parents is more powerful than anything they get from any other source." When my little girl expressed the wish to be white, my wife put aside her anguish and smilingly replied that she is bright and black and beautiful, a very special child. We'll keep telling her that until we're sure she loves herself as much as we love her.

Beyond the Pale

Why My 'Too-Black' Friends Want Light-Skinned Babies

Portia Williams

Portia Williams is a Maryland writer.

What with Michael Jackson's controversial color-change and the mulatto heroine of Alex Haley's TV mini-series, "Queen," people are talking again about the consequences of being a "dark-skinned" or "light-skinned" African American. Five years after Spike Lee's "School Daze" raised hackles by airing the issue outside the black community, this is a debate that will not die—for some of us. My 29-year-old friend Kate, on the other hand, doesn't bother herself with such discussions. She thinks that in 50 years being dark-skinned in America may be a non-issue. That's because an increasing number of dark-skinned women simply refuse to reproduce a dark-skinned child.

Let me explain.

Kate laid out this theory a few hours after I attended a party she gave her 1-year-old daughter. At the party, I had met several of her friends and their children; I happened to mention to Kate that I didn't recall meeting the mother of one little white girl.

"Oh," replied Kate. "You met her mother. The little girl is not white, but her father is. . . . You know, everybody wants a good-looking baby."

Come on, I said laughing. This is 1993; people don't focus on complexion anymore. "No, you come on," she said. "This is how it is. Nobody wants a dark-skinned, nappy-haired baby. . . ."

This statement, of course, is not true. Kate and millions of other black mothers not only want but adore their kids regardless of color. Yet after a moment I realized that indeed every dark-skinned mother at this party had a very light child. And now Kate was telling me that this was no accident. She said many of the women I met that day spoke openly about the necessity of having light-skinned children; that they had their children out of wedlock, and that the fathers of their children had not mattered as much as the lightness of their skin. "It's sad, and nobody wants to admit it," she said, "but even many educated, professional women of today don't want their babies to have to go through the same things they went through when they were growing up."

Suddenly I knew why this conversation so disturbed me. Not because it was outrageous; because it was plausible. For Kate and I weren't merely talking about light-skinned children or near-white partners, we were talking about the painful and contradictory effects of forced assimilation—the everyday struggle for social acceptance and against self-hate. If you're black, the struggle is hard enough. But if you're "too black," it can become your life. Color can mean everything; if you let it, it can consume you. It can dictate a woman's most fundamental choices.

In the neighborhood where I grew up, kids had a chant reserved espe-cially for me: "Portia was a *black* baby; Portia was a *thief*; Portia came to my house and *stole* a leg of *beef.*' " It was hardly the worst thing I heard as a child.

I am dark, like my mother and two of my brothers; dark unlike my father, my sisters and one brother. In short, I was the only dark-skinned girl in my family. Growing up, I was called tar-baby, nappy-head and black baby so many times that, for a period, I automatically looked up when a derogatory name was called.

I can remember with glowing clarity one of my brothers coming home from high school and noting how difficult it was to date dark-skinned girls. The guys at school joked about wanting only the light-bright-and-damn-near-white girls. If you're caught with somebody dark, he said, they'll trash you.

I already understood what he meant. I had been told by a light-skinned playboy that dark-skinned girls were only good for sex.

It wasn't just school-age kids who trashed dark skin, however; many children learned of their ugliness from figures of authority. I was in third or fourth grade when my Afri-can-American teacher told the class that beauty was high cheekbones, narrow noses and small lips—none of which the students had.

At home, however, my mother often told me to look in the mirror to see just how ridiculous these asser-tions were. "It is obvious to every-body but you," she'd say, "just how beautiful you are. There are different shades of skin and different grades of hair, but they are all beautiful. Especially yours."

While I didn't understand it then, my mother knew firsthand how difficult it is to love yourself while concurrently changing yourself to meet society's standards for acceptance and beauty. She knew why I had suddenly become interested in over-the-counter bleaching creams; she knew why I begged her to let me permanently straighten my hair. In short, my mother understood my conflict—the conflict that occurs when one strives for acceptance by rejecting everything that he or she is.

These feelings of conflict are foremost in my mind when I think of Kate's assertion that many women today refuse to reproduce what they perceive as their own ugliness. Because of my own experiences, I know where they are coming from, but at the same time, I have to wonder where we are going. To answer this question, I talked with several women about being dark-skinned in America. Not surprisingly, almost every person I spoke with told me of numerous painful experiences; in fact, many of them admitted their own desire to reproduce lighter children—children who could easily assimilate in a white American society.

Statistics show that black women are less likely to marry white men than black men are to wed white women. Still, my women friends believe that their careful selection process—planning the exact skin tone and hair texture of one's children—is practiced in households all over America. I have personally seen the anxiety some parents experience when their child is born a shade too dark; and I am fearful of what might

happen if that anxiety is transferred to the child. It has been suggested to me more than once that our jails are not only filled with more blacks, but more dark-skinned blacks: those who carry the double burden of blackness—being black in a white society, and too black in all of society.

Washington Post reporter Leon Dash spoke of this phenomenon in his 1989 book, "When Children Want Children." Several teenagers he interviewed made a direct link between skin tone and self-worth. He quoted one teenaged girl as saying, "Dark-skinned men lie more than light-skinned men," and wrote of another girl rejecting dark men because dating someone lighter "gave her higher status in the neighborhood."

Dash argues that this prejudice, which goes back to the time of slavery, exists especially "among poor urban blacks—those who were generally passed over by the internal self-evaluation [from] the civil rights movement of the 1960s and 1970s." For them, he says, "color consciousness, or being 'color struck' continues as an overt social consideration." But I know that it goes far beyond the urban poor.

I have often wondered what ever happened to such dicta as, "Black Is Beautiful," a phrase to which I clung desperately in the late '60s and early '70s. It helped me begin to discover my inner, as well as outer beauty; even so, I was 21 years old before I ceased to define myself through other people's eyes.

Four years ago I married a man whose mother is Ethiopian and whose father is half white, half Lebanese. He is light-skinned, but I did not fall for him because of his

child-producing ability. He was attracted to me. But more importantly, he was attracted to my dark skin. He thought me beautiful, and it was refreshing to be loved because of my darkness, rather than in spite of it. As far as children are concerned, my husband and I plan to adopt, and it will be someone who looks like me. Maybe that's because I want to make a difference in a child's life, or maybe, selfishly, I want to correct the paradox in my own.

Perhaps the practice of grabbing hold of a little piece of whiteness for one's children is in fact another way to rectify this paradox within oneself. Or perhaps it is an attempt to have control over one's own future. Perhaps it is the final form of assimilation. Either way, I can relate to it; and because of that, I refuse to judge these women.

What I do want is simply to share with them my own experiences and to tell them that there is another way to win that internal struggle between assimilation and self hate. We can start by recognizing our own natural beauty whether we are light, dark or one of the many beautiful colors between. We can say we will no longer alter ourselves to meet the European standards of beauty that have plagued black Americans since we were brought to this country—a country now our home. We can reject the notion that to validate our own existence, we must produce children with hair and eyes different from our own.

Identity, I have learned for myself, can be a hard thing to find if you are searching for it in someone else. So I no longer bother. Instead, I look in the mirror to see who I am and how beautiful I am. And, believe it or not, I have not been disappointed.

ENDANGERED FAMILY

For many African-Americans, marriage and childbearing do not go together.
After decades of denial and blame, a new candor is emerging as
blacks struggle to save their families.

Late on a sultry summer morning, Dianne Caballero settles onto her porch in the New York suburb of Roosevelt, bemused by the scene playing out across the street. Behind electric clippers, a muscular black man is trimming hedges with the intensity of a barber sculpting a fade; nearby, his wife empties groceries from the car. In most quarters, they might elicit barely a nod. But in this largely black, working-class community, the couple is one of the few intact families on the block. All too common are the five young women who suddenly turn into view, every one of them pushing a baby stroller, not one of them married. Resigned, Caballero says with a sigh, "Where are the men?"

A black child has only one chance in five of growing up with two parents

---

It's a lament she knows too well. Like her mother before her and her daughter after, Caballero, who is black, had a child out of wedlock at 16. Twenty-three years later, even she is astounded at the gulf between motherhood and marriage. When her mother got pregnant in the '50s, she says, she was considered unique. When Caballero had a baby in 1970, no one ostracized her, though it still wasn't something "nice" girls did. But by the time her daughter had a baby seven years ago, it was regarded as "normal." Now, Caballero says regretfully, it's commonplace. "And there doesn't

This article was reported by Farai Chideya, Michele Ingrassia, Vern E. Smith and Pat Wingert. It was written by Michele Ingrassia.

seem to be anything happening to reverse it."

That prospect troubles black leaders and parents alike, those like Caballero, who worries that her granddaughter is destined to be the fourth generation in her family to raise a child without a man. The odds are perilously high:

- For blacks, the institution of marriage has been devastated in the last generation: 2 out of 3 first births to black women under 35 are now out of wedlock. In 1960, the number was 2 out of 5. And it's not likely to improve any time soon. A black child born today has only a 1-in-5 chance of growing up with two parents until the age of 16, according to University of Wisconsin demographer Larry L. Bumpass. The impact, of course, is not only on black families but on all of society. Fatherless homes boost crime rates, lower educational attainment and add dramatically to the welfare rolls.

- Many black leaders rush to portray out-of-wedlock births as solely a problem of an entrenched underclass. It's not. It cuts across economic lines. Among the poor, a staggering 65 percent of never-married black women have children, double the number for whites. But even among the well-to-do, the differences are striking: 22 percent of never-married black women with incomes above $75,000 have children, almost 10 times as many as whites.

Nearly 30 years ago, Daniel Patrick Moynihan, then an assistant secretary of labor, caused a firestorm by declaring that fatherless homes were "the fundamental source of the weakness of the Negro Community." At the time, one quarter of black families were headed by women. Today the situation has only grown worse. A majority of black families with children—62 percent—are now headed by one parent. The result is what

Johns Hopkins University sociologist Andrew Cherlin calls "an almost complete separation of marriage and childbearing among African-Americans."

It was not always so. Before 1950, black and white marriage patterns looked remarkably similar. And while black marriage rates have precipitously dipped since then, the desire to marry remains potent: a NEWSWEEK Poll of single African-American adults showed that 88 percent said that they wanted to get married. But the dream of marriage has been hammered in the last 25 years. The economic dislocations that began in the '70s, when the nation shifted from an industrial to a service base, were particularly devastating to black men, who had migrated north in vast numbers to manufacturing jobs. The civil-rights movement may have ended legal segregation, but it hasn't erased discrimination in the work force and in everyday life. "When men lose their ability to earn bread, their sense of self declines dramatically. They lose rapport with their children," says University of Oklahoma historian Robert Griswold, author of "Fatherhood in America."

Some whites overlooked jobs and discrimination as factors in the breakdown of the black family. Back in the '60s, at the peak of the battle over civil rights, Moynihan infuriated blacks by describing a pattern of "pathology." Understandably, blacks were not willing to tolerate a public discussion that implied they were different—less deserving—than whites. The debate quickly turned bitter and polarized between black and white, liberal and conservative. Emboldened by a cultural sea change during the Reagan-Bush era, conservatives scolded, "It's all your fault." Dismissively, this camp insisted that what blacks need are mainstream American values—read: *white* values. Go to school, get a job, get married, they exhorted, and the family

Steep Rise in Out-of-Wedlock Births

Since the sexual revolution, the rate has shot up for both races. But the numbers are much higher for black women than white women.

Whites
Blacks

PERCENT OF WOMEN AGE 15-34 WHO HAVE FIRST CHILD BEFORE FIRST MARRIAGE

Year	Whites	Blacks
1960-64	9	42
1965-69	10	45
1970-74	13	55
1975-79	15	63
1980-84	16	68
1985-89	22	70

SOURCE: CENSUS BUREAU, 1992

NEWSWEEK POLL
WHAT BLACK ADULTS THINK

How important are the following reasons young, unmarried black people today are having children?

(Percent saying very important)

53% They don't understand sex or birth control

48% They won't use birth control or have abortions for personal or religious reasons

38% They want something all their own

37% They want to prove they are adults

35% They are following the examples of older people they know

THE NEWSWEEK POLL, AUGUST 12-15, 1993

will be just fine. Not so, liberals fired back. As neoliberal University of Chicago sociologist William Julius Wilson argued in "The Declining Significance of Race," the breakdown of the African-American family resulted from rising unemployment, not falling values. Liberals have regarded the conservative posture as "blaming the victim," a phrase that, not coincidentally, white psychologist William Ryan coined in a 1965 assessment of Moynihan's study. To this camp, any family structure is good, as long as it's nurturing. "Marriage is important in the black community, just not the most important thing," says Andrew Billingsley, the University of Maryland sociologist who wrote the pioneering "Black Families in White America." "It is not an imperative for black people who can afford it."

Who's right? Both sides are too busy pointing fingers to find out. "We're never going to get to where we need to be if we first have to settle whose fault it is," says writer Nicholas Lemann, whose 1991 book, "The Promised Land," chronicles the great migration of blacks from the rural south to the industrialized North. But if there is any optimism, it is that now, after more than two decades on the defensive and with a Democratic president in the White House for the first time in 12 years, the African-American community is beginning to talk a little more openly about its problems. "Because of all the debate about morality, social programs, individual responsibility, it became very difficult to have an honest discussion," says Angela Glover Blackwell, who heads the Children's Defense Fund's Black Community Crusade for Children. "I'd like to think we've

entered an era where we're willing to accept that there is a dual responsibility" between government and ordinary citizens.

Without question, government must do more to help. But increasingly, African-Americans are unwilling to wait for White America to step in. "During integration," says Virginia Walden, who owns a day-care center in Washington, D.C., "we kept saying that the white people did us wrong, and that they owed us. Well, white people did us wrong, but I tell my children, 'Don't nobody owe you anything. You've got to work for what you get'." In response, many African-American men and women have thrown themselves into a range of grassroots efforts from volunteer work in their communities to adopting children—stopgap efforts, perhaps, but to many, also cathartic and energizing. In many neighborhoods, the black church has led the awakening. Ministers began chastising themselves for sidestepping some basic moral issues. "We don't use 'family values' as an ax," says Wallace Smith, pastor of Shiloh Baptist Church in Washington. "But if someone is shacked up, we encourage them to get married." Smith is remarkably blunt about his own belief in the importance of a stable marriage. "Dan Quayle," he says, "was right."

At their kitchen tables and in their church basements every day, black families talk to each other, as they always have, about their fears. And part of what worries them is the growing tension between black men and black women, who are quick to blame each other for the massive retreat from marriage. "Black men say black women are 'Sapphires,'

trying to dominate," explains Harvard psychologist Alvin Poussaint, referring to the wife of Kingfish in "Amos 'n' Andy," who epitomized the bitchy, bossy black woman. But Boston anchorwoman Liz Walker believes that many black men mistake self-reliance for highhandedness. "I don't think black women have thrown black men out," says Walker, who sparked a controversy when she became pregnant out of wedlock six years ago, long before TV's Murphy Brown knew what a home pregnancy test was. "I think black women have been abandoned."

More commonly, though, black women feel the fallout of the economic and psychological battering the African-American male has taken in the last generation. Of course black women want love and commitment. But not with a man whose chief qualification for marriage is that he's, well, a man. The remarkable success of Terry McMillan's 1991 novel, "Waiting to Exhale," underscores that passion. The book's main characters are four strong-minded black women who can't seem to find men who measure up. They clearly struck a nerve. "When Terry McMillan wrote that book, the reason it was so popular was because it was us," says Walker, 42. Giddy one night from too much birthday champagne and pepperoni pizza, McMillan's quartet—Robin, Gloria, Bernadine and Savannah—get to the essential question: what's happened to all the men, they ask. Where are they hiding?

They're ugly.
Stupid.
In prison.
Unemployed.
Crackheads.
Short.
Liars.
Unreliable.
Irresponsible.
Too possessive . . .
Childish.
Too goddam old and set in their ways.

The litany drives the women to tears. But does marriage really matter? Or is a family headed by a single mother just as good as the nuclear unit? The evidence come down solidly on the side of marriage. By every measure—economic, social, educational—the statistics conclude that two parents living together are better than one. Children of single mothers are significantly more likely to live in poverty than children living with both parents. In 1990, Census figures show, 65 percent of children of black single mothers were poor, compared with only 18 percent of children of black married couples. Educationally, children in one-parent homes are at greater risk across the board—for learning problems, for being left back, for dropping out. Psychiatrist James P. Comer, who teaches at Yale University's Child Study Center, says that the exploding population of African-American children from single-parent homes represents "the education crisis that is going to kill us. The crisis that we're concerned about—that American kids don't achieve as well as European kids and some Asian kids—won't kill us because [American students are] scoring high enough to compete. The one that will kill us is the large number of

bright kids who fall out of the mainstream because their families are not functioning."

Statistics tell only part of the story. Equally important are the intangibles of belonging to an intact family. "Growing up in a married family is where you learn the value of the commitments you make to each other, rather than seeing broken promises," says Roderick Harrison, chief of the Census Bureau's race division. "It deals with the very question of what kind of personal commitments people can take seriously."

Boys in particular need male role models. Without a father, who will help them define what it means to be a man? Fathers do things for their children that mothers often don't. Though there are obviously exceptions, fathers typically encourage independence and a sense of adventure, while mothers are more nurturing and protective. It is men who teach boys how to be fathers. "A woman can only nourish the black male child to a certain point," says Bob Crowder, an Atlanta lawyer and father of four, who helped organize an informal support group for African-American fathers. "And then it takes a man to raise a boy into a man. I mean a real man." Mothers often win the job by default, and struggle to meet the challenge. But sometimes, even a well-intentioned single mother can be smothering, especially if her son is the only man in her life. Down the road a few years, she hears erstwhile daughters-in-law lament how she "ruined" him for every other woman. Like the street-smart New Yorker she is, Bisi Ruckett, who is Dianne Caballero's daughter, says flat out that she can't "rule" her boyfriend. And just as quickly, she concedes she can't compete with his mom. "If he tells her he needs a zillion dollars, she'll get it," says Ruckett, 23.

Without a father for a role model, many boys learn about relationships from their peers on the street. In the inner city in particular, that often means gangs; and the message they're selling is that women are whores and handmaidens, not equals. Having a father does not, of course, guarantee that the lessons a young male learns will be wholesome. But research shows that, with no father, no minister, no boss to help define responsibility, there's nothing to prevent a boy from treating relationships perversely. University of Pennsylvania professor Elijah Anderson, who authored a 1990 study on street life, says that,

among the poor, boys view courting as a "game" in which the object is to perfect a rap that seduces girls. The goal: to add up one's sexual conquests, since that's the measure of "respect."

Often, for a girl, Anderson says, life revolves around the "dream," a variation of the TV soaps in which a man will whisk her away to a life of middle-class bliss—even though everywhere she looks there are only single mothers abandoned by their boyfriends. Not surprisingly, the two sexes often collide. The girl dreams because she must. "It has to do with one's conception of oneself: 'I will prevail'," Anderson says. But the boy tramples that dream because he must—his game is central to his vision of respect. "One of the reasons why, when a woman

---

Wallace Smith, pastor of Washington's Shiloh Church, puts it bluntly: 'Dan Quayle was right.'

---

agrees to have a baby, these men think it's such a victory is that you have to get her to go against all the stuff that says he won't stick around."

For teenage mothers not mature enough to cope, single parenthood is not the route to the dream, but entrapment. They have too many frustrations: the job, the lack of a job, the absence of a man, the feeling of being dependent on others for help, the urge to go out and dance instead of pacing with a crying child. Taken to its extreme, says Poussaint, the results can be abuse or neglect. "They'll see a child as a piece of property or compete with the child—calling them dumb or stupid, damaging their growth and education to maintain superiority," he says. The middle class is not exempt from such pain. Even with all the cushions money could buy—doctors and backup doctors, nannies and backup nannies—Liz Walker says that trying to raise her son, Nicholas, alone was draining. "Certainly, the best situation is to have as many people in charge of a family as possible," says Walker, who is now married to Harry Graham, a 41-year-old corporate-tax lawyer; together, they're raising her son and his two children from a previous marriage. "I can see that now," she adds. "Physically, you *need* it."

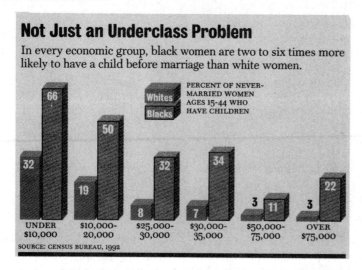

Not Just an Underclass Problem

In every economic group, black women are two to six times more likely to have a child before marriage than white women.

PERCENT OF NEVER-MARRIED WOMEN AGES 15-44 WHO HAVE CHILDREN

Whites / Blacks

UNDER $10,000	$10,000-20,000	$25,000-30,000	$30,000-35,000	$50,000-75,000	OVER $75,000
32 / 66	19 / 50	8 / 32	7 / 34	3 / 11	3 / 22

SOURCE: CENSUS BUREAU, 1992

More and more, black men aren't there to build marriages or to stick around through the hard years of parenting. The question we're too afraid to confront is why. The biggest culprit is an economy that has locked them out of the mainstream through a pattern of bias and a history of glass ceilings. "The economic state of the African-American community is worse in 1993 than it was in 1963," says NAACP head Benjamin Chavis Jr. He could be speaking, just as easily, about the black family, since the two fell in tandem.

A man can't commit to a family without economic security, but for many African-American men, there is none. The seeds of modern economic instability date back to the 1940s, when the first of 6½ million blacks began migrating from the rural South to the urban North as farm mechanization replaced the need for their backs and hands. At first, black men built a solid economic niche by getting factory jobs. But just as the great migration ended in the '70s, the once limitless industrial base began to cave in. And as steel mills and factories swept offshore, the "last hired, first fired" seniority rules disproportionately pushed black men out. During that time, says Billingsley, unemployment for blacks became twice as high as it was for whites, "and it has rarely dropped below that [ratio] since." Unarguably, economic restructuring hit whites as well as blacks, but the new service sector favored those with education—and there were many more educated white men than blacks in the '70s as vast numbers of baby boomers streamed out of the nation's colleges looking for jobs.

Ironically, just as the job market col-

lapsed for black men, it opened for black women, who went to college while black men went to war. Armed with the college degrees that black males didn't have and pushed by the burgeoning women's movement, growing numbers of black women found spots in corporate America. As with white women in the '80s, that bought them greater independence. But the jobs of black women came at the expense of black men. Throughout the workplace, says Yale's Comer, "there was a trade-off. The one black woman was a two-fer: you got a black and a woman." Since then, the gap between white women's income and black women's has disappeared—black women's salaries are the same as whites'.

But the chasm between black and white men has barely moved. In 1969, black men earned 61 cents for every dollar white men earned; by 1989, the number had increased to only 69 cents. And that's for black men who were working; more and more, they found themselves without jobs. During the same time, the number of black men with less than a high-school education who found jobs dropped from two thirds to barely half. And it's likely to worsen: in the last 25 years, the proportion of black men in college has steadily eroded. "America has less use for black men today than it did during slavery," says Eugene Rivers, who helps run computer-training programs as pastor of Boston's Azusa Christian Community.

Though he is scarcely 11, Lugman Kolade dreams of becoming an electrical engineer. But he already wears the grievous pain of a man who feels left out. Lugman is a small, studious, Roman Catholic schooler from Washington,

D.C., who will enter the sixth grade this fall, a superb student who won the archdiocese science fair with a homemade electric meter. Unlike most boys in the Male Youth Project he attended at Shiloh Baptist Church, his parents are married. His mother works for the Department of Public Works; describing what his father does doesn't come easy. "My father used to be a [construction] engineer. He left his job because they weren't treating him right; they would give white men better jobs who did less work. Now he drives an ice-cream truck."

Black men were hurt, too, by the illegal economy. As the legitimate marketplace case them aside, the drug trade took off, enlisting anyone lured by the promise of fast money. Ironically, says Comer, "you had to make a supreme and extra effort to get into the legal system and no effort to get into the illegal system." For many on the fringes, there was no contest. "It overwhelmed the constructive forces in the black mainstream," he says. Disproportionately, too, black men are in prison or dead. While African-Americans represent only 12 percent of the population, they composed 44 percent of the inmates in state prisons and local jails in 1991; and, in 1990, homicide was the leading cause of death for young black men.

The economy explains only one part of what happened. The sexual revolution in the '70s was the second great shift that changed the black family. Although the social tide that erased taboos against unwed motherhood affected all women, whites and blacks took different paths. White women delayed both marriage and childbearing, confident that, down the road, there would be a pool of marriageable men. Not so for black women, who delayed marriage but not children because they were less certain there would be men for them. In what they called a "striking shift," Census officials reported earlier this year that less than 75 percent of black women are likely to ever marry, compared with 90 percent of whites.

More dramatic is the childbearing picture. Between 1960 and 1989, the proportion of young white women giving birth out of wedlock rose from 9 to 22 percent, markedly faster than it did for blacks. The slower rate of increase for blacks was small comfort. Their rate—42 percent—was already so high by 1960 that if it had kept pace with the white race, ti would have topped 100 percent by now. As things stand, it's 70 percent.

Rejecting Marriage

Before 1950, young black women were actually more likely to get married than white women.

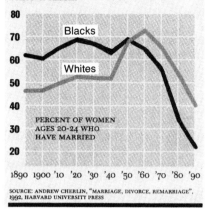

PERCENT OF WOMEN AGES 20-24 WHO HAVE MARRIED

SOURCE: ANDREW CHERLIN, "MARRIAGE, DIVORCE, REMARRIAGE", 1992, HARVARD UNIVERSITY PRESS

Traditionally, the extended family has served as a safety net. But the terrible irony of history is that it has also hurt the black family. While intended as a cushion, the network, in effect, enabled more single women to have children. And that helps explain why not only poor black women, but middle- and upper-class blacks as well, have had children out of wedlock at higher rates than white women. Historically, white women have had only themselves to rely on for child rearing, and so marriage became more of an imperative. For blacks, the network of extended kin is a tradition rooted in African customs that emphasize community over marriage. Although historians say that most black children grew up in two-parent households during slavery, as well as in the 19th and early 20th centuries, high rates of poverty, widowhood and urban migration reinforced the need for interdependence that continues today. The oft-repeated African proverb "It takes a whole village to raise a child" echoes back to that.

Now the extended family is breaking down. Yet the black family's expectations for it haven't diminished. Both sides feel the strains. With the soaring number of teenage mothers, grandparents today are getting younger and more likely to be working themselves. A 32-year-old grandmother isn't necessarily eager, or able, to raise a grandchild, especially when that child becomes a teenager and the problems multiply. And, after generations of no fathers, there are no grandfathers, either. What's more, the tradition of a real neighborhood is disappearing. "It used to be that everyone looked out for everyone else," said community activist Claudette Burroughs-White of Greensboro, N.C. "Now I think people are kind of estranged. They don't get involved. It's safer not to." Many families left in the inner city—the ones most in need of support—are increasingly isolated from relatives able to flee to the suburbs. "Not every poor black mother is in a strong kinship network," says Cherlin. "Many are living alone, hiding behind double-locked doors in housing projects."

What's the solution? Nearly 30 years after Lyndon Johnson launched the War on Poverty, experts on the black family return again and again to the same ideas—better education, more jobs, discouraging teen pregnancy, more mentoring programs. But now the question is, who should deliver—government or blacks themselves? Ever since the government started abandoning social programs in the '70s and early '80s, black families have been left on their own to find a way out. Those who would argue against funneling in more government dollars say we tried that, but "nothing works." Lemann, who believes that most of the positive social changes in Black America were sparked by government

intervention, dismisses the conceit that spending on social welfare failed. The War on Poverty, he says "threw out some untested ideas, some of which worked"—like Head Start, the Job Corps and Foster Grandparents—"and some of which didn't." Beyond the all-or-nothing extremes, there is room for solutions. Moynihan believes the nation has been in a collective "denial phase" about the black family for the last 25 years. But he says he's encouraged. "We're beginning to get a useful debate on this."

Will self-help do it? Though few African-American leaders expect what they call "White America" to come to the rescue, they're equally skeptical that the thousands of programs filling church rec rooms and town-hall meeting rooms can, on their own, turn things around. "People who are trying to salvage a lot of the children are burnt out, they think it's like spitting into the ocean," says Poussaint, who doesn't dispute the pessimism. "The problems are overwhelming. It's like treating lung cancer and knowing that people are still smoking."

There aren't many places left to look for answers. When black leaders peak with one voice, it is about the deep crisis of faith and purpose that came with integration: the very promise that African-Americans would be brought into the American mainstream has left many by the wayside. What's the penalty for doing nothing? "We could revert to a caste society," says Moynihan. Others are just as bleak. There are sparks of hope, says Comer, but he warns: "It's getting late, very late." The problems of the black family have been apparent for decades. And so has our collective understanding that we must take them on. What we need to find now is a voice to start the dialogue.

■ WHITE PATRIARCHAL SUPREMACY

The Politics of Family in America

JEWELL HANDY GRESHAM

The past is not dead. It's not even past.
                                            —*William Faulkner*

In April 1844, Secretary of State John Calhoun, the pre-eminent Southern philosopher of States' rights, directed a letter to the British ambassador in Washington attesting that where blacks and whites existed in the same society, slavery was the natural result. Wherever the states changed that providential relationship, the blacks invariably degenerated "into vice and pauperism accompanied by the bodily and mental afflictions incident thereto—deafness, blindness, insanity, and idiocy." In the slave states, in contrast, the blacks improved greatly "in number, comfort, intelligence, and morals."

To prove his point, Calhoun supplied statistics from the 1840 census. The data showed a shocking rate of black insanity in New England: one out of every fourteen in Maine, every twenty-eight in New Hampshire, every forty-three in Massachusetts, etc. The overall figure for the North was almost ten times the rate in the South, where only one "lunatic" for every 1,309 blacks was shown in Virginia, one in 2,447 in South Carolina, etc.

At the time Calhoun wrote that letter, one of the country's leading newspapers had just broken the scandal of the plot by President Tyler's Administration to annex Texas as slave territory—a potential constitutional crisis certain to inflame the bitter North-South conflict. In that context, Calhoun's statistics were intended less for the British than for Congress, to which he forwarded copies.

There was only one flaw in his argument: The figures were false. Dr. Edward Jarvis of Massachusetts General Hospital, a leading specialist in the incidence of insanity, immediately challenged them. Joined by the prestigious American Statistical Association, Jarvis conducted an exhaustive study of every town and county in the free states in which black insanity had been reported by the Census Bureau. In case after case, the number of "insane" blacks proved larger than the state's total black population!

The A.S.A.'s comprehensive study—forwarded to former President John Quincy Adams in the House of Representatives—concluded that "it would have been far better to have no census at all, than such a one as has been published" and urged Congress either to correct the data or "discard or disown" it "as the good of the country . . . and as justice and humanity shall demand." But when Adams, as recorded in his diary, confronted Calhoun at the State Department, the latter "answered like a true slavemonger. . . . He writhed like a trodden rattlesnake on the exposure of his false report to the House . . . and finally said that where there were so many errors they balanced one another, and led to the same conclusion as if they were all correct." The A.S.A. report—blocked by the Speaker the and proslavery majority in the House—never reached the floor.

While these developments unfolded, Southern slaves were of course in no position to challenge the claims in which their welfare was critical. Nor did the free blacks of New York City under the leadership of the distinguished black physician/abolitionist James McCune Smith stand a chance of having their memorial to Congress protesting the "calumnies against free people of color" recognized. For those who held political power, it was imperative that blacks simply not exist except as objects, and the truth or falsity of what was said was beside the point. What mattered, then as now, was not the *facts* but only that the semblance of "substance" be provided for a time sufficient to confuse the issue and carry the day.

'The Need to Segregate or Quarantine a Race'

After the Civil War, the Calhoun view of the inherent degeneracy of blacks, which held that they could not survive outside slavery, was tenaciously clung to by the outnumbered whites of Mississippi. In 1865 the *Meridian Clarion* asserted with unconcealed satisfaction that the black race

From *The Nation*, July 24-31, 1989, pp. 116-120, 122. © 1989 by The Nation Company, Inc.

was doomed: "A hundred years is a long time to one man; but to a nation or a race, it is but a limited period. Well, in that time the negro will be dead."

In due course, Mississippi produced figures to prove it: The 1866 state census showed a more than 12 percent decline in the black population. Unfortunately for the prophets, however, this data was as accurate as Calhoun's: The 1870 Federal census showed an *increase* of more than 7,000, which turned out to be an undercount of between 50,000 and 75,000, corrected in the 1880 Federal figures.

Nonetheless, in the 1880s, the Reverend C.K. Marshall, the most prominent preacher in the state, predicted that "by January, 1920 . . . except for a few old people [who] will linger as the Cherokees do on their reservation . . . the colored population of the south will scarcely be counted."

With the passage of more years without apparent visible diminution in black ranks, however, white theories of a built-in biological solution to the black "problem" obviously had to be augmented. In *The Plantation Negro as Freeman* (1889), the historian Philip A. Bruce used the black family as a device for attacking all blacks. Bruce, the scion of a former Virginia slaveowner, simply advanced Calhoun's thesis: With the end of slavery, the loss of white "supervision" led to a severe and menacing deterioration in blacks' social and moral condition. The black family as such did not exist, he announced; black children, accordingly, were born into a state of moral degeneracy.

Bruce viciously castigated black women. Alluding to the alleged propensity of black men to rape white women, he asserted that they found "something strangely alluring and seductive . . . in the appearance of a white woman" because of the "wantonness of the women of his own race." The "fact" that black women failed to complain of being raped by men of their race counted as "strong proof of the sexual laxness of plantation women as a class."

Herbert Gutman called Bruce's work perhaps the most important connecting link between the "popular" views of African-American degeneracy in the 1880s and the supportive pseudoscientific works of the ensuing decades before World War I. These latter writings rested heavily on the pseudoscientific data of Social Darwinism—the doctrine of survival of the fittest. The historian George Frederickson explains the relevance of such theories in his book *The Black Image in the White Mind*:

> If the blacks were a degenerating race with no future, the problem ceased to be one of how to prepare them for citizenship or even how to make them more productive and useful members of the community. The new prognosis pointed rather to the need to segregate or quarantine a race liable to be a source of contamination and social danger to the white community, as it sank ever deeper into the slough of disease, vice, and criminality.

The Device Updated

It was against these brutally repressive rationalizations still undergirding the Southern apartheid system after World War II that the civil rights revolution of the 1950s and 1960s erupted. And it was at the climactic stages of that struggle

that Labor Department official Daniel Patrick Moynihan conceived, in December 1964, his supposedly secret "internal memorandum" on the black family.

Whether Moynihan knew his history or not, his report served the time-tested purpose: Whenever the system is in crisis (or shows signs of becoming transformed); whenever blacks get restless (or show strength); whenever whites in significant numbers show signs of coming together with blacks to confront their mutual problems (or enemies), the trick is to shift the focus from the real struggle for political and economic empowerment to black "crime," degeneracy, pathology and—in Moynihan's innovative twist—the "deterioration" of the black family (previously defined as non-existent!).

Moynihan's report was subtitled "The Case for National Action." But just how much serious "action" it intended was made plain in the author's next "internal memo"—this time to Richard Nixon—counseling "benign neglect."

In the light of subsequent events it is interesting to discover in *Pat*, the Senator's biography, that it was presidential assistant Bill Moyers who, in May 1965, first brought the black family report, until then ignored, to Lyndon Johnson's attention and arranged for the President to deliver a major policy speech based on it.

Curiously, the Moyers-arranged speech bypassed all agencies of the government set up to aid the passage of the President's civil rights agenda. It was delivered at the graduation exercises of Howard University before an overwhelmingly black audience of thousands of students, parents, friends and dignitaries. Apparently few observers among the editors, journalists and scholars present found what Johnson did reprehensible. Howard was one of the colleges that had sent a sizable contingent of students into the revolutionary *nonviolent* Southern struggle which at that moment was galvanizing, inspiring and, in a thousand unforeseeable ways, transforming the nation. Before the young people whom he should have congratulated for the extraordinary example of sacrifice and heroism they were setting, the President emphasized the "historical" degenerate state of the families from which they came!

True, words of noble intent were there (as they were in Moynihan's original), and they heartened many. But so were the declarations of black degeneracy that reinforced the racism of many more and signaled the open-door policy for what was to come. Through the summer, however, the "secret" Moynihan report continued to be leaked to selected journalists. Then came the event that cemented its impact. Ten days after the August passage of the Voting Rights Act of 1965, Watts exploded—and in a mad scramble for instant wisdom, journalists turned to the black family report and drew on its conclusions as explanations for the violent civil disorders.

What did it explain? What were the causes of Watts and the succeeding ghetto rebellions? Not, as the Kerner commission concluded in 1967, the division of America into two societies, separate and unequal. Not historical white racism, Depression-level unemployment and the intolerable conditions of the ghetto that cut short the dreams and lives of millions of black men, women and children. Not at all. "Ours is a society," offered Moynihan, "which presumes male leadership in private and public affairs. . . . A subculture such as that of the Negro American, in which this is not the pattern, is placed at a distinct disadvantage." To overcome that disadvantage, he said, the malaise of the black family, characterized by the unnatural dominance of a "black matriarchy," had to be cured.

In contrast, Moynihan wrote: *The white family has achieved a high degree of stability and is maintaining that stability.* (Emphasis added.) Against the backdrop of the next twenty-five years, this declaration would be hilarious were it not for the fact that, for untold millions of *white* working women—divorced, single and joint providers—the idealized patriarchal structure held up as an icon had always been a myth! Indeed, even as Moynihan wrote the words, the modern women's movement for equal rights and a sense of selfhood, submerged under the centuries-old domination of that very model, was being forged in the crucible of the civil rights struggle.

MAMAS AND SUPERSTUDS

Raw and uncontrolled sex is at the root of the Black family problem. This is the most enduring of all lies about Blacks, and sociologists and historians froth at the mouth and strain at the leash of synonymity ("riotous debauchery," "unbridled passions," "wild and primitive emotions") in passionate attempts to express this academic and political voyeurism. For most, if not almost all, critics of the Black family, there is always at the back of the mind this myth, this image of Black America as Babylon, where the Studs and Sapphires are *always* making babies, where—in the words of the myth—"They do it, honey, right out in the middle of the streets." And one of the most challenging problems we face is confronting scholars, journalists and politicians, who have repeatedly used the Black family to exorcise the demons of their own sexuality and the guilt of their complicity in oppression. What makes this so difficult is that we are dealing here with a magical idea that is impervious to "facts." There are, in fact, no facts in this area, for there has never been a systematic analysis of the sexual differences between American Blacks and American Whites. And the few facts we have contradict the supersex theory of Black history and suggest that the differences between racial groups are relatively small, especially when you correct for economic and historical differences. More to the point, Blacks, according to the statistics, are not even in the running in the areas of wife-swapping and other experiments of the sexual revolution.

—Lerone Bennett Jr.
Ebony, August 1986

Those who found the Moynihan report useful were presumably unaware that the archetypal sexism on which it rests is inextricable from its racism. At any rate, the report signaled, at the very height of the civil rights movement, that Northern whites would pick up where the South was forced to leave off in blocking the long black struggle for parity with whites in American life.

Line of Descent

On January 25, 1986, Bill Moyers, Moynihan's original booster, invoked the full power of a prime-time, two-hour CBS Special Report to beam the old theme into millions of homes. The title: *The Vanishing Black Family—Crisis in Black America* (shades of the old Mississippi *Meridian Clarion*!). The East Texan, in sympathetic "liberal" guise, took cameras into a Newark, New Jersey, housing project for an "intimate" portrait of black teen-age welfare mothers, sexually irresponsible if not criminal youth, a smiling black male "superstud," and pervasive pathology all around. Moyers's report was directed not at the cause of the plight of the people whose confidences he elicited. Viewers were shown, rather, a pathology in black America so overwhelming and irredeemable as to leave the panel of blacks brought in at the end to "discuss" the subject helpless to dissipate the impact of the carefully selected imagery.

The result, whatever sympathy toward individual victims white viewers might have felt, and whatever responsibilities some might acknowledge that America has for its racist "past," could only be: First, to utterly terrify most as to the very nature of their fellow black citizens by reinforcing, with "liberal" authority, the most archetypal of racist myths, fears and stereotypes—a picture of "jungle" immorality and degeneracy, inarticulateness and sloth so rife that the onlookers could actually forget the terrible national corruption, wholesale public and private immorality, and other massive problems about them, in horrified fascination with the doings of these Others. And second, to make the situation seem so hopeless that "realistically" there is nothing to be done about it anyway. Racism is no longer the problem, self-destructiveness is. And if that is so, why continue to throw good taxpayer dollars after bad? In the words of the older black woman selected by Moyers to deliver the clincher at the end: "If Martin Luther King were alive, he would not be talking about the things I think he was talking about—labor and all that. He would be talking about the black family."

It is hard to believe that it was simply bad taste that led CBS to choose the very week of the first national celebration of King's birthday to televise his fellow Southerner's broadside. African-Americans had hardly had a moment to savor the honor to the martyred black minister before their psyches were so powerfully assaulted.

The extent of the commonplace manner in which deep-seated black response is blocked out from the larger society may be seen in several postscripts to the broadcast beginning when the National Black Leadership Roundtable, comprising the chief executive officers of more than 300 national black organizations, directed a detailed letter to CBS to protest the "untimely and indeed . . . suspect" airing of an "unbalanced, unfair and frequently salacious" documentary.

The N.B.L.R. challenged the implication "that the *only* legitimate and sanctioned family form is nuclear and patriarchal," and observed:

> One was left with the impression that black families generally do not have fathers in the home, but there was no serious examination of the reasons for the absence of the father within some black families. The unconscionable high levels of unemployment, underemployment, imprisonment, drug addiction and mortality among black men—effects of an economy which does not fully respond to the employment needs of all Americans—all play a role. . . . Single-parent families then, are not, as implied . . . the result of "immorality" or promiscuity, but rather are adaptive responses to economic and social forces.

Two months later CBS vice president of public affairs broadcasts Eric Ober, speaking for Moyers, replied. He refused to meet with Walter Fauntroy, N.B.L.R. president, or "any member of your group." And to the N.B.L.R. query as to what "experts" had been consulted within the black community, he replied that the "experts we consulted were primarily officials of *the Department of the Census*." (Emphasis added.) Little did he know the history.

The reinforcing white response was predictable. In early 1987, the Columbia University Graduate School of Journalism gave its highest award in broadcast journalism—the Alfred I. DuPont–Columbia University Gold Baton for the "program judged to have made the greatest contribution to the public's understanding of an important issue"—to CBS News for the Moyers Special Report on "the disintegration of black family life."

Moyers's contribution lies not only in his restoration to primacy of old images through the power of television but in his encouragement of the willingness, indeed the eagerness, of large numbers of white Americans to have all that he portrayed be true at any cost so that the victims might deserve their fate. Such is the depth of the entrenched white desire to avoid facing the society's culpability for creating and maintaining the two ever more unequal "societies" the Kerner report asked us to face up to a generation before.

Restraining the 'Darker Impulses'

In such a climate, it is not surprising that politicians like "centrist" Democrat Charles Robb, L.B.J.'s son-in-law and former Virginia Governor, now Senator, promptly picked up Moyer's cue. Once upon a time, black people were the victims of white racism, Robb conceded in his keynote speech to a conference on the Johnson presidency. But that time has passed. "It's time to shift the primary focus from racism, the traditional enemy from without, to self-defeating patterns of behavior, the new enemy within."

Approval by establishment opinion makers was swift to follow. A *New York Times* editorial endorsed Robb's brand of "hard truth," and journalists flung the name of the messenger into the public arena as a worthy candidate for President.

In such a climate, the level of public tolerance of the intolerable increased. Even years before, there had been little reaction when, at a speech in New Orleans to the International Association of Chiefs of Police, President Reagan had drawn "applause and some whoops of approval" for remarks that included the following:

> It has occurred to me that the root causes of our . . . growth of government and the decay of the economy . . . can be traced to many of the same sources of the crime problem. . . . Many of the social thinkers of the 1950s and '60s who discussed crime only in the context of disadvantaged childhoods and poverty-stricken neighborhoods were the same people who thought that massive government spending could wipe away our social ills. The underlying premise in both cases was a belief that there was nothing permanent or absolute about any man's nature—that he was a product of his material environment, and that by changing that environment . . . we could . . . usher in a great new era. The solution to the crime problem will not be found in the social worker's files, the psychiatrist's notes or the bureaucrat's budget. . . . Only our deep moral values and strong institutions can hold back that jungle and restrain the darker impulses of human nature.

Most black people knew immediately of which "jungle" and whose "darker impulses" Reagan was speaking, and that his words represented a not-so-subtle invitation to white-against-black terror.

Reagan's position was a *theological* one in the American Calvinist tradition, a division of the world into good and evil, with a scapegoat selected to serve as "sacrificial animal upon whose back the burden of unwanted evils is ritualistically loaded," in Kenneth Burke's definition. Through such projections, the culture thus expiates its sins and receives absolution.

The Reagan rhetoric directed to the assembled police officers was a direct corollary of his theological labeling of the Soviet Union as an "evil empire" (a remark now implicitly withdrawn in the case of the Russians, but not that of African-Americans!). It indicates how high is the level of responsibility for nationwide police practices of treating black Americans as if they are foreign enemies and, with sickening regularity, eliminating many. And it also indicates the treatment of a variety of foreign "enemies"—now mostly desperately struggling Third World countries—on the basis of a "moral" stance rooted in the myths of a fatalistically corrupt domestic system.

It is on this level that the politics of family—which is to say the politics of power and domination—threatens not only domestic but world social, political and economic order.

It is likewise on this level that the political manipulation of the intermingled race/sex/religion syndrome of the society is irrevocably wedded to violence; in its ultimate form, militaristic. For the identities of those who create the monsters in the mind (Toni Morrison calls the creations "grinning apes in the head") require ever vigilant attention to finding and confronting replicas in the external world.

It is this system of macho ethics that was successfully drawn upon in George Bush's march to the White House. True to tradition, the ultimate scapegoat tapped was a black male, the rapist Willie Horton (whether real or fancied does not traditionally matter), projected before millions via television and print.

Those who make use of such a repugnant and dangerous tactic—among them South Carolina's Lee Atwater, now chair of the Republican National Committee, and Texan James Baker 3d—know these traditions well. And they know further that it is not possible for the image of a black man accused of rape to be flashed before black Americans by white men independent of the psychic association for blacks with lynchings. After the election, *The New York Times* not only contributed the verdict to history that the Bush campaign was "tough and effective," this pre-eminent sheet augmented that judgment with strident editorial criticism of black students at Howard for their successful protest action when Lee Atwater was suddenly named to the University's Board of Trustees.

While white perception of black criminality is readily evoked, white awareness of black anger or anguish has been not only historically avoided but, on the deepest psychic levels, guarded against. Existentially, the concept of black people as vulnerable human beings who sustain pain and love and hatreds and fears and joy and sorrows and degradations and triumphs is not yet permitted in the national consciousness. Hence the constant need of the dominant society, in age after age, to reinforce linguistic and ritualistic symbols that deny black humanity.

Historically, white terror is the sustaining principle of the system. Whether overtly applied or covertly threatened, not only has this basic device of subjugation never been nationally rejected, it has, on the contrary, always been sanctioned.

The Family as Unifying Principle

A few weeks after his election, George Bush addressed the Republican Governors Association in Alabama where, some months before, several black legislators had been arrested for trying to remove the Confederate Flag from above the State Capitol, presided over by Republican Governor Guy Hunt. The theme of the conference—"Century of the States"—resurrected overtones of Calhoun's old brand of States' rights. To this audience, a smiling Bush announced that building more prisons was a major domestic priority of his Administration (on education, he emphasized that the initiative would be left up to the states).

Only a few weeks later a smiling Bush assured a black gathering celebrating the birthday of Martin Luther King Jr. that he is committed to the fulfillment of King's dream of America, just as they are. That King's dream does not include the construction of prisons is immaterial. In the prevailing political realm, language does not matter: Symbols are all.

However, the renewed focus on the black family has introduced a sleeper. For the very technology of communication which carries the message of black pathology to white people conveys to blacks the unmistakable message that once again the dominant culture needs the assurance that black pathology prevails. Clearly, we must bestir ourselves to face the threat. Ironically, we have been handed a mighty weapon. To millions of ordinary human beings the family is not a symbol to be manipulated by opportunistic politicians but the essential nurturing unit from which they draw their being. For African-Americans (and for hundreds of millions of others), it is the institution around which our historical memories cling. Through the extended family of mothers, fathers, sisters and brothers, uncles and aunts, cousins and unsung numbers of others who simply "mothered" parentless children, black people "got over."

It is unbelievable that on the eve of the twenty-first century those who are still fashioning the political formula for WHO and WHAT make a family remain overwhelmingly male!

But it is women who give birth, and children who represent the one essential entity which must exist if the family does. It is simply inconceivable that women, that society, can any longer allow men to retain almost exclusive domain over the vital process of defining the human family.

The concept of "family" can and should be a unifying, rather than divisive, principle. Given the weight of U.S. history that we uniquely bear, black women should step forth collectively not only as blacks but as women, in the name of our lost children throughout history—including most urgently the present generation. One of the first steps is to confront, in all their ramifications, the racist/sexist myths historically concocted by opportunistic, ruthless or naïve white males in the interests of white-over-black and male-over-female dominance.

Never again should the future of black children—or children anywhere in the world—be left in such hands!

Home Ownership Anchors The Middle Class

But Lending Games Sink Many Prospective Owners

Scott Minerbrook

It was the kind of house Donnell Cravens and his wife, Eugenie, had prayed for: a four-bedroom brick colonial with brown trim, hedges all around and an attached garage. They saw it for the first time in early July, and it was almost an apparition of earthly rewards. For him, a personnel director, there was a garden to raise corn, tomatoes and melons. For her, an accountant with the Detroit Symphony Orchestra, a green-sward of lawn manicured like a royal garden. True, West Bloomfield, Mich., didn't have many minority children for their kids to play with, but they'd somehow make do.

They almost didn't get it. They had $54,000 in the bank from the sale of their Detroit home and had been pre-approved for a $150,000 mortgage, complete with a letter of qualification from one financial institution. Then came the meeting with the seller's realtor. One look at the agent and Eugenie told Donnell, "She's going to give us trouble." The agent tried. She told the seller that the Cravens weren't qualified, even though she'd gotten a full rundown about the husband's finances — without his consent. The seller was about to pull out when the Cravens threatened to call in their lawyers. That seemed to do the trick. "It was a travesty," Donnell said. "I knew about the race game in real estate, but I wouldn't have believed it if I hadn't experienced it myself."

Welcome to the world of real estate, to seclusion and exclusion. It is a world where many minorities give up. Indeed, the very intent is to make minorities give up. "The ultimate humiliation for the black middle class is the denial of equal access to housing," said Charles Bromley, director for the Metropolitan Strategy Group in Cleveland, Ohio. For blacks, at all levels, the hoops are higher and smaller while for whites, they are wider and lower. It's discrimination with a smile."

For the black middle class, exclusion from better housing is the bitter fruit of a legacy of racial prejudice. In what scholars call the "inertia of segregation," millions of African-Americans who have climbed into the security of the middle and upper classes — about 12 per cent of all African-Americans now have earnings exceeding $50,000 a year — only to find that the dream of buying a home is a nightmare of miscues and obstacles. Nowhere is this fact of greater consequence than in the field of housing. Buying a home is not only part of the American Dream, it is essential to grasping it. But study after study reveals that those in the middle class are restricted in their choice of where to live and what to buy. They are treated differently by lending and insurance institutions simply because of the color of their skin. This has a profound impact on the wealth of generations to come.

More than two decades after the 1968 Fair Housing Act banned discrimination in the sale and rental of housing, blacks who try to move away from the disadvantages of city living often find themselves re-segregated into what sociologists call the "inner ring" or "near-in suburbs," such as Prince George's County or Silver Spring, in Maryland, which surround Washington, D.C. They find themselves hemmed in by housing practices that put them in close proximity to the poor and to lesser educational opportunities, despite the fact that they may be earning as much as their white counterparts. Steered there by discriminatory practices on the part of banks, insurance companies and realtors, middle-class blacks find themselves in areas where the demand for the houses they have purchased has already peaked, virtually ensuring a deflation in the value of their homes compared to those of the whiter suburbs beyond.

"The net result of segregation is that the black middle class loses the very freedom of movement that defines being in the middle class," said Douglas S. Massey, a sociologist at the University of Chicago.

Massey has a word for these collective experiences: hypersegregation. It is a term that defines the increasing spatial isolation of blacks from whites, not only in American cities, but in the suburbs that weren't built for blacks in the first place. In his recent book, *American Apartheid: Segregation and the Making of the Underclass*, Massey and his co-author, Nancy A. Denton, show just how deeply segregated America continues to be. A principal finding: Race, not class, is the main determinant of where blacks are allowed to live. According to the authors' data, a black person who makes $50,000 has fewer choices in where he or she can live and is more segregated than an Hispanic person earning $2,500. The authors say blacks earning $50,000 a year also experience the same degree of segregation as African-Americans earning $2,500 a year. And according to the National Research Council, it will take about six decades for blacks to achieve the minimal levels of economic security that integration with whites has already brought to Hispanics and Asians.

From *Emerge*, October 1993, pp. 42-48. Reprinted by permission.

6. AFRICAN AMERICANS

"This is the penalty of race," said sociologist George Galster, of the Washington-based Urban Institute.

It is a reality so widespread that it is almost never challenged. The bottom line, Massey said, is that blacks in many big cities are less likely to move to the suburbs than either Asians or Hispanics and are more likely to live segregated lives once they are there. In the Chicago area, for instance, fewer than 16 percent of blacks live in the suburbs, compared to 27 percent of Hispanics and nearly half of the area's Asians.

The numbers are just as stark when Massey compares where blacks live to where whites live. By 1980, when black economic progress was beginning to stall because of resistance to affirmative action, 71 percent of all whites lived in northern suburbs. Blacks then composed less than a quarter of all suburban residents. In the South, the suburbs were 65 percent white and 34 percent black. In the North and Midwest, blacks were even less likely to live in the suburbs of Indianapolis, Kansas City, Milwaukee and New York — all of which had black residential rates of less than 10 per cent. In the suburbs of Los Angeles, Pittsburgh and St. Louis, the black residential rates didn't approach that of whites.

But even these numbers are potentially misleading. While blacks began moving into the suburbs in the '80s, Massey said, this didn't mean the neighborhoods where they lived were integrated. In fact, many black "suburbs" were often simply sections of declining municipalities, replete with all the problems that have hobbled the economic growth of central cities.

Even if an African-American moved to the suburbs, various studies show high degrees of segregation — of blacks closer to blacks and whites closer to whites — were usually the rule.

And this does not bode well for blacks living there. Those suburbs where the numbers of blacks have increased have followed the old rule of real estate: Where blacks are, white homeowners stay away, fearful that the value of their homes won't increase. This may or may not be racism *per se*, scholars say, since racial attitudes are often indistinguishable from economic ones. One expert has estimated that between 30 percent and 70 percent of racial segregation is the result of economic concerns, such as home value. In large measure it is perception that becomes reality. In most instances, whites are reluctant to move to areas where housing approaches a 20 percent black ratio. Once this level is reached, white demand softens even as black demand increases. This often leads to re-segregation of an area. So set are white home buyers in their identification of the suburbs as being "white" that a 1985 study of white voters in Detroit by the Michigan Democratic Party found that whites believed that not being black is what, by definition, constitutes being middle class and that "not living with blacks is what makes a neighborhood a decent place to live."

This generally has devastating effects on the areas that have become integrated. Proud and comfortable as they may be, weakening white demand means blacks will find themselves stuck with homes they can't sell. Median home prices in the city of Detroit tell this story over time. The median home value of a single-family home in that city

dropped (in 1990 dollars) from $49,000 in 1970 to $36,000 in 1980 to $27,000 in 1990 — a 45 per cent drop in their equity as whites moved out over the 20-year period. As whites leave an area, a pattern of disinvestment that only hurts the areas where middle-class blacks are moving.

And that's for starters.

The inability of large numbers of blacks to buy homes in the suburbs reduces their ready access to jobs and increased income. Galster, at the Urban Institute, said that lack of access to markets in outlying areas where wages are higher than in the cities means lower savings rates, which diminish personal wealth.

Thus, the usual rule that has applied to virtually every immigrant European group — and now Asian — that political and economic power across generations can be secured through home purchase, has largely not been the experience of African-Americans. In 1970, 65 percent of whites owned homes. Today, that number is 69 percent. In 1970, 42 percent of blacks owned homes. That number increased to 45 percent in 1989, before falling back to 42 per cent two years later.

Instead of the crescendo of rising home values and economic viability, there is stagnation. "Realtors sense this weakness and begin offering forms of credit other than conventional mortgages," said Don DeMarco, executive director of the Fund for an Open Society, a Philadelphia-based fair housing group. "This tends to be a code for the fact that the neighborhood is no longer attractive to the majority population." Real estate agents jump into the breach by offering various federally-subsidized mortgage arrangements, including Veterans Administration and Federal Homeowners Administration loans that become a symptom of weakening market demand. And since the price of points and closing costs is generally higher for these deals, blacks who move into the neighborhoods offered are socked with a third whammy: neighborhoods of declining investment value where residents must deplete their funds to close, leaving less money to fix the homes.

The effect on black wealth is devastating. In 1988, the U.S. Census Bureau concluded that white families had 10 times the wealth of blacks in America. Crucially, 40 percent of that difference was the lack of home equity between black and white families. The latest numbers come from 1989. That year, the median value of home equity for all families—the vast numbers of whom were white—was $48,000. For blacks it was $37,000. Thus, while a white person can lean on their home-owning parents or relatives money needed for other investments—to buy a larger house the next time, to finance a child's education, a vacation—blacks do not enjoy this advantage. Some of this is the result of the historic legacy of segregation: since blacks have been barred in past generations from owning valuable homes, there is less money passed from the older generations to the new. "Wealth begets wealth and lack of wealth gets stuck," said Galster.

One of the most important consequences of these economic differences between blacks and whites, said Galster, is the number of blacks who would have enough money to cover the standard 10 percent down payment on a home and to finance a mortgage on a home at today's standard, about 9 percent. National figures show that 42 percent of white renters would be able to afford to purchase a typical starter home in a metropolitan area, while just 26 percent of blacks would be able to make that leap.

"What this means is that middle-class housing in America is bifurcated into two extremes," explained Bromley. "If you are white, you can trade up into a place in Chevy Chase [Md.], while a black family is sitting in a home in Shepherd Park in Northwest Washington, D.C., or in Silver Spring, Md., where demand isn't as great and the returns are low."

In 1989, *Money* magazine found that housing segregation tended to stifle the black middle class in its ability to build wealth through the appreciation of home values. The magazine illustrated the deflation in prices in black middle-class areas by comparing residential areas with the same income patterns. It found that price appreciation in middle-class black areas lagged behind those in white areas. For instance, in Washington, D.C.'s predominantly black Brookland/Catholic University area, housing prices rose 8 percent from 1985 to 1989. That was a 10 per cent drop in value (adjusting for inflation), the magazine reported. By comparison, in North Highland, which was 98 percent white, home prices increased nearly 100 percent. In Atlanta, prices in Ben Hill, about 97 percent black, appreciated 46 percent while those in North Highland, 93 percent white, jumped by 67 percent.

There are other costs to blacks as well. As a rule, blacks simply have far less wealth to give to their children. A 1984 Census Bureau study found that blacks who earned between $24,000 and $48,000 that year had net worths one-third as large as whites at the same income level. This means that whites will generally give their children a head start on blacks of the next generation. "That is generally the difference between going to the college of your choice and settling for a state or community college or no college at all," said Bart Landry, a sociologist at the University of Maryland and author of *The New Black Middle Class.*

In general, scholars are finding that these patterns of disparity and limitation of economic opportunity can be laid at the doorstep of racial discrimination by the real estate, banking and insurance industries. By far the most damaging evidence of discrimination by lenders is in how blacks and whites are treated when they try to obtain home mortgages. According to a study by the Federal Reserve Bank of Boston, published in 1989, even after accounting for differences in income and wealth, white neighborhoods received 24 percent more loans than black ones. The study looked at 3,000 mortgage application files from more than 300 lenders and found that people with identical credentials were rejected purely on the basis of race. Blacks were 56 percent more likely to be rejected than whites with similar credentials.

While whites were generally encouraged to learn about various mortgage plans, blacks were often discouraged through misinformation and lack of clear advice, for example, on how to clean up poor credit records.

The discriminatory behavior was not limited to the lending industry. Another study, by the Department of Housing and Urban Development, found widespread evidence of racially discriminatory practices in the real estate industry in 1989. The HUD report estimated that there were 2 million instances of housing discrimination annually against

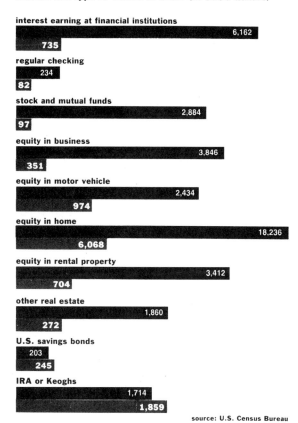

Assets and liabilities

total net worth

$43,164	$8,981
white	black

amount and type of wealth in 1988 (in 1990 dollars)

interest earning at financial institutions
6,162
735

regular checking
234
82

stock and mutual funds
2,884
97

equity in business
3,846
351

equity in motor vehicle
2,434
974

equity in home
18,236
6,068

equity in rental property
3,412
704

other real estate
1,860
272

U.S. savings bonds
203
245

IRA or Keoghs
1,714
1,859

source: U.S. Census Bureau

African-Americans and other minorities. Housing was systematically made more available to whites in 45 percent of all transactions in the rental market and in 34 percent of the sales market. Whites also received more favorable credit assistance in 46 percent of sales encounters and were offered more favorable terms in 17 percent of rental transactions.

In the sales market, the question of differential treatment boils down to behavior: how often a broker will call a buyer back; or if a buyer is called back, if the buyer be shown the preferred tree-lined streets and the cul-de-sacs.

"An agent will rely on code words, telling a white person, 'you wouldn't feel comfortable here,' while a black person will be told, 'there's nothing in your price range here,' " said Bromley. "Frequently, steering behavior consists of showing a black potential homebuyer a house priced at $150,000 after they've told the realtor to look for a house for no more than $125,000," Bromley said. "It's about the persistent feeling of being unwelcomed. It's about racism with a smile."

Often, the only time black home buyers get a chance to smile back is in the courtroom.

Under fair housing laws, any agent who has referred clients to banks or other lending institutions that discriminate, automatically become liable themselves. It was this leverage that Donnell Cravens used successfully when he threatened to sue the realtor and the banks in his attempt to buy a home in Bloomfield, Mich.

There are alternatives to the litigation threat for blacks who are seeking to break down the barriers of segregation. One of the best is offered by the Fund For An Open Society. It helped build a national model for resolution of the problems of segregation in Shaker Heights, Ohio, by trying to help address racial balance in both black and white communities. That unique approach allows individuals trying to find homes a low-interest loan as an incentive to integrate racially-segregated areas. Often, whites will be approached with the loan incentive to integrate black neighborhoods that appear to be in danger of losing their attractiveness because the density of black households is too high. Or, alternatively, the fund will approach blacks with the chance to integrate nearly all-white areas. Similar programs have been formed around the country, based on this model.

In the past, the real estate industry has been stuck in their basic way of thinking about human beings as economic objects. While whites have been encouraged to buy housing for its investment value because they are seeing them as "future-oriented people," blacks have been stigmatized by the industry which sees them as people who want to buy as much shelter as possible for the dollar, regardless of whether it is in an area that is losing its marketability to the majority population. One result is that blacks are forced to rely on mortgages from sources other than private lending institutions—falling back on government agencies such as VA and the FHA loans, where closing costs are higher, and additional points are required. "The result is that blacks are pushed by realtors into areas where private mortgages aren't even offered," Bromley said. "Breaking out of this pattern of inertia is difficult because there are so many higher costs."

The difficulty is overcoming the inertia of past generations. DeMarco said his program seeks to remedy this condition by involving the banks, real estate interests and home buyers in the process of keeping areas marketable through "integrative efforts." He explained, "You have to recognize that in this country, the majority simply has the money to determine supply and demand and unless minorities can link up with that system, they are in danger of losing out."

Massey proposed ending the crisis of inequality in black housing patterns by attacking racial discrimination in private housing markets, which comprise 98 percent of all dwellings in America. Public policies, he said, must interrupt the institutionalized process of neighborhood racial turnover, "which is the ultimate mechanism by which the ghetto is reproduced and maintained." That process depends on white prejudice and racial discrimination which restrict black access and channels black housing demand "to a few black or racially mixed areas." The federal government must insert itself into the housing markets, with HUD taking a greater role in enforcing Fair Housing Act directives, Massey said.

Whether the Clinton administration is willing to address the issue of housing segregation, meanwhile, is anybody's guess. There are strong indications that it may happen. HUD Secretary Henry Cisneros has promised stepped-up

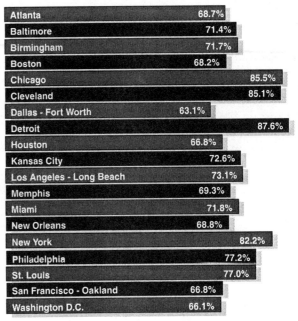

Percentage of blacks
who live in segregated neighborhoods in selected metropolitan areas.

Metropolitan Area	Percentage
Atlanta	68.7%
Baltimore	71.4%
Birmingham	71.7%
Boston	68.2%
Chicago	85.5%
Cleveland	85.1%
Dallas - Fort Worth	63.1%
Detroit	87.6%
Houston	66.8%
Kansas City	72.6%
Los Angeles - Long Beach	73.1%
Memphis	69.3%
Miami	71.8%
New Orleans	68.8%
New York	82.2%
Philadelphia	77.2%
St. Louis	77.0%
San Francisco - Oakland	66.8%
Washington D.C.	66.1%

source: Population Association of America, 1990

enforcement activities and the U.S. Justice Department appears to be increasing its monitoring of discriminatory practices in the real estate and banking industries.

But this isn't enough. One source of doubt about whether housing segregation will end any time soon comes from the black community itself, which appears to have lost faith in the benefits of integrated housing, despite widespread evidence that it is a powerful vehicle for joining the economic mainstream. There appears to be a kind of nostalgia that has settled in in many quarters of the minority community that support the idea that segregation in itself may not be such a bad thing. Even among African-Americans, who are most hurt financially by segregation, there appears to be little agreement on how to invest in the struggle against housing segregation with passionate commitment.

Recently, Massey was asked to discuss his book on a black Chicago radio station. He spoke of the problems blacks have with access to capital, about the real estate industry which blocks blacks from finding out how to exercise their options for a wider range of economically potent housing choices. "I was saying it was all about gaining access to greater opportunities, which basically means joining the mainstream, which means 'Are you willing to put up with white people to get what you want out of society?'"

A woman called the station and castigated those blacks who had moved out of the city. She said she didn't think blacks should be living near whites. The caller said blacks needed to "have pride in their communities." At another talk, Massey was confronted by a community activist who

Trends in black and white suburbanization
percentages of blacks and whites who lived in the suburbs in 1980 (the last year for which research was available).

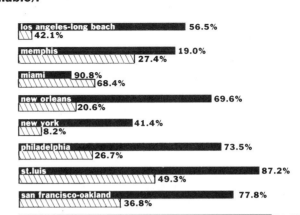

atlanta — whites 89.4% / blacks 44.7%
baltimore — whites 77.9% / blacks 21.3%
birmingham — whites 81.9% / blacks 72.0%
boston — whites 84.5% / blacks 20.8%
chicago — whites 72.8% / blacks 15.8%
cleveland — whites 80.1% / blacks 27.2%
dallas-ft.worth — whites 64.3% / blacks 15.3%
detroit — whites 87.8% / blacks 15.1%
houston — whites 58.5% / blacks 16.9%
kansas city — whites 60.2% / blacks 4.8%

los angeles-long beach — whites 56.5% / blacks 42.1%
memphis — whites 19.0% / blacks 27.4%
miami — whites 90.8% / blacks 68.4%
new orleans — whites 69.6% / blacks 20.6%
new york — whites 41.4% / blacks 8.2%
philadelphia — whites 73.5% / blacks 26.7%
st.luis — whites 87.2% / blacks 49.3%
san francisco-oakland — whites 77.8% / blacks 36.8%
washington, d.c. — whites 91.7% / blacks 46.2%

source: Douglas S. Massey and Nancy A. Denton, "Suburbanization and Segregation in U.S. Metropolitan Areas," American Journal of Sociology

told him that pursuit of integration by leaving the black ghetto was a dilution and betrayal of black political interests. Massey said he was stunned. "The bottom line is that I don't know of any story that begins with segregation and ends up with economic success. Segregation makes oppression easy and efficient. It allows disinvestment in the black community and it ultimately means the end of hope for the future."

FAIR HOUSING ADVOCATES:

NATIONAL FAIR HOUSING ALLIANCE
1400 I Street, N.W.
Washington, D.C. 20005
202-898-1661

FUND FOR AN OPEN SOCIETY
311 South Juniper Street, Suite 400
Philadelphia, Pa. 19107
215-735-6915

LEADERSHIP COUNCIL
401 South State Street, Suite 860
Chicago, Ill. 60605
312-341-5678

CINCINNATI COALITION OF NEIGHBORHOODS
6566 Montgomery Road, Suite 210
Cincinnati, Ohio 45213
513-531-2676

**FAIR HOUSING CONGRESS OF
SOUTHERN CALIFORNIA**
3535 West 6th Street, Second floor
Los Angeles, Calif. 90020
213-365-7184

D.C. FAIR HOUSING COUNCIL
1400 I Street, N.W.
Washington, D.C. 20005
202-289-5360

**TENNESSEE MID-SOUTH
PEACE AND JUSTICE CENTER**
P.O. Box 11428
Memphis, Tenn. 38111-0428
901-452-6997

**OAKLAND COUNTY CENTER
FOR OPEN HOUSING**
3060 Telegraph Road, Suite 1233
Bingham Farms, Mich. 48025
313-647-0575

The Ethnic Legacy

Ethnicity is often associated with immigrants and with alien importation of culture, language, stories, and food from foreign shores. Appalachian, western, and other regional ethnicities are evidence of multigenerational ethnic cultural development within the American reality. The persistence and ongoing process of humanity expressed in unique and intriguing folkways, dialect-languages, myths, festivals, and foods displays another enduring and public dimension of ethnicity. As this section's articles illustrate, ethnic experiences may be less foreign and alien than most imagine them to be.

The persistence of contributions and concerns of various ethnic immigrant groups over many generations provided a deep weave and pattern to the material and social history of America. There is a consciousness of ethnic tradition, exasperation and anger about stereotypes, and efforts to institutionalize ongoing attention to groups as the most relevant aspects of groups identity are ever present and clearly growing in interest and magnitude. Change and ethnicity are not contradictory, for each generation creates anew its ethnicity, which, alongside other affinities, affiliations, and loyalties, helps to guide our interaction with each other. Some present concerns of ethnic groups include language, preservation of neighborhoods, ethnic studies, and the rearticulation of historical claims to fairness, justice, and equity.

Perhaps the most obvious oscillation between celebration of achievement and concern about fairness is seen in the legacies of persons and groups that constitute ancestry-conscious populations. That such populations should be denied their distinctiveness through absorption into the mass of modernity and that their distinctiveness can accompany them into mainstream modern American identities are parallel lines of argument for their insistence that their ethnicity is not a form of diminished existence, but that they are "American Plus"—Americans with a multicultural affinity and competencies in more than one culture.

The winds of social change, whether in the American plains, Eastern Europe, or in the internal migration of populations reveal the varied texture of ethnicities in America. These articles explain the transmission of ethnic tradition in music and suggest linkages between religion and ethnicity. The story of the interaction of ethnicity and religion is curiously exposed in the etymology of the Greek word *ethnikos* (i.e., the rural, Gentile, or pagan people of the ancient Mediterranean world). Though such philological roots no longer drive our principal understanding of ethnicity, the experience of social affinity and cultural affiliation elaborated in the following articles about ethnics deepens our awareness and understanding of ethnicity—a changing yet persistent aspect of human identity and social cohesiveness.

Looking Ahead: Challenge Questions

Does ethnicity of an earlier era adequately suggest the tension between worlds of meaning discussed in this section?

Does the legacy of multiple ancestral origins and of the ethnic identities of European Americans from an earlier era in America argue for the passing relevancy of these ethnic populations and their marginality to the central ethnic issues of our time?

What is a central ethnic issue? By what criteria do we decide the importance and preferential protection of one ethnic group vis-à-vis another group?

What lessons can be learned from the immigration and settlement experiences of Eastern and Southern Europeans?

Unit 7

Early Italian Sculptors in the United States

Regina Soria

College of Notre Dame of Maryland, Baltimore, Maryland

Among constructive projects for the Bicentennial celebrations, a thorough and objective study of the cultural history of the United States, focusing on the Italian contribution to the artistic consciousness of this country, at least up to 1876, would surely be fruitful, and, for a great many Americans, quite revealing. During the Centennial celebrations, in 1876, the Exhibition at Philadelphia showed that the arts had progressed and flourished in America, to a sufficient extent as to make it plausible to talk of an American art. To those who visited the Exhibition it was quite evident that most of the native artists during the first one hundred years of the American republic had gone abroad, for shorter or longer periods, in order to acquire or perfect their skills. In fact most, especially the sculptors, had gone to Italy.

Writing in 1853 in *My Consulship,* Charles Lester, American consul at the Court of Savoy stressed "the mysterious tie which unites men born in this country with those born in the land that gave birth to Columbus and Vespucius."[1] He advocated that Italians be invited to come to America, to give the benefit of their way of life and genius in art, so as to help America create treasures for new museums, art galleries and palaces similar to those he admired in Italy. Travelling through that country, Lester was well aware that American sculptors such as Hiram Powers, the Greenoughs, and Thomas Crawford, who had worked in Florence and Rome in the second quarter of the nineteenth century, and who had received commissions from the U.S. Congress to decorate the Washington Capitol and many other public buildings in different states, derived much of their success from close relationship to Italian craftsmen. Indeed, they owed those early commissions to the desire of some of the founding fathers—especially Jefferson—to establish an artistic climate in America that would embellish her in a fashion to rival European cities. The particular style chosen by Jefferson was naturally one in keeping with the democratic ideals of the young Republic. The choice inevitably fell upon the nineteenth-century Neoclassical mode.

Neoclassical art, of which Antonio Canova is among the most important exponents, had a decisive influence on nineteenth-century American sculpture. Nonetheless, for a long time it was little known and even scorned as "academic." Now that a new long look is being given to nineteenth-century painting, it is time for the sculptors who brought so much art to America to be rescued from their oblivion. Their contribution should be reassessed and cleansed of the stigma of academic coldness. Cornelius Vermeule stated clearly:

> The artistic movement known as Neoclassicism which gripped Europe from 1760 to 1820, began for a group of reasons once defined with utmost simplicity and now told in increasingly complex terms. Pompeii and Herculaneaum were rediscovered and excavated. Stuart and Revett published their *Antiquities of Athens* (1762) and built structures comparable to the Propylaea and the little temples by the Ilissos in the English parklands. Winckelman's *History of Art Among the Ancients* (1764) gave literate substance to the notion of quality in ancient art. The French Rococo had run its course as a reaction to the Italo-French Baroque, and the artistic extravagances of the French court were associated with increasingly intolerable political beliefs and practices. Writers made these beliefs and practices seem inconsistent with the ideals of antiquity. When the new humanism of the American, French and Italian revolutions burst upon Europe, the classic purity, simplicity and spiritual containment of Greek art were associated with the democratic virtues of the Roman republic and . . . of the early ages of Greece.[2]

More recently and more specifically Wayne Craven has written:

> Neoclassical Art implanted in this country by such men as Ceracchi, Franzoni and Andrei, and their countrymen who followed them to America in the second and third decade of the 19th century . . . was thoroughly compatible with the political and philosophical foundation of the national government. The U.S. Capitol took a Roman revival form because this country could align itself politically with ancient Rome . . . thus was Neoclassicism successfully received in the early years of the Republic, and the Italian sculptors quite naturally carried the neoclassical style to America.[3]

How the Italian artists brought the Neoclassical style to America in the early days of the Republic, how they fared in this country, and what impact their works had on the development of art in America is a fascinating story.

Reprinted by permission from *Italian Americana*, Vol. 2, No. 1, Spring 1976, pp. 171-189.

If Giuseppe Ceracchi is not the first Italian sculptor to come to America, he is surely the most important one. Ceracchi introduced the portrait bust to America; it was to become the most significant form of American sculpture in the early nineteenth century. Everyone familiar with Houdon's statue of George Washington knows that it was done *de visum*, from life. Not many know that the only other sculptor to do the General *de visum* was Ceracchi. Houdon's statue of Washington in military dress enjoys much fame and is admired for its realism. Yet contemporaries and Washington's family said that Ceracchi's sculpture was truer to life.

Ceracchi persuaded George Washington to sit for a few hours and he modelled the bust in terra cotta, larger than life. Ceracchi did two marble renditions of his Washington; one is at the Metropolitan Museum of Art, the other at Gibbes Art Gallery, Charleston, South Carolina. Other marble versions of his original were later done by other hands. One is in Baltimore, one is at the White House (bought by President Monroe), and one is in the National Portrait Gallery. Another copy, ordered by the City of New Orleans, was put up for sale some years ago, for officials did not know who the portrait represented. It was purchased by James Lamantia, an architect and connoisseur of that city, who immediately recognized Washington by his prominent nose.

Ceracchi's bust of Washington—the terra cotta original is in the Nantes Museum in France—shows that this sculptor

> . . . is above all valuable as a portraitist, quick to seize the resemblance, to put in relief the characteristic traits of a person, capable of finesse in details, but unable to bring out completely the individuality of his models. The reason for this being that he put his gift of shrewd observer at the service of an aesthetic resolutely opposed to the portrait *ad vivum*. Having given life to his portraits, he then gives them lifeless eyes, a conventional posture, corresponding to a Greek-Roman type and with accessories from classical times. Faithful to reality at first, he then clothes his portraits with conventional idealization. In this, he belongs to the spirit of the times, which demanded rhetoric. It is style which also corresponds to his own personality of proud theoretician, imbued with republicanism.[4]

Born in Rome on July 5, 1751, son of Domenico, a goldsmith, Giuseppe Ceracchi studied at the Accademia di San Luca and received a prize in 1771. At this time he seems to have adopted Neoclassical aesthetics. He worked in Milan, Florence, and London, where he executed several important monuments and portrait busts, including one of Sir Joshua Reynolds. Ceracchi's work showed a combination of the nobility of Roman busts and the vivacity of expression suggested by his French contemporaries; he was also extremely faithful to the model's features. In Vienna, in 1779, he worked for Empress Maria Teresa. Returning to Rome, he did the portrait busts of Cardinals Albani and Riminaldi, as well as one of the poet Metastasio, originally destined for the Pantheon in Rome but now at the Pinacoteca Capitolina in Rome. In Berlin he did the portrait bust of Frederick II and in Amsterdam began the monument to Baron Van der Capellen, which, unpaid for, was to end up at the Pincio Garden in Rome.

Ceracchi arrived in America with his family in 1791. He brought with him a project for an equestrian monument to George Washington. This monument was to be a group sculpture sixty feet high with a base circumference of eleven colossal statues, six smaller statues of animals and other ornaments, the whole in marble—together with a bronze equestrian statue of the hero set on a large pedestal. The model of this monument was publicly exhibited in Philadelphia. Since the Continental Congress had voted for the erection of a monument to Washington, Ceracchi had come to bid for the commission. However, the sum of $30,000 was considered too large, and private subscriptions were not successful in raising the sum. The project was put off until after the death of the General.

It was left to another Italian, Enrico Causici, to execute the first Washington Monument in Baltimore in 1829. The commission for the Washington Monument in Raleigh, North Carolina, was given to Antonio Canova, who used the Ceracchi portrait bust for his larger-than-life Washington, portrayed in the dress of a Roman General and writing on a tablet; the inscription read: *"Giorgio Washington al popolo degli Stati Uniti 1796 Amici e Concittadini."*

Canova's statue arrived in November 1821 and was placed in the Raleigh State House. According to Craven, it was one of the most famous works of art in America, and "it played a large role in establishing monumental marble statuary in America."[5] Unfortunately it was destroyed by fire in 1830.

Ceracchi had brought art objects to present prominent Americans, including Washington, who felt obliged to refuse the gift because of his public office.

Ceracchi is considered, with the exception of Houdon, to be the greatest sculptor ever to have visited America. He modeled about two dozen busts of American founding fathers. Leaving America at the end of 1792 with his terra cotta casts as well as the model for the equestrian statue, he planned to carve them in marble in Italy. Ulysse Desportes, Ceracchi's biographer, wrote:

> A treasure trove of extraordinary interest to students of early American art and history may wait unrecognized in some storeroom in Florence. Over two dozen life portrait busts of America's founding fathers were left in the Tuscan capital by their author, Giuseppe Ceracchi, Roman sculptor and political exile. The busts, in terra cotta, were modeled in the United States in 1791–1792. Among the distinguished subjects represented were the first four presidents of the Republic, as well as Alexander Hamilton, General Henry Knox and David Rittenhouse. Ceracchi had been obliged to abandon them in Florence when he fled from the city under pressure from the local authorities. Also left behind was his model for an equestrian monument to George Washington.[6]

Ceracchi returned to the United States in 1794, bringing two of his marble busts of Washington and some of his other American portraits.

Ceracchi next began a project for a colossal group honoring the goddess Liberty. In his *Prospectus*, he wrote that Liberty was to be represented

> . . . descending in a chariot drawn by four horses, darting through a volume of clouds which conceal the summit of a rainbow. Her form is at once expressive of dignity and peace. In her right hand she brandishes a flaming dart, which dispels the mists of error and illuminates the universe; her left is extended in the attitude of calling upon the people of America to listen to her voice.

The project was dismissed, however, only to be realized about a century later, with a number of attempts made during the interval.

Meanwhile, Ceracchi became very busy doing busts of Jefferson, Franklin, Rittenhouse, and Alexander Hamilton. Desportes said of the Hamilton bust: "probably no example of neoclassical portrait sculpture ever proved to be as successful as this one." After Hamilton's tragic death in 1801, this bust enjoyed great commercial success, with hundreds of copies being executed. A thirty-cent U.S. stamp of 1870 carried Hamilton's bust by Ceracchi; in fact the bust has served as a model for most, if not all, the effigies of Hamilton. The painter John Trumbull, who had known Ceracchi and done his portrait, painted his Hamilton from Ceracchi's bust, and an engraving based on that portrait can be seen on our ten-dollar bill.[7]

On December 29, 1794, Ceracchi attended a meeting arranged by Charles Willson Peale to plan for the establishment of an academy in Philadelphia, then the foremost artistic center, where the arrival of a number of experienced painters and engravers (mostly from England) made the idea of an American academy seem possible. The agreement, adopted and signed by sixty-two artists, expressed the desire "to do our utmost effort to establish a school or academy within the U.S. to be called the Columbianum, or American Academy of Fine Arts." However, here the agreement faltered. The group split between the newly arrived artists from England, who proposed to offer honorary leadership to George Washington, thereby putting him in the same position as the King of England in regard to the Royal Academy, and the native artists, who felt the idea abhorrent. Ceracchi, "disputatious, sharp, uncompromising, heart and soul for freedom and democracy,"[8] was among the most vehement in protest.

Upon his return to France, Ceracchi became a very good friend of Napoleon, then a young general, of whom he did the first portrait bust, now known only in an engraving. He hoped that Napoleon would help him in his dream of freeing the Papal states and eventually the whole of Italy from foreign rule and bring about a democratic Italian republic. However, when Napoleon proclaimed himself first consul—obviously betraying the democratic ideal Ceracchi cherished above art and life—he took part in a conspiracy against him. By a strange coincidence, John Vanderlyn, one of the first native American artists to go to Europe to study, was in Paris on his

way to Rome when Ceracchi, "the celebrated sculptor," and his three companions were publicly guillotined on January 31, 1801. Vanderlyn witnessed the execution and was greatly moved, describing deaths in a tribute to the bravery of these lovers of freedom.[9]

We have seen Ceracchi at home in America, where he found his dream of freedom a reality. Eager to portray the founding fathers, he applied his ideals of Neoclassical purity and severity to his portrait busts and monumental plans. But America, into which he brought a style that was to last for the next seventy years, was not ready to give its financial support to the artist and his large family. Even those who posed for their portraits found it strange that they should pay for them.

Ceracchi, so celebrated during his life and considered second only to Canova, sank into oblivion. For over a century he was remembered chiefly because of his tragic death, or else he was dismissed rather contemptuously as unstable. Some art historians even were in error about his birthplace; as late as 1970, he was said to have been born in Corsica. A general confusion has existed regarding his works. Only recently, the art historian Desportes and the historian, De Felice,[10] have told the full story. We now see Ceracchi as an extraordinary product of that era of passionate ideals of democracy and freedom.

The parallels between Ceracchi and Vittorio Alfieri (1749–1803), Italy's foremost tragic playwright, who was almost an exact contemporary of Ceracchi, are irresistible. Like Ceracchi, Alfieri was an enthusiastic admirer of George Washington, to whom, in 1787, he dedicated his tragedy *Bruto Primo*:

> To the illustrious and free man,
> General Washington: Only the name
> of the liberator of America can
> stand before the tragedy of the
> liberator of Rome.

A presentation copy of the play, bearing Washington's signature on the page on which the dedication begins, is in the Boston Athenaeum. Alfieri had already hailed the American Revolution with a group of five odes, *L'America Libera* (1781–1783).

However, it is the *Bruto Secondo*, the play about the conspiracy against Caesar, which might have inspired Ceracchi. "I believe firmly that in the theater men should learn to be free, strong, generous, zealous followers of true virtue . . . devoted to their country . . . and in all their emotions and enthusiasms ardent, upright, and magnanimous,"[11] Alfieri had written. We do not know whether these two great Italians, both restless and rebellious against the foreign rulers of their country, men who travelled extensively around Europe, ever met. It is possible, however, that on fearlessly climbing the scaffold, Ceracchi's thoughts were on Alfieri's Brutus.

Ceracchi was not the first Italian sculptor to plan national monuments in the United States. The tomb of Montgomery, in St. Paul Church, New York City, executed in 1777, is considered the first national monument executed in this country, and it is the work of Caffieri. Other Italians who did Washington portraits (though not from life) were Trentanove, from the Stuart portrait, and Antonio Capellano, in 1828. Capellano also did the marble sculpture for the Battle Monument by Godefroy in Baltimore and probably many other works, not yet identified, for he was able to retire in wealth to a "small palace" in Florence, where his friend Rembrandt Peale, the painter, visited him in 1831.

Had Ceracchi stayed in the United States, he would surely have been called to decorate the U.S. Capitol. However, two other Italians, Giuseppe Franzoni and Giovanni Andrei, were the first sculptors called by Benjamin Latrobe to decorate the U.S. Capitol in 1806. The story of their fortunes was recorded by Charles E. Fairman, art curator of the U.S. Capitol.[12] He was given the opportunity to retell it in a speech to the House of Representatives in 1930, through the initiative of Fiorello LaGuardia, then a Congressman from New York.[13] It is worth retelling in part.

Fairman reminded the House of Representatives that, when these young Italian sculptors—Andrei and his brother-in-law Franzoni—arrived in Washington, on a cold February 24, 1806, with their wives, they were "people destined to exert a lasting influence upon the art of the Capitol of the United States." They had left Carrara and Italy, both so full of artistic wealth. Sailing from Leghorn, they had been at sea for 146 days. They contemplated the unfinished condition of the Capitol, "begun at a time when the country was entirely destitute of artists" and the meager settlement destined to be the capital city with an obvious feeling of disappointment. There were no people who spoke Italian, and they must have wondered why they had come at all. For these, as Fairman stressed, were not ordinary immigrants. Franzoni's father, Antonio, was a distinguished sculptor who had done extensive restoration and original work for the Animal Room of the Vatican Museum and was the president of the Carrara Academy. Andrei had studied at the Carrara Academy and decorated the balustrade of the high altar in Santa Maria Novella in Florence. Franzoni's uncle was a cardinal. They did not lack money or recognition in their native land. Why did they come? It must be assumed that the desire to contribute to the birth of sculpture in the budding Republic had persuaded them to undertake the venture. Instrumental in their enthusiasm was of course the personal persuasion of Thomas Jefferson, then president, who, in his determination to build the U.S. Capitol and to foster the arts in America, had appointed Benjamin Latrobe, as public architect, in 1803. Latrobe's first project was the completion of the House of Representatives. His plan called for extensive sculptural ornamentation. Philip Mazzei was asked to find suitable sculptors in Italy.

Although the name of Mazzei is surely familiar to a great many people in the United States today, it may be worth remembering that this physician from Tuscany had come to Albemarle County, Virginia, in 1773, to introduce the cultivation of grape, olive, and other Italian fruits in America. He was a neighbor of Thomas Jefferson, and in the course of their growing friendship he became his advisor not only in agricultural matters, but in democratic ideals and also in art. No wonder then that Jefferson advised Latrobe to ask Mazzei's help in securing sculptors. In Latrobe's *Journal* two letters to Mazzei carry explicit directions as to the quality of the sculptors and the financial arrangements proposed during their two-year contract with the U.S. government. Upon their arrival, Franzoni and Andrei found Latrobe a warm and helpful friend. He was also the only person who could converse in Italian with them. Interestingly, the Italian sculptors, as was customary in Italy, had brought marble articles as presents for Jefferson when they called on him. Like Washington, Jefferson also felt he could not accept them: "Be assured that I receive this mark of good will as thankfully as if I could accept it, but I have laid it down as a law to myself to accept no presents of value while I am in public life."[14] This he wrote to Franzoni, March 2, 1806. Jefferson assured the sculptor that he would "avail myself of every occasion to be helpful to you," and according to Fairman, he gave Mrs. Franzoni a silver dish for Christmas. Furthermore, it is reported by Franzoni's descendants (still living today in the United States) that he was often invited to dine at the White House on Sunday evenings.

One of the very first tasks for Giuseppe Franzoni was to do a huge eagle for the frieze of the House of Representatives. Since his design represented the classical Roman eagle, Latrobe asked Charles W. Peale for a drawing of the bald eagle (preserved in the Peale Museum) to acquaint Franzoni with the American variety of the species.[15] Although the Italian sculptors' two-year contract was to become a lifetime one, in 1808, due to Jefferson's budget economy, they found they needed more work. The architect Maximilian Godefroy, Latrobe's friend, asked them to come to Baltimore for about four months. There they did, among other works, a large lunette for the tympanum of the Union Bank, a piece which is now on the garden wall of the Peale Museum.[16] As Wayne Craven notes, after they returned to Washington, they did a great deal of sculpture in the Capitol, most of which, however, was destroyed when the English burned it in 1814.

Giuseppe Franzoni died in Washington on April 6, 1815, leaving a widow and six children, all but one born in America. At that time, his brother-in-law Andrei was sent to Italy by the government to procure Carrara marble for the Corinthian capitals in the Hall of the House of Representatives, since 1857 known as the Statuary Hall. Andrei returned in 1816, with Carlo Franzoni, a younger brother of Giuseppe, and a cousin Francesco Iardella. Iardella's work that has been identified so far consists of the tobacco capitals in the small rotunda north of the main Capitol rotunda. Andrei died in 1824. Carlo Franzoni's "Car of History" is believed to be the oldest example of statuary in any public building in the capital.

Another important Italian sculptor was Giuseppe Valaperta, of Genoa, who arrived from France in 1815 and enjoyed a considerable reputation, until his death under mysterious circumstances two years later. He too did an American eagle, "upon the frieze at the south side of Statuary Hall."[17]

All the sculptors mentioned so far came from the school of Carrara. According to Fairman they were the best. In his opinion, Capellano, of Florence, who did *Preservation of Captain John Smith by Pocahontas*, Causici, of Verona, who did *Landing of the Pilgrims* and *Daniel Boone and the Indians*, all in the Capitol, and Persico, of Naples, sculptor of the *Statues of Peace and War* and *The Discovery Group*, did not show great strength of inspiration in their attempts "to Americanize Italian art." Still, it is interesting to examine their attempts to express events that were so far from their own experience, and it is possible that a second look at their achievements might provide some insights into the power of adaptation of artists.

The 1820s brought a period of stagnation for the Capitol decoration. Latrobe retired and Bullfinch, the new architect of the Capitol took over. Fairman mentions Cardelli, another Italian sculptor of the time, and the letters in which he lamented the state of art in the capital. These letters were sold at auction in the early part of this century and surely ought to be retrieved and made available to the Archives of American Art and the Immigration History Research Center. However, thanks to the influence of the Italian sculptors, a new era in American sculpture was dawning—the native one. Congress began granting commissions to native sculptors, most of whom had gone to Italy to learn their craft. The first of this long series is of course Horatio Greenough, whose statue of Washington scrupulously modeled on the Phidias Zeus and intended for the rotunda, found little favor in the eyes of his fellow citizens; "the General looks so pale," a kindly old lady was heard muttering, after viewing the statue, which is now at the Smithsonian Institution.

The list of native sculptors who studied and even settled in Italy is a long one. Their interaction with Italian artists invites fruitful study. Lorado Taft noted in 1923:

> . . . at a recent meeting of the National Sculpture Society there were four candidates for membership—all Italians. On another occasion, among ten candidates four again were Italians. The catalogue of the great sculpture exhibit of 1923 seems to be half Italian. Masters of the solid attainments of the Piccirillis, the wizardry of Lentelli, and the imagination of Billotti, Salvatore, and Scarpitta enliven exhibitions of the academy and make their valuable contributions. . . . On the whole . . . the presence of this army of traditional sculptors is one of the most potent factors in America's artistic development.[18]

It would seem that the time has come for a systematic study of the interaction between Italian and American art. This brief sketch of the early Italian sculptors in America has been written in the hope that it will stimulate new generations of art historians, and especially those of Italian heritage, to undertake the exploration of this largely untouched field. The reward will be a rich one and a real contribution to the artistic and social history of America.

Acknowledgement: I wish to thank Ulysse G. Desportes, the Ceracchi expert, for his generous assistance in the preparation of the Ceracchi portion of my study. Painter, sculptor, and art historian, Professor Desportes is chairman of the Art Department of Mary Baldwin College in Staunton, Virginia. Since 1956, when he wrote his doctoral dissertation on Ceracchi for the Sorbonne, Professor Desportes has published a number of articles on the subject and has completed a definitive biography and catalogue raisonné *of Ceracchi's works.*

NOTES

1. Charles Lester, *My Consulship*, 2 vols. (New York, 1853), 1:301.

2. Cornelius Vermeule, *European Art and the Classical Past* (Cambridge. Mass.: Harvard University Press, 1964), p. 132.

3. Wayne Craven, *Sculpture in America* (New York: Thomas Y. Crowell Co., 1968), p. 59.

4. Gérard Hubert, *Les Sculpteurs Italiens En France Sous La Révolution L'Empire et La Restauration, 1790–1830* (Paris: Editions E. De Boccard, 1964), p. 28.

5. Craven, *Sculpture in America*, pp. 63–64.

6. Ulysse Desportes, "Giuseppe Ceracchi in America and His Busts of George Washington," *The Art Quarterly* 26, no. 2, (1963), ill. p. 141.

7. Ulysse Desportes, "Ceracchi's Bust of Alexander Hamilton," *The Currier Art Gallery Bulletin*, April–June 1969, ill. See also Desportes, "Great Men of America in Roman Guise Sculptured by Giuseppe Ceracchi," *Antiques*, July 1969.

8. Charles Coleman Sellers, *Charles Willson Peale* (New York, 1969), p. 269.

9. Marius Schoonmaker, *John Vanderlyn, Artist, 1775– 1852* (Kingston. N.Y.: The Senate House Association, 1950), p. 10.

10. Renzo De Felice, "Ricerche Storiche sul 'Giacobininismo' Italiano," *Rassegna Storica del Risorgimento*, Anno XLVII, Fascicolo 1 (Gennaio–Marzo 1960)

11. Ernest Hatch Wilkins, *A History of Italian Literature* (Cambridge, Mass.: Harvard University Press, 1954), pp. 371–73.

12. Charles E. Fairman, *Art and Artists of the Capitol of the United States of America*, 2d ed. (Washington: U.S. Government Printing Office, 1923).

13. "Art of the Italian Artists in the United States Capital." Extension of the remarks of the Hon. Fiorello H. LaGuardia of New York in the House of Representatives, January 29, 1930. An address by Mr. Charles E. Fairman, Curator of Art of the Capitol, *Congressional Record*. (I am deeply grateful to Ms. Florian H. Thayn, Head of the Art and Reference Division, Office of the Architect of the Capitol, for this publication, as well as for information regarding the Franzoni descendants still living in the United States today.)

14. *Congressional Record*, 1930, p. 2.

15. Sellers, *Peale*, p. 333.

16. Richard R. Borneman, "Franzoni and Andrei: Italian Sculptors in Baltimore, 1808," *The William and Mary Quarterly*, Third Series, 10, no. 1 (January 1953), pp 108–11. See also Craven, *Sculpture in America*. pp. 58–9.

17. Fairman, *Art and Artists*, p. 452.

18. Lorado Taft, *American Sculpture* (New York: Macmillan Co., 1924), p. 568.

THE NEW ETHNICITY

Michael Novak

The word "ethnic" does not have a pleasing sound. The use of the word makes many people anxious. What sorts of repression account for this anxiety? What pretenses about the world are threatened when one points to the realities denoted and connoted by that ancient word? An internal history lies behind resistance to ethnicity; such resistance is almost always passional, convictional, not at all trivial. Many persons have tried to escape being "ethnic," in the name of a higher moral claim.

There are many meanings to the word itself. I have tried to map some of them below. There are many reasons for resistance to the word "ethnic" (and what it is taken to represent). Rather than beginning with these directly, I prefer to begin by defining the new ethnicity.

The definition I wish to give is personal; it grows out of personal experience; it is necessitated by an effort to attain an accurate self-knowledge. The hundreds of letters, reviews, comments, invitations, and conversations that followed upon *The Rise of the Unmeltable Ethnics* (1972) indicate that my own gropings to locate my own identity are not isolated. They struck a responsive chord in many others of Southern and Eastern European (or other) background. My aim was—and is—to open up the field to study. Let later inquiry descern just how broadly and how exactly my first attempts at definition apply. It is good to try to give voice to what has so far been untongued—and then to devise testable hypotheses at a later stage.

The new ethnicity, then, is a movement of self-knowledge on the part of members of the third and fourth generation of Southern and Eastern European immigrants in the United States. In a broader sense, the new ethnicity includes a renewed self-consciousness on the part of other generations and other ethnic groups: the Irish, the Norwegians and Swedes, the Germans, the Chinese and Japanese, and others. Much that can be said of one of these groups can be said, not univocally but analogously, of others. In this area, one must learn to speak with multiple meanings and with a sharp eye for differences in detail. (By "analogous" I mean "having resemblances but also essential differences"; by "univocal" I mean a generalization that applies equally to all cases.) My sentences are to be read, then, analogously,

not univocally; they are meant to awaken fresh perception, not to close discussion. They are intended to speak directly of a limited (and yet quite large) range of ethnic groups, while conceding indirectly that much that is said of Southern and Eastern Europeans may also be said, *mutatis mutandis*, of others.

I stress that, in the main, the "new" ethnicity involves those of the third and fourth generation after immigration. Perhaps two anecdotes will suggest the kind of experience involved. When *Time* magazine referred to me in 1972 as a "Slovak-American," I felt an inner shock; I had never referred to myself or been publicly referred to in that way. I wasn't certain how I felt about it. Then, in 1974, after I had given a lecture on ethnicity to the only class in Slavic American studies in the United States,* at the City College of New York, the dean of the college said on the way to lunch, "Considering how sensitive you are on ethnic matters, the surprising thing to me was how American you are." I wanted to ask him, "What else?" In this area one grows used to symbolic uncertainties.

The new ethnicity does not entail: (a) speaking a foreign language; (b) living in a subculture; (c) living in a "tight-knit" ethnic neighborhood; (d) belonging to fraternal organizations; (e) responding to "ethnic" appeals; (f) exalting one's own nationality or culture, narrowly construed. Neither does it entail a university education or the reading of writers on the new ethnicity. Rather, the new ethnicity entails: first, a growing sense of discomfort with the sense of identity one is *supposed* to have—universalist, "melted," "like everyone else"; then a growing appreciation for the potential wisdom of one's own gut reactions (especially on moral matters) and their historical roots; a growing self-confidence and social power; a sense of being discriminated against, condescended to, or carelessly misapprehended; a growing disaffection regarding those to whom one had always been taught to defer; and a sense of injustice regarding the response of liberal spokesmen to conflicts between various ethnic groups, especially between "legitimate" minorities and "illegiti-

---

*This Slavic American course—in a happy symbol of the new ethnicity—is housed in the Program of Puerto Rican Studies, through the generosity of the latter.

From *Further Reflections On Ethnicity* (Jednota Press, 1977) by Michael Novak. Originally appeared in *Center Magazine,* July/August 1974, pp. 18-25. © 1974 by Michael Novak. Reprinted by permission.

mate" ones. There is, in a word, an inner conflict between one's felt personal power and one's ascribed public power: a sense of outraged truth, justice, and equity.

The new ethnicity does, therefore, have political consequences. Many Southern and Eastern European-Americans have been taught, as I was, not to be "ethnic," or even "hyphenated," but only "American." Yet at critical points it became clear to some of us, then to more of us, that when push comes to shove we are always, in the eyes of others, "ethnics," unless we play completely by their rules, emotional as well as procedural. And in the end, even then, they retain the power and the status. Still, the stakes involved in admitting this reality to oneself are very high. Being "universal" is regarded as being good; being ethnically self-conscious raises anxieties. Since one's whole identity has been based upon being "universal," one is often loathe to change public face too suddenly. Many guard the little power and status they have acquired, although they cock one eye on how the ethnic "movement" is progressing. They are wise. But their talents are also needed.

The new ethnicity, then, is a fledgling movement, not to be confused with the appearance of ethnic themes on television commercials, in television police shows, and in magazines. All these manifestations in the public media would not have occurred unless the ethnic reality of America had begun to be noticed. In states from Massachusetts to Iowa, great concentrations of Catholics and Jews, especially in urban centers, have been some of the main bastions of Democratic Party politics for fifty years. The "new politics," centered in the universities, irritated and angered this constituency (even when, as it sometimes did, it won its votes). Thus there is a relation between the fledgling new ethnicity and this larger ethnic constituency. But what that relationship will finally be has not yet been demonstrated by events.

Those who do not come from Southern or Eastern European backgrounds in the United States may not be aware of how it feels to come from such a tradition; they may not know the internal history. They may note "mass passivity" and "alienation" without sharing the cynicism learned through particular experiences. They may regard the externals of ethnic economic and social success, modest but real, while never noticing the internal ambiguity—and its compound of peace and self-hatred, confidence and insecurity.

To be sure, at first many "white ethnics" of the third generation are not conscious of having any special feelings. The range of feelings about themselves they do have is very broad; more than one stream of feeling is involved. They are right-wingers and left-wingers, chauvinists and universalists, all-Americans and isolationists. Many want nothing more desperately than to be considered "American." Indeed, by now many have so deeply acquired that habit that to ask them point-blank how they are different from others would arouse strong emotional resistance.

For at least three reasons, many white ethnics *are* becoming self-conscious. As usual, great social forces outside the self draw forth from the self new responses. First, a critical mass of scholars, artists, and writers is beginning to emerge—the Italians, for example, are extraordinarily eminent in the cinema. Second, the prevailing image of the model American—the "best and the brightest" of the Ivy League, wealthy, suave, and powerful—has been discredited by the mismanagement of war abroad, by racial injustice at home, and by attitudes, values, and emotional patterns unworthy of emulation internally. The older image of the truly cultured American is no longer compelling. Many, therefore, are thrown back upon their own resources.

Finally, the attitudes of liberal, enlightened commentators on the "crisis of the cities" seem to fall into traditional patterns: guilt vis-a-vis blacks, and disdain for the Archie Bunkers of the land (Bunker is, of course, a classy British American name, but Carroll O'Connor is in appearance undisguisably Irish). The national media present to the public a model for what it is to be a "good American" which makes many people feel unacceptable to their betters, unwashed, and ignored. Richard Hofstadter wrote of "the anti-intellectualism of the people," but another feature of American life is the indifference—even hostility—of many intellectuals to Main Street. In return, then, many people respond with deep contempt for experts, educators, "limousine liberals," "radical chic," "bureaucrats"—a contempt whose sources are partly those of class ("the hidden injuries of class") and partly those of ethnicity ("legitimate" minorities and unacceptable minorities). The national social class that prides itself on being universalist has lost the confidence of many. Votes on school bond issues are an example of popular resistance to professionals.

In my own case, the reporting of voting patterns among white ethnic voters during the Wallace campaigns of 1964 and 1968 first aroused in me ethnic self-consciousness. Descriptions of "white backlash" often put the blame—inaccurately I came to see—upon Slavs and other Catholic groups. The Slavs of "South Milwaukee" were singled out for comment in the Wallace vote in Wisconsin in 1964. First, South Milwaukee was not distinguished from the south side of Milwaukee. Then, it was not noted that the Slavic vote for Wallace fell *below* his statewide average. Then, the very heavy vote for Wallace in outlying German and British American areas was not pointed out. Finally, the strong vote for Wallace in the wealthy northeastern suburbs of Milwaukee was similarly ignored. It seemed to me that those whom the grandfathers called "hunkies" and "dagos" were now being called "racists," "fascists," and "pigs," with no noticeable gain in affection. Even in 1972, a staff advisory in the Shriver "trip book" for a congressional district in Pittsburgh called the district "Wallace country," though the Wallace vote in that district in 1968 had been twelve per cent, and the Humphrey vote had been fifty-eight per cent. I obliged the staff member to revise his account and to call the district "Humphrey country." It is one of the most consistently liberal districts in Pennsylvania. Why send this constituency the message that it is the enemy?

Jimmy Breslin was once asked by an interviewer in *Penthouse* how, coming out of Queens, he could have grown up so liberal. Actually, next to Brooklyn, there is no more liberal county in the nation. A similar question was put to a liberal journalist from the Dorchester area, in Boston. The class and ethnic bias hidden in the way the word "liberal" is used in such interviews cries out for attention.

One of the large social generalizations systematically obscured by the traditional anti-Catholicism of American elites is the overwhelmingly progressive voting record in America's urban centers. The centers of large Catholic population in every northeastern and north central state have been the key to Democratic victories in those states since at least 1916. The hypothesis that Catholics have been, second only to Jews, the central constituency of successful progressive politics in this century is closer to the facts than historians have observed. (Massachusetts, that most Catholic of our states, stayed with McGovern in 1972.) The language of politics in America is, however, mainly Protestant, and Protestant biases color public perception. Protestant leadership is given the halo of morality and legitimacy, Catholic life is described in terms of negatively laden words: Catholic "power," "machine politics," etc.

There are other examples of odd perception on the part of American elites with respect to Catholic and other ethnic populations. The major institutions of American life—government, education, the media—give almost no assistance to those of "white ethnic" background who wish to obey the Socratic maxim: "Know thyself." One of the greatest and most dramatic migrations of human history brought more than thirty million immigrants to this land between 1874 and 1924. Despite the immense dramatic materials involved in this migration, only one major American film records it: Elia Kazan's *America! America!* That film ends with the hero's arrival in America. The tragic and costly experience of Americanization has scarcely yet been touched. How many died; how many were morally and psychologically destroyed; how many still carry the marks of changing their names, of "killing" their mother tongue and renouncing their former identity, in order to become "new men and new women"—these are motifs of violence, self-mutilation, joy, and irony. The inner history of this migration must come to be understood, if we are ever to understand the aspirations and fears of some seventy million Americans.

When this part of the population exhibits self-consciousness and begins to exert group claims—whether these are claims made by aggregated individuals or claims that are corporate—they are regularly confronted with the accusation that they are being "divisive". ("Divisive" is a code word for Catholic ethnics and Jews, is it not? It is seldom used of others: white Southerners, Appalachians, Chicanos, blacks, native Americans, prep-school British Americans, or others who maintain their own identity and institutions.) Earl Raab writes eloquently of this phenomenon in *Commentary* (May, 1974): "Modern Europe . . . never really accepted the legitimacy of the corporate Jew—although it was at its best willing to grant full civil rights to the individual Jew. That, for the Jews, was an impossible paradox, a secular vision of Christian demands to convert . . . [And] it is precisely this willingness to allow the Jews their separate identity as a group which is now coming into question in America." Individual diversity, yes; group identity, not for all.

The Christian white ethnic, like the Jew, actually has few group demands to make: positively, for educational resources to keep values and perceptions alive, articulate, and critical; negatively, for an equal access to power, status, and the definition of the general American purpose and symbolic world. Part of the strategic function of the cry "divisive!" is to limit access to these things. Only those individuals will be advanced who define themselves as individuals and who operate according to the symbols of the established. The emotional meaning is: *"Become like us."* This is an understandable strategy, but in a nation as pluralistic as the United States, it is shortsighted. The nation's hopes, purposes, and symbols need to be defined inclusively rather than exclusively; *all* must become "new men" and "new women." All the burden ought not to fall upon the newcomers.

There is much that is attractive about the British American, upper-class, northeastern culture that has established for the entire nation a model of behavior and perception. This model is composed of economic power; status; cultural tone; important institutional rituals and procedures; and the acceptable patterns of style, sensibility, and rationality. The terse phrase "Ivy League" suggests all these factors. The nation would be infinitely poorer than it is without the Ivy League. All of us who came to this land—including the many lower-class British Americans, Scotch-Irish, Scandinavians, and Germans—are much in the debt of the Ivy League, deeply, substantially so.

Still, the Ivy League is not the nation. The culture of the Ivy League is not the culture of America (not even of Protestant America).

Who are we, then, we who do not particularly reverberate to the literature of New England, whose interior history is not Puritan, whose social class is not Brahmin (either in reality or in pretense), whose ethnicity is not British American, or even Nordic? Where in American institutions, American literature, American education is our identity mirrored, objectified, rendered accessible to intelligent criticism, and confirmed? We are still, I think, persons without a public symbolic world, persons without a publicly verified culture to sustain us and our children.

7. THE ETHNIC LEGACY

It is not that we lack culture; it is not that we lack strength of ego and a certain internal peace. As Jean-Paul Sartre remarks in one of his later works, there is a distinction between one's identity in one's own eyes and one's identity in the eyes of others. In the United States, many who have internal dignity cannot avoid noticing that others regard them as less than equals, with a sense that they are different, with uncertainty, and with a lack of commonality. It is entirely possible that the "melting pot" would indeed have melted everyone, if those who were the models into which the molten metal was to be poured had not found the process excessively demanding. A sense of separate identity is, in part, induced from outside-in. I am made aware of being Catholic and Slovak by the actions of others. I would be sufficiently content were my identity to be so taken for granted, so utterly normal and real, that it would never have to be self-conscious.

The fact of American cultural power is that a more or less upper-class, Northeastern Protestant sensibility sets the tone, and that a fairly aggressive British American ethnocentricity, and even Anglophilia, govern the instruments of education and public life. Moreover, it is somehow emotionally important not to challenge this dominant ethnocentricity. It is quite proper to talk of other sorts of social difference—income, class, sex, even religion. To speak affirmatively of ethnicity, however, makes many uneasy. Some important truth must lie hidden underneath this uneasiness. A Niebuhrian analysis of social power suggests that a critical instrument of social control in the United States is, indeed, the one that dares not be spoken of.

In New York State, for example, in 1974 the four Democratic candidates for the office of lieutenant governor (not, however, for governor) were named Olivieri, Cuomo, La Falce, and Krupsak. It was the year, the pundits say, for "ethnic balance" on the ticket. But all four candidates insisted that their ethnicity was not significant. Two boasted of being from *upstate*, one of being a *woman*, one of being for "the *little* guy. " It is publicly legitimate to be different on any other account except ethnicity, even where the importance of ethnic diversity is tacitly agreed upon.

If I say, as I sometimes have, that I would love to organize an "ethnic caucus" within both the Democratic Party and the Republican Party, the common reaction is one of anxiety, distaste, and strained silence. But if I say, as I am learning to, that I would love to organize a "caucus of workingmen and women" in both parties, heads quickly nod in approval. Social class is, apparently, rational. Cultural background is, apparently, counter-rational.

Yet the odd political reality is that most Americans do not identify themselves in class terms. They respond to cultural symbols intimate to their ethnic history in America. Ethnicity is a "gut issue," even though it cannot be

mentioned. A wise political candidate does not, of course, speak to a longshoreman's local by calling its members Italian American and appealing to some supposed cultural solidarity. That would be a mistake. But if he speaks about those themes in the cultural tradition that confirm their own identity—themes like family, children, home, neighborhood, specific social aspirations, and grievances—they know he is with them: he does represent them. In order to be able to represent many constituencies, a representative has to be able to "pass over" into many cultural histories. He may never once make ethnicity explicit as a public theme; but, implicitly, he will be recognizing the daily realities of ethnicity and ethnic experience in the complex fabric of American social power.

According to one social myth, America is a "melting pot," and this myth is intended by many to be not merely descriptive but normative: the faster Americans—especially white ethnic Americans—"melt" into the British American pattern, the better. There is even a certain ranking according to the supposed degree of assimilation: Scotch Irish, Norwegians, Swedes, Germans, Swiss, Dutch, liberal or universalist Jews, the Irish, and on down the line to the less assimilated: Greeks, Yugoslavs, Hungarians, Central and East Europeans, Italians, Orthodox Jews, French Canadians, Portuguese, Latins and Spanish-speaking. . . . (The pattern almost exactly reflects the history and literature of England.).

Now it was one thing to be afraid of ethnicity in 1924, in confronting a first and second generation of immigrants. It is another thing to be afraid, in 1974, in confronting a third and fourth generation. Indeed, fears about a revival of ethnicity seem to be incompatible with conviction about how successful the "melting pot" has been. Fears about a "revival" of ethnicity confirm the fact that ethnicity is still a powerful reality in American life.

What, then, are the advantages and disadvantages in making this dangerous subject, this subterranean subject, explicit?

The disadvantages seem to be three. The first one on everyone's mind is that emphasis on ethnicity may work to the disadvantage of blacks. It may, it is said, become a legitimization of racism. It may "polarize" whites and blacks. Nothing could be further from the truth. Those who are concerned about the new ethnicity—Geno Baroni (Washington), Irving Levine (New York), Barbara Mikulski (Baltimore), Ralph Perrotta (New York), Steve Adubato (Newark), Otto Feinstein (Detroit), Stan Franczyk (Buffalo), Kenneth Kovach (Cleveland), Edward Marciniak (Chicago), and others—have given ample proof of their concern for the rights and opportunities of black Americans. Many got their start in the new ethnicity through their work among blacks. The overriding political perception among those concerned with the new ethnicity is that the harshness of life in the cities must be reduced by whites and blacks together, especially in working-class neighborhoods. Present social policies punish neighborhoods that integrate. Such neighborhoods should be rewarded and strengthened and guaranteed a long-range stability.

But fears about ethnicity require a further two-part response. Racism does not need ethnicity in order to be legitimated in America. It was quite well legitimated by Anglo-American culture, well before white ethnics arrived here in significant numbers, well before many white ethnics had ever met blacks. Indeed, there is some reason to believe that, while racism is an international phenomenon and found in all cultures, the British American and other Nordic peoples have a special emotional response to colored races. Not all European peoples respond to intermarriage, for example, with quite the emotional quality of the Anglo-Saxons. The French, the Spanish, the Italians, and the Slavs are not without their own forms of racism. But the felt quality of racism is different in different cultures. (It seems different among the North End Italians and the South Boston Irish of Boston, for example.)

In America, racism did not wait until the immigrants of 1880 and after began to arrive. Indeed, it is in precisely those parts of the country solely populated by British Americans that the conditions of blacks have been legally and institutionally least humane. In those parts of the country most heavily populated by white ethnics, the cultural symbols and the political muscle that have led to civil-rights and other legislation have received wide support. Liberal senators and congressmen elected by white ethnics—including the Kennedys—led the way. Even in 1972, both Hamtramck and Buffalo went for George McGovern. McGovern's share of the Slavic vote was fifty-two per cent. Nixon won the white Protestant vote by sixty-eight per cent.

It will be objected that white ethnic leaders like Frank Rizzo of Philadelphia, Ralph Perk of Cleveland, and others are signs of a new racism on the part of white ethnics in the Northern cities, of a retreat from support for blacks, and of a rising tide of anti-"crime" and anti-busing sentiment. The proponents of the new ethnicity perceive such developments as a product of liberal neglect and liberal divisiveness. The proponents of the new politics talk well of civil rights, equal opportunity, economic justice, and other beautiful themes. But the new politics, in distinguishing "legitimate" minorities (blacks, Chicanos, native Americans) from "less favored" minorities (Italians, Slavs, Orthodox Jews, Irish, etc.), has set up punitive and self-defeating mechanisms. The new politics has needlessly divided working-class blacks from working-class whites, in part by a romance (on television) with militance and flamboyance, in part by racial discrimination in favor of some against others, not because of need but because of color.

The second part of this response is that the politics of "the constituency of conscience" (as Michael Harrington, Eugene McCarthy, and others have called it)—the politics of the liberal, the educated, the enlight-ened—is less advantageous to blacks than is the politics of the new ethnicity. The new politics is less advantageous to blacks because it is obsessed with racial differences, and approaches these through the ineffectual lenses of guilt and moralism. Second, it is blind to cultural differences among blacks, as well as to cultural differences among whites; and sometimes these are significant. Third, it unconsciously but effectively keeps blacks in the position of a small racial minority outnumbered in the population ten to one.

By contrast, the new ethnicity notes many other significant differences besides those based upon race, and defines political and social problems in ways that unite diverse groups around common objectives. In Chicago, for example, neither Poles nor Italians are represented on the boards or in the executive suites of Chicago's top 105 corporations in a higher proportion than blacks or Latinos—all are of one per cent or less.* In Boston, neither white ethnics nor blacks desire busing, but this highly ideological instrument of social change is supported most by just those affluent liberals—in such suburbs as Brookline and Newton—whose children will not be involved.

The new ethnic politics would propose a strategy of social rewards—better garbage pickup, more heavily financed and orderly schools, long-range guarantees on home mortgages, easier access to federally insured home improvement loans, and other services—for neighborhoods that integrate. As a neighborhood moves from, say, a ten per cent population of blacks to twenty per-cent or more, integration should be regulated so that long-range community stability is guaranteed. It is better long-range policy to have a large number of neighborhoods integrated up to twenty or thirty per-cent than to encourage—even by inadvertence—a series of sudden flights and virtually total migrations. Institutional racism is a reality; the massive migration of blacks into a neighborhood does not bring with it social rewards but, almost exclusively, punishments.

There are other supposed disadvantages to emphasis upon ethnicity. Ethnicity, it is said, is a fundamentally counter-rational, primordial, uncontrollable social force; it leads to hatred and violence; it is the very enemy of enlightenment, rationality, and liberal politics. But this is to confuse nationalism or tribalism with cultural heritage. Because a man's name is Russell, or Ayer, or Flew, we would not wish to accuse him of tribalism on the ground that he found the Britons a uniquely civilized and clear-headed people, thought the Germans ponderous and mystic, the French philosophically romantic, etc. A little insular, we might conclude, but harmlessly ethnocentric. And if it is not necessarily tribalistic or unenlightened to read English literature in American schools, just possibly

---

*Cf. "The Representation of Poles, Italians, Latins, and Blacks in the Executive Suites of Chicago's Largest Corporations." The Institute of Urban Life, 820 North Michigan Avenue, Chicago, Illinois 60611.

it would be even more enlightened and even less tribalistic to make other literatures, germane to the heritage of other Americans, more accessible than they are.

The United States is, potentially, a multiculturally attuned society. The greatest number of immigrants in recent years arrives from Spanish-speaking and Asian nations. But the nation's cultural life, and its institutions of culture, are far from being sensitive to the varieties of the American people. Why should a cultural heritage not their own be imposed unilaterally upon newcomers? Would not genuine multicultural adaptation on the part of all be more cosmopolitan and humanistic? It would be quite significant in international affairs. The Americans would truly be a kind of prototype of planetary diversity.

Some claim that cultural institutions will be fragmented if every ethnic group in America clamors for attention. But the experience of the Illinois curriculum in ethnic studies suggests that no one school represents more than four or five ethnic groups (sometimes fewer) in significant density. With even modest adjustments in courses in history, literature, and the social sciences, material can be introduced that illuminates inherited patterns of family life, values, and preferences. The purpose for introducing multicultural materials is neither chauvinistic nor propagandistic but realistic. Education ought to illuminate what is happening in the self of each child.

What about the child of the mixed marriage, the child of *no* ethnic heritage—the child of the melting pot? So much in the present curriculum already supports such a child that the only possible shock to arise from multicultural materials would appear to be a beneficial one: not all others in America are like him (her), and that diversity, as well as homogenization, has a place in America.

The practical agenda that faces proponents of the new ethnicity is vast, indeed. At the heights of American economic and social power, there is not yet much of a melting pot. Significant ethnic diversity is manifested in the proportion of each group studying in universities, on faculties, in the professions, on boards of directors, among the creators of public social symbols, and the like. In patterns of home ownership, family income, work patterns, care for the aged, political activism, authoritarianism, individualism, and matters of ultimate concern, group differences are remarkable. About all these things, more information is surely needed. Appropriate social policies need to be hypothesized, tried, and evaluated.

Ethnic diversity in the United States persists in the consciousness of individuals, in their perceptions, preferences, behavior, even while mass production and mass communications homogenize our outward appearances. Some regard such persistence as a personal failure; they would prefer to "transcend" their origins, or perhaps they believe that they have. Here two questions arise. What cultural connection do they have with their brothers and sisters still back in Montgomery, or Wheeling, or Skokie, or Pawtucket? Second, has their personal assimilation introduced into the great American superculture fresh streams of image, myth, symbol, and style of intellectual life? Has anything distinctively their own—formed in them by a history longer than a thousand years—been added to the common wisdom?

The new ethnicity does not stand for the Balkanization of America. It stands for a true, real, multicultural cosmopolitanism. It points toward a common culture truly altered by each new infusion of diversity. Until now, the common culture has been relatively resistant to internal transformation; it has not so much arisen from the hearts of all as been imposed; the melting pot has had only a single recipe. That is why at present the common culture seems to have become discredited, shattered, unenforceable. Its cocoon has broken. Struggling to be born is a creature of multicultural beauty, dazzling, free, a higher and richer form of life. It was fashioned in the painful darkness of the melting pot and now, at the appointed time, it awakens.

Irish-Americans Attack Beer-Ad Images

Joanne Lipman

On the eve of St. Patrick's Day, some infuriated Irish-American groups are lashing out at America's beer marketers for ads they say perpetuate the worst stereotypes about the Irish—and they are demanding that the ads be pulled.

Just in time for the holiday, the country's top beer marketers have been unrolling ad campaigns tying their brands to party-down leprechauns and three-leaf clovers. But a number of Irish-American groups are mobilizing to declare that the image of the Irish as excessive drinkers is nonsense. The ads sling ethnic slurs against the Irish, the critics say, reinforcing damaging stereotypes.

The groups are especially furious over a Budweiser spot starring Kathy Ireland, the bikini-clad model who graces the cover of Sports Illustrated's new swimsuit edition. **Adolph Coors,** too, gets its share of complaints for the way it is promoting its Killian's Irish Red brand with contests and other gimmicks; Irish Red drinkers will be offered such freebies as leprechaun ears and shamrock hats.

Even Miller Brewing comes in for criticism for a series of St. Patrick's Day ads that warn against drinking and driving. The **Philip Morris** unit's newspaper ads, for example, picture keys attached to a green shamrock keychain with the words, "A key thing to remember this St.

Patrick's Day. Think When You Drink." Sober enough—but critics say the ads unfairly associate drunken driving with the Irish.

The beer companies say they've heard no complaints. And some Irish-American ad executives say their outraged brethren are a little too sensitive. "Lighten up!" scoffs Sean Fitzpatrick, vice chairman of Interpublic Group's McCann-Erickson. As for himself, Mr. Fitzpatrick confides, "I never go to an Irish bar to drink on St. Patrick's Day—because I don't like to drink with amateurs."

But the National Ethnic Coalition of Organizations insists the ads are no laughing matter. Last week it fired off a letter to **Anheuser-Busch's** president, August A. Busch III, demanding that the company pull the Kathy Ireland spot. "We believe strongly that it is exploitative marketing and is tantamount to an ethnic slur when drinking and alcohol are equated with the celebration of the patron saint of Ireland," fumed William Fugazy, travel-company executive and chairman of the group, which represents 66 ethnic organizations.

"We have the same problems as the Italians with [stereotypes of] mafia ties and the Polish with jokes," Mr. Fugazy, who is partly of Irish heritage, said in an interview. An Anheuser-Busch spokesman said the company hadn't seen the letter and couldn't comment on it.

The Budweiser spot follows Ms. Ireland—unnamed and fully clothed—through a crowded neighborhood bar, all the while punning on the swimsuit model's name by suggesting Bud is the official beer of Ireland. The St. Patrick's Day campaign marks an ironic twist for Budweiser, the No. 1 selling beer: It comes as brand manager August A. Busch IV is proudly touting his effort to cut down on the use of sexy babes and assorted bimbos to sell brews in advertising.

The Irish-American groups, in any case, have already succeeded in pressuring other kinds of marketers to drop hard-drinking stereotypes. They organized protests against greeting-card companies in the past few years, and take credit for persuading them to abandon some of the most tasteless St. Patrick's Day cards. Between 40 million and 70 million Americans have some Irish heritage, and "they're saying all these people are drinkers? That's not the case whatsoever," says John Finucane, president of the American Irish Political Education Committee.

Marketers probably wouldn't dream of touting such stereotypes in Ireland itself, where St. Patrick's Day is a religious holiday. "It tends to be a very sober day," notes Ray O'Hanlon, national editor of the New York-based Irish Echo, the country's largest Irish-American weekly. "The pubs close earlier than usual."

Polish American Congress 1992 Convention Resolution Committee Report

Conceived during a devastating war, the Polish American Congress was organized in 1944 to unite and solidify the patriotic, political and social conscience of Americans of Polish descent or birth.

Poland had already been victimized by Nazi German brutality and bondage. The potential of Soviet oppression in the post World War II era was evident. Poland's geographical, historical and very cultural identity was threatened with extinction.

The establishment of the Polish American Congress as a strong, central force in the United States created a platform upon which Polish Americans could defend and advance Poland's right to freedom and independence as a sovereign nation. The Congress provided a ray of hope and rejuvenation to Polish Americans, inspired a renewed awareness of their ethnic heritage and aroused in them a renewed desire to elevate their status in the American mosaic of pluralism.

The emergence of the Polish American Congress as a unifying umbrella laid a firm base for the defense of the interests of Poland. It created the avenue for Polish Americans and encouraged visions of positive achievements that would be the driving force following the Second World War serving to elevate the good name and prestige of Poland, the Polish people and Americans of Polish heritage.

More than 2,600 delegates representing organizations from 26 states participated in our founding convention. Negative world events that ensued after World War II led to the eventual absorption of Poland into the Soviet Union orbit with Allied consent and the threat of Soviet inspired Communist domination of the world, including the United States. This development made the cause of Poland and struggle against fascism and communism the dominant issues on the Polish American Congress agenda.

Its people's tragic fate under Soviet domination caused the Congress to focus its energies on the work to free Poland.

As the years passed, generations of Americans of Polish descent lost interest in the Polish American Congress because of the lack of programs about their concerns. They became the invisible Polonia of largely assimilated citizens with Polish surnames, who knew little if anything about their ancestral roots.

We recognize the complexities of the dilemma that confronts and hurts Americans who trace their heritage to Poland. We are also aware that 383 years of Polish presence in America has fostered and evolved with a redefined heritage—the Polish American Heritage. The unfortunate fact is that Americans of Polish ancestry, especially the present younger generations, have had and continue to have very limited exposure to learning and knowing about the great accomplishments of Poles who immigrated here and Americans of Polish descent who have made contributions at the highest levels to the progress of the United States. Curriculums in schools do not focus on Poland and the Polish American heritage. Our many once Polish oriented parochial schools no longer emphasize any curriculum on Polish heritage, arts, music, etc. The Polish language in most cases was eliminated decades ago. There are very few qualified texts on Polish American heritage for primary and secondary schools.

We continue to have a very deep affinity and sympathy for Poland, her struggle and needs. Poland is free, but not totally secure. The latter has been a problem over centuries. The collapse of the Soviet Union, disintegration of Communist governments in Eastern Europe and the emergence of new free republics in the former Soviet Union may have led to overstated optimism. Former Soviet republics, whose politics are unpredictable, have access to or control of nuclear and conventional weapons. There is a rise in right-wing extremist attacks on ethnic immigrants in Germany. Most notable are the recent reports and investigation of "ethnic cleansing" and genocide in the former Yugoslavia, a grim reminder of the Nazi rise to power in the 1930's. Nonetheless, the Polish American Congress has attained one of its primary goals. Poland is free. The Polish American Congress Charitable Foundation is continuing its outstanding assistance. That effort is ongoing and highly successful. It should be encouraged and supported.

This is a historic convention because it is the first Polish American Congress convention held in a time of elation over a free Poland. It is a critical convention because Poland's emergence as a free nation places the Polish American Congress at the crossroads. The Congress played a lead role in the struggle for Poland's freedom and defeat of Communism in Europe. Ironically, it has yet to focus equivalent vigor and resources in meeting the challenges of domestic Polish American problems. During the years of actions for Poland's freedom, the issues affecting the esteem and quality of status of Polish Americans may have become the inadvertent casualties of that commitment and dedication.

A generation of Americans of Polish ancestry has been virtually left, unwittingly, to the assimilative structure of the melting pot, without any knowledge about their heritage, and, perhaps, feeling left out of its own ethnicity and regarded as second class.

There are very few Polish Americans in the highest levels of political, business, educational and governmental hierarchies. Polish Americans are out of the inner circle of power and influence. Compared to other ethnic groups, there are very few Polish Americans ascending to those lofty positions. Our successes have been unnoticed or, to be blunt, almost non-existent or very short termed.

Over the years, the Polish American Congress has built an effective lobby for Poland at the highest levels of influence. However, that influence has not translated into effective programs to help Americans of Polish ancestry to advance in politics, government, business, and other endeavors.

We have often heard the phrase: "Let Poland be Poland". Now is the time to put this into practice. Poland is a free and independent sovereignty. It has a duly elected government. Neither the Polish American Congress or any other private group is the government of Poland. Our current responsibility is to respect that sovereign status which the Polish American Congress helped attain, continue the caring humanitarian work of the Charitable Foundation, offer counsel when requested and encourage American government aid. Above all, we must place faith in the resolve and capability of the Polish people to succeed in their newly discovered free enterprise and remain vigilant to all ill-intended obstacles.

It is imperative that the Polish American Congress broaden its priorities toward a vigorous program that addresses and pursues solutions to the domestic concerns of Polish Americans.

Dedicated people have given years of devotion to Poland's freedom. The same type of concerted energies must now be exercised in creating and implementing positive actions for the benefit of Americans of Polish ancestry.

Consequently, having considered and thoroughly reviewed the record of the Polish American Congress and looking to the future, we, the delegates to the Polish American Congress Convention, assembled in Washington, D.C., do hereby recommend and resolve, with firm conviction, the following proposals for consideration by the National Council of Directors:

1. We recommend that the conduct of Polish American Congress affairs be pursued from a broad domestic concept which includes all efforts of Polish Americans or permanent residents of the United States in acting on behalf of our own ethnic community and Poland.

2. Our Polish American fraternal organizations, mainly the Polish National Alliance, the Polish Roman Catholic Union, the Polish Women's Alliance, and the Polish Falcons of America have been the resource lifelines of the Polish American Congress. Considering their financial and human resource commitments to maintain the work of the Polish American Congress on the national and international levels, we express our appreciation and commend their contributions.

3. One of the very serious and chronic problems facing the organization is its lack of sufficient funding. It is amazing that so much has been accomplished, almost unnoticed, on a very frugal budget. We recommend with urgency that the executive leadership and National Council of Directors appoint a qualified committee of individuals to address the PAC funding needs. We also recommend that this special committee include a review and consideration of suggestions made at the American Agenda Workshop on October 13, 1992, prior to the convention sessions.

4. We recognize the absence of Polish Americans in the hierarchy of political parties and actions. We recommend the establishment of a national political network to develop and enhance the progress of Polish Americans toward the highest levels of all major parties and government. The network should include all Polish American elected federal, state and local officials, regardless of political party affiliation.

5. We need effective initiatives and organized efforts to respond quickly and accurately to defamation and bigotry against Poland, the Polish people and Polish Americans. An organized network throughout the Polish American Congress districts should provide a united effort to respond and prevent such attacks.

6. One of the major problems in building an effective organization is communication. We urge the National Council of

Directors to appoint a qualified editor for the Polish American Congress Newsletter and ensure regular issuance of the publication on a quarterly basis. The newsletter costs can be covered by adding a publication fee to membership dues. The final responsibility for content would rest with the leadership of the Polish American Congress, the publisher.

7. Today, many Polish Americans have only a limited knowledge of their heritage. To help deal with this problem we recommend to the National Council of Directors that we consider pursuing the following course:

A. A close alliance is needed between the Polish American Congress and educators, and educational, historical and cultural organizations. We call upon the Polish American Congress state divisions to work with colleges and universities in their areas to create and promote workshops, courses and lectures on the Polish experience.

B. Establish a national network to promote and promulgate the inclusion of a Polish and East Central European studies curriculum either independently or as part of existing courses, in social studies, American history and multi-cultural studies at the public and parochial schools, so that children of Polish and other backgrounds are not "educated away" from their respective ethnic values, customs and heritage and can build esteem and pride from the accomplishments of their forefathers.

C. Organize national and regional conferences of primary and secondary educators to develop appropriate materials for a Polish and East Central Europe curriculum.

D. Encourage Polish American authors by promoting their publications among publishers and other communication outlets.

E. Utilize the capabilities and expertise of Polish Americans who are involved in higher education at the college and university level through existing qualified organizations such as the Polish Institute of Arts and Sciences and Polish American Historical Association. These resources, including the Kosciuszko Foundation and similar established groups, can be very productive and positive sources for addressing the problems Polish Americans face in getting a college or university education. Regarding higher education, we recommend creation of a national scholarship resource information bank utilizing appropriate professional expertise to help Polish American students attain grants and scholarships. The resource bank could be effectively organized with assistance of some well known groups already operating in our community.

F. We appreciate and commend the educational work of Polish Language Schools. We recognize the effort to teach immigrants English. Given today's societal structure and economic needs, we encourage bilingualism on the part of our people.

8. We encourage the creation of Polish American Centers for Culture and Heritage in local communities, and development of a cooperative spirit that assures their survival and growth. Such centers can be vital arms to the Polish American Congress in matters dealing with heritage, folklore, music, history and arts. They can be a very influential force in putting the younger generation in practical touch with the Polish American Heritage.

9. We recommend that the National Council of Directors utilize the spiritual leadership of the Polish American clergy to develop a program for strengthening the Polish American family. In these times of various concepts of family life, it is important that the traditional units of the Polish American Family be focused toward the values of unity and understanding.

10. On the occasion of the 14th anniversary of his elevation to the Papacy, we recommend that a communication be sent to Pope John Paul II wishing him well and expressing our happiness that he has recovered from his recent illness and continues his spiritual crusade for world peace and for the less fortunate who live in poverty and starvation conditions.

11. We commend and appreciate the President of the United States, the Congress, all other government agencies, and the private sector for their assistance to Poland during her ordeal under Communism and after her emergence as a free nation, and we urge its continuance in the future.

12. We are grateful to the United States Government for the revered care and respect provided for a half century to the memory of Ignacy Jan Paderewski, Polish Statesman, and for the honors bestowed during the ceremonies transferring his remains to Poland.

13. We acknowledge, with appreciation, that a delegation of Polish Americans participated in the historic Conference of World Polonias, the first held since prior to World War II. The conclave, sponsored by "Spolnota Polska", was held in Krakow, Poland, August 13–23, 1992.

We honor those who contributed toward the eventual freedom of Poland and the demise of Communist domination in Eastern Europe. We especially pay tribute to the memory of those who gave their lives on the battlefields, leaders and activists of the Polish American Congress who dedicated their lives to Poland's cause and who did not live to experience the joys of triumph.

We congratulate and appreciate the organizers of this convention for their hospitality and excellent arrangements.

This had been a crossroads meeting of diverse groups and individuals; the representation spans different ideas and concepts based on generational experience. It is evident that the Polish American Congress needs a healing process to bring itself together and a deeper understanding of its own diversity and organizational personality, and the broad generational constituency it represents. This convention can be the body that creates the moving force for a united community. Let us begin.

Long live the United States of America
Long live a fully Free Poland
Long live the ideals of the Polish American Congress.

Resolutions Committee

Hilary Czaplicki, Chairman
Donald Pienkos, Vice Chairman and Secretary
Frank Milewski
John Olko
Ewa Gierat

THINGS TO DO DURING
NATIONAL POLISH AMERICAN HERITAGE MONTH

—— SUGGESTION SHEET ——

1. Request the elected leaders in your area to present proclamations and greetings at a public event to leaders in the Polish American Community. Don't hesitate to ask them for a presentation that will honor the Polish American taxpayers during Polish American Heritage Month. (Sample proclamations are available upon request.) Invite the entire Polonia to attend as well as the news media.

2. Unite all Polish American organizations for a Mass for the intention of Polish Americans. Encourage each parish to have a Mass for the intention of their parishioners. Have a reception with Polish pastries and refreshments in the parish hall following the Mass. Ask all Polish American clergy to participate in your activities.

3. Sponsor an event to honor General Pulaski (October 11th is the anniversary of the death of Pulaski). Organize a wreath laying ceremony before a portrait of Pulaski and possibly award the coloring contest prizes during that event. Invite everyone from your area to attend along with the Polish American organizations and Polonia.

4. Display Polish and American flags in homes, organizations' headquarters, banks, businesses, etc. Ask your local organizations to fly the Polish flag alongside the American flag during the entire month of October. (Information on purchasing a Polish flag is available from the national committee.)

5. Organize an essay contest in your local schools. Award prizes during a school assembly or public event to encourage participation (you can obtain prizes from local businesses or organizations). Ask your area teachers to help organize and judge the essay contest.

6. Coloring contest on General Pulaski. This type of contest is very popular with the children. Ask some of the local art students to organize and judge the entries. Ask a local printer to reprint the artwork for your committee with the name of his business at the bottom as advertising.

7. Organize a library display of Polish books, arts and crafts, wycinanki and paintings by Polish American artists. Contact local artists and request them to display their works at the local library, parish hall, organization hall, public building or office building lobby.

8. Children's recital in local organization headquarters, school hall or recreation center. There are many children groups that would participate and appreciate this type of exposure for their students. Invite the public as well as the Polonia to attend the children's recital.

9. Display National Polish American Heritage Month posters. Posters are available by contacting the Polish American Heritage Month Committee at the address listed on this suggestion sheet. Ask all of your local stores, banks, supermarkets, churches and organizations to display Polish American Heritage Month posters throughout the month of October.

10. Contact your local radio, television and newspapers to tell them about Polish American Heritage Month and its activities in your area. If they are advertising the various activities, compliment them; if they have not complied with your request to advertise activities, call and complain about their lack of interest.

11. Ask all local radio programs to mention your local events in October as part of their community bulletin board or public service announcements. Press releases pertaining to the national celebration can be obtained by writing to the national committee.

12. Ask local organizations, banks, businesses and elected leaders to place "POLISH AMERICAN HERITAGE MONTH SALUTES" in local newspapers and on radio programs. Place a salute each week during the month of October in local newspapers, this will remind everyone about POLISH AMERICAN HERITAGE MONTH. (The national committee has an artwork for the newspaper salutes which is FREE upon request.)

13. Call upon your area high school students and college students of Polish descent to help with press releases and other activities. Polish American Heritage Month will he very successful if we get everyone involved. Members of your organizations have children and grandchildren that could volunteer some time for this very worthy cause.

14. Senior citizen groups could sponsor a Polish American Day Lunch or Dinner with a guest speaker or entertainment.

15. Local Polish American organizations could sponsor a lunch or dinner reunion day to get the people together for a Polish American Heritage Month celebration.

16. Hold a fundraiser to help the Polish American causes in your area or to help the needy children in Poland.

17. Sponsor a Polish American evening social with music, food and entertainment.

18. Contact the other Polish American organizations to see what they will be planning during National Polish American Heritage Month and possibly unite your efforts.

19. Solicit several area businesses to donate towards a highway billboard that reads "WE SALUTE POLISH AMERICANS DURING OCTOBER." List their names on the billboard, it's great advertising. (Sample billboard artwork available upon request)

20. Wear red and white or "Polish and Proud" buttons to your local events and encourage others to do the same.

21. Tell friends and family about National Polish American Heritage Month events and invite them to attend your local celebrations.

22. Encourage everyone you know to join a Polish American organization.

23. Encourage everyone to read a book about Polish American contributions or a book written by a Pole or a Polish American.

24. If there is a Polish American radio program in your area ask them to do something special during regular programming throughout the month of October.

WE ENCOURAGE ALL TO WRITE FOR INFORMATION ABOUT ANY OF THE SUGGESTIONS LISTED. ALL INFORMATION IS FREE. THE ADDRESS IS: POLISH AMERICAN HERITAGE-MONTH COMMITTEE, 308 WALNUT STREET, PHILADELPHIA, PA 19106; PHONE: (215) 922-1700.

LET'S GET TOGETHER AND CELEBRATE!

At the Gates of Nightmare

A New Museum Raises Old Questions About History, Evil and Ourselves

Henry Allen

Washington Post Staff Writer

Six million Jews died in the Holocaust, and who can name one of them?

Well, there's Anne Frank. And, if you're Jewish, there's a grandmother at Treblinka, a cousin at Auschwitz, and all the faces touched by forefingers in photo albums . . . *that was your mother's great-uncle George, he won medals for swimming and later he owned a factory that made mother-of-pearl brushes.*

After that, nothing but a number—the Six Million. As Stalin is said to have said, "A single death is a tragedy, a million deaths is a statistic."

The statistic—what does it mean?—is the companion of the images buried in your nervous system like herpes viruses: the barbed wire, the overcoats and soup bowls, the innocence of starvation eyes, trains, gas, children, experiments, smokestacks, the pornography of Nazi evil—swagger sticks, dogs, Hitler's frantic radio voice, torches—and then the Allies' bulldozers pushing slow piles of bodies into pits.

Whatever it means, this is our Holocaust, the memorial inside our heads. We've built it from television, books, movies, trials and college courses.

Now we have the U.S. Holocaust Memorial Museum, which opens Monday, just off Independence Avenue.

Why? Why put the Holocaust next to the Mall with its merry-go-round, moon rocks and other triumphs of the human spirit? If we want to commemorate a disaster, why not a museum of slavery or the slaughter of Cambodia?

"Fine," says Michael Berenbaum, head of the museum's research center. "Let's have them."

And, the argument goes, many slaves died indeed, but their owners wanted

them alive, not dead. Unlike the million or so Cambodians killed by Pol Pot, the Jews were not being killed for their politics, intellect or even religion, but for their race.

Why a museum dedicated almost entirely to the Jews who died in the Holocaust? The answer runs along the lines of: The Nazis slaughtered Gypsies, Jehovah's Witnesses, Poles, political prisoners, homosexuals, the insane and the enfeebled too, but not with the earnestness they brought to the Jews. The scope, intention and logic of the Jewish Holocaust make it unique.

Why have a memorial to a European genocide in the capital of the United States of America?

"I myself am not happy about having a building on the Mall. I belong to a generation that says a building cannot express this idea," says literary critic Alfred Kazin. "I don't think the Holocaust is part of American culture."

John Roth, a professor of Claremont McKenna College in California, says the museum belongs here. "Auschwitz and Treblinka—those death camps shadow American ground. They warn us never to take the Dream for granted."

More reasoning:

If we have museums of art from Asia, Africa and Europe, there's no reason to ban this museum because the Holocaust happened on another continent.

The museum illustrates American values by displaying their opposite.

The Holocaust is a moral absolute worth commemorating in an age of moral relativity.

The Holocaust gets used to denote an endless list of evils—the slaughter of the Ibos, AIDS, abortion and animal experimentation. Shouldn't we try to keep opportunists from misusing it?

On and on and on.

The Holocaust has been "corrupted by sentimentality, emotionalism and bathos," writes scholar Jacob Neusner.

"Now it's getting invoked when we're talking about Bosnia," says Peter Novick, a historian at the University of Chicago. "We're supposed to have learned the lessons of the Holocaust. This is especially dopey. What is the lesson? That killing 6 million men, women and children is wrong? We knew that! What the hell are these lessons?"

It doesn't matter. That fact is, the Holocaust Museum is here, a national monument. But what does it mean?

It is a brick and limestone building that reminds you of the factory on the edge of town when you were growing up, an industrial smugness about it. It has metal doors with big bolts in the frames. It has smokestacks, towers and blind niches. It has a lonely row of metal-shrouded security lights jutting from the wall. It overwhelms you with a sort of grim seniority, like a prison or like a railroad station in a bad memory. It looks like an old photograph of itself. Its indifference is crushing.

Inside, you feel as though you're being processed through the exhibit rather than strolling through it. A staircase narrows as it rises. Catwalks over the Hall of Witnesses provoke a Piranesian paranoia. You sense how industrial engineering and 20th century social engineering are the same thing, the same belief in rationality's ability to solve problems.

Zygmunt Bauman writes in "Modernity and the Holocaust" that "modern genocide is a grand vision of a better, and radically different, society." From the Nazi point of view, the killing of the Jews "was not the work of destruction, but creation. They were eliminated, so that an objectively better human world—more efficient, more moral, more beautiful—could be established."

It took the planning and machinery of the Holocaust—a work of mass genius in its way—to get the job done. The old pogrom techniques wouldn't do. For instance, *Kristallnacht,* when the Nazis went berserk and attacked Jews all over Germany, was a pogrom of the sort the Jews had endured for centuries. About 100 Jews were killed. As Bauman points out, at that rate it would have taken 200 years to kill the Jews who were killed by the Holocaust.

Reason, efficiency, a grand vision.

"Wouldn't you be happier if I had been able to show you that all the perpetrators were crazy?" writes historian Raul Hilberg.

Yes, indeed. By calling it madness, you absolve both the Nazis and yourself from responsibility for the Holocaust. You say it's not quite real. This is one of the many ways of explaining how it happened.

It cannot be understood. It must be understood. It is unique. It is universal. On and on.

It happened because of the glamour of evil.

It happened because of the banality of evil.

It happened because Hitler had intended the whole thing all along. (Known as the "intentionalist" position.)

It happened because Hitler was only looking for an answer to "the Jewish question," and Germany's bureaucracy, technology and culture created the death camps as the solution. (The "functionalist" position.)

It happened because mankind is inherently evil. (The Hobbesian or Original Sin position.)

It happened because mankind is inherently good, but corrupted by society. (The Rousseauian position.)

It happened because the Jews participated in their own destruction, from the Judenrates governing the ghettos to the Jewish kapos in the camps.

It happened despite brave and constant resistance, the Warsaw Ghetto uprising being the most famous.

It happened because the Allies didn't do more to destroy Auschwitz and other camps.

It happened because there was nothing the Allies could do—if the bombers couldn't take out the Third Reich's ball-bearing factories, how could they take out the camps?

It happened, and half a century later you take a small, grim elevator to the fourth floor, and descend through the permanent exhibit. In keeping with the latest museum technology, there are video screens everywhere, enough to prompt the feeling you get from the TV walls in electronics stores—as if you're being stared at by blind people, an unsettling blend of reality and unreality. Nazis salute Hitler with beefy tiptoe eagerness. They smash the windows of Jewish stores. And all the photographs: book-burning gleefulness, and an SS officer by the railroad tracks in Auschwitz, ordering people to the right or left, to death now or death later. As Tadeusz Borowski put it in the title of his Auschwitz memoir: "This Way for the Gas, Ladies and Gentlemen."

Holocaust photographs are nothing new. They hardly seem real anymore. But the sense of reality tingles quite vividly at the sight of the Hollerith machine. There, glowering with the bustling potential you remember from old sewing machines, is the IBM computer that sorted *lebensunwertes Leben,* life unworthy of life, into stacks of punch cards.

As you descend from floor to floor, things get even realer: A boxcar that hauled people to Treblinka—it smells like a bureau drawer in a summer house. A pile of shoes. The ovens. Then the newsreels of the liberation. The bulldozers. The eyes.

Carved into a museum wall is the testimony of Gen. Dwight Eisenhower.

"The things I saw beggar description. . . . The visual evidence and the verbal testimony of starvation, cruelty and bestiality were so overpowering . . . I made the visit deliberately, in order to be in a position to give first-hand evidence of these things if ever in the future there developed a tendency to charge these allegations merely to propaganda."

How strange. Who could forget something as real as the Holocaust?

Everybody could forget.

Or at least a lot of people didn't want to remember, or know.

Primo Levi, an Italian survivor of Auschwitz, describes the first Russian troops to reach the camp:

"They did not greet us, nor did they smile; they seemed oppressed not only by compassion but by a confused restraint. . . . It was that shame we knew so well, the shame that drowned us after the selections, and every time we had to watch, or to submit to, some outrage: the shame the Germans did not know, that the just man experiences at another man's crime; the feeling of guilt that such a crime should exist, that it should have been introduced irrevocably into the world of things that exist."

Irrevocably. What a triumph.

Simon Wiesenthal remembers SS troopers telling the prisoners:

"There will be no certainties, because we will destroy the evidence together with you. And even if some proof should remain and some of you survive, people will say that the events you describe are too monstrous to be believed: they will say that they are the exaggerations of Allied propaganda and will believe us, who will deny everything, and not you."

Who would believe the testimony of Jews whom an American liberator, Gen. George Patton, described as "a sub-human species without any of the cultural or social refinements of our time"? He also said no ordinary people "could have sunk to the level of degradation these have reached in the short space of four years."

Imagine thinking of four years in Dachau as "short."

Then again, who could imagine the reality of the Holocaust? From the beginning it has been a rumor, an incredible newspaper story, an idea, an impossibility, an invocation. Starting before World War II, newspapers were burying stories about it, if they ran them at all. Governments found it convenient to ignore what reports there were. Military strategists found it incidental to the main business of the war.

Toward the end of the war, the word "genocide" had to be invented to describe it. The word "holocaust" didn't enter general use until the 1960s—it started the decade as a common noun, and ended it capitalized. As if the words really mattered. Elie Wiesel has said: "The Holocaust in its enormity defies language and art, and yet both must be used to tell the tale, the tale that must be told."

Some have a tale of no Holocaust at all. For years, a small but thriving crowd of independent scholars, wackos and neo-Nazis has denied that the Holocaust ever happened. Some of them of course, are the very people who would have supported it.

Their books have titles such as "The Myth of the Six Million," "The Six Million Swindle" and "The Hoax of the Twentieth Century." A Frenchman and Buchenwald survivor named Paul Rassinier wrote in 1964 that exactly

4,416,108 of the 6,000,000 were alive. Another claim had it that the Holocaust was a propaganda coup created by a partnership of Nazis and Zionists.

The reality of the Holocaust grows, shrinks and metamorphoses.

"When we look back at World War II, the Holocaust stands out, but it didn't look that way at the time," says historian Peter Novick, who is writing a book on the shifting meaning of the Holocaust in American culture.

"From 1933 to 1938, there are hardly any Jews as Jews in concentration camps. They are communists, socialists, dissidents. For the first nine of 12 years of the Thousand-Year Reich a well-informed observer would conclude that while Jews were among the victims of Nazism, they didn't stand out. By the time news of the mass annihilation of the Jews comes out,it gets assimilated into this previous framework," Novick says. "Also, there was still a lot of isolationism on behalf of the American public. What we all know now comes from the pictures from the liberations. You have to remember that the Americans only liberated the western camps, and most people there weren't Jewish. You looked at those pictures then and saw victims of Nazism. You look at them now and you see Jews and the Holocaust.

"Back then it was the habit of journalists after the war to call a French Jew a Frenchman, a Belgian Jew a Belgian. To call them Jews was buying into Hitler's categories. What we call survivors now were DPs [displaced persons], people fleeing the Soviets, people fleeing the Nazis. In the struggle over immigration, there was a deliberate attempt by Jewish organizations to downplay Jewishness in order to avoid antisemitism in Congress.

"In the late '40s, we had a situation where we were going from being allied with Russia against Germany to being allied with Germany against Russia. The ones who talked the most about the Holocaust were the American Communists and pro-Communists."

Meanwhile, America wanted to put the war behind it. We were moving into the biggest get-rich economy in history. Progressive thinking disapproved of seeing ethnic differences, and the survivors who came here wanted to fit in—we hadn't yet invented the science of victimology to render them helpless.

"With the Cold War, the event was buried," says Raul Hilberg, author of "The Destruction of the European Jews."

In the 1950s the book, play and movie of "The Diary of Anne Frank" came out, and she became a sort of saint—not for her squalid death in Bergen-Belsen but for her happiness and confidence. In the play, her final words are: "In spite of everything, I still believe that people are really good at heart."

This prompted psychologist (and refugee) Bruno Bettelheim to say: "If all men are good, there was never an Auschwitz."

The hard facts grew harder to ignore in 1961, with the Israelis' trial of Adolf Eichman, who was a major architect of the Holocaust complex. Later in the '60s, says Novick, friction between blacks and Jews would lead the Jews to use the Holocaust as their credential of oppression.

"But the biggest single thing was the 1967 Arab-Israeli war," Novick says. "There was tremendous anxiety that the past history of the Holocaust had become the present. The invocation of the Holocaust was used to mobilize support."

Hilburg, on the other hand, dates the Holocaust we think of now to 1978, with the broadcast of the television series "Holocaust," the efforts of the Justice Department to find war criminals in this country and Jimmy Carter's decision to go ahead with a Holocaust memorial commission, not least because his poll numbers were bad among Jews. And the country was in search of a moral absolute after the ambiguities of Vietnam, he says. At the University of Vermont, where he taught a class on the Holocaust, "I got 50 students, then 80, then 120, and pretty soon we had to ask for a prerequisite to limit the numbers."

And the museum was going up in Washington.

What is the Holocaust in the American mind?

It's Nazis striding around with riding crops. It's a plea for sympathy, or a demand for respect. It's guard towers, "Sophie's Choice," the horrible *ee-oo* sirens of Gestapo Mercedeses and the old grandpa down the block who stayed in his room reading so you never got to see the number tattooed on his arm. It is Elie Wiesel's "Night." It was a technological inevitability, a moral probability, a freak of human nature. It's the boyman, a ghost, a historical event that someday will fade in students' minds like the Council of Trent or the Hanseatic League.

Yesterday, for instance, a Roper poll for the American Jewish Committee was released, showing that 53 percent of high school students and 38 percent of adults were unable to correctly define the word "Holocaust." A fifth said it was possible it never happened at all.

The Ethnic Factor: Challenges for the 1990s

The process of better understanding the multiethnic character of America involves the coordinated efforts of public and private sectors, educational institutions, and voluntary associations. This collection of articles addresses the sort of balances that are appropriate and required for education at various levels. Resistance to the challenge of incorporating approaches to learning about the cultural variety of America can be found in various sectors, and in behavior that indicates confusion, uncertainty, insensitivity, and violence toward and between ethnic groups. The persistence of these tensions calls for thoughtful examination of strategies for dealing with the reality of bias, hatred, and prejudice.

Examination, for example, of the legacy of the civil rights laws crafted during the 1960s and the process of shaping a society grounded in exclusionary habits and institutions involves assessment on many levels—the social, the political, the ideological, and the economic. Even on the most basic level of public perception, most agree that progress has been made toward a society of equality and social justice, with increased hopes for decreased segregation in schools and neighborhoods. Yet disparities of these views among ethnic and racial groups indicate that uniformity and a shared sense of the past and present are not generally common. The process of attempting to overcome such gulfs of misunderstanding that lead to more serious forms of conflict is among the great challenges of the present and the future.

Novel approaches toward the peaceful reconciliation of conflict should be explored more thoroughly. For example, unlike interethnic conflict between groups in the United States, conflict between the United States and Native Americans is regulated by treaties. The struggle over claims regarding the rights of nations and the interests of the U.S. government and its citizens defines a field of conflict that is no longer at the margin of public affairs. Does the definition of this conflict as an issue of foreign and not domestic policy provide a meaningful distinction? Should the claims of ethnic groups in defense of culture, territory, and unique institutions be honored and protected by law and public policy?

Questions on the future state of American ethnic groups raise even more profound issues. For example, understanding of the changing structure of the black family in America has stubbornly eluded researchers as well as parents who confront the realities of pride and prejudice. How does the continual redevelopment of an ethnic population enter public discussion, and what are the implications for public policy built upon alternative models of the family? Should public policy sustain an ethnic model of family or direct the formation of family life that is consonant with public purposes and goals?

The civil rights movement has been over for approximately 20 years, but many African Americans still face challenges in housing, employment, and education. Changing circumstances within the larger American society and the civil rights agenda itself have been affected by success and failure, as well as by movement from a time of clear issues and solutions to a time when issues have more complex structural, economic, and philosophical dimensions. The growing gap between blacks and whites in terms of education, financial status, and class, and the growing crime and death rates of young black men paint a daunting picture of the success of past policies and of this population's future. According to scales of mortality, health, income, education, and marital status, African Americans have emerged as one of the most troubled segments of American society. These problems also foreshadow grave difficulties for the African American family in the years ahead.

To be sure, African Americans have made advances since the civil rights movement of the 1960s. They have made dramatic gains in education, employment, and financial status. Unfortunately, they still are portrayed as being part of an urban underclass when only roughly one-third of their population could be considered part of this group. While not all African Americans are poor, those who are poor are in desperate situations. Will help come from the African American population that now constitutes part of the middle and upper classes of American society?

Scholarly differences of opinion concerning the composition of the urban underclass do not minimize the hardships that many poor people face. The growth of the underclass, its isolation from society, and society's inability to help it are tremendous obstacles that face our nation. Concrete strategies for improving this situation call upon the public and the private sector in areas of education, employment, and training. Suggestions for meeting future needs of this population and pragmatic policy responses also will help the general population.

Patent historical distortion and various forms of statistical evidence have been included in interpretations and rearticulations of race and ethnicity. The issues of race in the workplace and remedies for discriminating practices have been raised in the debate regarding the Civil Rights Act of 1991. Exploring the sources of ethnic and racial

Unit 8

THE UNIVERSAL DECLARATION OF Human Rights

WHEREAS recognition of the inherent dignity and of the equal and inalienable rights of all members of the human family is the foundation of freedom, justice and peace in the world,

WHEREAS disregard and contempt for human rights have resulted in barbarous acts which have outraged the conscience of mankind, and the advent of a world in which human beings shall enjoy freedom of speech and belief and freedom from fear and want has been proclaimed as the highest aspiration of the common people,

WHEREAS it is essential, if man is not to be compelled to have recourse, as a last resort, to rebellion against tyranny and oppression, that human rights should be protected by the rule of law,

WHEREAS it is essential to promote the development of friendly relations among nations,

WHEREAS the peoples of the United Nations have in the Charter reaffirmed their faith in fundamental human rights, in the dignity and worth of the human person and in the equal rights of men and women and ha

determined to promote social progress and better standards of life in larger freedom,

WHEREAS Member States have pledged themselves to achieve, in co-operation with the United Nations, the promotion of universal respect for and observance of human rights and fundamental freedoms,

WHEREAS a common understanding of these rights and freedoms is of the greatest importance for the full realisation of this pledge,

NOW THEREFORE THE GENERAL ASSEMBLY

mobility and the development of approaches and strategies that foster the breakdown of discrimination engages us in a web of baffling arguments and an array of social and political images and institutional forces' practices and procedures.

Since the breakup of the Soviet empire, ethnicity has reoriented the international arena. New national claims as well as the revival of ancient antagonisms are fragmenting Europe. War, the systematic expression of conflict, and its aftermath are also occasions for the use and misuse of ethnically charged political rhetoric. The presence of a politically relevant past and the invocation of religious warrants for group conflict have indicated the need for new approaches to peacekeeping and educational strategies for meeting and transcending group differences. The critique of diversity expressed in challenges to multiculturalism and the educational controversy regarding the dominant expressions of our human commonality and the shared values and virtues found in all ethnic traditions pose challenges for economic and socially turbulent times. Whether these moments are crises of growth or decline will be measured by a host of indicators. Which of these indicators are the most salient is, of course, to pose a another question that is often determined by our selec-

tive invocation of historical materials and ethnic symbols as guides for contemporary analysis of ethnic and racial factors in political action.

Looking Ahead: Challenge Questions

International events will continue to frequently affect the United States. In what respect do such events have special significance to ethnic populations?

Does the relationship of ethnic Americans to changes and challenges in the world arena provide a strength or a liability for the well-being of American interests? Does conflict between ethnic interests and national interests present real or imaginary fears about our activities in international affairs?

How will increased immigration, technological advances, and a more competitive world market affect the relationships between ethnic groups?

Unlike interethnic conflict within the United States, conflict between Native Americans and the national government is resolved through treaties. Should the claims of ethnic groups in defense of culture, territory, and unique institutions be honored and protected by law and public policy?

185

■ HISPANIC U.S.A.

The Mirror of The Other

CARLOS FUENTES

Carlos Fuentes is the author of The Campaign.

T he U.S.-Mexico border, some of those who cross it say, is not really a border but a scar. Will it heal? Will it bleed once more? When a Hispanic worker crosses this border, he sometimes asks, "Hasn't this always been our land? Am I not coming back to it? Is it not in some way ours?" He can taste it, hear its language, sing its songs and pray to its saints. Will this not always be in its bones a Hispanic land?

But first we must remember that ours was once an empty continent. All of us came here from somewhere else, beginning with the nomadic tribes from Asia who became the first Americans. The Spaniards came later, looking for the Seven Cities of Gold, but when they found none in what is today the southwestern United States, they left their language and their religion, and sometimes their blood. The Spanish empire extended as far north as Oregon and filled the coastal region with the sonorous names of its cities: Los Angeles, Sacramento, San Francisco, Santa Barbara, San Diego, San Luis Obispo, San Bernardino, Monterey, Santa Cruz. When it achieved independence, the Mexican republic inherited these vast, underpopulated territories, but it lost them in 1848 to the expanding North American republic and its ideology of Manifest Destiny: the U.S.A., from sea to shining sea.

L os Angeles is now the second-largest Spanish-speaking city in the world, after Mexico City, before Madrid and Barcelona.

So the Hispanic world did not come to the United States, the United States came to the Hispanic world. It is perhaps an act of poetic justice that now the Hispanic world should return, both to the United States and to part of its ancestral heritage in the Western Hemisphere. The immigrants keep coming, not only to the Southwest but up the Eastern Seaboard to New York and Boston and west to Chicago and the Midwest, where they meet the long-established Chicanos, the North Americans of Mexican origin, who have been here even longer than the gringos. They all join to make up the 25 million Hispanics in the United States—the vast majority of Mexican origin, but many from Puerto Rico, Cuba, and Central and South America. It is the fastest-growing minority in the United States.

Los Angeles is now the second-largest Spanish-speaking city in the world, after Mexico City, before Madrid and Barcelona. You can prosper in southern Florida even if you speak only Spanish, as the population is predominantly Cuban. San Antonio, integrated by Mexicans, has been a bilingual city for 150 years. By the middle of the coming century, almost half the population of the United States will be Spanish-speaking.

This third Hispanic development, that of the United States, is not only an economic and political event; it is above all a cultural event. A whole civilization with a Hispanic pulse has been created in the United States. A literature has been born in this country, one that stresses autobiography—the personal narrative, memories of childhood, the family album—as a way of answering the question, What does it mean to be a Chicano, a Mexican-American, a Puerto Rican living in Manhattan, a second-generation Cuban-American living in exile in Miami? For example, consider the varied work of Rudolfo Anaya (*Bless Me, Ultima*), Ron Arías (*The Road to Tamazunchale*), Ernesto Galarza (*Barrio Boy*), Alejandro Morales (*The Brick People*), Arturo Islas (*The Rain God*), Tomás Rivera (*Y No Se lo Trago la Tierra*) and Rolando Hinojosa (*The*

Valley); or of the women writers Sandra Cisneros (*Woman Hollering Creek*), Dolores Prida (*Beautiful Señoritas & Other Plays*) and Judith Ortiz Cofer (*The Line of the Sun*); or of the poets Alurista and Alberto Rios. Or consider the definitive statements of Rosario Ferré or Luis Rafael Sánchez, who simply decided to write in Spanish from the island of Puerto Rico.

An art has also been created here; in a violent, even garish way, it joins a tradition going all the way from the caves of Altamira to the graffiti of East Los Angeles. It includes pictures of memory and dynamic paintings of clashes, like the car-crash paintings of Carlos Almaráz, who was part of the group called Los Four, along with Frank Romero, Beto de la Rocha and Gilbert Luján. The beauty and violence of these artists' work not only contribute to the need for contact between cultures that must refuse complacency or submission to injustice in order to become alive to one another. They also assert an identity that deserves to be respected and that must be given shape if it is not visible, or a musical beat if it is inaudible. And if the other culture, the Anglo mainstream, denies Hispanic culture a past, then artists of Latin origin must invent, if necessary, an origin. And they must remember every single link that binds them to it.

For example, can one be a Chicano artist in Los Angeles without upholding the memory of Martín Ramírez? Born in 1885, Ramírez was a migrant railroad worker from Mexico who lost his speech and for this was condemned to live for three decades in a California madhouse, until his death in

---

The majority of Mexican immigrants are temporary and eventually return to Mexico . . . the differences between Anglo-America and Ibero-America . . . influence and clash with each other.

1960. He was not mad, he was just speechless. So he became an artist, and drew his muteness for thirty years.

No wonder that the Hispanic culture of the United States must manifest itself as forcefully as in a Luján painting; as dramatically as in a stage production by Luis Valdez; with a prose as powerful as that of Oscar Hijuelos with his mambo kings; or with a beat as life giving as that of Rubén Blades in his salsa songs of city woes and streetwise humor.

This vast flow of negation and affirmation forces newcomers as well as native Hispanics to ask themselves, "What do we bring? What would we like to retain? What do we want to offer this country?" The answers are determined by the fact

People and their cultures perish in isolation, but they are born or reborn in contact with other men and women.

that these people reflect a very broad social group that includes families, individuals, whole communities and networks, transmitting values, memories, traditions. At one end of the spectrum are 300,000 Hispanic businessmen prospering in the United States, and at the other is a 19-year-old Anglo-American shooting two immigrants to death for the simple reason that he "hates Mexicans." If one proudly spouts the statistic that Hispanic-owned businesses generate more than $20 billion a year, one can also, far less proudly, report that immigrants are shot at by Anglos with the paint-pellet guns used in mock warfare games. If one records that whole communities in Mexico are supported by the *remesas*, or remittances, of their migrant workers in the United States, and that these *remesas* add up to $4 billion a year and are Mexico's second-largest source of foreign income (after oil), then one must also record that many migrant workers are run down by vehicles on back roads near their campsites. And if, finally, one realizes that the majority of Mexican immigrants are temporary and eventually return to Mexico, then one must bear in mind the persisting differences between Anglo-America and Ibero-America, as these continue to oppose, influence and clash with each other.

The two cultures coexist, rubbing shoulders and questioning each other. We have too many common problems, which demand cooperation and understanding in a new world context, to clash as much as we do. We recognize each other more and more in challenges such as dealing with drugs, crime, the homeless and the environment. But as the formerly homogeneous society of the United States faces the immigration of vastly heterogeneous groups, Latin America faces the breakdown of the formerly homogeneous spheres of political, military and religious power through the movement of the urban dispossessed.

In this movement, which is taking place in all directions, we all give something to one another. The United States brings its own culture—the influence of its films, its music, its books, its ideas, its journalism, its politics and its language—to each and every country in Latin America. We are not frightened by this, because we feel that our own culture is strong enough, and that, in effect, the enchilada can coexist with the hamburger. Cultures only flourish in contact with others; they perish in isolation.

The culture of Spanish America also brings its own gifts. When asked, both new immigrants and long-established Hispanic-Americans speak of religion—not only Catholicism but something more like a deep sense of the sacred, a recognition that the world is holy, which is probably the oldest and deepest certitude in the Amerindian world. This is also a sensuous, tactile religion, a product of the meeting between the Mediterranean civilization and the Indian world of the Americas.

Then there is care and respect for elders, something called *respeto*—respect for experience and continuity, less than awe at change and novelty. This respect is not limited to old age in itself; in a basically oral culture, the old are the ones who remember stories, who have the store of memory. One could almost say that when an old man or an old woman dies in the Hispanic world, a whole library dies with that person.

And of course there is the family—family commitment, fighting to keep the family together, perhaps not avoiding poverty but certainly avoiding a *lonely* poverty. The family is regarded as the hearth, the sustaining warmth. It is almost a political party, the parliament of the social microcosm and the security net in times of trouble. And when have times not been troubled? The ancient stoic philosophy from Roman Iberia is deep indeed in the soul of Hispanics.

What else do Ibero-Americans bring to the United States? What would they like to retain? It is obvious they would like to keep their language, the Spanish language. Some urge them to forget it, to integrate by using the dominant language, English. Others argue that they should use Spanish only to learn English and join the mainstream. More and more often, however, people are starting to understand that speaking more than one language does not harm anyone. There are automobile stickers in Texas that read MONOLINGUALISM IS A CURABLE DISEASE. Is monolingualism unifying and bilingualism disruptive? Or is monolingualism sterile and bilingualism fertile? The California state law decreeing that English is the official language of the state proves only one thing: that English is no longer the official language of California.

Multilingualism, then, appears as the harbinger of a multicultural world, of which Los Angeles is the prime example. A modern Byzantium, the City of the Angels receives each day, willy-nilly, the languages, the food, the mores not only of Spanish-Americans but of Vietnamese, Koreans, Chinese, Japanese. This is the price—or the gift, depending on how you look at it—of global interdependence and communications.

So the cultural dilemma of the American of Mexican, Cuban or Puerto Rican descent is suddenly universalized: to integrate or not? to maintain a personality and add to the diversity of North American society, or to fade away into anonymity in the name of the after-all nonexistent "melting pot"? Well, perhaps the question is really, once more, to be or not to be? to be with others or to be alone? Isolation means death. Encounter means birth, even rebirth.

California, and especially Los Angeles, a gateway to both Asia and Latin America, poses the universal question of the coming century: How do we deal with the Other? North Africans in France; Turks in Germany; Vietnamese in Czechoslovakia; Pakistanis in Britain; black Africans in Italy; Japanese, Koreans, Chinese and Latin Americans in the United States: Instant communications and economic interdependence have transformed what was once an isolated situation into a universal, defining, all-embracing reality of the twenty-first century.

Is anyone better prepared to deal with this central issue of dealing with the Other than we, the Spanish, the Spanish-Americans, the Hispanics in the United States? We are Indian, black, European, but above all mixed, mestizo. We are Iberian and Greek; Roman and Jewish; Arab, Gothic and Gypsy. Spain and the New World are centers where multiple cultures meet—centers of incorporation, not of exclusion. When we exclude, we betray ourselves. When we include, we find ourselves.

People and their cultures perish in isolation, but they are born or reborn in contact with other men and women of another culture, another creed, and another race.

Who are these Hispanic "ourselves"? Perhaps no story better renders the simultaneity of cultures than "The Aleph," by the Argentine author Jorge Luis Borges. In "The Aleph," the narrator finds a perfect instant in time and space where all the places in the world can be seen at the same moment, without confusion, from every angle, in perfect, simultaneous existence. What we would see in the Spanish-American aleph would be the Indian sense of sacredness, communality and the will to survive; the Mediterranean legacy of law, philosophy and the Christian, Jewish and Arab strains making up a multiracial Spain; and the New World's challenge to Spain, the syncretic, baroque continuation of the multicultural and multiracial experience, now including Indian, European and black African contributions. We would see a struggle for democracy and for revolution, coming all the way from the medieval townships and from the ideas of the European Enlightenment, but meeting our true personal and communal experience in Zapata's villages, on Bolívar's plains, in Tupac Amaru's highlands.

And we would then see the past becoming present in one seamless creation. The Indian world becomes present in the paintings of Rufino Tamayo, who was born in an Indian village in Oaxaca and whose modern art includes an Indian continuity in the sense of color and the spirit of celebration, in the cosmic consciousness and in Tamayo's capacity to recreate on canvas the dream of a form that *can* contain dreams. A younger painter, Francisco Toledo, also from an Indian village in Oaxaca, gives the ancient Indian fear and love of nature their most physical and visual proximity to our urban lives, while the Cuban Wifredo Lam permits his African roots to grow in his pictures. The Mexican painter Alberto Gironella bitingly recovers the traditions of Spanish art and commerce: His Velázquez spinoffs are framed by sardine cans.

Culture is the way we laugh, even at ourselves, as in the paintings of the Colombian Fernando Botero. It is the way we remember, as when the Venezuelan Jacobo Borges imagines the endless tunnel of memory. But culture is above all our bodies, our bodies so often sacrificed and denied, our shackled, dreaming, carnal bodies, like the body of the Mexican artist Frida Kahlo. Our bodies are deformed and dreamy creatures in the art of the Mexican José Luis Cuevas. Indeed, like Goya, Cuevas offers the mirror of imagination as the only truth; his figures are the offspring of our nightmares, but also the brothers and sisters of our desires.

The union of Cuevas in the Americas with Goya in Spain also reminds us that when we embrace the Other, we not only meet ourselves, we embrace the marginal images that the modern world, optimistic and progressive as it has been, has shunned and has then paid a price for forgetting. The conventional values of middle-class Western society were brutally shattered in the two world wars and in the totalitarian experience. Spain and Spanish America have never fooled themselves on this account. Goya's "black paintings" are perhaps the most lasting reminder we have of the price of losing the tragic sense of life in exchange for the illusion of progress. Goya asks us again and again to harbor no illusions. We are captive within society. Poverty does not make anyone kinder, only more ruthless. Nature is deaf to our pleas. It cannot save the innocent victim; history, like Saturn, devours its own children.

Goya asks us to avoid complacency. The art of Spain and Spanish America is a constant reminder of the cruelty that we can exercise on our fellow human beings. But like all tragic art, it asks us first to take a hard look at the consequences of our actions, and to respect the passage of time so that we can transform our experience into knowledge. Acting on knowledge, we can have hope that this time we shall prevail.

We will be able to embrace the Other, enlarging our human possibility. People and their cultures perish in isolation, but they are born or reborn in contact with other men and women, with men and women of another culture, another creed, another race. If we do not recognize our humanity in others, we shall not recognize it in ourselves.

Often we have failed to meet this challenge. But we have finally seen ourselves whole in the unburied mirror of identity only when accompanied—ourselves with others. We can hear the voice of the poet Pablo Neruda exclaiming throughout this vision, "I am here to sing this history."

The Ends of History: Balkan Culture and Catastrophe

Thomas Butler

Thomas Butler is author of several books, including "Memory: History, Culture and the Mind," and "Monumenta Serbocroatica," a bilingual anthology of Serbian and Croatian texts.

Abuse of cultural memory—the manipulation of long-invalid past grievances to obtain present-day advantage—rules the day in the war-torn lands of Yugoslavia. Deliberate misreadings and misrepresentations of history are destroying the future in the Balkans.

The fundamental cause of Yugoslavia's terrible calamity is not just recent history, such as the infamous genocide by Croatians at the Jasenovac concentration camp during World War II. Nor is the cause rooted solely in the more distant chronicle of the Ottoman rule. Today's horrors are woven from strands of nothing less than the entire tapestry of history since the 6th-century Slavic invasion of the Balkans, with the subsequent division of Croats and Serbs between Catholicism and Orthodoxy and eventually Islam.

All these elements play a role in the minds of those destroying Bosnia. They are sick from history—from half-truths and ethnic prejudices passed from one generation to the next, through religion, political demagoguery, inflammatory tracts and even, through abuse of folk song and tales. More recently, the books of unscrupulous writers and the deliberately inaccurate speeches of unprincipled leaders have further contaminated the atmosphere.

Two years ago, at an international conference in Boston on cultural memory, I argued with an American scholar about the causes of the unfolding Yugoslav crisis. She felt that everything was traceable to 1941 and the Croatian killing of some 600,000 Serbs, Jews and gypsies at the concentration camp of Jasenovac. (Many of these Serbs were from the Krajina area of Croatia, which is now trying to merge with Serbia.) But I felt that the roots of the current conflict between Croats and Serbs ran much deeper, at least as far back as the schism between Catholic and Orthodox Churches in 1054 A.D.

It appears we were both right. She, in that the immediate cause of the fighting between Serbs and Croats in Croatia was Serbian fear of another Jasenovac. When Franjo Tudjman, author of a book stating that Serbian losses were only one-tenth what they claimed, became president of Croatia, Serbs in Croatia saw this as a sign that they were not to expect fair and unbiased treatment in the new state. Tudjman did not offer them concrete guarantees that would have allayed their worries.

Although it was the Serbs in Krajina who provoked the outbreak of hostilities, over the long run the fighting between Serbs and Croats in Croatia and Slavonia has been fueled by culturally derived feelings of "otherness" between Orthodox Serbs and Catholic Croats. Orthodox-Catholic prejudice is a powerful force. A few years ago, I visited the Orthodox monastery of Iviron on Mount Athos, Greece. While I was attending the early morning liturgy, a monk approached and asked whether I was Orthodox or Catholic. When I replied "Catholic," he told me to "go outside and pray."

The Greek Orthodox Church, like Rome, has a long memory: In the young monk's mind, I was excommunicated. The Schism in 1054 A.D. and the plundering of Constantinople in 1204 A.D. by the Fourth Crusade are alive in the Orthodox mind of today and continue to affect Orthodox–Catholic relations, including those between Serbs and Croats. Some of the doctrinal differences between the two churches seem ludicrous today. Take for example the "filioque" controversy: according to the Roman Catholic Creed, the Holy Spirit "proceeds from the Father and the Son" (*et filioque procedit*), whereas the Orthodox Church claims that according to the original Nicene Creed (325 A.D.), the Spirit proceeds from the Father alone.

The difference had already threatened to split the Church in the 9th century, with pope and patriarch hurling anathemas at each other. This is not to say that Serbs feel justified in shelling Dubrovnik because they believe its inhabitants are schismatics, but rather that they are affected in their relations with the "Latini" by negative feelings of "otherness," the residue of doctrinal disputes of long ago. The sense of "otherness" is further

 From *Washington Post*, August 30, 1992, p. C3. © 1992 by The Washington Post. Reprinted by permission.

exacerbated by the fact that the two peoples were ruled by different and opposing empires: the Croats by the Austro-Hungarian empire and the Serbs by the Ottoman.

As for Croatian and Serbian relations with Bosnia's Muslim population (who are actually Slavs), no one will deny that the Croats have the more harmonious dealings with their Islamic brethren. This may be because they see the Muslims as heretics, who can be saved through baptism. In fact, Tudjman was photographed a year ago, smiling benignly at the baptism of a group of Muslim children. This drove Bosnia's Muslim president, Alija Izetbegovic, into such a frenzy that he actually made a short-lived treaty with his arch-enemy, Serbia.

Serbs, on the other hand, take a different stance toward Muslims: They see them as *traitors,* as well as heretics. Scratch a Muslim, they believe, and you have a Serb whose ancestor went over to the Ottoman side four or five hundred years ago, in order to keep his land. The late novelist Mesa Selimovic, who was born and raised a Muslim but considered himself a Serbian writer, referred to himself and other Yugoslav Muslims as "renegades" in his autobiographical "Memories."

In a later edition he mentions that the lexicographer Abdulah Skaljic, a representative of the Reis-ul Ulema, the highest Islamic religious authority in Bosnia, objected to his use of the term "renegade" for those who had "taken the right road and the right faith."

(Actually, the adoption of the religion of the conqueror in order to maintain certain privileges such as landholding was common not only to the Ottoman Empire. A similar situation existed in Ireland, where one or two brothers, with the agreement of the rest of the family, sometimes joined the Protestant church in order to preserve the family's land.)

In the Bosnian case, the situation is further complicated by the fact that great numbers of those who converted to Islam were members of a heretical Christian sect called "Bogomils" ["pleasing to God"]. They were threatened by the Inquisition, and some historians have written that they invited the Ottomans in (1463), rather than face invasion by a Hungarian army blessed by the pope.

From all this came the saying: "Bosnia fell with a whisper." It wasn't until the rise of nationalism in the last decades of the 18th century that these converts to Islam and their descendants were branded "traitors." Particularly in Yugoslavia, much of the bloodshed of the 20th century may be traced to such reinterpretations of cultural memory by 19th-century historians.

The Serbian "purification" (*ciscenje*) of Bosnian villages of Muslim inhabitants reminds me of a similar action, described by the 19th century Montenegrin poet Njegos in his "Mountain Wreath." He sings of the events leading up to an early 18th-century extermination of Muslims in Montenegro, directed by Danilo, the Orthodox prince bishop of Montenegro, and motivated by fear of contamination from within. The same paranoia may be found in Serbia today.

Even 20 years ago, long before today's civil war, such views were common. My Belgrade landlady told me then that the Albanians (Shiptars), who are mainly Muslim, were lighting bonfires at night on the hills around the city, signaling to each other. She voiced fear of their high birthrate—warning that they would inundate the Serbs, as they already have done in Kosovo, the "holy ground" of the Serbian medieval empire.

In recent years, I heard worried talk of how Islamic fundamentalism was sweeping Bosnia and of Saudi Arabian money being used to rebuild mosques and Muslim schools. I used to smile at such stories, as indicative of excessive Serbian anxiety about Muslims. But I was wrong. Obviously, Serbian extremists played on fears of a revived Islamic state in Bosnia as a way to spur their savage war. The fact that the Bosnian president, Izetbegovic, was the author of the Islamic Declaration, a 1970 tract calling for the moral renewal of Islam throughout the world—for which he was jailed by the Yugoslav communist government in the early 1980s—hardly reassured the Serbs.

This oppressive preoccupation with Muslims—Albanians in particular—is vividly illustrated in the war diary of a Serbian reservist from Valjevo, named Aleksandar Jasovic, published in a Belgrade journal this year. Jasovic served as a medic in the Serbian ranks in the fighting for Vukovar in Croatia in 1991. While his battery was shelling the Croats in the northeast, he recounts in his diary, he actually was preoccupied with fears about Kosovo far to the south—the cradle of the Serbian medieval kingdom and the scene of the Serbs' fateful loss to the Turks in 1389.

He writes of the Albanian Muslims, who because of a high birthrate and immigration from neighboring Albania now are a huge majority in Kosovo: "Their Sarajevo mother supports them!" Westerners may find the phrase obscure, but it illuminates what in the medic's mind seems the powerful, irrefutable and threatening connection between the Muslims of Bosnia and those of Kosovo.

Of Slav Macedonians, who also occupy a former Serbian medieval province, he comments: "The Macedonians are continuing to play the fool. The time is near when we'll have to protect Kumanovo too [the scene of a major Serbian victory in the First Balkan War, 1912.] The Serbs there are being threatened more and more, the Albanians are continuing to act in their usual fashion [and] we know all we need to know about the Slovenes and Croats. Europe is against us and everyone is against us."

Fear of encirclement by all-powerful enemies grips the medic. Not once does Jasovic ask himself whether his worries—and by extension, the worries of millions of other Serbs—are justified by the facts. Elsewhere he borrows an apocalyptic line from Njegos: "Let there be what there cannot be!" i.e., Serbia may lose these ancient provinces, but not without a fight to the end. Such thinking is at the heart of Serbian aggression and terri-

8. THE ETHNIC FACTOR: CHALLENGES FOR THE 1990s

torial aggrandizement. Will Kosovo and Macedonia be next on the list for "purification" and "ethnic cleansing"?

Is there any way out of the gyre of death and destruction in the Balkans? There may be, but the failure of diplomatic efforts up to now have shown that without more active U.S. participation, nothing will happen. Western Europe's leaders seem incapable of seeing that they should act forcefully—with military power, if needed—to force a ceasefire. For those untroubled by the daily murder of innocents in Sarajevo, Gorazde and other Bosnian towns, I should point out the danger to Europe's economy posed by the permanent immigration of 2 or 3 million Balkan refugees.

The U.S. offer of air and naval support for the U.N. relief effort is a first step, but even if this should bring about a ceasefire, we shall have to prepare ourselves to play a very strong role in the overall negotiations. Several European powers, particularly Britain, Germany, Italy and Turkey, seem immobilized, perhaps by their own past history of invasion or involvement in the Balkans.

If there is ever to be a healing, it may be that it can only begin with the establishment of a unique, continuing conference of Serbian, Croatian, Muslim and other historians, to arrive at a core of mutually-agreed upon statements regarding each group's history. Ideally, this multicultural convocation would face shibboleths regarding "enemy" ethnic groups, examine national memories for their accuracy and rationality and separate truth from prejudice. The mediation of Western experts will be vital, since Balkan scholars always seem biased in favor of their own group.

In examining the more documented history of the 20th century, responsibility will have to be accepted for the crimes of one nation against the other. For example, Serbs will have to admit their nation's guilt for the dictatorship of King Alexander in the 1920s and '30s, which undermined the pre-war Kingdom of Slovenia, Croatia and Serbia. In the same way, Croatia will have to come clean on the holocaust of Serbs at Jasenovac. Only the admission of guilt on one side, and the granting of forgiveness on the other, can start the healing process.

The same is true for the Christian relationship with the Muslims (the "Turks"). The Muslims need to admit that their ancestors abused and lorded it over the Christians for centuries. And the Serbs especially, while granting them forgiveness, must ask in turn for *their* pardon for recent savagery. We have precedents for such national confessions of guilt, in the West German acceptance of responsibility for Nazi crimes against Jews and recently (June 21) in the French intellectuals' call for their government to condemn, in the name of "the French collective memory," the Vichy government's persecution of Jews.

If such a healing process is to take place in the Balkans, it will be best to keep it out of the hands of religious leaders and politicians. The liturgy of reconciliation should be written by the poet, aided by others of good will. Thus the Yugoslavia that many of us in the West truly loved for its diversity may pass peacefully into history.

Race and Urban Poverty

COMPARING EUROPE AND AMERICA

Margaret Weir

I n the past decade, a new specter has haunted Europe. The intertwining of race and poverty, once considered a distinctively American problem, has become a European concern as well. In the face of racial conflict and ethnic disadvantage, the press and some politicians have warned that Europe's cities are developing American-style ghettos populated by ethnic minorities cut off from the mainstream of social and economic life.

No one contends that Europe's cities today face the extremes of ethnic and racial segregation, violence, and poverty that blight American cities. But many fear that Europe is on the same trajectory as the United States, only a decade or so behind. And they have cause for concern.

Racial ghettoization does not "just happen." National political arrangements profoundly affect the way people and economic activity are organized spatially, either uniting or dividing people of different income levels and races. In the era after World War II, the forces shaping the way groups and economic activities sorted themselves out on the local level established distinct metropolitan spatial patterns in the United States, Britain, and France. American political structures invited extreme segregation within cities and the suburbanization of the white working and middle class, while British and French political structures tended to allow more mixing by race and income. But the sorting out was not immutable. Policy responses in the United States, Britain, and France since the late 1970s have influenced the development of concentrations of poor ethnic and racial minorities in each nation.

Margaret Weir, a senior fellow in the Brookings Governmental Studies program, is working on a book on race and poverty in the city. This article is drawn from a paper prepared for the Training and Research Workshop on Race, Ethnicity, Representation, and Governance, sponsored by the Harvard University Center for American Political Studies.

Are France and Britain now "10 years behind the United States"? In some ways the similarities are striking. Government promotion of homeownership and the ensuing suburbanization of the middle class, which took off in the 1950s in the United States, were simply delayed for a decade or so in Britain and France. Over the years poor minorities have become more concentrated in public housing in Britain and France. Likewise, the construction of highrise public housing has generated similar problems in all three nations.

Yet important differences in the design of housing policies and continuing distinctions in the political factors that shape population movements suggest limits on the process of "Americanization" in Europe. Despite significant policy changes during the 1980s in both Britain and France, neither is likely to develop the scope or the intensity of ghetto poverty seen in the United States.

America's Cities: Shaped after World War II

The political feature that most distinguishes the United States in the shaping of metropolitan spatial patterns is the power of local governments. Although municipalities in the United States lack formal constitutional recognition—they exist at the discretion of state governments—they exercise substantial powers. Among the most important is control over land use. Through zoning and other measures formally meant to ensure local health and safety, localities determine what kinds of people can live and what kinds of businesses can operate within their borders.

Not only are municipalities powerful, they are relatively easy to form. Areas often split away from existing jurisdictions to form new ones. By contrast, expanding existing jurisdictions, by way of annexation or consolidation, is usually much more difficult. And chief among many incentives to form separate political jurisdictions is the importance of local property taxes in financing public schools.

Precisely those features of American local political organization hailed by public choice analysts as allowing local residents to choose the mix of services and taxation they most desire—the organization of social policy, the power of local government, and the ease of forming separate political jurisdictions—provide powerful incentives for whites to separate out by income and by race.

Rather than counterbalancing local fragmentation, the federal government has reinforced it. Washington has supported suburban life by building highways, promoting automobile use, and subsidizing private homeownership, especially through the favorable tax treatment of mortgages. It has also engaged in practices that encouraged racial exclusion. Most significantly, until the late 1960s it sanctioned discrimination in housing markets by promulgating rules preventing blacks from receiving mortgages insured by the Federal Housing Administration.

Similarly, bowing to local opposition to subsidized housing that might promote integration, the federal government predicated its housing policies on local acceptance. Public housing, launched during the 1930s, remained a small program targeted on the very poor. Publicly subsidized housing currently comprises only about 4.5 percent of the U.S. housing stock. The opposition of the building industry to public spending in this area and the local option to accept or reject subsidized housing kept it in the cities—and out of the suburbs. Crucially, public housing was also racially segregated, ensuring that public housing for African Americans would be located in the already crowded and deteriorating inner city.

Together, the power of local governments and the federal underwriting of decentralization carved metropolitan areas into distinct jurisdictions defined by income and race. In this process of metropolitan fragmentation, cities were disproportionately left to shoulder the burden of metropolitan poverty. In addition, fragmentation spurred interlocal competition to attract well-off populations and business. Cities, increasingly, were the losers in these contests.

From Bad to Worse

Policy changes in the 1980s drove deeper wedges between cities and suburbs and made it increasingly diffi-

cult for cities to address the deepening poverty within their borders.

Since the 1950s, several federal government programs had cushioned the spatial inequalities that accompanied the suburban exodus. The urban renewal program helped local governments underwrite major physical renewals of their central business districts. In the 1960s, Democrats undertook new urban programs, such as Model Cities, that focused on improving the quality of life for poor urban residents. The creation of the Department of Housing and Urban Development in 1965 signaled the special place that urban aid would have at the federal level. With the election of Richard Nixon in 1968, assistance for poorer localities continued as a legitimate federal government responsibility. No-strings-attached revenue sharing and Community Development Block Grants enacted under Nixon used different approaches but reflected a similar sensibility that localities, and especially cities, required special aid from the federal government.

Until the 1980s, helping cities was good politics for Democrats. The urban vote, together with southern Democrats, had been the electoral core of the party since the New Deal. The dominance of urban interests within the party as a whole was clear in Congress, where Democrats from suburban areas in the North voted heavily in favor of aid to cities.

Demographic shifts during the 1980s contributed to the political eclipse of cities, however. In 1960 the nation's population was evenly divided among cities, suburbs, and rural areas. By 1990, both urban and rural populations had declined, with cities becoming poorer and more heavily composed of minorities. Nearly half the nation lived in the suburbs. The terms of partisan competition did not take long to register these changes. Republicans mobilized a distinctive suburban political identity. During the 1960s and 1970s central cities and suburbs in the North and Midwest had tended to vote in similar directions; by 1980 the suburban and urban vote had split sharply, with cities remaining the only Democratic stronghold.

The declining political importance of cities was reflected in the abandonment of many federal urban programs. The only programs totally eliminated during the 1980s were those that particularly benefited cities. In 1981 Congress ended the Comprehensive Employment and Training Act, which cities had used (unofficially) to bolster the ranks of their employees. General revenue sharing, which provided extra funds for localities, ended in 1986. Urban Development Action Grants were eliminated and subsidized housing severely cut. Overall, grants for cities were cut almost in half.

> Together, the power of local governments and federal underwriting of decentralization carved U.S. metropolitan areas into distinct jurisdictions defined by income and race.

Cities fared only slightly better at the hands of the states. Long dominated by rural interests, state governments instituted reforms during the 1960s and 1970s that equalized urban representation. But by that time, suburban influence overshadowed the cities in many statehouses. Although some states compensated cities for the withdrawal of federal aid in the 1980s, others took only limited steps or actually worsened cities' problems. State legislatures often rejected urban efforts to raise local taxes. States did little to guide the development that continued to spur the exodus from the cities, nor did they do much to improve possibilities for regional cooperation across city-suburban boundaries. Toward the end of the decade, recession-strained state budgets were simply unable to provide significant aid.

The Struggle to Survive

Cities were left alone to bear the twin burden of needy populations and a precarious economic base. To attract private development, urban leaders offered tax abatements and other incentives, in the process heightening interjurisdictional competition, draining future tax revenues, and reducing the scope for local public action. Other strategies, such as forming special taxing authorities within cities (with a variety of names such as Business Improvement Districts), further fragmented the public tax base.

The intergovernmental transfers that had helped sustain cities during the 1960s and 1970s represented a national recognition of the special fiscal burden cities carried because of the concentrations of poor within their borders. For the most part, the transfers did not directly serve the urban poor, or even appreciably stem the flight to the suburbs, but they did provide a cushion that allowed for high levels of public services such as libraries, police protection, and infrastructural maintenance to improve the quality of urban life. As these funds dried up, cities compensated by attracting private investment, often relying on tax abatements. This strategy increased private wealth in cities, but it precipitated a deterioration of urban public services that undermined efforts to rebuild an urban middle class and to stem the further decline of the poor.

Changes in industrial structure and the location of industry have also exacerbated the burden and political isolation of cities. The revolution in information technologies combined with the lack of metropolitan planning to deconcentrate economic activity. As new businesses and commercial centers appeared in suburban "edge cities," the connections between city and suburb further attenuated. In a recent poll, 51 percent of metropolitan New Yorkers said that events in the city had hardly any effect on their lives.

The story of social policy decentralization, the reduction of federal aid to cities, and the divisions between cities and suburbs can all be told without mentioning race. But the preexisting concentrations of poor minorities in cities meant that each of the policy decisions discussed above had racially targeted consequences. It also meant that racial concerns and conflicts would affect the fate of any proposed solutions to cope with urban poverty.

Britain's Cities: A Different Mix

In Britain, limited suburbanization and a vast public housing sector created quite different patterns of metropolitan development and population movements. County governments used their regional planning powers to restrict suburbanization at the same time that the central government underwrote public housing. Whereas the United States had sought to meet postwar housing needs by underwriting suburban homeownership, Britain rebuilt the housing stock with public housing. By the end of the 1970s, a third of British households lived in "council housing." The very size of the British public sector made some level of income mixing inevitable.

And council housing was not solely confined to the city. Most early postwar development was in the form of small units built in "new towns" well beyond areas of existing settlement. During the 1960s the government redirected public housing to the cities to combat suburban sprawl and deteriorating urban living conditions. Here, both spatial constraints and architectural fashion favored the highrise project. For the most part, the middle-class suburban boroughs of outer London were able to limit the amount of council housing built in their areas.

By the early 1980s, 43 percent of London's council housing was concentrated in poorer inner London, but 29 percent was still in the central business district and 23 percent in outer London. Compared with the United States, economically disadvantaged populations were still much more dispersed.

Britain's postwar sorting of populations did have some negative consequences for racial mixing, but it did not create sharp racial segregation. Initially the system for allocating public housing (one element of which was length of tenure in the borough) worked against members of racial minorities, most of whom were recent immigrants. Although this discrimination was substantially remedied by the Race Relations Act of 1968, minorities had missed out on the council housing built outside the central city. Minority populations therefore tended to concentrate in the inner city.

Yet the extent of segregation within the cities was tempered by integrated public housing. Because there were no preexisting racial ghettos, public housing was sited without racial considerations in mind. Much public housing was built in working class districts, which were not racially defined. Moreover, with the less favorable tax treatment of homeownership and without the abundance of financing that encouraged suburban homeownership in the United States, most of Britain's working class was not able to make its suburban exodus until the 1970s.

The lack of local government autonomy also stemmed the impulse to fragmentation and movement. In the highly centralized British political system, local authorities exist at the pleasure of the central government. Local authorities have access to only one independent source of revenue, the property tax, or "rate," which until recently was levied on property owners and businesses. Because local governments have so little autonomy and discretion in financing, the dynamic of interlocal competition so central in the

United States is far less evident. Throughout the postwar era, British cities remained poorer than their surrounding suburbs, but they continued to house a significant part of the British working class.

Moreover, the central government redistributed resources to reduce territorial inequalities. Most local expenditures were financed by the centrally provided rate support grant, calculated in part on the basis of local need. An "inner city" policy, modeled after that in the United States, offered special assistance to the poorest areas.

A Decade of Thatcherism

Prime Minister Margaret Thatcher's new brand of Conservative politics put an end to the postwar consensus. Her government reduced the equalizing role of the central government and left localities more on their own and less able to cope with the rising needs of their citizens. The government reduced the central grant and made it less redistributive. It limited the rates that local authorities could levy, thus hampering local efforts to compensate for the central government cutbacks. And Thatcher created new policymaking bodies to promote economic development, for example removing the power to undertake urban regeneration from local authorities and granting it to private Urban Development Corporations.

The 1980 Housing Act allowed council housing tenants of three years standing to buy their units, a measure that proved one of the most popular of Thatcher's administration. By 1990 one-fifth of the council housing stock had been sold to tenants, though most sales were in suburban areas, and very few in the inner city. Sales patterns followed existing lines of division and thus did not increase racial or income segregation. But reductions in expenditures on maintenance and construction of public housing have reduced its quality, making it less desirable than in the past. In addition, local authorities have often concentrated racial minorities in the worst of the deteriorated housing estates. Although levels of racial segregation do not approach those of the United States, the large dilapidated housing estates located in the British inner city and the urban periphery most closely resemble the isolation and hopelessness found in America's poor urban neighborhoods.

Although a decade of Thatcherism has transformed British politics in ways that will make it harder to assist disadvantaged areas, existing structures of policy and politics in Britain nevertheless hampered the government's ability to impose losses on poor places. Because localities can raise revenues only from the property tax, rich Conservative authorities joined poor Labour ones in opposing drastic reductions in the central grant. Unlike American middle-class localities that can make up for withdrawn central funds by raising local taxes or fees, all local authorities in Britain still depend heavily on central government support.

This dynamic led to the repeal of Thatcher's proposed "poll tax," opposition to which was central to Thatcher's resignation in the fall of 1990. The poll tax, proposed in 1986, would have replaced the local property tax by an equal tax levied on each voter, with the amount to be decided by the local authority. It replaced the local business rate with a uniform rate to be collected by the central government. A far more regressive tax on individuals, the poll tax would have sharply limited revenues of poorer localities. The new tax aroused enough opposition in Conservative constituencies to provoke a party revolt. Under Prime Minister John Major the poll tax has been replaced by a council tax, which promises fewer disadvantages for poor places.

The strong role of the central government has made it harder for British leaders simply to ignore the problems of the inner city. Throughout the 1980s, the Conservative government experimented with a string of policies aimed at revitalizing cities. Although these programs have redirected urban policies toward economic redevelopment, they have kept the problems of cities prominent on the national agenda, in striking contrast to the United States.

The Urban Landscape in France

In France, population sorting after World War II was even more centrally directed than in Britain. After an initial emphasis on industrial development, the central planning agency, the Commissariat Général du Plan, turned to housing. As in Britain, decades of depression and war had left a dilapidated and meager housing stock, and the French government looked to the fastest and cheapest means possible to address the problem. In the Parisian metropolitan area, this meant massive high-rise housing projects on new sites outside the city.

HLM housing, as the public housing program was called, came to serve 14 percent of the French population, far less than in Britain, though much more than in the United States. The suburban housing estates were conceived as workers' lodgings, located near (and often subsidized by) industries in the Parisian suburbs. As in Britain, rules governing access to public housing initially worked against immigrant racial minorities. In fact, HLM housing tended to serve the middle and lower-middle classes rather than the very

> A decade of Thatcherism has transformed British politics in ways that will make it harder to assist disadvantaged metropolitan areas.

poor, who lived in private rental housing in city slums.

By the 1970s, however, HLM housing had been opened to immigrant racial minorities, and the proportion of immigrants in HLM housing reached 30 percent in some estates. At the same time, national programs to promote homeownership prompted the exodus of many middle-class families from HLM housing.

During the 1980s, the French Socialists, with political aims and a constituency far different from that of Thatcher, also introduced sweeping changes in central-local relations. Their aim was to produce more local democracy and enhance local public powers.

Local government in France, as in the United States, is fragmented into many small units. Although the central government has the formal authority to reduce the number of units, in practice the penetration of central power by local authorities (who are allowed to hold multiple offices simultaneously) has blocked territorial rationalization. The central government exercised power over this fragmented political terrain through the departmental prefect, whose approval was necessary for most local actions.

Through a new system of block grants and the devolution of some social responsibilities to lower levels of government, the Socialists gave localities much more autonomy in urban planning and in allocating spending. Not surprisingly, however, well-positioned localities used their new autonomy to attract investment and enrich the local tax base, while poorer localities had to levy higher taxes and cut back on services. And an overall decline in public spending in France during the 1980s exacerbated these differences.

The myriad development decisions of local governments replaced the strong central hand that once allocated economic activities and populations among different regions and within metropolitan areas. And the central government's postwar power of siting social housing was sharply curtailed, while the local power to reject such housing, or to resist undesirable tenants, grew considerably. The least powerful and least well-off localities ended up with more social housing.

In response, the Socialists passed a series of laws aimed at reversing the new inequalities. One law transfers resources from rich localities to poorer ones. Another obliges localities to pay a penalty if they refuse to accept a certain percentage of social housing for the poor. A third seeks to remedy the housing problems of the extremely poor by helping them pay back-rent. Finally, the central government enacted a new minimum income financed by the central government for those not covered by existing social assistance. The new "Revenue Minimum d'Insertion" seeks, as its name implies, to insert the poor into French society by providing financial resources in exchange for which recipients seek work or training.

Many of the inequalities that the French government has sought to combat are closely linked to fears of developing American-style ghettos. In contrast to the short-lived shock experienced in the United States after the Los Angeles riots last year, the disturbances that have sporadically rocked French suburban housing projects since 1981 have provoked a national soul-searching about French identity. Government action has been aimed at preventing the consolidation of separate ethnic and racial communities.

The Socialist government has sought to combine the benefits of decentralization—greater local democracy, freeing of local economic initiative, and the reduction of central government responsibility for administering austerity—with a commitment to equalizing the territorial distribution of economic resources. By most accounts, the growth in the number of elected officials has not invigorated local democracy; it has merely increased the power of local notables. As such it introduces a dynamic into French politics familiar to Americans: representatives of localities with different resources may interpret not only the local interest but also the national interest quite differently. The changes introduced by decentralization have created political forces that may challenge equalization efforts now that a conservative political coalition has replaced the Socialists.

Building National Community
Concentrated, racially identified poverty presents a formidable challenge for liberal democratic regimes. The existence of such sharp racial and economic divisions has fostered a kind of "defensive localism" that corrodes any notion of a national community. The central challenge facing political leaders who wish to build national community in racially and ethnically diverse societies is to recreate a sense of common fate. To do that, they must understand how public policies and political institutions are contributing to the racially identified divisions that now form the subtext of politics across the West. Governments cannot erase social differences, but they can use policy to reduce the economic and political importance of such divisions.

The central task for policy is to reconnect the poor to the sources of vitality in the economy. Politically feasible starting points would fold initiatives for the poor into policies that also address the concerns of other sectors of society. Political leaders and policymakers must look for those points of connection and bear them in mind when making policy. That task is politically easier in the more centralized context of European politics, although it may be more culturally difficult in these once racially homogenous nations. In the United States, where long experience with ethnic diversity sits uneasily with a history of racial exclusion and a celebration of political localism, the political task is difficult indeed. But there are some possible points of departure, which include: dissatisfaction with the environmental consequences of deconcentrated patterns of metropolitan development, emerging strains in suburban public budgets, the growing needs of employers for better-educated entry-level workers, and the widely felt problems of combining work and family. The political structures and policies that have helped create concentrated racial poverty will not be easily or comprehensively transformed. But federal and state political leaders do have the power to initiate changes that will provide a foundation for asserting a broader collective interest in American political life.

ETHNIC CONFLICT

Andrew Bell-Fialkoff

Andrew Bell-Fialkoff, a former associate of the Center for the Study of Small States at Boston University, is completing his Ph.D. in ethnic conflict studies.

Lately one cannot open a newspaper or view the TV news without finding an item describing an attack on refugees in Germany or presenting the horrors of ethnic cleansing in the former Yugoslavia. Events such as these have stunned the civilized world. Aren't we supposed to have left such barbarity behind?

There is a common, widely held assumption that there is no place for ethnic nationalism in the modern world. Modernity and the concomitant urbanization, industrialization, and social mobility are deemed inimical to primordial attachments.

Clifford Geertz defined "primordial attachments" as those that "stem from being born into a particular religious community, speaking a particular language . . . and following particular social practices."[1]

In other words, all attachments engendered by ethnicity—those of kin, language, and custom—will gradually recede, lose their importance under the relentless assault of the all-pervasive modernity.

This assumption is based partly on the "liberal principle that people should be treated as individuals, and not as members of racial, religious, and other groups. . . . [Eventually] membership in ethnic groups must become increasingly irrelevant" and partly on the mistaken belief that increased economic and cultural integration of the global economy will diminish primordial attachments.[2]

■ A German Nazi poster, printed during World War II, meant to stimulate race hatred against both blacks and Jews.

Crudely put, if Serbs and Croats both like hamburgers they are less likely to kill each other.

That is why the recent explosion of nationalist passions in Europe and elsewhere caused such a shock. In fact, modernity is highly conducive to ethnic tensions. Nationalism was not an explosive issue when most people lived in small ru-ral communities where everybody belonged to the same ethnic group. But in the modern world, people of different ethnic backgrounds are increasingly concentrated in huge urban agglomerations, and compete against each other in a presumably meritocratic society in a Hobbesian all against all.

The very fact that mobile society offers a way to the top leads to fierce competition in which any weapon, but especially ethnic differences, lends itself to effective use. As Kautsky put it, "railways are the greatest breeder of national hatreds."[3] And airlines work even better, we may add.

CLASS AND ETHNICITY

The end-of-primordials assumption is shared by the Left, especially Marxists, but while liberals believe in the triumph of modernity, orthodox Marxists await the triumph of the working class.

To Marx, nationalism was part of the ideological superstructure arising on the foundations of economic self-interest. Like a true bourgeois, Marx was obsessed with monetary/economic relations of dominance and exploitation that reflected the ownership of the means of production. The main conflict pitted those who owned the means—the bourgeois—against those who did not—the proletariat. Everything else—culture, religion, ethnicity—was derivative.

Marx's hostility to nationalist movements also reflected his view that they served the interests of the middle classes and the bourgeoisie, diverting the proletariat from the really important task: the class struggle.

Actually, the relationship between nationalism and socialism was very complicated. In the nineteenth century they were allies in their struggle against autocracy and feudalism, at least in the semifeudal Austrian, Russian, and Ottoman empires. Marx himself distinguished between national movements that were progressive, that is, all those struggling against czarist Russia and Austria, and those that were reactionary, for example, Croats who allied themselves with Vienna in 1848 out of fear of Hungarian centralism. This artificial distinction led to strange ideological somersaults: Romanians of Transylvania who, like Croats, sided with Vienna, were reactionary, while Romanians of Bessarabia fighting against St. Petersburg were progressive.[4]

Once the feudal order was defeated and the old empires collapsed, in 1917–18, nationalism and socialism parted company. Nationalism, for example, ethnic nationalism, tried to absorb socialism and quickly evolved into national socialism, which emphasized adherence to one's ethnic/racial group, whose economic and ideological life was to be developed along socialist principles.

Socialism, that is, class nationalism (as opposed to ethnic nationalism), emphasized devotion to one's class within one's ethnic entity. It tried to suppress (ethnic) nationalism in the belief that it tied the working classes to their capitalist exploiters, thus blunting the class struggle.

The most principled socialists, such as Rosa Luxembourg, always insisted that there was no place for nationalism in a socialist society. She was even willing to give up hope for Polish reunification because, once Austria, Germany, and Russia turned socialist, national oppression would disappear and nationalism itself would become meaningless.

Once the Bolsheviks came to power,

PRÉCIS

The recent outbreak of fierce ethnic and nationalist passions in Europe and elsewhere has shocked many. Modernity's urbanization, industrialization, and social mobility were supposed to have crowded out ethnic nationalism and primordial attachments of kin, language, custom, and religion. Classical liberalism holds that people should be treated as individuals, not as members of racial, religious, or other groups. Marxists, seeing struggle in terms of economic classes, were hostile to ethnic and nationalist movements, and saw them to be serving the interests of the bourgeoisie. Socialism—class nationalism—was to lead to a one-class society.

But communist ruling elites did not actually destroy nationalism; instead, they often put it to their own use, so nationalism worked to undermine socialism. Fascism emphasized primordial attachments, and shared Marx's anti-Semitism; both promoted paranoid hate. Breakup of empires has historically allowed ethnic differences to emerge. Favoring one's ethnic brothers is part of any traditional social system. And modern mobility leads to competition, in which ethnic differences can be used as a tool of triumph. The melting pot works only sometimes.

Although the world knows and condemns it in South Africa, apartheid is one solution: Switzerland has such a system with its cantons. Other proposals include proportional democracy and territorial autonomy.

however, they quickly realized that nationalist passions were a powerful tool, particularly in Russia, which transferred its religious zeal from Orthodox Christianity to orthodox Marxism. When in 1941 the German armies were approaching Moscow, Stalin called for the defense of Mother Russia, not world socialism.

Contrary to commonly held opinion, communist ruling elites did not put nationalism on ice. Instead, they put it on the back burner, to be served to the presumably gullible public whenever an internal situation called for cohesion. They tried to domesticate it, to use it for their own purposes, as evidenced by government-inspired and -organized nationalist campaigns in virtually every socialist country, for example, Poland and Romania in the 1960s and repeatedly in Soviet Russia.

In the process, there occurred a nationalization of socialism that, in some aspects, moved it closer to the nationalist socialist mode. Thus, one hundred years after nationalism and socialism parted company, they joined hands again, this time with state socialism in the driver's seat.

Gradually, however, nationalism destroyed socialism from within and then slunk out of the old socialist skin. This is what happened in Eastern Europe in 1989. This is what accounts for nationalist virulence in the former communist countries.

NATIONAL SOCIALISM

While Marxism is a chiliastic movement striving for the yawning heights of a rational, scientific (perfect) society, fascism is representative of a whole class of antimodern ideologies that reject the anomie, the atomization and impersonal character, of modern society. It stresses social harmony, spiritual values, and cooperation that tilt it toward emphasizing primordial attachments, that is, ethnicity. Because "ethnicity ... implies affection based on intangible bonds and a belief in collective sustenance."[5]

That, incidentally, explains why, in a struggle of ethnic nationalism against class nationalism, ethnic nationalism always wins: It offers the additional comfort of kinship and affective ties, the warmth of community as opposed to impersonal class interests.

Fascism proclaims society's organic

unity, which Marxist class struggle and liberal individualism have destroyed. Urban environment and industry, by their very nature, destroy human and social solidarity. Therefore, where modernity promotes conflict and individualism, fascism offers unity and mutual support. And unity based on ethnic community is all the stronger. This may be one of the main reasons for fascism's success: It promised sup-

■ **Polish women being led to execution by German soldiers.**

port and solidarity to atomized, insecure, vulnerable masses. Communism did likewise but only to the working classes; fascism offered panacea to all.

Among things both movements share, none goes deeper than anti-Semitism. Marx, imbued with virulent German racism and Jew-hatred ("This Jewish Nigger Lassalle"[6]), redirected the hatred against an alien religious and ethnic group into the hatred of an economic class, the bourgeoisie. Jew the swindler and the moneybags became bourgeois-the-leech. Marx transferred the Jew-devil/Christian dichotomy of traditional anti-

Semitism into a bourgeois/proletariat dichotomy. "Marx's invention of the 'bourgeoisie,'" wrote Paul Johnson, "was the most comprehensive of [the] hate-theories and it has continued to provide a foundation for all paranoid revolutionary movements, whether fascist-nationalist or Communist-internationalist. Modern theoretical anti-Semitism [is] a derivative of Marxism."[7]

It is no accident that virtually all European communist countries have experienced periodic flare-ups of anti-Semitism: Russia repeatedly, Czechoslovakia in 1952–53 (largely Russian-inspired), Poland in 1967–68, and so forth.

ARE ETHNICITY AND NATIONALISM HERE TO STAY?

Attempts to define a nation are too numerous to be listed here. Perhaps the best known is that of Stalin, who listed four

LIBRARY OF CONGRESS

indispensable characteristics: a common language, a common territory, a common economic life, and a common mental makeup.[8]

However, one can always find ethnic groups that aspire to be called or to become full-fledged nations even though they lack one of these characteristics. Are Hispanics who barely speak English disqualified from being American? Do Transylvanian Hungarians cease being Hungarian because there is a stretch of Romanian ethnic territory that separates them from the bulk of their ethnic cousins? Was partitioned Poland no longer a nation? Wasn't Germany? And, of course "mental makeup" is too vague to be useful.

That is why many specialists despair.

"Thus I am driven to the conclusion that no 'scientific definition' of a nation can be devised; yet the phenomenon has existed and exists," wrote Seton-Watson.[9] And will continue to exist in the foreseeable future, we may safely add.

One of the most original explanations of why ethnicity is so persistent was provided by Pierre van den Berghe. It is based on notions derived from sociobiology and regards ethnicity as kin selection. "Ethnicity is common descent, either real or putative, but, even when putative, the myth has to be validated by several generations of common historical experience."[10] Ethnicity is thus perceived as something natural, rooted in the biological makeup of humankind. And favoring one's ethnic brothers (another kin term!) is part and parcel of any traditional social system.

This fact, of course, does not explain the many masks of nationalism. It was born in the struggle of the West European middle class against feudal privilege and absolutism. Later, it was used by the state for colonial expansion and imperialism (the "bureaucratic nationalism," as Anthony Smith calls it.[11]) Meanwhile, as it expanded (or contaminated) multinational empires of Central and Eastern Europe, nationalism was adopted by the nascent intelligentsias of ethnic minorities who sought freedom and development through self-determination and secession. As it penetrated the lower social strata, nationalism merged with populism and xenophobia to support us against them and provide structure and cohesion that the uprooted masses lacked. In short, nationalism can put on any number of masks, which explains why it has

"expanded and proliferated into the most powerful yet elusive of all modern ideologies."[12]

And there is no end in sight. The ideal of self-determination is now firmly established in the popular mind. Liberation movements of all kinds—ethnic, gay, women's, racial—have gained acceptance and respectability. Size no longer matters—Iceland, Luxembourg, and Malta proved that even very small states can be viable. Accession to economic unions, such as the European Community, gives even the smallest states access to huge markets. And successful conclusion of liberation struggles in former colonies gave a tremendous boost to ethnic political movements in the old countries in Europe.

Thus, smaller and more *ethnies*— the Basques and the Catalans, the Scots and the Flemings—are beginning to seek more autonomy and, eventually, independence, perhaps within a unified Europe.[13] And on it goes.

FROM VIENNA TO VERSAILLES

The gradual acceptance of the principle of self-determination can clearly be seen in the history of international congresses called upon to solve political problems after major wars.

Up until the nineteenth century, ethnicity got scant attention from statesmen and diplomats. As late as 1862, Lord Acton, in a flash of prescience, wrote that "nationality does not aim at either liberty or prosperity, both of which it sacrifices to the imperative necessity of making the nation the mould and measure of the State. Its course will be marked with material as well as moral ruin."[14]

Only an absolutist state ruled by an established dynasty was recognized as an acceptable international partner. Thus, at the Congress of Vienna, the Great Powers upheld the legitimacy of dynastic empire and confirmed the partition of Poland with total disregard for ethnic sentiment. However, even mighty empires could not withstand the spread of new ideas, including the idea of popular sovereignty. When applied to nationality, the principle of popular sovereignty implied that ethnically alien government was illegitimate.

As ethnic nationalism gained momentum, European powers could no longer ignore it. The Greek war of independence,

the conflict between Germans and Danes in Schleswig-Holstein, the Italian struggle for unification, Polish uprisings, all demanded settlement based on self-determination.

Once the Great Powers realized that they could not control or resist the rising tide of nationalism, they tried to use it for their own gain as, for example, Napoleon III used Italian struggle against Austria for his own purposes in 1859. At the Congress of Berlin in 1878 the Great Powers had to concede independence to various Balkan peoples who had broken away from the Ottoman Empire, but still felt free to carve up Bulgaria when it suited their interests.

It was only at the Paris Peace Conference of 1919 that the principle of nationality and self-determination was firmly established as the normative principle of a legitimate government. Thus, between 1814 and 1919 there occurred a major shift in the principle of settling international disputes. Since then, ethnicity has retained its importance.

Germany, Austria, and Turkey after World War I, Czechoslovakia in 1938, Romania in 1940, Yugoslavia in 1941—all lost territory or were dismembered along ethnic lines. (There are, of course, notable exceptions, as when Germany lost ethnically German territories after World War II, but even here populations were expelled to make sure that political and ethnic borders coincided.)

It was precisely for that reason (the lack of congruence between political and ethnic borders) that the settlement reached at Versailles proved so ephemeral: It left too many ethnic enclaves, too many ethnic problems unsettled.

SOLUTIONS: THE MELTING POT AND THE UNMELTABLE ETHNICS

Americans are probably most familiar with the notion of a melting pot. It could have developed only in a country of mass immigration, a country that had successfully absorbed millions of immigrants.

America, of course, is not unique in that sense. Other settler colonies—Canada, Australia, New Zealand, South Africa, to name a few—have also been settled in a similar pattern. And old countries like France after World War I also allowed and even promoted massive in-migration.

However, America has always been a classical land of immigration, so it is no wonder that the theory of assimilation and amalgamation of people of different ethnic stock was developed in this country. Basically, the theory postulated that assimilation was a four-stage process that included contact, competition, accommodation, and, finally, assimilation.

Since then the theory has been much tinkered with. For example, it has been suggested that white immigrants assimilate within large religious denominations. Some sociologists even ventured to predict that eventually large ethno-religious blocs of Protestants, Catholics, and Jews would develop.

The data on intermarriage seem to support this hypothesis. In the late 1970s, 40 percent of Jews and Catholics married outside their religion. And among certain ethnic groups high rates of intermarriage suggest the approach of complete meltdown: 70 percent for Germans and Irish, 50 percent for Poles and Italians, 40 percent for French Canadians.[15]

However, there are several cracks clearly visible in the melting pot. One is

that ethnic identification often persists even after all ethnic peculiarities have been lost. America is full of Italians whose Italianness finds expression in eating pasta and Poles whose Polishness is limited to kielbasa.

Second, it takes two to assimilate. Acculturation, in other words, changes in observable behavior, can be accomplished by one actor. But assimilation, that is, absorption into the social structure of another group, is impossible without at least a tacit approval of the assimilating group.

In a country like Australia, which was without significant racial minorities (until very recently), such assimilation may proceed relatively smoothly, but in the United States with its ethnic and racial diversity, complete amalgamation may have stalled, perhaps for good.

Does the melting pot work? There is no overall answer. We have to proceed country by country. In the United States, it worked for virtually all white immigrants although rates of assimilation and the degree of assimilation achieved vary from group to group. Some Asians, particularly second- and third-generation Japanese, have also achieved high rates of out-

marriage. It is quite possible that they will eventually dissolve, like other immigrants, in the American stew.

The question is more problematic with black and Latino populations. Although rates of outmarriage have begun to increase among these groups as well, the presence of large Latino populations south of the border and the sheer numbers of the black minority (thirty million) make absorption more difficult.

So the verdict is still out. The important thing to keep in mind is that a melting pot can only work in a settler country where ethnic groups lack territoriality. Whenever the territorial dimension appears—as in Quebec—the melting pot would not work.

SWITZERLAND: THE ADVANTAGES OF APARTHEID

The exact opposite of a melting pot is the concept of apartheid, in other words, a complete legal and structural separation of constituent racial or ethnic groups.

Various approximations of apartheid, though best known as it was practiced in

■ **Croatian guards talk with an elderly man who is demanding the return of Baranya territory from Serbian occupation.**

South Africa, can be found all over the globe, including Switzerland. (I can already see stares of incredulity on most readers' faces ... but wait.)

Even in South Africa, apartheid was never carried out to its logical extreme—the complete separation of racial groups from each other. In a developed industrial society dependent on cheap black labor that was impossible. So, even South Africa at the height of apartheid would not qualify as an example of pure apartheid. On the other hand, America, the classical land of a melting pot, never achieved complete melting. So, we have to keep in mind that we are talking about ideal types.

Romansh. In terms of religious subdivisions, 58 percent are Protestant and 42 percent Catholic.

If we now take a closer look at the cantons, we will find that of the twenty-six cantons (actually, twenty-two cantons and four semicantons), twenty-three are more than 80 percent monolingual and in the other three the percentage of people speaking the main language does not dip below 60. What's more, in seventeen cantons, monolinguals amount to 95 percent. The same pattern can be observed in the distribution of religious denominations. In eighteen cantons religious majority exceeds 70 percent; nowhere does it fall below 53 percent.[16]

man, two French, and one Italian (there is, however, a marked tendency for uneven income/religion distribution; thus, nine of the ten richest cantons are Protestant, nine of the ten poorest are Catholic, a clear indication of how Protestantism interacts with the spirit of capitalism).[17] In short, each canton has a large linguistic and religious majority, and this prevents fission based on language and religion.

A recently resolved problem in Jura is a hint of what might have happened if Swiss ethnic, linguistic, and denominational communities were mixed together.

The territory, predominantly Francophone and Catholic, was attached to Bern by the Vienna Congress of 1814 as

■ **Muslims fleeing India in 1947.**

Now, Switzerland is far from being a land of apartheid in its pure form because all Swiss citizens are equal before the law (at least in theory). However, its major linguistic and religious groups do not mix, for each one has a canton or cantons of its own. And this fact allows me to call it, tongue in cheek, a country that practices apartheid.

Swiss indigenous population is highly heterogeneous, consisting of 75 percent German speakers, 20 percent Francophones, 4 percent Italians, and 1 percent

One may add that religion has not been a political factor in Switzerland since a brief civil war in 1847 that pitted the industrialized, liberal, largely urban northwest against the predominantly rural, conservative southeast. But even then, divisions cut across both major linguistic communities.

The same felicitous balance is found in terms of income distribution. Of the ten richest cantons, seven are German and three are French. And among the ten poorest ones there are seven Ger-

a compensation for the loss of a dependent territory. Its inhabitants never reconciled themselves to this gunpoint marriage. They continued to struggle against the imposition until, in a series of referenda conducted in the early 1970s, the Catholic part was allowed to secede and form a new canton, Jura. Protestants stayed with Bern.

Does Swiss apartheid work? Apparently it does. Will it work elsewhere? (Incidentally, the Swiss model has elicited much interest in South Africa, which quite possibly will try to follow the Swiss path, rather than the American, as a road to a multiracial, multiethnic society).

CONSOCIATIONALISM

Consociational or proportional democracy is a last-ditch arrangement when all alternatives are worse than a precarious balance.[18,19] Under consociationalism the constituent ethnic groups remain distinct for an indefinite period of time within one political system, but do not form separate administrative units.

Such a system requires stability and cultural pluralism. It also needs a cleavage between constituent groups (to reduce interethnic contact and, therefore, conflict and competition), absence of hegemony by one of the groups, attitudes favorable to all-inclusive coalition governments, and lack of external threat. It also helps if there is a limited interpenetration of the ethnies (this makes partition more difficult), some intermarriage (to prevent extreme polarization), and functional interpenetration at the governmental level (the more they share the less need they would feel to separate).

Actually, there are two kinds of consociationalism: One is political, that is, a situation where several political or spiritual families (e.g., Catholics, liberals and socialists) share power. Political consociationalism is fairly stable, as is evidenced in Austria or the Netherlands. The second kind is ethnic consociationalism, which is extremely unstable. Belgium gradually evolved toward a federalized tripartite system, while Lebanon (it would be more accurate to call it denominational, rather than ethnic, consociationalism) collapsed into chaos and civil war.

AUTONOMY

Among various solutions to ethnic problems the first one that comes to mind is autonomy. Usually, it means territorial autonomy, although there is also personal and corporate autonomy as well. In the less-known personal autonomy, the autonomous status applies to the minority individual no matter where he lives, as long as he is willing to be officially assigned minority status. The status is given to the individual on the basis of a personal declaration, government ordinance, or court decision based on language, origin, or a national characteristic. Ultimately, this form of autonomy is based on a personal decision of the individual.

Historically, corporate autonomy was tried in the Moravian compromise of 1905[20]; it was cut short by the collapse of Austria-Hungary in 1918, but theoretically, this solution is very promising because it combines personal choice with protection of minority rights and does not lead to the creation of rigid territorial units.

Entitlement programs in the United States (e.g., affirmative action, financial assistance to minority students, etc.) come very close to the model of corporate autonomy. In this instance, autonomous status is given to the minority as a whole, no matter where its representatives live, but the personal decision is lacking. An individual is assigned to his/her group on the basis of origin, language, or religion and enjoys all the advantages or disadvantages of a minority, but only on a corporate basis. This pattern is less flexible from the individual's standpoint, but it gives more organizational muscle to the minority group.

Finally, the best-known type of autonomy is territorial. It can be applied to those ethnic groups that live in compact territory with clearly marked borders. When such borders are lacking, things can get very complicated, as witnessed by German (and now Russian) ethnic enclaves scattered throughout much of eastern Europe.

Territorial autonomy has been tried many times and in many countries, often to satisfy aspirations toward self-determination by a small but strategically located ethnic minority whose complete separation would be detrimental to the interests of the larger state. However, federal autonomy often proved to be a stepping-

stone toward a complete and final divorce. The Soviet Union and former Yugoslavia serve as good examples. Still, one has to keep in mind that in both cases autonomy was largely fictitious. Both states were ultimately held together by brute force.

What is usually overlooked, amid all the laments about fragmentation, is the fact that virtually all the newly established states aspire to join a united Europe. Thus, further unification of Europe, this time on the basis of voluntary association, rather than force, was impossible without the fragmentation of the old empires.

It is a dialectic that Marx had vaguely guessed, although he could not know that the new freedoms would bring the end of the proletarian hegemony. This was the ultimate victory of nationalism over its old ally.

NOTES

1. Clifford Geertz, *Old Societies and New States* (London: The Free Press of Glencoe, 1963), 109.

2. Arend Lijphart, "Political Theories and the Explanation of Ethnic Conflict in the Western World: Falsified Predictions and Plausible Postdictions," *Ethnic Conflict in the Western World*. Milton J. Esman, ed. (Ithaca and London: Cornell University Press, 1977), 53.

3. Karl Kautsky, *Neue Zeit* (1886), 522–5, cited in H.B. Davis, *Nationalism and Socialism*, (New York and London: Monthly Review Press, 1967), 142; ref. in A. Smith, *Nationalism in the Twentieth Century* (New York: New York University Press, 1979), 163.

4. Hugh Seton-Watson, *Nations and States* (Boulder, CO: Westview Press, 1977), 446.

5. Cynthia Enloe, *Ethnic Conflict and Political Development* (Boston: Little, Brown & Co., 1973), 67.

6. Paul Johnson, *Modern Times* (New York: Harper & Row, 1983), 117.

7. Johnson, *Modern Times*, 62.

8. Joseph Stalin, *Marxism and the National Question*, 1913.

9. Hugh Seton-Watson, *Nations and States*, 3.

10. Pierre van den Berghe, *The Ethnic Phenomenon* (New York: Elsevier, 1981), 16.

11. Anthony Smith, *Nationalism in the Twentieth Century* (New York: New York University Press, 1979), 169.

12. Smith, *Nationalism in the Twentieth Century*, 166.

13. A neologism borrowed from the French, now widely used by sociologists to denote a group that is ethnically, naturally, religiously, or otherwise distinct, so long as these groups claim ethnic particularity.

14. Lord Acton, "Essay on Nationality," reference in A. Smith, *Theories of Nationalism* (New York: Harper & Row, 1971), 9.

15. Pierre van den Berghe, *The Ethnic Phenomenon*, 228.

16. Pierre van den Berghe, *The Ethnic Phenomenon*.

17. Pierre van den Berghe, *The Ethnic Phenomenon*.

18. Arend Lijphart, *Democracy in Plural Societies* (New Haven: Yale University Press, 1977).

19. Gerhard Lehmbruch, "proporzdemokratie" Mohr, Tubingen, 1967.

20. Robert Kann, *The Multinational Empire* (New York: Columbia University Press, 1950), 194–5; and E.K. Francis, *Interethnic Relations* (New York: Elsevier, 1976), 98–99.

The walls that have yet to fall

Ulrike Helwerth and Gislinde Schwarz

Ulrike Helwerth, who lives in West Berlin, is a sociologist and journalist. Gislinde Schwarz, who lives in East Berlin, is a journalist. Helwerth and Schwarz have been commissioned by the Berlin Senate for Employment and Women to do research for a project called "Estranged Sisters: Differences Between East and West German Feminists." This article was translated from the German by Annegret Daiss and Zoran Minderović.

Picture a regular Lufthansa weekday flight from Berlin to Frankfurt. The four female flight attendants are wearing, on the lapels of their blue jackets, buttons that say, "We're foreigners every day." It's part of the company's public relations campaign against racism and xenophobia. One of the flight attendants is black. A businessman points at the button she's wearing, calling it "a capital idea." He then asks her, with a charming smile: "Excuse me, and where are *you* from?" "Heidelberg," she replies.

This is an everyday scene that mirrors Germany's great conflict: the inner contortions of a lily-white society determined to show that xenophobia and racism are not pervasive traits of the German national character, a society bent on proving that the images of refugee homes in flames, of screaming Nazi skinheads, represent merely an eddy in the wake of German unification.

Adama Ulrich, who grew up in the former East Germany, acutely feels the polarization. "I didn't use to be aware of the fact that I'm black. I was born and raised here. Roughly a year ago, however, I started noticing two distinct kinds of reactions from strangers. Some people now openly show their friendliness through glances and body language; others are standoffish or aggressive." Ulrich is the daughter of a German mother and a Nigerian father. She has become fearful. "Nowadays I carefully think where I go and I hardly ever use public transportation. The circle in which I feel safe is circumscribed by a wall of aggression and violence that is closing in on me." Ulrich and friends—female and male, black and white, Germans and foreigners—who formed human chains and organized candlelight vigils in Munich, Dresden, and elsewhere, have voiced their opposition to violence, racism, and xenophobia. What they want is a multicultural Germany. Any observer can notice that the majority of the antiracism protesters are women.

Do women feel less resentment toward "foreigners" and anything "un-German?" Is racism the problem of (young) men? According to a 1989 survey to determine the attitudes of West German youth toward authoritarian and nationalistic ideas, girls were less receptive than boys to extreme right-wing slogans such as "Germany for the Germans" or "Out with the foreigners." Studies conducted after unification showed similar results. Men constitute close to two thirds of the right-wing electorate—voting for such parties as the Republicans and the German Popular Union. Among card-carrying party members, women are an even smaller minority. Indeed, it is young men who roam around with chains and baseball bats, ready to "clobber foreigners" and throw Molotov cocktails into their homes.

But none of this can obscure the fact that there are some women behind the young thugs, standing, so to speak, in the second line. These women incite their friends to violent acts and reward them afterward with admiration. They are the ones who applaud those who will "finally create order." In late 1992 a group of young men attacked a home for asylum-seekers in the eastern German town of Thale. They fired tracer rockets, broke into the building, vandalized the furniture, and attempted to rape three Vietnamese women. There were also two young women who excitedly watched the assault.

Three years ago, 20-year-old Jessica moved from the West German town of Hamburg to East Berlin, where she started hanging out in a known skinhead haven. "I used to participate in the attacks," she says. "I feel good among the skinheads. I secretly rejoice when the asylum-seekers' homes are attacked. The foreigners must leave." Jessica doesn't dress like a skinhead anymore. "I had to find work, and nobody need know what I think. But what I do after work is nobody's business." Doreen, also 20, comes from a small town in eastern Germany. She is furious that nothing has "happened" after the firebombing attacks in Rostock and Mölln. "The government must close the border. But not only skinheads are against foreigners; some quite normal people are as well. We are at least doing something."

"Men practice violence; women are the victims." For many years this was the basic formula underlying feminist theory and practice in the West German women's movement. Everything could be explained from that standpoint. "By assuming the role of victim, one finds a way of legitimately rejecting an awareness of one's own unjust acts, as well as an awareness of the injustices committed by one's own society. In other words, the others are worse than we are." This was written by Christina Thürmer-Rohr in a recent article entitled "White Women and Racism." The Berlin professor and psychologist is one of the best known theorists of the women's movement in western Germany. Three years after the political and social upheaval in Germany and Europe, she is sending an urgent appeal to the "white, Western women's movement to reject the romantic Western view of the white woman as victim, to renounce the self-indulgent self-definition as helpless and incompetent." It's a harsh and sweeping criticism, but it hits home, revealing the weak point in the German women's movement. Already in the 1980s much of the West German women's movement had given up a global political vision in favor of a pragmatic "here and now" reformism. Feminists focused their energies on developing numerous social and cultural projects: they founded businesses, worked in political parties, unions, and state institutions, and fought for better status for women and for equal representation in government. Slowly but surely, the slogan "women's liberation" turned into "self-actualization." Internationalism lost ground and the issue of racism ceased to play an important role in discussions. Thürmer-Rohr writes: "Feminism became a limited intellectual model, a therapeutic instrument for the liberation of the white middle-class woman."

Then came November of 1989, a turning point in East Germany. Suddenly, at demonstrations and rallies of the citizens' opposition movements, feminist slogans appeared next to demands for more democracy—slogans such as "The country needs a new kind of woman" and "Those who don't fight end up in the kitchen." Seemingly overnight, a more political, activist women's movement emerged in East Germany. The movement participated in the process of change at all levels of society, demanding, in a radical and very imaginative spirit, a new, nonpatriarchal society. "It was a great feeling—we would change everything. We sat in grass-roots political committees, outlined a new constitution, sent our representatives to parliament; we even had a feminist cabinet minister for women's affairs." Ulrike Bagger, who in late 1989 helped found the Independent Women's Alliance of the GDR, today remembers those times as a dream. Within a few months, there were women's centers, cafés, and shelters, as well as municipal offices for women's rights in East Germany's larger urban centers. For a short while, there were indications that the awakening in the east might rejuvenate the women's movement in West Germany. "In many ways they reminded me of our own beginnings in the 1970s. What a fantastic impetus for us. But I also felt that all this wouldn't last long," says historian Ursula Nienhaus, a feminist activist from western Germany.

As soon as it became obvious that the former East Germany would be assimilated into the Federal Republic, the Cassandras from the east and west raised their voices. They warned of the consequences of unification, which for East German women meant the loss of previously unquestioned social rights, such as guaranteed employment, day care facilities, and virtually unrestricted abortion rights. In the west, women who during the past 20 years had managed to sensitize the society to gender

discrimination feared that in a "united Fatherland" feminist political discourse would gradually disappear from public life. Reunification meant more power to men, conservatism, nationalism—perhaps worse.

Feminists from the two parts of Germany are drifting farther apart.

The "united Fatherland" has been a reality for three years, and no unity has been achieved. Shortly after the Berlin Wall fell, both sides realized that they are not really "one people," that 40 years of separation produced two different histories, mind-sets, even linguistic differences, and, finally, that the social differences between east and west remained. The "sisters" are now separated by a new German wall: a tangle of disappointment, distrust, envy, and competitiveness. Feminists in the west say that their eastern counterparts haven't learned how to fight, that they have relinquished their rights. To the feminists in eastern Germany, their western sisters seem authoritarian, overbearing, and egoistic. Instead of organizing joint actions, feminists from the two parts of Germany are losing interest in one another and drifting farther apart. An oft-quoted saying goes: "Women are losers in the unification game." This is a seldom mentioned common denominator for all German women; common because women from both sides now find themselves in the familiar role of victim. With the loss of a broad-based political vision, there are now few signs—in either part of Germany—of an assertive and responsible women's movement. "I have a feeling that many women here are simply paralyzed. They are preoccupied with their personal problems. Women may still attend self-defense classes or carry Mace cans, but that seems to be it," says Ulrich, who remarks that she will not accept the victim role—because she knows "navel-gazing" renders many feminists incapable of reacting to what's going on in their country.

But some feminists have begun to react, especially after November 1992, when a group of extreme right-wingers set fire to a house in Mölln that was occupied mostly by foreign families. Two Turkish women and a small girl were killed. As a result, the subject of racism—to which Jewish, immigrant, and African German women have been trying to direct the attention of white feminists—suddenly acquired a terrifyingly concrete significance that could no longer be ignored. A growing sense of responsibility among white feminists has resulted in various actions that, although lacking in coordination and political impact, are a beginning. In November, the German Women's Council, an umbrella organization of women's groups, condemned all xenophobic and racist attacks. It also decided to work on integrating immigrant women into the concerns and activism of women's organizations in Germany. Around the same time, Berlin feminists created an antiracism group called Women's Action Alliance, modeled after the New York-based Women's Action Coalition. Other groups have set up hotlines to respond to calls for help when foreigners' homes are threatened

Campaigning Against "Frauenhass"

EMMA, Germany's leading feminist magazine, was the first of its kind in Europe when it was founded in 1978. It was also the first western German magazine to be distributed in the east, according to its founder and editor in chief Alice Schwarzer. *EMMA* has now initiated a campaign against *frauenhass,* or "hate of the woman," during a time when the country is struggling with *fremdenhass*—"hate of the other"—in hopes of illuminating the connections. "This violence is not, as is being reported, the violence of young *people,* because 99 percent of it is being committed by young *men,*" says Schwarzer. "The source of hatred of the 'other' is the hatred of men for women, because the woman is the first 'other' for man." She notes that in 1992, 12 people were killed because they were not German, while 800 women were killed because they were women, adding that "what we are seeing is the first generation that has been entirely 'pornographized,' that has its head full of the association of desire and violence." Schwarzer says that *EMMA,* having coined the term *frauenhass,* is lobbying the justice system to begin collecting statistics on hate crimes against women.

—Jana Meredyth Talton

and have organized protective vigils. Some women have taken refugees into their homes to help them adjust to life in a new country.

Feminists are also fighting to change the country's proposed constitution, due to be adopted this year. One of the principal demands is immediate asylum for women who have been persecuted because of their gender. In addition, activists are hoping to inundate the constitutional commission with letters from women requesting that Germany's citizenship requirements be revised. Activists say that every person born in Germany should, as a matter of course, be given German citizenship, and dual citizenship should be readily granted. "It's unacceptable that people who live beyond the Urals and do not speak a word of German but claim that their blood is German are instantly granted citizenship. Others who have been living here for 30 years, or who were born here and whose mother tongue is German, remain foreigners," says Emine Demirbuken, spokeswoman for the Association for Immigrants from Turkey.

Alisa Fuss is a 73-year-old antiracism activist, one who knows that racism and anti-Semitism are closely connected in Germany. In 1935, she fled from the Nazis to Palestine. She returned to Germany in 1976. In September 1992, the Jewish barracks of the old Sachsenhausen concentration camp were set on fire. Within hours, Fuss had assembled a few hundred people at the site of the camp. On another occasion, she organized a "solidarity" convoy from Berlin to Hoyerswerda—an eastern German town where, in 1991, asylum-seekers' homes were attacked for an entire week. She also set up protective vigils in front of refugees' homes. "There can only be a united struggle against racism and anti-Semitism. We know that this always starts with the most vulnerable group. Today it's the foreigners, the refugees, then we move on to the disabled and everybody else who is different. And finally, there are always the Jews."

One of the few feminist organizations that have for years been dealing actively with the connections between misogyny, racism, and anti-Seminitism is Orlanda Frauenverlag, a Berlin publishing house. In 1986 Orlanda, inspired by the African American writer Audre Lorde, published *Farbe Bekennen, Afro-deutsche Frauen auf den Spuren ihrer Geschichte [Showing Our Colors: Afro-German Women Speak Out].* African German women thus publicly confronted white German women with the following truths: racism in Germany cannot be neutralized by slogans including the word "xenophobia"; racism has nothing to do with nationality and everything to do with color; and white Germans, men and women, have a hard time accepting "others."

Discovering that racism is harbored not only by extreme right-wingers, Nazis, and men is a painful process for many white feminists. And this realization triggers feelings of guilt. But guilty feelings, as Audre Lorde once wrote, are "the stones of a wall against which we will all smash ourselves." Many walls must come down in today's Germany. Even among feminists.

Understanding Cultural Pluralism

The increase in racial violence and hatred on campuses across the country is manifested in acts ranging from hateful speech to physical violence. Strategies for dealing with this problem on a campus include increased awareness through mandatory ethnic studies classes, the empowerment of targets of violence, and fostering social and cultural interaction in festivals, folk-arts fairs, and literary and political forums. Systematic knowledge about ethnic groups has not been a central scholarly concern. In fact, mainstream literacy, humanistic, and historical disciplines have only recently begun to displace sociological attention to the pathologies of urban ethnicity as the primary contact and source of information and interpretation of ethnic traditions. The historic role that voluntary groups have played in the reduction of bias and bigotry also needs to be understood and revitalized. Voluntary associations can take part in a host of state and local initiatives that can improve intergroup relations. Schools and parents can help children understand commonalties and differences among and within ethnic traditions and groups. The incorporation of everyday experiences of families and a formal pedagogy rooted in accurate and locally relevant resources are essential building blocks for understanding diversity.

Educational efforts are necessary and productive, but it would be foolish to neglect the enormity of the issues of ethnocentrism and group hatred and prejudice that infect opportunities for better cultural understanding. Philosophical reflection on these dimensions of conflict, as well as recognition of the role of mass media in the social construction of cultures throughout the world, reveal the long-term need for attention to the nature of ethnically charged conflict.

There are many ways of measuring the development of wholesome relations among persons and ethnic groups. The evidence cited by various authorities in this chapter indicates contradictions that are probably caused by differences in assumptions and models of social processes used to frame the issues of group development. Important in this discussion is the role of government in the process of ethnic group relations. Progress in civil rights promoted changes in attitudes toward affirming the equality of all people. The development of this principle has been tracked by the National Opinion Research Center (NORC) from the 1960s to the 1980s. NORC findings include increased levels of acceptance for blacks and a decreased desire for segregated schools and neighborhoods and for laws prohibiting interracial marriage. Nonetheless, attitudes regarding frustration, powerlessness, racial distrust, and hostility reveal striking disparities in attitudes between blacks and whites.

Ethnic communities are also frequently in conflict with large-scale corporate powers and the media. What avenues of resolve are available to ensure that authentic cultural resources are preserved and presented in ways that enrich the overall legacy and endowment of America's multiethnic traditions? Can the promotion of pluralism and the enhancement of positive prototypes of ethnicity assist the shaping of our national self-image? Dialogue among conflicting parties about dilemmas that confront us all in a society driven by technological and economic changes is an essential feature of our freedom and of our responsibility to share and shape the burden of social change.

Although significant strides have been made in combating discrimination and defamation against Americans of various ethnic groups, much still remains to be done. Unflattering and often distorted stereotypes of ethnic Americans continue to appear in the media. In the national and local media in America, ethnic Americans still remain substantially underrepresented. Efforts to inform our fellow countrymen and women and our children of the history and culture of American ethnic groups through educational programs have suffered serious setbacks. Many of the institutions and foundations that were in the forefront of the struggle to create a genuine multicultural pluralism, to promote better understanding between various groups of Americans, and to end discrimination have adopted other agendas. Advocates of multicultural development, however, argue that to secure rights and justice for all Americans, we must address such tasks as:

1. Fairness and equal treatment under the law;
2. Compilation of full and accurate data on the ethnic composition of the American people; and
3. The promotion of corporate leaders and the appointment of public officials who are representative of and sensitive to America's ethnic diversity.

Looking Ahead: Challenge Questions

Have you seen signs of an increase in racist, anti-Semitic, anti-immigrant, and antiminority group acts that recent studies apparently confirm?

What explains the fact that large population studies confirm that in the areas of ethnic, racial, and religious differences, Americans are more tolerant than ever?

Why do teenagers commit eighty percent of all bias-related acts?

The public's reluctance to support programs for single groups is forcing ethnic advocates to adopt coalitional approaches to solving problems. As a result, coalition-building has been transformed from a crusade by utopian reformers, who once regarded ethnic advocacy as questionable, to a movement of rooted leaders and service providers who work together to meet the needs of diverse groups. Should ethnic communities formally train their leaders in the art and science of coalition-building?

Should ethnic groups meet regularly with other ethnic groups and engage in friendly "what's your agenda" meetings?

Does anyone benefit from the persistence of ethnic tension and conflict?

America: Still a Melting Pot?

Tom Morganthau

Few Americans remember Israel Zangwill, but he was a transatlantic celebrity in the years before World War I. Poet, novelist, dramatist and political activist, Zangwill was a founding father of the Zionist movement and an ardent suffragist. He knew Theodore Roosevelt, Oscar Wilde and George Bernard Shaw, and he was a prolific, if preachy, writer. Here is a bit of dialogue from Zangwill's greatest hit, a four-act melodrama that opened in Washington in 1908. The speaker is David, a young composer:

> *America is God's Crucible, the great Melting-Pot where all the races of Europe are melting and re-forming. . . . Germans and Frenchmen, Irishmen and Englishmen, Jews and Russians— into the Crucible with you all! God is making the American!*

The imagery comes from steelmaking, which was state-of-the-art technology then. The play is "The Melting-Pot," a phrase that has lived ever since. Zangwill, despondent at the eclipse of many of his political ideals, suffered a nervous breakdown and died in England in 1926. America had already turned its back on his optimism and, in an orgy of blatant racism, virtually cut off immigration. Two generations later, immigration is running full blast—and Americans once again are asking fundamental questions about the desirability of accepting so many newcomers and the very idea of the Melting Pot. They believe, with some justice, that the nation has lost control of its borders. They are frightened about the long-term prospects for the U.S. economy and worried about their jobs. They think, erroneously, that immigrants are flooding the welfare rolls and are heavily involved in crime. And

they are clearly *uncomfortable* with the fact that almost all the New Immigrants come from Latin America, the Caribbean and Asia.

The latest NEWSWEEK Poll reveals the public's sharply shifting attitudes. Fully 60 percent of all Americans see current levels of immigration as bad; 59 percent think immigration in the past was good. Fifty-nine percent also say "many" immigrants wind up on welfare, and only 20 percent think America is still a melting pot.

All this—an incendiary mixture of fact, fear and myth—is now making its way into politics. The trend is most obvious in California, where immigration is already a hot-button issue, and it is surfacing in Washington. Recent events like the World Trade Center bombing, the arrest of Sheik Omar Abdel-Rahman and the grounding of the

---

1600–1776

Seeking greater fortune and religious freedom, Europeans braved the Atlantic to settle in America before the Revolution

---

Golden Venture, an alien-smuggling ship crammed with nearly 300 Chinese emigrants, have revived the 10-year-old controversy about illegal immigration. "We must not—we will not—surrender our borders to those who wish to exploit our history of compassion and justice," Bill Clinton said last week, announcing a $172.5 million proposal to beef up the U.S. Border Patrol and crack down on

visa fraud and phony asylum claims. On Capitol Hill, the revival of an issue that many had thought dead is shaking both political parties, and Democrats such as Sen. Dianne Feinstein of California are scrambling to neutralize nativist backlash. "Some of the people who opposed me totally 10 years ago are now saying, 'What's happening to our country? We gotta do something!' " said Republican Sen. Alan Simpson of Wyoming, a perennial advocate of tougher immigration enforcement. "It's ironic beyond belief. Attitudes have shifted dramatically, and it's coming from the citizens."

This is not the 1920s—a time when most Americans regarded dark-skinned people as inherently inferior, when the Ku Klux Klan marched through Washington in a brazen display of bigotry and when the president of the United States could tell an Italian-American congressman, *in writing,* that Italians are "predominantly our murderers and bootleggers . . . foreign spawn [who] do not appreciate this country." (The president was Herbert Hoover and the congressman was Fiorello La Guardia.) The civil-rights revolution changed everything: it gradually made overt expressions of any ethnic prejudice into a cultural taboo. Almost accidentally, the moral awakening of the 1960s also gave the nation an immigration law that reopened the Golden Door. This law, passed in 1965 with the firm backing of Robert Kennedy, Edward Kennedy and Lyndon Johnson, has slowly led to a level of sustained immigration that is at least as large as that of 1900–1920. It inadvertently but totally reversed the bias in U.S. law toward immigration from Europe, and it created a policy so complicated that almost no one understands it. The policy, in fact, is a mess, whatever one thinks of the desperate Chinese on the

The Economic Cost of Immigration

IMMIGRATION HAS ranked with corn and cars as a mainstay of American economic growth. The traditional theory is simple: energetic workers increase the supply of goods and services with their labor, and increase the demand for other goods and services by spending their wages. A benign circle of growth uncurls as a widening variety of workers create rising riches for each other. Two hundred years of U.S. history seem to confirm this theory. Yet the perception today is that immigration is a drag on the economy, not a lift. In truth, it's both. "The short-term costs of immigration today are much higher," says Michael Boskin, formerly chief economist to George Bush, "but in the long run, immigrants are still great news for our economy."

The NEWSWEEK Poll shows that 62 percent of those surveyed worry that immigrants take jobs away from native-born workers. That can be true in times of high unemployment. In California, where the jobless rate is 9 percent, immigration is soaring and native-born Americans are actually leaving to find work in other states, some temporary displacement may be occurring. But in normal times, any job loss is more than offset by the creation of new jobs stemming from the immigrants' own work. The immigrants' new spending creates demand for housing, groceries and other necessities, and their employers invest their expanding profits in new machinery and jobs. "It is called competitive capitalism," says Tony Carnevale of the American Society for Training and Development, "and it works. It's how America got rich."

Two forces, however, have recently helped to undercut the benefits of immigration: the welfare state and the steep decline in the skill levels of immigrants since 1970. In the last great decade of immigration, 1900 to 1910, public education and a little public health were the only services provided to those migrating to New York and other Northeastern cities. One third of the new immigrants simply failed and moved back home. Today dozens of welfare programs—from food stamps to unemployment compensation—cushion failure and attract immigrants who might otherwise stay home. In California, children born to illegal parents now account for one in eight beneficiaries of one program alone, Aid to Families with Dependent Children (AFDC). The state-run Medicaid program provided $489 million in health care to more than 400,000 illegal aliens last year. Legal aliens got hundreds of millions more.

Donald Huddle, an immigration expert at Rice University, recently calculated that the 19.3 million legal, illegal and amnestied aliens accepted into the United States since 1970 utilized $50.8 billion worth of government services last year. They paid $20.2 billion in taxes. So the net burden on native-born taxpayers was $30.6 billion—a social-welfare cost per immigrant of $1,585. Huddle projects these immigrants will cost taxpayers another $50 billion a year on average over the next 10 years.

A decline in the skills of new immigrants helps to explain these numbers. Ninety percent of current immigrants arrive from Third World countries with income and social-service levels one tenth or even one twentieth those of the United States'. Their education levels relative to those of native-born Americans are steadily declining. So are their earnings. George Borjas of the University of California, San Diego, says that in 1970 the average immigrant actually earned 3 percent more than a native-born American but by 1990 was earning 16 percent less. "Each year the percentage is heading downward," says Borjas. What's more, welfare dependency has steadily climbed and is now above that of native-borns. In 1990, 7.7 percent of native Californians received

public assistance vs. 10.4 percent of new immigrants.

The welfare costs of immigration should dramatically decrease as the California and U.S. economies recover. The long-term benefits of immigrant labor and business enterprise will then be more apparent. But the age of innocence in the American immigration experience is over. The rise of the U.S. welfare state has placed a cushion under the immigrant experience—and diminished the benefits of immigration to the country at large.

RICH THOMAS *with* ANDREW MURR
in Los Angeles

Golden Venture or the young Latinos who scale the fence at Tijuana every night.

Bill Clinton's goal, like that of most defenders of continued large-scale immigration, is to drive home the distinction between legal immigration (good) and illegal immigration (very, very bad). Illegal immigration is undeniably out of control. Congress tried to stop it in 1986 with a law called IRCA, the Immigration Reform and Control Act, which was based on a two-pronged strategy. IRCA offered amnesty and eventual citizenship to an estimated 3.7 million illegal aliens and, at the same time, aimed at shutting down the U.S. job market by making it illegal for employers to hire undocumented aliens. The act has failed. Despite the amnesty, the estimated number of illegals has once again risen to between 2 million and 4 million people. "For the first two years there was a significant drop . . . because folks thought there was a real law here," says Lawrence H. Fuchs, acting chair of the U.S. Commission on Immigration Reform. "But the word got out" that IRCA had no teeth, Fuchs says, and the influx resumed. Fuchs concedes that as many as 500,000 illegals now enter this country each year, though he admits it is impossible to know for sure.

The concern over illegal immigration is fueled, in part, by two conflicting fears. Illegals are vulnerable to exploitation by employers and are often victimized—extorted, kidnapped, raped, tortured and sometimes killed—by crimi-

1820–1870
The potato famine of the mid-1840s sent the Irish scurrying to the promised land, while economic depression in Germany triggered an exodus

nals and smugglers. At the other extreme, in cities like Los Angeles, they flood the labor market and set off bitter competition with American workers and legal immigrants for jobs.

But the real problem is the subversion of U.S. law and policy, and that creates two dilemmas for the federal government. The first is what to do about the undocumented aliens who have made their way into this country since IRCA: another amnesty, obviously, would only encourage more illegal immigration. The second dilemma is worse. There is no particular reason to believe that the current influx of illegals cannot rise from 500,000 a year to 600,000 a year or even beyond. This is conjectural but not necessarily alarmist: as Fuchs says, the word is out. Looking around the world, "one can't find the natural forces that will bring down the flow," says Harvard University sociologist Nathan Glazer. "The first impact of prosperity will be to increase it. Look at China. These people don't come from the backward areas, they come from the progressive parts. As they learn how to run a business, they say to themselves, 'Why not go to the United States and do even better?' "

The same applies to Bangladesh, the Dominican Republic, Mexico or the Philippines. The dynamic, as Fuchs says, is rooted in powerful macroeconomic forces now at work all around the globe—rising birthrates and the conquest of disease, prosperity or the hope of prosperity, even modern telecommunications. (The glittery materialism of American TV shows is now being broadcast everywhere.) Much as Americans tend to regard the new immigrants as poor, uneducated and less skilled, the vast majority are surely enterprising. What they seek is opportunity—the opportunity to hold two jobs that no Americans want, to buy a television set and a beat-up car, to

start a family and invest in the next generation. Immigration is for the young: it takes courage, stamina and determination to pull up your roots, say goodbye to all that is dear and familiar, and hit the long and difficult trail to El Norte. Illegal immigration, with all its hazards, is for the truly daring: the Latino men who wait on Los Angeles street corners, hoping for daywork, have faced more risk than most Americans will ever know.

You can argue, then, that the distinction between legal and illegal immigration is nearly meaningless. Immigrants are immigrants: how they got here is a detail. And, in fact, the arcane system of regulation created by the 1965 law, together with its amendments and adjustments since, implicitly accepts this argument. The law recognizes three reasons to award immigrant visas—job skills, especially those that somehow match the needs of the U.S. economy; a demonstrable reason to seek refuge from war or political persecution, and kinship to an American citizen or a legal alien. This triad of goals replaced the national-origin quota system of 1924, which heavily favored immigrants from North-

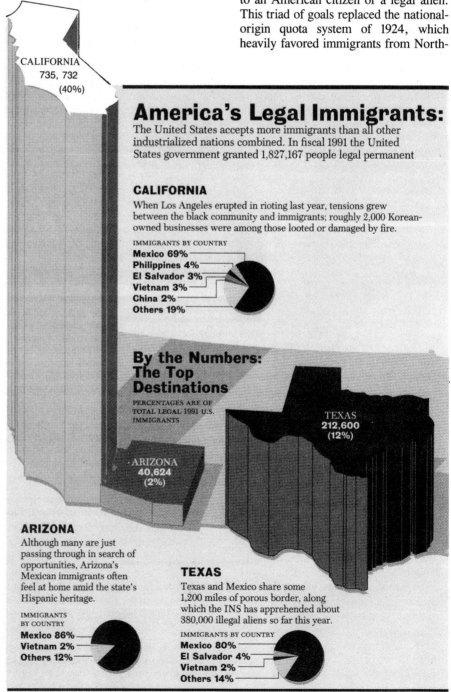

CALIFORNIA
735, 732
(40%)

America's Legal Immigrants:
The United States accepts more immigrants than all other industrialized nations combined. In fiscal 1991 the United States government granted 1,827,167 people legal permanent

CALIFORNIA
When Los Angeles erupted in rioting last year, tensions grew between the black community and immigrants; roughly 2,000 Korean-owned businesses were among those looted or damaged by fire.

IMMIGRANTS BY COUNTRY
Mexico 69%
Philippines 4%
El Salvador 3%
Vietnam 3%
China 2%
Others 19%

By the Numbers: The Top Destinations
PERCENTAGES ARE OF TOTAL LEGAL 1991 U.S. IMMIGRANTS

TEXAS
212,600
(12%)

ARIZONA
40,624
(2%)

ARIZONA
Although many are just passing through in search of opportunities, Arizona's Mexican immigrants often feel at home amid the state's Hispanic heritage.

IMMIGRANTS BY COUNTRY
Mexico 86%
Vietnam 2%
Others 12%

TEXAS
Texas and Mexico share some 1,200 miles of porous border, along which the INS has apprehended about 380,000 illegal aliens so far this year.

IMMIGRANTS BY COUNTRY
Mexico 80%
El Salvador 4%
Vietnam 2%
Others 14%

ern and Western Europe and severely restricted immigration from everywhere else. It is a matter of lasting national shame that Congress, throughout the 1930s and even after World War II, refused to adjust the law to admit the victims of the Holocaust. That shabby record outraged Jews and had much to do with the passage of [the] act of 1965. So did the old law's bias against Slavs, Poles, Italians, the Chinese and the Japanese.

But all three of these goals have been steadily distorted—chipped at, twisted out of shape—by the realities of immigration since 1965. Kinship to U.S. citizens, known as the "family-reunification policy," has become the overwhelming

1880–1920
Persecution and poverty throughout Europe unleashed the greatest flock of immigrants ever; no fewer than 12 million sought refuge here

favorite of visa seekers and the primary reason the pattern of immigration has shifted so hugely to the Third World. It was never intended to be: given the fact

that most immigration to the United States had always been from Europe, those who voted for the act of 1965 generally assumed that family-reunification visas would be used by Europeans. They also assumed that there would be no large increase in immigration to the United States. "Our cities will not be flooded with a million immigrants annually," Sen. Edward Kennedy told a subcommittee hearing. "Under the proposed bill, the present level of immigration [about 300,000 a year] remains substantially the same. . . ."

That is not what happened. Immigration from Latin America, the Caribbean and Asia, a trickle in 1965, has steadily widened so that it now comprises about 90 percent of the total. Legal immigration from 1971 to 1990 was 10.5 million people—but if 3 million illegals are (conservatively) added in, the total is pretty much the same as 1900–1920, the peak years in American history. Owing partly to a further liberalization of the law in 1990 and partly to the IRCA amnesty, the United States now accepts more immigrants than all other industrialized nations *combined*. (Upwards of 80 percent are persons of color: so much for the myth that U.S. policy is racist.) Proponents of further immigration argue that the current influx is actually lower than the 1900–1920 peak when considered as a percentage of the U.S. population. They are right: it was 1 percent of the population then and about one third of 1 percent now. But it is still a lot of people.

And the law is full of holes. A majority of those who get family-reunification visas (235,484 in 1992) come in with no numerical restriction at all: for them, at least, immigration is a form of entitlement program. Others game the system by forging documents, faking job histories and hiring smart American lawyers to get them eligible for resident visas and green cards. This is known in federal jargon as "adjusting status," and in most years it works for more than 200,000 immigrants. The asylum hustle is the newest wrinkle. By claiming political asylum, would-be immigrants circumvent the normal rules and, because the jails are full, are usually freed to stay and work. Many simply vanish into the underground economy. "We didn't [expect] the asylum problem," says Lawrence Fuchs. "We thought of it as the ballerina

Who They Are and Where They Go

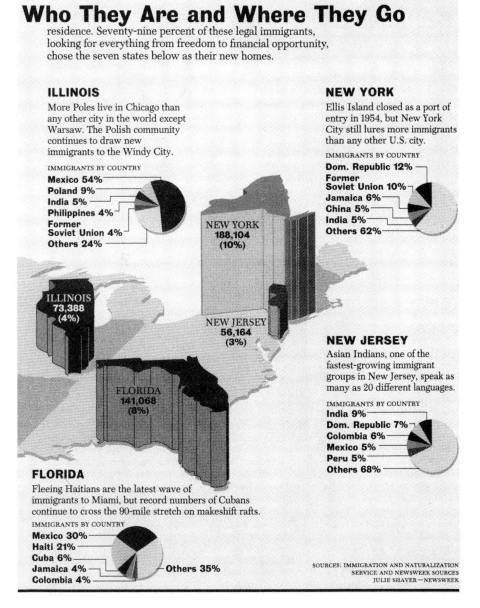

residence. Seventy-nine percent of these legal immigrants, looking for everything from freedom to financial opportunity, chose the seven states below as their new homes.

ILLINOIS
More Poles live in Chicago than any other city in the world except Warsaw. The Polish community continues to draw new immigrants to the Windy City.

IMMIGRANTS BY COUNTRY
Mexico 54%
Poland 9%
India 5%
Philippines 4%
Former Soviet Union 4%
Others 24%

NEW YORK
Ellis Island closed as a port of entry in 1954, but New York City still lures more immigrants than any other U.S. city.

IMMIGRANTS BY COUNTRY
Dom. Republic 12%
Former Soviet Union 10%
Jamaica 6%
China 5%
India 5%
Others 62%

NEW JERSEY
Asian Indians, one of the fastest-growing immigrant groups in New Jersey, speak as many as 20 different languages.

IMMIGRANTS BY COUNTRY
India 9%
Dom. Republic 7%
Colombia 6%
Mexico 5%
Peru 5%
Others 68%

FLORIDA
Fleeing Haitians are the latest wave of immigrants to Miami, but record numbers of Cubans continue to cross the 90-mile stretch on makeshift rafts.

IMMIGRANTS BY COUNTRY
Mexico 30%
Haiti 21%
Cuba 6%
Jamaica 4%
Colombia 4%
Others 35%

NEW YORK 188,104 (10%)
NEW JERSEY 56,164 (3%)
ILLINOIS 73,388 (4%)
FLORIDA 141,068 (8%)

SOURCES: IMMIGRATION AND NATURALIZATION SERVICE AND NEWSWEEK SOURCES
JULIE SHAVER—NEWSWEEK

in the tutu saying, 'I defect, I defect'."

Immigration policy is simultaneously a statement of America's relationship with the rest of the world and a design for the national future: it is, and probably should be, a mixture of altruism and self-interest. Current U.S. policy contains elements of both—but it is a blurry, heavily brokered policy that has been cobbled together over the decades to reflect the changing fads and competing interests of domestic politics. A purely selfish policy would accept only immigrants who could contribute to economic or social progress. But this idea—awarding visas on the basis of talent or skill—

has always been opposed by organized labor and other groups, and it is a minor feature of today's law, totaling about 140,000 out of 810,000 visas annually. Conversely, providing a haven for refugees is in the best tradition of the American conscience, and the United States has taken a lot of refugees since 1970—1.5 million Vietnamese, Laotians, Cambodians, Cubans, Russians and other oppressed nationalities.

But the vast majority of those who get here are ordinary folks pursuing a better life—and although this, too, is part of the American tradition, the question can and should be asked: What's in it for *us*?

What does all this immigration do for America and Americans? Julian Simon, a University of Maryland economist, says he knows the answer: more immigration means more economic growth—more wealth and more progress for all Americans, period. Pat Buchanan, the talk-show host and erstwhile presidential candidate, has a different answer: more immigrants mean more social friction and the slow erosion of the English-speaking, hybrid European culture we call "American."

There is a third issue as well: how many people, really, can the territorial United States support? Immigration now

Immigrant Schools: The Wrong Lessons

UNION AVENUE ELEmentary school, a dusty sprawl of concrete, asphalt and chain-link fence just west of downtown Los Angeles, bears all the scars of the inner city. Yellow caution signs mark the perimeter: NARCOTICS ENFORCEMENT AREA. RESIDENTS ONLY. In the distance a police helicopter circles over a crime scene. After school, parents anxiously hook their fingers through the fence and wait for their kids to emerge. But because Union Avenue draws from a heavily immigrant neighborhood, its 2,000 students have even more to surmount than the grim realities of crime and poverty. They also face the enormous obstacles, educational and societal, that stand in the way of foreign-born newcomers.

The student body is more than 93 percent Latino. The second largest group is Filipino, at 2.9 percent. A third of the students were born outside the United States, and well over half are not proficient in English. As many as half may be children of illegal aliens. There are as few Anglos as there are Native Americans: six. In the school library there are books in Tagalog, Korean, Vietnamese, Spanish and English. But

not even a third of the faculty can speak Spanish. The others rely on bilingual teacher assistants to translate the lessons. This is an explosive subject here. Many claim that bilingual education has done more to divide teachers than to help Spanish speakers. Defenders see it as a multicultural keystone. The faculty has been Balkanized by bilingualism: at lunchtime the two sides segregate themselves by table.

Most of the newest immigrants come from Central America, and many bring with them the trauma of war. Asked whether he had witnessed much fighting in his hometown of San Rafael, El Salvador, which he left three years ago, fifth grader Angel Alfaro nods but doesn't want to talk about it. Asked about his school and what he would do to fix it, he perks up and says in unaccented English, "Nothing. It's perfect."

The Union Avenue kids' eagerness to please, and to learn, is irrepressible. Yet it is hard to be optimistic about their future. For all of its inadequacies, the school is a relatively calm way station. Most of the kids will go on to Virgil Middle School, where education competes with gangs, graffiti tag-

gers and drugs. Fifth grader Reggie Perez, whose parents are Guatemalan, says he is going to go to a school in North Hollywood "because at Virgil there are just too many gangs." Out of 15 students interviewed last week (the school is in session year round), all but one said their parents were trying to get them into a parochial school or bused to a school in a better neighborhood. Still, most of the fifth graders will end up at Virgil.

Schools like Union Avenue are making a valiant effort. But as a recent report from the Rand Corp. says, "School systems that are beset by debt, declining and unstable revenues, dilapidated buildings and inadequate instructional resources cannot improve simply by trying harder." The federal government has all but ignored the needs of states with large immigrant populations like California, New York, Texas, Florida and Illinois. The single federal program that targets immigrant students is funded at $30 million a year—or $42 per child. In California, where budget tightening has hit specialized programs especially hard, state officials estimate that they are short 8,000 bilingual teachers.

Historically, a solid education has been the quickest road to assimilation. But today, during the greatest surge in immigration since the turn of the century, the schools are failing the 2 million children who have been part of the influx. Their education is isolating them from the mainstream, rather than helping them to join it, and exposing them to all of the pathologies of ghetto life. Meanwhile, as the NEWSWEEK Poll indicates, anti-immigrant sentiment is on the rise. Such a charged atmosphere "doesn't make the job any easier," said Lorraine M. McDonnell, coauthor of the Rand report. The kids, instead of getting the best that their new home has to offer, often get the worst.

STRYKER McGUIRE *in Los Angeles*

produces about a third of U.S. population growth, and projections for the future range from a population of about 383 million in 2050 to 436 million by the year 2090. All of these projections are shaky—based on complex assumptions about birth and death rates as well as immigration policy. Some environmentalists (and many Californians) think the United States should immediately halt immigration to protect the ecosystem and the quality of life. Fuchs says his commission has consulted environmentalists and population experts. "They persuaded us that the population growth is terribly serious on a planetary scale, but not in the United States," he says. "So migration to the United States perhaps has a beneficial effect on the global environmental problem." Still, Congress took no notice of this question when it voted to increase immigration in 1990—and given the wide disparity of current views, picking the "right" number of future Americans is ultimately a combination of taste and guesswork.

1965–1993
The face of immigration has changed over the last few decades, adding non-European cultures, languages and religions to the melting pot

The further question is one that troubles Pat Buchanan and many others: can America absorb so many people with different languages, different cultures, different backgrounds? The answer, broadly, is yes—which does not mean there will be no ethnic friction and does not mean that assimilation is easy for anyone. Assimilation is a generational thing. The first generation—the immigrants themselves—are always strangers in the land. The second generation is

halfway between or (kids will be kids) rejects the immigrant culture. The third generation is hyphenated-American, like everybody else, and begins the search for Roots. The tricky part, which worries Fuchs considerably, is that America's "civic culture" is unique in all the world. It is the belief, as embodied in the Constitution and our political tradition, "that it is individual rights, not group rights, that hold this country together." So here is the question for all of us, native-born and immigrant alike. At what point do policies like affirmative action and minority-voting rights stop being temporary remedies for past injustices and start being permanent features of the system? The whole concept of group rights, as Fuchs says, is tribalism—the road to Bosnia, not East L.A. And that, surely, is not what Israel Zangwill had in mind when he described America as the crucible of a new civilization.

With ADAM WOLFBERG and BOB COHN in Washington, ANDREW MURR in Los Angeles and bureau reports

Students talk about race

At Chapel Hill, N.C., racial tension runs high. A special report

On the basketball court in New Orleans last week, blacks and whites teamed together to win the national championship for the University of North Carolina. But back at Chapel Hill, togetherness is a description few would use to characterize relations between blacks and whites. "It has been brutal," says Associate Vice Chancellor Edith Wiggins. "There is blood all over this campus."

The reason: a proposal to build a privately funded, free-standing black cultural center on campus. When school opened last September, UNC Chancellor Paul Hardin opposed the project, fearing that—as has happened at some schools—the facility would promote separatism. In reaction, almost 300 students, most of them black, staged a disruptive late-night demonstration at Hardin's campus home. A few weeks later, supporters of the center held a rally during which several speakers spouted anti-white rhetoric. Adding to the confusion and turmoil: verbal attacks by militant black students on black faculty and administrators like journalism Prof. Chuck Stone, a well-known veteran of the civil-rights movement, who, although supportive of the center, questioned the demonstrators' tactics. Blustered one militant at Stone: "If you stand in the way of our progress, we're going to have to roll over you."

Signs of trouble. For a few months, tensions eased after a committee appointed by Hardin came out in support of the center, prompting the chancellor to change his mind about the project. But now black-white relations are strained once again, this time by conflict over whether the center should be built on the main campus or just across from it. Two weeks ago, supporters of the on-campus site began a sit-in at the main university administration building, vowing not to leave until the chancellor acceded to their demand.

Large institutions, where self-segregation is greatest, are more likely than other schools to have had racial incidents.

The continuing battle over the center is just one of many sources of tension between the races at an institution that calls itself "the southern part of heaven." In January, for example, a sign appeared in a residence-hall lavatory: "This bathroom is no longer desegregated. No niggers allowed except for housekeepers."

In an effort to understand the often complex relationships between the races at a university long admired for its liberal traditions, *U.S. News* recently conducted an intensive series of focus groups on the Chapel Hill campus. For two evenings, teams of *U.S. News* reporters discussed race relations with separate groups of 10 black students and an equal number of white students. On a third night, six members of each group came together for a free-ranging exchange about the attitudes and animosities shaping campus life at UNC, which, in many ways, typifies race relations on campuses throughout America. Following are three reports on the discussions at Chapel Hill.

THE BLACK EXPERIENCE
Strangers in a strange land

Being black at Chapel Hill means shouldering a heavy burden. In addition to satisfying personal academic ambitions, black students feel they must be "defenders of the race." Outsiders in a white world, they feel they are subject to an exquisite racial etiquette that sees black-ness and whiteness as opposing forces. And all share the same distress at the bleaker dynamics of race relations, whether it's racial epithets scrawled on bathroom mirrors or assumptions about their academic qualifications because of their skin color.

One source of nearly universal discomfort: being constantly singled out to represent the views of all black people. Jasme Kelly, 19, a sophomore from Durham, N.C., who attended a predominantly white high school, says, "I know every time I go somewhere with a white person, something is going to come up racial." That is why one of Kelly's black friends refuses to associate with whites. "She says, 'crackers ain't good for nuthin' but cheese.'" Asked if this isn't an example of black bigotry, Kelly and others said it is more a summary of resentment.

At half of the large schools, white students feel that blacks receive special treatment that is not warranted.

That resentment has its roots in experiences like that of Philip McAdoo, a 22-year-old senior from Haw River, N.C. When he stopped to visit a friend who worked in a campus building, the receptionist asked if he would sign her son's basketball: Because he is tall and black and was wearing sweat pants, "she just assumed that I was on the basketball team." Kelly tells a similar tale of stereotyping. When she went to a fraternity to see a friend, the student who answered the door asked her, "Are you here to apply to be the cook?"

Michelle Thomas, a 23-year-old senior from Laurinburg, N.C., suffered an indignity of a different kind. When she arrived at Chapel Hill, she recalled, white "friends" from her high school treated her like a stranger. It was three years before she made her first white friend at Chapel Hill. Philip Charles-Pierre, 19, a sophomore from New York City, added that when he is with white friends they seem unwilling to enlarge the conversation beyond their own world.

Often, black students—just over 10 percent of all undergraduates at Chapel Hill—feel isolated from the intellectual environment because of what they perceive as subtle bias. Not long ago, for instance, the university provided space for a statue that showed a black man twirling a basketball and white students with stacks of books. African-Americans were insulted. Eventually, the statue was moved to a less central location. There are individual slights, as well. Before Carolynn McDonald, 20, a sophomore from Goldsboro, N.C., changed her major from premed to international studies, she told an adviser she wanted to take a second-semester calculus but was informed she didn't need to; the adviser seemed to assume McDonald would not apply to a top-notch medical school.

More "black." Not all blacks, of course, have such perceptions. Kenneth Allen, a 20-year-old National Merit Scholar from Havelock, N.C., said his faculty adviser invited him to take his course in English and was helpful in other ways, because Allen had taken pains to distinguish himself as an individual. If there is racial bias, Allen argued, it stems from black students themselves. He feels quite confident in his abilities and said the criticism he gets usually comes from blacks who feel he should speak differently or be interested in "other things or have more black friends." In other words, they think that he should act more "black."

Economic differences are a particularly sore point. Jasme Kelly told the group that while she worries about where to find $30 for the week's groceries, she sees white fraternity members spending freely on drinking sprees. And Vikki Mercer, a 20-year-old sophomore from Farmville, N.C., said that her financial life is a slow dance with penury, while white parents "pay for everything and their children drive new cars every semester. It's just unreal." Mercer is upset not because whites have money but be-

cause "they have no concept of what this money means." In their own minds, several students clearly identified *whiteness* with *success* and couldn't see themselves fitting into it.

True or not, blacks also believe that whites have greater access to university financial aid, although Allen and two others revealed that they are on full scholarships. Three of the students turned down full scholarships to other elite schools to attend UNC.

At 1 out of 3 large schools, most whites have a physical fear of black students, while the reverse is true at fewer than 1 in 10.

Curiously, despite its divisive impact on the campus as a whole, the students felt that the controversial black cultural center was a force for greater understanding. Many agreed that it did more to unite blacks and like-minded whites than any campus issue in years. And, said Philip McAdoo, the BCC provides the incentive for blacks who often aren't very tolerant of differences among themselves to unite behind a shared purpose. At first, McAdoo said, he hadn't marched for the BCC and was criticized for it by black friends who questioned his "blackness." But then he recognized an opportunity to educate others about African-American history and to heal divisions within the black student community. Those are goals that transcend the immediate controversy. As Carolynn McDonald puts it: "We are trying to educate not only ourselves but the larger community as well."

THE WHITE EXPERIENCE
The double-standard perplex

For white students at UNC, the lofty view of the university as a bastion of reason where even the most contentious matters can be calmly debated is simply a myth. They live in a world where discussions about race can be a dicey proposition except among very close friends. It is a world where nerve endings lie close to the surface and where tolerance for dissent is in short supply.

White students in the *U.S. News* focus group said that even the simplest conver-

sation with a black classmate can be fraught with anxiety. Jenny Johnson, a 20-year-old junior from Kernersville, N.C., worried about offending black acquaintances "and having them jump at my throat because I used the word 'black' instead of African-American. There is just such a huge barrier that it's really hard . . . to have a normal discussion."

Lee Hark, a 21-year-old senior from Rome, Ga., who is president of the Interfraternity Council, said that writing a letter to the school newspaper criticizing the September march on the chancellor's house got him "stamped as a racist." Hark, who views himself as a political moderate, said he was simply "trying to voice an opinion, but the feeling [among blacks] is that if you're not with us, you're against us, and that alienates me."

At 53 percent of the large schools, editors say blacks feel that white students are hostile and aloof toward them.

Trey Ezzell learned an even harsher lesson. When the 21-year-old junior from Hillsboro, N.C., wrote a sarcastic letter to the *Daily Tar Heel* about a planned rally in support of the black cultural center, two black students knocked him to the ground. "Immediately, I knew the letter got published," he said wryly. During the next several days, Ezzell, who calls himself "very conservative," got nasty phone calls at his off-campus apartment. He even started checking his car before driving to school. "When someone is telling you they're coming after you, a lot of things change," he explained.

"White boy." Patrick Herron, a 21-year-old senior from Malvern, Pa., was among a small number of white supporters of the black cultural center who took part in the march on the chancellor's home. As the demonstrators joined hands, the black woman next to Herron turned and said: "I refuse to hold your hand, white boy." Herron was upset, but said "you have to realize [that given] the history of race relations in this country . . . she's entirely rational to distrust me." Besides, other blacks made it clear that she did not speak for them.

Like Herron, some in the focus group argued that whites need to make a greater effort to understand the anger of black classmates. Jim Copland, a 20-year-old junior from Burlington, N.C., who is the elected president of the student body, said that blacks "feel as if they're not given the same respect, and to a large extent that feeling is justified." Copland, former editor of a conservative campus magazine, has become sympathetic to black activists. They have to use tough tactics, he argued, to get whites to pay attention. For example, said Copland, "for year after year, there has been an effort on the part of leaders pushing for a free-standing black cultural center to communicate in a civil forum with the administration. And year after year, they have been unsuccessful." Only when they turned up the heat, he said, did the administration respond.

But for some, the tactics used by the campus demonstrators were a turn-off. "If you can't go through proper channels like I have to do every day, then I can't be supportive," said Lee Hark. Backers of the center counter that focusing on the tactics misses the point. "It's kind of scary that what determines support for or against the center is the actions of those trying to achieve it," said Valerie Halman, a 20-year-old senior from Montreal.

No bonds. Many of the students think the animosity between the races is exacerbated by their relative isolation. Most blacks choose to live on the south campus, instead of the more convenient north campus, because that is where they have a feeling of community. "If you do not live with people of other races, then you don't form friendships and bonds," said Julie Davis, a 21-year-old junior from Atlanta. Lili Stern, a 19-year-old sophomore from Oriental, N.C., proves the point: She has made a number of black friends because she lives on the south campus. "If you want to learn about black culture, then the south campus is where you have to be," she says. Still, there are real cultural gaps. White students, the group agreed, tend to center social activities on alcohol, while blacks make music the center.

Many of the students believe that blacks who try crossing racial lines to socialize are pressured to back off. Culley Carson, a 21-year-old junior from Durham, N.C., said that a friend who has a white and a black parent was told by blacks: "You're gray. What are you doing over there at that white fraternity?" Said Carson:" "It was basically people saying we

don't care what your background is, this is what we want you to do.' "

Jill Jacobs, 22, a senior from Goldsboro, N.C., said "freshman African-American students feel a lot of pressure initially to be black. . . . I'm not suggesting that there is anything wrong in identifying with your culture and finding that there are other people who feel the same way that you do, but there is something wrong in saying 'you're here, we're going to take care of you and you can separate yourself from all that other stuff.' "

Then there is dating. "Most of the couples that are interracial are not out in the open about it," said Stern, "because they are just so afraid." Black male friends have told Stern that "if they were ever to date a white female, they would just be closed off from the black female population of the school."

Athletes seem to be the only ones who can comfortably defy campus mores. Hark said his often intolerant fraternity brothers view it as "cool" when a black basketball player has a white girlfriend. "I guess it's just pointing to a double standard."

Many whites deeply resent what they see as a double standard in admissions. Jim Copland told of a white high-school classmate whose admission to Chapel Hill was denied and another whose entry was deferred, while a black with weaker credentials was admitted. "A lot of friends from my hometown know the people who've gotten in and the people who haven't, and it's a big issue with them," said Copland. About 68 percent of black applicants are admitted, compared with a 60 percent admission rate for in-state students and a 12 percent rate for out-of-staters. "I definitely think there's a feeling that the affirmative-action system admits people who are not qualified," said Julie Davis.

Yet, despite all the tension, students in the group are surprisingly optimistic. Valerie Halman sees the campus turning the corner very soon. She anticipates "a surge in education, awareness and communication between groups" arising from the debate over the black cultural center. "And that," said Halman, "is really going to make the difference."

BLACK AND WHITE TOGETHER
"What do you want us to do?"

When the two groups of students came together on the third night, it was quickly

evident that the gulf of mistrust and misunderstanding between blacks and whites was wide indeed. Its vastness was dramatically demonstrated by several intense exchanges.

Many whites, for example, were angered when Philip Charles-Pierre said he was not "too convinced that those who are white and liberal, who think that they are so open, are truly very open." Too many liberals, he said, suffer from a "messiah complex," believing that they are the only ones who can save blacks—a view he deemed "subconsciously racist." In a retort filled with anger, Lee Hark said: "Philip, that infuriates me when you say stuff like that." His anger was scarcely acknowledged.

Eighty-eight percent of the newspaper editors at all schools believe that it is possible to improve the racial climate on college campuses.

Many of the black students, most of whom would not be considered militants by Chapel Hill standards, said they wished they could be blind to color differences but that the reality of race always intrudes. Vikki Mercer told the joint group: "I start from the fact that my great-grandfather used to be a slave. Then I try to put that out of my mind. For a while, that works really well. Then I turn on the television and see there was a Ku Klux Klan march in town. That takes me right back."

History's legacy. For Philip McAdoo, the best efforts of well-meaning whites cannot heal the wounds of racism. "Because of what's happened in the past, there's always going to be white people who consider black people 'niggers' and there'll be black people who are going to hate white people," he said. "Do you understand that? That's not going to go away."

Why then, Trey Ezzell wondered, "are you trying to educate white people if, realistically, it's just never going to work?" If it doesn't - work, replied McAdoo, it would not be for lack of effort on his part. But, he explained, "I can be Mr. UNC or Mr. Whatever and still walk around the street and get called 'nigger.' '' Such experiences, he said, make him wonder "what's the purpose of my accomplishments?"

"Do the rest of the black students have that same fatalistic viewpoint?" Lee Hark interjected, and Jill Jacobs then asked plaintively: "What do you want us to do?"

Jasme Kelly tried to make the whites understand the depth of her racial hurt. She explained that when she becomes friends with whites they unfailingly ask her to come onto their turf but are unwilling to come onto hers. "Why don't you come to church with me? Why don't you come to my grandma's house?" she asked of no on in particular. Adding to her frustration is a fact of campus life she confronts when visiting predominantly white sororities. "Every house I've ever been to, the cook and the housekeeper have been black," said Kelly. "That's too 'Gone With the Wind' for me."

When the conversation turned to the success of a rally in support of the black cultural center held earlier that day, the racial rift manifested itself again. Ezzell, among the most conservative whites in the group, noted that the rally began with "hip-hop" music. He compared the event with an earlier silent protest that "just seemed much more intelligent than a rally where people are rapping."

This provoked Philip McAdoo: "It was so obvious to me when you said there should have been a more intelligent way that you just totally degrade this part of black culture and call it nonintelligent because it's not part of white culture. . . . And you can't tell me that's not what you meant. I don't think it's the responsibility of black people to step outside of who we are when you're not willing to step outside of who you are."

But Lee Hark didn't see it that way: "The theme that I've gotten from the get-go of all the rallying and marching is, 'We're going to do our black thing, and if you don't understand it—and if you can't be with it—then screw you.' " That's how "the vast majority of white students on this campus feel," added Julie Davis.

"You say to them, 'You're white and you don't understand.' "

To be sure, not all the blacks in the group are as frustrated as McAdoo, nor all the whites as frustrated as Davis and Hark. Yet it is these exchanges that reveal the real chasm between the races on the Chapel Hill campus—and in much of the world beyond. They illustrate, in ways that rallies, slogans and speeches simply cannot, just how much race has transformed student life at Chapel Hill. They show the magnitude of the challenge facing not only that campus but higher education as a whole. Unfortunately, for all the progress of the past decades, race relations today still remain what they have been for generations: an American dilemma.

By Alvin P. Sanoff and Scott Minerbrook with Jeannye Thornton and Elizabeth Pezzullo in Chapel Hill

DIVERSITY: A PROGRESSIVE APPROACH

Organizational programs to celebrate racial and ethnic diversity hold great promise for promoting respect for human dignity, values of tolerance, and appreciation of difference.

John I. Gilderbloom and Dennis C. Golden

John I. Gilderbloom is an Associate Professor of Urban Policy at the University of Louisville, Louisville, Kentucky. Dennis C. Golden is Vice President for Student Affairs at the University of Louisville, Louisville, Kentucky.

D iversity programs to fight racism and bigotry have generated a great deal of controversy. Detractors of diversity programs claim they cause "a simmering backlog of resentment"[1] and "division,"[2] while producing "fraudulent"[3] and "ugly"[4] results. The University of Louisville's experience with organizing a large-scale, campus-wide diversity program offers no lessons that support these inflammatory charges. While certain diversity programs have emphasized a separatist and hostile theme which has polarized groups, the University of Louisville's Celebration of Diversity emphasized the themes of integration as opposed to segregation, tolerance as opposed to intolerance, heterogeneity as opposed to homogeneity, and inclusiveness rather than exclusiveness.

Diversity is ... one of the most neglected elements of our democracy.

Universities can play a major role in molding community consciousness and influencing a generation of young adults by sponsoring Celebration of Diversity programs. The success of the University of Louisville's diversity program serves as a model that others should emulate.

DIVERSITY: A PROGRESSIVE APPROACH

Diversity is one of the most important aspects of the development of citizenship, and yet it is often one of the most neglected elements of our democracy. It is important to develop informed, accepting and tolerant people. If we do not meet this challenge, we will fail as a nation. Valuing diversity means recognizing that individuals need to be accepted, understood, valued, nurtured, cherished, and well utilized. Ernest Boyer argues that we must strive to create a purposeful community, an open community, a just community, a disciplined community, a caring community, and finally, a celebrative community.[5] Boyer's thoughts served as the cornerstone of the University of Louisville's first annual Celebration of Diversity.

BACKGROUND[6]

The University of Louisville is considered the oldest municipal college in the United States; its origins date back to 1778. Up until 1970, U of L was a private, city-funded institution. Because of budget constraints, the University of Louisville merged formally into the state system in 1970 and was assigned an "urban mission." At this time the university's enrollment totalled less than 10,000 students and had fewer than 200 African-

American students. The University of Louisville has a statewide admission mandate that provides for the admission of any student who graduated from an accredited high school in Kentucky. The tuition rate was also lowered to make college more accessible to minorities.

Within ten years of its merger with the state university system, the University of Louisville's enrollment had increased from 10,000 to 20,000 students. Meanwhile, African-American student enrollment had skyrocketed from 200 students in 1970 to 2,000 students by 1980. This increase in African-American students was not matched by an increase in minority faculty. The percentage of African-American faculty remained unchanged from 1978 to 1980.

In 1989, a radical incident occurred that galvanized the university campus into combatting racism.

In 1980, the university experienced a change in leadership. Dr. Donald Swain from the University of California system was hired as president, and brought a progressive perspective and vision. He embarked upon a strategic planning course to help meet the Kentucky Council of Higher Education's mandate to carry out an "urban mission." President Swain charged every academic and administrative unit with the responsibility to develop individual unit-level plans to address urban issues. A Ph.D. program in urban and public affairs was initiated which is now ranked among the nation's top ten programs.

In 1989, a radical incident occurred that galvanized the university campus into combatting racism. A young female African-American student came forward and alleged she was called a "nigger" by a white fraternity member. The university community was outraged. African-American students presented a list of demands to the president.[7] The University of Louisville was committed to a proactive strategy in dealing with racial friction between whites and blacks. Dr. Swain appointed a committee to take the lead role in planning a "Celebration of Diversity" to heal the racial animosity and division on campus.

LEADERSHIP

The Celebration was planned and implemented by a combined student, faculty and administrative committee in accordance with the university president's charge. The effort was coordinated under the leadership of the vice president for student affairs, who chaired the committee, and the director of minority

services, who served as vice chair. The initial committee of nine members was expanded to 17 because of the tremendous amount of work involved in planning, coordinating and implementing the complex details of a program of this breadth and consequence.

The hand-picked committee consisted of members with a demonstrated record of concern for minority needs and ability to organize events. Specific tasks included contacting speakers, negotiating contracts, organizing logistics, scheduling, informing the media, conducting outreach, and writing and publishing program brochures. Task force members were encouraged to "think big." The committee chair required strong consensus-building skills. Committee members needed commitment to openness, inclusivity and genuine progress.

PROGRAM DESCRIPTION

For ten days in the early fall of 1990, the University of Louisville campus went into a whirlwind of activity focusing on diversity issues. The Celebration of Diversity program fused over 35 separate events into a coordinated exploration of important racial issues and concerns. The purpose of the event was to promote human dignity, tolerance and appreciation of humankind.

Events included more than 20 lectures and workshops, forums, films, discussions, entertainment events, and social programs designed to meet the university president's goal to "increase awareness and appreciation of the different races and ethnic groups represented on the university campus." The speakers included some of the nation's leading spokespersons, including Derrick Bell, Jr., Dr. Harry Edwards, Jaime Escalante, Dr. Jacqueline Fleming, Dr. Edward J. Nichols, Michael Woo, and Giancarlo Esposito.[8]

For ten days ... the university ... campus went into a whirlwind of activity focusing on diversity issues.

Topics discussed by speakers ranged from entertainment, gender, hiring practices, and professional athletics to politics and education. These issues generated much discussion among the participants both during and after the lectures.

In addition to a major lecture series, workshops offered an opportunity for discussion of issues relating to race and cultural diversity. Discussion participants ranged from College Republicans to black Muslims. The films presented were portrayals of minority life which were designed to sensitize individuals on racial and cultural issues. Among the movies shown were *Do the Right Thing, Leadbelly, My Left Foot, El Norte,* and *Stand and Deliver.* Social events included a football half-time show that recognized the theme of diversity, an ethnic heritage festival, performance of the Black Diamond Gospel Choir, an Interfaith Celebration, and Jamaican Reggae dances.

SYMBOL AND COVENANT

In order to establish and maintain a unified focus, a symbol defining diversity was needed. The symbol used at the University of Louisville was the Covenant of Justice, Equity and Harmony, which originated with the Council of Churches in Boston, Massachusetts in the late 1970s at a time of enormous racial tension and strife. The graphic incorporates the olive branch, representing peace and harmony; a red background, representing the blood relationship that exists between and among all people; a green branch, symbolizing hope and the common dignity shared among all human beings; and colored leaves, corresponding to the major races of people.

In order to establish and maintain a unified focus, a symbol defining diversity was needed.

The university's student government association and student senate purchased thousands of T-shirts bearing the inscription "Celebrate Diversity" and the multicultural logo described above. Huge banners with the symbol were placed on the academic building and in front of the new student activities center. The covenant symbol was also printed on book markers which were distributed throughout the University of Louisville campus. In addition, thousands of covenant buttons were given out and people proudly wore them around campus, and are still doing so many months after the actual Celebration. The goal was to establish a diversity symbol, adopt it, maintain momentum, and proudly display the symbol as a statement of unity and an ethic of care and concern.

When the University of Louisville football team played in the 1991 Fiesta Bowl, the diversity symbol was proudly worn by the coach, the players, the band, the cheerleaders, and thousands of fans at Sun Devil Stadium in Tempe, Arizona. The statement of commitment to diversity and its celebration, in conjunction with honoring the legacy of Dr. Martin Luther King, Jr., was seen by millions of people watching football on New Year's Day, 1991. As the theme so proudly proclaimed, "The Dream Lives On," the symbol allowed the participants to identify who we were and what we were about. That symbol carries a message of bonding, friendship and affiliation.

IMPACT OF DIVERSITY PROGRAMS

Does a celebration of diversity make a difference? Who goes to these programs and why? How do people react to programs such as the University of Louisville's Celebration of Diversity? How are people impacted? These are important questions that deserve answers.

Nine major lectures were selected and phone numbers were gathered from participants who attended the program. A questionnaire, which included a mixture of open-ended and forced-choice items, was administered to 220 randomly selected Celebration of Diversity participants. The response rate was a respectable 70 percent, which is considered excellent for survey research.

Counting attendance at each event, a total of 3,500 people participated. Who attended the events held in association with this program? Roughly 63 percent of the people in attendance were white. Thirty-two percent were African-Americans. Sixty percent were women. Breaking down participants by status, 50 percent were students, 15 percent were faculty, 30 percent were staff, and ten percent came from the surrounding community. People who attended these events were liberal: only one out of eight voted for George Bush in 1988. Approximately 50 percent of the participants were involved in 1960s-era protest movements (e.g., civil rights, antiwar, etc.), women's issues, and disabled and tenants'-rights issues. One out of every two attended religious services regularly.

When asked whether they had experienced racism in the past year at the University of Louisville, 31 percent of the blacks and 13 percent of whites felt that they had experienced some sort of racism or bigotry. Examples of racism on campus were typically graffiti in restrooms, a professor using the word "Negro" in the classroom, or an African-American basketball player being described as a "natural-born athlete" or a "real thoroughbred." Perceptions of racism cover a broad continuum of different actions and thoughts. One out of every two participants had experienced racism in the community during the past year. Our survey of participants found very little difference between how blacks and whites felt about integration. "How do you feel about living in the same neighborhood with a person of another race?" One hundred percent said no problem at all. "Living next door to someone of another race?" Again, no difference between blacks and whites. "Working with someone of another race?" One hundred percent said no problem. "Sharing a friendship with someone of another race." One hundred percent said fine. In other words, no fundamental differences were identified. "Inviting a person of another race to your home?" Ninety-nine percent reported no problem.

Some disagreement arose with the question of dating or marrying someone of another race; 76 percent of whites and 75 percent of blacks approved inter-racial dating and/or marrying.

One out of every two participants had experienced racism in the community during the past year.

The Celebration of Diversity was widely perceived as a timely, educational and relevant program. Participants felt it was a positive step on the part of the university administration toward creating greater understanding and acceptance of the diverse populations comprised by the university community. Our survey revealed the following:

- "Helps increase awareness of diversity"–95 percent agreed
- "Helps increase understanding of people of other cultures"–67 percent agreed
- "Is educational"–96 percent agreed
- "Speakers were prepared, knowledgeable and enthusiastic"–95 percent agreed
- "Relevant to society"–96 percent agreed
- "Relevant to the respondent"–92 percent agreed
- "Is timely"–96 percent agreed
- "Will improve racial harmony"–61 percent agreed
- "Promoted positive change in the respondent"–69 percent agreed
- "Offended by the program"–five percent agreed
- "Program was a waste of time"–four percent agreed

There was no major difference between blacks and whites on these items.

The central message of the Celebration of Diversity program was characterized by interviewees as follows: "Everyone needs to make an effort to know and understand each other." "Differences are something to celebrate ... they are positive and not negative!" "The university is willing to deal with issues of race ... and will deal with them now before they become a problem." "We should respect other ethnic groups because everyone is different and everyone has something to contribute." "We need to get out and learn about other people and other ways of life." "We should evaluate people by what is on the inside and not on the outside." And finally, "The university is committed to offering an environment that recognizes and honors difference."

For a faculty member, the program "increased my fervor to help my students be more open and more tolerant." For another it provided "concrete ideas for restructuring courses and curriculum. I was ready to make changes ... now I have the information." A student remarked that the program caused him to "re-evaluate myself and become more conscious of racial prejudices I have." And perhaps most to the point, "I will be more understanding of different cultures. I won't label people."

Interviewee after interviewee expressed praise and appreciation to the university for taking "a lead in the community by addressing issues of diversity" and "taking steps to make a change." While there was skepticism expressed by some–"I think this is a passing phase, one week, a lot of noise, and then it will pass"– others were looking to the future: "This is not an answer, only the beginning. This is the frosting but the cake is yet to be baked."

The Celebration of Diversity program has fundamentally changed the University of Louisville.

Fifty-four percent of the participants in the program felt that their behavior and attitudes had been changed as a result of the Celebration of Diversity program. That percentage is impressive. One out of every two participants–1,750 people–claimed that they had been changed by a progressive program calling for integration, tolerance and understanding, not hate or separatism. Diversity leaders are seen as hateful. The University of Louisville program contradicts the conventional media view of diversity programs as being hateful, separatist, and sometimes violent.

OUTCOMES

The Celebration of Diversity program has fundamentally changed the University of Louisville. The faculty, students, administrators, and staff are more sensitive to and concerned about racial issues. While we are able to demonstrate empirically that greater sensitivity to minority needs has been realized, other positive outcomes can be attributed to the Celebration of Diversity program:

- Greater scholarship aid to minorities;
- A mandate for annual Celebration of Diversity programs;
- Administrative expectations to address diversity issues in the academic curriculum;
- More aggressive hiring of minority faculty and staff;
- The director of the Office of Minority Services has more help in dealing with all student populations with particular emphasis on African-American students;
- The university-wide enrollment-management plan will be strengthened, both in recruiting and retention efforts, for all needy and under-privileged students;

- The athletic department has enhanced its involvement in the academic performance of student athletes;
- The concept of a "campus community"–particularly for students–both inside and outside class, is becoming more of a reality;
- The essence of racism, both direct and indirect, is being challenged frequently and effectively;
- The 1991 Fiesta Bowl team displayed the diversity symbol to millions of television viewers as they honored the memory of Dr. Martin Luther King, Jr.;
- There will be ongoing research to analyze and foster diversity programs in a timely and helpful fashion;
- A multi-cultural center was established; and
- Hundreds of college administrators and community groups from around the country have received presentations on the University of Louisville program.

UNRESOLVED ISSUE: INCORPORATION OF DIVERSITY INTO THE CURRICULUM

In the fall of 1991, the university provost led an initiative to encourage diversity in the curriculum.[9] While most agree that it is important, differences exist concerning content. Some faculty members committed to diversity in the curriculum argue that academics should only be party to truth and not worry that facts might be upsetting to students. Others believe that diversity in the curriculum means material is uplifting and encourages minorities to feel better about themselves.

The Athletic Department has enhanced its involvement in the academic performance of student athletes...

It seems absurd to mandate that a race or culture be portrayed only in positive or uplifting ways. Academics describe these kinds of depictions as biased instead of objective. Does someone of German background feel awkward, embarrassed or depressed when Hitler and Nazism are discussed in History classes? Do white Americans take offense when southern slavery is taught? Perhaps, but no one is calling for these topics to be removed from the curriculum because some people might feel ill at ease. Truth over sensitivity must prevail in any university classroom. After all, research that reflects negatively on a particular minority is also subject to challenge. As writer-activist Randy Shilts notes, "There is a fundamental fallacy in preaching diversity but rejecting the most important form of diversity of all, which is diversity of thought."[10]

Participants in the Celebration of Diversity program are nearly unanimous on the need for greater diversity in the curriculum. Ninety-five percent agreed with the statement "minority perspectives should be included in appropriate courses," and 94 percent agreed that professors should provide competing perspectives. A proportionate number felt that we must be tolerant of competing perspectives. As one white male faculty member expressed it: Faculty members need to explore and examine the issues of race and gender in the classroom. However, we must also have tolerance for perspectives that challenge the liberal agenda. A student is not racist if he or she opposes affirmative action or sexist if he or she opposes abortion.

Participants in the Celebration of Diversity Program are nearly unanimous on the need for greater diversity in the curriculum.

One out of every five participants felt that research reflecting negatively on minorities should be prohibited from the classroom. A white male professor explained: "The issue of 'research' reflecting negatively on minorities is loaded because much so-called 'research' is tendentious, false, sometimes falsified, and not subject to independent verification or questioning. For example, Holocaust studies appearing in the journal of the neo-Nazi Institute of Revision, when represented as research, would violate norms of responsibility attaching to academic freedom."

A white faculty member summed up the prevailing attitude when he said, "The university leadership needs to send a signal that diversity must be part of the curriculum, but only when we tolerate competing viewpoints: Truth is more important than sensitivity to minority groups."

RECOMMENDATIONS

Kentucky's largest newspaper, *The Courier-Journal,* declared in an editorial, "U of L aimed to get racial concerns on the table with a celebration of diversity. The Celebration of Diversity is only a beginning in the minds of many respondents. As one member of the university community stated, 'It's not enough to say that we're going to have a week-long celebration—we must continue to explore and work toward respect for one another.'"

Indeed, this Celebration of Diversity can be a basis for future programs which are richer, deeper and even more inclusive. Important considerations for future programming should include the following:

■ Diversity programs should not be narrowly defined as attempting only to ameliorate racism directed against African-Americans. The theme of diversity should embrace the broad range of race and ethnicity (African-American, Hispanic, Asian, Arabic, etc.), religion, sexual orientation, disability, age, and gender. Non–African-American minorities and whites should participate as speakers and panelists. Issues common to all these groups are the need to fight harmful stereotyping and demonstrate the significant array of contributions they have made to American society and culture. The theme of diversity is humanistic in tone, imploring society not to judge by physical characteristics, but to view all community members as individuals with unlimited possibilities.

Diversity programs should not be narrowly defined as attempting only to ameliorate racism directed against African-Americans.

■ Invited speakers must have "cutting edge" credentials, particularly in the eyes of university faculty and students. When faculty supported or required student attendance at events, the auditoriums would be filled; when this did not occur the rooms would sometimes be virtually empty. An effective way to marshall faculty and student support is to seek their input in the selection of speakers and involve them in event planning.

■ A result of elective as opposed to mandatory participation (less than 20 percent of the survey respondents indicated attendance due to requirement) was a liberally oriented audience. Of those who attended the program, only 17 percent voted for President George Bush while 51 percent voted for Dukakis. Over half of the attendees participated in protest movements for civil rights, empowerment of women, and anti-war activity. This could indicate that the program was "preaching more to the choir" and perhaps not reaching those most in need of the message. Administrators should consider mandating attendance or exploring other methods of achieving a more representative pattern of attendance at such events.

■ Diversity programs should be opened to include a variety of perspectives and stimulate lively debate. Most of the University of Louisville's Celebration of Diversity had a 1960s-era liberal perspective. This might have alienated conservative students from the program. Diversity programs also should recognize the steady rise in conservatism among minorities,[11] and include minority conservative speakers in the program.

CONCLUSION

During the ten-day Celebration, students, faculty, staff, guests, presenters, alumni, and community leaders shared heart-felt concerns with disarming candor. There was silence, there were smiles, and indeed there were sparks. Clearly, acknowledging, accepting, respecting, enhancing, and eventually celebrating diversity is a difficult, demanding and at times agonizing business. The Celebration of Diversity at the University of Louisville went from a typical business-as-usual opening of the academic year to a whirlwind of activity focusing on issues of diversity and multiculturalism. The Celebration of Diversity fused over 35 separate events into a coordinated exploration of important cultural and racial values and traditions. The purpose of the program was the promotion of human dignity, tolerance and appreciation of diversity. The events were designed to meet the university president's goal of "increasing awareness and appreciation for the different races and ethnic groups represented on the university campus."

The purpose of the program was the promotion of human dignity, tolerance and appreciation of diversity.

We are encouraged by the Celebration of Diversity's ability to address the following: 1) the undergraduate curriculum; 2) the president's incentives to meet the mandate of an urban mission; 3) undergraduate and graduate minority student recruitment, admission, financial aid, and retention; 4) student life; and 5) staff recruitment, hiring and development. Further, we are pleased that university leaders are now stating vigorously to students the importance of concepts such as diversity, pluralism and appreciation of difference. Incoming students now hear these themes articulated during the freshman orientation and at regular intervals throughout their undergraduate careers. The Celebration of Diversity program is a credible vehicle for the deeper understanding of the basic value of respect for our fellow human beings.

NOTES

1. S. Goode, "Efforts to Deal with Diversity Can Go Astray," *Insight,* 10 September 1990, pp. 15–19.
2. W. West, "Out of Many Comes Division," *Insight,* 17 December 1990, p. 64.
3. B. Timmons, "Fraudulent 'Diversity,'" *Newsweek,* 12 November 1990, p. 8.
4. A. Sullivan, "Racism 101," *New Republic,* Vol. 22 (1990), pp. 18–21.

5. E. L. Boyer, *College: The Undergraduate Experience in America* (New York: Harper & Row, 1987).

6. The authors thank Ralph Fitzpatrick for providing the history of the University of Louisville. Additional thanks are extended for the contributions of Phyllis Webb, Linda Wilson, Denise Fitzpatrick, Adam Matheny, Patricia Gilderbloom, and Jim Van Fleet. Special assistance and funding for this project was contributed by Dr. Donald C. Swain, President of the University of Louisville. Additionally, Ralph Fitzpatrick, director of the Office of Minority Services of the University of Louisville, is recognized for his leadership, cooperation and support.

The following graduate students participated in the research study of the University of Louisville's Celebration of Diversity program, and prepared preliminary reports of the findings: William P. Friedlander, Gary Dennis, Mary Henderson, Gracie Wishnia, Greg Bucholtz, Samantha Israel, David A. Collins, Mike Burayidi, Sheila Thompson, Pat Bailey, Dennis J. Golden, David W. Parrott, Karen King, Manuel McMillan, Mark Buchter, Stephen L. Wagner, and Frances Campeau (see Gilderbloom, et al., below).

7. The demands submitted to the university president by the Black Student Alliance are as follows:

1. The campus housing office is to begin the development of a plan to end the segregation of the Panhellenic dormitory immediately, and complete the plan by Thursday, November 16, 1989.

2. The campus housing office is to increase the number of resident assistants to a level directly proportional to the number of black students living in campus housing.

3. The campus housing office is to reimburse Ms. Dawn Ones [the racially slighted student] for her dormitory fees and inconvenience during the incident of racial bias.

4. The University of Louisville is to develop a facility for black students, similar to the Martin Luther King Cultural Center at the University of Kentucky.

5. The university must end its plans to separate upperclassmen from lowerclassmen in housing; the plan is genocide for the younger black students on campus, acting as a role model drain for black students.

6. The university must change the name of the Confederate Apartments and the campus street where it is located, Confederate Place, to the name of a black leader.

7. The university must develop a race consciousness course and require all resident assistants to attend it. If the course is not developed, resident assistants should be required to take a minimum of six credit hours of instruction in black history.

8. The university must adopt a policy of automatic expulsion of anyone who is convicted of racist intimidation or harassment. This includes defamation of private or school property characterized by racial slurs and/or repeated verbal abuse by a person or persons on the university campus directed at specific persons of another race which causes emotional duress. Emotional duress is defined as the need for a victim to report specific victimizers directly to resident directors, the university administration or concerned student organizations. Such reports of victimization would become written public information.

8. **Derrick Bell, Jr.,** is among the nation's leading experts in civil rights law and a former Professor of Law at the Harvard University School of Law. His demands for more tenured African-American and female law professors at Harvard University School of Law led to recent front-page news stories around the nation. **Dr. Harry Edwards** is a prominent sociologist at the University of California at Berkeley, as well as a leading social critic, author and activist. At the forefront of the movement to increase black participation in coaching, management and ownership of professional sports teams, he is a special advisor to the commissioner of major league baseball. **Jaime Escalante** is the East Los Angeles barrio calculus teacher immortalized in the recent motion picture *Stand and Deliver*. Escalante's minority students rank near the top in the nation in mathematics test scores. **Dr. Jacqueline Fleming** is an expert on how personality sparks individual motivation differences and an instructor of undergraduate courses on the psychology of racism and human motivation at Barnard College. She also serves on the Advisory Committee of the United Negro College Fund. **Dr. Edwin J. Nichols** is a psychologist recently retired from the National Institute of Mental Health where he held various positions, including Section Chief for Special Populations and Chief of the Center for Studies of Child and Family Mental Health. **Michael Woo** is the first Asian-American to serve on the Los Angeles City Council, representing an unusually diverse constituency of 198,000 people who speak 54 separate languages and dialects. A leader in ethics reform, he is widely considered a strong prospective candidate to replace outgoing Los Angeles Mayor Tom Bradley. **Giancarlo Esposito** is an actor and screenwriter best known for his recent role as "Buggin' Out" in Spike Lee's film *Do the Right Thing*. He is a winner of the OBIE and Theater World Awards.

9. This section is adapted from a recently completed report on the University of Louisville's Second Annual Diversity Celebration program (J. Gilderbloom with W. Friedlander, *Building Diversity in the Curriculum: Charting the Course* [Louisville, Ky.: Office of the Provost, University of Louisville, 1992]).

10. J. Gross, "Gay Journalists Gather to Complain and Celebrate Progress at Work," *The New York Times,* 29 June 1992, p. A7.

11. "A Bowlful of Opportunity," *The Louisville Courier-Journal,* 30 December 1990, p. D2.

OTHER SOURCES

Chafetz, J., "Hispanics in the United States," *New Republic,* Fall 1990, pp. 15–18.

DePree, M. *Leadership is an Art* (New York, Dell, 1989).

Gilderbloom, J. et al. *Attitudes and Reactions to the University of Louisville's Celebration of Diversity Program* (Louisville, Ky.: University of Louisville School of Urban Policy, unpublished report, 1990).

Green, M. F. *Minorities on Campus: A Handbook for Enhancing Diversity* (Washington, D.C.: American Council on Education, 1989).

Steele, S., "White Guilt," *American Scholar,* Autumn 1990, pp. 487–507.

Blood and irony

How race and religion will shape the future

Henry Louis Gates

Henry Louis Gates is head of the department of Afro-American studies at Harvard.

WE LIVE in confusing times. Communism, we now know, was the opiate of the nationalities. As its stuporous influence wore off, assertive and sometimes clashing national aspirations swept from the Baltic states to the Transcaucasus. Separatist movements have left the former Yugoslavia a bloody jigsaw: what communism had joined, nationalism has been all too eager to put asunder.

In the industrialised West, though, things look very different. In fact, never in this century has the western project of supranational unification seemed closer to realisation. The long-deferred idea of genuine European community appears, fitfully, to be acquiring an aura of inevitability. Meanwhile, the countries of North America have been hammering out a free-trade compact. Isn't economic integration supposed to be the handmaiden of political integration?

Today, in short, both the forces of fragmentation and the forces of consolidation are abundantly on display. Just which side is history on, anyway?

I am not so sure. The forces of supranational community have merely economic reason on their side; ranged against them are heart and home, *Blut und Boden*—all those sticky, uncouth, thoroughly pre-modern attachments that liberal rationalists find so irksome. In 1796 that illustrious French reactionary, Joseph de Maistre, scornfully dismissed a central enlightenment creed when he avowed: "in the course of my life I have seen Frenchmen, Italians, Russians; I even know, thanks to Montesquieu, that one can be a Persian; but *man* I have never met." In de Maistre's hard sense, there are no men in Bosnia. Are the rest of us really so much more enlightened? The secular creed of the technocrats and planners may yet founder on the home-style politics of identity.

More than 100 new nations have come into existence in the past 50 years, and yet the proliferation of new national identities may prove less important, in the long run, than the transformation of old ones. To be sure, the phenomenon sometimes known as the "browning" of the West is not without its own ironies. For while the West worries about being inundated by migrants from the third world, many in the third world continue to worry about the westernisation of the globe.

Still, even as the economic apparatus of Euro-unification is being assembled, the countenance of Europe itself is changing in unprecedented ways. In present-day Western Europe, there are perhaps 10m legal immigrants from the third world; the number of illegals can only be guessed at. Hundreds of thousands of asylum-seekers from Eastern Europe have joined them. The human tide now moves not just from south to north, but from east to west. Indeed, some argue that the past few years have witnessed the largest peacetime movement of peoples in Europe since the Middle Ages.

The short-term consequences, at least, are plain to see. West European states, France and Germany in particular, are buffeted between the pressures of the demographic influx on the one hand and of native reaction on the other. The force of neither can be gainsaid. The resurgence of the racist right in Germany has been a matter of widespread attention and concern—but Germany, (which has had, in some respects, a singularly generous policy of asylum) has no unique claim to it. "By the year 2000," roared Jean-Marie Le Pen of the French far-right National Front this spring, "the majority of the population of Paris will be foreign!"

In 1992 he got a robust 14% of the vote in regional elections. Judging from electoral returns this past March, his support seems to be ebbing. But that is because his tough line on immigration has, in no small measure, been absorbed by more mainstream parties. Meanwhile, in Belgium's national elections last year, the Vlaams Blok party called for the outright expulsion of all of the country's 400,000 immigrants and was rewarded with a fairly robust 10.7% of the vote.

And what of America? "We are not a nation," Herman Melville avowed of his country a century ago, "so much as a world." Never has his description seemed more apt. In the 1980s 8.6m people emigrated to the United States, more than in any decade since the first decade of the century. According to one estimate, by 2020 the number of non-white or Hispanic inhabitants of America will have doubled, while the white

Melville's world
Immigrants entering the United States, by country of origin, %

1992 total: 973,977

Other 0.4
Other America 11.6
Caribbean 10.0
Mexico 22.0
Canada 1.6
Africa 2.8
Asia 36.7
Europe 14.9

Source: Immigration and Naturalisation Service

population will remain essentially unchanged. By 2050 the percentage of Asian-Americans will have quintupled, with the total reaching 40m. Already in New York state, 40% of school children are classified as ethnic "minorities." Already in Los Angeles, the most popular radio station is a Spanish-language one. And within just a decade or so, Muslims will be more numerous in America than Presbyterians or Jews.

But then America is fairly backward in this respect. For historical reasons, the Muslim presence in the former colonial powers of France and England has long been much more pronounced. And indeed, it is the Muslim factor, first and foremost, that arrests the attention of many Europeans. For them, transfixed by the ancient rivalry between Musselman and Christian, Europe's very identity hangs in the balance.

The anxiety is nothing very new. Surely such a Manichean vision infused the peculiar prophecy that Ernest Renan, France's pre-eminent theorist of nationalism, offered in the fateful year of 1848. "Since the Aryan race and the Semitic race . . . are destined to conquer the world and restore unity to the human species," he wrote, "the rest of the world counts, alongside these races, only as experiments, obstacles, or auxiliaries."

Almost a century and a half later, Patrick Buchanan, a leading spokesman for American nativism, made a similar prediction in characteristically apocalyptic tones. "For a millennium, the struggle for mankind's destiny was between Christianity and Islam; in the 21st century, it may be so again. For, as the Shiites humiliate us, their co-religionists are filling up the countries of the West."

The old story, with new twists

And so the question naturally arises: will these concerns be unabated 150 years hence? Will the nativists' direst prophecies be

fulfilled? At this point, it might be worth distinguishing between two, not wholly consistent, sources of concern.

First, there is the charge that these immigrants cannot be truly integrated into western societies, so inimical are their mores and collective allegiances. They are happy to take the services and benefits of their prosperous host countries, we are warned, but fail to extend their loyalties to them. As Mark Almond, an Oxford historian, expresses the apprehension: "It is one thing to deal with immigrants, even great masses of them, who see the new host society as admirable and the place of their future prosperity, as scores of millions of new arrivals over the last 200 years have viewed the United States; it is quite another to come to terms with newcomers who reject many of the basic tenets of the society into which they are entering."

It will not do to dismiss these concerns out of hand, but it would be mistaken, I think, to make too much of them. A tug of allegiances? Of course—but this is hardly anything new in the manufacture of the modern nation. Gascon or French? Welsh or British? Catalan or Spanish? The answer has not always been obvious; for some, it still isn't.

Then, too, the terms of argument about the "Muslim factor" are reminiscent of the language in which the "Jewish question" was debated in England a century and a half ago. Thomas Babington Macaulay's swingeing 1831 essay, "On the Civil Disabilities of the Jew," can be read today with a sense of *déjà vu*: "It has always been the trick of bigots to make their subjects miserable at home, and then to complain that they look for relief abroad; to divide society, and to wonder that it is not united; to govern as if a section of the state were the whole, and to censure the other sections of the state for their want of patriotism."

One thing to remember: most of those third-world Muslims who are in the West chose to be there. Intruders in our midst? The 1989 Gulf war provided a test whose results should not be lost on us. It was a time when French officials surveyed their large Arabic population, with so many unemployed youths, and worried about violent acts of protest, sabotage, terrorism. The fears proved groundless. A perfect proving ground was Marseilles, a city where 100,000 residents are classified as "immigrants", and where unemployment among young adult Arabs hovers around 40%. Both support for Saddam Hussein and opposition to the war ran high among its Arab population. Yet the crisis passed without so much as a demonstration.

But if some fear that the West's new Muslim communities will prove to be social immiscibles—gravel in the ethnic soup—for others, it is the prospect of integration itself that alarms. Since integration, historically, is a two-way street, genuine integration would seem to entail the transformation not only of the immigrant, but of the "host" nation as well. This is the second sort of concern we face, and, I think, a deeper one. In Britain, Charles Moore gave voice to an undoubtedly widespread sentiment when he wrote in a *Spectator* editorial in 1991: "Britain is basically English-speaking, Christian and white, and if one starts to think that it might become basically Urdu-speaking and Muslim and brown, one gets frightened and angry." All of this speaks to the West's growing identity crisis: to the question of who "we" are and will be.

Undoubtedly the Islamicisation of the West, to the degree that it happens, will usher in changes. But they will not all be of the sort that conservatives fear. Most immediately, in the perennial *Kulturkampf* between faith and secularism, the growth of Islam will fortify the side of faith—the side with which many cultural conservatives in the West have allied themselves. In this sense, the Muslim from South Asia or the Maghreb has more in common with his God-fearing Christian opposite from the Home Counties than with his secular compatriot.

An unexpected pattern of alliances, then, may be in store. In American cities, many Muslims of third-world origins staunchly support vouchers for private school tuition and an array of key "family-values" issues, including opposition to abortion, pornography, homosexuality and sexual promiscuity. So the mordant irony is that cultural conservatives like Mr Buchanan may find their best hope for expanding their political base lies with those brown-skinned Muslims whose growing numbers they find so unsettling.

There are other ways in which anxious westerners misapprehend the likely impact of Muslim immigration. Again, though, it is important to proceed carefully, for there are dangers on both sides. One is to overestimate the assimilative capacity of western culture; the other is to underestimate it. We should grant that a blithely triumphalist view of western culture simply is not born out by history. It will not do to ignore the obduracy of cultural differences; yet to exaggerate their obduracy would be equally mistaken. Those who spend time among the Muslim communities of France's cities find that while the older generation tend to be poorly educated and devoutly religious, their children, the young women especially, are inclined to be as irreligious as their "western" counterparts. Most of France's second-generation Arabs seek protection against discrimination, not sponsorship of Muslim worship. What these unlikely evolués want, first and foremost, is to be allowed to be French.

What is more, western apprehensions of the impact of Islam on the West tend to be blinkered by an unduly monolithic, static conception of Islam itself. For in the longer term, there is reason to think that Islam is poised to undergo significant internal changes, changes that must prompt a re-examination of the putative clash between Islam and liberal democracy.

Actually, many Muslim intellectuals have been arguing for "Islamic modernism" since at least the mid-19th century; but increasingly, these modernists are moving away from the framework of the traditional sharia, which was developed between the 7th and 9th centuries, and seeking instead to develop a new, more humane, version of sharia based on new interpretations of Islamic texts. These clerics and intellectuals know that secularism is doomed to irrelevance for most Islamic societies, and that the most important project they can pursue is the reformation of Islam from within.

"An Islamic reformation cannot be a belated and poor copy of the European Christian model," argues Abdullahi Ahmed An-Na'im, executive director of Africa Watch, a human-rights group, and a major theorist of this movement. "It will have to be an indigenous and authentically Islamic process if it is to be a reformation at all." Dr An-Na'im courageously carries on the reformist project of his teacher, M. M. Taha (executed by the Sudanese authorities in 1985 for his opposition to sharia), and he is joined by growing numbers. They go about their work quietly, without fuss; they issue no fatwas, capture no headlines. Maybe these are not the "Islamic spokesmen" favoured by the western media, but their message of tolerance may carry

more weight in the long run. For all the undoubted strength of the fundamentalist revival, they are making headway too. Islam will remain Islam: but the transformation of Islamic tradition cannot long be deferred.

Now, what Muslims are to Europe, Hispanics are to the United States. They have, we are told, demography on their side: between birth rate and immigration, they are the single fastest-growing component of the population. For large parts of the country, the doomsayers insist, English will become an extinct tongue: it is just a matter of time.

So what must come as a surprise to them—and what confounds nativist stereotypes—is that the overwhelming majority of Hispanics in the United States actually believes that the country permits too much immigration. (Of course the impulse to close the door behind you makes a kind of economic sense: the competition for labour that immigration poses is most acute for those who have just immigrated themselves.) An even greater majority of Hispanics believes that all residents of the United States should learn English. On key issues, the newcomers are more nativist than the natives.

The nationalism vaccine

None of this is meant as an adjuration to, as it were, stop worrying and love the population bomb. What western intellectual and political leaders can properly concern themselves with is not the conservation of complexion, but the preservation, indeed, expansion, of democratic culture. And while transnational flows can be regulated responsibly, harshly exclusionary policies—the creation of "Fortress Europe"—would be extremely hazardous to that culture's health. If nationalism we must have, and in some measure we must, let us plump for a modulated, liberal, embracive, self-conscious nationalism—debilitated but therapeutic, like the virus in a polio vaccine. Surely nationalism red in tooth and claw is not the only kind.

Indeed, what is striking about the dark conviction of Charles Moore and his co-religionists that national cohesion requires the preservation of racial homogeneity is how utterly unhistorical it is. In the last century, Ernest Renan went so far as to venture that "the noblest countries—England, France, Italy—are those where the blood is most mixed. Germany is no exception." And in the first century of American independence, the great advocates of American exceptionalism, from Crèvecoeur to Margaret Fuller, found the diversity of its intermingled tribes to be its foremost asset. Mixing and hybridisation—what French thinkers like to call métissage—is the future, as it was our past.

At the end of the day, we cannot long escape the simple logic of demography. While Africa, for example, has an annual birth surplus of 15m, the European Community has an annual birth deficit of 1.2m. According to UN estimates, in just 30 years the population of sub-Saharan Africa will exceed the combined population of all western nations. "Most men in this world are coloured," the great black American intellectual W. E. B. Du Bois once observed. "A belief in humanity means a belief in coloured men. The future will in all reasonable possibility, be what coloured men make of it."

'Ask Not'—'90s Style

National Service: NEWSWEEK went behind the scenes for 10 months as Clinton's dream smashed against the politics of race, class and selfishness

Steven Waldman

When Bill Clinton thinks of National Service, this is what he sees:

A roomful of earnest young people talking about how, as part of a program called City Year, they have cleaned the apartments of frail seniors, tutored in inner-city schools and fixed up community playgrounds. As Clinton campaigned for the New Hampshire primary in December 1991 and listened to these stories, he was struck by the racial and social mix of the young workers. Yes, there was a former drug dealer from Boston, but alongside him was a prep-school student from Texas and a working-class white from South Boston. One by one they talked about how serving together had forced them to shed prejudices and opened up new worlds. Visibly moved, Clinton told them, "You make a statement every day that there is an American Community."

Here is a reality Clinton must deal with:

Last June the White House launched the Summer of Service to demonstrate what service could do. Seventy-five percent of participants at the training retreat near San Francisco were minorities. By the third day the 1,500 young people from around the country had split into black, Hispanic, Native American and gay/lesbian/bisexual caucuses. Some of the African-American groups debated whether whites should even be allowed to attend their meetings. Vegetarians complained that organizers hadn't attended to their needs. Students berated Eli Segal, the head of the White House Office of National Service, about gays in the military, the failures of the federal government and the need for the program to politically organize poor people to demand benefits. "I almost thought we were going to have a riot," said one official who helped organize the retreat.

In Bill Clinton's ideal world, all things are possible. You can help the middle class and uplift the poor, convince blacks and whites to serve side by side, and make government work without wasting the taxpayers' money. But the political reality is that the great liberal ideals of the Democratic Party have been soured by the persistent divisions of race and class. In many precincts, hope and idealism have been replaced with cynicism and isolationism. Clinton tried to replace Washington's prevailing "got mine" attitude with the message he took from John F. Kennedy's "ask not what your country can do for you." But the demands of class and race kept intruding into his plans. A compromiser at heart, Clinton in the end had to settle for less. Last week Congress passed Clinton's national service plan. Even after all the dealmaking and ducking, the president achieved something significant: a plan that will ask thousands of young Americans to perform some national service in exchange for help with their college education. And his program will rely on a burgeoning collection of successful local service corps. But the program is far from what Clinton once promised. Many have noted its modest size. More important, it is not the engine for social and racial integration that he envisaged as he listened to the young work mates of City Year.

Ten months ago NEWSWEEK launched a special project designed to track the national service initiative's dramatic but barely reported journey from campaign applause line to law. The obstacles Clinton faced along the way show how difficult it will be for "New Democrats" to "reinvent government" and restore the idealism that moved Clinton as a young high-school student shaking JFK's hand 30 years ago.

During the early months of the campaign, Clinton's political advisers rolled their eyes whenever the candidate started talking about a national program to encourage young people to serve their country. "Every candidate has one of these things," James Carville said later, speaking as if it were a bad habit, like bingeing on Big Macs. "You humor him and you move on."

The joking stopped once the aides heard the applause. Clinton's plan—to reward service with a college scholarship—was the most consistent crowd-pleaser in his stump speeches. Clinton had melded two controversial ideas into a proposal designed to please everyone. Just asking for service would have appealed to a narrow sliver of do-gooders. On the other hand, just offering bundles in college aid would have seemed like profligate "tax and spend" liberalism. But put the two together and Clinton sounded like a New Democrat who preserved the best of his party's past while junking the worst. Yes, Clinton was saying, government *does* have a role to play in improving society. But people can't just ask for handouts. They should have to give something back.

Crowds loved Clinton's stock speech line about his "domestic GI Bill." There was only one problem: it was wildly expensive. If he really allowed *all* students to wipe out *all* of their loans, the program could cost as much as $40 billion. Of course, not everybody would want to serve, but even if just 3 percent of those with loans did—as the campaign predicted—it would still cost $8 billion, more than the government now spends on the entire student-loan program.

During the campaign, reality did not intrude. Aides who gingerly asked about the true cost of the program were told to be quiet. But when Clinton as president had to produce his first federal budget, he shrank his promise considerably: $3.4 billion by 1997. That would fund 70,000 students—four times as many, Clinton liked to point out, as were enrolled by the Peace Corps during its heyday—but hardly the scholarships-for-all he had initially promised. So before Clinton's plan was even introduced to Congress, it had been radically scaled back. And the real fight, over the true mission of national service, had not yet begun.

At its core, Clinton's proposal changed the government's approach to helping people go to college. For the past 30 years Congress has given out financial aid based almost entirely on who needs it most. Income, not ability, has been the criterion. Attempts to tie aid to academic merit were viewed as anti-democratic. Clinton's national service program contained a new message: the government will still give aid according to need but will give *more* money to those who serve their country.

A seemingly worthy ideal, but it was deeply worrisome to the colleges and universities that rely on—and lobby for—federal education aid. The significance of Clinton's shift was not lost on former congressman William Gray III, the president of the United Negro College Fund. Gray believed the approach seriously threatened his schools and their students, many of whom survive on Pell grants, the no-strings attached scholarships for the needy. On March 25, Gray summoned other leaders of higher education to a summit at the American Council on Education offices. "It's American pie, you know, national service," he said dismissively, "doing something for the country, shades of JFK, the whole bit. Wonderful images of Americana et cetera." But the ultimate goal of national service, he warned, was to replace Pell grants, which aid 4.4 *million* low-income students, in order to give a nice experience to 100,000 middle-class kids.

The New Program at a Glance

Service Jobs: The government will create 20,000 full-time service slots by fall 1994. High-school graduates or anyone working toward an equivalency diploma can apply through local programs.

College Loan Forgiveness: For each year of full-time service, participants will earn a $4,725 scholarship. They can use it for future schooling, including job training, or to pay off past loans. They will receive a stipend (probably minimum wage) and health care.

Flexible Loan Repayment: As of the 1994-95 school year, students can repay loans as a percentage of future income, instead of in fixed payments. The goal: to spur people to take low-paying public-service jobs by easing burden of debt.

A practicing Baptist minister, Gray pounded the table, warning that when members of Congress have to decide between a middle-class program like national service, or one for the poor like Pell grants, "I can tell you right away which they're going to pick. They're going to pick the one for the people who vote! Middle-class Americans. Middle class vote! Poor folks don't!"

In a private meeting the next day with officials from the American Council on Education, Bud Blakey, the counsel for the United Negro College Fund, turned up the heat. "If we end up trading the interests of upper-income whites for low-income blacks and Latinos . . ." He didn't finish that sentence, adding: "If the race card has to get played to stop this bull—— from happening, then the race card is going to be played here!"

By making "service" a criterion for aid, the White House had backed into the dangerous arena of racial politics. In times of scarcity, giving money to white middle-class kids—even those who've earned it through good works—can mean taking money away from poor kids. The White House tried to reassure colleges that it would support Pell grants but undermined its credibility by simultaneously cutting millions of dollars from other student-aid programs.

Until Summer of Service awakened them, White House negotiators were oblivious to the fact that their notions of race were deemed by some to be naive, antiquated and condescending. Clinton wants to solve racial troubles through aggressive integration—an approach admired when he was memorizing Martin Luther King's "I Have a Dream" speech but out of touch with sentiment in the streets today. King and busing to achieve school integration are out; Malcolm X and Afrocentric curricula are in. Clinton implicitly assumes that low-income blacks will benefit more from exposure to affluent whites than from working in their own communities. And affluent whites are more likely to drop their prejudices if forced to work on an equal footing with blacks than if they watch "In the Heat of the Night" in their homogeneous suburbs. National service "is one of the things we *have* to do," Clinton says, "to re-establish the ability to talk to one another."

But some groups that work with minorities view these assumptions with contempt. Kathleen Selz represents local service corps mostly comprising low-income blacks and Hispanics and believes that race-mixing proponents overstate the magical ability of Yuppie whites to transform the lives of the underclass. "These girls from [affluent] Bethesda at the D.C. Service Corps are always saying things like, 'Oh, it opened our horizons!' " says Selz, mimicking the syrupy voice of an earnest suburbanite. "Well, you notice the welfare mother doesn't say much like that."

If money were unlimited, Clinton could give aid to programs that celebrate unifying ethnic groups and minority self-help programs that emphasize separateness. But the White House had to decide: should the legislation favor local programs that share the same vision as Clinton? Early on, as White House negotiators worked with congressional staff, they considered listing "diversity" as a criterion when giving out money; programs that sought to mix whites and blacks would be more likely to get funding than those that didn't. But the staff of the House Education and Labor Committee feared that such a preference might sink the all-minority programs popular with black and Hispanic members of the committee. After all, if the government funds a program with 50 blacks and 50 whites, it has less money to fund the program with 100 blacks. "Every time 'diversity' would come up [in legislative negotiations, the committee's staff] would say, 'Well, the House is going to have some problems with that' and we'd say, 'OK, OK, we'll take it out'," one White House official said. The White House did not put up much of a fight, severely underestimating how hard it will be to produce mixed programs. They even casually agreed to set aside at least one third of the money for programs that recruit mostly "disadvantaged" youths, further reducing the pot of money that will go to truly diverse programs.

There were other ways of encouraging race- and class-mixing without requiring it—but these methods threatened to alienate key interest groups. Clinton believed that if he offered to wipe out large chunks of college-loan debt, the service program could attract white middle-class kids. In a Feb. 24 meeting, he argued that college graduates had genuinely greater skills and could therefore contribute more than a 17-year-old just out of high school. And, he told aides, the college grad would be making a sacrifice by taking two years to teach, "a real gift to society." Seventeen-year-olds, on the other hand, have fewer skills and expenses, since many live at home. Clinton decided to offer a $10,000 benefit to college graduates and $5,000 in aid to those who serve before college or don't intend to go to college.

But advocates for the non-college-bound hated Clinton's idea. "The whole message is we value people who go to college more than those who don't," longtime low-income advocate Sam Halperin told While House officials at a private meeting sponsored by the umbrella group Youth Service America. Clinton couldn't bear undervaluing the non-college-bound. He agreed to have one smaller benefit of $6,500, which seemed to settle the issue. What other group could possibly object? April 28, two days before they were scheduled to unveil their plan, they found out who.

Veterans. These were the men who *did* service in Vietnam, who really don't much like this gays-in-the-military idea—the last group in America with which Clinton could pick a fight just then. The veterans argued, using some slightly deceptive arithmetic, that the $6,500 benefit was more than GIs get as college aid. White House staff at first debated how hard to fight, but the debate came to an abrupt close when top adviser George Stephanopoulos entered the discussion, incredulous at the political naiveté of his colleagues. He knew the veterans could sink the entire bill, shaky statistics or not. Segal's staff cut the benefit to $5,000 faster than you can say "political viability." Clinton lost what he considered a key tool for luring a broad range of young people into service, but at least he seemed to have cleared the remaining obstacles to swift legislative passage.

Republicans in Congress were not about to make it that easy. As the legislation journeyed through Congress, they proposed a series of changes that struck the Democratic Party's exposed nerves. In both the Senate and the House they offered killer "trigger" amendments forbidding the government to spend a penny on national service until it had first boosted Pell grants. One by one, Republicans rose to accuse Clinton of insensitivity to the poor. "You want to help young kids, then double and triple the Pell grants. Reach out to millions!" Sen. Al D'Amato shrieked on the floor of the Senate. "This bill is a turkey; we should shoot, kill it, now!" This Republican righteousness was too much for Sen. Edward M. Kennedy, a key national service advocate. "Tonight at 8 o'clock we hear how some are absolutely indignant about what is happening to these programs. Where were they when the appropriations were coming out over the last 12 years? Where were they?"

Behind the scenes, though, Kennedy himself was furious about the administration's other student-aid cuts. "This is crazy!" he wrote in thick marker atop a memo from a staffer. Although much of the Republican attack was cynical posturing, critics had a legitimate point: national service did pose a threat to Pell grants and need-based financial aid. If national service continues to grow, it will be very difficult to increase grant aid.

Clinton was partly to blame for the Republican attack. For all his criticism of the "politics of entitlement," he could not resist pitching the re-

Give Up the 'Self-Centered' Life

President Clinton discussed service [August 1993] in the Oval Office with NEWSWEEK's Steven Waldman:

NEWSWEEK: Looking back on your own life, what made you interested in service?

CLINTON: When I became governor I saw all kinds of unmet needs in every community that, hell, we simply couldn't raise the taxes to pay for. I also became convinced that a lot of problems in this country were highly personal in nature—that the culture had changed in ways that broke down the traditional bonds of community. They suffered internally—not just economically, but emotionally from having insufficient order and emotional support and role models.

You really think [a national service program] can address that?

I think it can make a huge difference . . . I watched how the systematic attempt to affect people individually was making a difference in [schools] far beyond what could otherwise be predicted. Then I started seeing the same sort of potential happening in service projects.

The Summer of Service program had about 75 percent minorities. Would you be disappointed if that was the makeup of the rest of the program?

I would be disappointed if we didn't have a lot of white kids, middle-class white kids, in there, too. And I think we will. I fought very hard to keep the means testing [which targets aid toward the needy] out of the program because I want all kinds of people.

In a time of scarce resources, you're giving educational benefits, potentially, to the son of a millionaire.

Only if they really do something for their country. You know, wealthy people may go into the military, but if they do they're entitled to the GI Bill.

Some Republicans attacked comparisons between domestic service and military service. I'm curious about your reaction. On a personal level, if there had been a civilian-service option available during Vietnam, would you have chosen that?

Probably.

Why?

I mean, who knows what I would have done? I always thought I was going to be drafted. But I think

that most people would like the feeling of serving their country.

I think all these kids doing drugs, shooting guns, dropping out of school, going to jail, changing the culture of life in a destructive way and losing their opportunity to have a good life—I see that as a national-security issue.

You often speak about the plan as opening access to college. Yet the loan forgiveness will affect a very, very small percentage of people with loans. Isn't it misleading to talk about it that way?

No, because when I was in the campaign I always . . . saw reformation of the student-loan program as an important part of this, too. This income-contingent loan business [in which people can repay loans in small installments as a percentage of their income] is, I think, very important. It is my belief that if you know that the burden of repaying your loans is not a problem, then you are free to take a job that might pay somewhat less but be somewhat more rewarding. I talked to a young couple that had a combined college-loan repayment schedule of $1,000 a month. Both of them said they would like to have been doing something a little bit more community oriented than what they were doing. But it's all they could do to scramble and put together $1,000 a month.

During the campaign, you promised that anyone could wipe out their loans with service. Obviously, the [law] is far from that. Wasn't that really a pretty unrealistic campaign promise to make?

Well, I don't think you can do it overnight. There was a limit to how fast you could start and expand a program effectively.

How do you respond to the argument that you're not asking much of young people if you're offering them a stipend and a generous college benefit—that it's almost like bribing people to serve?

I just don't agree with that. You're still asking people . . . to give up what in almost every case will be an easier life and a more self-centered one to devote a significant period of their lives to primarily helping other people with their problems. You're rewarding them for serving their country, for doing something that most people their age won't do, don't do.

ward—college benefits—more than the sacrifice. Casting national service as a student-aid program inevitably forced the comparison with Pell grants. And viewed as a student-aid program, national service is laughably inefficient—roughly $1,300 per person for Pell grants; $15,000 to $22,000 per person for service. Longtime supporters of

national service such as Sen. Harris Wofford privately pleaded with Clinton to stress the benefits to communities of service. Sen. David Durenberger, a Republican who strongly supported Clinton's legislation, feared that the president's hyperbole would jeopardize the entire bill. "Everything the president has done and said is an exaggeration," he complained as other Senate Republicans mounted a brief but aggressive filibuster in July. "The rhetoric is destroying the reality—and the Republicans took advantage of it."

But Clinton's political advisers such as Mandy Grunwald and pollster Stan Greenberg still believed that lofty service rhetoric wouldn't win over middle-class voters—and Clinton sided with them. "I want my national service plan to pass; that will open the doors of college education to millions of Americans," Clinton said in a staggeringly misleading statement on "Larry King Live" the same week the Senate was considering his legislation.

The White House was able to defeat the lethal "trigger" amendments by restoring some of the money that had been cut from student aid and promising future generosity to Pell grants. It avoided a rift the old-fashioned way—papering it over with money.

But the Republicans weren't done. They launched another attack from the left, this time proposing to forbid rich kids from receiving national service benefits. Again, they were trying to drive a wedge through the Democratic coalition with an argument designed to appeal to liberals: shouldn't money for national service scholarships be given according to need? The notion had some immediate appeal—particularly to members of the House Education and Labor Committee, which is, in the words of one staff member, so far to the political left it "would pass the Communist Manifesto if it had jurisdiction." The committee's chairman, Bill Ford of Michigan, was a Lyndon Johnson protégé who had disliked national service in past years and always fought hard for targeting aid to the poor.

This time was different. Ford had decided to help Clinton out. In part, it was out of personal affection. Clinton had helped Ford win re-election narrowly by campaigning in his suburban Detroit district six times in 1992. Ford also rediscovered his own political inner child—values not from the 1960s but from the 1940s. He had gone into the navy during World War II, met people of many different backgrounds, gone to college on the GI Bill and discovered "Christ, I'm just as smart as these rich guys. It changed my whole life." Ford, in essence, saw Clinton's New Democratic approach as a return to the FDR/Truman Democratic Party, the party of old World War II movies in which Joey Brooklyn learns to love Tex Hayseed because he throws himself on a grenade.

On June 16 Segal called Clinton to tell him that the House committee had voted with the president—that is, against targeting the money toward the poor. Clinton—the man attacked by Republicans as a Carter-Mondale-Dukakis liberal—clenched his fist and pumped it in the air. Next time Clinton saw Ford, the president of the United States went over to the gruff, authoritarian committee chairman . . . and gave him a hug. "Damn good victory," Clinton said, lifting Ford off the floor with his embrace. "The guy is a really enthusiastic young man," Ford says.

In the end, the White House did win a key test—allowing middle-class and rich kids to get the same benefit as the poor. They won a partial victory on the size of the scholarship; the final amount was $4,725 per year, a far cry from the $10,000 they originally sought, but probably generous enough to attract a variety of kids into the program. As a result, Clinton may get middle-class families to feel invested—literally, financially invested—in improving their communities and understanding people who are different from them. The White House also succeeded in structuring a highly flexible program that can subsidize existing charities like the Red Cross or Habitat for Humanity; urban and environmental corps; professional corps like Teach for America, which sends recent college graduates to teach in disadvantaged communities; and even "service learning" efforts that incorporate service into high-school curricula. By August, the Summer of Service had illustrated the tremendous potential of the approach: volunteers in Atlanta set up an after-school program for 250 poor kids; 87 volunteers in south Texas went door to door and brought 100,000 school kids in for immunizations.

But the White House lost, without even fighting, on the critical issue of whether to favor local programs that mix races. As Summer of Service showed, racial and economic diversity won't happen unless organizers make it a prominent goal. The administration passed the legislation swiftly, but merely postponed the day when Clinton will have to decide: does he want racial progress to be central to his national service program, and is he willing to take the heat from those who disagree?

For all his inspiring rhetoric, John F. Kennedy attracted to his Peace Corps a narrow group of mostly white, well-educated Americans. Clinton's plan is far more ambitious, seeking to regenerate fragmented American communities and break down rock-hard barriers of the heart. Because Clinton must confront the emotional issues of race and class, he is more likely to fail. But should he succeed, Clinton will have accomplished something far more significant than his hero ever did.

THE VALUE OF THE CANON

Irving Howe

Irving Howe is at work on a book about the novel titled Selected Short Subjects. *His* Selected Writings: 1950–1990 *was published in 1990 by Harcourt Brace Jovanovich.*

I.

Of all the disputes agitating the American campus, the one that seems to me especially significant is that over "the canon." What should be taught in the humanities and social sciences, especially in introductory courses? What is the place of the classics? How shall we respond to those professors who attack "Eurocentrism" and advocate "multiculturalism"? This is not the sort of tedious quarrel that now and then flutters through the academy; it involves matters of public urgency. I propose to see this dispute, at first, through a narrow, even sectarian lens, with the hope that you will come to accept my reasons for doing so.

Here, roughly, are the lines of division. On one side stand (too often, fall) the cultural "traditionalists," who may range politically across the entire spectrum. Opposing them is a heterogeneous grouping of mostly younger teachers, many of them veterans of the 1960s, which includes feminists, black activists, Marxists, deconstructionists, and various mixtures of these.

At some colleges and universities traditional survey courses of world and English literature, as also of social thought, have been scrapped or diluted. At others they are in peril. At still others they will be. What replaces them is sometimes a mere option of electives, sometimes "multicultural" courses introducing material from Third World cultures and thinning out an already thin sampling of Western writings, and sometimes courses geared especially to issues of class, race, and gender. Given the notorious lethargy of academic decision-making,

there has probably been more clamor than change; but if there's enough clamor, there will be change.

University administrators, timorous by inclination, are seldom firm in behalf of principles regarding education. Subjected to enough pressure, many of them will buckle under. So will a good number of professors who vaguely subscribe to "the humanist tradition" but are not famously courageous in its defense. Academic liberalism has notable virtues, but combativeness is not often one of them. In the academy, whichever group goes on the offensive gains an advantage. Some of those who are now attacking "traditionalist" humanities and social science courses do so out of sincere persuasion; some, from a political agenda (what was at first solemnly and now is half-ironically called p.c.— politically correct); and some from an all-too-human readiness to follow the academic fashion that, for the moment, is "in."

Can we find a neutral term to designate the anti-traditionalists? I can't think of a satisfactory one, so I propose an unsatisfactory one: let's agree to call them the insurgents, though in fact they have won quite a few victories. In the academy these professors are often called "the left" or "the cultural left," and that is how many of them see themselves. But this is a comic misunderstanding, occasionally based on ignorance. In behalf of both their self-awareness and a decent clarity of debate, I want to show that in fact the socialist **and Marxist traditions have been close to traditionalist views of culture. Not that the left hasn't had its share of ranters (I exclude Stalinists and hooligans) who, in the name of "the revolution," were intent upon jettisoning the culture of the past; but generally such types have been a mere marginal affliction treated with disdain.**

Let me cite three major figures. Here is Georg Lukacs, the most influential Marxist critic of the twentieth century:

> Those who do not know Marxism may be surprised at the respect for *the classical heritage of mankind* which one finds in the really great representatives of that doctrine. (Emphasis added.)

9. UNDERSTANDING CULTURAL PLURALISM

Here is Leon Trotsky, arguing in 1924 against a group of Soviet writers who felt that as the builders of "a new society" they could dismiss the "reactionary culture" of the past:

> If I say that the importance of *The Divine Comedy* lies in the fact that it gives me an understanding of the state of mind of certain classes in a certain epoch, this means that I transform it into *a mere historical document.* . . . How is it thinkable that there should be not a historical but *a directly aesthetic relationship* between us and a medieval Italian book? This is explained by the fact that in class society, in spite of its changeability, there are certain common features. Works of art developed in a medieval Italian city can affect us too. What does this require? . . . That these feelings and moods shall have received such broad, intense, powerful expression as to have raised them above the limitations of the life of those days. (Emphasis added.)

Trotsky's remarks could serve as a reply to those American professors of literature who insist upon the omnipresence of ideology as it seeps into and perhaps saturates literary texts, and who scoff that only "formalists" believe that novels and poems have autonomous being and value. In arguing, as he did in his book *Literature and Revolution*, that art must be judged by "its own laws," Trotsky seems not at all p.c. Still less so is Antonio Gramsci, the Italian Marxist, whose austere opinions about education might make even our conservatives blanch:

> Latin and Greek were learnt through their grammar, mechanically, but the accusation of formalism and aridity is very unjust. . . . In education one is dealing with children in whom one has to inculcate certain habits of diligence, precision, poise (even physical poise), ability to concentrate on specific subjects, which cannot be acquired without the mechanical repetition of disciplined and methodical acts.

These are not the isolated ruminations of a few intellectuals; Lukacs, Trotsky, and Gramsci speak with authority for a view of culture prevalent in the various branches of the Marxist (and also, by the way, the non-Marxist) left. And that view informed many movements of the left. There were the Labor night schools in England bringing to industrial workers elements of the English cultural past; there was the once-famous Rand School of New York City; there were the reading circles that Jewish workers, in both Eastern Europe and American cities, formed to acquaint themselves with Tolstoy, Heine, and Zola. And in Ignazio Silone's novel *Bread and Wine* we have a poignant account of an underground cell in Rome during the Mussolini years that reads literary works as a way of holding itself together.

My interest here is not to vindicate socialism or Marxism—that is another matter. Nor is there anything sacrosanct about the opinions I have quoted or their authors. But it is surely worth establishing that the claims of many academic insurgents to be speaking from a left, let alone a Marxist, point of view are highly dubious. Very well, the more candid among them might reply, so we're not of the left, at least we're not of the "Eurocentric" left. To recognize that would at

least help clear the atmosphere. More important, it might shrink the attractiveness of these people in what is perhaps the only area of American society where the label of "the left" retains some prestige.

What we are witnessing on the campus today is a strange mixture of American populist sentiment and French critical theorizing as they come together in behalf of "changing the subject." The populism provides an underlying structure of feeling, and the theorizing provides a dash of intellectual panache. The populism releases anti-elitist rhetoric, the theorizing releases highly elitist language.

American populism, with its deep suspicion of the making of distinctions of value, has found expression not only in native sages (Henry Ford: "History is bunk") but also in the writings of a long line of intellectuals—indeed, it's only intellectuals who can give full expression to anti-intellectualism. Such sentiments have coursed through American literature, but only recently, since the counterculture of the 1960s, have they found a prominent place in the universities.

As for the French theorizing—metacritical, quasi-philosophical, and at times of a stupefying verbal opacity—it has provided a buttress for the academic insurgents. We are living at a time when all the once-regnant world systems that have sustained (also distorted) Western intellectual life, from theologies to ideologies, are taken to be in severe collapse. This leads to a mood of skepticism, an agnosticism of judgment, sometimes a world-weary nihilism in which even the most conventional minds begin to question both distinctions of value and the value of distinctions. If you can find projections of racial, class, and gender bias in both a Western by Louis L'Amour and a classical Greek play, and if you have decided to reject the "elitism" said to be at the core of literary distinctions, then you might as well teach the Western as the Greek play. You can make the same political points, and more easily, in "studying" the Western. And if you happen not to be well informed about Greek culture, it certainly makes things still easier.

I grew up with the conviction that what Georg Lukacs calls "the classical heritage of mankind" is a precious legacy. It came out of historical circumstances often appalling, filled with injustice and outrage. It was often, in consequence, alloyed with prejudice and flawed sympathies. Still, it was a heritage that had been salvaged from the nightmares, occasionally the glories, of history, and now we would make it "ours," we who came from poor and working-class families. This "heritage of mankind" (which also includes, of course, Romantic and modernist culture) had been denied to the masses of ordinary people, trained into the stupefaction of accepting, even celebrating, their cultural deprivations. One task of political consciousness was therefore to enable the masses to share in what had been salvaged from the past—the literature, art, music, thought—and thereby to reach an active relation with these. That is why many people, not just socialists but liberals, democrats, and those without political tags, kept struggling for universal education. It was not a given; it had to be won. Often, winning proved to be very hard.

Knowledge of the past, we felt, could humanize by promoting distance from ourselves and our narrow habits, and this could promote critical thought. Even partly to grasp a significant experience or literary work of the past would require historical imagination, a sense of other times, which entailed moral imagination, a sense of other ways. It would create a kinship with those who had come before us, hoping and suffering as we have, seeking through language, sound, and color to leave behind something of enduring value.

By now we can recognize that there was a certain naïveté in this outlook. The assumption of progress in education turned out to be as problematic as similar assumptions elsewhere in life. There was an underestimation of human recalcitrance and sloth. There was a failure to recognize what the twentieth century has taught us: that aesthetic sensibility by no means assures ethical value. There was little anticipation of the profitable industry of "mass culture," with its shallow kitsch and custom-made dreck. Nevertheless, insofar as we retain an attachment to the democratic idea, we must hold fast to an educational vision somewhat like the one I've sketched. Perhaps it is more an ideal to be approached than a goal to be achieved; no matter. I like the epigrammatic exaggeration, if it is an exaggeration, of John Dewey's remark that "the aim of education is to enable individuals to continue their education."

This vision of culture and education started, I suppose, at some point in the late eighteenth century or the early nineteenth century. It was part of a great sweep of human aspiration drawing upon Western traditions from the Renaissance to the Enlightenment. It spoke in behalf of such liberal values as the autonomy of the self, tolerance for a plurality of opinions, the rights of oppressed national and racial groups, and soon, the claims of the women's movements. To be sure, these values were frequently violated—that has been true for every society in every phase of world history. But the criticism of such violations largely invoked the declared values themselves, and this remains true for all our contemporary insurgencies. Some may sneer at "Western hegemony," but knowingly or not, they do so in the vocabulary of Western values.

By invoking the "classical heritage of mankind" I don't propose anything fixed and unalterable. Not at all. There are, say, seven or eight writers and a similar number of social thinkers who are of such preeminence that they must be placed at the very center of this heritage; but beyond that, plenty of room remains for disagreement. All traditions change, simply through survival. Some classics die. Who now reads Ariosto? A loss, but losses form part of tradition too. And new arrivals keep being added to the roster of classics—it is not handed down from Mt. Sinai or the University of Chicago. It is composed and fought over by cultivated men and women. In a course providing students a mere sample of literature, there should be included some black and women writers who, because of inherited bias, have been omitted in the past. Yet I think we must give a central position to what Professor John Searle in a recent *New York Review of Books* article specifies as "a certain Western intellectual tradition that goes from, say, Socrates to Wittgenstein in philosophy, and from Homer to James Joyce in literature. . . . It is essential to the liberal education of young men and women in the United States that they should receive some exposure to at least some of the great works of this intellectual tradition."

Nor is it true that most of the great works of the past are bleakly retrograde in outlook—to suppose that is a sign of cultural illiteracy. Bring together in a course on social thought selections from Plato and Aristotle, Machiavelli and Rousseau, Hobbes and Locke, Nietzsche and Freud, Marx and Mill, Jefferson and Dewey, and you have a wide variety of opinions, often clashing with one another, sometimes elusive and surprising, always richly complex. These are some of the thinkers with whom to begin, if only later to deviate from. At least as critical in outlook are many of the great poets and novelists. Is there a more penetrating historian of selfhood than Wordsworth? A more scathing critic of society than the late Dickens? A mind more devoted to ethical seriousness than George Eliot? A sharper critic of the corrupting effects of money than Balzac or Melville?

These writers don't necessarily endorse our current opinions and pieties—why should they? We read them for what Robert Frost calls "counterspeech," the power and brilliance of *other minds*, and if we can go "beyond" them, it is only because they are behind us.

What is being invoked here is not a stuffy obeisance before dead texts from a dead past, but rather a critical engagement with living texts from powerful minds still very much "active" in the present. And we should want our students to read Shakespeare and Tolstoy, Jane Austen and Kafka, Emily Dickinson and Leopold Senghor, not because they "support" one or another view of social revolution, feminism, and black self-esteem. They don't, in many instances; and we don't read them for the sake of enlisting them in a cause of our own. We should want students to read such writers so that they may learn to enjoy the activity of mind, the pleasure of forms, the beauty of language—in short, the arts in their own right.

By contrast, there is a recurrent clamor in the university for "relevance," a notion hard to resist (who wishes to be known as irrelevant?) but proceeding from an impoverished view of political life, and too often ephemeral in its excitements and transient in its impact. I recall seeing in the late 1960s large stacks of Eldridge Cleaver's *Soul on Ice* in the Stanford University bookstore. Hailed as supremely "relevant" and widely described as a work of genius, this book has fallen into disuse in a mere two decades. Cleaver himself drifted off into some sort of spiritualism, ceasing thereby to be "relevant." Where, then, is *Soul on Ice* today? What lasting value did it impart?

American culture is notorious for its indifference to the past. It suffers from the provincialism of the contemporary, veering wildly from fashion to fashion, each touted by the media and then quickly dismissed. But the past is the substance out of which the present has been formed, and to let it slip away from us is to acquiesce in the thinness that characterizes so much of our culture. Serious education must assume, in part, an adversarial stance toward the very society that sustains it—a democratic society makes the wager that it's worth supporting a culture of criticism. But if that criticism loses touch with the heritage of the past, it becomes weightless, a mere compendium of momentary complaints.

Several decades ago, when I began teaching, it could be assumed that entering freshmen had read in high school at least one play by Shakespeare and one novel by Dickens. That wasn't much, but it was something. These days, with the disintegration of the high schools, such an assumption can seldom be made. The really dedicated college teachers of literature feel that, given the bazaar of elective courses an entering student encounters and the propaganda in behalf of "relevance," there is likely to be only one opportunity to acquaint students with a smattering—indeed, the merest fragment—of the great works from the past. Such teachers take pleasure in watching the minds and sensibilities of young people opening up to a poem by Wordsworth, a story by Chekhov, a novel by Ellison. They feel they have planted a seed of responsiveness that, with time and luck, might continue to grow. And if this is said to be a missionary attitude, why should anyone quarrel with it?

II.

Let me now mention some of the objections one hears in academic circles to the views I have put down here, and then provide brief replies.

By requiring students to read what you call "classics" in introductory courses, you impose upon them a certain worldview—and that is an elitist act.

In some rudimentary but not very consequential sense, all education entails the "imposing" of values. There are people who say this is true even when children are taught to read and write, since it assumes that reading and writing are "good."

In its extreme version, this idea is not very interesting, since it is not clear how the human race could survive if there were not some "imposition" from one generation to the next. But in a more moderate version, it is an idea that touches upon genuine problems.

Much depends on the character of the individual teacher, the spirit in which he or she approaches a dialogue of Plato, an essay by Mill, a novel by D. H. Lawrence. These can be, and have been, used to pummel an ideological line into the heads of students

(who often show a notable capacity for emptying them out again). Such pummeling is possible for all points of view but seems most likely in behalf of totalitarian politics and authoritarian theologies, which dispose their adherents to fanaticism. On the other hand, the texts I've mentioned, as well as many others, can be taught in a spirit of openness, so that students are trained to read carefully, think independently, and ask questions. Nor does this imply that the teacher hides his or her opinions. Being a teacher means having a certain authority, but the student should be able to confront that authority freely and critically. This is what we mean by liberal education—not that a teacher plumps for certain political programs, but that the teaching is done in a "liberal" (open, undogmatic) style.

I do not doubt that there are conservative and radical teachers who teach in this "liberal" spirit. When I was a student at City College in the late 1930s, I studied philosophy with a man who was either a member of the Communist Party or was "cheating it out of dues." Far from being the propagandist of the Party line, which Sidney Hook kept insisting was the necessary role of Communist teachers, this man was decent, humane, and tolerant. Freedom of thought prevailed in his classroom. He had, you might say, a "liberal" character, and perhaps his commitment to teaching as a vocation was stronger than his loyalty to the Party. Were such things not to happen now and then, universities would be intolerable.

If, then, a university proposes a few required courses so that ill-read students may at least glance at what they do not know, that isn't (necessarily) "elitist." Different teachers will approach the agreed-upon texts in different ways, and that is as it should be. If a leftist student gets "stuck" with a conservative teacher, or a conservative student with a leftist teacher, that's part of what education should be. The university is saying to its incoming students: "Here are some sources of wisdom and beauty that have survived the centuries. In time you may choose to abandon them, but first learn something about them."

Your list of classics includes only dead, white males, all tied in to notions and values of Western hegemony. Doesn't this narrow excessively the horizons of education?

All depends on how far forward you go to compose your list of classics. If you do not come closer to the present than the mid-eighteenth century, then of course there will not be many, or even any, women in your roster. If you go past the mid-eighteenth century to reach the present, it's not at all true that only "dead, white males" are to be included. For example—and this must hold for hundreds of other teachers also—I have taught and written about Jane Austen, Emily Brontë, Charlotte Brontë, Elizabeth Gaskell, George Eliot, Emily Dickinson, Edith Wharton, Katherine Anne Porter, Doris Lessing, and Flannery O'Connor. I could easily add a comparable list of black writers. Did this, in itself, make me a better teacher? I doubt it. Did it make me a better person?

We still lack modes of evaluation subtle enough to say for sure.

The absence of women from the literature of earlier centuries is a result of historical inequities that have only partly been remedied in recent years. Virginia Woolf, in a brilliant passage in *A Room of One's Own*, approaches this problem by imagining Judith, Shakespeare's sister, perhaps equally gifted but prevented by the circumstances of her time from developing her gifts:

> Any woman born with a great gift in the sixteenth century would certainly have gone crazed, shot herself, or ended her days in some lonely cottage outside the village, half witch, half wizard, feared and mocked at.... A highly gifted girl who had tried to use her gift for poetry would have been so thwarted and hindered by other people, so tortured and pulled asunder by her own contrary instincts, that she must have lost her health and sanity....

The history that Virginia Woolf describes cannot be revoked. If we look at the great works of literature and thought through the centuries until about the mid-eighteenth century, we have to recognize that indeed they have been overwhelmingly the achievements of men. The circumstances in which these achievements occurred may be excoriated. The achievements remain precious.

To isolate a group of texts as the canon is to establish a hierarchy of bias, in behalf of which there can be no certainty of judgment.

There is mischief or confusion in the frequent use of the term "hierarchy" by the academic insurgents, a conflation of social and intellectual uses. A social hierarchy may entail a (mal)distribution of income and power, open to the usual criticisms; a literary "hierarchy" signifies a judgment, often based on historical experience, that some works are of supreme or abiding value, while others are of lesser value, and still others quite without value. To prefer Elizabeth Bishop to Judith Krantz is not of the same order as sanctioning the inequality of wealth in the United States. To prefer Shakespeare to Sidney Sheldon is not of the same order as approving the hierarchy of the nomenklatura in Communist dictatorships.

As for the claim that there is no certainty of judgment, all tastes being historically molded or individually subjective, I simply do not believe that the people who make it live by it. This is an "egalitarianism" of valuation that people of even moderate literacy know to be false and unworkable—the making of judgments, even if provisional and historically modulated, is inescapable in the life of culture. And if we cannot make judgments or demonstrate the grounds for our preferences, then we have no business teaching literature—we might just as well be teaching advertising—and there is no reason to have departments of literature.

The claim that there can be value-free teaching is a liberal deception or self-deception; so too the claim that there can be texts untouched by social and political bias. Politics or ideology is everywhere, and it's the better part of honesty to admit this.

If you look hard (or foolishly) enough, you can find political and social traces everywhere. But to see politics or ideology in all texts is to scrutinize the riches of literature through a single lens. If you choose, you can read all or almost all literary works through the single lens of religion. But what a sad impoverishment of the imagination, and what a violation of our sense of reality, this represents. Politics may be "in" everything, but not everything is politics. A good social critic will know which texts are inviting to a given approach and which it would be wise to leave to others.

To see politics everywhere is to diminish the weight of politics. A serious politics recognizes the limits of its reach; it deals with public affairs while leaving alone large spheres of existence; it seeks not to "totalize" its range of interest. Some serious thinkers believe that the ultimate aim of politics should be to render itself superfluous. That may seem an unrealizable goal; meanwhile, a good part of the struggle for freedom in recent decades has been to draw a line beyond which politics must not tread. The same holds, more or less, for literary study and the teaching of literature.

Wittingly or not, the traditional literary and intellectual canon was based on received elitist ideologies, the values of Western imperialism, racism, sexism, etc., and the teaching of the humanities was marked by corresponding biases. It is now necessary to enlarge the canon so that voices from Africa, Asia, and Latin America can be heard. This is especially important for minority students so that they may learn about their origins and thereby gain in self-esteem.

It is true that over the decades some university teaching has reflected inherited social biases—how, for better or worse, could it not? Most often this was due to the fact that many teachers shared the common beliefs of American society. But not all teachers! As long as those with critical views were allowed to speak freely, the situation, if not ideal, was one that people holding minority opinions and devoted to democratic norms had to accept.

Yet the picture drawn by some academic insurgents—that most teachers, until quite recently, were in the grip of the worst values of Western society—is overdrawn. I can testify that some of my school and college teachers a few decades ago, far from upholding Western imperialism or white supremacy, were sharply critical of American society, in some instances from a boldly reformist outlook. They taught us to care about literature both for its own sake and because, as they felt, it often helped confirm their worldviews. (And to love it even if it didn't confirm their worldviews.) One high school teacher introduced me to Hardy's *Jude the Obscure* as a novel showing how cruel society can be to rebels, and up to a point, she was right. At college, as a fervent anti-Stalinist Marxist, I wrote a thoughtless "class analysis" of Edmund Spenser's poetry for an English class, and the kindly instructor, whose politics were probably not very far from mine, suggested that there were more things in the world, especially as Spenser had seen it, than I could yet recognize. I mention these instances to suggest that there has always been a range of opinion among teachers, and if anything, the American academy has tilted more to the left than most other segments of our society. There were of course right-wing professors too; I remember an economics teacher we called "Steamboat" Fulton, the object of amiable ridicule among the students who nonetheless learned something from him.

Proposals to enlarge the curriculum to include non-Western writings—if made in good faith and not in behalf of an ideological campaign—are in principle to be respected. A course in ancient thought might well include a selection from Confucius; a course in the modern novel might well include a work by Tanizaki or García Márquez.

There are practical difficulties. Due to the erosion of requirements in many universities, those courses that survive are usually no more than a year or a semester in duration, so that there is danger of a diffusion to the point of incoherence. Such courses, if they are to have any value, must focus primarily on the intellectual and cultural traditions of Western society. That, like it or not, is where we come from and that is where we are. All of us who live in America are, to some extent, Western: it gets to us in our deepest and also our most trivial habits of thought and speech, in our sense of right and wrong, in our idealism and our cynicism.

As for the argument that minority students will gain in self-esteem through being exposed to writings by Africans and black Americans, it is hard to know. Might not entering minority students, some of them ill-prepared, gain a stronger sense of self-esteem by mastering the arts of writing and reading than by being told, as some are these days, that Plato and Aristotle plagiarized from an African source? Might not some black students feel as strong a sense of self-esteem by reading, say, Dostoyevsky and Malraux (which Ralph Ellison speaks of having done at a susceptible age) as by being confined to black writers? Is there not something grossly patronizing in the notion that while diverse literary studies are appropriate for middle-class white students, something else, racially determined, **is required for the minorities? Richard Wright found sustenance in Dreiser, Ralph Ellison in Hemingway, Chinua Achebe in Eliot, Leopold Senghor in the whole of French poetry. Are there not unknown young Wrights and Ellisons, Achebes and Senghors in our universities who might also want to find their way to an individually achieved sense of culture?**

In any case, is the main function of the humanities directly to inculcate self-esteem? Do we really know how this can be done? And if done by bounding the curriculum according to racial criteria, may that not perpetuate the very grounds for a lack of self-esteem? I do not know the answers to these questions, but do the advocates of multiculturalism?

One serious objection to "multicultural studies" re-mains: that it tends to segregate students into categories fixed by birth, upbringing, and obvious environment. Had my teachers tried to lead me toward certain writers because they were Jewish, I would have balked—I wanted to find my own way to Proust, Kafka, and Pirandello, writers who didn't need any racial credentials. Perhaps things are different with students today—we ought not to be dogmatic about these matters. But are there not shared norms of pride and independence among young people, whatever their race and color?

The jazz musician Wynton Marsalis testifies: "Everybody has two heritages, ethnic and human. The human aspects give art its real enduring power. . . . The racial aspect, that's a crutch so you don't have to go out into the world." David Bromwich raises an allied question: Should we wish "to legitimize the belief that the mind of a student deserves to survive in exactly the degree that it corresponds with one of the classes of socially constructed group minds? If I were a student today I would find this assumption frightening. It is, in truth, more than a license for conformity. It is a four-year sentence to conformity."

What you have been saying is pretty much the same as what conservatives say. Doesn't that make you feel uncomfortable?

No, it doesn't. There are conservatives—and conservatives. Some, like the editor of *The New Criterion*, are frantic ideologues with their own version of p.c., the classics as safeguard for the status quo. This is no more **attractive than the current campus ideologizing. But there are also conservatives who make the necessary discriminations between using culture, as many have tried to use religion, as a kind of social therapy and seeing culture as a realm with its own values and rewards.**

Similar differences hold with regard to the teaching of past thinkers. In a great figure like Edmund Burke you will find not only the persuasions of conservatism but also a critical spirit that does not readily lend itself to ideological coarseness. Even those of us who disagree with him fundamentally can learn from Burke the disciplines of argument and resources of language.

Let us suppose that in University X undergoing a curriculum debate there is rough agreement about which books to teach between professors of the democratic left and their conservative colleagues. Why should that trouble us—or them? We agree on a given matter, perhaps for different reasons. Or there may be a more or less shared belief in the idea of a liberal education. If there is, so much the better. If the agreement is momentary, the differences will emerge soon enough.

A Little Epilogue

A NEW REPUBLIC reader: "Good lord, you're becoming a virtuoso at pushing through open doors. All this carrying on just to convince us that students should read great books. It's so obvious . . ."

I reply: "Dear reader, you couldn't be more right. But that is where we are."

Credits/ Acknowledgments

Cover design by Charles Vitelli

1. Race, Ethnicity, and the Law

Facing overview—AP/Wide World Photos.

2. Immigration and the American Experience

Facing overview—Reproduced from the collections of the Library of Congress.

3. Native American Groups

Facing overview—Reproduced from the collections of the Library of Congress.

4. Hispanic/Latino Americans

Facing overview—United Nations photo by Heidi Larson.

5. Asian Americans

Facing overview—New York Convention and Visitors Bureau.

6. African Americans

Facing overview—Reproduced from the collections of the Library of Congress.

7. The Ethnic Legacy

Facing overview—Sula Benet.

8. The Ethnic Factor

Facing overview—United Nations photo.

9. Understanding Cultural Pluralism

Facing overview—United Nations photo by Y. Nagata.

ANNUAL EDITIONS ARTICLE REVIEW FORM

■ NAME: _____ DATE: _____

■ TITLE AND NUMBER OF ARTICLE: _____

■ BRIEFLY STATE THE MAIN IDEA OF THIS ARTICLE: _____

_____

_____

_____

_____

■ LIST THREE IMPORTANT FACTS THAT THE AUTHOR USES TO SUPPORT THE MAIN IDEA:

_____

_____

_____

_____

_____

_____

■ WHAT INFORMATION OR IDEAS DISCUSSED IN THIS ARTICLE ARE ALSO DISCUSSED IN YOUR
TEXTBOOK OR OTHER READING YOU HAVE DONE? LIST THE TEXTBOOK CHAPTERS AND PAGE
NUMBERS:

_____

_____

_____

_____

_____

_____

■ LIST ANY EXAMPLES OF BIAS OR FAULTY REASONING THAT YOU FOUND IN THE ARTICLE:

_____

_____

_____

_____

■ LIST ANY NEW TERMS/CONCEPTS THAT WERE DISCUSSED IN THE ARTICLE AND WRITE A
SHORT DEFINITION:

_____

_____

_____

_____

*Your instructor may require you to use this Annual Editions Article Review Form in any number of ways:
for articles that are assigned, for extra credit, as a tool to assist in developing assigned papers, or simply
for your own reference. Even if it is not required, we encourage you to photocopy and use this page;
you'll find that reflecting on the articles will greatly enhance the information from your text.

ANNUAL EDITIONS:
RACE AND ETHNIC RELATIONS 94/95
Article Rating Form

We Want Your Advice

Here is an opportunity for you to have direct input into the next revision of this volume. We would like you to rate each of the 51 articles listed below, using the following scale:

1. **Excellent: should definitely be retained**
2. **Above average: should probably be retained**
3. **Below average: should probably be deleted**
4. **Poor: should definitely be deleted**

Your ratings will play a vital part in the next revision. So please mail this prepaid form to us just as soon as you complete it.
Thanks for your help!

Annual Editions revisions depend on two major opinion sources: one is our Advisory Board, listed in the front of this volume, which works with us in scanning the thousands of articles published in the public press each year; the other is you—the person actually using the book. Please help us and the users of the next edition by completing the prepaid article rating form on this page and returning it to us. Thank you.

Rating	Article	Rating	Article
	1. *Dred Scott v. Sandford*		25. Asian Americans Don't Fit Their Monochrome Image
	2. *Plessy v. Ferguson*		26. The Victimization of Asians in America
	3. *Brown et al. v. Board of Education of Topeka et al.*		27. Spicier Melting Pot: Asian Americans Come of Age Politically
	4. *University of California Regents v. Bakke*		28. Black-Korean Conflict in Los Angeles
	5. Freedom of Religious Expression: *Shaare Tefila Congregation v. Cobb* and *Saint Francis College v. Al-Khazraji*		29. 10 Most Dramatic Events in African-American History
	6. Historical Discrimination in the Immigration Laws		30. Black Americans: The New Generation
	7. Immigration Reform: Overview of Recent Urban Institute Immigration Policy Research		31. Growing Up in Black and White
			32. Beyond the Pale: Why My 'Too-Black' Friends Want Light-Skinned Babies
	8. New Americans Weather and Survive		33. Endangered Family
	9. Census Bureau Finds Significant Demographic Differences Among Immigrant Groups		34. The Politics of Family in America
			35. Home Ownership Anchors the Middle Class: But Lending Games Sink Many Prospective Owners
	10. Lifestyle 2000: New Enterprise and Cultural Diversity		36. Early Italian Sculptors in the United States
	11. Paupers in a World Their Ancestors Ruled		37. The New Ethnicity
	12. Bolivia's Vice President, First Indian in High Office, Waits for Change		38. Irish Americans Attack Beer-Ad Images
			39. Polish American Congress 1992 Convention Resolution Committee Report
	13. Struggling to Be Themselves		40. At the Gates of Nightmare: A New Museum Raises Old Questions About History, Evil, and Ourselves
	14. Return of the Natives		
	15. Crimes Against Humanity		
	16. Gadugi: A Model of Service-Learning for Native American Communities		41. The Mirror of the Other
	17. American Indians in the 1990s		42. The Ends of History: Balkan Culture and Catastrophe
	18. Lakhota Sioux Hutsul		
	19. Seeking Lost Culture at a Powwow		43. Race and Urban Poverty: Comparing Europe and America
	20. U.S. Hispanics: To Be and Not to Be		44. Ethnic Conflict
	21. What Does "Hispanic" Mean?		45. The Walls That Have Yet to Fall
	22. "La Raza Cosmica"		46. America: Still a Melting Pot?
	23. There's More to Racism Than Black and White		47. Students Talk About Race
			48. Diversity: A Progressive Approach
	24. Not Much Cooking: Why the Voting Rights Act Is Not Empowering Mexican Americans		49. Blood and Irony
			50. 'Ask Not'—'90s Style
			51. The Value of the Canon

(Continued on next page)

ABOUT YOU

Name_____ Date_____

Are you a teacher? ☐ Or student? ☐

Your School Name _____

Department _____

Address _____

City_____ State _____ Zip _____

School Telephone #_____

YOUR COMMENTS ARE IMPORTANT TO US!

Please fill in the following information:

For which course did you use this book? _____

Did you use a text with this Annual Edition? ☐ yes ☐ no

The title of the text? _____

What are your general reactions to the Annual Editions concept?

Have you read any particular articles recently that you think should be included in the next edition?

Are there any articles you feel should be replaced in the next edition? Why?

Are there other areas that you feel would utilize an Annual Edition?

May we contact you for editorial input?

May we quote you from above?

ANNUAL EDITIONS: RACE AND ETHNIC RELATIONS 94/95

BUSINESS REPLY MAIL

First Class   Permit No. 84   Guilford, CT

Postage will be paid by addressee

The Dushkin Publishing Group, Inc.
Sluice Dock
DPG **Guilford, Connecticut 06437**

No Postage
Necessary
if Mailed
in the
United States